THE FREE PRESS

New York   London   Toronto   Sydney   Singapore

From
WEST
to
EAST

CALIFORNIA

and the Making
of the American Mind

STEPHEN SCHWARTZ

THE FREE PRESS
A Division of Simon & Schuster Inc.
1230 Avenue of the Americas
New York, NY 10020

Designed by Carla Bolte

Manufactured in the United States of America

10 9 8 7 6 5 4 3 2 1

Library of Congress Cataloging-in-Publication Data

Schwartz, Stephen, 1948–
    From west to east : California and the making of the American mind
  / Stephen Schwartz.
        p. cm.
    Includes bibliographical references and index.
    ISBN 0-684-83134-1 (alk. paper)
    1. California—History.   2. California—Intellectual life.
  I. Title.
F871.S34   1998   97-44882
979.4—dc21   CIP

*Writings by Robert Duncan quoted by permission of the Literary Estate of
Robert Duncan. Materials by Kenneth Rexroth quoted by permission of
The Kenneth Rexroth Trust.*

**For my mother
and for Claire Fraschina**

She wears the birth of physics as a jewel,

And of the maritime empires as a flower.

—William Empson, "Thanks for a Wedding Present,"

in *Collected Poems* (1949)

Contents

Part IV. Red Years 205

Wherein surviving California radicals are overtaken by a wind from the Russian steppes; Communists set up shop locally and begin spying, agitating, and organizing the least advantaged; a great strike shakes the coast, reviving unions; radical intellectuals gravitate between Communism and modernism; a naive but sincere hero attempts a ballot-box revolution, and nearly succeeds at it; labor crusading succumbs to infighting; and the California Communists, after dominating the scene, turn sour under the impact of Stalinism

Part V. Charon's Shore 287

Wherein World War II begins in the shadow of the Hitler–Stalin Pact; literature and music contend with deeper social issues in California; Japanese Americans suffer a terrible injustice, but find a few white defenders; U.S. entry into the war mobilizes democratic intellectuals; other racial conflicts emerge involving Blacks and Hispanics; Soviet spies invade a California-originated project with the potential to destroy the world; Hollywood Communists test the limits of film as a propaganda medium, while hunting imaginary enemies; and a tiny group of mystical-anarchist poets, all unknowing, begins (but only begins), from California, to change the American and world intellect forever

Part VI. In Defense of the Earth 391

Wherein Communist influence in California leads to division and suspicion throughout society; government investigators and Hollywood Stalinists confuse the nation and the world with their bad manners; painters bring about the most profound, if the least known, of all the California revolutions; a poet sees idols and friends die, some horribly, and produces a manifesto of outrage; and the intersection of anti-totalitarianism, a new poetics, and the revival of dissidence makes California a laboratory of an authentic worldwide revolution

Epilogue: Thirty Years After 509

BEGINNING IN INVERNESS

*T*his book is a history of the California intellect and the California cultural identity, and seeks to explain, by examining those aspects of the California experience, the impact of California on the United States and the world; better yet, its conquest of the world.

It is appropriate to begin such a work in the place that is, in my view, the most Californian of all California places: the tiny hamlet of Inverness, in west Marin County.

Inverness is everything the great California cities, San Francisco and Los Angeles, are not. It is too small to rate even the status of a municipality, with no more than 300 permanent residents, although it swells in summer when the upwardly mobile from elsewhere come for the season. It has almost no business district. It seems little more than a main street with a bakery, a restaurant or two, a post office, an old-fashioned "all and everything" market, and a couple of bed-and-breakfast inns. Behind the little street a mountain is visible, cloaked with redwood trees; on the other side of the street, a thin band of water called Tomales Bay, and on the other side of that, dairy country: rolling hills covered with grass, often brown. Inverness is isolated, usually silent, tranquil, scorchingly hot sometimes, dank and foggy at others.

And yet one has a sense there, ever so difficult to discern, of expectation. Inverness sits at the north end of the Point Reyes peninsula, a scrap of land that juts out of the Pacific coast like a breast with a reversed underside. Point Reyes, the most prominent landmark on this littoral, was the original goal of the Spanish explorers who established California more than 200 years ago.

The inlet separating redwoods from grassland also sets the peninsula off from the mainland geographically and even ecologically, for the fjord, as it is also called, is nothing but the watery face of the San Andreas fault line, mother of great California earthquakes. Tomales Bay and the Point Reyes peninsula, like "the San Andreas," are products of the grandest and mightiest of all the impressive components of the Pacific landscape—components invisible to human eyes. These are the forces that, under the ocean and deeper, beneath the earth's crust, drive gigantic geological plates against one another, supporting the beautiful breast that is the peninsula, and, not far away, tearing open the earth to create San Francisco Bay and thrusting upward the Sierra Nevada and other mountain chains.

California's form is reminiscent of a human body as depicted in the mannerist paintings of Arcimboldo: Marin and San Francisco are the head; industrial Richmond and Oakland the arms; San Jose, where the Hispanic world and even the so-called "Third World" begin, the lungs. Then there is the most productive valley in the world, and finally, farther down, the sturdy legs.

Somehow "the San Andreas" seems more like the heart of California than, say, Silicon Valley. At its north end, in Inverness, where the fault line leaves the land and dives down, the human inhabitants swear that the Point Reyes peninsula is another continent, or, at least, a minicontinent, situated on its own tectonic plate, distinct from the mainland. And so it seems, with the woodland on the west side of Tomales Bay so utterly different from the pastures on the opposite shore. The concept of a minicontinent rubs off on the inhabitants; farther down the peninsula, in Bolinas, the residents repeatedly take down highway signs to prevent tourists from finding the town.

One may follow "the San Andreas" to San Juan Bautista in San Benito County, a town of about 1,500 people with a beautiful mission, a tourist attraction but still largely unspoiled. Two of the greatest lyrical works about California, Frank Norris's novel *The Octopus* (1901) and Alfred Hitchcock's film *Vertigo* (1958) include scenes set there, or rather set in fictionalized and transformed versions of San Juan Bautista that nonetheless seem true to its character. In the narrow defile of "the San Andreas" one feels an eternal tension, a watchfulness—as if the land itself knowingly awaited new tremors.

The grandeur of geological collisions is reflected elsewhere in the landscape: in high cliffs the length of the coast (California, unlike the Atlantic states, has few sheltered ports); in the redwoods; in the great Central Valley; in mountains that although not the highest in the world are among the most beautiful; in the deserts that may be the most inhospitable north of the Mexican border.

Along with these wonders come massive fires, devastating snows, frightful heat spells and droughts, floods and landslides. In the (nonhuman) animal realm, it is unsurprising to find that the state's symbol is the grizzly bear; and if the grizzly be extinct in the state, California nonetheless boasts untamable sharks, resurgent mountain lions and coyotes, horrifically venomous spiders, and rattlesnakes.

In its human dimension, California is known for equally wild and terrifying species: radicals and intellectuals, entertainment stars larger than life, brutal gangs and bizarre cults. And its southern border seems so much more than a mere geographical demarcation line.

―――――――

MOST AUTHORS WHO have dealt with California in this century have written about it from the outside in, from the midwest and east of the United States westerly, and outward into the Pacific. In this book I shall go in precisely the opposite direction: from west to east, from the Pacific basin shoreward, aiming toward the American heartland and the Atlantic coast; from Mexico north, and, above all, from the inside out.

In response to Bishop Berkeley's eighteenth-century prediction— "Westward the course of empire makes its way"—commemorated in the naming of the great University of California campus in his memory, I shall endeavor to show how a society, already fully formed when it came under American sovereignty, expanded in the opposite direction. Something was there in California from the beginning, its later power anticipated by such visitors as the Barcelonese cartographer Miquel de Constançó in the eighteenth century and the Russian revolutionary Dimitrii Zavalishin early in the nineteenth. But what was it that allowed this reversal of the tide of history?

California was radical from the beginning. It was not simply new, it was the newest society ever to have reached full development. Like its elder brothers New Mexico and Texas, and its "newer" cousins Hawaii and Alaska, but unlike the rest of the United States, it has a cultural identity of its own. Yet it stands apart from New Mexico, Texas, Hawaii, or Alaska, in that its cultural identity is that of radicality; not based on a radical ideology or ism *per se* but, experientially rather than conceptually, ever embodying the new. California's role in a series of "cutting-edge" historical developments, in which it always occupied a forward post, its favorable geographical situation, and its instant rise to immense wealth during the Gold Rush have made it unique in the world. All societies undergo periods of radicalization; California has never known anything else—it has *always* been radical, and has never really undergone a period of pure stability and institutional conservatism. Of no other human aggregation in history can the same be said.

The San Francisco radical and literary historian William McDevitt stated this point in 1944 when he printed, in a crank orthography intended to simplify office shorthand, a reminiscence of the turn-of-the-century labor agitator Carl Browne. Since the 1850s the community "specialized in producing 'free spirits,'" McDevitt wrote. "It nurtured individuality," in people and in careers; "it spawned eccentrics." It is perhaps a matter of irony that so many individualists would embrace collectivist social theories.

THIS BOOK IS coming out, fortuitously, at the intersection of three anniversaries: those of 1697, when the Spanish first colonized Baja California; 1846–48, when California was wrested from Mexico, and 1898, when America's conquest of the Philippines ended the Spanish Pacific empire and commenced an attempt to build an American empire in its place. But this book is not a story of Spain, of Baja, of the Mexican mainland, or of the Philippines, no matter how echoes from those places may intrude. Indeed, I have acceded to the general indifference of the American reading public to the 1898 Spanish-American war, leaving it mainly untouched—with some regret. This volume is intended as a counterargument to conventional histories of American expansion, in which California is described as a mere pawn of such. This book is also, necessarily, less about California's relationship with its neighbors, near or far, than about its relationship with itself and with the wider world. In the Pacific, Hawaii—annexed by the United

States in 1900 and soon to have its own anniversary—has been California's closest "relative" in psychological terms. But to have discussed the Spanish-American war, and the Philippines or Hawaii in the modern period, would also have required more discussion of Alaska, Washington, Oregon, British Columbia, Nevada, Arizona, and perhaps also Utah and Colorado. That would be far too much. The great unavoidable presences in the treatment of California's history have involved the southern border and Mexico, along with Russia and Japan. These have proven the enduring political powers in California's rise to its destiny, as much as New York or Paris have been cultural powers.

Similarly, where I have nothing new to offer, I have chosen not to retell the whole of certain events or the full biographies of certain prominent figures, such as Mark Twain or William Randolph Hearst. This book is not "booster" history, concerned to include everybody and everything that ever happened, or a recital of official legends. Rather, it is an account of a "hidden" or "secret" history.

The story told here is that of the California Republic, something that is almost, but not quite, a separate nation, a mirror for the world that ended up changing the face of human society forever.

PART I

BORDERLANDS AND OTHER EXTREMES

It is from the ideas of you that you emerge . . .
I return to you from my longing,
You a second image in longing . . .
I shall never reach you—
Between me and thee.

— Robert Duncan, "Correspondences"

Wherein Spanish sailors coasting along a maritime borderland encounter a place rich with flora and fauna, inhabited by peaceful natives; rivalries between distant powers lead to the foundation of a clerical-military colony with Utopian overtones; a faraway revolution overturns the universal order; American sailors and trappers infiltrate the lost paradise, and a new kind of society is born in California

*O*n the afternoon of August 23, 1542, a Friday, two ships stood at anchor in a sheltered bay on the coast of what today is northern Baja California. They were small vessels, rudely built and launched, and meagerly provisioned, hundreds of miles southward on the Pacific mainland of New Spain, as Mexico was then known. The larger was christened Holy Savior or *San Salvador;* the smaller, an escort frigate, was called *Victoria* or Victory.

They had come into the bay on the Monday before under command of a Portuguese navigator, João Rodrigues Cabrillo, and his Spanish chief pilot, Bartomeu Ferrer. On the second day of their visit to the bay, Cabrillo had gone ashore and claimed the land for King Carlos I of Spain, who was also Holy Roman Emperor, ruling as Charles V. Cabrillo named the bay Puerta de la Posesión, further asserting the claim; it is now called Bahía San Quintín. The crews remained at the site for a week, taking on water and repairing the sails. The sailors examined the country on foot; a *Relación* or account of their voyage, possibly by Ferrer and perhaps a copy at second hand, described the bay as "a good port . . . suitable for making any kind of repairs on ships, by placing them out of the water." The interior terrain, the writer said, was "high and rugged," seemingly fertile land with fine valleys, although the landscape was bare of vegetation.

The explorers observed some local inhabitants, called Indians here as brown people were throughout the Spanish American and Asian empire: first a group of fishermen, who fled at sight of the mariners; then a much larger group, who stood their ground. The two sides of the encounter, Indians and Spaniards, sought to communicate through hand signs. The natives showed the sailors a pool of fresh water and a large deposit from which salt could be gathered. They indicated that they did not live on the coast but inland, and that they were numerous.

Later that day, five brown men suddenly approached the foreigners on the beach. "They seemed to be intelligent Indians," the author of the *Relación* wrote. Their bodies painted with white slashmarks, the natives came aboard the *San Salvador* and counted the Europeans. The Indians then demonstrated their intelligence by telling the Spaniards, still using signs, that they had observed similar interlopers, bearded, accompanied by dogs and bearing swords and crossbows, who were now five days' march to the east.

This dialogue, two months before the fiftieth anniversary of Columbus's arrival in the New World, marked the historical birth of the California we now know. The Indians were correct in their commentary: the white men they had previously seen were members of an expedition led by another Spanish nobleman, Francisco Vázquez de Coronado. Under Coronado, between 1540 and 1542, three hundred Spanish soldiers and a large party of Mexican Indians had marched north, commissioned to search for the legendary "seven golden cities of Cíbola." Coronado and his companions wandered around the northern Mexican frontier, ranging from the vicinity of the Gulf of California as far as central Kansas; they were the first Europeans to see the Grand Canyon.

Cabrillo and Ferrer's Indian encounters on the Baja coast are full of meaning for those who have since lived in California. The Spanish sailors stood at a borderland of the imagination and the intellect. The indigenous Californians clearly had a sophisticated knowledge of their physical environment, more than many who came after would expect. Communication was helped by the linguistic unity of the Indians of northern Baja with those of the Lower Colorado River, all of whom spoke languages of the Yuman family. News of Coronado's invasion seems to have traveled fast and far; it was known as far north as Ventura on the Upper (Alta) California coast.

Certainly, Cabrillo's first, limited interchanges provoke us to wonder how much more might have been learned from the California Indians. Paradoxically, California is so modern that any trace of the pre-Spanish past seems almost absent, and Indians are almost never a topic of public discourse save among a few experts. Yet California has the second largest Indian population in the United States, and modern Indian reality is encountered relatively easily outside its cities.

Indeed, the landscape where the California Indian and European cultures first collided, from San Quintín on the Pacific coast northeast to and beyond the Colorado River, has changed remarkably little in four hundred years, and is still mainly wild. We have no trouble, walking the beaches and hills of Baja California, visualizing it as it then was; here history disappears like water in desert sand. Settlement of the region remains thin today, and even where the population is dense it seems superficial and even more recent than it is, whether that of the Anglo cities to the north, the immense slums of Tijuana and Mexicali, or the gaudy, brittle Baja resorts.

And there, right there, is The Border.

The sailors of the *San Salvador* and the *Victoria* had departed from the

Mexican port of Navidad on June 27, seven weeks before their encounter with the Indians at San Quintín. By September 28 they reached what is now San Diego. There, with autumn turning into winter, they suffered bad weather. The meteorological hazards of the Alta California coast would become notorious, but the splendid natural harbor at San Diego, one of the best in the world, protected them.

The explorers sailed on, soon passing the large islands of Santa Catalina and San Clemente. At Ventura, in the week of October 12, fifty years after Columbus's world-transforming landfall, they saw a Chumash Indian town, or *pueblo,* with houses that were as large as those in Mexico. Their ships were surrounded by "many very good canoes," each carrying a dozen or so Indians, who repeated the earlier declarations to the explorers about white men traveling through the interior. The Coronado expeditionaries were hundreds of miles away, but Cabrillo may have sent two of his men eastward by land, as scouts; we know, at least, that he asked Indians to carry letters inland for him.

Although they claimed the coasts for Spain, Cabrillo, Ferrer, and their company, unlike the Coronado party, were not *conquistadores.* Nor were they missionaries, traders, or pirates; they were seaborne surveyors, using their maritime skills to expand geographical knowledge. The author of the *Relación,* whether he was Ferrer or Juan Páez, another member of the crew, was a talented observer of some eloquence. Their specific mission was to seek the Straits of Anián, an imagined northwestern sea route from Europe to Asia.

Of course, such efforts made conquest, missionization, trade, and piracy possible. But it would be a mistake to imagine that the Spanish colonial enterprise was unrelievedly genocidal. In the same year 1542 (as in 1500 and 1512), the Spanish Crown declared the freedom of the Indians, with new ordinances calling for Indian customs to have the force of law as often as possible.

Early in November the Cabrillo-Ferrer party was halted by heavy winds that prevented them from using their sails and forced them back south, where they sought shelter on the coast. They resupplied themselves with wood, fresh water, and sardines provided by the Chumash, who previously furnished them with great quantities of the fish. These Indians lived in a group of towns near the present Gaviota, ruled by an elderly woman who slept two nights aboard the Spanish ships with numbers of her people.

The sailors had further difficulty making progress after passing Point Concepción. As they continued northward, more bad weather—strong northwest winds, storm upon storm—was complemented by dramatically high mountains, which overshadowed the shore and allowed the ships no easy harborage. "All this coast . . . is bold and entirely without shelter. All along it runs a chain of very high mountains. It is as high at the seacoast as it is in the interior, and the sea beats upon it," the author of the *Relación* commented.

Forced out to sea for a week by the weather, they completely missed Monterey Bay, Half Moon Bay, the Golden Gate, and Drake's Bay, and the two ships became separated. The *San Salvador* found its companion vessel and made landfall again in mid-November, near what would become Fort Ross. The coast of today's Marin and Sonoma counties, seeming so inhospitably mountainous, greatly impressed the author of the *Relación,* who commented that the sailors had "proceeded along the coast to see if there were any port where they might take shelter. So great was the swell of the ocean that it was terrifying to see, and the coast was bold and the mountains very high."

They now turned back south deliberately, impelled by strong north winds. The *Relación* continues, regarding the Coast Range visible from the Gulf of the Farallones, off the San Francisco peninsula, "All the coast . . . is very bold; the sea has a heavy swell, and the coast is very high. There are mountains that reach the sky, and the sea beats upon them. When sailing along near the land, it seems as if the mountains would fall upon the ships."

Fleeing this dizzying vision, the mariners landed on San Miguel, the westernmost of the Santa Barbara islands, and spent two winter months of unrelieved wind and rain. There Cabrillo, who had fallen and broken his arm on an earlier visit to the island, died.

Ferrer assumed command, and in a second northward attempt, reached as far as Point Arena. The sea was "so high they became crazed"—a portent of California's history—before they again turned back, with Ferrer guiding the party to Mexico. The companions of Cabrillo and Ferrer had established, for later travelers, the reality of California, which had previously existed in a half-world of vague maritime knowledge mixed with fantasy. The first California—which meant, for hundreds of years, all land from the southern tip of the Baja peninsula to the northernmost point where a Spanish claim could be asserted—may have been named by Hernán Cortés, the conqueror of Mexico.

Cortés was committed to shipbuilding on the Pacific coast of New Spain, beginning soon after his conquest of Mexico in 1519. In 1522, at Zacatula, a village near where the River Balsas flows into the Pacific, he established a shipyard. It was manned by forty Spanish carpenters, joiners, blacksmiths, and sailors, and Cortés ordered naval stores to be transported there from Veracruz on the Caribbean coast. However, no sooner had the supplies arrived at Zacatula than the warehouse caught fire, sparing nothing but nails and anchors.

Such problems could not deter Cortés. He ordered new supplies, and sought to obtain artillery from Spain, against firm opposition from a group of influential figures including the archbishop of Burgos in Castile, who had been named president of the Spanish empire in the Indies. "I place a value on these ships beyond all expression," Cortés wrote to King Carlos I, as cited in an English version from the eighteenth century.

> I have been at immense expenses, and contracted vast debts for [this] service both by sea and land . . . yet have I determined to send three caravels and two brigantines for this end; though I reckon it will cost me above ten thousand gold crowns. . . . By the intelligence I have received of the countries on the upper coast of the South Sea, the sending of these ships along it, will be attended with great advantage. . . . I have laid aside all other profits and advantages, of which I have the most certain knowledge, in order to follow entirely this course.

Cortés had hoped to send an expedition along the north Pacific coast as early as July 1524. However, royal approval for his maritime ambitions was not forthcoming until 1526, and the Spanish and religious authorities in Europe declined to allow him to proceed at his own discretion; in 1529 Cortés agreed that any future seafaring expedition would be financed out of his own pocket. Still he continued to commission the launching of ships from the Mexican west coast.

Most scholars today believe the name California was bestowed by Fortún Ximénes, a native of the Basque country and the pilot of the *Concepción,* a ship built at Cortés' order and sent north nine years before Cabrillo and Ferrer, in 1533, seeking yet earlier, lost pioneers. The master of the *Concepción,* Diego Becerra, seems to have been an exceptionally cruel and capricious individual, "of a haughty, choleric disposition" according to an eighteenth-century Jesuit priest and California historian, Father Miguel

Venegas. The crew of the *Concepción*, led by Ximénes, mutinied and killed Becerra, and then sailed across the Gulf of California to the bay at today's La Paz.

This mutiny was another omen of California's turbulent and radical life to come. Most of the rebel sailors, including Ximénes, were killed by Indians, but the few who escaped returned the short distance to the Mexican mainland in possession of some black pearls. Cortés, seeking the source of the treasure, led an exploring party to the Baja peninsula in 1535. Since then the Gulf of California has also been called the Sea of Cortez (the Anglicized spelling), though for a time it bore the name Vermilion Sea, perhaps because of a reddish tint caused by fish or algae, perhaps because of a resemblance to the narrow Red Sea separating Egypt and Arabia.

The Pacific coast to the north of the peninsula was soon well known as Alta California, a name that has persisted among Mexicans. California, on the furthest border of New Spain, was—and still is—a borderland of many dimensions. The eastern Pacific is a grand frontier between the Euro-American world and Asia, and the *idea* of California, as represented on maps and in literature, engaged the fascination of many.

The very name *California* was emblematic of exploration, drawn by Ximénes, it is said, from a popular novel of chivalry, a variety of literature to which the Spanish *conquistadores* were addicted: *Las sergas del muy esforzado caballero Esplandián, hijo del excelente rey Amadís de Gaula (The Exploits of the Very Zealous Knight Esplandián, Son of the Great King Amadis of Gaul)* by Garcí Rodríguez de Montalvo.

Around 1500, Montalvo had assembled a Spanish version of a neo-Arthurian epic, *Amadis of Gaul,* and supplemented it with the lengthy tale of Esplandián, derived entirely from his own powers of invention. In Chapter 157 of *Esplandián* Montalvo described the then-imaginary country:

> [A]t the right hand of the Indies there was an island called California, very near the Earthly Paradise, which was peopled by black women, without any man among them, so that their style of life was almost like that of Amazons. They had valiant and forceful bodies and burning hearts and great strength; the island itself had the highest crags and wildest rocks found anywhere in the world, the arms they had were made of gold, as were the fittings of the beasts they tamed and rode; for there was no other metal on the island.

A little further on, Montalvo adds that their weapons were covered with precious jewels, found as commonly as rocks in California.

The black Amazons, according to Montalvo, were ruled by a queen, Calafía, who was "very large of body, a very beautiful example of her people . . . desirous in her being of creating great things." She led them to besiege Constantinople, supported by a flying fleet of tame griffins—a beast which abounded on the island, according to Montalvo. Montalvo sang the exploits of the queen:

> Calafía, with a sword in her hand
> Worked a great damage with her Amazon troops
> And there put to death very many persons
> From among the faithful, and more of the pagans.

Her forces captured men to take back to their island, some to feed to the griffins, a few to keep for labor and reproduction. (It is small wonder that Calafía has become an icon of contemporary black and feminist advocates in the state.) The origins of the name Calafía have never been authoritatively established, although some have traced it to the Greek καλλιφυισ, or beautiful stature. *Califerne,* which resembles it, occurs in the *Chanson de Roland.*

There is an obvious similarity between Montalvo's fictional California, with its "highest crags and wildest rocks found anywhere in the world," and the land observed by Cabrillo and Ferrer, where "it seems as if the mountains would fall upon the ships." California merited the name bestowed upon it. But enthusiasm for Montalvo's "bastard" work was not uniform; in Cervantes's *Don Quixote,* Montalvo's version of *Amadís* is praised, but *Las sergas de Esplandián* is burned as worthless. A work on the margins of the new secular literature, and an irreplaceable landmark in the development of the novel as we know it, *Esplandián* became intertwined with the birth of an innovative model of human society in California.

REFLECTING THE SLOW and contradictory progress of physical exploration in contrast to Montalvo's racing fantasy, California was long believed to be an island. It so appeared on European maps through the sixteenth century as attention to this maritime frontier grew, and as navigators, mainly under Spanish patronage, continued probing the empire's limits.

An illustrious intruder, Sir Francis Drake, landed on the Alta California coast in 1579, somewhere near the bay now bearing his name. He had made a career of his hatred of the Spanish, who were the outstanding rivals to English ambitions in the Elizabethan Age. Before entering the Pacific Drake had fought his way through the Spanish colonies in the Caribbean and along the Atlantic coast of South America. In Chile and Peru he captured a great gold and silver treasure, and he repeated his success in plundering the west coast of New Spain.

Drake came to the area in June 1579. Finding a good harbor in which to refurbish his hundred-ton ship, formerly the *Pelican* but now the *Golden Hinde*—at a location which has never been established—he anchored and stayed for more than a month.

During his visit (as described in two accounts of his voyage, neither from his own hand) Drake had various encounters with Coast Miwok Indians. Among other details his chroniclers noted their reed-weaving, which produced baskets usable for carrying water. They also described large herds of deer, a multiplicity of rabbits, and the probable presence of gold and silver.

Drake believed the Spanish had ignored the Upper California coast, and convinced himself that the Indians he met had offered their sovereignty to him. Drake declared the territory a possession of Queen Elizabeth, naming it New Albion, or New Britain. But Upper California, joined at the hip to Baja, is not New Albion; its history would remain consistently Mediterranean, never fully surrendering, like the other New England on the Atlantic coast, to Anglo-Saxon, Celtic, and other northern European traditions.

Drake, we are told, called the country Albion for its "white banks and cliffs, which lie toward the sea," perhaps those observed by Cabrillo and Ferrer 37 years before, but also in the hope that "it might have some affinity with our country in name, which sometime was so called." The white cliffs bring to mind the famed White Cliffs of Dover and the Latin word *albus,* or white.

Drake's "Albion" was as fantastical in its way as the borrowing of "California" from Montalvo's romance. A recent historian, Dora Beale Polk, has persuasively argued the influence on Drake of the "Albion" described in the works of an Elizabethan mathematician, mystical philosopher, and maritime historian, Dr. John Dee. Like Montalvo, Dee was an experimental figure on the frontiers of the European intellect. Famed as an alchemical investigator, he was a founding fellow of Trinity College at Oxford, the personal occult adviser of Queen Elizabeth, and astrologer to the Spanish king Felipe II, the son of Carlos I. He was also a companion of the great martyr to the flames of Catholic intolerance, Giordano Bruno, and mentor to the love poet and adventurer Sir Philip Sidney, author of the *Defense of Poesie.* Another comrade of Drake, Dee, and Sidney, Sir Edward Dyer, wrote the poem *My mind to me a kingdom is,* which could stand as a motto for Californians.

Drake had undertaken his world-encompassing voyage with secret counsel from Dee, who possessed a description of the epochal voyage into the Pacific via the tip of South America made in 1521 by Fernando Magalhães or Magellan, a disgraced Portuguese who entered Spanish service. The account, a copy of which Drake very likely carried with him, may have been obtained by Dee during a visit to the court of the Holy Roman Emperor Maximilian II, to whom Dee dedicated his occult *Hieroglyphic Monad.*

The chimerical British claim to New Albion had no real future, save as a source of anxiety for the Spanish. However it remained a subject of commentary by writers in English. A fictive "map" of New Albion, with Cape Blanco, Cape Mendocino, "port Sir Francis Drake," and the port of Monterey clearly marked appeared in Jonathan Swift's *Gulliver's Travels,* first published in 1726; it was shown to be south of Brobdingnag, the land of giants.

If the European consciousness that focused on the eastern Pacific at California's historical beginning had a hallucinated quality, this seems curiously appropriate when we examine the culture of its indigenous peoples. Pre-European California was densely occupied, with an Indian population estimated between 100,000 and a half million, speaking a remarkable variety of languages.

Indian California was also a borderland. The lower tier of the grandiose religious system, elaborate material culture, and complex social relationships identified with the "potlatch" civilization of the Northwest Coast Indians may be discerned among the Hupa-Karok-Yurok, near today's Eureka. This large grouping of communities at Hoopa Valley survived the white invasion and continues to function. An eloquent exemplar in the mosaic of California Indian societies, Yuroks, who may have come to the area from the north within the last 1,000 years, were sophisticated woodworkers, building houses and canoes, weapons and fishing gear, and accomplished basket and basketry-hat weavers. There and elsewhere in pre-European northern California, ritual healing by women as *shamans* was widespread.

More importantly, indigenous Californians lived on the northern frontier of a Mexican Indian culture in which the use of powerful psychedelic drugs was widespread; indeed, southern and central California represented a kind of spur extending north out of the Mexican culture zone.

Although modern, nonnative knowledge of California Indian culture before the arrival of Europeans is in some respects limited, it is known that (put simply) much of indigenous California was awash in psychedelic drug use, mainly involving the violently hallucinogenic and poisonous plant *Datura stramonium,* which is known by its Nahuatl (Aztec) Indian name as *toloatzin* or *toloache*. For a recent observer, one of the most provocative features of the California Indian culture is the religious order of sungazers, a group of Central Miwok Indians that lived in the southern Sierra Nevada, who used *toloache* as a mystical weapon. Each subgroup of the order symbolically "killed" the other in ritual observances; for this and other reasons, the *toloache* religion in California has often been called the "death cult."

Toloache appears in California from July through September, a prickly grayish plant with purple-tinged, white flowers. *Datura* is widely known as the thorn-apple and angel's trumpet; it is also called jimsonweed in other parts of the United States where it grows wild. It is a member of the *Solanaceae,* plants whose risk of fatality to human users is indicated by their "common" name: the nightshade family. Its active poison is atropine, which paralyzes the nervous system; the smallest overdose may cause coma and death. *Datura stramonium* is a cousin of tobacco and belladonna, and is also related to the potato, the eggplant, the tomato, and the bell pepper. The wild potato classified with the family played a major role in the development of the potato in South America before European contact. The use of *Datura stramonium* as a psychedelic narcotic was of overwhelming significance in indigenous Californian botany, religion, and curing practices.

The importance of *toloache* derives not only from the powerful, colorful visions it fosters in the user but also from its toxicity. The Indian capacity to moderate the dose and keep users of the drug alive constituted "a significant technological achievement," in the words of the anthropologists Lowell Bean and Sylvia Vane. They note, "even when (*datura* is) taken in safe dosages, the psychedelic state that results can be frightening, and those who took it needed to be watched and guided carefully through the experience." The *datura* religion is apparently very old in those California areas where the plant is commonly found—the Sacramento and San Joaquin river basin, the coastal valleys of Southern California, and the desert from Death Valley to and across the Colorado River. With or without a complex set of beliefs and practices that would merit description as a full-fledged cult, *datura* was used as far north as San Francisco Bay.

In the first two decades of the twentieth century, according to the founder of modern California Indian ethnography, Alfred L. Kroeber, "The Luiseño and Diegueño [were singing] nearly all their *toloache* songs in the Gabrielino language without concern at not understanding the words issuing from their mouths." While the Indian use of *datura* does not explain the mass drug-taking that emerged in California in the late twentieth century, it provides a remarkable antecedent of the practice, and there are historical links, slender but real, between the two phenomena.

SPANISH PENETRATION NORTHWARD from Mexico and westward into the Pacific had an irresistible geographical logic. Magellan in 1521 had led his crews as far as the islands that would become known as the Philippines; he was killed there, and his successor as captain, the Basque Juan Sebastián Elcano, completed the first European circumnavigation of the globe. In 1525, a Spanish fleet had left La Coruña in Galicia and passed the tip of South America, reaching the Moluccas, where they refused Portuguese orders to stay away. Four years later, however, King Carlos I sold any Spanish rights in the Moluccas to the Portuguese.

A Spanish expedition explored the coasts of Papua New Guinea in 1536, and in 1542, the same year as the Cabrillo-Ferrer voyage, Ruy López de Villalobos left the port of Navidad in New Spain and sailed to the Hawaiian archipelago, the Caroline Islands, and the San Lázaro Islands, which he renamed the Philippines after the regent of Spain who would become King Felipe II.

Spanish navigation in the south and western Pacific ended its pioneering period with the close of the sixteenth century. In 1564 four ships, with

380 men aboard, left Navidad under the command of Miguel López de Legázpi. This *conquistador* laid claim to Guam and the Mariana Islands, and spent six years establishing Spanish rule over the Philippines. In 1565, the first Spanish trading ship departed the Philippines for Mexico. It was the 500-ton *San Pablo,* with a small cargo of cinnamon, but the main task assigned its officers was to find a usable route eastward across the Pacific. The ship proceeded north from the Philippines to the Japan Current, which carried the sailors over the ocean to the California coast.

A Spanish party led by Álvaro de Mendaña surveyed the Solomon Islands in 1567, and in 1595 he reconnoitered the nearby Santa Cruz (La Pérouse) islands, as well as the Marquesas. Remarkably, after Mendaña died at sea his wife, Doña Isabel Barreto, took command of the expedition and brought it back to the Philippines. By then there was a significant trade between the Philippines and Mexico, based on the annual dispatch of the "China ships," also known as "Manila galleons." These vessels, loaded down with such Asian products as Ming porcelain and silk, as well as Mexican silver and gold on their return trips, began following a course across the ocean to the area of Cape Mendocino, first seen by a European in 1584, during a voyage from Manila by the Catalan navigator Francesc de Galí. The Manila galleon traffic drew new attention to the Alta California shore and quickly became a target for English pirates, the successors of Drake, who exercised their daring by raiding Spanish Pacific waters.

Worse than pirates for the trans-Pacific crews was illness. After weeks at sea, mariners suffered exhaustion, weakness, irritability, weight loss, and pain in muscles and joints. Fingernails broke; gums swelled up, turning purple and spongy, then crumbled, and finally bled freely. Eventually secondary infections occurred, along with gangrene and loosening of teeth. Taking food became nearly impossible. Old scar tissue would break down, new injuries would not heal, and hemorrhages would spread under the skin and around the body.

This was scurvy, caused by a deficiency of vitamin C, a legendary bane of seafarers. Fear of pirates and hope in the possibility of a port where seamen could recover from scurvy impelled the Spanish imperial authorities to cast their eyes repeatedly toward Alta California. In 1595, Sebastián Meléndez Rodríguez Cermeño was directed from Manila to sail down the California coast looking for a suitable site for a station. But his ship, the *San Agustín,* was wrecked at Drake's Bay. (Its possible recovery has recently fascinated California treasure hunters.) Cermeño and his surviving sailors made their way back to Acapulco in a *viroco,* a small open boat made up of a dugout log with one or two square sails and plank bulkheads, which had been brought prefabricated from the Philippines to be assembled for a survey of the coast.

While Cermeño was sailing to investigate California from the west, Sebastián Vizcaíno, a veteran of the Manila trade and entrepreneur, was preparing to head north from the Mexican mainland by sea, to La Paz and farther. In 1596 Vizcaíno explored much of the east coast of the Baja peninsula. He began planning in 1599 to go north again, with a royal mandate to explore the outer, Pacific coast of the Californias north to Cape Mendocino. He departed in May 1602, passing Cape Mendocino and reaching as far north as Cape Blanco.

Vizcaíno found the coasts crowded with Indians, who came down to the beaches *en masse* to observe the Spaniards. On Santa Catalina Island the foreigners bartered with the indigenous Californians, who offered them ropes of high quality, skins, and other items. Elsewhere on Santa Catalina the Spaniards found Indians in possession of Chinese silk, proof that they had become used to visits by passing ships. There is also evidence, though sparse, that Filipino and African sailors and servants aboard the Manila ships had already run away to live among the Indians.

Vizcaíno and his voyagers returned to Mexico "crying aloud" with sickness and hunger, in a ship that seemed no better than a hospital. All his companions had fallen ill; at least forty men, of two hundred who began the trip, had died. "Some died talking, some sleeping, some eating, some while sitting up in their beds." Inexperienced seamen, if they could leave their bunks, took turns at the wheel and in the galley alike; soon none were fit to handle the sails.

But notwithstanding these travails, Vizcaíno furnished the Spanish with the first *derrotero,* or periplus, which named and described San Diego, Santa Barbara, Monterey Bay, and other major features of the California shore, but Vizcaíno missed San Francisco Bay, like others before and after him. A letter sent to the King by Vizcaíno in 1603 was printed and published, and caused considerable interest in Europe. It included an enthusiastic description of the port, forests, and fauna at Monterey:

[A] harbor protected from all winds, while near the port there are many pine trees large enough to use in building ships, as well as live and white oaks, rose-mary, rockroses, and Alexandria rosewood trees. There is a great supply of game, including rabbits, hares, partridges, and other kinds and species found in Spain, but in greater abundance even than in the Sierra Morena [a wild area of Andalusia], and flying birds of different sorts. This is a land of agreeable climate and good water, very fertile for the growth of trees and plants, particularly chestnuts and acorns, which are larger than those in Spain.

Translated, embroidered, and read far and wide, Vizcaíno 's account was the first to create in the European mind the idea of a real California that was something like a paradise on earth.

As noted, the belief that California was an island then had wide currency. Indeed, many contemporary writers still treat California as, in effect, a geographical and cultural island. Certainly a sense of isolation and insularity contributed to California's image as a unique and exotic location. Meanwhile Spanish expansion into New Mexico, on a meridian parallel to Alta California, began and proceeded apace. As the great California historian Herbert E. Bolton wrote, the Spanish explorations "on the Pacific coast at the turn of the [seventeenth] century, as exemplified by the two expeditions of Vizcaíno, were preceded and stimulated by a new advance into the northern interior." Seeking to exploit mines and raise cattle, the rulers of New Spain had colonized Zacatecas, Durango, and Chihuahua in the mid-1500s. In 1604–05, Juan de Oñate explored the region from Zuñi west to the mouth of the Colorado River. De Oñate sought a land route to the upper California coast, but succumbed to the island theory of California geography. Santa Fe was founded in New Mexico in 1610, and missions were established among the Pueblo ("town-dwelling") Indians in a broad and deep belt from Taos and other communities on the upper Rio Grande.

The Pueblo Indians, led by the *shaman* Popé, rose in a successful revolt against the Spanish in 1680. The chief effect of this rebellion was the freeing of horses, which invaded the Great Plains and multiplied. Decades later this brought about the "horse revolution" in the cultures of Plains Indians, who gave up their previously sedentary existence, tamed the animals, and became superlative riders. The Spanish fought to reestablish control, succeeding on the Rio Grande but failing to regain the Hopi mesas.

These Spanish imperial ventures, navigational, missionary, and military, were not cheap. The Jesuit Venegas stated that measures taken in the year

1700 to safeguard Pensacola, in Florida, from the French had cost more than a million Spanish dollars. "Great advantages were also expected from the conquest of Texas, which was carried on without any regard to expense," he wrote, complaining that both enterprises had diverted the interest of the Spanish authorities from California.

But the various projects for the exploration and settlement of California were also lucrative for some. Venegas wrote, "[T]he former expeditions to California, though unsuccessful, had served to enrich great numbers, either by the large sums of the royal revenue that had been expended, or by fishing and trading for pearls." Report and rumor revived the California excitement in Europe as the eighteenth century began, along with resentment at the interest of Jesuit missionaries in these resources. The Society of Jesus had established a mission at Loreto on the east coast of Baja California in 1697; this was the first permanent European settlement in the Californias.

The entry of the Jesuits into Baja California had been preceded, beginning in the last decade of the 1500s, by a slow but steady missionization of the northwest coast of New Spain, through Sinaloa and Sonora. A new phase began in 1687 with the exploration of Pimería Alta, the region between the Gila River and the present Arizona border with Mexico, by a brilliant German Jesuit, Father Eusebio Francisco Kino, a former mathematics professor and talented astronomical observer. Setting up missions as far north as San Xavier del Bac (today still a gorgeous monument) at Tucson, Kino repeatedly explored the Gila, and made two trips down the Colorado River. He crossed into California and satisfied himself that only the Colorado separated Upper California from Pimería Alta, that is, from "the continent." Kino composed an account demonstrating that California was not an island and that Alta California could be reached by land from northern Mexico. In his 1710 *Relación* describing his proselytizing work in Sonora and Arizona, Kino repeated that California was "not an island," and described Baja California as a peninsula. Bolton among others considered Kino, for his geographical efforts, to have been the region's outstanding European pioneer.

———

THE FRANCISCANS UNDER Junípero Serra, who eventually accomplished the missionary task in Upper California, shared a common ethnicity—they were mainly from the island of Mallorca, where Serra was born.

As we shall see, the Franciscan affiliation and Mallorcan identity of Serra and his leading colleagues gave a distinct character to their evangelizing effort. But to better understand the origins of their California, it is well to first analyze more extensively Spain and its American empire during the eighteenth century.

What kind of society was then expanding north from Mexico? It was a many-faceted one, characterized by competing religious, secular, local, and commercial interests. A Spanish priest, Alfredo Martínez Albiach, wrote in 1968, "The Spanish church, during the Bourbon period from 1700 to 1868 . . . repeated the same historical error of Christianity in the fourth century, under the emperor Constantine: a euphoria based on the social and religious peace of 1492 and on the reign of the Catholic kings fostered the belief that the Spanish monarchy was the image and even the realization of the kingdom of God in this world." However, neither Spain itself nor New Spain was culturally unified; nor in any other way did either embody this ideal Christian-universalist wholeness.

Indeed, the royal state in Spain was not much older than the imperial order in the New World. Both the concept of Spain as a single polity and the overseas empire were creations of the personal union of Fernando of Aragón (Fernando V, 1474–1504) and Ysabel of Castile during a period of continuous upheaval. The brutal conquest of New Spain and the destruction of Indian empires was carried out by Castilian adventurer soldiers who saw their actions as the legitimate and necessary completion of the wars their forebears had waged against the Muslims.

The year 1492 is known in the rest of the world mainly for Columbus's voyage. But that year saw three dramatic events in Spain, in a rising crescendo of importance for world history. On January 2 the last Muslim territory in Spain, the Nasrid kingdom of Granada, surrendered to Christian armies. The reconquest of Spain had taken 781 years. Then, three months later, Fernando and Ysabel, although they had negotiated the capitulation of Granada on a promise of religious tolerance, decreed the immediate conversion to Christianity of Spanish Jews, on pain of expulsion. The deadline for the Jews' departure was set at the end of July, giving them time to decide on conversion and settle their affairs.

The fall of Granada, the expulsion of the Jews, and Columbus's voyage, which began in the autumn of the same year, were all "birth traumas." The first "unified" Spain, at least geographically. The second inaugurated a new and enormously significant phase in Jewish history, that of the post-expulsion *Sephardim,* or Jews from *Sepharad,* a Hebrew name for Spain. The last produced new civilizations in the Western Hemisphere.

In both the Iberian peninsula and the New World, the Spanish Church and State struggled to establish a unitary order. The authorities in Spain sought to impose a single Christian religious identity on thousands upon thousands of converted Jews and Muslims and their descendants, through the Spanish National Inquisition, or Holy Office, and further sought to repress the regional and linguistic differences between Castilians, Catalans, Basques, and others. The rulers of New Spain paralleled this effort by pursuing the conversion of the Indians and their assimilation into the community of Spanish speakers. Neither effort succeeded fully, though New Spain may be said to have accomplished more in this direction than Spain itself. The Inquisition played a role in this effort from the beginning; a representative of the Holy Office, the Catalan Benedictine Bernat Boïl, accompanied Columbus on his second voyage. In 1508, the Spanish royal power decreed that immigration to the island of Hispaniola, and by extension, the whole of the New World, be forbidden to "children or grandchildren of renegades, Jews, or the children of those burned, or reconciled (i.e., 'confessed'), by the Inquisitors." The rule was overturned in 1511 and reinstated in 1518.

The Inquisition was a state instrument intended to create order, by terror, out of the chaotic Spain that emerged from the reconquest. Like the totalitarian ideological police of modern times, the Inquisition needed enemies as grist for its mill. Thus, although the Jewish *conversos* were the first concern of the Holy Office, they were by no means the last or even the most significant, at least in quantity. An eventual steep decline in the number of *conversos'* descendants remaining to be accused of practicing secret Judaism did not deter the Inquisition from continuing its savage work, even expanding its scope. The Holy Office went on to pursue other real and imagined internal enemies of the Spanish state. It had begun its persecutions with Jews and *conversos,* the Muslims who remained in Spain after the fall of the Arab power, Muslim converts to Christianity *(Moriscos),* and their children, but then found victims among alleged witches, Protestants, sodomites, and various other classes considered either nonconformist or simply inconvenient. Of the total, the Muslims and *Moriscos* may have occupied the largest place.

The Mexican writer Octavio Paz has emphasized in his book *Sor Juana* that Latin America, in contrast with the United States, was founded in the interest of an expanding religious orthodoxy, not by religious dissidents seeking a refuge from such. As indicated, that unifying crusade was more successful, in many respects, in the New World than it had been in the Old, at least in forging a single cultural identity.

In Peru in 1548, the Inquisition held the first *auto de fe* in the New World, followed by a similar spectacle in Mexico City in 1574. In the latter instance a Frenchman and an Englishman were burned alive as Lutherans while eighty others were punished as secret Jews, witches, or bigamists. More such executions followed in Mexico. Most importantly, however, a sense of distinct and disunited communities persisted; Paz writes that the inhabitants of New Spain, particularly the *criollos,* or whites born in the New World, were viewed with no less distrust by the Castilian authorities than were the heterogeneous masses in Spain itself. The fundamental contradiction in New Spain was "not based on the antagonisms between rich and poor or between subjected natives and European oppressors," he writes, but between the competing *criollo* and Spanish-born (peninsular) factions.

Paz has analyzed Mexican history as "abrupt and tortuous," as if reproducing its mountainous, often hostile landscape; but he has also described New Spain as "an enormous land, prosperous and peaceful. In spite of occasional uprisings, hunger, epidemics, and riots, it was public order, not turmoil, that prevailed during three centuries." The mind of New Spain "had as its ideal neither change nor the modern consequence of change, the cult of progress. Rather, its ideal was stability and permanence; its vision of perfection was to imitate, on earth, the eternal order." But this was, of course, an ideal and not a reality, as in Spain itself.

In its pursuit of this ideal, New Spain benefited from a shift in allocation of financial resources with, as shown by the Hispanist John Lynch, the colonial authorities retaining a major part of the public funds for their own needs and those of the Philippines, thus diminishing the quantity of money sent to Spain. Two later historians, John J. Te Paske and Herbert S. Klein, have confirmed that whereas in 1611–20, 55 percent of public monies in New Spain were remitted to the mother country, the percentage fell to 21 percent in 1700, even as the proportion reserved by New Spain for the Philippines continually increased.

Thus New Spain became a global financial center: its capital, Mexico City, had 100,000 residents in the seventeenth century and was then, as it is today, a megalopolis. It was also a place filled with radical questionings in literature, philosophy, theology, mysticism, and science. Between 1650 and 1699, let it be noted, exports of paper from Spain to the American possessions grew forty times, far surpassing increases in exports such as wine (which declined), olive oil, brandy, ironware, and textiles. Governed by appointees from the mother country, New Spain nonetheless remained an Indian civilization at the core of its being; Paz has called it "a unique society." Each of the succeeding phases of Mexican history involved a negation of what went before: New Spain represented the negation of the indigenous world, but New Spain was negated in turn by modern Mexico. And yet, Paz writes, "[E]ach negation contains within it the negated society—usually as a masked, a veiled presence. . . . These breaks and interruptions do not exclude a secret and persistent continuity."

We shall see how the history of California reproduces this model, in which competing European and other distant interests repeatedly erupted into the Mexican and Californian borderlands and there were transformed. Above all, Paz argues, deep social rivalries present in "old" Spain were long absent from New Spain. Such conflicts and their consequences were alluded to in a limited fashion by the English admiral and pirate Baron George Anson, who raided the Spanish Pacific coasts in 1740 during the War of Jenkins' Ear, and who left a widely read narrative of his circumnavigation of the globe, including significant comments on the Californias. Lurking at Tinian Island in the Marianas, Anson seized a Manila galleon with a treasure of four million Spanish dollars, and triumphantly returned with it to London.

Anson had found, to great effect, that the old Spanish galleon route, north past Japan to the area of the trade winds, had been abandoned. He described the insistence of the Spanish authorities, after almost two hundred years of navigation in the Pacific, that in sailing from the Philippines to Mexico their shipmasters go no further north than the lower end of the Japanese archipelago, on a line parallel to San Quintín in Baja. On such a course, they would presumably still encounter westerly winds, filling their sails and propelling their vessels to Cape Mendocino, thereby crossing the ocean in weeks rather than months. But, according to Anson, the Spanish authorities "were more apprehensive of too strong a gale, though favorable, than of the inconveniences and mortality attending a lingering and tedious voyage."

Whatever the justification for such orders, the consequence for seafarers was dire, for voyages remained long and brought the domination of scurvy. Establishing a port on the Alta California coast would at least ameliorate the problem of illness, since it could furnish the mariners "medicines, provisions, and other refreshments" at the end of the passage. Such was the advice derived from Anson's account by a Spanish commentator.

Of further interest is Anson's discussion of tensions between protectionist merchants in Spain and their colleagues in New Spain and the Philippines. The Philippine trade was condemned by some in Spain as unfair, for Chinese silk and Indian cottons transported in the Manila galleons were cheap enough to drive competing products from Valencia, Cádiz and other peninsular cities out of the market in New Spain.

According to Anson, some Spaniards had demanded the abolition of the Philippine commerce for this reason, but it was perpetuated because of the Jesuits. Thus the Spanish colonies enjoyed some autonomy in trade as well as in fiscal matters. Still, the Spanish policy of operating only one annual galleon between the Philippines and the New World contrasted with Britain's exuberant trade with the East Indies, which employed vast numbers of ships and flooded the world with silk, cotton, and every other kind of dry goods. The Dutch, French, Swedes, Danes, and Prussians, like the English, had aggressively joined the Far Eastern trade; none of these nations shared the Spanish complaint that domestic exports would suffer.

Notwithstanding the justice of such claims by peninsular manufacturers and traders, in some cases considerable, Adam Smith wrote in *The Wealth of Nations* that the London merchants had no hope of matching the personal riches of those in Cádiz—then the major Spanish port serving the empire—thanks to the gold and silver of the New World. This advantage in the exploitation of precious metals persisted even while the Spanish trade monopoly in its empire was reduced to utter fiction by English and American smugglers, who replaced the pirates as a continuing menace.

Anson's narrative assailed the Jesuit missionaries in Baja California, whom he accused of monopolizing the Manila commerce for their own financial gain. But the Jesuits were directly involved in neither the Manila trade via Cabo San Lucas nor the lucrative Baja pearl fisheries. Nevertheless, being the only Europeans present, they fully controlled the remaining economy of that peninsula, which then involved little more than export of a small wine production to the mainland of New Spain. Or so a Jesuit commentator replied to Anson.

Anti-Jesuit arguments such as Anson put forth were exaggerated, but attracted great attention in Europe. The Jesuits' protorationalism, energy, and intellectual elan (which led many of them, like Kino, to dedicate themselves to scientific research), irritated some, while others were scandalized by the Society's supposed political manipulations, its purported wealth and corruption, and its "Utopian" ideology.

As Paz has written in *Sor Juana,* Jesuit enterprises were based on a belief that history was "a gradual unfolding of a universal and supernatural truth." Seeking to realize an earthly expression of such an order, a Jesuit, Roque González de Santa Cruz, established a renowned system of "reductions" or Indian colonies in Paraguay in 1609. González founded nine villages, and the community grew to encompass fifty-four settlements with 150,000 indigenous residents. Spanish civil and military authorities were excluded from the Jesuits' realm. The Paraguayan "reductions" were credited with the preservation of the Guaraní Indian language, which is still widely spoken in the country. The Jesuits propounded assimilation of native cultures through missionization from above, while maintaining the government of local rulers and even syncretizing, or merging, Christian and pagan beliefs. This conception favored the survival of local autonomy and identity, and in Europe seemed enormously threatening to absolutism.

The Jesuits were expelled from Spain and its dominions in 1767. By then they had established fifteen missions in Baja California. In 1773 Pope Clement XIV, a Franciscan but formerly considered among their friends, disbanded the Society of Jesus altogether. Only Protestant Prussia and Orthodox Russia, remarkably enough, refused to honor the papal bull, and sheltered the Order. It was officially revived by Pope Pius VII in 1814.

The Spanish empire that sought expansion on the Pacific coast of North America in the eighteenth century was an enlightened despotism. But, both in Europe and in the New World, it was still riven by differing local and global interests. Its Bourbon rulers had committed themselves to a contradictory "reform." Not for the last time California, although still more a concept than a reality, was the coveted prize in a world-spanning ideological rivalry. At the moment of their expulsion, as noted, the Jesuits maintained an extensive network of missions in Baja California, mainly on the east coast of the peninsula, beginning at Loreto and continuing south to San José del Cabo as well as north. The Baja missions were turned over to the Franciscans, who governed them until 1773 when they were transferred to the Dominicans. The Franciscans' eyes now turned north, to the virgin territory of Alta California.

The division between Baja and Alta California reflected geographical logic and practical decisions by the civil authorities in New Spain; but the "intellectual" split between the authority of the Franciscans, from an area near San Diego north, and that of the Dominicans, southward from that point, had a more subtle and more lasting effect. It *created* The Border, a phenomenon that was never imposed from outside but developed organically. Obviously The Border is exceptionally significant today, even as the line between the United States and Mexican Californias seems extraordinarily permeable, with some 30 million people crossing it each year.

IN 1767, Gaspar de Portolà i de Rovira, a middle-aged nobleman and captain of dragoons from Balaguer, near Lleida in western Catalonia, was sent to Baja California with secret orders to remove the Jesuits and assume governorship over the peninsula. The changes at the Baja missions, along with the origins and local activities of Portolà and his soon-to-be companion, the Franciscan missionary Junípero Serra, would prove of transcendent importance for the history of modern California.

The following year another event occurred that was also destined to considerably alter the historical development of Mexico and California: the Spanish authorities received reports that foreign ships had appeared in the far north Pacific. The new seafarers were Russians. In 1768, two master mariners from the imperial Admiralty College in St. Petersburg, captains Pyotr Krenitsyn and Mikhail Levashov, sailed to the Aleutian Islands, where they wintered.

These navigators' voyages followed a series of expeditions that began in 1728 with the voyage of a Dane, Vitus Bering, to the Asian side of the strait later named for him. In 1733, the Russian empress Anna ordered a second north Pacific expedition under Bering, which confirmed the existence of the northern Kuriles and the Aleutian Islands. Bering had been sent in search of furs, increasingly exploited by Russian trappers.

There were many such fur-hunting expeditions to the north Pacific islands between the 1740s and the end of the century. News of these explorations led the Russian governor of Siberia, Denis Chicherin, to call for a formal survey in 1763. Empress Catherine supported the proposal, and mandated that naval officers be assigned to the effort, in government ships. The Russians had as yet accomplished little in their colonization of Alaska, but even their minor presence in the north Pacific caused an uproar in Mexico. Bourbon reforms for improved defense of the empire were under way, and the Russian threat added urgency to them.

Late in 1768, Portolà was ordered north, to fortify the ports of San Diego and Monterey in Alta California. This Catalan nobleman had been joined in Baja by a group of Franciscans sent to take over the missions from the Jesuits. The missionaries took ship in the nearby harbor of San Blas, a small port below the Tropic of Cancer, scorched by relentless sun and filled with screaming birds, that had just been established as the main Spanish naval station on the Pacific coast of Mexico, also in response to anxiety over the Russians. Like Portolà, the leading figures among the clerics, who came originally from Mallorca, spoke Catalan.

Nearly all the military and nautical personnel serving with Portolà and Serra were Catalan and Mallorcan, as well. The founders of Spanish California were therefore neither Castilian nobles nor *criollos* from Mexico. The distinct cultural background shared by these soldiers, priests, and mariners, who were men apart from their fellows, is of considerable interest.

A diverse and tumultuous intellectual environment produced the men whose names are found so prominently in our California: Portolà, Serra, Palou, Crespí, Moraga, Font, and others. These Catalans and Mallorcans who created California came from one borderland to another, with a distinctive consciousness as outsiders, as new men bursting with a truly Californian sense of intellectual enterprise, reinventing themselves on an unknown terrain. They had been chosen to defend the furthest outposts of empire, including the route to the Philippines, from "northern" aggressors, Russians and English speakers, in a remarkable concatenation of circumstances. For them the Americas represented a sanctuary of opportunities, as it had for the English settlers on the Atlantic—in pursuit of economic and ideological ambitions that were different from the goals of north European religious dissenters, yet partially resembled them. To the indigenous Californians and to local patriots of New Spain, such distinctions among peninsular "Spaniards" may have seemed irrelevant; yet California, from its beginning, shared the cultural dynamism that has historically characterized the Catalan lands in contrast with the stagnant obscurantism of Castile. The Catalans and Mallorcans, whether commercial or clerical, always searched for "new ways, new roads," in the phrase of the Catalan historian Carles Martínez Shaw.

We have reached the threshold of California's real history. None of the individuals so far discussed could be called an authentic Californian, notwithstanding their characters and their role in California's origins. Before proceeding to account for the men and works, headed by Portolà and Serra, that created the first European settlement in Alta California, it is well to discuss a personage whose existence cannot be fully confirmed, but who was the first "resident" of whom we know something, and who best deserves the title of First Californian.

This is Chingichnish, the central figure in a new form of the *toloache* religion that emerged among southern California Indians almost simultaneously with the arrival of Portolà and Serra. The Chingichnish religion was a "reformed" version of the ancient cults based on *Datura* use. Some of its beliefs resemble those of Christianity; according to the anthropologists Bean and Vane, it may have developed out of sporadic contacts between indigenous Californians and visiting Europeans, including Christian survivors of shipwrecks and runaway seamen.

Chingichnish, a "*shaman*-like hero," was said to have appeared in the Gabrielino area, near today's Long Beach. (Some early accounts traced his cult to Santa Catalina Island.) His teachings demanded "obedience, fasting, self-sacrifice," according to the anthropologist C. G. DuBois, and featured both an elaborate ritual and utter secrecy. Chingichnish, a new divinity, had come to supplant the previously worshipped god. He was said to be omnipresent, to live in the sky, and to have turned humans into spirits.

Chingichnish brought a new array of religious institutions to the people, and supplied a group of rather frightening "avengers"—rattlesnakes, bears, and tarantulas, among others—to maintain the loyalty of the communicants and punish transgressions. Ravens served Chingichnish as messengers, reporting to him when humans violated ritual practice and community rules. Kroeber wrote that in the Luiseño versions of the cult "trials of endurance followed the general drinking of the Jimson weed. The novices were blistered with fire, whipped with nettles, and laid out on anthills." Here the cult shows a parallel with the mortification, along with an apocalyptic world outlook, that characterized the Franciscans—a remarkable coincidence.

Kroeber wrote of the Chingichnish phenomenon,

> [I]f it were not for the wholly native flavor of the ideas connected with the cult, and the absence of European symbols, it might be possible to think of missionary influence. . . . The idea of a present and tremendously powerful god, dictating not only ritual but the conduct of daily life—a truly universal deity and not merely one of a class of spirits or animals—is certainly a remarkable phenomenon to have appeared natively among any American group north of Mexico.

Indigenous prophets whose preachings anticipated either the arrival or the doctrines of Christian invaders are an old affair in American Indian studies. The most fascinating such phenomenon is that of Chilam Balam, or the priest Balam (Jaguar), who lived in the village of Maní, in the hinterland of Yucatán, *circa* 1500–1520.

Balam predicted the imminent arrival of bearded men from the east, bringing with them a new religion—meaning priests of a returned Kukulcán or Quetzalcoatl, a Toltec-Mayan culture hero. When the Spanish invaders appeared on schedule, Chilam Balam became the most famous Mayan of the time, his reputation continuing to the present day. In the late seventeenth and early eighteenth centuries "books of Chilam Balam" surfaced in towns throughout Yucatán. These were manuscripts in the Mayan language, recorded in Latin letters by Indians who had become Christian scribes and priests while continuing to participate in their own people's culture. They included ritual texts and calendrical data from the pre-European Mayans, prophecies, and other valuable documents.

The *toloache* religion came to California from Mexico, as did the Christianity that supplanted it (although the Christian missionaries, as previously noted, were not Mexican). It is perhaps therefore understandable that parallel figures such as Chingichnish and Chilam Balam would appear. Chingichnish is our Chilam Balam: he is a true Californian not only in his origins and his psychedelic practices, but in the content of his revelation as a reaffirmation of indigenous culture and an implied protest against encroaching European imperialism. He was also the pretext for the first European-style intellectual work produced wholly in and of California, an account of his worship at San Juan Capistrano, recorded by a Mallorcan priest, Father Jeròni Boscana Mulet. Boscana Mulet's account of "Chinigchinich" was translated into English and published in New York in 1846, as *Chinigchinich: A historical account of the Origins, Customs and Traditions of the Indians of the Missionary Establishment of San Juan Capistrano, Alta California, called the Acagchemen Nation.* Extremely obscure, this item was the real beginning of California literature.

Kroeber described the continued diffusion of the Chingichnish cult inland as late as 1850. From Bean and Vane we learn that the secrecy of the cult was so thorough that little of its inner doctrine was known until few adherents remained; grown very old and alone and fearing it would disappear altogether, these surviving elders sought to record it by informing anthropologists. The Chingichnish cult was observed until the 1970s at the Rincon and Pauma reservations, two small Luiseño reservations in San Diego County. Today the Rincon reservation, like many others around the country, operates a rather poor casino offering card games and bingo.

IN JANUARY 1769, with his new orders to strengthen Spanish influence on the Alta California coast, Portolà headed north as chief of a Sacred Expedition made up of four parties. Two groups were to proceed by sea: one aboard a barkentine with eleven sails, the *San Carlos,* captained by Vicenç Vila, the other in two ships, the *San Antonio,* whose master was a distinguished Mallorcan navigator, Joan Perés, and the *San José,* a small packet boat carrying supplies.

Two other groups were to march up the peninsula: a vanguard under the officer Ferran Ribera i Montcada, accompanied by Fathers Joan Crespí Fiol and Fermín Lasuén, a Basque from Vitoria (Gasteiz), and a main detail commanded by Portolà himself and joined by Serra. The four expeditions were to meet at the port of San Diego.

The sailors aboard the *San Carlos* were accompanied by some twelve to twenty "Catalan Volunteers" under a 35-year-old officer named Pere Fages Beleta, a self-described minor aristocrat from Guissona, a place in western Catalonia not far from the birthplace of Portolà. These soldiers belonged to a body of 1,200 men recruited in the 1760s from the ranks of the Second Regiment of Light Infantry of Catalonia, stationed in Barcelona, to form a

"Mountain Riflemen's Company of Catalonia." Their name was changed to the *Compañía Franca de Voluntarios de Cataluña,* or Free Company of Catalan Volunteers, and led by captain Agustí Callís they had come to Baja California by way of Cádiz, Cuba, and a military action against Indians in Sonora. Fages Beleta was to play a part in the early history of the new colony as significant as that of his commander, Portolà.

In addition, Fages Beleta and the Catalan Volunteers were assisted by a brilliant military engineer and cartographer, a Catalan from Barcelona named Miquel de Constançó. Commissioned to choose sites and design fortresses and other structures at San Diego and Monterey, de Constançó was one of the outstanding intellectual figures in the Spanish imperial administration. The provisions carried by the explorers were considerable, including quantities of olive oil, wine, and brandy, seed and plants for cultivation, as well as farming tools and, of course, arms and ammunition.

The first party, in the *San Antonio,* reached San Diego in April 1769, just before the arrival of the *San Carlos.* Both vessels were filled with sick men, struck down by scurvy. The Catalans and Mallorcans built shelters at San Diego and awaited the Ribera i Montcada party, coming by land. Ribera i Montcada arrived within two weeks, his men fit but hungry. After five more weeks, Portolà's group joined them. Soon Portolà, spurred by the passing days and fearful of an unknown style of winter, led Ribera i Montcada, Fages Beleta, de Constançó, Crespí Fiol, and assorted Catalan Volunteers and California Indians north by land to locate Monterey, where they expected to meet the packet boat *San José* with fresh provisions. Along their route deer, shellfish, and geese were plentiful sources of food, along with nuts and grains obtained from natives.

Serra had come up the Baja peninsula on foot, doing without a horse even though he suffered from an infected leg; this was an expression of his Franciscan dedication to simplicity, sacrifice, and poverty. He remained at San Diego and began work at the first of the Alta California missions, named for St. Didacus, a fifteenth-century Franciscan lay brother famous for his healing powers. Crespí Fiol, a fellow Mallorcan who was Serra's dearest friend and his partner in religious study, proceeded north. On July 27, 1769, in the hills of today's Orange County, Crespí Fiol commented on a quintessentially Californian experience: he was the first European to record an earthquake on the territory of Upper California. Crespí Fiol described the temblor as "horrifying," with four shocks in as many hours.

The Catalans and Mallorcans increasingly interacted with Indians in their march north. Above Ventura the soldiers named Pitas Point for the whistles (*pitos*) blown by dancing Indians, who kept the invaders awake and fearful all night. Carpintería (the carpentry shop) was so called after the Spaniards observed some Indians working on a canoe. Gaviota received its name from a seagull killed by a soldier. Fages Beleta, Crespí Fiol, and de Constançó surveyed and named many more locations, on the coast and later inland.

The party reached Monterey in October, but had missed Monterey Bay itself; they had been misled by the discrepancy between the descriptive accounts left by Manila-galleon pilots and the actual coastal configuration. They continued north, and "discovered" a far greater natural landmark. De Constançó observed the Farallones Islands on October 31, or Halloween, appropriately enough considering the later history of the region. The explorers believed that the Gulf of the Farallones, outside the Golden Gate (of which they knew nothing), and with Point Reyes visible just to its north, was the Bahía de San Francisco of which many had spoken but which few could locate. Then the group came upon the inland sea that is the true San Francisco Bay.

This journey laid the foundation for the Spanish colonial advance into Alta California. In 1770, the Catalans and Mallorcans returned to Monterey and Serra officially established the mission of San Carlos Borromeo (named for a major figure in the Catholic Counter-Reformation), and the *Presidio* or military headquarters of Monterey.

Portolà returned to Mexico, leaving Fages Beleta as *comandante.* The hardy Fages Beleta conducted extensive reconnaissance trips into the interior. He led a group of his men from Monterey to the eastern shore of San Francisco Bay in a failed attempt to find Point Reyes by land. One of his soldiers, the Catalan sergeant Joan Puig, was probably the first European to see the opening of the Golden Gate from inside the bay, but their path to Point Reyes was blocked by the bay itself and its northeastern river delta. On a second trip in the same direction, in 1772, they followed the delta waters upstream to the great Central Valley. Later that year, Fages Beleta led a group from San Diego through Cajón Pass into the Mojave Desert, returning via the lower end of the immense valley.

Monterey was to become the capital of Spanish California. Serra would live the rest of his life and lie buried at the mission of San Carlos Borromeo. He moved the mission from its original site near the *Presidio* to the Carmel Valley, mainly to escape the conflicts created by the sexual attentions of the Spanish troops to Indian women whose souls Father Serra hoped to save.

Serra remains an enigma; today's Californians know nothing meaningful about the Mallorcan missionary. What we think we know is a function of our narcissism, derived only from his fifteen years in California and lacking any awareness of his social context or his authentic thoughts and motivations.

Almost from the beginning, Serra has existed in California historical consciousness in two parallel and equally caricatural forms. One image of Serra's reality is found at the heart of a sentimental civic myth, fostered in the early twentieth century by Californians who sought to match the colonial past of the eastern United States with a distinguished European legacy of our own. In this accounting, the Spanish mission fathers introduced civilization to their Indian converts, who were viewed as naked and ignorant—nearly subhuman.

In the alternative view, which was favored by nineteenth-century Protestants and which reappeared in the 1970s, Serra is portrayed as a tool of pure Spanish imperialism and a brutal enslaver of the Indians. Indigenous life before the Europeans arrived is presented as ecologically balanced, idyllic, and humane.

Both versions are fantasies, and there is little to be gained by trying to extract grains of truth from either. Certainly Serra was a Catholic missionary of his time, with all the limitations that suggests. He had sworn to having no Jewish or Muslim ancestry when he took his vows as a Franciscan. However, his maternal grandmother's family names were Abraham, on her father's side, and Isaac, on her mother's. The Pere Serra family of Petra, Mallorca (his birthplace), to which he perhaps belonged, may have been descended from Arab slaves freed after their conversion to Christianity. In addition, the name Serra appears on a roster of nearly a hundred names of Mallorcan families converted from Judaism, with members later accused of secret Jewish worship. Curiously, Serra had been turned down for seminary study when he first applied, supposedly because of his small stature. Even such long-standing forms of discrimination, however, began to disappear in the late eighteenth century; descendants of *conversos* in Palma de Mallorca were freed from limits on their right of residence in 1782 by the reforming Bourbon king Carlos III.

Serra may well have come under Inquisitorial scrutiny; but he was himself named an Inquisitorial commissary in Mexico, and as a missionary in
the Sierra Gorda of Mexico, before coming to Alta California, he denounced some Mexicans as witches. Nevertheless, and aside from the issue
of possible Jewish or Muslim ancestry, it is obvious that the minds of Serra
and his companions were far more complex than either of the two myths of
Serra would suggest.

Serra did not deal easily with his colleagues in the organization of Spanish Alta California; but then, it was not easy to keep the peace between and
among soldiers and missionaries. Serra early on grew to dislike Fages Beleta—
first for his refusal to turn over naval stores for missionary use, later for his alleged violent outbursts, general arrogance, discrimination against non-Cata-
lans in soldierly ranks, hoarding of the best food for himself even when his
men suffered dire illness, and myriad interferences with the missionary effort.

Yet Fages Beleta was a man of considerable parts. In addition to his surveys of the internal territories, he became known as *El Oso* or The Bear because of his fondness for hunting, and his ability in pursuit of predators
won him favor with the Indians at Monterey. But he was also among those
whose interest in the indigenous inhabitants went beyond the casual to assume an ethnographic cast: his reports to Mexico City included word lists
for Indian languages in addition to descriptions of flora and fauna. Nevertheless, in 1774 he was sent back to Mexico. There he married Na Eulàlia
Callís, daughter of his military superior, Agustí Callís. In 1782 Fages Beleta
returned to Monterey, serving as governor of Alta California for nine years.

Fages Beleta brought his wife back to Monterey, and there ensued one
of the least known and most interesting episodes to foreshadow the California to come. Conflict erupted in the governor's household: Na Eulàlia,
known as *la gobernadora,* attacked her husband, accusing him of adultery,
separating from him, even, according to some sources, demanding a divorce. This incident could be seen as a beginning, or at least a harbinger, of
feminism in California. Or, as with the Indians devoted to the *toloache* religion, the mutineers and others who read Montalvo, and the mariners who
nearly went mad on the high seas while serving Cabrillo and Ferrer, it may
simply be that there have always been some people who find contact with
California deranging, as they still do.

Na Eulàlia Callís—she typically appears under her own rather than
her husband's name—"seems to have been either a lady of too high and ex-

acting a spirit or to have been sadly abused in her new home," according to the nineteenth-century California historian Theodore Hittell. She was "loud and boisterous in her complaints. There was great scandal." When an officer and friend of both parties met with Na Eulàlia and sought a reconciliation, he compared the encounter with a fire in a powder magazine, indicating, as Hittell wrote, "that the materials with which he was called upon to deal were exceedingly explosive." Na Eulàlia was even threatened with shackles. Finally, however, her family, which included children, was reunited.

———

SUCH PERSONAL RIVALRIES and controversies were characteristic of the obvious stresses caused by isolation in and fear of an unknown land, and were compounded by the cultural and other strains beneath the surface of colonial life. Yet the Spanish enterprise in California might seem to have fulfilled the promise Octavio Paz discerned in New Spain, that of an order based on peace.

For the California Indians, however, the European invasion was a disaster, largely because of diseases, which preceded the Spanish missions: venereal illnesses first, followed by respiratory afflictions, diphtheria, and measles. Obviously, the arrival of Christianity qualitatively changed the environment of California Indian civilization. Still, it is manifestly unfair to imagine that the Spanish missionaries were entirely or even mainly responsible for the cultural and spiritual decline of the California Indian.

As the anthropologists Bean and Vane have written,

[S]ome native Californians were Christianized only by force, [but] others accepted the new religion apparently because the Spanish demonstrated possession of kinds of power that appeared desirable. The acceptance of Christianity did not mean that native religious systems disappeared. Native religious ceremonies persisted alongside Catholicism, often tolerated by the priests under the guise of "secular" events, but sometimes carried out secretly. The extreme decrease in native population in the last part of the nineteenth century and the concomitant "melting pot" philosophy on the part of the Anglo-Americans were more destructive to native religious systems than Catholicism.

The coming of the Anglos, eighty years after Portolà and Serra appeared at San Diego, brought California Protestant missionaries who, in contrast with the Catholic priests, were completely intolerant of any syncretism of Christian and indigenous beliefs and sought the obliteration of Indian spirituality.

Thus Indian California reacted variously to the missionary presence. The promise of peace, central to the Christian faith, induced mass conversion at, for example, the mission of San Luís Rey, where the local Quechla Indians were tired of endemic warfare with their neighbors. The Chingichnish cult, however, became a form of resistance to the missionaries. Another was flight, and many new converts or "neophytes" were reported as "runaways" from the missions over the decades. Finally there was open revolt.

Nine villages near San Diego rose up and destroyed the mission in 1775, killing a Mallorcan priest, father Lluís Jaume Vallespir, who had been nicknamed "the sermonizer" by the Indians. Serra, let it be noted, successfully appealed to the Spanish authorities to pardon the perpetrators, offering them "eternal life" as Christians in place of execution. Ten years later, the Indians at the mission of San Gabriel rebelled under a chief's daughter and medicine woman, Toypurina (who was also pardoned after her capture). A three-year insurrection broke out in 1793 at San Francisco Bay, and similar incidents were reported at the missions of Santa Clara and San Juan Bautista between 1790 and 1800. Priests were also poisoned and otherwise assassinated.

The greatest of the California Indian revolts occurred in 1824, at the missions of La Purísima Concepción and Santa Barbara; thousands of natives seized La Purísima and armed themselves. After the movement spread to Santa Barbara, the Indians attacked the *Presidio* and then retreated into the countryside. It took the Mexican authorities four months to suppress the movement.

Abuses inflicted on the missionized Indians were protested by some among the Spanish from very early on. A priest at the mission of San Miguel, father Antonio Horra, denounced the Franciscans to the authorities in Mexico, alleging wholesale cruelty involving persistent application of the whip, chains, and stocks. Horra was unfortunately declared insane and deported from Alta California with an armed escort. But word of the disciplinary régime at the missions had spread throughout the indigenous population, and already in 1787 the missionaries had begun employing military help in obtaining conversions.

Father Serra died in 1784, having overseen the establishment of nine large and solid missions, the last, San Buenaventura (named for the Franciscan philosopher known as the "Seraphic Doctor") in 1782. They included the mission and *Presidio* at San Francisco, founded in 1776 mainly through the efforts of the Catalan captain Josep Joaquim Moraga and the Franciscans Francesc Palou Amengual, Tomás Eixarch, and Pere Font. Font, a Catalan from Girona, accompanied the explorer Juan Bautista Anza with a party of Catalan Volunteers, Mexican colonists of both sexes, and Indian interpreters, on a long and roundabout trail from Tubac, near Tucson, overland to the San Gabriel Valley and thence north to the Bay. The group totaled some 240 people: in addition they drove with them nearly 700 horses and mules, and more than 300 head of cattle intended as food. The *pueblo* or civil settlement of Los Angeles—*El Pueblo del Río de Nuestra Señora Reina de los Ángeles de la Porciúncula,* or The Town on the River of Our Lady Queen of Angels of the Little Portion—was founded in 1781.

In 1786 the Alta California missions had their first known European but non-Spanish visitor, the French admiral Jean-François de Galaup, Comte de La Pérouse, who had been sent on a global voyage by King Louis XVI, and who stands as the greatest eighteenth-century Pacific navigator after James Cook. At the moment of La Pérouse's arrival in Alta California, ten missions were operating. His reports include numerous piquant details: at Monterey, he found that "the sound of the sea, rolling in upon the foot of the sand dunes along the coast, can be heard more than a league away." The French observed the bay covered with pelicans, and also saw spouting whales, the ancient guardians of the Pacific coast; they were puzzled by the stench emitted by the water the cetaceans discharged.

The French explorer also noted the considerable economic superiority of Alta California when compared with the Baja peninsula. La Pérouse's vision of the landscape was paradisiacal in the familiar Mediterranean manner:

> [T]he healthfulness of the air, the fertility of the earth, and last but not least, the abundance of every species of fur-bearing animal, which assures a profitable trade with China, have given this part of America an infinite advantage over Lower California, whose unhealthful climate and sterile ground cannot be compensated by a few pearls which have been torn from the bottom of the sea. No country has a greater abundance of fish and game of every kind. All the aquatic birds are found in the greatest number on the ponds and the seacoast. The earth is incredibly productive. It is perfect for growing

vegetables. The harvests of corn, barley, wheat and peas can be compared only with those of Chile. The average return on wheat is about 75 to one. Finally, the climate is very similar to that of the provinces of southern France.

With Spain and France allied in the Family Compact between their Bourbon rulers, La Pérouse, unlike later foreign visitors, was welcomed by the priests to the San Carlos mission at Carmel. His description of the mission mentioned the numerous copies of paintings by Italian masters that decorated the church; many portrayed "scenes of heaven and hell especially calculated to impress new converts." He was less flattering when discussing the "wretched" huts in which the Indians lived—although, he said, the Indians insisted they preferred simple structures open to fresh air which, once their human occupants inevitably grew tired of sharing them with vermin, could be burned and replaced in a few hours.

La Pérouse is significant to California's intellectual history for his revulsion at the clerical repression of the Indians. He warned that restrictions on Indian rights, as well as on the ownership of private property by non-Indians, could retard the growth of population. His critique of the mission régime was echoed by many more visitors to Alta California. Clear-sighted in his sentiments, La Pérouse has been credited with a rationalist conception of the Indians' humanity.

In 1788, two years after the visit of La Pérouse, the authorities in New Spain were alarmed by fresh reports of Russian commerce in Aleutian and Alaskan waters. This news may have originated in the voyage of the *Tri Svyatityelya (Three Saints),* which had sailed from a Russian base at Kodiak Island to explore and claim the Alaskan mainland. A scouting expedition to the region made contact with the Russians, who informed the Spanish of their intention to place a colony at Nootka Sound on the west coast of Vancouver Island. The next year, a party was sent to Nootka to preemptively found a Spanish outpost, but there encountered even more troubling outsiders: one ship under British colors and two flying the proud Stars and Stripes of the world's newest maritime contender, the recently independent United States. The appearance of American ships was to some extent unsurprising to the Spanish, for the empire had fought a war with Britain, beginning in 1779, over Madrid's support of the rebellious Atlantic colonies. The peninsular authorities imposed a war tax on all their subjects, collected in Alta California under the supervision of Serra and amounting to one peso paid by each Indian at the missions and two pesos levied on each Spaniard or Mexican.

Autumn of 1789 saw a further Spanish decision: an eighty-member force of the Catalan Volunteers was dispatched to Nootka under captain Pere d'Alberni Teixidor, a 44-year-old from Tortosa in Catalonia. Coming to Mexico as a sublieutenant of Callís and Fages Beleta, d'Alberni Teixidor had enjoyed a series of more or less accidental career advances. But he was also a remarkable figure reminiscent of La Pérouse, admittedly on a lesser scale, and his biography provokes one to wonder how different the history of the Spanish in the New World might have been if more individuals of his caliber had participated in the imperial venture.

Pere d'Alberni Teixidor was, first, a conscientious and dedicated professional officer. He shared in every task; when trenches were to be dug he marked out guidelines, then worked alongside his men until they were completed. He demanded warm clothing and new weapons for his troops for their passage to Nootka. His soldiers went to San Blas to await ships, but d'Alberni Teixidor delayed his own departure, remaining in Guadalajara to care for four sick troopers. He was named commandant at Santa Cruz de Nútka; small groups of Catalans would fan out through the far northern Pacific, surveying and assessing local conditions between Nootka and the Strait of Juan de Fuca to the south and the Aleutians to the northwest. They left names on the coasts, including Port Alberni on Vancouver Island and, in Alaska, Cordova and Valdez. The harbor of Valdez, on what today is known as Prince William Sound, crowned by Valdez Glacier and the Chugach mountains, is among the most beautiful in the world.

D'Alberni Teixidor was also a figure of controversy, as befits a California pioneer. He had the range of contradictory traits widely ascribed in the Hispanic world to Catalans: vigor, loyalty, efficiency, and personal modesty along with, by contrast, a considerable excitability and sense of outrage when subjected to perceived injustice, as was previously seen in the case of Na Eulàlia Callís. Such attitudes run very deep in Catalonia, which has undergone repeated national and political uprisings throughout its history, and which in the nineteenth and twentieth centuries produced a remarkable anarchist labor movement as well as important radical nationalists.

Indeed, d'Alberni Teixidor had gone to foggy Nootka with a clouded reputation. In 1789, just before his trip to the north, he had been charged with insubordination because of an incident in San Blas that has been notably described by the historian Joseph Sánchez. D'Alberni Teixidor's troops had not been paid for two months, and when he went to military headquarters to press an inquiry over the delay he was treated disrespectfully, driving his temper to explosion. He raged at commissary chief Antonio Villaurrútia, his superior, threatening and charging him with discrimination against the Catalan soldiers. D'Alberni Teixidor was ordered to place himself under arrest, and refused. He was punished by 70 days' house arrest, so that when he led his men to Nootka, facing all the risks and sacrifices implied by such a project, he did so under legal sanction.

The historian Joseph Sánchez describes d'Alberni Teixidor as "unusually talented," inventive, and imaginative. His relations with the Indians at Nootka—among the greatest canoe builders in the world, also known for their magnificent contributions to the "Northwest Coast" style of art—proved excellent, even though they had been mistreated by and grown suspicious of the Spanish who came before him. D'Alberni Teixidor studied their language, compiling a word list of more than six hundred entries, and he even composed a song in Nootka and Spanish, set to an Andalusian tune, in praise of the local chief, Macuina. He trained his Catalan personnel to perform it in chorus, to the chief's delight. D'Alberni Teixidor also completed extensive observations of the weather and some successful farming experiments, analyzing the potential of various crops. His linguistic and meteorological studies remain of great value. More importantly for him and his soldiers, d'Alberni Teixidor grew so popular with the Indians that fresh fish and deer meat, gifts from the natives, regularly graced his garrison's mess table.

The Russians met with the masters of three Spanish ships in Prince William Sound in 1791, and a Russian representative whose name would be of great importance in California history, Aleksandr Baranov, sought to communicate with them through a South Slav interpreter aboard one of the Spanish vessels. The Spanish officers, according to Baranov, had been sent out to complete the survey of Nootka and its surroundings, and they emphasized their intention to establish Spanish authority there. But they also expressed sympathy for Russian claims as a buffer against the British, and indifference to the fur trade, given that furs had no market in the Spanish empire. The British, on the other hand, were making quite a profit on otters. The Russian interest in Nootka diminished, for they were by now established at Kodiak and were actively colonizing the Alaska mainland.

Nootka was a well fortified and armed but frigid and very isolated Spanish post where, in the beginning, many men fell to the blade of scurvy. D'Alberni Teixidor left Nootka in 1792, returning to Alta California and then to Mexico, and the northernmost colony of the Spanish empire was abandoned. Notwithstanding his earlier difficulties, he became the top officer of the Catalan troops in the Pacific zone, succeeding Callís, who died in 1782.

The personality of Pere d'Alberni Teixidor, whom we shall encounter again in California, was emblematic of something far greater than he or his contemporaries could have imagined. In him the cultural difference that set Catalans against Castilians was both accentuated by the entrepreneurial energies let loose among the Catalans by Bourbon trade reforms and combined with a rationalist attitude that reflected a deeper division within Bourbon Spain and Europe at large. Under the surface of society, an archaic and exhausted monarchical and clerical absolutism was giving way slowly, so slowly, to the growing self-consciousness of the incipient revolutionary ruling class, the commercial *bourgeoisie*. The French Revolution was beginning as d'Alberni Teixidor and his colleagues were preparing to colonize distant Nootka. Ideas of individual enterprise and responsibility, citizenship, and the general welfare of the nation would burst apart the brittle structures of imperial Spain and New Spain as if they were dry wood, and the kindling would light a fire destined to burn long and hot. The exploits of the Catalans and Mallorcans in Alta California—Portolà, Serra, Fages, Crespí, d'Alberni, and the rest—were the swan song of the Spanish empire.

PARADOXICALLY, THE REVOLUTION in France would have a greater immediate effect on the politics of New Spain, and therefore on the intellectual history of California, than the geographically nearer American War of Independence, although the latter altered economic relations in the Pacific with great suddenness. The American ships the Spanish found anchored at Nootka in 1788 were among many sent to the Northwest Coast by New England merchants—the "Boston men"—engaged in the international fur trade, beginning in the 1780s and continuing for at least forty years.

In the twenty years after 1769, Spanish Alta California became a settled society. The Mallorcan origin and Franciscan communitarianism of Serra and his colleagues may have accelerated this process by creating a sense of unity and coordination among the missions that seems to have been absent in the Jesuit establishments in Baja. Furthermore, the Alta California missions remained under the control of a succession of Catalans. But the idyll enjoyed by the Spanish in Alta California was doomed by the triumphant World Idea embodied, soon enough, in the person of Napoleon. In truth, the Spain created by the empire—since the empire transformed Spain no less than Spain did the New World—rested on a defective economic base from the beginning, and the collapse of Spanish power had begun three hundred years before it became manifest. As Manuel Fernández Grandizo, a twentieth-century Mexican historian, wrote,

> Nowhere but in Spain did the dead so thoroughly obstruct the works of the living. . . . In no European country was there so dizzying and profound a decline. . . . Its prostration was so great that Spain remained far behind the rest of western Europe, and hardly contributed at all to the progress of humanity beginning in the seventeenth century.

The enormous and complex internal contradictions within the mother country and the effort of the Inquisition and other institutions to effect an illusory unification of Spanish society imposed severe and deeply resented limitations on the entrepreneurial intelligence of the Catalans and other merchants in Spain. These problems seemed much diminished within such colonies as New Spain. But even as life in Mexico, according to Octavio Paz, seemed far more vital and offered much greater opportunities for individual reward, the colossal mineral wealth exported from the New World, which excited the envy of Adam Smith, fatally clogged the arteries of Spain. To again cite Fernández Grandizo,

> No European power was as thoroughly prepared as Spain to launch itself into the storm of capital accumulation that followed the discovery of America and the securing of the sea route to India via Africa; while no other country came out of the experience so broken down. . . . Holland and England, France and even Germany to a degree, became rich and made their worldwide commerce the basis for prosperity and dominance in later centuries, while Spain ruined itself, depopulated itself, lost its technical capacity, saw its industry disappear and its fields lie fallow, its cities losing inhabitants or, on the coast, overcrowded.

None of this came about by chance. Put at its simplest, Spain choked on the gold and silver of the New World. Given the country's flimsy industrial base, the precious metals looted from the Indian civilizations of Mexico, Panamá, and the Andes had an irresistibly destructive impact on the economy of the mother country. The immediate consequence of the first shipments of gold and silver to Spain was one of the worst inflationary cycles on record. The value of money fell and the prices of commodities rose throughout the country, and the effects extended to the rest of Europe, including faraway Russia. In the 250 years after Columbus's voyages, the price of wheat in Spain rose nearly 1,000 percent. Every Spanish product reflected the same catastrophic inflation, made even worse by rising demand. The internal market was permanently and increasingly undermined. The main effects of this long crisis were degradation of the quality of goods and the deterioration of agriculture, which came to be widely replaced on the central Spanish plateau by grazing of sheep. Trades and crafts were impoverished. And, of course, taxation also grew with inflation.

The wealth of the New World was usurped by the political requirements of the aristocratic class—including, frankly, such projects as the expansion into California—rather than being employed as productive capital. Speculation in Spanish metals and goods became an international phenomenon, exceptionally harmful for the Spanish economy, and exacerbated by a negative balance of payments. Spanish money was worth more outside the country than within its borders, and the grotesque disparity between the enormous quantity of gold and silver in the country and the low level of output of goods made money the chief export.

Above all, as Fernández Grandizo concludes, "A manufacturing Empire with no manufactures, a nationality without a nation as its base, are chimeras."

In Spain the French Revolution at first had little visible impact, which is not surprising considering the ill-health in the Iberian Peninsula of the bourgeoisie, who were the decisive element in the Parisian upheaval. But there was much greater intellectual excitement in New Spain at the revolutionary developments in Europe, as Paz has described. This excitement was a function not only of the more sophisticated commercial activity in the New World but of the growth in the Americas of the same conflicts that characterized regional interests in Spain, now expressed in open hostility between the *criollos* and the peninsular aristocrats at the top of the pyramid. In 1800, of 17 million inhabitants of the Spanish American empire, 13 million were deemed white—but of those only 30,000 were true Spanish *peninsulares.*

Most importantly, a Bourbon liberalization of trade, which spurred the Catalans to come into the New World, had a truly disastrous effect on the economy of New Spain. Local products could not compete with the sudden influx of cheap goods either made in or reexported from Spain. Further, the immense quantity of items imported into New Spain drove prices even lower, making trade unprofitable, in turn, for the peninsular exporters. The merchants of Barcelona, echoing their earlier peninsular colleagues whose complaints were known to the pirate Anson, demanded that the Spanish ports in the New World be even more rigorously closed to foreign commerce and that industries in the colonies be shut down. Discontent about these restrictions spread throughout the society of Spanish America. Many priests, even some born in Spain, sided with the *criollos* in their emerging struggle with the mother country. Churches, convents, and religious colleges from Mexico to Buenos Aires became hives of discussion, then of dissension, then of conspiracy.

The crisis of the old order in Europe predictably stimulated wholesale anxiety in the Spanish settlements on the California coast. Along with fear of universal disorder, the Spanish became increasingly concerned about immediate foreign incursions. Smuggling raged unabated. Colonists were needed in Alta California, and although the numbers of "runaway" sailors from foreign as well as Spanish ships continued to grow, they were hardly enough to make the huge area militarily self-sufficient.

In 1794 the Barcelonese engineer-cartographer Miquel de Constançó composed a summary of defensive issues in California that showed close study of the colony's strategic situation but also revealed the impact of European events on the Pacific coast. De Constançó, like his predecessors, enthusiastically enumerated the assets of the region, including rich fisheries and forests suitable for shipbuilding, while repeating the habitual warnings about the British. As they were then penetrating China, he wrote, the British could easily land thousands of colonists on the California shore while also pursuing their fur business.

While de Constançó doubted that the Russians, for their part, represented much of a threat to the Spanish in the Pacific, he also observed that "the revolutions of the world are very strange." He insisted, "Strange are, in their effects, the revolutions of this world, and although for some we discern presentiments or firm antecedents, which allow a margin on which to make predictions . . . regarding the way things happen, or accidents, prophecies end up being very illusory." De Constançó saw no rational limits to economic development in the north Pacific on either the Siberian or the American littoral, although he was naturally pessimistic about the former.

But de Constançó, an Enlightenment Catalan, also saw that economic improvement of California could not be left in the hands of the Church. "There are missions (in the Americas) that have behind them more than a hundred years' history," he wrote, "and we see them still in the hands of preaching ministers who maintain the same escort of soldiers as at the beginning." Something further was required: the introduction of more reliable colonists. With asperity, de Constançó pointed out that for more than ten years a royal order had called on the masters of the Manila ships, on their annual voyages, to land discharged Mexican-born soldiers finished with service in the Philippines at Monterey if they chose to become settlers. But although the practice had been observed in the first three or four years, on pain of a fine for those captains who ignored it, it had fallen into neglect.

A solution to the problem of defensive colonization developed beginning in 1795, and again involved the Catalan Volunteers and Pere d'Alberni Teixidor. This was the "planned society" or *villa* of Branciforte near the mission of Santa Cruz, the first ideal colony conceived in California, a place eventually known above all for its Utopian spirit. Branciforte was to be a community of soldier-farmers from the ranks of the Catalan Volunteers, who were ordered to settle there in the belief that, in the words of Joseph Sánchez, "the Catalonians would promote prosperity."

Branciforte was intended as a genuine town rather than a haphazard village, inhabited by a hundred families drawn from San Francisco, Santa Barbara, San Diego, Los Angeles, and San Blas. They were to be organized in three classes: experienced cold-weather farmers, building workers such as carpenters and blacksmiths, and craft workers including tailors, millers, tanners, weavers, and mechanics. Indians were also to live in Branciforte, integrated with the Europeans. The houses were intended to be larger, cleaner, and more comfortable than the squalid structures in San José or Los Angeles, so that its appeal anticipated those of the housing developments of modern California.

D'Alberni Teixidor, now a lieutenant colonel, returned to Alta California with his Catalan Volunteers in 1796. They were first assigned in detachments divided between Monterey, San Francisco, and San Diego. D'Alberni Teixidor was then commissioned to choose a site for the Branciforte experiment. Drawing on his experience at Nootka, he examined the terrain around the missions at San Francisco and Santa Clara, but rejected them in favor of a tract near the mission of Santa Cruz. He argued that enough land was unused there that the local Indians would not feel resentful at a part of it being occupied by a town, and he proposed that the authorities underwrite the cost of buildings and farming needs for the colonists. These subsidies would supplement annual payments, incentives, and similar benefits usually provided to *pueblo* settlers. Indeed, the entire *pueblo* economy including Branciforte resembles nothing so much as a modern welfare system. However, recruits were to be strictly limited to experienced and hard workers accustomed to an adverse climate.

Branciforte was launched, with d'Alberni Teixidor in charge of military construction, hydraulic works, quarries, lumber cutting, and wheat planting. It was the third *pueblo* established by the Spanish in Alta California, after San José (the first, in 1777) and Los Angeles, and was supported by the Spanish from 1797 on. But Branciforte was an unsuccessful project, along with nearly all the Utopian ventures that succeeded it in California and elsewhere. The specific reasons for this outcome are unclear today but probably had much in common with those generally seen in the failure of state-sponsored communities.

In the annals of early California, Branciforte has a strange, almost sinister reputation as a gathering place of work-shy undesirables, but little detail on this fascinating topic is available to us. In 1802 d'Alberni Teixidor died, and the next year the Catalan Volunteers, who had been expected to sustain Branciforte by taking up residence there on their retirement from service, were mainly withdrawn from Alta California to Mexico, although a unit of them remained at San Diego for some years. In any case a scheme like Branciforte, even had it been more successful, could hardly by itself fill the colonizing requirements of the Spanish. In 1798 a policy of sending convicts to Alta California was introduced; it remained in force until at least 1834.

In the year 1808, the European revolutionary crisis that had begun in France nineteen years before finally burst open the gates of the Spanish empire. The armies of Napoleon Bonaparte served as history's battering ram. Napoleon placed his brother Joseph on the Spanish throne, where he was supported by the Inquisition and part of the Bourbon court, while introducing a derisory constitution. The Bourbons themselves, King Carlos IV and his son Prince Fernando, abdicated and were exiled to France. Joseph Bonaparte warned his brother that Spain would be a graveyard of his hopes, and he was right: the Spanish people rose up as a single force, from one end of the country to the other, with thousands upon thousands of men and women forming irregular bands to fight the *guerrilla* or "little war." Karl Marx wrote nearly fifty years later in the *New York Daily Tribune,*

> Napoleon, who, like all his contemporaries, considered Spain as an inanimate corpse, was fatally surprised at the discovery that when the Spanish State was dead, Spanish society was full of life, and every part of it overflowing with powers of resistance.

The classic Spanish author Benito Pérez Galdos put it more concisely: "Napoleon came and the whole world awakened."

The Napoleonic invasion and its unintended subversion of the Spanish régime had immediate echoes in New Spain. In September 1810 a Constituent *Cortes,* or assembly, met at Cádiz. In the *constituyentes* of Cádiz the Third Estate, or bourgeoisie, had a large majority over the aristocracy and clergy, and representatives of the colonies were seated. This was the high point of early Spanish liberalism, and remained a beacon for Spanish reformers and radicals across several succeeding generations. British troops landed in Spain and assisted in the anti-French struggle. But political development was halted with the defeat of Napoleon's armies and restoration of the Bourbon régime under King Fernando VII, the formerly abdicated prince, in 1814–15.

However, the Constituent *Cortes* of Cádiz had coincided with an event in Mexico in September 1810 that in the long run was still more significant for California history. A *criollo* priest, Miguel Hidalgo y Costilla, who had participated in a revolutionary secret society, rang the church bells in the village of Dolores in Guanajuato. With this celebrated act he summoned his parishioners to rise up against the "heresies" introduced into the empire by Napoleon. He called for death to the Spanish-born rulers: *"¡Mueran los gachupínes!"* employing an insult derived from an Aztec (Nahuatl) word meaning "a man with spurs." This *grito de Dolores* or "outcry of Dolores" marked the commencement of the Mexican War of Independence; Hidalgo's partisans took up arms under the image of the Virgin of Guadalupe, a syncretism of the Christian Mother of God with the Aztec goddess of rain and childbirth, Tonantzín-Coátlicue. Between then and 1814, when the royal restoration allowed Spain to send fresh troops for their suppression, the Mexicans fought valiantly for their freedom, although Hidalgo and his disciple Morelos were defeated and executed.

———————

IT WAS DURING this period of great uncertainty that the long-feared Russians appeared in San Francisco and then abruptly planted a colony, Ross, on the California coast. Their first party showed up in 1807, under Nikolai Rezanov, a highly educated and intellectually acute chamberlain of the Tsar's court and a roving representative of the Russian American Company, which had taken over the Tsar's Pacific enterprise. Rezanov had come to San Francisco in search of provisions—especially grain for bread—to feed his Alaska colonists. Rezanov was also interested in hunting fur-bearing animals. To the Russian authorities he had proposed several options to remedy the hunger and illness endemic in Russia's Alaskan outposts, including purchase of grain in the Philippines and imports from "New Albion," the name the Russians rather disingenuously used to refer to the extensive territories north of Alta California. It is clear that their gambit was to utilize, at least abstractly, the old claim of Drake as a foil against the Spanish, if such were needed.

Rezanov's visit came at a time when Spain was still an ally rather than a victim of Napoleonic France, which had broken off relations with Russia, stirring some concern among the Spanish at San Francisco. But Rezanov dispelled all suspicion of hostile intent and became involved in a romantic episode widely celebrated in the literature of California (and also in that of modern Russia). He made a promise of marriage, which was never carried out, with Doña Concepción de Argüello, daughter of the Spanish commandant at San Francisco, José Darío Argüello. Rezanov was middle-aged; Doña Concepción, only 15, has been praised as the most beautiful and energetic European woman then in California. The story of the couple has inspired the imagination of many, for as a Roman Catholic woman and a Russian Orthodox man they could not wed without the permission of, according to a Russian account, the Pope, and according to the Spanish version, the Tsar.

Rezanov was not above using the affections of Doña Concepción and her influence with the Spanish authorities to gain his business ends. She secured him the grain he sought and he departed, promising to come back for Doña Concepción's hand and to take her to the court at St. Petersburg, where she would share the opulent life of a chamberlain to the Tsar. But Rezanov never returned to California; he died only a year later, on the road to St. Petersburg, in the Siberian town of Krasnoyarsk. Doña Concepción waited for him, but finally entered a convent.

Rezanov's trip was the beginning of a significant commerce between the Spanish missions and the Russians, as well as of the exploitation by the latter of the fur resources of the California coast. Simultaneously with Rezanov's voyage, an American shipmaster, Nathaniel Winship, had contracted with the Russian American Company to sail to Trinidad Bay with a large group of Aleuts, seeking otters. Thus began the wholesale and uncontrolled harvesting of otter furs that would lead to the animals' extinction in California. In the five years that followed, the Russians also began cooperating with American fur-trading posts on the Columbia River, and sent an expedition to Hawaii.

The Russians pressed the Spanish court in Madrid for official permission to trade with the California settlements; the directors of the Russian American Company pointed out how much commerce in California was clandestine and conducted in American ships. However, impelled by the continuing problem of feeding their Alaskan colonies, which could not grow their own grain because of weather, the Russians decided to act on their own and establish a post "on the coast of New Albion adjacent to the Russian colonies," in the words of the official historian of the Russian American Company, Pyotr Tikhmenev.

This interpretation of the location of "New Albion" and of the borders of the Spanish, British, and Russian spheres of influence was, as noted, deliberately ambiguous: the Russians argued that the failure of the Spanish colony at Nootka, and the Spanish condominium with the British north of Alta California, had vitiated any Spanish claim above San Francisco Bay. Russian navigator Ivan Kuskov, supported by Aleksandr Baranov, surveyed a location for a colony at Bodega Harbor, which the Russians called Rumyantsev Bay. His first attempt to place settlers there failed, since Russians, Kodiak Islanders, and Aleuts alike thought only of an increasingly familiar California notion: running away. In 1811, Kuskov founded a settlement north of that site, named it Ross, and fortified it with ten cannon.

The local Kashaya Pomo Indians, who feared the Spanish, eventually became quite friendly and helpful to the newcomers. A major watercourse halfway between Ross and Bodega Harbor was called the Slavyanka, or Little Slav River, today's Russian River. Soon Russians, Kodiak Islanders, and Aleuts were living on both its banks. Already, *comandante* Luis Antonio Argüello, at the Royal Presidio of San Francisco, had begun issuing cash payments as aid to Anglo-American, Russian, and Aleut-Kodiak Island mariners stranded there. In his account book for 1809 he entered his first such reference to the Slav intruders, noting, "Three Russians, from the first of March to the 24th of June, were helped." In accord with the practice observed for the Anglo-Americans, they had been paid one and a half Spanish *reales* per day.

The Ross settlement included, in addition to housing and administrative structures, a dockyard, a smithy, and vegetable plots. Potatoes grew in quantity, although many were lost to gophers and other rodents. Kuskov stationed some Russians and Islanders on the Farallones Islands, where they collected fur seals, whose meat was eaten, seabirds and their eggs, and other sources of food. The Spanish barred them from hunting otters in San Francisco Bay. Only six years after the Russians showed up, otters had disappeared the length of the north coast, and fur seals were extinct in the Farallones.

The directors of the Russian American Company, in St. Petersburg, did not share Baranov's carefree attitude about Spanish sovereignty; above all, they felt that Ross was too close to San Francisco to be adequately defended. Their pessimism was somewhat justified, for soon Spanish troops, under the command of the Catalan officer Josep Joaquim Moraga, had gone to Ross and rather politely asked for an explanation of Russian intentions. The Russians insisted their only interests were to feed their people in Alaska and to promote trade, which would provide the Spanish colony with desirable goods. The Spanish demonstrated a friendly attitude, but their anxieties were revived soon after as British and American sea captains, according to the Russians, began spreading rumors that the latter aimed to seize San Francisco. The Spanish demanded that the Russians quit the settlement and arrested several Russian officials. The Spanish continued to tolerate low-level trading, but insisted that the colony be disbanded.

The Russian American Company had to contend with another limit on its ambitions in California, posed by individuals whose influence in St. Petersburg rivaled its own, and whose visit in 1816 brought to California one of the most remarkable sojourners in its history. This was a Russian oceanic survey under Lieutenant-Captain Otto von Kotzebue, aboard the brig *Rurik*. Kotzebue's father A. F. von Kotzebue was a critic of the Romantics and became the victim of a student assassin, in an incident well remembered in the nineteenth century but largely forgotten today. The younger von Kotzebue was accompanied to California by the Franco-German Romantic author and naturalist Adelbert von Chamisso, the first European with a truly inspired outlook, the first *radical traveler,* to come to California.

Chamisso, like de Constançó and La Pérouse, was a son of the rationalist age, but was also a personality of exceptional versatility and an authentic genius. He had been detailed to the *Rurik* as its botanist; his researches included the typology of the California poppy, which would become the state's official flower. Somewhat like La Pérouse, Chamisso complained that supplies to Monterey from Mexico consisted in a single ship sent from San Blas each year, and he predicted that "a little liberty would make California the granary and market of the north coast of these seas."

Chamisso also resembled La Pérouse in criticizing the Spanish attitude toward the Indians: "None of them appear to have troubled themselves about [the Indians'] history, customs, religions, or languages. 'They are irrational savages, and nothing more can be said of them. Who would trouble himself?'" In truth this judgment was unfair, since at the time Chamisso wrote, Father Boscana Mulet, also something of a rationalist, was at work on his account of the Chingichnish cult. Father Lasuén, often considered Serra's greatest successor, and other priests had compiled word lists for Indian languages and translated the Catholic catechism into some of them.

Chamisso was, however, a much more acute analyst than most of the priests in California. He had observed a contrast between Polynesia, where a single language family united the dispersed island communities across vast distances from west to east, and California, where the very numerous indigenous groups, living as neighbors or intermingled with each other, had completely different languages belonging to unrelated families. He therefore called for a greater study of California Indian languages, a task left incomplete even now, when many of these languages have disappeared.

But Chamisso is justifiably more famous in world literature for an amazing work, *Peter Schlemihl,* published three years before his arrival in California. *Peter Schlemihl* introduced into German, Yiddish, and several other idioms the now universal term for a victim of one's own ineptitude. Although Chamisso, a scion of French aristocrats who had fled to Prussia during the revolution, was not Jewish, he is said to have admitted borrowing the term *schlemiel* from the argot of Berlin Jews; however, its provenance in Jewish sources cannot be established. *Peter Schlemihl* is more significant for its fantastical account of a man who sells his shadow to the Devil, but learns that a shadow is more valuable than gold. A scholar of German literature, August C. Mahr, wrote of Chamisso that, with mixed origins and adventures on both sides of the Franco-German border, he always suffered a feeling of rootlessness, symbolized by Schlemihl's shadowless situation. "Chamisso actually had the desire to wander into faraway countries where it would make little difference whence a man came," Mahr wrote. This comment may be read with recognition and emotion by many Californians, whose experience has often been stated in almost identical terms.

Of greater immediate importance for California history, von Kotzebue's visit of 1816 angered the directors of the Russian American Company, because he compelled Kuskov to officially recognize the Spanish claim on the Pacific coast all the way to the Strait of Juan de Fuca; Kotzebue also protested that Kuskov had set himself up in Ross and Bodega Bay without official authorization. Chamisso agreed, pointing out that Kuskov's establishment of a fortress equipped with cannon could only be considered provocative in a time of peace between Spain and Russia.

This is not to say that von Kotzebue was an uncritical admirer of the Spanish; he expressed great irritation at hearing a sermon at San Francisco that seemed to put St. Francis on an equal level with Christ. As for the Ross effort, it was uneconomical, but Kuskov and his companions resisted disbanding it and continued to advocate better coastal trade relations, even though the depletion of furs and the near-moneyless economy in Spanish California at that time made any business there, aside from provisioning, only marginally worthwhile.

A final point regarding the von Kotzebue-Chamisso expedition is merited: their accounts of California were published in various European languages, with illustrations by the expedition's artist, Louis Choris. Choris was a significant figure in his own right who, unfortunately, was killed by bandits in Mexico. He transcribed Indian music from Mission Dolores, which he called *"trembloté et mystérieux"*—trembling and mysterious. But above all Choris deserves honor for his exquisite paintings of California Indians, which remain a most important record of them, as well as his beautiful renditions of California and Northwest Coast Indian art and of the landscapes he encountered.

IN 1815 THE only Spanish colonies in America to successfully oppose the restoration of imperial rule had been on the Río de la Plata, and the next year Argentina, calling itself the United Provinces of South America, declared its independence. Simón Bolívar landed in Venezuela and resumed a struggle he had begun after the Constituent *Cortes* of Cádiz; in another year the flames of revolution had swept the southern continent.

In 1816 and 1817 rumors of an imminent attack on Alta California by Argentine rebels were continuously heard, and in 1818 seaborne insurgents from Buenos Aires appeared at Monterey and demanded that the Californians join the revived war on monarchical power. In St. Petersburg, the Russian American Company was informed that California had been occupied by insurrectionists, which was an exaggeration although desultory fighting between the rebel forces and local militia had taken place.

Liberal revolt exploded again in Cádiz in 1820, in protest against orders for peninsular troops to suppress the independence movement in South America. The resumption of civil conflict in Spain saw a great outburst of rage as bourgeois reformers and liberal soldiers fought desperately against the monarchy. This set Mexico ablaze once more, and in 1821 it became free. Early the next year a Mexican federal force arrived at Monterey and, to the enthusiasm of most local residents, proclaimed Alta California subject to the new authorities. After 280 years the Spanish imperial dominion over California had ended.

Mexico declared itself a republic in 1823, and adopted a constitution in 1824 that made Baja and Alta California two of four territories affiliated with the nineteen Mexican states. The Californias were to be administered by a single governor from Monterey, and Alta California was granted one deputy and one alternate in the Mexican Congress.

The first and unquestionably most important consequence of Mexican independence for California was the opening of its commerce to the shipping of all nations. The Russians, for their part, were not pleased by this outcome: they complained that taxes on California grain, as well as on imports to the Mexican colony, had risen drastically, and that increased competition by other ships made acquisition of supplies in San Francisco more difficult. The Russians began seeking grain in Chile, offering Russian-produced goods—mainly heavy textiles—in exchange. British traders immediately began purchasing hides, tallow, and other products from the missions; priests, officials, soldiers, and Indians threw themselves into an entrepreneurial frenzy. But the government of the Mexican republic soon ordered trade to be limited to San Francisco, Monterey, Santa Barbara , and San Diego, and reinforced the ban on contact by foreigners with the more remote missions.

In September 1823, Alta California was visited by another remarkable Russian naval figure, Dmitrii Zavalishin. As an emissary to the formerly Spanish, now Mexican authorities, and a speaker of Spanish, Zavalishin spent some time in San Francisco, engaging in a series of picaresque adventures. He raided Mission Dolores to locate some runaways from his ship, the frigate *Kreyzer.* The fugitives were musicians; the Catholic priests looked jealously at the Russian vessels, which carried musical bands aboard, and hoped to lure their members away to play in the churches, which lacked organs.

Zavalishin became convinced that both the Hispanic élite and the native population would look with gratitude at conquest by the Russians—the Spanish and Mexicans to escape the advancing Anglo-Americans, the natives to escape the Spanish and the Mexicans. Having entertained extensive conspiratorial fantasies, he formulated a plan for the Ross and Bodega Bay colony to immediately annex Alta California. Returning to St. Petersburg, he lobbied the highest authorities, including the Tsar himself, for the plan, to no avail. Zavalishin then joined in the first Russian democratic revolt, the Decembrist uprising of 1825, in which he played a leading role, even though he had misgivings about an insurrection and the probable replacement of monarchical despotism with revolutionary dictatorship. The rebellion was suppressed and he was exiled to Siberia, where he remained the rest of his life. He never abandoned his belief in the possibilities of Russian expansion in the Pacific, particularly his fantasies of what might have happened in California. However, Tsar Nikolai I, whose reign followed the Decembrist revolt, feared the outside world and contamination by radical ideas, and initiated a withdrawal from foreign colonization.

In Mexico proper, the former Hispano-Indian commonwealth of New Spain had embarked on a search for its political soul, which continues today. Octavio Paz has lamented the failure of the Mexican élite, after the achievement of independence, to search through the history of their Iberian forebears and to emulate the traditions of local autonomy, legal continuity, and individual enterprise that characterized the Catalans and other regional bourgeois elements in Spain. Instead, successive Mexican leaders have floundered between personalist dictatorship and a doomed adoption of American and French liberalism in a society that, without a strong bourgeoisie but burdened with all the cultural baggage of the former empire, could not sustain such a transplantation of political concepts.

The Mexican ruling class was faced with a range of challenges. Although Alta California was distant from the center of power at Mexico City, the missions and their Indian subjects became a major topic of debate, particularly as anticlericalism burgeoned. Mexican intellectuals soon demonstrated a ferocity against the Church that, at least in the form of opinion and prejudice, remains a feature of the country's public life today. The Californias, where the missions were exempt from taxation yet claimed title to virtually all the territory within their sight, were seen by Mexican liberals as a preserve of priestly exploitation.

For these reasons, dissension between the religious and civil authorities in the Californias emerged almost immediately after Mexican independence. This conflict created a troubled atmosphere in Alta California that seemed to lead directly to the great California Indian revolt of 1824. Anticlericals became even more exercised, believing that the Spanish priests would stir up Indian resistance to the Mexicans, who were also bent on expanding their large inland estates. The liberals, echoing the rationalist doctrine of citizenship associated with the French Revolution, condemned the Indians' state as near-slavery and called for the indigenous population to be emancipated.

In the meantime, whaling captains from the ever more enterprising United States of America discovered the "Japan grounds," an exceptionally rich area for their activities, in the 1820s, and their ships began to fill the Pacific. Hawaii became "the emporium of the Pacific," as sea lanes between the Islands and California were increasingly used by American vessels. In 1824, along with the Mexican constitution and the great Indian revolt, Alta California saw the establishment at Monterey of the first American hide-trading business.

Numerous foreign settlers began to appear in Alta California, provoking an early protest by the former chief administrator of the missions, the Catalan Franciscan Vicenç Sarrià, who had previously railed against the new government and who now denounced the importation of "immoral" books and periodicals. The territory saw a revival of Inquisitorial practices, including the seizure and burning of scientific and literary works and a campaign against dancing the waltz, a fashion that had overtaken Mexico.

The Mexican Congress in 1829 finally legislated the expulsion of all Spaniards, not sparing clerics who had sworn allegiance to Mexico, from the Californias and New Mexico. The order was extremely unpopular among Californians, and the municipal authorities at San José opposed it in the name of their whole community. Father Boscana Mulet, the Mallorcan writer on the Chingichnish cult at the mission of San Juan Capistrano, was dumbfounded by the decree; in the quaint words of Cora Older, the widow of a distinguished California newspaperman and an expert on mission lore, "Snuff-taking was his only solace." (Cora Older herself professed a belief in Chingichnish—but we shall encounter her more amply in her due time.)

In any event, the expulsion warrant was not immediately enforced. The settled population of Alta California was still too small; in 1826 a census counted no more than 24,614 Mexicans, Spaniards, Christian Indians, and others, aside from the uncounted masses of non-Christian Indians. An increase of 2,000 over the numbers of the same classes recorded ten years before partially reflected new conversions at the missions of San Rafael and San Francisco Solano as well as fresh arrivals at Monterey that included many convicts from Mexico.

A new *diputación* or regional government began meeting in Monterey, and the issue of Indian dependency remained at the forefront of concern for Californians involved in the territory's political evolution. One expression of this interest was a proposal to change the name of Alta California to "Moctézuma," after the Aztec ruler defeated by Cortés and known to Anglo-Americans as Montezuma. Its capital would be Los Angeles and its coat of arms would depict an Indian man armed with a bow crossing the straits from Asia to America; this indigenous image had revolutionary associations as well, calling to mind that of the Virgin of Guadalupe carried as a banner by Hidalgo's insurrectionary forces.

This conception marked the first open expression of an emerging California patriotism, and even a separatist resentment of Mexican rule; in any event, it was never discussed further. But it is noteworthy that the grievances of Californians against Mexico had more to do with resentment over restrictions on commerce than with the racial enmity that set Mexico against Spain; in this sense California's relation to Mexico resembled that of the thirteen Atlantic colonies with Britain.

At that time, Baja California had a reputation as a reactionary, antirepublican clerical redoubt, and occasional tensions emerged between the upper and lower territories over such issues as the placement of the border between them. Civil war broke out anew in Mexico, this time between two factions identified with competing rituals in Freemasonry, which in France and Spain had come to exercise a considerable influence over liberal opinion. "Federalists" (those for a loose confederation of states) were associated with the York Masonic rite, while "centralists" were known as adepts of the Scottish rite. This division fueled the rise of Antonio López de Santa Anna, who made himself a full-fledged dictator.

Among the liberal élite of Alta California the secularization of the missions became a source of continuous controversy. In 1833, with the appointment as governor of José Figueroa, a progressive figure under whose administration the first printing press was established in Alta California, serious civil measures began to curb the Church's dominion over the Indians. A pronounced anticlerical, Figueroa was incensed at reports that priestly abuses had so alienated the natives at the north end of San Francisco Bay that considerable numbers of converted Indian men and women had fled from the mission of San Rafael to take refuge with the Russians at Ross. He ordered an immediate end to punishment by flogging, then called elections in which emancipated Indians were granted the vote. Most importantly, the same year saw the Mexican Congress act to secularize the missions, thereby transforming them into ordinary church parishes in fulfillment of a principle first put forward by the Spanish liberals of 1813 but previously ignored. The Indians became free individuals; the missions were now simply Indian towns.

Tragically, the main consequence of this secularization was a wholesale looting of mission resources by the local Mexican ruling class. This brought down a new disaster on the mission Indians, who, formerly residents of close-knit, self-sustaining communities, were now offered the meager rewards of labor in the towns or on the expanding Mexican estates. Some of them became *peones,* bound to the land. Emancipation typically brought to the mission Indians a poverty and spiritual oblivion far worse than any they had suffered previously.

But the vast majority of Californian Indians remained in the interior of the territory, escaping Mexican control, and some mission Indians fled into the mountains. Clashes between Mexicans and unconquered Indians multiplied in the Central Valley, where Mexican landholdings rapidly spread. Indian raids on livestock did not abate although military measures were increased. Indian resistance to imported illness was, as in the past, less effective. In the wake of the emancipation the roster of epidemics brought by the Europeans, which had already partially devastated Indian California, grew to include smallpox, scarlet fever, cholera, and tuberculosis. In the period ending with the coming of American rule in the late 1840s, up to 60 percent of the non-Christian California Indians perished from disease— five times the number that died by violence.

In 1835 the shores of California welcomed an American whose writing would become truly classic in its simple but eloquent presentation of the rigorous life at sea and on land in the Pacific: Richard Henry Dana, author of *Two Years Before the Mast,* the greatest work of early California literature.

A New England university student, at the age of 19 Dana shipped to the Pacific coast in the brig *Pilgrim.* His magnificent narrative provides a fascinating look at California in the heyday of the hides trade, evoking the landscape and inhabitants in absorbing and occasionally surprising detail. For example, Dana recounted how the American shipmasters operating between Hawaii and California had planted colonies of Polynesian boatmen in the California towns to guard the hides stored in American-owned warehouses.

Dana passed four months with the Polynesians as a hide-curer. The tradition of diversity among seafarers was visible in San Diego, where Dana's group included "out of forty or fifty, representatives from almost every nation under the sun: two Englishmen, three Yankees, two Scotchmen, two Welshmen, one Irishman, three Frenchmen, one Dutchman, one Austrian, two or three from Spain, half a dozen Spanish Americans, two native Indians from Chile, one Negro, one Mulatto, about twenty Italians, as many more Hawaiians, one Tahitian, and one Kanaka from the Marquesas."

Dana's exquisite powers of observation, as shown in his many sketches and anecdotes, revealed a stunted California economy in which few goods were produced. Grapes were plentiful but no wine was pressed; the Californians preferred "bad wine made in Boston and brought round by us, at an immense price." The Californians even bought shoes from the Americans that were, "as like as not, made of their own hides, which have been carried twice round Cape Horn." In addition to wine and shoes, the *Pilgrim* brought trade goods including other spirits, sold by the cask, tea, coffee, sugar, spices, raisins, molasses, hardware, crockery, tinware, cutlery, every kind of clothing and textiles, jewelry, combs, furniture, "and in fact, everything that can be imagined, from Chinese fireworks to English cart wheels—of which we had a dozen pair with their iron rims on."

Dana was impressed by the amount of silver in Monterey; there was no currency in Alta California aside from silver coin and hides, which the sailors called "California bank notes," and no credit, banks, or investments except in cattle. He had never seen "so much silver at one time in my life, as during the week we were at Monterey." He found a number of Anglo-American colonists; because Protestants had no civil rights in Mexico, many of the immigrants had to "leave their [religious] conscience at Cape Horn." But they had succeeded in amassing property and gaining control of commerce. Already, the chief municipal officers at Monterey and Santa Barbara were, Dana said, "Yankees by birth" who became Catholics, married local women, and adopted the Spanish language, teaching their children no English.

DANA'S BOOK PASSED lightly over the internal politics of California, which underwent a major upset at the time of his visit. Under Santa Anna, the Mexican Congress adopted a centralist constitution in late 1835, dividing the country into departments on the French model rather than states and territories. Power was concentrated in Mexico City, with departmental governors appointed by the president. Under such a system Alta California and other outlying areas would suffer a loss of whatever political liberty they had previously enjoyed, or so many Californians believed.

California was therefore avidly "federalist." That term, it should be noted, meant the opposite of what it stood for in the United States; that is, Mexican federalists were fighting for a loose association of highly autonomous states rather than a strong federal authority. Revolutionary tendencies were soon visible in the Alta California towns.

Juan Bautista Alvarado, a 26-year-old California-born customs auditor, then treasurer of the custom house at Monterey and a member of the Alta

California *diputación,* was considered the outstanding leader of California youth. Alvarado was self-educated in the rationalist tradition, to the extent that such was possible on the California coast, and had been excommunicated for reading the seventeenth-century French thinker François Fénelon's *Télémaque.* He then sought out and secretly devoured every "impious" book to be found in the territory, including works of Rousseau and Voltaire.

Alvarado found many such texts kept safe in the large library of his uncle—a prominent military officer and rancher, Mariano Guadalupe Vallejo—even as the priests were busy burning scientific and other volumes brought from Mexico by a luckless physician. Alvarado was also widely known for having been, as a boy of 11, the initiator of a new and interesting custom in Alta California. Local men had habitually let their hair grow luxuriantly down their backs, but Alvarado was the first California lad to adopt a new fashion: short-cut hair, in rejection of a style he considered unmanly and above all useless. What was at first seen as a bizarre affectation soon became the standard men's hair style.

In summer 1836, Alvarado, who had been harassed by the civil authorities, suddenly rode to Vallejo's residence at Sonoma and called on his uncle to join a rebellion against the centralist regime. Vallejo demurred, and Alvarado returned south, but while riding back to Monterey he learned that the *rancheros* along the road, which followed the Sacramento River delta, the east shore of San Francisco Bay, and San José, were aware of his intentions and eager to join in an uprising. They sharpened their old swords and cleaned their ancient muskets, and Alvarado found himself leading an army. Its ranks soon included foreign seamen as well as some American hunters who were, naturally, expert sharpshooters.

The insurrectionists arrived at Monterey in great numbers and with even greater enthusiasm, accompanied by drums and trumpets and supplied with more weapons from the missions. Alvarado, the customs auditor and secret radical intellectual, was now a revolutionary chieftain. A single cannon shot fired by an artilleryman from the Philippines brought about the surrender of Monterey. The centralist governor Nicolás Gutiérrez was deported to the Mexican mainland.

In November 1836 Alvarado assembled the *diputación* at Monterey and issued a proclamation: *"¡Federación o muerte!"*—"Federation or death!" was his watchword. "California is free and will end all relations with Mexico until that country ceases to be tyrannized by the present dominant faction, which calls itself the central government." Alvarado wrote a declaration of independence in which the territory became "The Free and Sovereign State of Alta California," separate from Mexico until a federative regime was restored there. Although the new nation would recognize Catholicism as its official creed, individual religious opinions would no longer be subject to scrutiny. The *diputación* would become the legislature and Vallejo would assume command of military forces.

"Citizen Alvarado" as he titled himself in the best French Revolutionary manner, was at first named Secretary of the new régime under the presidency of José Castro, revolutionary director of the operational vanguard. Castro issued a stirring manifesto, declaring "If the time must come when another race shall occupy our rich and fertile soil, let them, looking with admiration and compassion to the past, say 'Here was California, whose people preferred destruction to the dominion of tyrants! . . . ' *¡Viva la federación! ¡Viva la libertad! ¡Viva el estado libre y soberano de Alta California!*" ("Long live federation! Long live liberty! Long live the free and sovereign state of Upper California!")

The defense of the State was placed in the hands of a citizen militia, the government was purged of corrupt elements, and the state was divided into two cantons, one with its capital at Monterey, the other ruled from Los Angeles. Each cantonal administration would be headed by a *jefe político* or commissioner, with the State governor serving as the *jefe* at Monterey and appointing a subordinate for Los Angeles. The two *jefes* would have the right to make land grants to settlers, subject to approval by superior authorities. Alvarado then became "higher *jefe político* and governor," and as "colonel of the civic militia" replaced his uncle, Vallejo, as military commander.

This first California revolution was successful, in great part because in Mexico Santa Anna's attention was diverted by the war against American settlers and their partisans in Texas, a conflict which bankrupted his government. The radical "citizen Alvarado" in the name of federation became a dictator, although his character was widely viewed as benevolent. His only significant opposition came from the citizens of Los Angeles, for whom, as noted by the nineteenth-century historian Hittell, "probably no system not recognizing it as the capital and no governor residing in the northern part of the country would have been acceptable."

Here was the first major sign of the North-South competition that would become familiar in the California that came after. Los Angeles defied Alvarado on two main points: they rejected full independence from Mexico, even though the Angeleños insisted on their federalist principles, and they repudiated any tolerance toward non-Catholics. Hatred for the "Monterey principles of religious toleration" became the alleged pretext for counterrevolutionary agitation in Los Angeles led by municipal officer José Sepúlveda; this was not the last time the southern part of the state would embrace a more conservative outlook than the north. Alvarado marched down the coast in arms, and Los Angeles capitulated.

The Free and Sovereign State of Alta California survived only until July 1837, when "citizen Alvarado" recognized its reaffiliation with Mexico as the department of Alta California. In the meantime, the Mexicans had decreed the reunification of the two Californias as a single territory, and Santa Anna had been captured by the Texans.

Alvarado's revolution, as well as the secession of Texas from Mexico, led, among the growing number of Americans in Alta California, to seditious disturbances in which some who had helped his movement became involved. The ranks of the new immigrants had been swelled by Germans, Scandinavians, and other Europeans previously scarce on the coast; these included such notable figures as the Dane Peter Lassen and the Swiss-German Johann Augustus Sutter. Reputedly the nephew of a famous radical propagandist, Sutter established an ambitious colony, New Helvetia, at the confluence of the Sacramento and American Rivers in 1840. Like Dana's employers, Sutter imported workers from the Hawaiian Islands.

The only unqualifiedly bright spot in this panorama, from the Mexican viewpoint, came in 1841 when the Russians abandoned Ross. After thirty years' effort the settlement was judged a failure, even though its farms had developed enough to make purchase of grain from the Mexican territory less frequent. Rust caused by humidity ruined the wheat; cultivation was moved from the coast to the hills, but could not escape "the destructive influence of the fog." Wild oats outgrew the wheat, requiring that cattle graze the fields for up to three years and depriving the colonists of cultivable farmland during that time. In addition, field vermin ate up the grain. In 1835 crops failed throughout California, and in 1836 not one grain of wheat was exported from Ross. Cattle wandered many miles away, to all compass points, seeking pasturage after that at Ross was exhausted or destroyed by the burning sun. The valuable fur-bearing mammals had by now become extinct. The products of the settlement sold to the Spanish and Mexicans, such as small boats, wheels, and dishes, had been profitable until the California trade was taken over by British and American ships, whose low prices could not be beaten. The dampness of the wood cut at Ross made it rot easily, and the cost of transporting lumber to the coast was prohibitive; therefore shipbuilding at the settlement ended.

The Russians had sought to expand the colony by annexing an inland valley of great attractiveness, but such plans were still blocked by Mexico's refusal to recognize Russian sovereignty over the settlement. Spain's establishment of the mission of San Rafael and Mexico's emplacement of the mission of San Francisco Solano effectively cut the Russians off from the rest of California, seriously diminishing the small influence they had enjoyed. By 1836 the zone between Ross and Point Reyes was occupied by American ranchers. Any strategic value to Russia was negated by the distance between Alaska and Ross and the unfavorable character of the harborage at Bodega Bay. Finally, the status of Ross was made even more confused by the political chaos in Mexico. Ross was a burden, and an increasingly expensive one, and in April 1839 Tsar Nikolai ordered the settlement abandoned.

The land, livestock, and structures at Ross were sold to Sutter two years later. The official historian of the Russian American Company, Tikhmenev, writing in the early 1860s, found one consolation in the colony's end: had the Russians maintained Ross until the Gold Rush of 1849, all the workers at the settlement, without doubt or exception, would have run away to the goldfields.

THE SUCCEEDING FIVE years, from 1841 to 1846, were filled with disquiet in Alta California. The Mexican department showed greater development as cultivation and other land uses expanded. But the same economic growth bore within itself the destruction of Mexican authority over Alta California as settlement by Americans increased. More and more of these newcomers availed themselves of large land grants, which were registered as far as the northern extreme of the Sacramento Valley, in the foothills of the Sierra Nevada, and in a wide belt inland from the Sonoma coast to San Diego.

Aside from the missions, these Mexican land grants are the most enduring institutional legacy of Hispanic rule. The Spanish had allowed
twenty-five land concessions for grazing and other purposes, but title remained with the Crown. The grants that followed under the government of
Mexico have been viewed as the predecessors of big agribusiness in California, and have also been blamed for the emergence of a mammoth title-in-
surance industry in the state. Of 813 land grants made by the Mexican
authorities (453 of them between 1841 and 1846), 42 percent were claimed
by non-Mexicans, in a boom of occupancy that could not but hasten the
eventual military occupation of the territory by U.S. forces.

During the same period attempts were made to improve relations with
and economic activities in the Baja peninsula, which remained under the
jurisdiction of the *excelentísima asamblea departamental* of Alta California.
But factional dissension between Alvarado and his opponents flared up
anew, and in 1845 a new revolution brought a divided administration to
power. It was made up of Pío Pico, a Los Angeles political leader, as governor and the northern revolutionary and companion-in-arms of Alvarado,
José Castro, as militia commandant.

Pío Pico was the last governor of Mexican California. The year 1846
saw the greatest wave of immigrants yet to come overland from the United
States across the Sierra Nevada to the Sacramento Valley. The recent arrivals
gravitated to Sutter's Fort, where they joined with other American and foreign malcontents, some of whom had taken up arms against Pico and Castro. Rumors of a Texan-style conspiracy to unite Alta California with the
United States swelled to new proportions. Alta California was clearly un-
raveling in the face of the American advance.

The Anglo-Saxon conquest of the territory was an outcome foreseeable
from the beginning of American independence; the United States and California were like distant cousins who know little of each other but whose
lives are parallel. The year 1769, in which Portolá and Serra embarked on
their Sacred Expedition, was the same year in which Jefferson and his colleagues in the Virginia House of Burgesses decided on a revolutionary boycott of British goods. The mission and *Presidio* at San Francisco had been
founded in 1776, the year American independence was declared. The ambition of the English-speaking colonies on the Atlantic to foster emulation
of their insurrectionist path by the inhabitants of the French and Spanish
possessions in the Americas was debated by the First Continental Congress

in the very sessions that adopted the Declaration of Independence. Jefferson's two administrations encouraged such sentiments in South America.

Most significantly, the same Napoleon who inadvertently overthrew the Spanish empire threatened to occupy and fortify Louisiana, but was unable to assert his power there owing to the revolution of Toussaint L'Ouverture; this former slave's troops definitively defeated Bonaparte's army in what is now Haiti in 1802. Napoleon then offered Louisiana for sale to a United States quite unprepared for such a massive windfall. Once the Jefferson Administration had completed the purchase of Louisiana in 1803, the United States had a common border with New Spain. As a result, American "manifest destiny," meaning inevitable expansion to the Pacific coast, now made a leap the logic of which was as irresistible as that of the Spanish mariners in the Pacific 300 years before.

Still, California's social history is about far more than the state's location at the end of the American frontier, closing off a continent filling up with English-speaking residents. This aspect of its history—its place "at the edge of the world" to borrow from an Indian lyric—has explained, for many, the original impetus for the creativity, enterprise, and tolerance found in California. Nevertheless, at least one historian, Norman Graebner, has argued that the acquisition and the character of California have had more to do with its settlement by sea rather than by land, and its potential as "a prosperous and independent maritime republic," which was widely discussed in American journalism at the time of California's conquest.

Graebner comments:

Manifest destiny persists as a popular term in American historical literature to explain the expansion of the United States to continent-wide dimensions in the 1840s. Like most broad generalizations, it does not bear close scrutiny. . . . The vistas of all from Jackson to Polk were maritime and they were always anchored to specific waterways along the Pacific Coast. . . . Any interpretation of westward extension beyond Texas is meaningless unless defined in terms of commerce and harbors. Travelers during the decade before 1845 had created a precise vision of the western coasts of North America. It was a vision born of the sea. . . . Historians have tended to exaggerate the natural urge of the American people to expand in the forties. For that reason they have attributed an unrealistic importance to the impact of pioneers. . . .

American frontiersmen never repeated the role they played in the annexation of Texas. In time they might have secured possession of California, but in 1845 hardly a thousand had reached that province. . . . What mattered far more in the definition of American purpose were the travelers who toured the Pacific coasts and recorded the location and significance of waterways. These men, not pioneers, formulated the objectives of American officials from Adams to Polk.

In 1846 U.S. President James Knox Polk, possibly in clandestine concert with the Mexican dictator Santa Anna, initiated the bizarre and desultory conflict between the two most populous North American nations that we know as the Mexican War. Abraham Lincoln, among others, denounced the highly unpopular war, which was viewed by many as, in James Russell Lowell's words, *"a damned war . . . a war for the spreadin' o' slavery."* The hostilities began over the Texas boundary, but California was no less significant a prize. Thus in June 1846, a decade after Alvarado's rebels briefly declared the Free and Sovereign State of Alta California, Anglo-Saxon colonists at Sonoma proclaimed a California Republic, symbolized by the Bear Flag still in use by the state.

The Bear Flaggers come down to us as forerunners of a separatist spirit that occasionally seems relevant today. As their most articulate member, William B. Ide, stated, the Bear Flag rebels sought "a republican government, which shall secure to all religious and civil liberty, which shall encourage virtue and literature; which shall leave unshackled by fetters agriculture, commerce, and mechanism," the last a contemporary term for technology.

Ide's words were prophetic, and were soon to be fulfilled. However, the Bear Flag venture and the related enterprises that effected the American conquest of California were in reality a sordid undertaking. Mexico's power was clearly overextended in the North, very little of which had been systematically exploited; once the Mexican War began the seizure of California by the United States was obviously imminent. The Bear Flaggers, their hero John C. Frémont, his bloodthirsty sidekick Kit Carson, and the assorted military adventurers who assisted and occasionally opposed their assertions of American sovereignty appear to have been little more than marauding bands of opportunistic ne'er-do-wells. The California Republic whose peculiar legend appears on the state flag never came into existence; within a month the Bear Flag had been superseded by the raising of the Stars and Stripes on California soil.

Many Hispanic Californians, or *Californios* as they had come to be called, sympathized with the American cause—at least until they learned of the brutal conduct and attitudes of the crew of truculent vagabonds that had descended upon them. Anti-American resistance broke out, led mainly by José Castro, Andrés Pico (brother of Pío, who had fled to Mexico), and José María Flores. The Hispanic Californians administered a series of substantial defeats to the aggressors. But the 1848 Treaty of Guadalupe Hidalgo, which ended the Mexican War, transferred the entire northern Mexican territory, from the California coast to the upper Rio Grande and Colorado Rivers, to the United States. The fate of the *Californios* was sealed by this action of two distant governments.

Fate is not the same as destiny. Peace between Mexico and the United States was negotiated in February 1848. A month earlier James Wilson Marshall, an employee of Sutter, was engaged in building a new mill on the American River to saw lumber cut in the vast nearby forests. Marshall was concerned to make the river site adequate for milling use, and repeatedly pumped streams of water along the banks to widen the channel. He found a substantial quantity of gold washed up by his work.

By April news of the discovery had spread to the coastal towns, and by the end of the summer had emptied them. It soon reached the Atlantic coast, as well. The long gestation of the California we know today had come to term. With a cosmopolitan identity that would remain utterly different from that of the other West Coast states, Oregon and Washington, as well as from that of Texas, Arizona, or New Mexico, California seemed to burst whole into the consciousness of the United States—and then, gifted with the wealth of the Gold Rush, onto the world stage. As an American possession it soon demanded full status as a state, which was granted almost immediately.

Because of California's sudden emergence the adoption of Minerva, the Greek goddess who sprang full-grown from the head of her father Zeus, as the main element in the state's seal seemed appropriate to the leaders of the new American California. Today's Californians paradoxically view both the Spanish founders and the American conquerors almost the way the California Indians did, as more than ordinary men, as legendary figures whose character and actions were both heroic and unfathomable. But California was not the product of a virgin birth, attended by the Gold Rush. It had its birth trauma in the form of the Mexican War, yet it also boasted a distinguished intellectual lineage. Child of Indian and European hallucinations; of Bourbon reform, Franciscan millenarianism and the Enlightenment; of English piracy and smuggling, Mexican federalism, and American commerce, the new California was uniquely modern.

PART II

A RUNAWAY SOCIETY

That's history, Leroy. They don't teach it in school, but it's American history, just the same.

—Robert Young as Detective Finlay in *Crossfire* (1947)

Wherein Hispanic and Native California cultures vanish in the sudden rise of California to wealth and power; patterns of world commerce change as misfits and malcontents rush to find new lives as gold miners; seafaring customs continue to influence the lives of shorebound folk; land, railroad, and immigration controversies convulse the state; the labor movement emerges and grows immensely; and California comes into its own as a landscape of high culture

*T*he discovery of gold in California worked "a marvelous change," the pioneering labor historian Ira B. Cross wrote some sixty years later, in one of the great examples of historiographic understatement. For Cross, studying the origins of the West Coast maritime unions, the experiences of "runaway sailors" furnished a major element in the Gold Rush epic. As we have observed, California had long seen its settler population swelled by runaway seamen from ships under every visiting flag as well as from Spanish vessels, servants of various races from the Manila and other trading operations, Russian colonists, and similar fugitives in search of opportunity, even as the Indian neophytes "ran away" from the missions.

The historian Neal Harlow has summarized the runaway phenomenon concisely: "Army, navy, and commercial vessels on the coast had been plagued by desertions even before the discovery of gold." U.S. Navy captain John B. Montgomery, for whom San Francisco's financial thoroughfare is named, complained in 1846 that California offered "peculiar facilities" for sailors to escape from both trading ships and whalers, and he called on the local authorities to exercise every possible means to secure their detention and return them to the vessels on which they had served.

In 1847 attempts to capture runaway merchant seamen, as well as deserting Army and Navy personnel, were expanded, with rewards for those who turned them in and fines for anybody harboring them. Cross states that crews aboard the hide- and tallow-carrying vessels that tied up in the South Bay before the Gold Rush typically jumped ship. A local ordinance passed in October 1847 mandated a six-month prison sentence at hard labor for desertion from a merchant ship, with a $50 reward for each runaway apprehended.

Such efforts were notably unsuccessful, as Captain Montgomery glumly admitted. With news of Marshall's gold find, crews departed ships *en masse* and posthaste. Photographic and hand-drawn images of San Francisco at the end of 1849, its harbor crowded by nearly four hundred empty, abandoned ships, remain the archetypal symbol of the California Gold Rush. Many of the ships stood empty and rotting until they were scuttled, turned into piers, and transformed into buildings; their hulls have repeatedly been located and excavated in the process of filling and construction on the San Francisco waterfront. The lure of the precious metal was so great that the American naval officer Thomas ap Catesby Jones reported that eight of his crew rushed off his ship on its arrival in Monterey in October

1848. He offered considerable sums for anybody who might return them to service—$500 each for the first four men—to no effect.

However, the posted bounty for runaway sailors soon drew the interest of another class of enterprising spirits in San Francisco: groups of ruffians who formed up as "sailor-catchers." They found the task more daunting than they had thought; they evolved into the first major criminal gang in San Francisco history, the "Hounds," specializing in street terror against ordinary residents, particularly against the increasing numbers of "Chilean" miners, a generic term for newly arrived South Americans. A civic reaction against the Hounds led to the formation of the city's first popular tribunal and the gang's banishment.

Behind these curious demographic developments lay real tragedy aboard ships. As Cross wrote, "It is impossible to do justice to the brutality shown to the sailors in those days." The very existence of American laws, in force since 1790, that defined abandonment of a shipping contract as desertion and those who left ships as runaways subject to a reward, showed that the civil status of the U.S. mariner was not a great deal better than that of slaves held in the American South. Sailors' pay stood at the low end of the wage scale, quarters were cramped, and the food was dreadful, whether in the hides trade and whaling vessels, or aboard ships voyaging to China. U.S. seamen had organized and called strikes from the earliest years after the proclamation of American independence.

The gravest problem faced by American seamen was not specifically economic but rather psychological, and resulted from the extraordinary cruelty habitually visited on them by captains and mates. The first American author to cast light on this horror was Richard Henry Dana, already familiar to us as a chronicler of shore life in Mexican California, but indeed better remembered as an outstanding early advocate of seamen's rights. Dana's account in *Two Years Before the Mast* of the flogging of the sailor Dana called Sam, followed by the similar beating of his friend John the Swede for having questioned Sam's punishment, shocked his readers. Dana recounted how the insane captain screeched, "If you want to know what I flog you for, I'll tell you. It's because I like to do it!—Because I like to do it!—It suits me! That's what I do it for!" The American public was as yet unfamiliar with what we today would recognize as sadism, and the very concept was frightful.

Given the long-lasting importance of shipping to the California economy, it was perhaps predictable that issues of sailors' rights would be the starting point for much of California's nineteenth-century labor history, extending into the twentieth—but that is a tale better told later on, in appropriate order. Suffice to say that the first seamen's strike on the West Coast occurred in August 1850, after wages had fallen because of a sudden return to San Francisco of men disillusioned by their failure to make their fortune by mining. The strikers marched through the town for three days, headed by a drum corps flying the Stars and Stripes. But the strike was defeated by the sheer number of ex-miners prepared to serve as marine strikebreakers.

Shipboard abuses were denounced in eloquent terms not only by Dana and later Herman Melville but also by one of the first writers in English to become well known in California, J. Ross Browne. Born in Ireland in 1821 and brought to Kentucky as a boy of 11, Browne was also the first known authentic intellectual eccentric to take up permanent residence in California.

In 1846 Browne published his *Etchings of a Whaling Cruise,* an account of a trip to the Indian Ocean that was to prove doubly important, both as a landmark denunciation of shipborne cruelties and as a source for Melville in the composition of *Moby Dick.* Browne's works are almost unknown today, and Browne had the misfortune of providing unintended research material for other authors in addition to Melville, notably Mark Twain. Browne later remarked of Twain, "He made plenty of money on his books, some of it on mine."

Unlike Melville and Twain, however, Browne was radical in both his opinions and his habits. Son of an Irish rebel, he carried with him a lively sense of outrage and protest against human injustice. This had led him to expose the brutality suffered by seamen, but it also drove him to investigate and denounce the condition of the California Indians. He further shared with Melville and other leading American writers of the time the combination of a literary career with government service.

In 1857 Browne was named a special confidential agent of the U.S. Treasury Department for Indian affairs on the West Coast. He enjoyed his secret status, and his delvings turned up evidence of governmental corruption, forced labor, and impoverishment of the Indian population. The Spanish mission system, which at least had established a semblance of orderly life by European standards, had completely collapsed. Following the American conquest, the California Indians had been reduced from the citizenship granted them by Mexican and Alta California authority to the status of "wandering savages." Browne's exposé led to widespread criticism of U.S. Indian policy in California.

Browne wrote that Indian history in American California was "a melancholy record of neglect and cruelty." Of course, the main work of Indian extermination was carried out by the least enlightened representatives of our civilization, namely the raw mass of miners who poured into the foothills of the Sierra Nevada. The occasional rage of the miners was also visited on Spanish-speaking California natives as well as on the increasing number of Chinese miners, both of whom became victims of lynchings and other atrocities in the gold camps. Gold Rush California was filled with such violence: it was a "runaway society" in addition to being a society of runaways.

Browne's anger at the bad treatment of the California Indians would,be echoed by other writers decades later, most notably by Helen Hunt Jackson. But if radicals like Browne were as yet rare in the California of the 1850s, eccentrics were not. In 1855 Browne moved into an Oakland residence that would later become famous as a folly, "Pagoda Hill." It stood at the northeast corner of Ross Street and Chabot Road, in the present-day upscale Rockridge neighborhood; sadly, no trace of it remains. He later served as an American diplomat in China. His individualistic character resembled that of several other seemingly bizarre personalities that emerged from the Gold Rush in California—mainly, it must be said, in San Francisco—out of the social maelstrom created by that influx of enterprising and extraordinary folk.

Every nation on earth seemed to have sent its misfits and failures to the California mines, where each might, by the sweat of his own brow, attain riches undreamed of in the class-bound societies of the American eastern seaboard as well as of Europe. Gold Rush California was in general a remarkably classless, open society in which all stood as equals before the god of Ore. Getting gold did not necessarily bring an enduring change in one's social status; today's rich man was often tomorrow's pauper, while hopeless, desperate, hungry men who had never known any life but that of hard labor—sailors, Chinese peasants, European proletarians—could become wealthy at a stroke.

Further, even among the rough inhabitants of the mining camps, with their bigotry and love of quick "justice," there were a great many political refugees from the failed European revolutions of 1848–49; such men gave up their subversive postures when they arrived on the Pacific Coast but continued to espouse a liberal and tolerant view of the world. Some miners were past denizens of failed Utopian movements, including the French disciples of Charles Fourier, who rubbed shoulders in San Francisco with the Mormons who had succeeded them in the quest for an ideally organized society. The excitement of the California Gold Rush retained its allure for European fortune-seekers over some seventy years; that attraction is powerfully expressed in the wonderful first novel of the world-traveling Swiss writer Blaise Cendrars (Frédéric Sauser), *L'Or (Gold)*. Written between 1910 and 1924 and still in print in French, *L'Or* outlines the saga of Cendrars's compatriot Sutter, like Cendrars a Swiss who reinvented himself; it remains the greatest imaginative work about the California idea yet produced by a foreign writer. (It was also adapted for an unproduced film project by the Russian director Sergei Eisenstein.) Cendrars was the outstanding European experimental writer to be concerned with the California myth.

Two figures whose nonconforming nature made them exemplars of the California of that legendary time were "Emperor" Joshua Norton and William Walker. "Emperor" Norton remains a favorite San Francisco personality to this day, more than a century after his death. Born in London in 1818, he had come to San Francisco in 1850 as a commercial agent. A failed attempt to corner the market in rice left him bankrupt and bereft of reason. He soon began appearing on the streets of the city in a military uniform with epaulets and plumed hat, with his two dogs Lazarus and Bummer. He was welcomed and fed in bars and restaurants, though he sought to pay with scrip of his own issuance, on which he was styled "Norton I, Emperor of the United States and Protector of Mexico." His dogs were almost as well loved as he, and the demise of each, ruler as well as pets, was an occasion for real mourning.

A much less benign kind of madness was found in William Walker. This Tennessee-born physician, with his piercing eyes and undeniable charisma, was a man of real intelligence but also of unmistakable evil. He landed in San Francisco in 1850, aged 26, and worked for a time in journalism before launching himself as a "filibuster," that is, as a *gringo* conqueror of hitherto Latin lands to the south, in emulation of the American

victors in the Mexican War. Where Norton proclaimed himself, imaginar-
ily, as Mexico's "protector," Walker sought to transform such idle boasts
into reality.

Walker led an expedition to Baja in 1853, seizing La Paz and proclaiming an independent republic, then declaring his annexation of the Mexican
state of Sonora, on the other side of the gulf. That adventure failed rather
quickly and he returned to San Francisco, where he was tried for violation
of American neutrality laws but was acquitted. He then moved on to the
enterprise that would make him infamous: a revolution in Nicaragua. That
Central American nation loomed large in the minds of Californians, for
vast numbers of emigrants had passed through it in their journey to the
gold fields. Such traffic was also the beginning of a significant Nicaraguan
colony in San Francisco.

Walker's Nicaraguan invasion, in 1855, was backed by discontented
American officials of the Accessory Transit Company, established by transportation magnate Cornelius Vanderbilt to carry travelers from the Atlantic
shore of Nicaragua to the Pacific. More important, Walker was also supported in the beginning by Nicaraguan Liberals, then at war with the country's Conservative faction. The Liberal party was centered in León, the main
town of northern Nicaragua, which had an agricultural and clerical history.
Here, as elsewhere in Latin America, the priestly class was frequently reform
minded, and the Nicaraguan Liberals saw nothing wrong with seeking
American assistance. Indeed, resistance to American influence was led by
the Conservative party, centered in the southern city of Granada on Lake
Nicaragua. That area had grown rich on commerce with the Atlantic via the
San Juan River, and because of the prosperity it derived from trade re-
mained loyal to monarchical and traditional institutions.

Walker arrived in Nicaragua as a supporter of the Liberals, but with a
distinct agenda, that of making Central America a slaveholding dominion
associated with the American South. He assumed all power for himself but
was defeated by armies raised by Nicaragua's Central American neighbors.
He returned to the United States in 1857 but invaded Nicaragua anew and
finally turned up in 1860 in Honduras, where he was arrested by the British
and handed over to the local authorities; they executed him by firing squad.
Without doubt the most vicious action of his ominous career was the destruction by fire of beautiful Granada, known as *La Gran Sultana,* the oldest Spanish city in Nicaragua, graced with many lovely churches and other

structures. Nicaraguans have never forgiven Walker. His ignominy made any association with such ventures highly suspect in California thereafter, and the very term "filibuster" became a loaded political insult.

———————

GOLD RUSH CALIFORNIA, in which such flamboyant Anglos as Norton and Walker flourished, also produced a heroic myth of Hispanic resistance, personified by Joaquín Murieta. The very existence of this putative bandit and guerrilla leader is doubted by many historians. While it is certain that a reward was offered for a brigand named Joaquín, five different suspects bore that given name. The bounty was collected by a deputy sheriff and Mexican War veteran named Harry S. Love, who killed a Hispanic male and severed the victim's head. Joaquín was said to have become an outlaw to avenge a rape or other atrocity suffered by his family at the hands of Anglo miners.

The story or legend of Joaquín Murieta was mainly the work of the poet John Rollin Ridge, also known as Yellow Bird. Ridge was born on a Georgia plantation, the grandson of a Cherokee chief, and was the only survivor of a tribal massacre of the Ridge family carried out by another Cherokee leader, John Ross. Ridge followed the killers to California, then settled there and emerged as a poet and essayist. He composed *The Life and Adventures of Joaquin Murieta, The Celebrated California Bandit,* first printed as a pamphlet in 1854. The saga of the revolutionary avenger of wrongs suffered on account of color carried within it a considerable degree of Ridge's own pain and quest for justice, along with a notable dose of anti-Chinese prejudice, but also served as a depiction of California unease over the conditions of the U.S. conquest.

Murieta became the object of a kind of cult: a certain Cincinnatus Hiner Miller renamed himself after the bandit, to whom he dedicated some poetry. As Joaquin Miller he became the leading nineteenth-century California bard and all-around wild man, with an influence extending into the twentieth century: Ambrose Bierce, Frank Norris, Jack London, and many others counted themselves his friends. The tale of Murieta continues to excite; the Chilean writer Pablo Neruda constructed a version of the myth in which Murieta became a Chilean martyr to *gringo* imperialism. This fantasy, however, is unlikely as much because of the broad-brush identification of "Chileans" in the California of the time as for Neruda's embroidery of the oft-retold story.

Murieta as a symbol embodied both the ambivalence felt by Americans occupying the land and the real impoverishment and other oppression felt by the Hispanic population in American California, whether they were native *Californios,* Mexicans, or "Chileans." The first group was soon deprived of its extensive land grants; the second was reduced to an agricultural laboring class; the last found themselves driven from the gold camps. A fault line in California's social conscience between the Hispanic legacy and an Anglo-Saxon "future," the latter conception carrying all the intimidating power implied by that term, persists today.

But if such an ambiguity was unarguably present among Gold Rush Californians themselves, other observers, of varying temperaments, simply rejoiced at the American conquest. Abraham Lincoln, still a minor political figure, called California "the far best part of our acquisition from Mexico." Karl Marx demanded to know, in an 1849 polemic, "Is it perhaps a misfortune that magnificent California was snatched away from the lazy Mexicans, who did not know what to do with it?" In the succeeding two years Marx grew yet more enthusiastic about California. In late 1850 he and his collaborator, Friedrich Engels, wrote,

> [T]he Californian market itself is unimportant compared to the continual expansion of all the markets on the Pacific coast, compared to the striking increase in trade with Chile and Peru, western Mexico and the [Hawaiian] Islands, and compared to the traffic which has suddenly arisen between Asia, Australia, and California. . . . It may be said that the world has only become round since the necessity has arisen for global steam shipping. . . . No matter how many companies go bankrupt, the steamships—which are doubling the Atlantic traffic, opening up the Pacific, connecting up Australia, New Zealand, Singapore and China with America and are reducing the journey around the world to four months—the steamships will remain.

Marx further noted that the growth of the American market in the aftermath of the conquest of California and the Gold Rush had restored an economic prosperity to the German states that the local ruling classes naïvely ascribed to the restoration of order after the failed 1848 revolution.

A favorite polemical target of Marx at that time, the Russian anarchist and Slavic nationalist Mikhail Bakunin, would come to personally experience the advantages of the expanded Pacific ship traffic that so excited Marx. Bakunin came to San Francisco in 1861, for only six days, but his arrival caused tremendous excitement far away in Europe and especially in his native Russia. Bakunin had been arrested in the German states in 1849, deported to Russia, imprisoned in fortresses there, then banished to Siberia. In June 1861 he left his place of exile in Irkutsk and made his way to the Russian Pacific coast, traveling by sea to Japan. He sailed from Yokohama to San Francisco on an American vessel. The eminent historian of anarchism, Paul Avrich, notes the excitement in Russian radical circles at the news of Bakunin's arrival in California: *Kolokol (The Bell),* the leading journal of Russian democratic opinion, edited from exile in London by Aleksandr Gertsen [Herzen], reported, MIKHAIL ALEKSANDROVICH BAKUNIN IS IN SAN FRANCISCO—HE IS FREE!

The "Pacific rim" relationships (as they would be called today) that illuminated Marx's vision also brought about a demographic development with great influence on California society: the growth of the Chinese immigrant population. Chinese migration to California during the nineteenth century was far exceeded by that of non-Asians; nonetheless it was an extraordinary phenomenon, second in quantity only to the rush of Anglo-Americans to the Pacific Coast, and probably superior to it in rate of expansion. Dana omitted the Chinese in his multicultural panorama of Mexican California, which included considerable numbers of Polynesian Islanders and assorted European nationals. But some Chinese were resident in Alta California as early as 1815, and by 1849 there were 780 in the San Francisco Bay Area. By the next year, the Chinese population in San Francisco had risen to 4,018, and many had gone to the gold fields.

Their situation was not the best, but neither was it the worst. Soon after the admission of California to the Union a state court barred Chinese from serving as trial witnesses in cases involving whites, and the imposition of a Foreign Miners' Tax in the state fell especially heavily on the Chinese gold seekers. Yet prejudice and, particularly violence against the Chinese were notably less in the first twenty years of the state than later on, in the period of class turbulence and economic rivalries from 1870 to 1900. Frank Bailey Millard, a newspaperman and local historian, observed that "Sentiment against the Chinese [in the 1870s] was in strong contrast with that held in California in 1850 as well as at the present day [i.e., in the 1920s], for in both the earlier and the later periods Californians have had a feeling of tolerance for them which at times . . . evinced itself as genuine affection."

Indeed, Mark Twain wrote admiringly of the Chinese, describing their

situation as he saw it in the mid-1860s in *Roughing It,* a book filled with evidence of his genius:

> They are a kindly-disposed, well-meaning race, and are respected and well
> treated by the upper classes, all over the Pacific coast. No Californian *gentle-
> man or lady* [Twain's emphasis] ever abuses or oppresses a [Chinese], under
> any circumstances. . . . Only the scum of the population do it—they and
> their children; they, and, naturally and consistently, the policemen and
> politicians, likewise, for these are the dust-licking pimps and slaves of the
> scum, there as well as elsewhere in America.

Most importantly, Twain observed the high level of civic responsibility and
education found among the Chinese immigrants. Disorderly behavior was
rare, laziness unknown; "[W]hite men often complain of want of work, but
a [Chinese] offers no such complaint," Twain wrote. He further noted that
all of them could "read, write, and cipher with easy facility," skills rare
among the Anglo-American yeomanry—who, although illiterate, possessed
an asset denied the Chinese: the vote.

The enviable level of learning found in the Chinese community was
matched by remarkable capacities for self-governance. The great bulk of
Chinese immigrants came from the city of Guangzhou [Canton] and the
Pearl River delta, a focus of Arab sea trading for centuries and a cosmopolitan borderland like California. They came for gold, certainly, and as laborers in other trades, but also to escape the chaos that was engulfing the
Celestial Empire, as it was then widely called in the West, during the Tai-
ping rebellion of the 1850s and 1860s. Once arrived in California, the Cantonese immediately produced a wide range of durable social institutions of
which the non-Asian settlers, once they understood them, became somewhat jealous. The Chinese were, in general, outstanding in their devotion
to community self-help, mainly developed through regional associations
(huiguan) that grouped colonists coming from the same villages and counties in the province of Guangdong. By the end of the 1850s the main
huiguan had federated in a virtual autonomous government, the Chinese
Consolidated Benevolent Association or Chinese Six Companies, which
long served as the leading political organ of the Chinese in America and
which survives nearly intact today.

The *huiguan* functioned as burial societies, an important matter in a
culture that profoundly honored departed ancestors, but also operated in

the same manner as the mutual benefit societies, fraternal orders, and similar organizations that flourished for a time throughout the United States. They offered the new arrival lodging, loans, and references for work. While the *huiguan* were limited to people from a particular geographical district, their activities were supplemented by other groups, including surname or family associations, and some recruited on a less restricted basis, such as commercial associations, Christian churches, and the secret orders known as Triads. Many Triads were conspiratorial bodies directed against the Qing dynasty, of Manchu origin, which then ruled over China's Han majority.

As the nineteenth century wore on, the Chinese were driven from California's countryside, from mining and agriculture, and forced to mass together in Chinatowns. With the passage of various discriminatory laws, which we will discuss further on, the number of Chinese in California, which once stood near 100,000, or nearly a quarter of the state's population, dropped by half. Instability in Chinese California was also heightened by cruel legal bars to the entry of Chinese women, which left the Chinese men desperately lonely and melancholy, and often made them the victim of gambling, prostitution, and other vices, in addition to the infamous opium habit. Naturally, the illegality of female Chinese immigration also restricted the normal rate of population growth that would have existed if marriage and childbirth were not effectively banned. But the Chinese continued to come, for even in an environment of prejudice and discrimination, within their own communities they knew political freedoms in California (and, to a lesser extent, in Hawaii) that were unknown anywhere in Asia. This great paradox of Asian life in nineteenth-century California—for similar experiences later marked the Japanese and Korean communities—brought forth a series of unanticipated radical developments, with greater impact in Asia itself than in California. As it had been for the Hispanic world and for the United States, California was an Asian borderland.

No sooner was it admitted as a state to the American Union than California illustrated its borderland character with regard to another issue: that of slavery and the festering North-South conflict in the eastern United States. Throughout the 1850s, as the Gold Rush lost its momentum and Pacific Coast society stabilized, the topic of slavery was debated.

Blacks had probably lived in California since the beginning of Spanish exploration, with servants and seamen aboard imperial ships escaping inland when vessels stopped to search for fresh water. The first English-speaking African American of note in Alta California was Allen Light, a marine steward who left the ship *Pilgrim,* in which he sailed in the company of Richard Henry Dana, at Santa Barbara in 1835. Light became a Californian, working as an otter trapper, and was authorized by Mexican governor Juan Bautista Alvarado to suppress otter poaching on the Santa Barbara shore.

Another notable Black figure was William A. Leidesdorff, an Afro-Dane from the Virgin Islands who operated a ship between Hawaii and California, then settled on the American River. He was named American vice consul in Alta California in 1845, and was an active protagonist in the passage of the territory from Mexican to American sovereignty. He was described as the "most valuable resident" of the town of Yerba Buena, the future downtown San Francisco, at his death in 1848. Leidesdorff was also very likely the first open homosexual to live in San Francisco, for his "wife" was a "girl-like" Russian from Alaska.

Many Blacks came to California after gold, and set about founding churches and other community institutions. The generally classless nature of the society made non-Black Californians remarkably sympathetic to them and antipathetic to the slavery cause. For example, Bailey Millard notes that the *Morning Call,* a leading San Francisco newspaper from the Gold Rush era to the end of the century, lost a $5,000 libel judgment for using the word "darky" in a headline. Millard ascribed the decision to "feeling running very strongly in California in sympathy with the negroes of the South." A California Fugitive Slave Law, in effect from 1852 to 1855, was widely resented and seldom enforced; some magistrates held that Mexican law, under which slavery had been abolished in California, had precedence over American law.

In the presidential election of 1856, northern Californians rallied to John C. Frémont, the so-called hero of the Bear Flag events, who came forward as the standard-bearer of the new national Republican Party on an anti-slavery platform. Republican voters "back east" brandished Bear Flags to recall their candidate's California exploits. However, Frémont was unpopular in southern California, where native Hispanic Californians, many of whom hated him, retained considerable political influence. There the Republican standard was borne locally by Francisco P. Ramírez, a writer for a Spanish-language weekly one-sheet newspaper, *El Clamor Público.*

As the Civil War approached the hot, harsh, and hallucinatory hamlet of Los Angeles, which barely supported regular communications with the metropolis of San Francisco, began to ring with anti-Unionist arguments. Some called for a division of California into two, the southern entity to become a slave state. As the rumblings of war grew louder, there was new debate over the concept of a Pacific republic. Surprisingly, even in Unionist San Francisco this fascinating option was not wholly excluded but simply criticized as too far in advance of the times. The *Alta California,* a San Francisco daily, argued that a maritime republic on the West Coast of North America might become a possibility with the growth of wealth and population in the region, but warned that it would take at least three generations, and probably more, for such a result to take place.

Once the Civil War began, northern California became rather excitably loyalist, and southern California deepened its pro-Confederate reputation. This was hardly surprising; Los Angeles was distant from the gold fields, and most of the Anglos who settled there came from the American South. Their mentality was entirely different from the open-minded attitude that bloomed elsewhere in the state.

Nevertheless, from the very first decade of American rule Los Angeles sheltered religious and spiritual cranks: the first book printed in the town was a pamphlet on reform of the Christian churches by one William Money, an incoherent visionary who claimed to have been born with four teeth in his head and a right eye colored like the rainbow. Like Emperor Norton for San Franciscans, William Money seems a powerful archetype for Angeleños, with the distinction that San Franciscans were accepting of Norton whereas Angeleños have consistently seemed enthusiastic, rather than merely tolerant, about characters like Money. Money's sectarian organizational efforts went on for some years, and his preachings were printed in both English and Spanish.

Notwithstanding their distaste for Frémont, some California Hispanics rallied to the Republican cause in 1860 when Abraham Lincoln was the party's nominee. *El Clamor Público,* the Los Angeles weekly, was condemned by pro-Confederate elements as the most violent Abolitionist organ in the state. Spanish journalistic enterprises in Los Angeles provide a remarkable look into a highly contradictory bilingual society that had already produced separatist tendencies as well as cultural harbingers of the later distinctive culture of southern California.

For example, Francisco Ramírez, the editor of *El Clamor Público* and a

Republican politician, had become famous before the age of 17, in the early 1850s, as an editor of the Spanish pages of the weekly *Los Angeles Star,* the first newspaper in southern California. A youthful prodigy such as Ramírez looks like an archetype in the local landscape alongside an eccentric like William Money. Again in the latter category, Los Angeles became famous during the Civil War because of the antics of Peter Biggs, a barber who was arrested for shouting "Hurrah for Jeff Davis!"—and who was Black.

The *Los Angeles Star* also printed the first literary works of a teenager, Ina Coolbrith, a great-niece of the Mormon prophet Joseph Smith. She had come across the Sierra Nevada as a tiny child in the company of the Black pathfinder, guide, and mountain man James Beckwourth. Coolbrith much later was named state poet laureate and became the mentor of Jack London. But regardless of its literary distinction, the *Star* was widely attacked during the Civil War as a "secesh" organ for its pro-Southern diatribes. San Franciscans feared throughout the war that Los Angeles would serve as the staging area for secessionist plotting. The "City of Angels" was already declared a "City of Demons" by one religious observer.

The *Star* was briefly banned from the mails and express delivery services in 1862 for having been "used for the purpose of overthrowing the government of the United States." It was not the only California newspaper to be censured for its proslavery stance. The *San Jose Tribune,* which called Lincoln an "illiterate backwoodsman" and labeled his government "galling military despotism," was similarly sanctioned, along with two papers in Stockton and others in Tulare, Visalia, and Placerville. Sometimes Unionist sentiment led to the use of physical force. Some soldiers smashed the press of the Visalia *Equal Rights Expositor* for its pro-Southern editorials; two weeks later the same fate was visited on the *Banner of Liberty,* published in Solano County. In 1865, news of the assassination of President Lincoln was met in San Francisco by the sacking of the "Copperhead" or alleged pro-Confederate dailies, an action recorded with some glee by the newly established *Daily Dramatic Chronicle* (later the *San Francisco Chronicle*), which was founded as a throwaway entertainment sheet by two teenaged Jewish brothers, Michael and Charles de Young.

WITH THE UNION victory in the Civil War southern California separatism died out. Although Union partisans contributed funds to the war and even enlisted, the fighting itself had no direct impact in the state. But the Civil War brought with it a development of great moment for Californians in the form of the legal foundation of the transcontinental railroad system.

The "Pacific railroad"—universally believed by settlers on the Pacific Slope to be the means for real prosperity to emerge, at least in the beginning—was also seen by many as a "Republican," Unionist, and Northern conception. In 1860, the state had elected a Republican governor, Leland Stanford, who would play a considerable role in the history of the state and the railroad. The federal authorities in 1862 chartered the construction of the Union Pacific railroad, to run from the Missouri river to the border of the territories of Utah and Nevada. The Central Pacific Railroad Company, which was to build eastward from the Sacramento Valley to meet the Union Pacific, had been incorporated in 1861 by Stanford and three associates named Mark Hopkins, Collis P. Huntington, and Charles Crocker. All four were moderately successful merchants in Sacramento.

The four partners almost immediately decided on a policy with deep and traumatic effects: construction of the trackage from the Pacific coast eastward would be carried out by contract laborers from China, who were widely praised for their commitment to work and reduced economic requirements. The mainly Irish Union Pacific construction crews and the Chinese gangs of the Central Pacific blasted and built their way across deserts and mountain ranges, finally meeting at a negotiated junction point in Utah in 1869. The completion of the transcontinental railroad was cause for voluble celebration in California. The economic advantages, in terms of the traffic of goods as well as ease of travel for residents and future newcomers, could not be questioned. But the Pacific railroad also left a legacy of discontent that marked public life in the state for some forty years, involving five issues: race, land ownership, political corruption, abuse of the transportation monopoly, and labor relations.

The racial aspect of the Pacific railroad controversy was the most obvious. Skilled laborers of all races in California had from the commencement of the Gold Rush enjoyed high wages and social status owing to the scarcity of experienced workmen in a free labor market, given the attractive alternative of the mines as well as the distance from the rest of the country. A certain layer in the non-Asian working class, mainly Irish and often without regular trades, saw the importation of Chinese contract workers as a threat to these advantages. Others viewed the phenomenon in grimmer terms, fearing that the Chinese on the Pacific Slope would become a kept labor force like the Blacks of the prewar South. As we have noted, real racial violence against the Chinese had been comparatively rare in California before this period, and was to become so afterward. But now class anger at the new power of the railroad, and at the allied ocean steamer companies which also employed Asian contract workers, fueled anti-Asian resentment.

The great wealth and influence of the Pacific rail combine fostered other economic and political conditions that stirred up opinion against the corporation. As an incentive to railroad construction, the combine had been furnished with vast public-land grants across the Sierra Nevada and down into the Central Valley. The Central Pacific builders were not satisfied with such generosity; once the road was under construction they demanded cash payments from towns along the proposed right of way, declaring that if no funds were forthcoming the line would bypass the town and leave it to wither and die. By these methods they gouged $848,000 out of Sacramento and Placer Counties alone; when the Southern Pacific line was built from San Francisco to New Orleans, Huntington demanded 5 percent of the assessed valuation of all land in Los Angeles County, and the eventual payoff to the railroad combine amounted to $100 for every man, woman, and child in the county, Indians included.

In addition to their extraordinary land manipulations, which left the Central Pacific-Southern Pacific system the biggest landlord in California for generations, the Pacific rail combine found other ways to feather its nest. The federal government reimbursed the combine on the basis of track mileage, so the main line was built over the peaks of the Sierra Nevada rather than through the passes. In the final reckoning, the blackmailing of resources from local communities, the swindling of the national government by inflating costs, and the accounting schemes of the Contract and Finance Company, which administered the construction work (and which had an equally unsavory parallel in the form of the Crédit Mobilier, associated with the Union Pacific), had an amazing result: the Central Pacific Railroad from Sacramento to Utah was completed without the expenditure of a single penny from the pockets of Messrs. Stanford, Hopkins, Huntington, and Crocker, its owners.

As if this successful experiment in wholesale financial abuse was not enough, Californians also found that their state government had become an invertebrate servant of the railroad corporation's interests; given Stanford's statehouse career this was doubtless predictable. But worst of all, once the railroad commenced full operation it was clear that the habit of extortion from the community employed in building the line would continue to characterize the railroad's business practices: farmers, merchants, and other shippers saw that the costs of transportation, far from easing the producers' burden, were set by the railroad for the convenience and profit of the railroad. Farmers began joining a secret order, the Grange, to oppose the railroads, and soon appealed to labor for "war upon monopolies."

This constellation of problems—Chinese contract labor, land tenure, political domination, and the pricing of its services, made enemies of the railroad out of thousands of Californians.

The ensuing struggle to limit railroad power consumed California political life for decades, but the railroad itself had an irremediable constitutional weakness in the form of its own workforce. The army of employees hired to operate the system—engineers and firemen, conductors and brakemen, telegraphers and clerks, shop and roadway workers, switchmen—produced a distinctive subculture of common sentiment and unity in feeling that was stronger than any previously known in America's industrial working class. Railroad workers were more than simply replaceable human parts in an industrial apparatus; they had a sense of community, of a shared mission in the mastery of a new and wonderful technology, of pride and self-respect. Most of their work had a professional, rather than a proletarian character. Throughout the nineteenth century the "mechanic" epitomized the socially conscious workman; and the railroad was a vast force of mechanics. These aspects of railroad life would, inevitably, bring about a powerful labor upsurge that, even more than the reform campaigns of antirailroad politicians, imposed limits on the power of the railroad combine.

Stanford and his ring soon understood that something had gone wrong with their plans for empire. The Central Pacific began quarreling with the federal authorities over freight charges, which the railroad unpatriotically assessed on government traffic. In September 1873, Stanford and Hopkins, the president and secretary-treasurer of the Central Pacific, appeared at the line's Sacramento car and locomotive shops to defend themselves before their employees. Stanford declared that railroad service had been made cheaper in California than anywhere else in the country "by this overgrown and dangerous monopoly that they tell so much about." The San Joaquin Valley had been worthless except as cattle pasture until the completion of the line, he argued. Indeed, according to Stanford the railroad was anything but a monopoly—rather, it was the "breaker-down of monopolies," preventing anyone from cornering the market in basic commodities such as sugar, soap, and molasses. Further, he insisted, the railroad had forced the monopolistic Western Union Company to lower its rates for telegraph service. The railroad had even improved the competitiveness of the newspapers, he said. After Stanford completed this oration, Hopkins came forward to explain that because of the financial obstacles facing the railroad company construction of further lines would cease—and, most significantly, payroll would be reduced and men would be discharged. "With apparently deep emotion [Hopkins] said he felt much disappointed that the people of Sacramento should recently have voted against the friends of the railroad company there."

Thus the years following the Civil War remained turbulent in California. It was an unstable time globally; the Paris Commune of 1871, which began in the wake of France's defeat in war by Prussia, shocked the world with the return of bloody conflict to the country still considered the homeland of revolution. However, the atrocities that attended the suppression of the Commune were aimed less at the abstract, almost mythical concept of revolution than at the militant working class. The small-scale "civil war in France" was a powerful harbinger of growing class conflict in every major country, and left many anxious about the future of European society as a whole. In addition, the Irish nationalist revolutionary movement had entered a phrase of greater aggressivity in its struggle against Britain.

These distant events were followed with great interest and emotion on the Pacific Coast. A survey published in autumn 1873 in the *San Francisco Chronicle* called California "the most cosmopolitan state in the globe," and described San Francisco as "a city of a hundred tongues." Unsigned, it began, "San Francisco is one of the few cities which present in miniature a picture of the world, where, as in a kaleidoscope, may be viewed its varied inhabitants—where new manners and habits of thought are encountered every day." The writer noted that ancient Rome and modern Britain both derived their power from the admixture of peoples, and predicted a similar outcome for the United States.

Basing his observations on the 1870 census, the *Chronicle* writer
pointed out that of the 190,000 inhabitants of San Francisco half were foreign-born. Chinese made up a quarter of the latter, about 25,000, but because of the ban on entry of Asian women, Chinese men constituted a third
of the foreign-born males in the city, and a full quarter of all men over 21.
The leading ethnic groups, aside from the Chinese, Americans, Irish, and
Germans, were the French, English, Scots, Italians and Italian Swiss, Mexicans, "Chileans," Portuguese, and Scandinavians. They were followed by
Canadians, Spaniards, Australians, and Hawaiian Islanders. Still, "every nation has a representative among the remainder," including Japanese, Hin-
dus, Eskimos, and Aleuts—the last, of course, having a history on the coast
predating that of most Anglos.

Nearly a third of the non-Asian residents of San Francisco were Irish,
and they made up a powerful social and political force. They were chiefly
employed at physical labor, but could be found in nearly every trade, and
had flourished in tailoring. However, notwithstanding their effectiveness
in politics, their organizational talents were widely deemed inferior to
those of the next-largest white immigrant group, the Germans, who possessed a variety of mutual-aid and other voluntary societies that were
wealthy and varied in their activities. Germans mainly worked as wholesale merchants, mechanics, and grocery dealers, although some German
Jews were prominent in the dry-goods and fancy-goods businesses. The
Italians, typically Genoese, were known as fishermen, with a hundred
boats working the Bay in 1873. The Scandinavians were nearly all sailors.

San Francisco in 1873 had a lively ethnic press in addition to its
leading English-language dailies, which then included the *Morning Call*
and the *Bulletin* (both considered antilabor after a bitter strike by the Typographical Union in 1870), the *Alta California,* the *Chronicle,* the *Examiner,* and the *Post.* Four weeklies catered to the Irish interest; three
others came out in Spanish. Two German papers appeared daily, supplemented by two literary and humorous weeklies in the same language.
The Italian community also supported two dailies, one monarchist and
one, *La Voce del Popolo,* favoring a republic. The French press consisted
of a conservative paper, *Le Courrier de San Francisco,* and the radical *Le
Petit Journal;* a paper called *L'Internationale,* which supported the revolutionary program of the Commune, was issued for a time, but disappeared. Finally, local Russians could read items in their language printed

in the *Alaska Herald.* The foundation of a Chinese newspaper was still in the future.

————————

READERS OF SO varied a mass of print were treated to a series of epical and provocative dramas unfolding across the state in 1873—a year that also featured a major financial panic. The first such tale was that of the Modoc War, the last and greatest battle in the armed resistance of the Native Americans in California. By this time, twenty-five years after the arrival of Americans in large numbers, and twenty years after the warnings of J. Ross Browne about the injustices done to them, California Indians had been in the main wiped out by the most brutal methods of massacre, or had been pushed deep into the mountains and wastelands on the margins of settled society. Repeated so-called "Indian wars" were exercises in wholesale killing by whites for sport; in an era when the telegraph had made daily newspapers true organs of mass communication, these spectacles attracted the interest of the whole world.

Remarkably enough, the unsettled California of the Indian Wars also saw a major disturbance involving its Hispanic population, some of whom felt a resentment at Anglo authority as bitter as that of Indians. The same journals that reported breathlessly on the dénouement of the Modoc "rebellion" expended considerable ink on a "bandit," the California native Tiburcio Vásquez, who raged up and down the valleys of the state. Unlike Murieta before him, Vásquez was a real person whose existence cannot be doubted, given that he was hanged, at the age of 39, in San Jose in 1873. Vásquez was an effective guerrilla marauder who used the badlands of San Benito County as his base; California still had plenty of places to hide. Born in Monterey, Vásquez seems to have been associated in an obscure way with the missions, but was convicted of various crimes and served a prison sentence at San Quentin. On his release in 1863, it was said, he took up banditry, ranging from Pleasanton to Visalia, occasionally hiding in Mexico but generally preferring refuge in the foothills and ridges of the Coast Range. He was put to death after being found guilty of murder. The *San Francisco Chronicle* declared with satisfaction, "[B]y the execution of that sentence California has been rid of one of the bloodiest scoundrels of the century."

Indian rebels and Vásquez's banditry underscored the resentments of disenfranchised nonwhites in California. But the conscience of the state's laboring population was soon outraged anew by the abuses practiced aboard American ships.

On Saturday, September 27, 1873, the ship *Sunrise* arrived in San Francisco from New York after a five-month voyage. As was common at the time, a mass of "runners" employed by boardinghouses and saloons catering to sailors rowed out to the ship in fast boats and swarmed aboard, enticing the crew to patronize their establishments and looking for mariners who might quickly fill a berth for an outbound trip. What the "runners" learned aboard the *Sunrise* was "fearful," according to the journalism of the day. The *Sunrise* was a fairly typical Yankee "hell-ship," ruled by seemingly crazed officers who got the work aboard done by the application of continuous physical abuse, and who enforced their power by shortening what were already insufficient rations. But this trip was different: the sailors were reported to be seeking a charge of triple murder against the *Sunrise*'s first mate, a certain Harris, who fled the ship.

The *Sunrise* case quickly gripped the attention of the public. Three crew members had died on the voyage. The first report held they had been forced overboard at the point of a gun by Harris; then it was said they had committed suicide. The ship's captain, Robert K. Clarke, was interviewed by reporters and explained each of the three deaths by the alleged bad qualities of the victims. The first man to jump overboard, Charles Brown, was "very dirty" as well as incompetent, the captain said, noting that Brown had "no clothes to go a voyage of 18,000 miles." Brown simply vanished from the foredeck, according to the captain.

The second victim, John Condiff, was also incompetent and dirty, the captain declared. He was incapable of climbing the rigging, scraped the deck in the wrong direction, and went to sleep while on lookout duty. Furthermore, Condiff was so filthy and snored so loudly that the rest of the seamen had forced him to sleep alone outside their forecastle. Condiff had, the captain said, "slipped overboard" from the bow.

The third suicide, Francis Carrigan, was a mere youth of 17 or 18. He had apparently slipped and fallen from the rigging, Captain Clarke said; but Harris, the mate, told a newspaper reporter before his disappearance that Carrigan was a liar and had been put in irons by the captain.

The incapacity of the three men was easily explained, according to crew members who came forward to denounce the officers. Brown, Condiff, and

Carrigan were not sailors at all, but unfortunates "shanghaied"—that is, kidnapped—in New York. They knew little about the sea and Brown spoke English poorly. Enraged by the victims' unpreparedness for shipboard labor, the first mate, the boatswain, and the captain had beaten and otherwise tormented the men throughout the passage. The three were forced to work through the night as well as the day, deprived of sleep, kicked awake by the heavy boots of the first officer, hit with fists, pieces of rope, and any other handy object, taunted, starved, and denied water.

Kept awake on deck for twenty-four hours straight without food or water, beaten hourly so that he was rendered a virtual cripple, Brown had stood only eleven days of such treatment, and had jumped overboard in "madness and desperation," according to a letter signed by sixteen crew members and printed in the *Chronicle*. Condiff, a grocer, defiant and complaining, was pummeled into a state where his legs had swollen to double their normal size and his body was covered by scabs and bruises, and was then forced to sleep with hogs. He was harassed by Captain Clarke, who called him a coward for not immediately following Brown over the side. Condiff suffered for another month before he did, at last, follow Brown and leap to his death. Carrigan, similarly beaten, forbidden food and sleep, may have fallen from the rigging, according to one of the protesting sailors, but only because he was exhausted by ill treatment; but whether he fell or jumped, they charged, the officers were responsible for his death.

Furthermore, the rest of the crew detailed similar abuses. The sailors never had more than four out of twenty-four hours to sleep; the food allowance had been reduced for six weeks, with the men denied adequate bread. Yet two dogs kept aboard by the captain were given loaves to chew on, and were provided with a large tub of water while the men were suffering thirst. "I have stolen a drink from that tub often," one of the crew told a *Chronicle* reporter. These atrocities had been enacted in the presence of the captain's wife and children who, rather than softening the officers' aggressive attitudes, laughed at their mistreatment of the crew.

One of the protesting sailors, Thomas Furt, summarized the situation: "We want to know if there *is* any law to protect the sailor." Indeed, the weight of American maritime law at that time denied any recognition of the sailor's rights. Paul S. Taylor, husband of the documentary photographer Dorothea Lange and himself an outstanding California economic historian, wrote that "the revolutions and emancipating decrees of Europe, and the thirteenth amendment in the United States [which abolished Black slavery] passed the sailor by. The passage of time . . . not only failed to remove his bondage to the vessel but statutory enactment further stamped his status as peculiar and unfree." In 1872, the year before the *Sunrise* scandal, a federal Shipping Commissioner's Act reinforced the legal sanction on "deserting" sailors who, if they quit the ship before a voyage was completed, could be arrested, imprisoned, and forcibly returned to the vessel.

Other cases of shipboard brutality had come before the California public, but the *Sunrise* case seemed to have a life of its own. Captain Clarke bristled at the insistence of newspaper reporters in pursuing the matter. The protesting sailors had no means apart from a fickle press and expensive courts to air their grievances, and were soon dissuaded from prosecuting their claim before the law. Newspapermen found that Furt and others who had denounced the officers of the *Sunrise* were silenced by cash payments from the captain. Hundreds of West Coast seamen waited to see if the outcome of this case would be any different from those that came before, and newspaper readers continued to make the *Sunrise* the main topic of daily conversation in the city. Then, as reported in the *Chronicle,* a warrant was sworn out for the arrest of Captain Clarke in the death of Charles Brown. The warrant had been obtained by a private citizen named Henry George.

THE *CHRONICLE* NEGLECTED to mention that Henry George, then 34, a man with red hair, an open countenance, small hands, and a delicate complexion, was the editor of a rival daily, the *Evening Post.* George had founded the *Post* in 1871; from the beginning it stood as a defender of labor. George was a gifted journalist but seemed unable to remain in one place for very long. Born in Philadelphia, the son of a publisher of Episcopal literature, he had himself shipped out to sea at 15, traveling to Australia and India; he became an advocate for sailors' rights out of his own experience. When he returned home, however, he was apprenticed to a printer, and learned to set type.

Nonconforming through and through, George was destined to become the first California thinker to move the world thanks to his book *Progress and Poverty,* begun in 1877. After his first trip to sea, he had become an active Abolitionist, and wrote a few immature essays before unemployment in Philadelphia drove him back to sea. He sailed to San Francisco in 1858 aboard the *Shubrick,* a steamship operated by the U.S. Lighthouse Service. Once landed in California, he worked as a printer, along with other menial jobs, since demand for typesetters was unstable; however, although undersized (he stood on a riser to set type) he qualified as a journeyman. He married and settled into family life, but encountered obstacles to lasting success wherever he turned. He went from newspaper to newspaper, from San Francisco to Sacramento and back, briefly joining others in the trade in attempts to establish new journals and printshops. He, his wife, and the children who were soon born contended with near starvation.

George began to despair, but at the very bottom of his difficulties he discovered he could write articles as well as set them in type, and that his writings, as well as the type he set, could be printed. He began by sending letters to the editors of the San Francisco dailies, dealing with the condition of seamen and the need for working men to take up social questions. Soon he was published in the company of Mark Twain and Bret Harte, the California literary aristocrats of the moment. In 1865, while working as a part-time typesetter for the *Alta California,* he learned of the assassination of Lincoln, joined a mob that sacked the pro-Southern daily *News-Letter,* then wrote an impassioned eulogy of the dead president that led to the *Alta*'s editor calling him from the composing room to an assignment as a reporter.

George's professional situation stabilized a very little bit, although his personality could not. He joined an expedition to assist the Mexican partisans of Benito Juárez in their struggle against the French, who had invaded Mexico and installed an Austrian prince, Maximilian, as its ruler. The venture was quickly headed off by the U.S. authorities, but George became a leading member of the ephemeral Monroe League, which unsuccessfully tried to launch a second such attempt. Although the intentions of George and the Monroe League had something in common with the filibustering of Walker ten years before, their political attitudes, at least as publicly stated, were different. George's Mexican adventures were followed by more vagabondage in the company of his incredibly patient wife, including a position with the state printing office in Sacramento, new jobs with San Francisco newspapers, and the establishment of the *Evening Post.*

A year before the completion of the Pacific railroad, George traveled East. He went to New York to find a way around the exclusionary practices of the Associated Press, which discriminated against new papers. He had already become, along with his California compatriots, a critic of growing monopoly; some of his early printed pieces had been signed "Proletarian." Writing on the coming of the transcontinental railroad to California, he warned,

> The completion of the railroad and the consequent great increase of business and population, will not be a benefit to all of us, but only to a portion. . . . [T]hose who have, it will make wealthier; for those who *have not* it will make it more difficult to get. Those who have lands, mines, established business, special abilities of certain kinds, will become richer for it and find increased opportunities; those who have only their own labor will become poorer, and find it harder to get ahead.

These words were prescient to an extreme. As George traveled the East Coast he found that the railroad companies there had practiced extortion of industry through rate-gouging and the buying and selling of legislative officials on a scale impossible in remote, provincial California. He experienced other abuses of the new civilization: while Californians worshipped sudden riches gained or lost at mining, which at least involved some hard labor, Easterners reveled in the legal gambling offered by the parasites of Wall Street. Denied a franchise by the Associated Press, he launched a new wire service from Philadelphia, but was prevented by the monopolistic Western Union from using their facilities, first by a ban, then by rate manipulation.

George returned to San Francisco, outraged at the grotesque miseries he had seen piled one upon the other in the clogged tenements of the great Eastern cities. He wrote on the matter of Chinese contract labor in California, taking a predictably negative position, though he noted that the race issue on the Pacific Coast was, at bottom, a labor problem. The article provoked wide comment when it elicited a letter from the British political economist John Stuart Mill, which George printed with his reply. (Mill, by the way, defended the Chinese and called for their assimilation, rather than their exclusion from California.)

Soon afterward, Henry George received his "ecstatic" revelation, which would mark the rest of his life and make him world famous. Riding on horseback in the Oakland hills, he heard that a local man was offering land at $1,000 per acre. Suddenly George perceived that the basis of all social injustice lay in the inevitable growth of land values, particularly the value of unused land—not because of human labor and improvement of the property but because of the broader expansion and development of the community. Profits on land should properly accrue to the whole of society, not to the individual titleholder, who might play no role at all in their creation except to hold title. Social development increased the worth of land, but while the community taxed the workman and the employer to support public services the landlord evaded paying his fair share. Land, necessary for progress, came to benefit the speculator rather than the producer. And in California there was no more offensive and abusive speculator than the state's biggest-ever landlord, the Pacific railroad combine, or, as it was soon nicknamed for its unchallenged expansion of branch lines throughout the state, "the Octopus."

George began agitating against the railroad almost as soon as it opened for traffic, and by 1871 had completed his first extensive work, a pamphlet titled *Our Land and Land Policy.* He called for a tax to be levied on land alone, not on the improvements to it, with the revenue collected used for social purposes. Labor should not be taxed at all, he wrote. The tax on land would be the same whether its owner kept it unused for speculative purposes, or built a house on it and lived in it, or collected rent from it. The outcome of his tax plan, he said, would be a fall in the price of land, and an end to speculation and monopolization in land. The removal of the tax burden from the producers and sellers of goods alone would stimulate demand colossally, boosting employment and securing prosperity.

George's conceptions, which would be finalized in his theory of the Single Tax, were complex, but offered answers to enemies of the railroad. At the time of the *Sunrise* incident, the bulk of George's writing in this field, as well as his political activities (including a climactic intervention in the Irish revolutionary movement), remained ahead of him; but the main effort of the seamen to organize for their common interest was also delayed for another dozen years. The captain and first mate of the *Sunrise* were tried and punished, in great part thanks to George's persistence. And the truly desperate matter of sailors' rights was again dramatized, two years after the *Sunrise* events, by the affair of the schooner *Jefferson Borden.* But regardless of the outrage over such tragedies that seized radicals like George as well as ordinary working men and women, labor organization proceeded very slowly until the depression year 1877, when a bloody convulsion changed the nation completely, "back East" as well as on the Pacific coast.

The global unrest that began with the Paris Commune of 1871 had yet to abate. From the domestic American perspective, the year 1877 is mainly known for the political compromise worked out by the Republicans and Democrats over the future of the formerly rebellious Southern states. Put simply, the compromise of 1877 assured that a Republican president, Rutherford B. Hayes, who had lacked a majority of the popular votes but enjoyed a one-vote advantage in the electoral college, would suspend the Reconstruction laws and other post-Civil War measures that white Southerners, who were uniformly Democratic, believed had victimized them while they enfranchised Black citizens. The compromise called forth extensive debate, but the upheaval it caused in the press was as nothing compared with the fear and trembling occasioned by the great strike that broke out in the summer of that year.

The strike began in the Cumberland Valley, among railroad workers whose wages had been cut, although a depressed business cycle had already brought the specter of "hard times." Within days the work stoppage had spread through Maryland, West Virginia, Pennsylvania, and Ohio, and had sparked numerous riots. The city of Pittsburgh was destroyed; Baltimore, Philadelphia, Wheeling, and many others were devastated. Hundreds of people were killed or wounded. Volunteers were raised and militia sent to do battle with the strikers, their families and supporters. In the view of most, the horrors of the Paris Commune had come to America.

Yet popular feeling against railroad power was so great that even while it reported "a fearful slaughter" in Reading, Pennsylvania, with militia in Buffalo firing on rioters, the *San Francisco Chronicle* thundered, pointing to the prewar South, "those old slaveholders were models of mildness compared with the average railway corporation in the treatment of its employees." Strike violence seemed to be confined, fortunately, to the East and Midwest; the Central Pacific workers were quiet for the time being, if only because, as explained by railroad officials in San Francisco, a pay cut like that posted in the East had been rescinded.

Given the sympathies of San Franciscans for the Eastern strikers, it was not surprising that about noon on Monday, July 23, 1877, an obscure labor figure named A. J. Starkweather, described in the *Chronicle* as a "peddler," appeared on Montgomery Street with a banner calling for support of the workers of Pittsburgh and Baltimore. Starkweather was arrested and his banner confiscated; but a similar notice had appeared in all the dailies that morning, following a meeting Sunday evening at which anti-Chinese opinions had been heard, mixed in with calls for support to the railroad strikers. Throughout Monday rumors circulated that a proposed demonstration might turn into an anti-Chinese riot. Although anti-Chinese bloodshed had occurred during the Gold Rush and Chinese had been forced out of rural California into the urban Chinatowns, most anti-Asian aggression in California since the Civil War had remained verbal, except for common street assaults habitually carried out by young white hoodlums.

Nevertheless, precautions were taken, and almost all the police in the city were sent to protect San Francisco's Chinatown. By 8:00 P.M. Monday night as many as 8,000 people had gathered at a sandlot south of the new City Hall, at a spot where many anti-Chinese orations had been delivered in recent times. Speakers addressed the crowd, but limited themselves to arguments in favor of the Eastern rail strikers, leavened with disapproval of mob action. A resolution was read and passed in which the working men and women of San Francisco declared their "heartfelt sympathy to the families and friends of those who have been shot down while fighting the battle of oppressed labor," condemned the depression as a product of capitalist greed, protested the railroad land grab, and decried the failure of Congress to address the plight of hundreds of thousands of unemployed who had been forced into poorhouses, prisons, and vagabondage by the economic downturn. The resolution was, indeed, filled with a spirit of class war, calling for withdrawal of troops from the Eastern strike zones and extensive antimonopoly reforms, and warning of a corporate conspiracy to reduce free labor to servitude. But nowhere did it mention the Chinese.

The assembly was mainly peaceful until 8:15, when shots were fired at the crowd by a drunken man. A suspect was arrested, but a half hour later about fifty people rushed the building from which the shots had been fired, and a riot was prevented only when others at the scene claimed the gunfire had originated elsewhere. Some in the crowd were now unsettled, and the majority of the participants began leaving. "Ruffians" had, however, infiltrated the meeting, and interrupted the moderate speakers with anti-Chinese catcalls. Individuals offered such diplomatic suggestions as the bombing of Chinese theaters, and fights broke out. A boy was arrested and then freed from the police by hoodlums. The ranks of the labor demonstrators had thinned considerably when, about 9:00 P.M., an "anti-coolie club" marched up Market Street with a musical band and a banner proclaiming

"SELF-PRESERVATION IS THE FIRST LAW OF NATURE." This body had its own orators, who harangued the remaining persons present, with the last speaker calling for patience in the face of police and military—but also demanding that the anti-Chinese forces organize secretly for a "clean sweep" that would soon take place, and threatening any politician who did not answer to the demands of the voters with hanging from a lamppost.

Within minutes a riot had begun. A section of the crowd, loud with encouragements, headed toward Chinatown. A Chinese laundry two blocks north of City Hall was attacked, its windows broken, its operators forced out the back door, and two policemen overcome by the mob, with one seriously injured. A neighboring laundry was also ruined, but the Chinese within again escaped, and the angry rioters turned on a non-Asian-owned grocery, which they looted for whisky. Soon the first fire had been set, in another laundry, which burned fiercely, with flames high in the air. The crowd swelled with bystanders, most of whom remained watchful as a band of hoodlums continued its work. The arrival of police from City Hall, detailed to assist the firefighters, caused the mob to disappear briefly, but it formed up again and, now plentifully armed with kerosene, attacked more laundries. Throwing bricks and cobblestones, the mob emptied adjoining non-Asian businesses, including an Italian fruit stand and an artificial-flower shop, and set fire to a residential building. The mob cut the fire hoses in several places, and even briefly seized a hose. The rioters reached the edge of Chinatown but were held back by a double rank of police, who then charged and charged again, driving them away. About twelve laundries had been destroyed in a crescent around Chinatown, from the vicinity of City Hall to North Beach, where another police charge with clubs readily employed had vanquished a section of the mob.

The main gang of laundry assailants began at a strength of about three hundred, but by midnight had dwindled to a couple of dozen, who nevertheless continued marching, yelling, and tussling with police. A curfew was declared along Dupont Street, the main thoroughfare of Chinatown, which today is known to English speakers as Grant Avenue although Chinese residents still call it "Dupont-gai." Fewer than a dozen people were arrested, and the *Chronicle* noted that some Chinese had saved their laundries by dousing lights and removing signs. In an unrelated but significant incident, some sailors that same day had beaten up a man who appeared in the local Shipping Commissioner's Office offering to ship a crew of Filipino sailors aboard the vessel *Indiana,* bound for Ireland. As an incentive, he had offered the "Manila" seamen $18 per month, well below the prevailing wage of $25 per month for American mariners.

Rioting continued for days. Much of the later violence came from teenage and subteenage boys, and parents were urged to keep them home. More laundries were demolished, buildings were torched, several Chinese were killed, the Central Pacific sent its superintendent to the police to remind them that it had rescinded its wage cut, and two hundred prominent merchants and property owners met to consider reinstating the Vigilance Committee, which had administered rapid justice during the lawless years just after the Gold Rush. Twenty-four of their members were constituted as a General Committee of Safety. City officials insisted that responsible labor had nothing to do with such depredations; labor representatives said the same. A National Guard colonel warned that the real issue was not the Chinese but unemployment, particularly among the young.

As the days wore on, new and terrible incidents occurred. On the night of Wednesday, July 25, an anti-Chinese meeting was held, again in the sandlot adjacent to City Hall, and in its aftermath twenty more laundries were sacked. An open attempt was made to burn the Pacific Mail Steamship wharf, on the pretext that the company had a boatload of Chinese on its way to San Francisco. Police who arrived at the dock faced hours of combat with the mob, but the safety committee elected the day before turned out 3,000 men to patrol the streets, and, armed with pick-handles, they swelled the ranks of the regular officers. Several rioters were killed in this mêlée. By this time the Chinese themselves had begun organizing for self-defense and had accumulated stones as well as an occasional firearm. Meanwhile the excitement had spread to Oakland, San Jose, and the mines in Virginia City, Nevada, where unionism was strong.

The effective revival of vigilante rule in the city brought the disorders to an end, with numerous arrests, an unknown number of dead and wounded, and a considerable loss of property. Assaults and arson attempts continued, but in very reduced number. By the end of the week the Pacific Mail Steamship Co.'s *City of Tokio* had landed its 188 Chinese passengers, who rode to Chinatown in express wagons, accompanied by a party of sixty-five police. By then, even the anti-Chinese political groups in the city had denounced the riots. A brisk decline in anti-Chinese enthusiasm may also have had something to do with reports in the newspapers that China-

town had been transformed into "a complete arsenal," with enough new rifles on hand to arm every male Chinese. According to the *Chronicle,* the
mood in Chinatown was wary but unsubdued; the Chinese did not seek
vengeance, the paper assured its readers, but they would not be unhappy at
an assault on Chinatown itself by the hoodlums, who would receive a long-
awaited lesson.

If there was a moral to the episode, it was that the greater part of white
opinion in San Francisco, although prejudiced against Asian immigrants,
found the hard-working and mainly inoffensive Chinese far preferable as
neighbors to the destructive element in the white proletariat, some of
whom would go to any lengths to avoid regular employment. In the wake
of the 1877 riot, the rising California labor movement briefly veered away
from race issues, although not wholly, for more anti-Asian atrocities were to
come, backed up by exclusionary laws. The anti-Chinese spirit among the
San Francisco Irish, in particular, led to the emergence of a so-called Workingmen's Party under a demagogue named Dennis Kearney, who had stood
with the vigilantes in July 1877 but within two months had changed his attitude when he perceived a political advantage. Kearney held his first anti-
Chinese sandlot meeting in September 1877. His party won control of City
Hall on an anti-Chinese ticket, but the chief exploit of Kearney's puppet,
the elected mayor Isaac Kalloch, was to bring about the assassination of
Chronicle cofounder Charles de Young.

Some labor advocates never lost their antipathy toward the Chinese,
Henry George among them. But George had undertaken another task: In
the year of the anti-Chinese outbreak, he began writing his masterwork,
Progress and Poverty, and in spring 1879 he began circulating the manuscript to publishers. Around him, clerical workers were contending with inventions, including the typewriter and the telephone, that, like the railroad,
transformed daily work; meanwhile industrial workers, the railroaders in
the van, were joining a semisecret "order," the Knights of Labor. *Progress
and Poverty* first came out in an author's edition, and appeared commer-
cially in March 1880.

Only two months later, on May 11, at an obscure spot in the southern San
Joaquin Valley then called Mussel Slough, later renamed the Lucerne Valley,
an event occurred that illuminated George's criticism of railroad land
abuses like a bolt of lightning. The Mussel Slough incident, or massacre, re-

mains one of the pivotal events in California history. It took place in a remote location, and reports on it remained confused; no proper inquiry was ever held. To this day, it is impossible to determine exactly what transpired. But some facts are beyond dispute.

On the morning of Tuesday, May 11, the *San Francisco Chronicle* printed a one-paragraph item:

THE MUSSLE [*sic*] SLOUGH TROUBLES

United States Marshal Poole has gone to Mussle [*sic*] Slough to serve writs of ejectment upon the settlers on the railroad lands in Tulare and Fresno counties, Judge Sawyer having affirmed the Southern Pacific Railroad Company's patent to the land in question.

The outcome of this matter, minor to *Chronicle* editors (who could not be bothered to check the spelling of the place name) as well as, doubtless, to many of its readers, was anything but trivial. The next day, the *Chronicle* reported A COLLISION. BLOODY TRAGEDY IN TULARE COUNTY. SEVEN PERSONS KILLED AND WOUNDED.

Bulletins from Mussel Slough were as confused as the legal issues in the dispute. A considerable community had grown up in the vicinity of Hanford, drawn by Southern Pacific company pamphlets encouraging land occupancy even before the railroad was completed—and promising first right of sale to the settlers already living on it, at costs reflecting the value of the property before any improvements were made. Railroad literature priced the lands at $2.50 to $5 per acre if they were not wooded.

Farmers and ranchers had in fact established themselves on the properties, which, as Leland Stanford himself had bragged a decade before, were empty but for wild cattle and horses and hardly worth even $2.50 per acre. But the settlers had irrigated the land, planted their crops, and developed a thriving agricultural district. In the fateful year of 1877, however, the railroad registered more than 200,000 acres in the Hanford area and then offered the land to the settlers on it at $22 to $27 an acre. Moreover, the land was thrown open to the general public at that price, so that earlier settlers who could not pay might well find their farms purchased out from under them.

Henry George himself could hardly have imagined a clearer example of the problems of land valuation that he had analyzed. Soon the railroad had sold parcels to outsiders and attempted to establish them as *bona fide* owners.

A committee of the settlers had gone to Sacramento to meet with Stanford; accompanied by settlers, Stanford had visited Tulare and Fresno Counties to inspect the properties. But Stanford stood by the new valuations. The farmers organized a Settlers' Grand League, which announced their readiness to pay the full value of the land at the time it was acquired by the railroad, and even the full value in 1880 without the improvements they had made, which would render a price no higher than $2.50 an acre. "But we are not willing, and look upon it as an injustice without parallel in the United States, that we should have to pay the enhanced value made by our own industry and toil," they asserted. The leading figure in the league was a former Confederate cavalry officer, "Major" Thomas Jefferson McQuiddy.

The railroad claimed that the settlers "refused to recognize the title of the company in any way," and that in 1878 the company had sold properties in the Mussel Slough district, entirely legally, to Perry Phillips, Mills D. Hartt, Walter J. Crow, and others. The settlers sued, but the court found for the railroad. The new owners clamored for the railroad company to secure their occupation of the land. The company was reluctant to take extreme action, but finally turned over writs of ejectment to the U.S. Marshal. Perry Phillips had taken over the land he bought, but his house was burned and he was driven off by the "League." On the morning of May 11, Marshal A. W. Poole accompanied Hartt to take over two parcels he had bought a year and a half before. An encounter with the settlers turned into a battle.

The *Chronicle* reported that the telegraph office in Hanford had been taken over by the settlers. Details directly from the scene were at first scarce. About 11:00 A.M., according to the paper, Poole and Walter Clark, a railroad land grader, followed by Hartt and Crow, the most aggressive new owners, had gone to the ranch of one Storer aiming to evict him. When the four arrived at the Storer property they were confronted by a group from the Settlers' League, who demanded they surrender their arms. They refused, and shooting broke out in which five settlers were killed. On the other side, Hartt was also mortally wounded, and Crow was found dead some distance away. Poole and Clarke had been escorted from the scene by the Leaguers, who had occupied the telegraph office and ordered the operator out. Marshal Poole wired the railroad's head office in San Francisco from another station, declaring that Storer had discussed a compromise with Crow but then rode away to consult with his partner, a man named Brewer, about the matter. Forty mounted men then appeared and drew weapons. "Am not certain who fired first," Marshal Poole said. He, embarrassingly enough, had been knocked down by a kick from a horse, but was unhurt. "Great excitement prevails at Hanford," the paper concluded.

The *Chronicle* noted that five officials of the railroad had appeared at the paper's office shortly after the first dispatches were received from Tulare County to offer their explanations, which were duly printed. But the paper editorialized in the familiar anticorporate style:

> The course of the railroad company in precipitating the issue cannot be too severely condemned. . . . No excuse can be suggested for a resort to measures to dispossess these men of the lands they had so long occupied, which they had improved by their hard labor, and on which they had created homes for themselves and their families. . . . Whatever might be their strictly legal rights, it is undeniable that all the equities were in favor of the settlers.

Public opinion leaped to the side of the settlers. The latter's statements, printed in the papers, were militant. They denied the railroad's title, given that it had neither built the line nor accounted for its work as required by the provisions of the federal law granting the land. Even so, they were willing to come to a fair agreement with the railroad—but they wanted to wait for a judgment by the U.S. Supreme Court. In the meantime, "they consider it gross oppression on the part of the company to eject them . . . and they announce their determination to resist such attempts by all the means in their power." The *Chronicle* noted a widespread belief that the new occupants were puppets of the railroad employed to force the issue, and "a suspicion that they and not the settlers opened the fight, went there with that intention, concealing their purpose from the Marshal; and that the settlers fired back in self-defense."

The settlers held meetings attended by hundreds, and listened to radical speakers like Thomas Chevers, who "urged the settlers to stand together for mutual protection and, if need be, to die for their homes, and never allow the railroad company to get one dollar nor one bushel of grain for the lands claimed by the soulless corporation." The funerals of the five dead settlers, Harris, Henderson, Kelly, Knutson, and McGregor, provided "an imposing demonstration." Later reporting revealed other elements in the picture. The telegraph office had not been invaded, although the railroad company ordered that no outside messages were to be accepted, and the operator had left his post only because his wife was ill.

Hartt, near death, described how railroad agent Clark successfully pleaded for his life, and how Crow, who fled, was supposedly hunted through the tules and finally brought down by a single shot. Hartt and Crow were well known to the settlers, and suspected by all of serving in a test case. They had received anonymous orders to leave the district, according to the Visalia *Delta,* which noted that local residents had anticipated a clash between the settlers and the railroad for some time. Marshal Poole now came forward to say that it would take "two hundred disciplined men . . . at least" to beat the settlers.

The settlers answered with their own detailed version of the tragedy. Marshal Poole had already evicted one settler, William Braden, before proceeding to the Storer-Brewer place. The settlers, getting there some time afterward, presented the marshal and his posse with a protest note, warning that "it will require an army of 1000 good soldiers against the local force that we can rally for self-defense, and we further expect the moral support of the good, law-abiding citizens of the United States." Hartt began the shooting, they said, by killing the unarmed Knutson. Poole and Clark had been "greatly alarmed" when the gunfire ended, "as they could see the settlers coming in almost every direction." Nonetheless, Clark was given his guns back, and he and the marshal were taken across the Fresno County line by a guard of four settlers on orders from "Major" McQuiddy.

An account in the *Chronicle,* signed "Settler," concluded, "We think that this collision was the result of a deep-laid plan by the Southern Pacific Railroad Company to frighten the settlers off. The people were never in such a state of mind as at present." An anonymous resident of Mussel Slough complained to the paper that the Southern Pacific was falsely attempting to paint the fight as a settlers' insurrection against the federal authorities in which the railroad's property was greatly endangered. The settlers would offer no resistance to duly constituted authorities, but simply called on the populace for support. The railroad, however, stopped service to Hanford until the affair died down.

The settlers paid the bill for Mussel Slough: five of them went to jail for obstructing a federal marshal in the performance of his duty. "Major" McQuiddy escaped and was never tried, but he became an antirailroad hero to the whole state during a long period in hiding. Henry George, who had anticipated such hostilities, seems to have known nothing of Mussel Slough; he had departed for New York upon the commercial release of *Progress and*

Poverty. An extraordinarily similar "land war" was under way in Ireland, between rent-gouging landlords and dispossessed tenants organized in radical "Land Leagues." George's adoption of the Irish cause made him a hero in that country. Soon he was a figure known to the whole world, for *Progress and Poverty* became a long-term best-seller and a classic of populist economics. Although George was proud to be called "the prophet of San Francisco," he never returned there.

Mussel Slough burned in the memory of two generations of Californians. The affair was reflected in novels by, among others, the philosopher Josiah Royce (*The Feud of Oakfield Creek,* 1887), but not until twenty years after the events, with the publication of a much greater work, did the story find its greatest teller. That book, which we will treat in its time, was *The Octopus,* written by a former *Chronicle* reporter, Frank Norris.

Josiah Royce was among the first native Californians to rise to literary prominence in America. He was born in Grass Valley in 1855. His mother was a pioneer woman of 1849, strong-willed and community-minded. His father, a businessman, was frequently absent. Royce was taught at home until age 10. Royce never lost a deep sense of the very youthfulness of American California, a newness in its people mixed with a natural tendency to mythify the past, even the very recent past. He studied at the University of California at Berkeley, then spent a year in Germany before receiving a Ph.D. from Johns Hopkins. He came back to Berkeley and joined the faculty as an instructor in rhetoric and logic. His thinking was particularly marked by German idealist philosophy.

In *The Feud of Oakfield Creek,* with apparent satirical intent, Royce made the fictional Alonzo Eldon, an oppressive millionaire landowner, a fan of Henry George. His portrayal of a hypocritical California élite, violently driving "squatters" off their lands while embracing radical fads, was a brilliant premonition of a later, decadent California liberalism. George, for his part, was frequently mocked for his obsession with the land question. But Royce had an obsession of his own, which grew out of a profound ambivalence, and which was revealed in his first book, begun in 1883. This was an essay on the history of the state, entitled *California: A Study of the American Character.* It was commissioned by Houghton Mifflin & Co., in a series called "American Commonwealths."

Royce began writing his *California* from a refuge at Harvard College, where he had been appointed an assistant professor of philosophy, originally as a temporary replacement for his mentor William James. Although, like Henry George and others, Royce saw injustices in land tenure as the poisoned fountain causing much discord in the state, he repudiated a radicalism that would lead, he feared, to anarchy. His *California* was not a study of the state's economic history; nor, in truth, did it have much to do with the "American character." In an exceedingly Californian manner that many would associate with eccentricity and crank interpretations, but with fruitful antecedents in intellectual history (such as the work of Carlyle), Royce made his volume in this otherwise anodyne series of state histories a detailed and devastating criticism of the conditions under which California had been conquered by the United States. The narrative was increasingly concerned with the claims and reputation of Frémont; in a phrase reminiscent of many nonconformist historians, Royce wrote that he had begun work on the book with "a very high opinion of the work of the gallant Captain Frémont in the acquisition of California," but had become disillusioned as he proceeded.

Royce's essay on California history became what may be fairly described as an anti-imperialist jeremiad. Frémont was, at the very best, an unreliable witness, Royce believed after interviewing him; at worst, Frémont was no more than a "filibuster" (and therefore could be put in the same disreputable class with William Walker), abusing what little authority he had as an American military officer. As the historian Kevin Starr has indicated, the blood of Indians and Hispanic Californians spilled by Frémont and his companions was the essence of the "birth trauma" of American California, if not indeed the symbol of its fall from paradise. For Royce, although he would have denied it, greatly romanticized pre-1846 Alta California as a place of gentle charm and rustic pleasures. California had offered the United States, according to Royce, the possibility of peaceful assimilation of a Spanish-speaking community in a way that would contribute to American greatness. But the "Bear Flag" adventurers had rejected that option, choosing instead to inflict bloodshed that bitterly alienated Anglo and Hispanic Californians from each other from that day forth. Royce's hatred of the Bear Flaggers was a marvel to behold, particularly given the cult that then surrounded them as Anglo California's founding patriots.

Royce's comments caused an outcry among California boosters and Anglo chauvinists, leading to its author's widespread condemnation as a traitor to his native state. Like George, Royce never returned from Harvard. In reality, he had merely told the truth, if in an exaggerated and histrionic fashion.

THESE FIRST MAJOR intellectual works (George's and Royce's) produced by American California were, then, ambivalent and questioning about progress. But if both writers found dark aspects of the California idyll, there was no author of that time who combined the celebration of California's romance with anguish over the tragic chapters of its brief history more thoroughly than Helen Hunt Jackson, the author of *Ramona*. This novel attained immense popularity, inculcating a fundamental California myth. The critic Susan Sontag has rightly described *Ramona* as the key to California consciousness even today.

Helen Maria Fiske, as she was christened, was born in Amherst, Massachusetts, in 1831. Her father was a professor at Amherst College. She was a lifelong friend of the poet Emily Dickinson. In her twenties Helen Fiske married an army officer, Edward B. Hunt, the designer of an unsuccessful submarine prototype. Hunt died and left her a widow in 1863; after the death of a son two years later she turned to writing to relieve her anguish, encouraged by Dickinson, whose work she later championed. Helen Hunt's poetry, essays, travel sketches, and other works, mostly appearing over the bare initials "H.H." almost immediately gained enormous success. She produced dozens of books, and became socially prominent and a world traveler. In 1875 she married William S. Jackson, financial administrator of the Denver and Rio Grande Railroad, and went to live with him at Colorado Springs.

Helen Hunt Jackson had a vague interest in the spiritualism popular in the William James circle, which she frequented after she became famous. She was originally anything but a reformer—indeed, her first husband hated Abolitionists, and while living with him she leased a slave girl. But her personality changed completely in 1879 when she attended a program on the removal of the Ponca Indians from Nebraska to the Indian Territory, later Oklahoma. Almost overnight, she became a fanatic for the Indian cause. "I cannot help it," she confessed. "I cannot think of anything else from night to morning and from morning to night."

Over the next two years, beginning with the defense of the Poncas, Helen Jackson undertook an ambitious campaign of advocacy and research culminating in the 1881 publication of her biting survey of the American government's treatment of Indians, *A Century of Dishonor.* The book had an explosive impact on the public, for this well-off literary woman had no incentive to defend the Indians—hitherto widely portrayed as primitive scoundrels—other than her sincere belief in their victimization.

A Century of Dishonor led to her appointment as a commissioner of Indian Affairs along with Abbott Kinney, later the creator of the town of Venice, California. The pair were mandated to, in effect, follow in the footsteps of J. Ross Browne thirty years earlier by investigating the condition of Indians in California. Jackson and Kinney recommended that the government improve medical services to Indians, provide legal aid, and send women to their communities as teachers. But they warned that too much time had passed for a real redress of the deplorable situation of the Native Americans: "With every year of our neglect the difficulties have increased and the wrongs have been multiplied, until now it is, humanly speaking, impossible to render to them full measure of justice."

Helen Jackson soon began writing *Ramona.* It is a complicated, at times saccharine tale of cruelty, love, and race oppression in nineteenth-century southern California. Jackson wove many anecdotes collected during her work as an Indian commissioner into the story, which is set in an area she had come to know well. The tale centers on a California girl, Ramona Ortegna, born of a "squaw" and a drunken Scotsman, Angus Phail. Phail, prevented from marrying a childless woman of the California Spanish élite, Señora Ortegna, leaves the baby girl in her foster care. When Señora Ortegna becomes ill, Ramona is handed over to another aristocratic foster parent, Señora Moreno, a classic evil stepmother.

Ramona and Alessandro Assis, a handsome and charismatic Indian who is the boss of the Indian laborers on the Moreno *hacienda,* fall in love. Even though she is herself part Indian, the secret of her blood has been hidden from Ramona, and her plan to marry an Indian provokes loud and unceasing conflict. In the authentic nineteenth-century cliff-hanging style, the book is replete with melodramatic interludes. Alessandro leaves the *hacienda* and does not return when promised; meanwhile the truth of Ramona's origin is revealed, and when he does not come back she takes sick. When he does, it is to tell her that his native Indian village, Temecula, has been attacked by brutal Americans.

The couple escape the evil stepmother and flee through the canyons to

San Diego, where a priest marries them. They continue their search for the lost paradise of Indian California, going deeper and deeper into the hinterland until Alessandro goes insane. In the end, although "a part of her is dead," Ramona finds a kind of happiness.

Published in 1884, *Ramona* was a landmark work, hailed as an achievement in defense of the Indians greater than Harriet Beecher Stowe's antislavery classic *Uncle Tom's Cabin*. Suffering medical problems, Jackson came to San Francisco to recuperate; she died there only a year after *Ramona's* publication. She was active in the Indian cause to the last, sending an appeal to the White House from her deathbed. Strangely enough, considering its corrosively antiwhite tone, *Ramona* became a standard text in the California public schools, and its tradition was adopted by boosters in southern California. For decades, holiday parades in many towns featured figures in Ramona dress, and several versions of the story were brought to the motion-picture screen. A *Ramona* pageant is still held today at Hemet, in the Mojave Desert.

George, Royce, and Jackson were radical in their context, and the writings of Royce and Jackson resonate for later Californians who opposed American imperial power and who protested the Indian holocaust. Yet the three were really no more than nineteenth-century liberals. George, who inveighed against monopoly and advocated labor's cause, remained a believer in individualism and free enterprise and was an active promoter of free trade. In the five years between Mussel Slough and the death of Helen Hunt Jackson, however, something new was noticeable in the intellectual atmosphere of California: the arrival of socialism.

The earliest English-speaking socialists on the Pacific Coast are found in a small but influential group around Burnette Gregor Haskell, a young man with a sad mien who was a failed lawyer, a brilliant but erratic journalist, the unsuccessful organizer of a Utopian colony, and a general misfit; but he turned out to be an inspired labor leader. Haskell was born in 1857 in Sierra County, California. He was admitted to the California bar and began practicing law in San Francisco in the early 1880s, but was considered too much of an idealist to prosper in the courtroom. In 1882 he discovered socialist and anarchist ideas and began to disseminate them through a newspaper he founded, modestly titled *Truth*.

Haskell established a circle of collaborators drawn from the labor scene that included a Polish Jew, Sigismund Danielewicz, who had a command of several languages, and Haskell's political mentor, William C. Owen, an Englishman born in India in 1854 who also studied law but failed admission to the bar. Owen came to San Francisco to make his fortune but became a radical. His political transformation, he later wrote, originated

> not from books, or any reading about economic determinism, the class struggle, or all that exceedingly dubious philosophy with which we fret our brains, but from the poverty of a great city that stank beneath my nose. . . . It did not take any profound reasoning or erudite scholarship to convince me that, fix the thing which way I could, there was no genuine happiness under existing conditions.

Haskell and Owen's encounter with socialism was timely, to say the least. Both had become prominent union advocates, Haskell as a lawyer for various locals and Owen as an organizer of a successful boycott by the San Francisco public against the anti-union *Call* and *Bulletin* newspapers. The Knights of Labor, the order of working men that had organized secretly for some years past, now emerged in the light of public attention as a powerful mass movement. A new depression brought more strikes. Radical workers back East, many of German origin at a time when that ethnic group dominated the mechanics' trade, were agitating for the socialist program that in Europe would lead to foundation of the Socialist (Second) International in 1889. Ideological war between Marx and Bakunin had split the First International, or International Working Men's Association, between the former's followers, known as "Reds" or Social Democrats, and the anarchist or "Black" partisans of the latter. In 1872, the Marxian wing had transferred its operation to the United States, where it held its last convention in 1876; it was made up of only American delegates, but many of them still spoke German as their main tongue.

The Bakuninist faction, which already led masses of workers in Spain and Italy, held its own American congress in Chicago in 1881, followed by a second conclave in Pittsburgh in 1883. The latter meeting set up a new radical entity, the International Working People's Association or I.W.P.A. As described by Paul Avrich, the Pittsburgh convention of the I.W.P.A., whose German members were enthusiasts of rifle clubs formed to prepare the workers for struggle, heard a group of social revolutionaries from Chicago outline a new conception of labor organization. This was the "Chicago idea," according to which unions would "shun political action, distrust all central authority, and guard against betrayals by self-important leaders. All . . . faith was to rest in the direct action of the rank and file."

At about the same time, Haskell took it into his head to set up an orthodox Marxian group, based in San Francisco, called the International Workmen's Association (I.W.A.) Haskell, probably thanks to Owen, had corresponded with the British socialist H. M. Hyndman, but the I.W.A. had no other known contact with the socialists in Europe. Nevertheless, filled with the strange audacity that conflicted with his melancholy soul, Haskell pressed ahead, declaring his group the "Red" faction, opposed to the "Black" Bakuninists of the I.W.P.A., while also calling for unification of the two tendencies. Haskell's loyalties in matters of ideological detail were inconsistent; Avrich views Haskell as a partial Bakuninist. He had a pamphlet printed, titled *What the I.W.A. Is,* and advertised book editions of writings by the Russian anarchist Peter Kropotkin, Hyndman, and William Morris, the outstanding British designer and social theorist. Haskell also wrote the introduction to an 1884 book titled *Socialism,* written by A. J. Starkweather (the "peddler" arrested on Montgomery Street in July 1877 for carrying a placard supporting the Eastern railroad strikers) and S. Robert Wilson. Both Starkweather and Wilson, as well as Haskell and Owen, had been involved with the anti-Chinese movement.

Haskell's I.W.A. borrowed the name of the First International, but its membership remained restricted to the United States and northern Mexico. Remarkably enough, his grand ambitions were almost immediately rewarded. The United States was undergoing the greatest working-class upsurge in its history, with thousands joining the Knights of Labor; its adherents paraded the streets during strikes, roaring their anthem, *Storm the Fort! Ye Knights of Labor!* Railroad workers affiliated with the Knights *en masse,* particularly on the Missouri Pacific and Wabash lines owned by Jay Gould in the Midwest. The I.W.A. became far more successful than its "Black" rival, the I.W.P.A., in recruiting adherents, and the Haskell group's inaugural membership certificate, or "red card," was soon detected among laboring people throughout northern California, Oregon, the Washington Territory, and the Rocky Mountains. In Colorado, led by another labor pioneer, a typesetter named Joseph R. Buchanan, the I.W.A. briefly became a true mass movement.

In 1884 Haskell began dreaming of a socialist Utopian colony in California, a project that would eventually exhaust him. But in 1885 a series of events took place that guaranteed his stature in California's labor history. A depression was on; the flashpoint of a new labor crisis ignited among sailors. With the financial downturn, seamen's wages had dropped to $20 per month for deepwater voyages and $25 per month for sailors in the coastal trade. The latter mainly carried lumber in schooners, under notably difficult conditions: loads were stacked high on the decks and the small coastal ports, many of which had unprotected harbors, typically had no longshoremen; thus sailors entering such ports but still practically out at sea worked the cargo. The coast lumber trade was dominated by highly skilled Scandinavians, who made up 40 percent of West Coast seamen; they were difficult to replace, and many were highly militant in their views on labor and society.

In the first week of March 1885 a group of coasting sailors in San Francisco began to discuss a strike. A national fight was under way for the eight-hour workday, a major walkout had begun on the Gould rail lines (mainly the Missouri Pacific), and spirits were high among the laboring class throughout the West. Attempts to form a sailors' union had been made at various times but had failed or had dissipated after participants had become inveigled into anti-Chinese agitation—a predictable outcome in that the West Coast steamship companies had tenaciously maintained a policy of hiring Asian crews.

The group of mariners in San Francisco resolved to publish a notice calling on seamen to leave their jobs. The next morning, crews were walking off ships and little groups of strikers appeared. A meeting was held at the Howard Street Wharf on the night of March 4, followed by an assembly at Garibaldi Hall on March 5. On the afternoon of the fifth, I.W.A. leader Sigismund Danielewicz, who had just returned from Hawaii, passed a group of striking sailors on the waterfront and called on them to assemble the next night at the Folsom Street Wharf.

The meeting of March 6 was held in darkness and intermittent rain, behind a lumber pile, and "their existence was only revealed by the tones of their voice[s]," according to a report the next day in the *San Francisco Chronicle*. The first entry in the Minute Book of the Coast Seamen's Union noted the presence of an organizing committee from the I.W.A., including Haskell, Danielewicz, and Joseph Kelly, a participant in the anti-Chinese movement. The minutes recorded, "The meeting was addressed by various speakers who advocated unity of action and resistance to oppression in any and every form. Great enthusiasm prevailed."

At the instance of Haskell, the organizers repaired to a street-lamp, took down the names of 222 seafarers enrolled on the spot, and collected $34.60 in contributions. Haskell was charged with organizing another meeting for Saturday, March 7, at Irish American Hall. Before the participants left the Folsom Street Wharf, "Three cheers were given for the International." At the next night's meeting at least a hundred more men joined the new Coasting Sailors' Protective Association, as it was first called. Men were sent to the ships along the waterfront to discuss wages and to the many boarding houses where sailors lived to find new recruits. An office was to be rented on Eddy Street. All unknowing, Burnette Gregor Haskell and his comrades in the I.W.A. had overseen one of the most momentous undertakings in the history of international unionism.

———————

THE CONDITION OF the seamen remained abysmal twelve years after the *Sunrise* case. In today's money $25 per month, the typical wage in coast shipping in 1885, might be worth ten times as much, but that would still be far below a poverty-line wage.

The enthusiasm that had kept the sailors meeting night after night to establish their organization did not ebb in the months that followed. Haskell was in his element, finding new tasks for himself and his associates in the I.W.A.; they constituted an official Advisory Committee to the Coast Seamen's Union, or C.S.U. At the fourth meeting, George Thompson became the first president, with Rasmus Nielson as secretary and Haskell as treasurer. The strike for higher wages continued for some time and, after little more than a week, ships were leaving San Francisco with union crews, deepwater sailors had begun showing an interest in the movement, and wages had returned to $30 per month. By the end of the month the C.S.U. boasted a thousand members, and "colored" seamen had been invited to join. Haskell and Nielson began planning the opening of a union hiring office, with preference for those who had gone the longest without a ship.

Shipowners, brutal officers, and, particularly, corrupt shipping agents and boardinghouse keepers known as "crimps" were not pleased at the new developments on the waterfront. Police began arresting union members who went aboard ships to demand removal of nonunion men. But after only five weeks the union shipping office opened, and secretary Nielson recorded that "[W]e would rather die in our tracks than retreat one inch." Soon the union had appointed agents as its representatives in San Pedro and Eureka in California and at Port Townsend in the Washington Territory.

Late in 1885 the Coast Seamen's Union came to grips with the matter of the Chinese. This was inevitable, given that Haskell and other figures prominent in its founding had also been involved in race agitation. An emergency assembly of the C.S.U. was held to begin discussion of the anti-Chinese movement. At an I.W.A. meeting in the C.S.U. hall, Danielewicz spoke against any participation in such activities; he suggested that instead the I.W.A. attend a coming anti-Chinese convention with a socialist program for class solidarity of all races and then withdraw. The preeminent historian of the anti-Chinese labor movement in California, Alexander Saxton, has described how, although many in the I.W.A. and the C.S.U. strongly disagreed with him, Danielewicz was allowed to speak at the anti-Chinese convocation in December 1885. He argued that he could not, as a Jew, support the persecution of Asians, and reminded the Irish and Germans in the audience of their own experience with ethnic injustice. Unfortunately he was met with jeers. Saxton has noted that Haskell and the rest of his comrades fought to swing the emphasis of the convention away from race to class, but without success. The anti-Chinese movement developed its own internal dissensions, which weakened it as an organized force, but California labor remained anti-Asian for a long time afterward.

The first great tests of the Coast Seamen's Union came in 1886. The C.S.U. called for a boycott against the Spreckels steamship line, but "scabs" were provided to Claus Spreckels, the company's founder, by the most notorious crimp, a one-eyed man named John Curtin. In June of that year waterfront employers established a Shipowners' Association of the Pacific Coast, which announced that its members would hire crews only through their own shipping bureau, and that sailors would be required to keep "grade books" listing their qualifications and employment record. To obtain his grade book a sailor would have to surrender his C.S.U. membership book. Then, on August 25, 1886, after discussion with the Council of Federated Trades in San Francisco, the union called the first coast-wide maritime strike, in all ports from Puget Sound to San Diego.

The coast seamen's strike was closely reported in the San Francisco dailies. The main targets of the struggle were Curtin and his allies, the worst of the crimping boarding-house masters. The *San Francisco Chronicle* reported that about twenty other boarding masters, a majority by far, had sided with the union, being infuriated at Curtin and his peers, who had become infamous for "shanghaiing" not only seamen but even ship's officers. But the coastwide work stoppage was also directed against the Shipowners' Association and its so-called "pool," or shipping bureau, which was run by Curtin's band, who formed themselves into a boarding masters' alliance. The spirit of organization was well and truly abroad in California! The strike emptied ships, spreading even to deepwater and foreign vessels, as soon as they reached San Francisco.

San Francisco took sides in the strike. The *Chronicle,* which described the Coast Seamen's Union as "one of the most powerful labor unions on the coast," was immediately branded as "biased" in favor of the strikers. A bunch of sailors who administered a beating to Curtin were tried for assault with intent to commit murder, and during the proceeding the union's oath of allegiance was denounced by prosecutor W. W. Foote as "un-American, unlawful, dictatorial, and outrageous." The Federated Trades, a body mainly composed of metalworkers, wanted the strike to spread, and its members lobbied the other waterfront unions to join the walkout. Ironworkers were just then fighting the importation of strikebreakers to the Bay Area, in disputes at the Pacific Nail Works and the Union Iron Works, and hoped the union seamen would prevent the Pacific Mail Steamship Company from contracting for repairs at struck facilities. Solidarity was also forthcoming from crews aboard English deepwater ships tied up at Oakland, who published a notice promising "to assist our organized brothers against our common enemy."

The shipowners and Curtin and their friends began taking men off deepwater vessels to man the struck coastal ships, enticing them with the unarguable fact that work on the coast was easier, with better food aboard ship and more time ashore. An order was posted at C.S.U. headquarters: "Do not engage or set foot upon any vessel leaving port." Men were joining the strike at the rate of at least fifty per day, and numbered 700 after only a week in San Francisco alone, with a total of 1,000 striking on the coast. The Maritime Officers' Protective and Benevolent Association agreed to walk off ships as well, "till justice is done." Crews on the pilot boats at San Francisco joined the strike. Bay boatmen began leaving the scows that served the inland waters. Strikers were assigned to patrol the length of the San Francisco waterfront. California was suddenly in the vanguard of labor's world-wide uprising.

The Shipowners' Association and the Curtin gang were, however, unmoved. The former declared that its members refused "all the [union's] propositions, and have none of their own to offer, and proposed to run their business as it pleased." The Association hired Chinese and Japanese labor as well as English apprentices as strikebreakers, and was accused by the C.S.U. of employing hoodlums in the dirty work of "shanghaiing" men, whatever their color. In one instance, reported by the *Chronicle,* two crimps' runners, finding the strike patrol briefly absent from the 'front, were dragging a deepwater sailor into the crimps' shipping office when a woman passerby gave the alarm and he was rescued. The shipowners attempted to gull long-shoremen into sailing up the coast, without much success. Curtin's name appeared in the papers repeatedly; three weeks into the strike he was arrested for firing a revolver at a union man. Five days later, six sailors came into his establishment and began arguing over what card game to play, then jumped him and "beat him so badly he had to be carried upstairs," according to the *Chronicle.* About that time, a riot in Arcata, California, near Eureka, left twenty strikers in jail after they had rushed aboard the schooner *Mary and Ida* and forced strikebreakers off.

Unlike some San Francisco papers, the *Chronicle* stood by the C.S.U., repudiating claims of excessive union violence, playing up news of shipboard brutality, and denouncing cases where sailors who quit in protest of physical abuse were charged with desertion. Men seemed to walk off the ships as fast as they entered the Golden Gate. The C.S.U. opened a new shipping office, and declared a victory—but in expression of a false hope, for no negotiation with the shipowners took place, and after five weeks the strike collapsed. Union members signed up to ship through the shipowners' hiring bureau, except for about 150 who went to work on the railroad.

Defeat in the 1886 strike did not destroy the Coast Seamen's Union, but it changed it considerably. Haskell and most of his socialist associates, though valued as supporters, were somewhat discredited by the loss. At the end of the year Rasmus Nielson was voted out as the union's secretary, and replaced by a Norwegian, Anders (later Andrew) Furuseth, a man of a completely different kind from the flamboyant Haskell. The new C.S.U. leader was a single-minded partisan of the sailors' cause, fanatically dedicated to the liberation of the seamen. Under his leadership, which continued until the 1930s, the Coast Seamen's Union (which soon absorbed other maritime labor bodies to become the Sailors' Union of the Pacific or S.U.P.), succeeded, at least temporarily as we shall see, in emancipating the American sailor. For this reason, the establishment of the Coast Seamen's Union must be viewed as California's greatest contribution to labor history.

The Coast Seamen's Union had come into existence thanks to a peculiar alignment of circumstances: the radicalism of Scandinavian-born sailors, the special character of labor in the coast trade, and the activity of the I.W.A. But the C.S.U. also benefited from the nature of California, and especially San Francisco, as an environment for social and political innovation. It was the first clear example of a distinctly *Californian* radicalism.

Haskell's attention became concentrated on his dreams of a Utopian colony, which he conceived as, among other things, a means to give financial support to unemployed sailors. He planted such a colony in Tulare County, near Visalia some 45 miles due east of Mussel Slough, in the Sierra foothills. The land was densely wooded and Haskell imagined that lumber could be exported in ships manned by the C.S.U. Under the name of Kaweah Cooperative Commonwealth, the experiment was launched as a tent city until a logging road was opened by the colonists in 1889. Eventually Kaweah included a community center, dining and assembly halls, a store, print shop, smithy, barn, and sheds. Haskell induced several C.S.U. founders to join Kaweah, and it was alleged that many union members contributed to its treasury.

Kaweah failed, in great part for reasons that would have been obvious to Henry George and the Mussel Slough settlers: the colonists neglected to file their land claim in proper fashion, and the federal authorities investigated the colony for timber fraud as soon as claims were entered. The fraud charge was based on the signing of the claim by seamen who, as "transients," had given their addresses as the C.S.U. boardinghouse in San Francisco. But Kaweah may have been doomed from the start by the main flaw that seems to appear in all such efforts: high principles could not overcome personal differences within the community. Finally, the actual logging operation was inefficient.

Haskell and his companions were then accused of mere plundering of the redwoods at Kaweah, and the colony became the target of a scandal-mongering press. In 1890, the U.S. government established Sequoia National Park, encompassing the colony's land, and federal troops were sent to the scene. Understandably, Tulare County locals, who were touchy about land issues given their recollections of Mussel Slough, sided with Haskell, and soldiers were jeered in the streets and fired on in the woods, according to the historian Paul Kagan. The next year the colonists were charged with poaching lumber from federal property, and in 1892 they were served with a mail fraud indictment. In a curious coincidence, that same year saw the foundation of the Sierra Club by the nature writer John Muir, also following the creation of Sequoia and Yosemite National Parks. Its immediate purposes were seemingly opposed to those of Kaweah, but in times to come it would play a more effective role in pursuit of an environmentalism that shared some of the conceptions of the Kaweah colonists. Meanwhile, Kaweah disbanded.

The Kaweah utopians had inaugurated their work by naming the highest redwood tree they found the Karl Marx Tree. It was renamed the General Sherman Tree by park authorities and bears that title today. Kagan has described Kaweah as a focus of enthusiasm for radicals throughout the country, including Lawrence Gronlund, the author of a popular book, *The Co-operative Commonwealth*. Kaweah maintained a complex system of accounts and payments using coupons and tokens based on time measurement. Artists, musicians, and writers gave the commune a high intellectual atmosphere. Burnette Gregor Haskell had been viciously hounded by certain newspapers, and after the Kaweah experiment ended he fell into obscurity, dying in 1907. He remains one of the most remarkable California thinkers.

———————

HASKELL HAD BEEN the special victim of an especially nasty journalist, Ambrose Bierce. Brilliant but deeply cynical, if not downright misanthropic, Bierce had come to San Francisco some years after the Civil War and there began writing for humorous and literary weeklies, of which San Francisco boasted several in the late nineteenth century. His talent for the entertaining insult made him an obvious candidate for employment by a publisher who had entered the newspaper field with limitless self-confidence. William Randolph Hearst in 1887 convinced his father, George Hearst, a mining magnate and a United States Senator from California, to purchase the *San Francisco Examiner* for him. Hearst was 24, an "unearthly child" in Bierce's description, and the satirical genius was one of his first hires.

"Billy" Hearst's story has become, in a sense, the California story without peer, and has been told and retold. Like Bierce, who seemed to have no politics apart from a general contempt for humanity, Hearst was no radical, although many people over the years believed otherwise; he merely had an exceptional understanding of the public consciousness—or lack thereof. He made the *Examiner* the most exciting daily paper in the country by dishing out in highly spiced form the by now predictable Pacific Coast menu: a nearly demented hatred of the Southern Pacific Railroad as the main course, followed by titillating yarns that often had nothing to do with news as it was previously known. Circulation ballooned from about 20,000 to 60,000 in the first year of Hearst's ownership. The *Examiner,* and the chain of copies Hearst set up in nearly every major American city, later became known as "jazz" newspapers, selling shock and amusement rather than the staid analysis traditionally purveyed in other broadsheets. Hearst would posture as a near-atheist, an advocate of labor, and a foe of monopoly while popularizing the color comic strip, "women's features," and other novelties; most importantly, he paid the highest wages to reporters, and was a bold raider of rival news staffs.

Hearst's *Examiner* was soon locked in a war for scoops and circulation with the *Chronicle,* which had hitherto prided itself on being the biggest and best daily in the West. One opportunity to outshine the competition came in 1892 when the *Examiner* claimed to have gotten an interview with two men wanted by the law, Christopher Evans and John Sontag.

Evans and Sontag had become heroes to many Californians, not unlike the Mussel Slough fugitive, "Major" T. J. McQuiddy. Much of their fame was easily understood: they lived in Tulare County, where the evil memory of Mussel Slough was still vivid, and were known as enemies of the Southern Pacific railroad. According to one account Chris Evans had come from Vermont in his twenties and, after a fling in the mines, settled in the lower San Joaquin Valley on a parcel he thought was priced at $2.50 per acre, only to be offered it by the railroad at $10 per. He was unable to find the money, and lost the farm. The familiar grievance was only exceeded in its symbolic quality by that of his friend John Sontag. A former railroad brakeman, Sontag had suffered a badly injured ankle, and had been treated incompetently, he claimed, at the Southern Pacific hospital in Sacramento. While in his hospital bed he had grown disgusted with the company and cursed the doctors and the railroad, and was thrown out. The company offered him only such work as was clearly impossible in his state of health.

Evans and Sontag embodied the rage against the railroad of thousands of farmers and workers, as well as the local attitude of resistance that had produced both the Settlers' Grand League and support for Kaweah. In an extraordinary sequence of events, the two men came under suspicion for a series of train robberies. The trains were owned by Southern Pacific. Suspicion led to a shootout with railroad police, escape, and a manhunt.

For almost a year Evans and Sontag hid out in the hills above Visalia, evading their pursuers with the support of the railroad's myriad local antagonists. The pair became legendary figures, whose myth survives even today in Tulare County; among the railroad's challengers, they occupy the romantic place of the guerrilla, living off the land and enjoying the warm sympathies of the populace. Railroad police, deputies, and Indian scouts combed the foothills and almost caught them, but a bloody gun battle left two deputies dead, while Evans and Sontag again fled successfully. The imperious Southern Pacific's executives poured money into the hunt, but Evans and Sontag had the guerrilla's ability to hide in broad daylight.

Newspapers sent reporters to scour the area, and on October 7, 1892 the *Examiner* came out with an interview obtained by a staffer who pestered everybody in Visalia until finally he was conducted to the fugitives' mountain stronghold. He found them living in a small house overlooking the southern valley. The pair denied any involvement in the robberies and denounced the railroad, thus providing Californians with exactly what they expected to read in their newspapers. The other dailies claimed the interview was a hoax, but internal evidence supports its authenticity.

The two men were nothing if not daring. In April 1893 they openly returned to the Evans house, which was ringed with deputies, but were left unmolested and again got away. Several days later, however, they were caught by a United States marshal and a considerable body of armed men; shooting again broke out and Evans was badly wounded. The two took shelter and kept up defensive fire. Sontag, who (let us not forget), was already lame, was hit in the right arm and in his side, but continued shooting. Evans was struck in the back, his left arm, and his right eye, and could no longer hold a gun. Sontag was hit again, but continued reloading and firing until he passed out.

Evans then crawled *six miles*—without the use of his arms, blind in one eye, and with buckshot in his cranium—to a farmhouse.

The deputies were so intimidated by the pair that they waited through the night before attempting to ascertain the men's condition. Sontag was still breathing, and was taken not to a hospital but to jail in Fresno, where he died within a few days.

Evans negotiated his surrender from the farmhouse. He lost his left arm, but after recuperation was tried in the death of one of the deputies. To raise money for his defense, Evans's daughter Eva appeared in a fabulously popular melodrama performed in San Francisco, *The Collis Train Robbery*. Christopher Evans was convicted and sent to jail to await sentencing, but after fifteen days escaped yet again with the help of a Fresno waiter named Morrell. Evans and Morrell, the former with a prosthetic arm and a missing eye, took up the struggle anew and stayed free for several weeks. But they were captured by deceit: a rumor was floated of illness affecting one of Evans's children, and when he came back home a regiment-sized posse grabbed him.

Christopher Evans was sentenced to life in prison, and remained in Folsom from 1894 to 1911. He was then paroled and went to live in Oregon, after a campaign by his family that gained the endorsement of the poet Joaquin Miller among others. He died in 1917.

In the year 1894 the attention of Californians radical and otherwise was also drawn to a drama played out on the other side of the continent, in the form of a mass march, mainly of unemployed men, known as Coxey's Army. This national demonstration against government indifference and corporate power began in Ohio, but among its leading protagonists was a Californian, Carl Browne, a former anti-Chinese agitator who had gone to the Chicago World's Fair in 1893 and then attended a national convention of money reformers in the same city. There he met J. S. Coxey, whose son-in-law he would become. Together Browne and Coxey drafted a "Good Roads Bill" embodying a scheme to combat joblessness through public works programs.

Coxey's Army brought together virtually every form of dissidence visible in America at the time. Browne, a highly talented cartoonist, painted a banner of Christ to be carried in the march. At the same time, he proclaimed himself a Theosophist, but organized the marchers according to the structure of Haskell's Marxian "international," based on groups of "communes." Thousands of Coxeyites arrived in Washington on May 1, 1894. The mass protest collapsed, however, after Browne and Coxey were arrested, the former for "treading on the grass." Browne returned to California and launched a pioneering mimeographed journal, the *Labor Knight*. Nicknamed by his admirers "the Don Quixote of California," Browne was, like Burnette Haskell, a particular target for the insults of Ambrose Bierce. Some veterans of Haskell's Kaweah project had joined the march, including a young San Franciscan, George Speed.

THE SAN FRANCISCO whose residents thrilled to the popular stage pageant of Evans and Sontag and were amused by the cartoons of Carl Browne had, at the same time, become a sophisticated cultural center. The creative lights of the past—Mark Twain, Bret Harte, Helen Hunt Jackson, and others—had been exceptional figures in a society mainly concerned with acquiring and enjoying wealth. But now proof of the city's intellectual maturity came with the eruption of Bohemianism in its literary life. The first warning tremor was felt when the city woke up one morning in 1894 to find that someone had thrown ropes over a statue, at the important intersection of California and Market Streets, of temperance advocate Dr. Henry Cogswell and pulled it off its plinth. Cogswell had placed monuments throughout the city with fountains in their pedestals dispensing spring water. The vandalism had been done in apparent emulation of the French painter and revolutionary Gustave Courbet, who during the Paris Commune directed the tearing down of the Vendôme Column.

This act of highbrow destruction had been organized by Gelett Burgess, a young man who had come to California in the 1880s. He first worked for the Southern Pacific as a draftsman before joining the faculty of the University of California. With the fall of Dr. Cogswell Burgess lost his job at Berkeley, but the times were such, and the energies coursing through the intellectual atmosphere worldwide so intense, that Burgess seems to have laughed at his situation. He began designing new-style furniture for a local dealer, but in 1895 joined with his friends, the architect Willis Polk and two youths named Porter Garnett and Bruce Porter, to launch an entirely new literary enterprise, *The Lark*, price five cents.

The Lark was more than modern, it was modernist, echoing and also anticipating experimental literary trends in Europe, which remained the focus of intellectual attention of the whole Western world and a growing part of the Far East. As the *New York Times* described it, *The Lark* was "incredibly, even impossibly, 1895." Everything about *The Lark* had to be innovative: its general tone of flippant humor, its inclusion of articles and sometimes baffling verse chosen almost spontaneously, cheap and flimsy but exotic paper found in Chinatown and printed on only one side, often uneven lines of type, strangely colored inks. It was a one-stop revolution in the arts.

San Francisco at first tried to ignore the *The Lark's* erratic flights, but the bizarre little journal had an asset that, as elsewhere in the world, lifted modernism from mere experimentalism to intellectual greatness: its high quality and the undeniable ability of its exponents. The original circle was joined by other outstanding talents, including the painter Maynard Dixon, who would dominate the art scene in California for nearly fifty years, the poet Yone Noguchi, a protegé of Joaquin Miller, and the painter Ernest Peixotto. Paris-style, they were dubbed *Les Jeunes* or The Young by the *New York Times*. It was a title in which they reveled.

By the end of its first year, *The Lark* had a press run of 3,000. Of the original *Jeunes,* Burgess remains known today for his nonsense book *Goops and How to Be Them,* which is still today a children's classic. Burgess later described the origins of the *The Lark:* his group "had been watching the literary movements of the time very narrowly, and the impulse to strike for California grew in us. . . . There was a new note of personal expression then becoming dominant." Burgess had been influenced by a London review, *The Yellow Book,* still famous today if only for its illustrations by Aubrey Beardsley, and the even more distinguished French journal of revolutionary art and politics, *La Revue blanche,* to which the greatest French writers and painters contributed. But he declared, "we must demolish Decadence and its 'precious' pretensions."

Burgess's main partner in the venture, whose work remains contemporary, was Porter Garnett. A San Franciscan by birth, Garnett, aged 24 when *The Lark* appeared, also worked for *The Argonaut,* a leading San Francisco weekly that provided a platform for such writers as Bierce and Ina Coolbrith and, later on, Frank Norris and Jack London. *The Argonaut* and its main rival *The Wasp* both come to us with stained reputations: *The Argonaut* tenaciously supported the Southern Pacific in politics, to the outrage of many; *The Wasp* opposed it, but published grotesque anti-Chinese cartoons and articles. *The Lark* expired in two years, its founders having decided they had made their point, but Burgess and Garnett had also produced *Le Petit Journal des Refusées* [*sic*], which like many ambitious *avant-garde* journals to come, saw only one number, in 1896.

Porter Garnett's intentions, for his part, did not at all include limiting himself to either weekly journalism or Bohemian experimentation. Although he also produced excellent daily journalism, mainly for the *Morning Call,* Garnett's eyes were turned to an exemplar of cultural revaluation greater than any other at that time: William Morris, whose socialism had also inspired Burnette Haskell. Garnett took up the work of Morris and his disciple T. J. Cobden-Sanderson in the design of printed books. But Garnett did not follow Morris into a cult of late-medieval craftsmanship; rather, he looked to the Renaissance, which had more to teach typographers and other makers of books. Porter Garnett was a man more of the twentieth century than of the nineteenth. He later directed The Laboratory Press at the Carnegie Institute of Technology in Pittsburgh. He seems not to have been very well appreciated there; but for printers in California, a place that soon became a world capital of book arts, he remained the leading figure for decades.

Burgess, Garnett, Polk, Porter, and others in the group achieved much for California, contributing immensely to its rise to international intellectual leadership. As Burgess wrote, *The Lark* had "made its pages known in the East as no California publication has ever been known before. It has stood for the reaction against decadence—and prophesied the renaissance." For present-day San Franciscans perhaps the best monument to the spirit of *Les Jeunes* is the beautiful Swedenborgian Church on Lyon Street. Built with the participation of Polk, William Keith (another in *The Lark*'s nest), and Bruce Porter, who designed its stained glass, the church remains a favorite for weddings.

The greatest member of the circle of *Les Jeunes,* however, was the writer Frank Norris, who was not an active participant in *The Lark.* Born in Chicago in 1870, Norris had come to California with his parents in 1884. A *fin-de-siècle* intellectual writ larger than even Burgess or Garnett, he had gone to Paris for two years at the end of his teens, and was a fanatical advocate of the new tendencies in French art and literature. Correctly, he saw that the Parisian writers of the nineteenth century had transformed poetry, prose, and criticism while its painters had done the same for art. He returned to the Bay Area so imbued with a Parisian spirit that he seemed peculiar to his fellow students when he enrolled at the University of California. He was a dandy, affecting elegant dress and filling his off-campus room with pieces of armor, a skeletal and shackled human wrist, and his own drawings of nudes.

Norris's passion for France made him an obvious candidate for *Les Jeunes.* He, after all, had been to the City of Light, had seen *La Revue blanche* on its café terraces, had breathed the air of the place that then embodied modernity more than any other. Norris seemed at first to have a very French and especially modernist dilettante quality. He stayed at the University for four years but left without a degree. But he found, like others after him, that once he published some short stories that showed, in whatever limited manner, his gifts, a college diploma was unnecessary.

He went East for a time and oversaw publication of his first novel in print, *McTeague,* about the struggle for success of a San Francisco dentist. The book sold well; by then he had already attained some fame as a journalist. The *San Francisco Chronicle* sent him to cover the Boer War in South Africa. He was captured by the Boers and, in that war at least, ceased to be effective as a correspondent. When he came back to San Francisco, enjoying the fruits of a promising career, Norris and his beautiful wife Jeannette haunted the cafés of North Beach and the parties thrown by his illustrious friends. His second book in print, *Blix,* which appeared the same year as *McTeague,* is a tribute to the couple's love and the charm of the Bohemian life they shared. He then covered the Spanish-American war as a correspondent before hiring out with Doubleday, Page and Company, his publisher, and again going to New York.

Norris' work attained greatness, above all, thanks to his fixation on Paris. He had long since read Émile Zola, whose naturalism had wholly conquered first the French, and then the worldwide reading public; he signed his letters "The Boy Zola." *McTeague,* which would be his favorite of his books, had been written in that spirit. But Norris resolved to tell a great story, frightening and disturbing like Zola's mighty *Germinal,* an epic of class struggle among coal miners. Norris took as his subject wheat, the commodity that, above all others, had turned the land over which the Southern Pacific and the settlers had fought into a cornucopia of financial gain. He worked with the patient research methods of Zola himself, gleaning much from the files of the *Chronicle.* He composed a narrative that gave voice to the courage and terror and martyrdom of the men of Mussel Slough: he wrote *The Octopus. The Octopus* was more than a work of authentic genius; it was immortal Literature.

A barely fictionalized account that paints the whole social landscape of California at the end of the nineteenth century, *The Octopus* was the first volume in a projected trilogy, *The Epic of the Wheat*. It was to be followed by *The Pit* and *The Wolf*, each volume illustrating a different aspect of the grain industry, from its growth to its financial allure as a commodity to its consumption by the world's masses. Norris did not live to see complete publication of the series; he died in 1902 at 32, in San Francisco, a year after *The Octopus* came out.

The Octopus is marred by late-nineteenth-century sentimentalism and is clumsy in places but it remains the book that, more than any other, expresses the contradictions that faced California at that time and anticipates the issues which would determine the course of California society in the future. It even depicts the supernaturalist tendencies then influential, and melds the waning presence of Hispanic traditions, Baroque and romantic, with an occult sense of the California landscape. One beautiful passage, "The Mission," based on the gorgeous San Juan Bautista, is informed with meaning, reminding the reader of a noble and mysterious past. Like Josiah Royce, though more darkly, Norris romanticized Spanish California. A leading character in *The Octopus*, the "sheep herder and range rider" Vanamee, his life twisted by inexplicable tragedy, goes to the Mission to "pass the night in the deep shadow of the aged pear trees. . . . Until this moment Vanamee had not trusted himself to see the Mission at night."

Behind its tale of a brutal corporation and disenfranchised settlers, as behind the economic critique of Henry George, many critics have chosen to see in *The Octopus* a reaction to the "closing of the frontier" described by Frederick Jackson Turner not long before. But this view is more than a little simplistic, and even evasive, for the eloquence of *The Octopus* is much more clearly grounded in a deep class anger. *The Octopus* is not without flaws, including a certain note of anti-Semitism. Yet it remains a powerful and beautiful piece of writing, a perfect distillation of the times, fully relevant to today's readers. It is the great testament of nineteenth-century California radicalism.

THE SOUTHERN PACIFIC railroad had, by 1899, begun to find its power restricted by competition. Although Leland Stanford and his three cronies, Mark Hopkins, Collis P. Huntington, and Charles Crocker, had done their best to make railroad transportation in the Far West their preserve, they had to some extent failed. The main challenge to the Southern Pacific's monopoly would come from the Atchison, Topeka & Santa Fe Railway, a tough corporation in its own right. Stanford's ring had prevented one railroad builder, Tom Scott, from entering southern California via Yuma, on the Colorado River, by sending Huntington to successfully buy off the politicians in Washington. Scott abandoned the field to New York's magnate Jay Gould. Gould came to an agreement with Huntington, who had assumed executive direction of the corporation, that left the S.P. in joint control of rails to the Texas Panhandle. Congress, disturbed at the probability that Stanford and his pals would end up in monopolistic possession of both the central and southern transcontinental railroad routes, denied a transfer of land grants in the Arizona and New Mexico territories to the S.P. However, the combine pressed ahead and built a through route to New Orleans. With the S.P. operating the Morgan steamship line in the Gulf of Mexico and the Atlantic, the company now offered its own service all the way from San Francisco to New York.

The relentless expansion of the Southern Pacific's position was not accomplished without overcoming numerous political and financial obstacles, especially since railroad stocks and bonds had become so notorious for being diluted by reissue, or "watered," that they were nicknamed "melons." The Santa Fe, however, was a different breed of cat; it would not go away. Under the management of two hardheaded Midwesterners, Thomas P. Nickerson and W. B. Strong, through the 1870s and 1880s, the A.T.&.S.F. built from Kansas south into Texas and New Mexico, conducted a lengthy bidding war for access to Colorado, and then began pushing, pushing at the edges of the S.P.'s domain. Jay Gould, whose lines competed with the Santa Fe, was no happier about this than Huntington, and the two of them worked together consistently to maintain their dominance. Gould took over railroads across the Southwest, while the S.P. held every rail line to the West Coast except the Northern Pacific.

The Santa Fe was granted rail access to California at Needles in 1884, but that was not much, since it depended on an agreement with the Southern Pacific. Given their enterprising, expansionist, and no-nonsense mentality, it is not surprising that the Santa Fe's executives found an extraordinary way around the problem, one which still demonstrates the amazing extent of the S.P.'s influence. To get to California, the Santa Fe built a line south across The Border, into Mexico! The S.P. at last capitulated, and allowed the Santa Fe to operate its own trackage in southern California. The A.T.&S.F. constructed a respectable network of lines serving the region, reaching tidewater at Los Angeles and San Diego. And in the 1890s it got to the Bay Area.

Jay Gould meanwhile had died, and his properties were inherited by his son George, who considered himself a great railroad king but who could hardly fill the old man's shoes. Indeed, even in an era that boasted great capitalists of the Stanford breed, Jay Gould had been a phenomenon unto himself. In 1900 Huntington also died, and the Southern Pacific system was sold to the investment banking firm of Kuhn, Loeb, and Company and Edward H. Harriman, proprietor of the Union Pacific. The combined S.P.-U.P. system was the greatest railroad operation of its time. Seeking at all costs to compete with it George Gould, whose base was in the Missouri Pacific, purchased the Denver & Rio Grande line; this gave him a route to Ogden, Utah, where, along with the Union Pacific, the D.&.R.G. handed over California-destined cars to the S.P.

George Gould decided to build into California. The project required absolute secrecy. Gould was frankly afraid of Harriman, realizing that the latter could destroy the entire Gould empire if he wished. A risky scheme proceeded in utter clandestinity: as a first step, an unknown relative of one of Gould's agents bought land in the Sierra Nevada to build a logging railroad. A challenge to the S.P.'s central-route monopoly was finally under way.

California at the end of the century remained, then, a society in turmoil. The early radicals, here as elsewhere in the country, had evolved into programmatic socialists. In 1894 Eugene Victor Debs, a former official of the Brotherhood of Locomotive Firemen and Enginemen, had led a national railroad strike directed against the paternalistic Pullman Palace Car Company, which produced passenger railroad coaches in a company town where George E. Pullman regulated every aspect of his employees' lives. The strike was called precipitately, under the aegis of Debs's new American Railway Union, which aspired to bring all railroad workers into a single body (although it barred Blacks, who then made up a quarter of the railroad workforce, mainly as locomotive firemen). The "Debs strike" shocked the nation, and was finally crushed, and the A.R.U. disappeared, but its leader, who was jailed, became a saint to working people in all parts of the country. Debs turned to politics, and emerged as a leader of the Social Democratic Party, which became the Socialist Party. He ran for president, the first of four times, in 1900. He was credited with about 88,000 votes, or less than one per cent, in a contest won by the Republican McKinley.

Socialism had become a popular topic among Californians. Of the personalities who, as 1900 drew nigh, became involved with it, none is more significant than Jack London. The life of this world-renowned author has been so thoroughly studied it seems almost absurd to try add to his biography, and the Londonian work most relevant to this inquiry came after 1900. But something happened to him in his twenties that merits comment here.

Born in 1876, Jack London had experienced extreme poverty and had entered into a quasi-vagabond existence as a fisherman and oyster pirate on San Francisco Bay. He went to sea, traveled around the country as a hobo, and, at 17, joined Coxey's Army in its march on Washington. As a result he seems to have had his first experience in print; the *San Francisco Chronicle* published an account of an unnamed "Oakland youth" who had traveled across the country riding the brake-beams of railroad freight cars. He became a Socialist, and was a radical even among them. Soon he had encountered the mentor who, for the rest of his life, he credited with making him a writer: Ina Coolbrith, the poet who by then had assumed a sedate position at the Oakland Public Library. Coolbrith could see what the lonely young man was about and loaded him down with books, every one of which he read. Thanks to this coaching, London was able to get into the University of California; but, rather like Norris before him, he learned that for a writer a college degree was of scant importance and he left after one semester.

London took to active street speaking and polemical argument in the Bay Area Socialist milieu, and this eagerness has typically been described by writers on him as an outcome of his childhood poverty and his experiences as a wanderer on the road. But Jack London seems to have also found out something that many young men and women would similarly learn in the century to come: for an isolated, alienated but brilliant youth the Socialist movement offered opportunities that seemed available nowhere else, above all a chance to gain skill in the use of words and ideas. At the same time, Socialist comradeship offered the young militant a means to self-esteem. London may have become a Socialist out of conviction, but his enthusiasm reflected another matter: he had, for the first and probably the last time in his life, found a home. In 1897 London went to Alaska, where the Klondike Gold Rush was on, and in 1900 he published his first book of stories. The skill with language he had honed as a speaker on street corners served him well when he put pen to paper.

California radicalism also stimulated others to undertake new paths. Paradoxically, the growing labor strength on the Pacific coast was felt in Asia, notwithstanding the evil that had been done to Asian immigrants. The first product of this influence was visible among the Chinese. San Francisco was visited in 1896 by Sun Yat-sen, a Christian Hakka ("untouchable") from Guangdong province who had left China for Hawaii two years before. An enemy of the ethnic Manchu dynasty of the Qing, Sun had founded a conspiratorial group, the *Hsing-Chung hui* or Revive China Society. In 1894, China was defeated by Japan in the First Sino-Japanese War of 1894–95—the mother of classic East Asian culture was, in so many words, raped by an upstart descendant—and the trauma this caused in the Chinese political conscience stirred that nation to rebellion.

In Hawaii Sun raised almost $10,000, recruited about 120 members for his movement, and selected a handful of youths to be militarily trained. He went back to China in 1895, prepared to launch a revolution with less than half a dozen partisans. He organized a coup at Guangzhou, but it failed. He came to the United States after a stop in Hawaii, and toured the country, speaking in halls maintained by anti-Qing triads, of which Sun was a member. He recruited a little more than a dozen new followers, mainly San Franciscans and Christians.

Unknown to Sun during his first American tour, an eccentric white student at Stanford University named Homer Lea was fascinated by China. Lea was himself a remarkable individual, a hunchback and a dwarf, born in Denver in 1876, who had made himself an expert in military affairs. At Stanford he impressed his fellow students and his professors with his knowledge of ancient warfare, while spending most of his time with Chinese students. As Bailey Millard notes, notwithstanding anti-Chinese laws in California, "no bar ha[d] ever been placed upon Asiatics in the universities of California; they were welcomed at both Berkeley and Stanford."

Lea joined another Chinese society, the Chinese Empire Reform Association, which had been founded in British Columbia. Within that organization Lea stood on its radical wing. He organized military training of some Chinese students, then went to China just as the so-called Boxer Rebellion of 1900, an antiforeign conspiracy based in martial arts societies, took place. He came back with a price set on his head by the imperial régime, and eventually threw in his lot with Sun. But Sun's moment had yet to arrive.

Bailey Millard also observes that "the antipathy entertained by the people of the bay region and all California toward the Chinese transferred in the course of time to . . . the Japanese." China was viewed as a threat to white labor in California. But a rising Japan, which had become a major power in the aftermath of its forcible "opening" by American ships in the 1850s and an artificially imposed but successful "bourgeois revolution" beginning in 1868, was perceived as a threat to the entire white world, the worst exemplar of the "Yellow Peril." For this reason, it is particularly remarkable that labor politics entered Japan in emulation of the California labor movement through the work of a man named Sen Katayama. Born in 1859 on a farm in Okayama prefecture, the son of a Buddhist priest, Katayama had worked as a farm laborer and at many other unskilled occupations before becoming a primary-school instructor at age 18. At 22, he had gone to Tokyo to complete his education, and there toiled as a printer. He landed in San Francisco in 1884 with only one Mexican silver dollar in his pocket, and studied English for three years while earning a living as a houseboy (the common occupation of Japanese in San Francisco in that era), a restaurant worker, a farmhand, and at other jobs.

Katayama, who had become a Christian, entered a school in Oakland in 1887 but in the face of racial harassment left after eleven months. He went to Tennessee to study, then to Grinnell College in Iowa, where he was awarded his bachelor's and master's degrees. A glutton for education, he went on to gain a divinity degree from Yale University. In the summer of 1895, he sailed to England to observe the church administration of charitable work, to which he had chosen to dedicate his life. He returned to Japan in 1896 to find a country filled with triumphalism over its mauling of China and its seizure of Korea and Formosa (Taiwan) in the recent war. He launched a Christian social institution, Kingsley Hall, in Tokyo. But soon he had plunged into labor organization.

Katayama joined with a journalist named F. Takano; a tailor, H. Sawada; and a shoemaker, T. Jo, to form a provisional Brotherhood of Labor. These three had come to San Francisco in 1890 to study the American Federation of Labor; notwithstanding the anti-Asian prejudice the latter embraced, the Japanese learned lessons from its methods and successes as well as from its failures. Late in 1897 the first authentic Japanese labor organization, the Iron Workers Union, was established, with 1,100 members and with Katayama as its paid secretary. He launched a journal, *Labor World*, in both Japanese and English.

The *Labor World* published a statement of principles that read:

> The people are silent. I will be their advocate in their silence.
>
> I will speak for the mute; I will speak for those who are silent from despair.
>
> I will interpret stammering; I will interpret the grumbling, murmurs, the tumult of crowds, the complaints, the cries of men so degraded by suffering and ignorance that they have no strength to voice their wrongs.
>
> I will be the people's word.
>
> I will be the bleeding mouth from which the gag has been snatched.
>
> I will say everything.

As the nineteenth century ended, California radicalism had come into its own and, internationally, its voice had already generated one of its loudest and clearest echoes.

PART III

BLOOD ORANGES

California is honeycombed with the Socialistic spirit.
—Brigadier General Tasker H. Bliss, U.S. Army (1911)

Wherein class conflict produces gigantic and dramatic crises; corruption makes San Francisco infamous, but is at last defeated; rich and poor battle for the soul of Los Angeles; bombs explode in both cities, and a revolution breaks out nearby; Wobblies and other labor radicals challenge civic boosterism; and World War I transforms the world, but especially California, where radicalism is largely suppressed

*T*he California labor movement that inspired foreign imitators entered the twentieth century with a militancy and an influence unmatched in the United States. In booming San Francisco, where the unions were centered, wages were high and membership grew. The period was marked by class conflict throughout the country and the world, and a local contest between unionists infected by a triumphalist spirit and employers increasingly reluctant to accept the "closed" union shop was inevitable.

The showdown between labor and capital in San Francisco came in 1901. The national scene was then dominated by an unsuccessful campaign for union recognition at the U.S. Steel Corporation in Pittsburgh. In San Francisco, January of that year saw the founding of a City Front Federation uniting sailors, longshoremen, teamsters, marine officers, and related workers. In April, fifty of the city's business leaders set up a secret Employers' Association in the hope of suppressing the "closed" shop, and were publicly represented by a lawyer, M. F. Michael.

Soon a strike by culinary workers was met by clandestine action; the Employers' Association blocked delivery of oysters, bread, and meat to union restaurants. Wholesalers to the wagon-delivery industry boycotted union firms and beer bottlers fired members and announced their adherence to the nonunion, or "open," shop.

Organized Labor, the new weekly paper of the San Francisco Building Trades Council, warned, "Faster and faster the city is moving toward the most critical period in its history. Broad minds and coolness only can avert a general strike." *Organized Labor* was edited by Olav Anders Tveitmoe, a former teacher, journalist, and leader of the Cement Workers' Union, who like his fellow Norwegian, the Sailors' leader Andrew Furuseth, left a deep impress on California labor politics for more than a generation.

The breaking point arrived in July when Teamsters' Union members were locked out of work for refusing to handle nonunion baggage, and drayage companies in the Employers' Association announced that Teamsters must leave the union or lose their jobs. These workers were the key to all freight delivery in a city where, at the time, few docks had railroad connections. The Teamsters struck, 6,400 strong. On the night of July 29, ten days after the lockout began, the City Front Federation met and announced that its membership, of 16,000 more, would cease work on the docks of San Francisco, Oakland, and Port Costa.

With a rhetoric reminiscent of Burnette Haskell fifteen years before, Furuseth's weekly *Coast Seamen's Journal* declared,

> The City Front Federation of San Francisco now holds in its hands the fortunes of the entire labor movement on the Pacific Coast and, to a considerable extent, of the labor movement throughout the country. The result of the present struggle in San Francisco will either strengthen or weaken the forces of labor now aligned to meet the onslaught of concentrated capital against the liberties and the common manhood of the American people. The result lies with ourselves. The workers, united and firm in the demand for decent conditions of employment, are supreme and invincible . . . no employers' association or other array of opposing forces can subjugate them.

Although the Teamsters were led by the charismatic Michael Casey, Furuseth emerged as the "manager" of the massive strike. In the years since the Coast Seamen's Union had first organized, it had fulfilled Haskell's hopes, becoming the recognized leader of West Coast labor; many union advocates who began in its ranks had later organized other trades. Alongside Furuseth in 1901 stood Walter Macarthur, the editor of the *Coast Seamen's Journal;* Ed Andersen, veteran of the radical I.W.A. set up by Haskell, a founder of the Coast Seamen's Union, and a leading figure in the City Front Federation; and Ed Rosenberg, a Furuseth partisan in the Sailors' Union who served as secretary of the San Francisco Labor Council.

For much of the previous decade Furuseth and his union had battled for reform in the status of the seaman. The organization's *Journal,* established in 1887, began by publishing essays by Karl Marx, and went on to become one of the most literate and thoughtful weeklies in the United States. Furuseth also oversaw the union's issuance of "The Red Record," a landmark pamphlet detailing the worst incidents of shipboard brutality by "bucko" officers. In 1895 a federal law alleviating the sailors' condition, the Maguire Act, was passed.

In May 1895, however, a scandalous case erupted. Four seamen who quit the barkentine *Arago* at a Washington port were arrested, imprisoned, and carried back aboard in irons. When the ship arrived in San Francisco, they were rearrested. This, the first major test of the Maguire Act, was lost by the seafarers, for in 1897 the U.S. Supreme Court upheld the imprisonment of sailors for "desertion." Furuseth and his men responded with great bitterness, declaring that they could not participate in a Fourth of July celebration that year. Again in 1898 the sailors declared, "The spectacle of a slave worshipping his chains would be less ludicrous than that of the American seamen celebrating Independence Day." The sailors' combativeness and determination were becoming legendary; their legal efforts continued, and at the end of 1898 a federal law aimed at corrupt shipping agents, the White Act, was passed.

Understandable it was, then, that in July 1901 the decision of waterfront labor to "walk" in support of the Teamsters was greeted by unionists with delirious enthusiasm. But the *San Francisco Chronicle,* which had come a long way from the days when the de Youngs gave the paper a pro-union tone, reported somberly on the crisis: "During the day there was an air of expectancy everywhere over the city. Not only in labor circles, but even in the homes of all classes there was a feeling of anxiety over the coming of the [City Front Federation] meeting which was to be fraught with so much for the good or ill of the business interests of San Francisco." Sinister news came from the police, who were cleaning and oiling their full complement of riot guns and pistols. Meanwhile, Hearst's *Examiner* was conspicuous in its sympathy for the strikers.

Ed Rosenberg declared, for the Labor Council, "There is no demand for an increase of wages or the shortening of hours. . . . The issue is clearly defined; the battle is for and against the principle that labor has the right to organize." His superior as council president, Walter H. Goff, emphasized, "The organized labor of this city will make a great struggle for its rights."

The Employers' Association, supported by such major corporations as Levi Strauss & Co., was no less confident of victory. Mayor James D. Phelan had offered to mediate the controversy, to no avail. The Employers' Association demanded a universal "open" shop and union abandonment of sympathetic strikes and boycotts. Strikebreakers were recruited in considerable numbers. By the morning of the strike's second day, the press reported that the police had granted 100 concealed weapon permits to employees of the struck firms, several of them vouched for by M. F. Michael. The police commission also granted the infamous crimp John Curtin, the union sailors' longest-standing enemy, credentials for forty men to operate as special patrol officers. But public opinion was distinctly on the side of the unions, and the strike spirit was infectious: Japanese and Chinese workers at the Federal Salt Works in the southeast portion of the Bay walked off the job, demanding an increase in wages to $1.50 per day. The city's Board of

Supervisors sided with the strikers, calling on the police to remain strictly impartial. Rank-and-file patrolmen were clearly unhappy with orders from the police brass to act forcefully against the unionists.

Labor was militant, but could hardly be described as radical. A massive Labor Day parade brought out over 20,000 union members in a disciplined, sober march extending four miles. By September 8, after seven weeks on strike, the unions counted 192 ships tied up, with nine hundred strikebreakers on the docks; the Employers' Association only admitted that 100 vessels were out of operation, and claimed that 2,100 nonunion longshoremen were at work. The Employers' side also insisted, in an assertion brusquely denied by labor, that five hundred strikers had secretly resumed work.

Nevertheless, the struggle had become incredibly violent. In two months, according to union sources, 336 assaults were recorded, with 250 requiring medical aid; five men were killed. Even the assassination of President William McKinley in September 1901 did not divert San Francisco's attention from the waterfront labor epic. Indeed, the conflict was so great in its intensity and extent that a clear victory by either side became an impossibility, and the battle turned into a stalemate, with neither side capable of backing down. Short of open and declared civil war, which many feared was looming, there seemed to be no way out of the impasse.

Finally, at the beginning of October 1901, with both camps still breathing fire and discharging lead at each other, Governor Henry T. Gage stepped in and imposed a truce. Neither contender could claim overwhelming victory, and the unions had gained nothing new; they had simply preserved the right to continue representing their members. Then, anticlimactically as in many other such strikes, the confrontation dissipated into nothingness, like a nightmare vanishing at daybreak. But one thing was certain: the unions were still in place, and San Francisco had become the nation's outstanding "union town."

The strike saw the founding of a municipal Union Labor Party, on a thirteen-point platform that called for public ownership of utilities, including street railways, gas, electric, light, and water services, and telephone and telegraph systems. The party program further demanded "rigid enforcement" of the eight-hour workday for all labor performed under municipal contract and the union label on all supplies bought by the city; free garbage removal; the construction of new brick schoolhouses; establishment of a free farmers' market, and arbitration of labor disputes. Reflecting the prejudices of the times, the Party also called for separate schools for Asian children.

The Union Labor Party nominated Eugene Schmitz, the president of the Musicians' Union and a Catholic of mixed German and Irish origin, for mayor. Schmitz and three Union Labor supervisors were elected. With this outcome, California entered into a ten-year political convulsion that completely transformed local society. Out of the legal proceedings, debates, strikes, assassinations, bombings, demonstrations, and lesser upheavals of the period, San Francisco emerged mature, California gained a new and amazing institutional health, and Los Angeles rose to a place as one of the country's major cities.

Yet it was a time of great confusion and contradiction, much of which has yet to be sorted out or fully understood, even nearly a century later. Factions proliferated, established roles and reputations were rendered irrelevant, and conspiratorial explanations for otherwise inexplicable events abounded. Honest reformers were slandered as tools of the entrenched interests; strikers were denounced as pawns of their corrupt employers. Labor rose to the heights of power and fell to the depths of scandal before participating in an astonishing civic renewal.

The triumph of the Union Labor Party was deeply flawed. Although it was reelected to office again and again, almost from its beginning some union leaders and their friends in journalism mistrusted it. And their suspicions were justified, for neither Schmitz nor the rest of the party leaders acted on their own. Schmitz was under the control of a lawyer, Abraham Ruef, hitherto a Republican. Ruef and Schmitz left a legacy in San Francisco politics debated long after they were removed from the scene.

Ruef was a "fixer." He assembled a network of favored clients, business associates, union functionaries, and ancillary individuals who fed off city contracts awarded by Schmitz. In addition, Ruef soon began to skim vast quantities of cash from two illicit industries that had long been prominent in San Francisco life: prostitution and gambling. No political leader had ever attempted to curb the satisfaction of these vices in San Francisco, a city famous throughout the world for the jollity of its gaming tables and the beauty of its women for hire. But Ruef, who had become prosperous as an attorney for prostitutes and their masters, went beyond their protection to extortion: he demanded the owners of "French restaurants" pay him directly and continuously for the right of operation.

"French restaurant" was, in San Francisco, a euphemism for a genteel kind of brothel. Many of the "French restaurants" were small two- and three-story hotels, with meals offered on the first floor, sometimes served family style. On the upper floors prostitutes lived in "cribs," tiny rooms with little more than space for a bed and a sink, as well as in small apartments. The food and wine were typically excellent in the "French restaurants"—as so often in San Francisco, then as later.

Schmitz was reelected in 1903. By the middle of his first term, however, civic leaders had begun to perceive something rotten in San Francisco. Ruef was visibly enriching himself, and public opinion recognized that he was doing so by selling licenses and protection through his influence with Schmitz. A scandal-mongering editor, Fremont Older of *The Bulletin*, found evidence of Ruef's blackmail of the "French restaurant" owners and began to print exposés of the administration with bold headlines on one front page after another. Older demanded a full legal inquiry, seeking the aid of President Theodore Roosevelt, who granted help under a veil of secrecy. But while the corruption of Tammany Hall in New York City stood as a cautionary example, and while civic reform was a popular slogan for many San Franciscans, criticism of the Ruef-Schmitz régime also impelled some unionists to the defense of the "pro-labor" political machine.

Nationally, the labor movement was heading in a direction more radical than had been seen since the 1880s. As San Francisco labor, having been tested and benefited by the weapon of the mass strike in 1901, now tried electoral methods, a revived militancy was visible in the ranks of other unions around the country.

In 1903 Joseph Buchanan, the Denver labor journalist and comrade of Haskell in the I.W.A., published a stirring volume of memoirs, *The Story of a Labor Agitator*. Buchanan looked back to a younger union movement— one that was firmly united, idealistic, and unafraid of aggressive action; one that even encompassed, however briefly, an open challenge to the basic relation of capital and labor. A minor classic of the period, marred only by rather subdued anti-Chinese comments, his book appeared at a time when American labor organizations, although not yet completely domesticated, had settled into certain predictable routines, occasionally interrupted by great struggles like that of 1901. After all, the fundamental role of unions was to negotiate wages and working conditions, and they tended to do serious battle only when the opportunity for negotiation was denied them. Buchanan was also disillusioned by the sectarianism and lack of personal generosity he found in the Socialist movement. But above all, he yearned for the old days "under the red flag," the days of radical innovation and bold hopes.

The flame of the Haskell-Buchanan revolution had never really died in the American West. Buchanan's successors in the Rockies organized the Western Federation of Miners, soon the most radical element in the American union movement. The W.F.M. dropped out of the American Federation of Labor, believing the federation had compromised itself, but some unions that remained in the A.F.L. were nearly as militant: the United Brewery Workmen had long acted as a frankly revolutionary section of the labor movement. Mainly German-speaking and socialist in "old-country" style, they inscribed on their union label, "Workingmen of All Countries, Unite." Like the railroad union leader Debs, the Brewery Workmen looked toward an industry-wide unionism, in contrast with the A.F.L.'s devotion to organization by craft. On the West Coast the Brewery Workmen were led by Alfred Fuhrman, a socialist and former member of the Coast Seamen's Union. The Brewery Workmen were debating in 1904 whether to follow the Western Federation of Miners out of the A.F.L.

A meeting held in Chicago in June 1905 heralded an entirely new stage in America's labor history, and many dramatic incidents in California's: the founding convention of the Industrial Workers of the World (I.W.W.). This uncompromisingly revolutionary labor organization began by adopting as its slogan, "The working class and the employing class have nothing in common." Prominent figures in the creation of the I.W.W. included William Dudley "Big Bill" Haywood, a leader of the W.F.M., and William Trautman, former editor of the Brewery union paper, the *Brauer-Zeitung,* who had been deposed from his editorship for endorsing the gathering. Delegates also attended from the Debs Socialist group and from a competing, more radical faction, the Socialist Labor Party, which was led by an eccentric New York law professor named Daniel De Leon. A "preamble" adopted at the inaugural conclave of the I.W.W. declared, in an echo of Karl Marx, "instead of the conservative motto, 'A Fair Day's Wage for a Fair

Day's Work,' we must inscribe on our banner the revolutionary watchword, 'Abolition of the Wages System.'"

It would be hard to imagine a program that, in appearance at least, offered a greater contrast with the "bread-and-butter" unionism of the San Francisco trades. Yet men like Furuseth and Tveitmoe, then the outstanding minds in San Francisco labor, in spite of their inborn caution and general disdain for ideological speculation, were, culturally at least, more than a little susceptible to its appeal. The birth of the I.W.W. was part of a worldwide phenomenon known as "syndicalism" that had its earliest full incarnation in France in the 1890s. The American anarchist Emma Goldman became an outspoken defender of the new trend, which she defined as "the revolutionary philosophy of labor conceived and born in the actual struggle and experience of the workers themselves." Syndicalism, as described by Goldman, rejected political activity in the pursuit of union demands, emphasizing radical economic measures: "direct action" and, above all, the general strike. For the syndicalists, "economic emancipation of the workers must be the principal aim . . . to which everything else is to be subordinated."

The year 1905 had been marked by other events that contributed to a general atmosphere of uncertainty in California. The most significant of these was a boycott of American goods in China, which led to a relaxation of the U.S. laws that excluded Asians. But the most remarkable and shocking news came from Russia. In a war beginning in 1904, the tsarist empire was stunningly humiliated at the hands of Japan, feeding the anxiety of whites in many places about the rise of a "yellow" military power. The events that followed had longer and larger consequences than almost any other in the twentieth century for the Pacific Basin. President Roosevelt communicated with both the belligerents, appealing for a peace conference. But in defeated Russia, political turmoil burst into the open with the Bloody Sunday massacre. California papers ran banner headlines reporting the carnage as imperial troops killed two thousand peaceful petitioners and wounded five thousand more.

The Russian revolution of 1905 deeply frightened the world as the cruelty of the Paris Commune had thirty-five years before, but on a wider scale, with a brutality that seemed both more sustained and more atrocious. At the end of January rioting in Warsaw, capital of Russian-ruled Poland, left three hundred dead; in June bulletins came of a worker insurrection in Łodz, which turned into a massacre by the Cossacks, and of increasing outrages against Jews. On each of these occasions, the American press groped for superlatives: no such terror had been seen in modern times, no such uprising, no such wanton killing. The infant twentieth century was undergoing a baptism by wide streams of blood.

Again triumphant in war, Japan was also the scene of limited but important radical political developments. Sen Katayama had continued his labor agitation there, but returned to the United States in 1904. He toured the Japanese communities of the Pacific Coast, fiercely denouncing the Russo-Japanese war and defending the Socialist program. Branches of the Japanese Socialist movement were established in the major California cities. Katayama's stand in favor of collaboration with Russian socialists, the supposed enemies of the Japanese, made him an internationally known figure. He maintained a great interest in the United States, and even briefly considered launching a Utopian colony of Japanese rice farmers in Texas.

The municipal election of 1905 in San Francisco brought out an anti-Schmitz, anti-Ruef fusion ticket, allying Republicans and Democrats behind mayoral candidate John S. Partridge. As the November balloting approached, the local dailies interspersed investigative attacks on the Ruef "labor" machine with further lurid headlines from Russia. Partridge called for "a great uprising of the people" of San Francisco against graft while, as if in irony, the worst rioting yet broke out in Russian cities.

The 1905 mayoralty race saw Partridge offer himself as the candidate of the "fireside lamp," against the "red light" of the brothel-keepers who backed Schmitz; if Ruef's man lost, the *Chronicle* predicted, "the Red Light District will go into mourning." After two Union Labor administrations, San Francisco was infamous for its municipal graft; its bonds could not be sold and its credit had dived. Los Angeles and Seattle increasingly drew Eastern investors, who now avoided San Francisco. In case after case recorded in the press, Schmitz and Ruef had been paid off for protection, for city contracts, for the right (according to the reformers) to sell tainted meat and milk and run tenements with broken sewers and plumbing, and to leave the streets filthy. Schmitz was denounced as "the idol of the criminal element," a mayor fearful of a city audit, a patron of fraudulent elections.

Labor leader O. A. Tveitmoe and his main associate, Patrick H. Mc-

Carthy, had once opposed Schmitz and Ruef, but now attacked the anti-Ruef reformers. As president of the Building Trades Council, McCarthy knew the union vote could be delivered for the machine; by contrast, the reformers ineffectually called on union workers to repay a city that had always supported their demands for higher wages and greater dignity by contributing to its improvement. The reformers warned that Ruef was merely using labor for his personal advantage and would lead the unions to destruction. The *Chronicle* reprinted letters condemning Schmitz and Ruef that McCarthy and Tveitmoe had published in 1903; Tveitmoe had described Schmitz therein as a "prattling parasite" and a "traitor," and inveighed, "Are we to have two years more of this Schmitz-Ruef regime? If so, then God help the working people of San Francisco."

But in the intervening two years the machine had gotten to McCarthy and Tveitmoe, the dailies charged, with offers of municipal jobs. Other radicals' support for Schmitz and Ruef was less easily explained. For example, the veteran protestor Carl Browne drew cartoons for their electoral literature. Nevertheless there were people in the labor movement who could not be bought. Walter Macarthur, a prominent critic of Ruef and Schmitz, considered by some a notorious labor agitator, was the close associate of Furuseth and an editor of the *Coast Seamen's Journal.* Schmitz was rebuked by Austin Lewis, a leader of the growing local branch of Debs's Socialist Party, as "the promoted proletarian," creator of "the vile corruption, the infamous degradation, this rotten administration." Lewis, who had come to California from England in 1890 at age 25, was a prolific writer on labor and socialist topics and a friend of Fremont Older and Jack London. Lewis railed at Schmitz, who, he said, "went into power under the guise and upon the pretense as the champion of the workingman, [but] organized a gigantic scheme for graft."

Schmitz responded with well-crafted phrases, accusing the reformers of acting as a front for an anti-union group, the Citizens' Alliance, and prophesied, in recalling the mass strike of 1901, that "the time of the Teamsters' strike, when policemen were used as teamsters and shipping clerks, when the blood of the union man was held as cheap as dirt and there was no safety on the streets, were sweet and peaceful compared to what you will see here if the Citizens' Alliance, or the fusion ticket, which is the same thing, is allowed to prevail." Schmitz knew his supporters. The entire Union Labor ticket was reelected overwhelmingly, to the despair of the reformers. Meanwhile in New York Billy Hearst, campaigning for mayor on a Municipal Ownership ticket, and in the full flight of his supposed radicalism, was defeated. He then alleged fraud by Tammany Hall; Hearst had become used to getting what he wanted.

————————

THE YEAR 1906 was destined to be remembered, always, for the great San Francisco Earthquake and Fire. Mayor Schmitz responded to the destruction of the city with immediate, aggressive measures, including orders that looters were to be shot on sight and a two-month shutdown of saloons—a considerable innovation in San Francisco. Gathering the city's business leaders to his side, Schmitz began to shed Ruef's influence; some said his post-earthquake career, brief as it was, was unblemished by his prior habits. The reconstruction that followed the earthquake saw further bounty accruing to the unions, with opportunity for building-trades workers in particular.

But the problems facing Schmitz and Ruef did not go away in the aftermath of the earthquake. Some unionists said Schmitz had become too close to business interests after the disaster. Fremont Older, leading the reformers, allied with Rudolph Spreckels, son of old Claus (whose antilabor reputation did the reformers no good), as well as with a former mayor, James D. Phelan, and the district attorney, William J. Langdon, who had been elected on the Union Labor ticket. The group was joined by Francis J. Heney, a federal investigator appointed a deputy district attorney and charged with investigating Ruef. Heney had verbally pilloried Ruef during the 1905 election, promising he would bring him to justice if given the power of a grand jury.

Schmitz suddenly left town for Europe. Ruef then boldly removed Langdon and Heney and named himself district attorney. Community outrage led San Franciscans to gather on October 29, 1906 at Temple Sherith Israel, where Ruef had worshipped and which, after the earthquake, was temporarily put to public use. Judge Thomas Graham, using the synagogue as a courtroom, would rule on whether Ruef or Langdon would serve as district attorney.

The synagogue demonstration was menacing. Some anti-Ruef elements brought ropes; Ruef's police at first threw out the newspaper reporters who appeared at the building. Rabbis joined the businessmen and Christian clergy in the anti-Ruef faction milling around outside the synagogue. Jews had been a highly assimilated, successful, and respectable section of the city's residents from the beginning of the Gold Rush; still, a taint of anti-Semitism diluted the reform campaign against Ruef.

The tension broke when Heney and Older, with their assembled thousands of supporters, suddenly pushed past Ruef's gunmen into the synagogue. Judge Graham arrived, and issued his decision: Langdon would remain as district attorney. Ruef was arrested and charged with extortion of "French restaurants"; promised immunity except in the restaurant cases, he confessed. He testified against Schmitz, who came back from Europe, and against other accomplices, who were then indicted for bribery; chief among these was Patrick Calhoun, an "Eastern capitalist" and the head of the United Railroads streetcar system, but other utility officials were also charged. Ruef and Schmitz were now accused of receiving bribes to permit the installation of overhead trolley-car wires and to allow a rise in gas rates. Ruef declared under oath that he had received a payment of $200,000 from Calhoun's chief attorney and kept $50,000 for himself, giving Schmitz the same amount and furnishing $85,000 to the Board of Supervisors.

It was then that one of the most remarkable incidents in California's mythic history of intrigue, corruption, double-dealing, and conspiracy took place: simultaneously with the indictment of Patrick Calhoun and his top officers, a thousand carmen on the United Railroads, demanding a 25-percent wage increase, launched the bloodiest strike in the annals of San Francisco. The walkout began in May 1907, amid a national depression, and was led by Richard Cornelius, a Schmitz crony who had become a supporter of the antigraft campaign. Patrick Calhoun, who had avoided a strike late in 1906 by importing a thousand strikebreakers by express train from the East, similarly hired an armed legion to run cars and to protect his company's facilities. An unrestrained war of the classes ensued.

Patrick Calhoun was a grandson of the Southern politician John C. Calhoun and a protegé of the financier J. P. Morgan. His antistriker mercenaries were trigger-happy; from the first day of the strike they freely shot at demonstrators, bystanders, and even the police. Strikers and their supporters fired their own revolvers and pelted the cars with bricks, planks, and scraps of metal. Enraged police, seeing the strikebreakers shooting their colleagues, rushed the streetcars, with some falling wounded in the crossfire. Chief of Police Jeremiah Dinan announced, "Policemen armed with riot

guns will shoot down any strikebreakers on the company's cars we catch firing a shot." But Calhoun proclaimed, in so many words, his own police
power. If the regular police were armed with riot guns, he would provide his
men with repeating rifles. For many on labor's side, the ultimate horror of
corporate power had finally come to pass: Patrick Calhoun had completely
usurped public authority in the interest of United Railroads profit.

The Citizens' Alliance, much baited by Schmitz, announced a reward
of $100 to owners of the new Kodak hand-held camera who might capture
"good, clear snapshots of those caught in the act of committing violence"
and $1,000 for evidence securing a murder or arson conviction. Schmitz
had seemingly paid off on his promise that police would not interfere with
strikers, and even antilabor journalists admitted that the city's majority was
on the unions' side. Calhoun claimed that the strikers had used the graft
prosecution as a cover for pure aggression against him; but some saw in the
strike a secret maneuver by Calhoun to shift attention away from the reform campaign. Fremont Older believed Calhoun had nurtured and controlled the strike; Spreckels accused Calhoun of deliberately inciting the
strikers by his manner. Day after day Calhoun issued new declamations of
defiance, insisting that his armed men would replace the derelict police in
maintaining order and defending his right to operate the streetcars with
strikebreakers. Day after day new storms of bricks, metal, and wood assailed
the cars, and men were killed and wounded. The struck carbarns, although
offering a fortress-like bulwark during the daylight hours, were lit up by
bright electric lights at night, making them excellent targets for raids by the
strikers. The police, most of them Irish, many former union men or related
to current members, repeatedly fought pitched battles—not with the strikers, as elsewhere in America, but with the strikebreakers.

Meanwhile, the graft prosecution continued. Thanks to the imaginative Older, it added new terms to the English language: *higher-up,* originally
used to describe Calhoun; *boodler,* attached to Ruef's ring, and even *gangster,* first referring to criminals who preyed on the city after the earthquake.
Violent incidents occurred even in the investigators' realm; the home of a
witness against Ruef was dynamited, followed by three apartments he
owned. Schmitz was convicted and driven from office; but, though sentenced to five years in prison, he served none of it. The 1907 strike ended in
"absolute failure [and] complete disaster" for the carmen's union, according
to I.W.W. leader William Trautmann, who blamed the defeat not on Cal-

houn but on the division of the workforce between many small craft unions. The final toll included at least thirty-nine strikers dead and 701 strikebreakers seriously injured. No full accounting of the strike was ever made; no resolution of the charges about its manipulation ever came forth.

With Schmitz out of office a successor, Dr. Edward R. Taylor, a leading attorney and poet, was hand-picked by Fremont Older. The *Bulletin* editor now turned to the man who, above all, symbolized "the higher-ups." Calhoun became the chief target of reporters; but limits on the graft prosecution emerged as the city's business leaders drew back from a proceeding that would touch the streetcar boss.

Fremont Older, the chief reformer, was a dramatic personality. Born in Wisconsin in 1856, he was, like Henry George and Joseph Buchanan, a typesetter who became a newspaper publisher. Until the graft prosecutions, he was merely a brilliant practitioner of newspaper competition through sensationalism; a typical Older headline in *The Bulletin* was POLICEMAN CAUGHT ROBBING DYING MAN'S POCKETS. The anti-Ruef campaign made him a hero, but his pursuit of Calhoun saw him turned overnight into a troublemaker, in the eyes of civic leaders. It also made him the target of serious threats.

On one occasion in 1907, Older was grabbed off the street, shoved into a car by gun-toting heavies, and taken aboard a southbound Southern Pacific passenger train. Told he would be killed, he believed it; he was in the hands of Calhoun attorney Porter Ashe and a Calhoun-employed detective. The train crew barred other passengers from entering the coach where he was kept, but his captors took him into the dining car. There he was seen by a San Francisco lawyer, who perceived what was afoot. The lawyer left the train at King City and wired San Francisco. Rudolph Spreckels obtained a writ of *habeas corpus* by telephone to Santa Barbara, where extras came off the newspaper presses screaming that Older had been kidnapped. When the train eased into the Santa Barbara S.P. station at 8:30 the next morning, hundreds of people surrounded the tracks. Older's tormentors, baffled, imagined that a wedding reception was in progress. But then a group of deputy sheriffs burst into the compartment and liberated the *Bulletin* editor. The crowd cheered, and more cheered again when Older returned in triumph to San Francisco. The story was reported throughout the country.

Older stood out from his contemporaries in journalism for his genuinely complex personality. Aside from his dedication to getting scoops and readers, he was a man of intense enthusiasms. He was sensitive to ideas and to literature, and was the only prominent newspaperman of his time to frequent San Francisco's Bohemia, which had begun with *Les Jeunes* a decade before and which still flourished. Sadly, Frank Norris, the city's great writer at the century's end, had died young. But new talents appeared, many of them politically as well as artistically rebellious. Painters, poets, and similar folk flocked to the Montgomery Block, nicknamed the "Monkey Block," a fading office building in downtown San Francisco where studios were available at cheap rents. The "Monkey Block" continued in this role until the 1950s. On its ground floor, a fabled restaurateur, Giuseppe "Poppa" Coppa, dispensed Italian dinners as well as his own experimental dishes such as chicken Portola, which consisted of a half-bird baked in a coconut, proving that the *nouvelle cuisine* of more recent times was nothing new at all.

Older joined the crowd from Poppa Coppa's, along with Ambrose Bierce, the poet George Sterling, Jack London, and other such spirits in the Bohemian Club, a men's society that much later became known as a core institution of the highest California and American financial and political élite. In the aftermath of the 1906 earthquake the interlocking circles of Bohemians, whether members of the Club or not, began congregating away from San Francisco at Carmel, which became the epitome of the rather-precious kind of "artist's colonies" that also gathered at Taos, New Mexico, and Provincetown, Massachusetts.

The Carmel intellectuals were by no means exclusively concerned with esthetic issues: some embraced radical political views, and socialism was debated through many a bonfire-lit night on the picturesque shore of the central coast. Older and the Carmel cenacle were joined by a Californian who, leaving the state, had become nationally celebrated: the "muckraker" journalist Lincoln Steffens. Born in San Francisco in 1866 and a graduate of the University of California, Steffens made his reputation as a magazine writer in New York. He had turned the journalistic attack on urban corruption into a national crusade, publishing his most famous book, *The Shame of the Cities,* in 1904; he was drawn back to California by the Schmitz-Ruef graft prosecution.

THE BOHEMIANS STOOD like a phalanx around the man who was unarguably the outstanding California radical of his time: Jack London. In the ten years since he abandoned his studies at the University of California, London had lived many lives, published a considerable amount of writing, and become rich and admired. Yet he had not given up his socialism. His Alaska tales, elaborated in a world of pure animal survival, gained him national acclaim, and his stories of Bay sailors and oyster pirates were similarly successful. But "social problems" ate at him. In 1902, well along on his career, London published a detailed, and for readers of the time appalling, study of the London slums, *The People of the Abyss;* in 1903, influenced by a beautiful Socialist woman, Anna Strunsky, he brought out *The Kempton-Wace Letters.* Also in 1903 *The Call of the Wild* appeared, destined to be his enduring favorite as a children's book. He had also issued an exposition of *The War of the Classes* in 1905; but in 1906 London embarked on the work that would immortalize him as a socialist, *The Iron Heel.*

Published the next year, *The Iron Heel* remains the most famous work of revolutionary socialism by an English-language author. It is among London's masterpieces, absurdly sentimental but compelling, poorly developed but impossible to put down once begun. In it, London distilled his own and the world's amazement at the horrors and glories of the Russian revolution of 1905, and, above all, at the revolutionaries of 1905—desperate conspirators, fomentors of destruction, terrorists. He added to this fictional tapestry a deep tint of "social Darwinism," the doctrine of "survival of the fittest." Nikolai Bukharin and Leon Trotsky, the most brilliant of the Russian Communists, adored *The Iron Heel,* seeing in it less a portrayal of the epic they themselves had experienced than a powerful anticipation of new and frightening developments in society, specifically the ruthless, oligarchical form of dictatorship known as fascism. But *The Iron Heel* was composed in the direct aftermath of the 1905 struggle against the Tsar, during which newspaper readers in California absorbed many poignant details: Polish schoolchildren kissing the red flag and swearing to die for freedom in the corpse-filled streets of Łodz; the Jewish youth of Odessa going house to house, urgently collecting *kopecks* to buy firearms for their defense.

It was a time of extraordinary revolutionary romanticism. Yet London's social Darwinism also had a racist aspect, with socialism frequently viewed as a white man's ideal from which the "weak" and "unfit" Asians and other nations of color would be barred, at least until they "developed further." The early radicals never learned, and Californians in general did not find out for at least another seventy-five years, that the fundamental values and even the institutions of Chinese and Japanese society, both in their home-lands and in the diaspora communities of the American West Coast, were a good deal fitter, healthier, and more capable of survival than their Anglo-Saxon counterparts.

Nonfictional San Franciscans were, nonetheless, still devoting their time to strengthening such municipal principle as survived the debacle of the Schmitz-Ruef scandals. The graft prosecution wore on into 1908, and continued supplying garish material for the dailies. Ruef found out that the immunity agreement that secured his confession was not to be hon-ored; he was tried again. During that proceeding special prosecutor Heney was shot down in court by Morris Haas, a saloon-keeper and ex-convict excluded from the jury. Heney survived, but the opinion was widely held that Haas had sought a position on the panel to obtain an acquittal for Ruef. Haas and Ruef, whose bail was immediately revoked, were both in jail the day after Heney was shot; there Haas died of a gunshot wound in his cell, perhaps a suicide. Two weeks later police chief William J. Biggy, a reform appointee blamed for Haas's death, vanished from a police boat at midnight while on his way back to the city from Belvedere in Marin County; two weeks later his body floated to the surface of the Bay. His death remained a mystery, but San Francisco had reached the furthest depths of its civic disgrace.

With Heney recovering from the shooting, his place was taken by a hitherto obscure lawyer for the Teamsters' Union named Hiram W. John-son. A native of Sacramento, the son of local politician Grove Johnson, Hiram had moved his small law practice to San Francisco in 1902. He pur-sued an undistinguished career until, at 42, he took over the graft prosecu-tion. The change in command was momentous; it began California's political regeneration, for which Johnson is still honored after almost ninety years. Within two weeks of the Haas-Biggy affair's end, and after an impres-sive courtroom summation by Johnson, Ruef was convicted of bribery and sentenced to fourteen years in prison.

For his part Fremont Older, who had distinguished his newspaper, *The Bulletin,* by its pursuit of Ruef, experienced a truly astonishing change of heart once he saw Ruef in prison stripes. The man who had hounded Ruef now returned to *The Bulletin*'s office from a visit to San Quentin and inau-gurated an entirely unexpected campaign in Ruef's favor. It was not Ruef, he argued, but "the System," a term Older adopted from his friend Steffens, that was at fault; Older, a true "bleeding-heart liberal," could not stand to see Ruef in jail. Most people assumed and repeated for years after that Older had been bought off by Ruef. Some who did not consider Older a "press prostitute" believed he was, at the very least, mentally ill. The great editor spent much of the rest of his life contending with the ups and downs of his reputation; as we shall see, it was not the last time he faced such accusations. It may be for such reasons that San Francisco today lacks any public monument to Fremont Older.

With the end of the recent depression, San Francisco decided the time had come to celebrate its tremendous work of post-earthquake reconstruction, its wealth, hospitality, and the fashionableness and wit of its residents. The city announced a "Portola Festival," celebrating the arrival of Gaspar de Portolà in 1769, for October 1909. The countries of the world and the cities of America were solicited to send delegations, warships, and other tokens of honor, and, on the day the festival opened, to drink toasts to San Francisco wherever they were. Some cities organized parallel festivals; in Chicago it was announced that 300,000 children would rise from their school desks to chant, "Three cheers for San Francisco and the public school children!"

Publicity for rebuilt San Francisco was effected through, among other media, some rather gorgeous examples of Art Nouveau color rotogravure printing by the dailies. The Portola Festival also marked the full-fledged arrival of the period when twentieth-century California, a society wholly different from its predecessors, sought to match the historical traditions of the Atlantic states, symbolized by the Pilgrims, Captain John Smith, and similar Anglocentric icons, with a strictly European, "noble" origin of its own, traced to the Spanish missionaries and military that originally established Alta California. It was a civic myth filled with ambiguities, both culturally open and racist, recognizing the Spanish to the barely concealed detriment of the California Indians as well as that of the other Hispanics, both Californian and Mexican.

WE NOW MUST turn to the City of Devils, Los Angeles. Until the end of the twentieth century's first decade the southern rival to San Francisco played little role in the state's economic and intellectual affairs. But an additional irony of the Portola Festival in San Francisco was that, just as Portolà's exploit was the last gasp of empire, so did the Festival named for him mark the end of San Francisco's domination of the state, if not of the entire eastern Pacific region. In 1910, the modern history of Los Angeles begins.

Los Angeles had lately gained an advantage over its northern rival thanks to the 1906 Earthquake and the bad reputation with Eastern financiers that San Francisco earned under the Union Labor Party. In addition, the Southern Pacific stood behind the Los Angeles boom; the corporation favored that city's line to New Orleans over its more northerly central route for hauling freight; it supported citrus growers by promoting oranges and orange juice; and it built the world's most extensive transit system, the Pacific Electric Railway, in the Los Angeles basin. The fate of Los Angeles was also in great part determined by the role of a single newspaper, the *Los Angeles Times,* and its publisher, Harrison Gray Otis. General Otis, as he styled himself, had moved to Los Angeles in the 1880s, and was fanatical about the promise of sunshine and the profits of real estate. Backed by railroad land promoters, and then favored by the discovery of oil fields, Otis presided over a series of municipal economic booms, as the century turned, that made Los Angeles grow prodigiously. The community attracted thousands of emigrants from the American South and Midwest who sought a new environment and fresh opportunities as the Gold Rush pioneers had fifty years before them. Kevin Starr has shown how the lure of cheap land, orange juice, and sun complemented and confirmed the booster propaganda that, even more than San Francisco's Portola Festival, evoked the gentility of the Spanish past, the mission bells and archaic shadows of the adobe legend. In this context, Helen Hunt Jackson's *Ramona* became semiofficial folklore.

The dark side of Otis's boosterism was his ferocious hatred of that quintessential feature of late nineteenth-century American life, labor organization. In 1890 he had beaten the Typographical Union in a strike, and he never forgot it or let anybody else forget it. Otis comes down to us as a man whose biography should perhaps wait another hundred years, or until the consequences of his bizarre career have become less difficult to assess. The social historian Mike Davis, whose widely acclaimed *City of Quartz* is incoherent and replete with mistakes, is nonetheless correct when he identifies a "Forty Year War" between capital and labor—a phrase taken from the pages of the *L.A. Times* itself—as the confirmation rite of contemporary Los Angeles. From 1910 on, the city lived permanently on the edge, contending with unpredictable and therefore threatening change. Davis is also correct in crediting the earliest major insight about this phenomenon to Lav Adamic, a brilliant Slovenian intellectual who made a career in American literature as Louis Adamic.

Adamic, then 24, came to Los Angeles in 1923, more than a decade after the height of Otis's power. Even so, because of his Slovene background with its peasant, labor, and anticlerical traditions, he comprehended Otis and his dominion better than almost anybody that came after. Adamic was the opposite of everything Otis esteemed: a foreigner, a radical, and, worse, a relentless skeptic in the face of boosterism. As a Slovene, he had grown up with a contempt shared by the folk around him for the exaggerated pretensions of the Austrian empire that ruled over them. The "imperialism" of Otis and his Los Angeles could not have seemed very different in its absurd gigantism; in any event, it was inferior, particularly with Los Angeles as its presumptive Vienna. In his early books Adamic painted Otis as the chief of demons in the "City of Angels" and above all as "the most savage and effective enemy of unionism in the country."

The conservative Otis was no less a social Darwinist than Jack London and many other radicals. Otis did not wait for unionists to challenge him; he hunted them down and destroyed them. His goal was to make Los Angeles the great metropolitan example of a serene, nonunion, low-wage future. In the pages of the *Times,* union members were uniformly baited as thugs. Otis established a Merchants' and Manufacturers' Association that was far more effective than its counterparts in San Francisco. According to author Geoffrey Cowan, in Otis's Los Angeles an employee could only get a job with a letter of recommendation from a constituent body of the Association, and, if he or she were to quit a job without permission, would be barred from future employment in Los Angeles.

Otis thus made Los Angeles the ultimate, nightmare Company Town. But his enemies were many and tenacious; far more Midwesterners and Southerners than might have been expected were populist in bent, haters of corporate arrogance, and eager for a new brand of politics, as represented by "insurgents" such as Hiram Johnson. Admired for his victory over Ruef, Johnson became the Republican candidate for governor in 1910, and described Otis as follows:

In [San Francisco] we have drunk the dregs of the cup of infamy; we have
been betrayed by public officials; we have been disgraced before the world by
crimes unspeakable; but with all the criminals who have disgraced us, we
have never had anything so degraded, so disreputable, and so vile as Harrison Gray Otis and the *Los Angeles Times.*

In May 1910, a group of San Francisco unionists, led by the combative
Olav Anders Tveitmoe, went down to Los Angeles to see if something
could be done to improve the situation from labor's perspective.

But if the condition of the labor movement was bleak in Los Angeles, there
was another element of the community whose situation was even worse: the
large Spanish-speaking population. Disenfranchised during the nineteenth
century and increasingly isolated and suppressed with the coming of the
Midwestern hordes in the twentieth, by 1910 they were a source of serious
anxiety. Neglected by such historians as Adamic and Davis, Mexican issues
are as crucial as Anglo labor history to the development of modern Angeleño society.

In August 1910 Spanish-speaking Los Angeles welcomed three Mexican revolutionaries who had just been released from an Arizona prison to
which they had been sent for their exceptionally dedicated effort, from
north of the border, against the Mexican dictatorship of Porfirio Díaz. Like
the Asian revolutionaries we have previously discussed, these Mexicans—
Ricardo Flores Magón, Librado Rivera, and Antonio I. Villareal—had
learned that although the situation of their ethnic community was difficult
under *gringo* rule, they could avail themselves of political freedoms in the
United States that were unknown in their own country. Or so the Mexicans
believed.

Unfortunately, there was a considerable difference between the Chinese
regime fought by Sun Yat-sen from California and that of Mexico. China
was far away, its decadent government less than influential, and events
within its borders, even major ones like the 1900 "Boxer" martial-arts rebellion, had a delayed and somewhat abstract impact in the United States
that amounted to little more than minor fluctuations in immigration. But
Mexico being next door, the consequences of an upheaval there would immediately be felt in the form of massive numbers of refugees, gun-running,
and the temptation of Americans to go "filibustering." Most important, the

Mexican régime was in a position, not only due to its proximity but thanks to the great extent of American investment in the country, to demand that U.S. authorities suppress the seditious activities carried out by north-of-The-Border exiles. Such petitions met with enthusiastic U.S. cooperation.

Ricardo Flores Magón became the most famous victim of this American policy. Born in Oaxaca in 1874 of a Zapotec Indian father and a *mestiza* mother, he was sent to jail for five months at 18 for sedition after joining an anti-Díaz demonstration in Mexico City. Nevertheless, he was admitted to the Mexican bar while still studying law; then he was expelled from law school for political reasons. In 1900, he was joined by his brother Jesús and a friend in launching a newspaper, *Regeneración*.

Librado Rivera, 10 years older than Ricardo, founded a Liberal Club in his native San Luís Potosí, with a mainly anticlerical program. Soon a hundred such clubs were operating in Mexico, and in 1901 Ricardo attended their first congress, where he passionately denounced the Díaz regime. Ricardo and his brother were arrested, yet *Regeneración* continued to appear, filled with attacks on Díaz. Threatened with execution, Ricardo Flores Magón decided to shut the paper down. The next year, he and two associates took over an anti-Díaz humor sheet. This was soon confiscated and Ricardo and a third brother, Enrique, were locked up for five months; but Ricardo had meanwhile procured the Spanish-language pamphlet publication of Kropotkin's anarchist classic *The Conquest of Bread.* Once out of jail, they took up the struggle again. Díaz attempted to co-opt Ricardo into his government, but without success. Soon Ricardo was rearrested and his writings were completely banned. At the beginning of 1904 Ricardo, his brother Enrique, and a comrade moved to Texas. *Regeneración* was revived in San Antonio.

There a Díaz agent entered their house and tried to kill Ricardo; the local police arrested the victim and released the assailant. *Regeneración* moved to Missouri. In 1905 the Díaz regime obtained an agreement from the U.S. Post Office to monitor Ricardo's mail. At the same time, the *Partido liberal mexicano* or Mexican Liberal Party was officially established with Ricardo as president. Its slogan was "Reform, Liberty, and Justice."

Regeneración was raided by detectives in St. Louis and its assets were confiscated and sold. Ricardo decided to move to Canada. The group of revolutionaries was pursued from Toronto to Montréal, putting out the paper as they went. But Mexico was beginning to feel the tremors of an approaching overturn. In the first week of June 1906 copper miners at an American-owned mine in Cananea, Sonora, just below the Arizona border, declared a strike. The movement, led by Liberal Party supporters, was crushed by a force of 275 American rangers; a hundred strikers were killed. The Cananea strike was among the most traumatic of all the events leading to the Mexican Revolution, for it seemed to demonstrate that Díaz's government had turned over Mexican sovereignty to American business interests. It produced an enduringly famous *corrido,* or popular revolutionary ballad, *La Cárcel de Cananea (The Cananea Jail),* known even today to virtually all Mexicans as an anti-*gringo* anthem.

With Cananea, the Flores Magón brothers and their Liberal Party captured the attention of thousands of Mexicans. Ricardo returned to Texas, planning an uprising in Mexico from a base in El Paso. Meanwhile, a colleague of the Flores Magón brothers had approached an anti-Díaz landowner, Francisco I. Madero, proposing an armed revolt. Madero, for now, refused, although insurrectionary incidents had begun to flare up here and there, with tiny groups seizing tiny towns for as long as they could hold out. In El Paso the membership roster of the Liberal Clubs and the subscription list for *Regeneración* were confiscated and turned over to the Mexican government. Hundreds of Mexican Liberals were rounded up on both sides of the border.

Ricardo Flores Magón headed for Los Angeles. His first visit to California, in late 1906, was filled with danger. Hunted by the authorities to the home of a supporter, he evaded arrest, but was soon found anew and fled in women's clothing. California lawmen chased him around the state, to Sacramento and San Francisco, then back to Los Angeles. A reward of $25,000 was offered for his capture; unfazed, he started a new journal in Los Angeles with the subtle title *Revolución* and resumed organizing for the overthrow of Díaz. After a series of maneuvers by the Los Angeles authorities, Ricardo, Rivera, and Villareal were tried, for the first but not the last time, for violation of American neutrality. Their defense was handled by a local labor lawyer and Socialist, Job Harriman, and American anarchists and Socialists began an aggressive defense of the Mexican revolutionists. But the three were ordered returned to Arizona to be tried again in the jurisdiction where the alleged crime took place.

Through the rest of 1907 and all of 1908, Ricardo Flores Magón and his two companions sat in jail in Los Angeles, waiting to be "deported" to

Arizona. In May 1909 they were taken to Tombstone, where they were tried and sentenced to eighteen months. They served time in state penitentiaries at Yuma and Florence and were freed in August 1910. They immediately proceeded to Los Angeles and a tumultuous greeting at the railroad station followed by a mass meeting of supporters. *Regeneración* resumed publication. In the meantime, many more armed clashes had taken place in Mexico, American journalists, some with links to *Regeneración,* began reporting on the atrocities of the Díaz government, more Mexican Liberals were arrested in the United States at Díaz's behest, and Madero had decided to challenge Díaz in a presidential election set for that year. But Díaz had Madero arrested, and in October 1910 Madero fled north across The Border, calling for a full-scale revolution to begin in Mexico on November 20.

On October 1, 1910 the California public was horrified by other news from Los Angeles: at 1:00 in the morning, an explosion and fire had devastated the *Times* building. At least twenty people, mainly nonunion typesetters, were killed; twenty-two more were hospitalized. The newspaper's managing editor, Harry Andrews, immediately declared, "The *Times* building was destroyed by dynamite this morning by the enemies of industrial freedom. The *Times* itself cannot be destroyed. It will soon be reissued from its auxiliary plant and will fight its battles to the last."

Otis feared an attack on the plant by unionists, and was assiduous in training extra nonunion workers to operate linotype equipment. He returned to Los Angeles from Mexico, where at the behest of U.S. President William Howard Taft he had joined Díaz in celebrating Mexico's independence centennial. Two bombs had been found unexploded, one at Otis's home and one at that of the head of the Merchants' and Manufacturers' Association. Dynamite was the explanation for the *Times* disaster offered by newspapers around the country; huge rewards were offered for the capture of those responsible. But many in Los Angeles disbelieved Otis. Workers in the printing plant had complained for weeks, it was said, of the smell of gas; an explosive leak was a more likely explanation than a radical's bomb. Some argued that Otis had arranged the blast himself, to collect insurance. In the six months following, Los Angeles wrestled with charges and countercharges.

Meanwhile, Hiram Johnson had been elected governor of California as the champion of a Republican reform group, the Lincoln-Roosevelt League. Chosen as candidate and groomed by Fremont Older, Johnson ran as a declared enemy of the Southern Pacific, which on top of all its other abuses had maintained a "political bureau" of lawyers who pulled the strings of the state legislature—or better, plucked them, as if the body were not even a legislature, responsible for laws affecting millions, but rather a mere instrument on which the railroad played whatever tune it chose. Johnson emerged as an open foe of corporate interests in general; he believed that the way to cleanse local and state politics of abuse by big business was to simplify the political process through a system of voter initiatives, referenda, and recall of elected officials, for which California politics has been famous ever since.

A more direct form of popular government was also the aim of the Mexican opponents of Díaz. Within weeks of Johnson's victory, on the appointed day in November 1910, Madero's supporters rose up and the old Mexico came to an end. American troops were soon ordered to The Border. Madero called for support from Flores Magón and his followers, but Ricardo warned that although they would fight alongside him, Madero's program, mainly concerned with fair elections, was far less extreme than theirs. Already, in October, the Liberals had changed their slogan to "Land and Liberty!" and Ricardo had declared, in the pages of *Regeneración,* "The Land! shouted Bakunin, The Land! shouted Ferrer, The Land! shouts the Mexican Revolution."

As 1911 began Johnson took office as governor, to fabulous enthusiasm. His inaugural address was described as radical in the press, with some accuracy. Johnson's practical recommendations were simple. The voter initiative and referendum, and the direct primary ballot, would "arm the people," in his words, to impose the policies they desired; the recall system would facilitate removal of any corrupt official, including such judges as had quashed the graft prosecution in San Francisco. The press stood in awe of his audacity. Past streams of tears and blood, in the long shadow of Mussel Slough, and stirred by the memory of Francis Heney shot down in a San Francisco courtroom, Hiram Johnson had pronounced the most powerful words ever spoken by the state's political tribune. California was free.

––––––––

MANY, INCLUDING WILLIAM F. HERRIN, the railroad lawyer who was E. H. Harriman's unofficial governor of the state, later said the fight had gone out of the Southern Pacific by then. The mainstream railway-labor brotherhoods had accomplished a great deal toward humbling the S.P., and the Santa Fe Railway had taken over a significant share of the rail traffic in southern California. The S.P.'s other challenger, George Gould, had been ejected from his railroad empire by Wall Street financiers, but his associates, beginning in secret as we previously noted, had built an alternate central route, the Western Pacific Railway, operating from Salt Lake City to the Bay Area through the Feather River Canyon. However, no competing rail ever came near the S.P. Coast Line from San Francisco to Los Angeles via Santa Barbara. Even the powerful Santa Fe showed serious weaknesses in California. Because so much land was held by S.P., Santa Fe was unable to construct many branch lines, and they are the moneymaking foundation of a railroad.

As for the Western Pacific, it fought a great campaign and got access to the Oakland waterfront thanks to further subterfuges and the assistance, it was said, of men armed with rifles to keep S.P. sharpshooters from killing its roadway crews. Harriman, the S.P. boss, had availed himself of every means to block the new road. *Collier's* magazine reported in 1907 that Patrick Calhoun had met with Harriman and proposed a deal. The S.P. had built interurban streetcar systems in the East Bay, in Los Angeles, and elsewhere around the state, and had begun laying tracks in San Francisco itself. But Calhoun told Harriman, "You want to block the Western Pacific. You want to get your lines in position to handle all the traffic before the Western Pacific is in operation." Calhoun offered Harriman political backing if Harriman would give up any interest in streetcar service within San Francisco. The agreement was made, and Calhoun's cars began running on the heavy, freight-gauge S.P. rails; where S.P. spurs had been laid across the United Railroads' right-of-way they were removed.

Understandably, the opening of the Western Pacific brought jubilation in San Francisco, although both it and the Santa Fe were barred by the S.P. from direct access to the city and had to deliver cars and switch engines to San Francisco by water, across the Bay. (Both the W.P. and the A.T.& S.F. maintained local freight-tug and ferry services on San Francisco Bay until the 1980s.) By the time the Western Pacific was completed, the cost of building a main-line railroad was so great that the company was bankrupted and never recovered. It, too, was prevented from constructing branch lines; in later years it was contemptuously referred to as the "Wooden Rail" and the "Wobbly Pacific." The latter nickname may have derived from the term "Wobblies," commonly applied to members of the Industrial Workers of the

World, whom the S.P. blacklisted but the W.P. hired. Or it may have come from the willingness of the W.P., which lacked the resources to employ many railway police or "cinder dicks," to let hoboes, often carrying the I.W.W. "red card" or membership book, ride its freight cars.

In May 1911 a voice from the past summed up the long struggle of Californians against the S.P.: Christopher Evans, the Tulare County anti-railroad guerrilla of the 1890s, was paroled from prison. That he was not forgotten was demonstrated by the many offers he received to appear on stage as a lecturer. Evans refused, but granted an interview to Fremont Older's *Bulletin*. "I was a rebel, not a thief," he said. "I fought a robbing corporation. . . . In my time the railroad owned the courts, the Legislature, the ballot box—everything. It owned the State. So I started my 44-caliber protest. . . . Because I was alone in my fight, I was an outlaw. If I had a few regiments with me, the newspapers would have called me what I was—a rebel." Evans praised Governor Johnson, Francis Heney, Older, "and every man who took up the fight where I left off. I am still an insurgent," he proudly declared. It was clear to all in California, however, that the old order had definitely passed. Aside from the turbulent matters we have described, the women's suffrage movement was marching for voting rights, and Governor Johnson's extensive agenda of political innovations included securing them the ballot.

Meanwhile, as Johnson embarked on the fulfillment of his program, Ricardo Flores Magón and his comrades had been carried by the Mexican Revolution to new heights of exaltation. At the end of January 1911, a *Magonista* group, including numerous American I.W.W. members and immigrant Italian anarchists, crossed the border and seized the town of Mexicali, in Baja, in one of the most remarkable incidents in California history. Liberal groups were also fighting Díaz's troops in six mainland Mexican states. In February, another Liberal column crossed the border from New Mexico into Chihuahua. An American associate of Flores Magón, the journalist John Kenneth Turner, began an ambitious solidarity effort appealing to Americans and demanding, above all, that the United States refrain from sending troops to back up Díaz.

In mid-February Francisco Madero returned to Mexico and took over command of the revolutionary forces. Alarmed at the *Magonistas'* strength and seeking to divide them, he soon denounced a *Magonista* leader in Chihuahua, Gabino Cano, to the U.S. authorities for taking wounded men back across the border. Cano, who had fought jointly with the *Maderistas,* was arrested in the United States and charged with a neutrality violation. Madero next ordered one of his supporters, Pancho Villa, to detain the other principal *Magonista* in Chihuahua, Prisciliano G. Silva, and disarm the *Magonista* fighters for wearing red badges rather than the Mexican green-white-red tricolor; some joined the *Maderistas,* some were killed. The *Magonistas* fighting in Baja warned that if Madero came there to establish a provisional government they would oppose him, and in *Regeneración* Ricardo Flores Magón bitterly charged Madero, who proclaimed himself Mexico's provisional president, as a "traitor to the cause of liberty."

Ricardo's break from Madero's leadership led some Americans to end their support for the Flores Magón brothers, but the revolution in Mexico was gathering strength with such speed that such concerns seemed of little immediate import. In March 1911 Emiliano Zapata, an Indian peasant in the Mexican state of Morelos, began his rebellion, and sent emissaries to Flores Magón in Los Angeles. The previous month had seen a visit to The Border by Brigadier General Tasker H. Bliss, commander of the U.S. Army's California department. Bliss was dispatched by the War Department in Washington to investigate the *Magonista* insurrection in Baja. Bliss reported that the whole population on both sides of the border supported the *Magonistas,* adding, "California is honeycombed with the Socialistic spirit." General Bliss was especially perturbed that "'Labor Unions' which make Socialism their basic principle are strong here. These are the men who are particularly active in their sympathy with the present insurrection."

Two months later, in May, the *Magonistas* occupied Tijuana and Tecate, giving them full control over the thinly populated urban area of northern Baja California; among their immediate measures was an appeal to establish agricultural cooperatives. At the end of the month Díaz resigned, having sued for peace with Madero. The *Magonistas* refused to end their struggle until the peasants and workers achieved control over the land and the means of production. Still, the Baja movement was isolated, and in June the *Magonistas* were driven out of Tijuana by Madero's troops; some fled back into the United States but were interned.

Díaz was gone, but the U.S. government continued to persecute Flores Magón and his followers; although the armed phase of *Magonista* activity soon ended, Ricardo's movement was far from dead. Already in April, an individual had come forward to replace the faint-hearted *gringo* socialists who had deserted him: William C. Owen, friend of Burnette Haskell and a founding member of the Coast Seamen's Union. In 1886 Owen had left California for Oregon as a C.S.U. organizer. In the intervening twenty-five years he continued in a career that, even considering the unorthodox adventures of most of his colleagues, was remarkably varied. During much of the Kaweah controversy he edited a paper in Los Angeles, the *Weekly Nationalist,* which preached in favor of the popular movement created by Edward Bellamy's Utopian socialist novel, *Looking Backward.*

Owen moved to New York in 1890. There he was introduced to the Italian anarchist Erico Malatesta, and in line with the social Darwinism that so influenced the radicals of the time he published a book, *The Economics of Herbert Spencer.* He then returned briefly to England, where he met Kropotkin. Like Haskell, Owen was subjected to despicable press attacks, including a libelous assault by the *New York Times.* Nevertheless, he came back to the United States, where he discovered the work of the American individualist anarchist Benjamin R. Tucker, whose "cold logic," he wrote, "saved me from what threatened to become chronic Kropotkinist hysteria." He frequented, off and on, the anarchist circle of Emma Goldman. He went to the Klondike in search of gold, but failed as a miner; once back in California he worked for newspapers, mainly as a crime and police reporter, and eventually wrote a book, *Crime and Criminals,* which was published in Los Angeles in 1910 by the Prison Reform League.

Owen was drawn to the *Magonista* cause by the writings of John Kenneth Turner. With an energy that seemed unlimited, Owen had become a fluent journalist and, as in the past, had considerable competence as a political organizer. While the fortunes of Ricardo Flores Magón seemed to have taken a downturn, Owen provided the Mexican Liberals with an English-language advocacy far more articulate and extensive than that offered by their previous, hesitant Anglo collaborators. Owen began editing the English-language section of *Regeneración,* which now had a press run of 17,000 and was known throughout the Hispanic world. Owen brought to its English pages his own truly unique style of radical lyricism; unlike John Kenneth Turner, who was entirely concerned with illuminating the abuses of the Díaz tyranny, Owen dealt with broad ideas and abstractions, often letting his mind and pen wander experimentally. In this regard he was certainly closer to the spirit of Flores Magón; literary flair was the main thing

Ricardo and Owen had in common. But Ricardo's stories and parables are today widely read and admired in Mexico, while Owen's writings seem to have sunk without trace.

Aged 57, Owen had not joined Flores Magón in search of glory, or even out of complete ideological agreement with him; rather, Owen was impelled by his obsession with the land issue. "My own experience," he wrote, "is that if you attempt to discuss politics with the Mexican proletarian he shows no interest, but that the moment you mention the word 'land' he becomes alert." Still, he did not see the Mexican Revolution as "a subject on which the various camps of the international revolutionary movement should take sides, and never have I felt myself called on to endorse the particular creed of the Magóns or other Mexican agitators. From the first I have regarded it as a struggle by many millions of the disinherited to win back their heritage; as a battle for the right to live."

Owen shared fully in the daily life of the *Magonista* revolutionaries. More than a gifted polemicist, he was also indefatigable in helping produce and distribute leaflets and manifestos. On September 11, 1911, from Los Angeles, the Mexican Liberal Party issued a new program ending with the slogan, *Land and Liberty!* Within two months, Zapata had risen anew, now against Madero, with the same motto, and with a platform, the Plan of Ayalá, that showed the influence of *Magonista* literature. The Mexican Revolution entered its legendary period, which continued for a decade. But Mexico was not alone in its radical upsurge. A fresh revolutionary wind simultaneously struck the Pacific Coast from China. The insurrection of 1905 in Russia had inspired Jack London and influenced radicals throughout the world, but in Asia its impact was direct.

On October 10, 1911, forever after celebrated as "Double Ten" by anti-imperial Chinese, revolution began in Hubei province. Within days a republic was declared and the imperial family left the country. By December the 250-year-old ethnic Manchu régime had fallen.

Asian revolutionaries affected by 1905 in Russia had not gone to Russia, where the revolution had failed but, as in the past, came to California. Sun Yat-sen's movement had reorganized and was now mainly based in San Francisco, where he had overseen the foundation of a daily newspaper, *The Young China (Shaonian Zhongguo Chenbao).* Sun's brother, Sun Yu, was in Hankou as fighting began there, and was elected president of a provincial assembly. Sun Yat-sen himself was touring the United States when "Double Ten" occurred, and he was immediately named in the American press as the inspirer of the revolution and probable leader of the new republic. He returned to China via Europe, seeking negotiations with the powers that dominated China after the failure of the "Boxers." At the end of December an assembly of provincial representatives named Sun as provisional president of the Chinese Republic.

This hemispheric and Pacific-wide panorama of discontent vied for the attention of Californians with the onward march of Governor Johnson's reforms. "Double Ten" in China came the same day as a California state election in which Johnson's program was submitted for direct approval by the voters. Some items on Johnson's long list of abuses worthy of correction had been adopted by the legislature without much controversy, such as a bill abolishing the state's fugitive-sailor law. Others were thorny indeed, and thorniest of all was the matter of women's voting rights.

Women's suffrage appeared on the state ballot as Constitutional Amendment 4, and after false reports that it would lose, it passed. The *Chronicle* sarcastically described an atmosphere that "vibrated with joy" at suffrage headquarters in San Francisco, as congratulatory telegrams poured in from the East. A leading figure in the campaign was Anita Whitney, president of the College Equal Suffrage League, a graduate of Wellesley and member of a distinguished old American family. Although she was rich, an encounter with the misery of the New York slums, which she first saw in 1893, stimulated her to take up social work.

Johnson had applied the principle of popular sovereignty in its broadest form. Amendments to the state constitution were ratified providing authority for all his fundamental conceptions: the initiative and referendum (Amendment 7), the recall of officials by the voters (Amendment 8), and workers' compensation for on-the-job injuries, to be paid for by the employer (Amendment 10). But the vote also established as law, by enormous majorities, the principles of railroad rate regulation and municipal ownership of public utilities.

JUST WHEN CALIFORNIA radicals might have exulted at the local triumph of reform and the international advance of revolution, a devastating blow fell on the Los Angeles labor movement. In April 1911 a break had come in the investigation of the *Los Angeles Times* explosion and fire. William J. Burns, a private detective hated by Otis for having assisted Older, Heney, and the other San Francisco reformers in battling the grafters, raided the Indianapolis office of the International Association of Bridge and Structural Iron Workers. The union's secretary-treasurer, John J. McNamara, was arrested and charged with involvement in dynamiting the *L.A. Times* plant. His brother James B. McNamara, who held no union office, had also been arrested in Detroit, along with a man named Ortie McManigal who confessed, implicating the McNamaras. The Detroit arrests had been kept quiet by Burns; all three accused were then whisked by fast train across state lines to Los Angeles. The labor movement, throughout the country, labeled it a "kidnapping," and asserted the innocence of the trio.

The Structural Iron Workers were unquestionably a "bomb-throwing" component of the union movement. Experienced users of explosives on bridges and related projects, their members employed "direct action" against nonunion construction. Great numbers of Angeleños, however, were then, as before, unimpressed. "General" Otis, who they believed had either allowed the building to blow up or planted a bomb in it to implicate labor, was obviously capable of securing the false arrest of the McNamaras, who insisted on their guiltlessness. It was then that the *Times* explosion assumed its full importance as a pivot of Los Angeles history. Each side, capital and labor, rallied its partisans and accused the other of lawlessness, with Otis further impeaching the union movement as murderously violent and labor accusing Otis of seeking to murder innocent labor advocates. National union leaders such as Samuel Gompers of the American Federation of Labor set to work on the McNamaras' defense. Millions of union members, their families, and sympathizers were called to action. Clarence Darrow, the most esteemed radical lawyer in the whole country, was hired as the McNamaras' attorney.

The *Times* affair took on an electoral dimension as a race for the mayoralty approached, with the incumbent, an urban reformer named George B. Alexander who was no friend of "General" Otis, mainly challenged by the Socialist leader Job Harriman, Ricardo Flores Magón's attorney. As in San Francisco during the graft prosecutions, political tendencies were blurred; but Job Harriman campaigned on a platform of, first and foremost, support for the McNamaras. Meanwhile, Darrow had come to town in a tornado of publicity, and on October 11, the day after Johnson won his vast plebiscite, the trial of the McNamaras began. Jury selection was slow, as the immense controversy had made impartiality almost impossible.

At the end of October Job Harriman led the municipal primary, with a 12-percent lead over Alexander, and the two headed for a runoff. Something then happened that has never been fully understood or explained. On December 1 the McNamara brothers, shepherded by Darrow, suddenly entered guilty pleas, J. B. for the *Times* attack, J.J. for ordering McManigal to commit a later bombing at the Llewellyn Iron Works in Los Angeles. Sentencing was set for the day of the mayoral election.

The effect of this turnaround on the local and national labor and radical movements cannot be overestimated; it was an unparalleled disaster. The worst consequences were felt by rank-and-file union workers who had committed themselves to the McNamaras' innocence and were suddenly exposed as dupes. Gompers was reported by venomous journalists to have broken down in tears, which made him the object of widespread ridicule, as it was believed he had foreknowledge of the *Times* atrocity. The glee of Otis and his allies was, as was to be expected, unrestrained.

The outlines of a deal supported by Lincoln Steffens, who was also on the scene, soon emerged: although they pleaded guilty, neither J. B. nor J. J. would face the hangman. But for radical Angeleños, this was small consolation, particularly since it was obvious that the main casualty of this legal maneuver would be neither J. B. nor J. J. but Job Harriman, as the Socialist candidate for mayor; Harriman was too closely associated with propaganda for the brothers' innocence. A week later, J. B. McNamara was sentenced to life imprisonment in San Quentin, with J. J. receiving fifteen years, and Harriman lost the municipal election by a margin of 62 to 38 percent. Women, voting for the first time in Los Angeles, overwhelmingly backed Alexander. The Socialists were swept aside.

The *Times* bombing, or the McNamara case, was the first and worst major battle in the Forty Year War between capital and labor described by Mike Davis and other historians of Los Angeles. Being such a mighty victory for the anti-union forces, it guaranteed that the war would long continue. But Los Angeles liberalism had remarkable powers of resistance: for example, Clarence Darrow was soon acquitted of jury-tampering in the *Times* bombing case. As previously noted, Lav Adamic, in Los Angeles a decade later, was the first to understand the full significance of these events; he made the bombing the centerpiece for a book on class war in America,

Dynamite! which assigned considerable blame for the affair to Olav Anders Tveitmoe and other San Francisco militants.

Tveitmoe, whose six feet of height justified his nickname, "The Viking," was called a "gorilla" by Adamic, and the characterization has been repeated in academic works. A social Darwinist *par excellence,* he was so disgusted with Steffens's attempt at "Christian" labor relations in the McNamara case that he threatened to kill him. But "Tveit" was no gorilla. He was a real intellectual who believed, too much, in the doctrine of survival through strength. He was convicted of complicity in the bombing campaign in a 1912 proceeding in Indianapolis involving the Structural Iron Workers, but on appeal his sentence was reversed.

The debacle suffered by Job Harriman and his comrades in Los Angeles did not halt the increase in ballots cast for the Socialist Party and its national standard-bearer Eugene V. Debs. Harriman's campaign had followed a series of Socialist municipal victories in California, including places as unsurprising as Berkeley and as surprising as Pasadena. Socialists racked up big totals, again unsurprisingly, in Santa Cruz in 1911. But they also earned a majority in 1912, after the McNamara affair, in Daly City, a working-class San Francisco suburb, and they even won votes in the higher-class community of Hillsborough. In 1912 Johnson was reelected governor, while in the presidential election California was carried by Theodore Roosevelt, running unsuccessfully as the candidate of a "third party," the Progressives. But Debs gained 12 percent of the state's presidential vote that year, which saw his highest ever national tally, at nearly a million votes. Four years before, his California share had been only 7.5 percent.

However, like the many union workers disillusioned, after the McNamara scandal, by the intrigues of liberals such as Darrow and Steffens, some radicals viewed Debs with suspicion. In 1913, Ricardo Flores Magón and W. C. Owen published a collection of essays in Los Angeles entitled *Land and Liberty* to explain the Mexican Revolution to American readers. The book included seven of Owen's distinctive polemics. Already in 1911, in the pages of Emma Goldman's periodical, *Mother Earth,* Owen had accused the Socialists of wasting time on the Harriman campaign to the detriment of support for the Mexican Revolution. Owen and Flores Magón had been deeply wounded by Debs, who, Owen wrote in fury, "proclaimed that Mexicans were too ignorant to fight for freedom and prophesied their pitiful scourging at the hands of the possessing class."

Of the individuals we have examined, Owen saw furthest beyond his time, although his anarchist extremism left him in glorious isolation with Flores Magón. Owen's final response to Debs's criticism was simple but, again, far-sighted: "Labor's Solidarity Should Know Neither Race nor Color." Owen himself had once been an anti-Chinese agitator; yet he went further than nearly all his contemporaries, as well as his past associates, in repudiating race prejudice to defend, in Goldman's *Mother Earth,* a white woman hounded by mobs in Oregon for seeking to marry a Japanese. Ever original, ever mordant, Owen claimed to perceive a similarity between the oppressive government that meddled in the relationship of such a couple and the governmental power acclaimed by statist Socialists such as Debs.

INTO A CALIFORNIA bemused by these competing radical philosophies, the I.W.W., now widely known as Wobblies, had erupted not long before. Their organizational methods were improvised and only won, at best, temporary improvements in wages and conditions. But the I.W.W. had begun attracting numerous "wage slaves," particularly those agricultural, lumbering, maritime, and other transient workers whose mode of existence was nomadic and who therefore had been neglected by the established unions. That the mainstream unions, which depended above all on the stability in employment, residence, and family arrangements of their members, had not overlooked so footloose and unpredictable a work group as the sailors seemed owed exclusively to the dedication of Andrew Furuseth. For seamen, unionism offered the only possibility of a life as a normal member of society as opposed to a lingering death on its margins.

The Wobblies took on California in its heartland, and challenged the most fearsome guardians of the booster mentality: they went to Fresno in October 1910 and to San Diego in February 1912 to fight for their constitutional right of free speech. Authorities in both towns had curtailed the street-speaking and other activities of the Wobblies, beating and jailing them. The Fresno confrontation ended quickly, but the San Diego conflict was more serious. Vigilantes appeared; two men were killed, and Ben L. Reitman, an associate of Emma Goldman, was tarred and feathered and run out of town. Eighty I.W.W. members and Socialists were locked up as the hysteria grew, with rumors of plots to kill San Diego police chief J. K. Wilson and other leading citizens. A Free Speech League was formed and its

supporters prevailed on Governor Johnson to send Colonel Harris Weinstock, a state commissioner, to investigate vigilante activities in San Diego.
Weinstock's report did little to satisfy the ostensible forces of law and order
in the town; in it he asked, "Who are the greater criminals, who are the real
anarchists, who are the real violators of the Constitution, who are the real
undesirables—these so-called unfortunate members of the 'scum of the
earth,' or these presumably respectable members of society?"

Governor Johnson backed up Weinstock, ordering state attorney general Ulysses S. Webb to San Diego to enforce the law. Webb told city officials that their duties included protecting the public from vigilantism, and
that if they could not handle the task martial law would be declared.

On June 2, 1912, 1,500 Wobblies and their partisans filled a hall in San
Francisco to protest the situation in San Diego; speakers included Cora
(Mrs. Fremont) Older, who excited wide comment for the sharpness of her
remarks, and Socialist Mayor J. Stitt Wilson of Berkeley. I.W.W. "free
speech fights" were seldom if ever successful; their only accomplishment
was to give the state a long-lasting reputation as a place where the Bill of
Rights was under constant threat, if only from local peace officers, even as
Californians continued to enjoy the benefits of Johnson's administration.
The Wobblies could be imprisoned. They could even be killed. But they
could not be ignored.

For his part, the prickly William C. Owen, who had been unafraid
to lambaste the radical idol Debs, also looked askance at the campaigns
for free speech. In one of his essays, "Free Speech Crushed! What Else
Could You Expect?" Owen wrote, reflecting the experience he and the
Flores Magón brothers had in Los Angeles, "As a consequence of the increasing frequency with which radical speakers are arrested, meetings
suppressed, headquarters raided and objectionable agitators run out of
town, a great cry is going up from all the labor and semi-demi-revolu-
tionary press." But he bitterly condemned the passivity of the majority of
workers. Owen had been among the first to detect the growth, especially
in southern California, of a middle-class and quasi-intellectual radicalism, supplanting the proletarian revolt that had long set the tone for socialism. He saw in this phenomenon an unhealthy influence of the "New
Age" (the term was already in use); that is, of spiritualist and other "self-
improvement" experiments and cults, with which southern California
was already widely identified.

Owen was observing the end, at least temporarily, of social Darwinist radicalism in California and the onset of a new Enlightenment, although he did not clearly understand it. This change in mentality paralleled a shift of gravity in the radical movement: a shift away from labor. This was a development in which California stood in advance of the rest of the United States, if not the world. But the veteran revolutionist had seen many such fads come and go; the Nationalist movement in which he participated in the late 1880s and the 1890s grew out of Theosophical activities in Boston. For much of the nineteenth century, before the great wave of labor organization in the United States, spiritualism and Socialism were intertwined; California seemed a natural haven for all such innovations. Northern California, home of Joaquin Miller, whose circle had a cultish air, also boasted a Utopian colony, Fountain Grove near Santa Rosa, harboring a full-fledged, "theo-socialist" sect.

Thomas Lake Harris, a prolific versifier and pamphleteer, established Fountain Grove in 1875 and ran it until 1892. He crafted a doctrine of trance communication with the Divine, out of the writings of the esoteric philosopher Emanuel Swedenborg and the various spiritualists. Harris's theories centered on the suppression of sexual impulses and the apprehension of an androgynous principle: Masculine Love and Feminine Truth. His disciples included Edwin Markham, whose poem "The Man with the Hoe," based on the famous painting of the same title by Jean-François Millet, appeared in the *San Francisco Examiner* in 1899 and gained an enormous readership. Lawrence Ferlinghetti and Nancy Joyce Peters in their book *Literary San Francisco,* note that Harris influenced Markham toward a "mystical insurgency" in which he composed a "book of darkness." "The Man with the Hoe," an outcry against the eternal degradation of the toiler, made Markham the great "people's poet" of his time; he was a partial model for Presley, the protagonist of Norris' *Octopus.* Harris's successors at Fountain Grove turned the place into a winery.

Fountain Grove and Haskell's Kaweah were not the only Utopian socialist ventures attempted in California; Icaria Speranza, based on the teachings of the French socialist Étienne Cabet, briefly functioned in the 1880s near Cloverdale in the northern section of the state, and ten years later the Altruria colony appeared, again near Santa Rosa. According to Ferlinghetti and Peters, California produced more Utopian colonies than all the other American states combined. However, northern California had yet to generate the *frenzy* for the new that was visible in the south of the state. As early as 1895, a Mrs. Charles Stewart Baggett had commented, "I am told the millennium has already begun in Pasadena, and that even now there are more sanctified cranks to the acre than in any other town in America." As the twentieth century began, San Diego was host to an occult colony, Point Loma, headed by Katherine Tingley, known as the "Purple Mother." One of her followers, Albert P. Warrington, founded a splinter community, Krotona, in Los Angeles in 1911. Theories, pamphlets, and mass meetings based on bizarre styles of dress, diet, and healing all proliferated in southern California.

In the cynical streets of San Francisco, the nearest thing to a cult then in existence was the Hellenic revivalist movement of Raymond Duncan, brother of the renowned dancer Isadora. Both were born in San Francisco; Raymond had attained an ambiguous celebrity in his home town as a dandy and a reciter of verse, but they then left the city. In 1910 he returned from Europe. There he had adopted ancient Greek culture, symbolized by a modified toga made of hand-loomed fabric, worn as daily apparel by him, his wife Penelope, and his son. He had caused a considerable uproar wherever he went. Recalling Duncan's arrival in Athens, the Greco-Italian aesthete Alberto Savinio, born Andrea de Chirico and brother of the surrealist painter of genius Giorgio de Chirico, described how "bewilderment paralyzed the city" at the news that *an ancient Greek* [emphasis in the original] had been observed in Parliament Square. Savinio wittily imagined the city's police chief, hearing that the "ancient one" had saluted the Chamber of Deputies building, exclaiming, "No doubt about it, it's an ancient Greek. He mistook the Chamber of Deputies for the Temple of Apollo. That's the trouble with neo-classical architecture."

The modern Greeks were not long to be fooled, especially when they realized that these "ancients" spoke English among themselves, with an American accent. But Raymond Duncan saw no obstacles anywhere to his ambitious plans for the reintroduction of Classical styles of dress, theatre, gymnastics, and music, to the great merriment not only of the contemporary Athenians but also of San Franciscans, who also failed, sadly, to treat Raymond Duncan with the respect he desired. Isadora, at work on the same principles through her school of dance, knew better than to come back; she loathed San Francisco and its philistinism and, once departed, never saw California again.

The Duncans represented the purest form of the self-improving enthusiasm that provoked Owen's suspicion (although perhaps because of
his obsession with the recovery of the land Owen spared the various
Utopian colonies his critical wrath). However, Flores Magón and Owen
had come to understand that Revolution by itself was not enough. In
both China and Mexico the "provisional presidents" were quickly neu-
tralized: Sun Yat-sen was shunted aside in March 1912 after only three
months in power, and Francisco Madero was killed in Mexico City in
February 1913. Their places were taken not by stern radicals but by
mediocre warlords and politicians: General Yuan Shih-kai in China,
Venustiano Carranza in Mexico; it was not the fittest who survived, but
the most devious and ambitious.

Apparently the Sinophile Homer Lea, who had become Sun's military
deputy, had also experienced a certain disillusion. He was widely credited
with making Sun's temporary success possible, and came back to San Francisco loaded with Chinese honors, including the title of General. But the
hunchbacked dwarf died suddenly in November 1912, aged 35. The San
Francisco English-language dailies, which had never treated Lea very
kindly, expressed further contempt for him when they discovered that his
estate was minuscule, even though he had entertained lavishly and driven a
splendid motorcar—paid for, it was assumed, by his Chinese admirers.

Many in California sought or at least dreamed of exploits like those of
Homer Lea. The opportunity to enter into a great cataclysm, from which
only the fit would supposedly escape, presented itself sooner than most
people anticipated. A new brutality was visible everywhere, or so it seemed.
Ghastly atrocities were reported daily from both Mexico and China.

The First World War, although far from the Pacific Coast, posed immense challenges for radicals. Jack London, in *The Iron Heel,* had expressed
the belief that a general strike could successfully block hostilities between
the United States and Germany, and promises of just such an action had repeatedly been made by the leaders of the giant European Socialist parties.
But when war came late in 1914, the French, British, German, and Austrian Socialists rallied patriotically to their own governments. Even the old
anarchist Kropotkin came out for the Allies—that is, for revolutionary and
democratic France, but also for the tsarist régime—against imperial Germany. Only the Serbian Socialists and most of the Russian Marxists, joined

by individuals in the other belligerent countries, called for revolutionary opposition to the conflict.

At first there was no thought of American involvement in the European fighting. Nevertheless, San Francisco labor radicals such as Olav Tveitmoe were outspoken in their pacifist sentiment, although Tveitmoe was among those who saw the war as a conflagration in which humanity would be purged, redeemed, and transformed. As an antiwar speaker in the Bay Area, Tveitmoe shone; this was perhaps his greatest moment. He was joined in this activity by Paul Scharrenberg, the new editor of the *Coast Seamen's Journal* and the secretary of the California Federation of Labor.

Andrew Furuseth, Scharrenberg, and their comrades in the Sailors' Union viewed the European war with dismay, but were then more occupied with a definitive campaign for the legal emancipation of seamen. A progressive U.S. senator from Wisconsin, Robert M. LaFollette, had repeatedly introduced a Seamen's Bill into Congress, drafted under Furuseth's guidance and calling for abolition of all "fugitive sailor" laws. In 1915, the Seamen's Act was finally passed. Furuseth hailed the Act as the legal basis for foreign as well as American seamen to pursue their demands; like the Mexican and Asian revolutionaries, he operated internationally from his base on the Pacific Coast, working closely with European maritime unions in far-flung and ambitious organizing efforts.

Among California liberals, Furuseth's unremitting crusade made him labor's greatest local hero, although the rank-and-file in his union observed that government and the shipowners found ways around some of the law's provisions as soon as it was signed by President Woodrow Wilson. Working sailors complained that "Old Andy" was expending too much energy on legislation and not enough on the economic struggle "at the point of production," to use a favorite Wobbly phrase. He had grown too fond of Washington, when San Francisco was where he was needed.

THE EUROPEAN WAR was greeted with elation by Ricardo Flores Magón: "Behind the catastrophe, Liberty smiles," he wrote. Ricardo was no social Darwinist; rather, he was a thoroughgoing enlightener. But the Flores Magón brothers were already at war with the world as it was. They, Owen, and *Regeneración* had not been spared the unfriendly attention of the *Los Angeles Times*. The insults of Debs and other Socialists could not be forgotten, while the *Regeneración* group had also come under increasing attacks from former comrades who had gone over to the *Maderistas*. Owen had published articles in the European anarchist press publicizing the Flores Magóns' struggle, and gained support from Kropotkin himself against those who claimed that the Mexican Revolution was a product of Ricardo's imagination. In June 1912 the brothers Ricardo and Enrique, along with Librado Rivera and another comrade, were again tried for neutrality violations in Los Angeles and sentenced to ten months' imprisonment at McNeil Island, in Washington state. A courthouse demonstration on the day of their sentencing turned into a serious clash with police, in which many supporters of the Flores Magóns were injured and jailed. The defendants remained on McNeil Island until January 1914, when they were welcomed back to public life by Owen, who organized a speaking tour for them in the Pacific Northwest.

Throughout the next two years the group concentrated on the Mexican situation. For a while, the group's poverty forced *Regeneración* to shut down but Ricardo and Enrique, along with Librado Rivera, their families, and a few collaborators, moved to Edendale, a suburb of Los Angeles, where they set up a communal farm, obtained a hand press, and began producing *Regeneración* once again. Owen, for his part, decamped to Hayward, on the eastern shore of San Francisco Bay, and produced a new journal, *Land and Liberty,* during 1914–15. In it, he provoked fresh controversy by adopting an anti-German position in line with that of Kropotkin, and thus coming out for the Allies in the World War. The Edendale idyll was of short duration; in February 1916 the Flores Magón brothers and Owen were indicted by a grand jury on three counts of using the mails to incite murder. The charge was based on statements in *Regeneración* condemning the usurper Carranza and advocating continued Mexican revolutionary action. Federal marshals, supplemented by Los Angeles police officers, went to Edendale and arrested Ricardo; Enrique resisted and was beaten badly enough to send him to the hospital.

Owen, luckily, was absent from the scene; he had left for the Northwest. He was reported to be at Home Colony, an anarchist community in Tacoma, but evaded the law. He went underground and continued sending articles to the comrades in Los Angeles and elsewhere. But the center of radical activity had shifted back to San Francisco, where one of the most remarkable personalities in the history of anarchism, Alexander Berkman, arrived in the autumn of 1915.

Save for his close associate Emma Goldman, Berkman was the most notorious anarchist in the United States. Born in Vilna, then in Russian Poland, in 1870, Berkman had come to the United States at 17. He became unforgettably infamous to the American press in 1892 when, a week after the massacre of a group of strikers at the Carnegie Steel works in Homestead, Pennsylvania, he tried to kill Carnegie executive Henry Clay Frick. Berkman gained entry to Frick's office and shot him twice, then stabbed him twice, but Frick survived. Anarchists, including Owen, rallied to his defense, but Berkman served some fourteen years in prison for the assault.

Almost ten years after his release, Berkman went from Denver to Los Angeles in spring 1915, on behalf of a small revolutionary group, the International Workers' Defense League (I.W.D.L.), to assist David Caplan and Matthew Schmidt, two alleged accomplices in the *Los Angeles Times* bombing case, who had just been arrested after evading capture for five years. In October 1915 Berkman came north to San Francisco on the Southern Pacific "Lark" with a plan for a "revolutionary labor weekly," to be called *The Blast.* The first number appeared at the beginning of 1916, and was welcomed by a small but fervent readership.

Berkman lectured in San Francisco on such topics as homosexuality in prison, which he had personally observed and on which he held an unprejudiced view. He also helped set up a Current Events Club that held weekly meetings, sometimes in collaboration with an Italian anarchist faction, the *Gruppo Anarchico "Volontà."* The latter maintained a popular hall on Stockton Street overlooking Washington Square in the Italian section of North Beach. Such affairs would typically attract audiences of a couple of hundred. In February 1916, as soon as he heard of the arrests of the Flores Magóns, Berkman, who considered Ricardo "the Kropotkin of Mexico," called a protest meeting in San Francisco. Emma Goldman went to Los Angeles to speak in defense of the Flores Magón brothers, and, with Berkman, raised cash for the defendants' bail.

Owen, from his hiding place in the Northwest, wrote in *Mother Earth* assailing the monopoly status of the U.S. Post Office and its use against the revolutionary press. The Flores Magón brothers were again convicted, but were released and appealed; unfortunately, the U.S. Post Office canceled *Regeneración's* second-class mailing permit, doubling the cost of production. Ricardo was now showing the ill effects on his health of his long self-denial. Owen, after six months' clandestine existence, escaped to England.

Although Europeans like Kropotkin and Owen succumbed to the appeals of the belligerent powers, most Californians remained opposed to the war and to any United States involvement in it. Partisanship for the Allies had, however, become a noticeable element in much of the American press, which began to emphasize a need for American "preparedness." Such views were denounced as militarist propaganda by Tveitmoe, Scharrenberg, and other leaders of the San Francisco labor movement. Rudolph Spreckels, the reformer who by then had publicly broken with his father Claus, and become quite a radical, also spoke out against "preparedness." The vocabulary he employed was exceedingly blunt, especially considering he was president of the First National Bank.

A Preparedness Day was proclaimed for July 22, 1916 in San Francisco, with a parade to march down Market Street. Employers encouraged workers to join the demonstration, but the event was criticized by the San Francisco Labor Council and Tveitmoe's Building Trades Council, which declared in unison, "Labor is opposed to the fostering of the war spirit by 'preparedness parades,'" and warned, "An attempt may be made by the enemies of labor to cause a violent disturbance." The unions urged their members to boycott the parade, insisting, "Do not march. . . . Do not let your employers coerce you." On July 20, labor held a giant peace rally, chaired by George A. Tracy, head of the San Francisco Typographical Union.

William McDevitt of the Socialist Party, a bookseller and city electoral commissioner, spoke boldly at the peace meeting. He quoted advice given to military recruits by the pacifist playwright George Bernard Shaw: "Shoot your officers and come home," then continued,

> If I thought the people in the preparedness parade on Saturday afternoon were in a heroic humor and could take sound advice, I might be tempted to say to them: "Shoot in the back of the neck, or somewhere else, in this parade, all of the corrupt corporation officials and minions, all of our corrupt bankers, all of the representatives of those powers whose greed is lust for war, shoot them and call it a good day's work and come home" . . . I prefer . . . that all the flags of all the world were made into one. . . . I would favor one color, the color of the human heart's blood, to indicate that we stand for life.

To those who insisted on marching, McDevitt declared,

> Get ready to march for [J. P.] Morgan, march for the gun makers, march for the ammunition makers, march for those who will never do anything for themselves so long as the common people are willing to fight their battles for them.

The *San Francisco Chronicle* observed that Rabbi Jacob Nieto of the American Union Against Militarism ended the meeting to "roars of laughter," with a satirical eulogy to the courage of participants in the scheduled parade. "Those present were advised to stand silent as the paraders passed," the *Chronicle* added.

On July 22, 1:30 P.M., the Preparedness parade began. Most of the marchers had entered Market Street when, at about 2 P.M., the Civil War Union Army veterans' group, the Grand Army of the Republic, began proceeding along Market from the corner of Steuart Street. At 2:06 P.M. a bomb exploded at the intersection, killing nine people and injuring at least forty more.

This atrocity, as much as the *Los Angeles Times* bombing, horrified the country. Suspicion quickly fell on a group of labor radicals linked to Berkman and his ill-titled periodical. Within a week five suspects had been arrested: Thomas J. Mooney, his wife Rena Mooney, Warren K. Billings, Edward D. Nolan, and Israel Weinberg. All five asserted their innocence and had detailed alibis, which were ignored. *The Blast* was raided by investigators, but Berkman was not arrested.

One aspect of the case could not be denied: the architect of the arrests, district attorney Charles M. Fickert, and his colleagues in the city's leading circles sought an eye for an eye. Whether Mooney and his cohort had anything to do with the bomb itself was irrelevant; they were hostages from radical ranks taken in revenge. The bomb seemed, above all, to serve the needs of a Law and Order Committee, backed by the Chamber of Commerce, then crusading against labor extremism. The atmosphere in the city may be judged by a minor but significant incident. An uproar broke out over William McDevitt's remarks at the July 20 antipreparedness meeting, and he was attacked by the Chamber as an anarchist unfit to serve on the city electoral commission. (This was ironic, in that McDevitt had been called a traitor by the Socialists for accepting the post!)

Summoned to a municipal hearing, McDevitt claimed his comments had been purely humorous, and he had intended only to entertain the crowd. But McDevitt was not removed; indeed, the incident did little more than demonstrate that, even with the blood and bodies left by the explosion fresh in everybody's minds, some San Franciscans would not be cowed. Scharrenberg came before the hearing in a combative mood and declared that the Chamber had no business accusing McDevitt, considering that one of its own leaders, steamship capitalist Robert Dollar, had lately called for violence against waterfront strikers. According to Scharrenberg, Dollar's attitude was "anarchistic" but had not been disowned by the Chamber. It should be noted that only four days after the bomb went off, Scharrenberg had printed the full text of his own uncompromising speech at the July 20 meeting in the *Coast Seamen's Journal.* Scharrenberg had also been active alongside Cora Older and the other labor figures who stood up on behalf of the I.W.W. in the free-speech fights, and he had supported strikers with whom Mooney and Billings were identified, in a walkout at the Pacific Gas and Electric Company.

Berkman received much rougher treatment from the law and press, but he also responded pugnaciously. He sent out a notice in mid-August, declaring, "The reaction is rampant in San Francisco. . . . We may be arrested at any moment but *The Blast* must be kept up at all costs." Much of the day-to-day work of managing both the paper and the Mooney-Billings defense effort was taken up by an artist in his thirties, Robert Minor, who had come to San Francisco in response to the arrests. A Texan and the son of a judge, Minor was a successful cartoonist for such newspapers as the *San Antonio Gazette,* the *St. Louis Post-Dispatch,* and the *New York World;* like Jack London, he had a second career as a radical speaker and organizer. Minor began in the Socialist Party, but later studied art in Paris and adopted the anarchism popular in French intellectual milieux.

The International Workers' Defense League was revived and Minor issued a stream of bulletins in its name, denouncing the arrests. His propaganda steered away from the "social war" vocabulary favored by Berkman, and raked Fickert for his association with Patrick Calhoun, invoking the shooting of Francis Heney and other events of the previous decade. "Those who cowered before the outraged citizenry of 1907 have now usurped the courts, and through professional jurors and police-controlled witnesses, hope to strangle Billings and his co-defendants," a *Weekly News Letter* issued by the I.W.D.L. declaimed, calling Fickert a "lickspittle of the Calhoun-Mullaly United Railroads gang, whom he refused to prosecute."

Billings was the first to be tried, in September. Two people claimed to have observed him carrying a suitcase on the roof of a building at 721 Market Street, almost a mile from the bomb explosion, and others said they had seen him soon afterward, at Steuart and Market Streets. Supposedly, he had brought the bomb to the first location and then taken it to the second. The witnesses against Billings consisted of a prostitute, Estelle Smith; her mother, Mrs. Alice Kidwell, whose involvement in the proceeding was motivated by her desire to free her husband and brother from state prison; a morphine addict, John McDonald, who said he saw Billings placing the bomb "as if in a dream," and an alleged male prostitute and thief, John Crowley. Billings' defense that he was nowhere near either 721 Market Street or the site of the explosion, was supported by credible (and respectable) witnesses, to no effect. At the end of two weeks, he was convicted of first-degree murder and sentenced to life imprisonment.

Berkman had seen various such cases in his career as a revolutionary; but even he found the Billings trial shocking, and he was not alone. A letter from Berkman to Frank P. Walsh, a noted liberal lawyer, revealed that Billings' lawyer, Maxwell McNutt, was "broken down with nervous strain" by the experience. The San Francisco Bar simply did not comprehend that the five defendants were casualties in the war of the classes, or that the trial was something other than an ordinary proceeding. Bewildered by the spectacle, some newspaper reporters who had cried for the defendants' blood now voiced alarm at an obvious miscarriage of justice. After weeks of silence, the Building Trades Council endorsed the defense campaign, and was expected to be joined by the rest of the San Francisco labor leadership.

Yet however timid the unionists became in the wake of the bombing, California by and large preserved its skepticism about American involvement in the World War. British intelligence sources complained that the *San Francisco Chronicle* and the Hearst papers were pro-German, an absurd exaggeration. But to the degree that they left British interests dissatisfied the papers reflected considerable local sentiment. In the 1916 presidential election, soon after Billings's trial, incumbent Democrat Woodrow Wilson, who it was said had kept the United States out of war, was challenged by the Republican Charles Evans Hughes, who also opposed American entry. Hughes had excluded Hiram Johnson from the vice-presidential slot on his ticket, and this decision was widely believed to have lost the state for the Republicans. Indeed, a British parliamentary source referred to 1916 as the year of a political "discovery of California"; it was the first example of the state determining the outcome of a presidential race.

On the evening of November 22, 1916 Jack London was found dead of uremia at his Glen Ellen home. His income had been swelled by motion-picture royalties, but he had found no satisfaction in wealth, fame, or the magnificent landscape where he lived. Californian reactionaries as well as Reds were saddened. The radical writer Upton Sinclair, speaking in Pasadena where he was spending the winter, recalled that his career had taken off after London wrote in praise of *The Jungle,* Sinclair's novel about Lithuanian Socialists in the Chicago meatpacking industry. Sinclair noted that London had already achieved great esteem abroad, perhaps greater than in his own country. London "is and will remain one of the great revolutionary forces in American letters," Sinclair avowed, adding "I have Jack London's own support for my opinion that the finest of his writings are the socialist essays which he wrote for love only." Sinclair settled in Pasadena permanently, and in the coming decades became, even more than London, a symbol of the uniquely Californian mixture of literary and political radicalism.

———————

BERKMAN, ANOTHER EXAMPLE of the California mix, had little time to ponder such matters. He considered the Preparedness Day bomb case a parallel to the 1886 Haymarket trial, which had stained American justice for a generation; eight of the most active and radical labor organizers in Chicago had been convicted in a bombing, and four of them hanged. Berkman wrote bitterly of "that dabbler in radicalism, Fremont Older," who had refused to defend Mooney and Billings. Emma Goldman had come to San Francisco to lecture, but her audience was sparse, reflecting fear of the authorities in the aftermath of the bomb; still, raiding *The Blast* failed to intimidate its publishers, and Berkman brought together groups of Russian, Jewish, and Italian anarchists to defend the movement's reputation.

But the situation in San Francisco was grave enough that by December 1916 Berkman had left for New York. There he and Goldman addressed a Carnegie Hall meeting on the San Francisco trials, sponsored by the United Hebrew Trades and chaired by the radical poet Max Eastman. Berkman's main wish was that *The Blast* continue to resound. At the beginning of 1917, Berkman sent out another solicitation for subscribers, in which he characterized the obstacles to its success as "Chicken-hearted printers, fearful of what their respectable customers would say; sly underhand wire-pulling opposition by grafters high and low; bitter opposition by Mother Grundies in silk skirts & overalls; arbitrary, stupid postal censorship & deprivation of second-class [mailing] rights; police terroriz[ing] newsdealers, open persecution & Hidden malice." However, this array of forces prevailed, and *The Blast* expired. Once in New York, Berkman ceased to play a significant role in the San Francisco drama. Fickert sought to extradite him in mid-1917, but by then it was too late: Berkman was in Atlanta Penitentiary, sentenced to two years for obstructing the newly reinstituted draft.

In San Francisco, all eyes were on Mooney as he went to trial in January 1917. Fickert's case still rested on the questionable witnesses who had testified against Billings. The prosecutorial theory was unchanged. Only one element of the Mooney trial was new: a cattleman named Frank C. Oxman swore that he had seen Mooney come to Steuart and Market in Weinberg's jitney, accompanied by Rena Mooney and Billings. The suitcase had been placed, he said, and he then watched the group drive away. Once again an array of reputable defense witnesses was heard, but seemed to leave no impression. After four weeks in court, the jury found Mooney guilt of first-degree murder. The "mercy" extended to Billings was absent: Mooney was sentenced to hang, and appealed.

The verdict echoed all over the world, and San Francisco, considered not long before the most corrupt city in the country, was again tainted as the home of an alleged frame-up. The situation grew even more dramatic when, after only two months, an acquaintance of Oxman, F. E. Rigall, provided the Mooney defense with letters showing that the cattleman had tried to get Rigall to perjure himself as a witness in the trial, even though Rigall had been halfway across the country when the bomb exploded. This was a strong indication that Oxman's own sworn testimony had been false. Fremont Older had supported the anti-preparedness campaign, but he disliked Mooney and Billings intensely, and believed in their guilt. Then Andrew Furuseth came to Older with the Rigall letters, and Older printed them in *The Bulletin.* He began an inquiry into the case that turned into an international crusade to save Mooney from the gallows. Soon Rena Mooney was tried, and acquitted; Weinberg was also found innocent, in September 1917. Nolan was never tried.

Between Mooney's sentencing and the Rigall revelation, radicals had been greatly heartened and equally discouraged by even larger events. In March, a democratic revolution overthrew the tsarist régime in Russia; the war had finally produced the outcome awaited by so many, and the process that followed in the former Russian Empire would prove more significant for California intellectuals than any local development for decades. Only weeks later, at the beginning of April, President Wilson, elected in 1916 as a lover of peace, led the United States into the World War. At first, California's enthusiasm for Wilson's decision remained limited.

American entry into the World War brought a great transformation of California, along with the broader American and global society. Though acclaimed by some radicals as a forging furnace from which a new world of superhumans would be born, the war left the social Darwinist outlook discredited. Yet America, for which the World War was a novelty, was not immediately touched by the sense of moral collapse that the war, after three years' slaughter, had brought to Europe. Rather, the United States was soon swept by war enthusiasm and a demanding, suspicious, and violent patriotism. With American soldiers ready to die on the other side of the Atlantic, radicals, religious pacifists, and ethnic Germans were suddenly perceived as scheming traitors and spies, and were so represented by government and the press. Berkman, as previously noted, had been imprisoned almost immediately, as was Goldman. But nobody suffered as much as the I.W.W. membership, who were accused of wholesale sabotage in the service of the Kaiser.

How much of the ensuing hysteria was artificially created, in an excessive effort to counter American ambivalence about the war, was and is a matter of opinion. Still, patriotic rage did not fully prevail. A wave of I.W.W. strikes occurred; it was then that a ferocious, nationwide campaign against the radicals began. The suppression of the I.W.W. in California assumed a savagery never seen before or after in America, in any antiradical effort. Many Californians became obsessed with the fear that Wobbly farm workers would rise up like Zapata's peasant soldiers, or like the agricultural rebels of southern and eastern Europe, to devastate property. In a state overwhelmingly devoted to agriculture, the press was filled with charges of conspiracy to burn crops, to destroy whole cities, to rouse armies of Wobblies marching in all directions, spreading destruction.

Much of this fear may be traced to a bloody clash between Wobbly-inspired hop pickers and local authorities in 1913 at Wheatland, California, an incident that greatly resembled an old-world rural outbreak—and after which an investigator appointed by Governor Johnson blamed the grower, rather than the I.W.W. In San Francisco, George Speed, secretary of the Wobbly branch and a popular local figure whose radical career went back to the Kaweah colony and Coxey's Army, was now arrested and charged with obstructing the war. But the Wobblies were nothing if not ingenious; allegedly, when their main hall on Third Street was raided they conducted meetings on the lower deck of a Bay ferry, adjourning before the vessel reached its slip and police could come aboard.

The Wobblies had gained particular strength among the Western metal miners and timber workers. Thousands of miners went on strike in Arizona, many of them Mexican and, ideologically, the offspring of Flores Magón's movement as well as of the Wobblies. In Bisbee, in July 1917, more than 1,200 copper miners were rounded up and "deported" in freight cars, first to New Mexico, and then along the border with Mexico. Similar incidents occurred in other Arizona and New Mexico towns, as well as in Nevada and across the border in Sonora, after I.W.W. organizers visited Cananea, again in the footsteps of Flores Magón's movement. In Butte, Montana, miners' strikes practically shut the copper industry down for good; I.W.W. leader Frank Little, famous in the Fresno "free-speech fight," was hanged by a secret posse for his alleged unpatriotic remarks.

Amid this environment of crisis, Tom Mooney was fighting for his life, supported by Fremont Older. New disclosures further undermined the state's case in the Preparedness Day bombing. First, it was established that the prosecution had suppressed evidence by refusing the defense copies of sequestered photographs showing Tom and Rena Mooney on the roof of their own residence at 975 Market Street, with a clock face visible in the background proving they were there when the bomb went off. Second, more letters emerged about Oxman, who had been brought into the case after the revelation of the photographs, and who was now shown to have, indeed, perjured himself. Finally, it was demonstrated that Fickert and his staff knew the witnesses in the two trials were unreliable, but used them anyway.

Older was not the "dabbler" he had been labeled by Berkman. As in the Ruef case, once he felt he had to correct a course of conduct he had followed, he did so vehemently. He became a fanatic for Mooney's vindication. His passion for the case was especially inflamed when the management of *The*

Bulletin, the newspaper he had loved and made truly great, ordered him to drop his Mooney fixation. Older would not be silenced; no job was worth that ignominy. But where could he turn?

There was one man in the newspaper business who had long tendered a standing offer to employ Older, but whom Older despised: Billy Hearst. Finally, in July 1918, Older went to Hearst's man in San Francisco and told him he had left *The Bulletin,* where he was replaced as managing editor by former Hearst journalist and historian Bailey Millard. Within two weeks, Hearst hired Older to run *The Call,* which he bought, and granted him complete freedom to pursue the Mooney affair as far as Older deemed appropriate. Once again, Older was called a sellout, who in his decline had gone helplessly to the man he hated, begging for security; again, he was derided by some as an inconsistent, unpredictable crackpot.

But if Mooney and Billings were framed, and there is every reason to believe they were, who placed the bomb? Berkman, Older, and others recalled that in the week preceding the explosion propagandistic letters had been sent to newspapers and civic leaders threatening such an act. Did Mooney, Billings, and Nolan know the identities of the real bombers, and keep the information to themselves? Only very recently has anything new or plausible emerged from the Mooney debate. In 1991, the historian Paul Avrich argued persuasively that the Preparedness Day bomb was the work of a group of Italian ultra-anarchists led by Luigi Galleani.

The U.S. government was under pressure about Mooney, but the problem was only one of many on a global roster of difficulties created by the World War. In November 1917, news came from Russia that an obscure group of extreme Socialists had seized power in the capital, Petrograd. Bolshevik-ruled Russia left the war and commenced negotiations with the Germans; this seemed to confirm the argument that antiwar radicals were agents of America's military foes, and antirevolutionary hysteria continued to rise in the United States. But increasing dissension also brought some concessions from the ruling powers; in January 1918 President Wilson, after a federal investigation into the Mooney affair, wrote to California Governor William D. Stephens urging that Mooney's death sentence be stayed pending a new trial. Finally, Stephens (a Progressive and the successor to Hiram Johnson, after Johnson was elected to the U.S. Senate in 1916) granted the stay. But both labor militants, Billings as well as Mooney, remained behind bars.

No compassion of any kind was shown to the Flores Magón circle in Los Angeles. On March 16, 1918, Ricardo Flores Magón and Librado Rivera were arrested for sedition, based on a Spanish-language manifesto they had published in *Regeneración*. In August, they were found guilty and sentenced, Ricardo to twenty years, Rivera to fifteen. They were sent back to McNeil Island, but the bad health of Ricardo led to their transfer to Leavenworth Penitentiary in Kansas.

Ricardo Flores Magón never again saw the light of day as a free man. But the heroic period of the Mexican Revolution had already ended, as the combat degenerated into an extended contest between warlords, interrupted by sporadic U.S. military intervention that was both ineffective and extremely unpopular, in California as elsewhere.

Unlike W. C. Owen, who eventually backed the Allies, Flores Magón held no brief for either side in the war, and would have indignantly rejected any involvement with German interests in his battles with the American authorities. But other revolutionaries were not so fastidious. In 1907, as part of the series of developments in Asia following the Russian uprising of 1905, an anti-imperialist movement, the Gadar Party, had been founded in the Punjab, in then-British India. The leading spirit of the party, the anarchist and rationalist Har Dayal, came to California in the footsteps of Sun Yat-sen and Sen Katayama and launched the party's local branch in 1913. Har Dayal appealed mainly to the large population of (Asian) Indians, most of them Sikhs, in the Sacramento Valley. He became an instructor at Stanford University and a close friend of Jack London, and, with Owen, set up the Bakunin Institute in Oakland. However, he left the United States in 1914.

In November 1917, 105 men and women were indicted in San Francisco for plotting an anti-British revolt in India with the backing of German diplomats. Most of them fled, and the list of defendants was reduced to 32, including Franz Bopp, the former German consul-general in San Francisco, and more than a dozen Gadar advocates. After five months, and the longest trial ever seen in California up to that time, 29 of them, including Bopp, were found guilty of establishing an illegal military enterprise. The verdict was announced on April 23, 1918, a day otherwise memorable because a Gadar associate entered the courtroom and shot dead a Hindu witness against the group. The assassin was killed in turn by a bailiff. Although this sensational act may have been moti-

vated by revolutionary principles, it was said that the two men had disagreed over money donated to the Gadar party. The party itself continued its activity in California for a long time afterward, and its traces are
detectable here today.

The repression of radicals grew; at the end of 1917, 100 members of
the I.W.W., including "Big Bill" Haywood, were sent to prison for obstructing the war. Federal authorities began arresting young men for evading draft registration; in April 1918, twenty-five of them were taken into
custody in a raid on the San Francisco premises of the Young People's Socialist League, the youth wing of the Socialist Party. The branch changed its
name to the Jack London Memorial Institute, and continued holding meetings and classes, while launching a magazine, *The Proletariat,* "dedicated to
International Revolutionary Socialism," in May 1918. The inaugural issue
included several fascinating items, including a highly sophisticated essay by
Leon Trotsky, commissar of foreign relations in Russia's new Bolshevik
regime, on "Prospects of a Proletarian Dictatorship."

Trotsky and the other Russian extremists wrote in a sociopolitical
idiom that California radicals, used to the idealistic and often poetic discourse favored by the Wobblies as well as the mainstream Socialists,
found unfamiliar but compelling, even dazzling. Social Darwinist fantasies, no less than lyrical and satirical flights, seemed to have given way,
in the international socialist movement, to a modern, analytical style of
revolutionary rationalism. Above all, Russian Bolshevism bespoke a military kind of discipline which many equated with commitment but which
had been inconceivable in the socialism of the past, even among the comrades of Burnette Haskell and Joseph Buchanan, who wore uniforms and
marched in arms.

The Jack London Memorial Institute was an ambitious enterprise. It
boasted of its library, which held one of the largest socialist collections in
the country, and was open daily from 9:00 A.M. to 11:00 P.M. It taught
drama and presented a "Radical Play" every other Saturday. It maintained a
school along the lines developed by Francesc Ferrer in Spain, with high-
school level "children's" classes in ethics, "history of civilization," economics, socialism, current events, and dance (classical as well as folk). A
Montessori day school was planned. The Institute's evening classes offered
instruction in public speaking, economics, industrial history, English,
and—a clear sign of the times—Russian. Its instructors included several in-

dividuals whose names we will encounter again: Emanuel Levin, Benjamin Ellisberg, Jack McDonald, and the Reverend Robert Whitaker.

THE WORLD WAR ended in November 1918, with the Allies victorious. But the antiradical campaign continued, although it had already nearly destroyed the revolutionary political culture that had existed in America. Eugene V. Debs was sent to Atlanta Penitentiary in September 1918 for a remarkably moderate antiwar speech at a convention of the Ohio Socialist Party. During his address, federal agents entered the hall and arrested fifty-five Socialists who lacked draft cards. Even more than the Mooney frame-up, the imprisonment of Debs, universally considered an idealist of the purer kind, embarrassed the United States. Meanwhile, Washington state, where the Wobblies had organized the majority of timber workers, saw a real reign of terror, including lynchings, as triumphant patriots sought to clear the lumber industry of agitators.

The repression, although severe, was deemed insufficient by some, particularly after the Bolshevik Revolution. The San Francisco press began featuring sensational tales of Bolshevik doings in the city, first in the Russian colony on Potrero Hill, where it was said that the children were so Red they refused to salute the flag at Patrick Henry Elementary School! In addition, 1919 saw one of the greatest periods of industrial unrest in the history of the United States, and of the world. The first general strikes in North American history broke out in Seattle in January, and in Winnipeg, Manitoba, in May and June. A spontaneous strike by trainmen shut down the rails in southern California in August, following similar unauthorized work stoppages by railway shopmen, the new leaders of railroad radicalism, around the country. In September the Boston police struck, a development that surprised the whole nation. A massive walkout in the steel industry was met by martial law. Finally, in November, almost half a million coal miners struck.

Californians soon got their first taste of the new revolutionary dispensation. In mid-1919, two conventions in Chicago launched competing factions, the Communist Labor Party and the Communist Party, which quarrelled for some time before uniting to form a single Communist Party, the American section of the Communist International, or Comintern. The Communist Labor Party mostly drew its adherents from the English-speaking sections of the Socialist Party Left Wing, while the original Communist

Party mainly consisted of foreign-born members of the so-called "language federations" in the Socialist Party. Some of these Socialist ethnic federations were quite wealthy; the Jewish (Yiddish-speaking) federation published the *Forverts,* the largest foreign-language newspaper in the United States, in New York City (where it was known as the *Jewish Daily Forward*) with a press run in the hundreds of thousands. The Jewish federation, however, remained loyal to the established Socialist Party. By contrast, eight Slavic, Baltic, Hungarian and Finnish federations, all in the orbit of the Russians, wholly joined the Communists. Of these, the Finns, although a tenth of the size of the Jewish Socialist federation, were also quite prosperous, possessing considerable property around the United States, including three daily newspapers.

In California, however, the ethnic federations were weak, except for the Finns, and the Communist movement began with a convention of the Communist Labor Party in Oakland on November 9, 1919. The sixteen delegates came from the Bay Area, Santa Cruz, Fresno, and other California cities. Max Bedacht, a German-born barber in his mid-thirties who edited an Oakland Socialist weekly in German, *Vorwärts der Pacific-Küste,* and who was a popular leader of the Socialist Party Left Wing, became the new party's organizer. Another founding participant was Anita Whitney, the suffragist leader, social worker, and former president of the Oakland Center of the California Civic League, the successor to the College Suffrage League. Whitney, now aged 53, had joined the Socialist Party in 1914, and her views evolved in an exceptionally radical direction; she served as treasurer of the regional branch of the antiwar People's Council, and aided the legal defense of the I.W.W.

The Communist Labor Party established branches in San Francisco, Santa Barbara, Oakland, Richmond, San Jose, Santa Cruz, Lodi, Fresno, and other towns, and opened a headquarters in Oakland, which was immediately raided by police and then by World War veterans who had joined the equally new American Legion. The veterans dragged the furniture and radical literature out of the office and burned it in the street. But even before that, Anita Whitney was charged with "criminal syndicalism" for her membership in the party, on a warrant secured by Fenton G. Thompson, an inspector in the Oakland police "loyalty bureau" who conducted a minor reign of terror in the East Bay city. The circumstances were dramatic, for she was arrested at the end of November at a downtown hotel, after delivering a speech on "The Negro Problem in the United States" before a session of the women's club of which she was the former president. The incident nearly turned into a riot, since Whitney had many admirers among East Bay women.

In January 1920, while Whitney awaited trial, Alameda County authorities indicted ten others associated with the new Party under the "criminal syndicalism" law. These included James Hulse Dolsen, J. E. Snyder, editor of another Oakland Socialist paper, *The World*, which was now described as the local Communist Labor organ, and Max Bedacht. Soon the bulk of the party's cadre, including the San Francisco Communist Labor leader, J. A. Ragsdale, had been jailed.

Whitney's speech on "the Negro problem" had shown a genuine prescience about the challenges facing American society; but the circumstances of her trial were premonitory as well, and indicated the outlines of much California history that came after. Unlike the Wobblies, Anita Whitney was neither a vagabond wage-worker, nor a marginalized rebel. She was a rich, sophisticated, and widely admired woman who moved in a social circle with which most Wobblies never had contact. Her women friends, all of them as respectable and many as well off as she, had nearly prevented her arrest by their riotous protests; indeed, the club that sponsored her speech had defied demands for its cancellation by the police, in the form of Fenton Thompson. One of her close associates was Meta Erickson, known as "the only woman railroad president in the world," the head of the tiny Amador County Railway in the Sierra Nevada, described as "the shortest railroad in the United States."

Whitney's case could not be disposed of with ease. When she was tried, some fifty "fashionably-gowned society women" attended in force, according to the press coverage, and showed their support for her by hissing prosecution witnesses. Soon a so-called "silent jury" of American Legionnaires had adopted the same tactic, appearing daily in court to stare down the defendant and her Amazons. The Legionnaires had done the same thing before, but Whitney's trial was the first where two such bodies came face to face. The Whitney trial was held during a worldwide influenza epidemic, and the illness and death of various lawyers, jurors, and other figures in the trial gave the proceeding a "hoodoo" or jinxed reputation.

At the end of February 1920 Anita Whitney was found guilty and sentenced to one to fourteen years in San Quentin, the first woman convicted of "criminal syndicalism." Her Amazons, crowding the courtroom, wept, wailed, and kissed her as she was led out; one was heard to call her "another John Brown." Her case was appealed in a process that proved long. The significance of the Whitney case was important in its demonstration that, somehow, the San Francisco Bay Area was truly different from the rest of the state and the country. No matter how outraged its citizens might have been at the Preparedness Day bomb, no matter how violent the campaign against the Wobblies and antiwar Socialists, liberal opinion would rally to a personality like Anita Whitney, if only because true Californians could not resist a new fad.

James Hulse Dolsen, for his part, though neither rich nor a clubwoman, gave a remarkably similar lesson in his trial, which began at the same time as Whitney's. Dolsen was the only defendant to appear without a lawyer, but his arguments were so provocative and effective that he obtained a hung jury—after fifty failed ballots! The clever Dolsen had, among other antics, announced that in fifty years the prosecution's anti-Communist views would be considered treasonous; he questioned the jurors as to whether they would oppose a Soviet government in America if it were established peacefully, and each answered "No." In 1922, Dolsen, J. E. Snyder, J. A. Ragsdale, and three other Communist defendants were subjected to a second attempt at a trial, but the charges were dropped.

Max Bedacht was not tried in Oakland but was extradited to Illinois, where he was convicted and served time for conspiracy to overthrow the government. He became one of the top Communists in America; Whitney and Dolsen, who remained Communists for the rest of their lives, were inducted into the Party's second-level leadership.

The new model of revolutionary action appealed to many other radicals. Sen Katayama, leader of the Japanese Socialists, worked underground in America, took refuge in Russia, and became one of the Comintern's highest officials. Lincoln Steffens observed the early stages of the Russian process firsthand, and was pleased to serve as a leading American defender of the Bolshevik regime. By contrast Berkman and Goldman were deported to Russia at the end of 1919; although they were initially enthusiastic about a country gripped by what seemed an unstoppable revolution, they soon became deeply disheartened and left it. They were barred from returning to the United States and wandered Europe instead.

Parallel with the birth of the Comintern, the Wobblies continued to gain strength, although subjected to their incredible mass martyrdom, shot, hanged, jailed, tarred and feathered, and otherwise punished for refusing to conform. Beginning in 1921, the main area of I.W.W. activity shifted from the Northwest timber industry to the seas, where the I.W.W. waterfront section, known as the Marine Transport Workers Industrial Union or M.T.W., grew enormously. The explanation for this was simple: the Sailors' Union lovingly built by Andrew Furuseth had been crushed by an offensive of the federal authorities and the shipowners.

Furuseth and his union had grown incautious during the World War. Once the United States was a belligerent, the American merchant fleet burgeoned beyond all previous expectation. The Wilson administration adopted a kind of "state capitalism" for the duration of the conflict, with unions awarded a share in running the system for the sake of stability. The sailors gained a union shop aboard government vessels, along with high wages and an eight-hour workday—the three-watch system. Furuseth paid for these benefits by endorsing the war, with moderate vocabulary, and by trying to chase the Wobblies out of the union. In this latter endeavor he failed.

Unfortunately, the West Coast shipowners saw Furuseth as a dangerous radical, whatever his vituperations against the Wobblies. In April 1921, the United States Shipping Board set about breaking the Sailors' Union by locking its members out, and the task was completed by the end of July. A member of the Union, Charles Lesse, wrote in its *Journal,* "The battle is fought and lost. The hired brains of the shipping trust have been successful. . . . They are marshaling all their forces to put the union out of business. They are fighting us with scabs, police, injunctions, courts and press, with other institutions held in reserve." He concluded with a phrase that reflected the Wobbly tendencies of many union members, calling for the unification of *"all industrial unions into One Big Labor Alliance the world over"* [italics in original]. In shipping, at least, the hour had struck for the Wobblies. Seamen were welcomed into the M.T.W. by many "two-card" men; these had remained in the Sailors' organization while also carrying the I.W.W. red card. The historian Hyman Weintraub wrote that the M.T.W. stood "in the midst of the anti–I.W.W. persecution with a strong, militant, and thriving maritime union." The Wobblies called "job actions" (later known as "wildcat" strikes), from ship to ship, to restore the three-watch system and boost pay. In San Pedro the shipowners capitulated. The

M.T.W. imitated Furuseth in using the Pacific Coast as a base for international organizing.

WHILE COMMUNISTS AND Wobblies anticipated new and bigger revolutionary skirmishes, other effects of the World War and the decline of the old socialism were felt among radical intellectuals in California. A figure whose biography anticipates much that came later is that of a then-obscure radical, Jaime de Angulo.

Of Castilian heritage, born in Paris in 1887, de Angulo arrived in America in 1905. He became a cowboy in Colorado, and, after amassing a financial stake, traveled to San Francisco, where he stayed in a small French-owned proletarian hotel in North Beach, fascinated by the Italian-French-Spanish-Mexican-Basque community surrounding him. He grew interested in language, or rather in linguistics. However, he was academically trained as a physician. He studied at Cooper Union in New York City and at the Johns Hopkins University in Baltimore, where he met and married a doctor, Cary Fink. Under her influence, he joined the Baltimore branch of the ultraradical Socialist Labor Party. Soon he had in hand his first written work, a pamphlet on the role of the Catholic Church in the repression of the radical movement in Spain, The "Trial" of Ferrer. Thus began one of the most important, fruitful, and controversial intellectual careers ever seen in California.

In 1921, de Angulo embarked on an enterprise as innovative as Bolshevism, but in a different context and direction. In a log he kept, he wrote on September 23 of that year, "Going out." He was headed for Alturas in Modoc County, to record the language of the Achomawi (Pit River) Indians.

De Angulo, a cowboy Socialist and physician, while long fascinated by variations of language, had come to California Indian linguistics by a circuitous path. He had read Lewis Henry Morgan's Ancient Society, a nineteenth-century analysis of the Iroquois Indians, ancient Greece and Rome, and other "tribal" cultures, which had an enormous reputation among Socialists. (The Socialist Labor Party, to which de Angulo belonged, has kept the book in print to this day!) Marxists loved Morgan's work because it presented a triune historical sequence of savagery, barbarism, and civilization, which Marxists believed pointed to the inevitability of Socialism. Few if any anthropologists ever took the book seriously. But de Angulo became a fanatic for it, and handed copies around to his friends even after he met the professional anthropologist Robert Lowie, also a Marxist, who scoffed at Morgan.

Returning to California with his medical degree, Jaime de Angulo and his wife Cary frequented the Bohemians. One of his first new friends was an experimental composer, Henry Cowell, whom we shall encounter again, then "in his teens and already quite eccentric," according to de Angulo's daughter and biographer, Gui de Angulo. Cowell produced a composition dedicated to Jaime, *The Freak de Concert,* in 1912. Jaime and Cary began visiting Carmel, and there met a man who invited him to become part-owner of a Modoc County ranch. De Angulo went there and was welcomed into the companionship of the Achomawi people who worked for the local white ranchers. But the Alturas enterprise ended unsatisfactorily, and he returned to Carmel.

Then, south of the artists' colony, he came upon Big Sur. Writing two decades later, he described the excitement of the moment, which he never forgot:

> You never saw such a landscape! . . . I did not imagine it was possible . . . like a dreamland, somewhere, not real . . . imagine: only a trail, for a hundred miles, bordering the ocean, but suspended above it a thousand feet, clinging halfway up the side of the sea-wall, and that wall at an incredible angle of forty-five degrees, a green wall of grass and canyons with oaks, redwoods, pines, madroños, blue jays, quail, deer, and to one side the blue ocean stretching away to China, and over all that an intense blue sky with eagles and vultures floating about . . . and nobody, no humans there, solitude, solitude, for miles and miles.

Jaime de Angulo, of Castilian background, had rediscovered the wonder of the central California coast, expressed hundreds of years before by the companions of Cabrillo and Vizcaíno. He was invited by a local resident, a Spanish-speaking descendant of the original settlers, to "esquatar"—to squat on unoccupied land as a homesteader. His neighbors still wore old-style rowel spurs on the fine horses they rode along the dizzying trails. He settled down; perhaps because of his Spanish origin and language, he had the opportunity to become the first intellectual to live at Big Sur. His marriage to Cary began slowly to fall apart, although they remained friends for some time. Soon he met the woman who became his second wife, Lucy Freeland, nicknamed Nancy. Jaime gave her a copy of Morgan's *Ancient Society.*

The gift of a book betrayed the intellectual passion that increasingly occupied his thoughts, but its fulfillment was delayed while he pursued the vagaries of his distinctive existence. In 1915 he drove a herd of horses across California, from Modoc County to Big Sur. But in mid-April 1917, as soon as he learned that the United States had entered the war, he enlisted in the Army Medical Corps. He hated militarism, but a reading of *Under Fire (Le Feu),* an antiwar novel by the French writer Henri Barbusse, made him intensely curious about the experience. And Jaime de Angulo was nothing if not curious. His service was (fortunately) uneventful beyond a few minor personal adventures. He came back to Big Sur in December 1918 and, in Carmel, met two of the leading anthropologists of the time, Alfred Kroeber and Paul Radin.

Kroeber and de Angulo shared an interest in psychiatry, and although de Angulo had no formal ethnological training, Kroeber invited him to lecture at Berkeley on psychology and anthropology. There de Angulo began reading linguistics, and was intrigued; he met a Pomo Indian man, William Bronson, with whom he completed his first research on a living language. He remembered the friends he had made in Modoc County, and there he went, in 1921, to begin his fieldwork in California Indian linguistics, paid for by a private patron.

Jaime de Angulo's first linguistic fieldwork marked the commencement of a career totally apart from his political radicalism, but which, in its humanism and solidarity with the California Indians, put him decades ahead of his time. In the next fifteen years he published 35 articles, reviews, and papers, beginning with a study of nasal sounds in Mexican Indian languages and continuing with surveys of kinship terms in Indian languages, religion among California Indians, and numerous other topics, including many traditional narratives collected in the field. He reviewed the early work of Georges Dumézil, one of the most influential figures in anthropology today. His work offered indisputable proof that California Indian culture was not dead but alive, at least for the time being. Perhaps inevitably he soon broke with Kroeber, who utterly lacked de Angulo's verve and spontaneity. Meanwhile, Cary left him in 1921 and went to Switzerland, where she too opened a new chapter in intellectual history as one of the first Americans interested in the work of C. G. Jung.

California Indians would have benefited from more friends like Jaime de Angulo in those years. The standard anthropological view of Indian culture as a nearly vanished phenomenon seemed all too appropriate, given the continuing degradation of the indigenous population. Things had only gotten worse since Helen Hunt Jackson's time. The 1920s saw a renewed campaign to compensate Native Californians for lands stolen from them during the Gold Rush. But litigation was slow, unproductive, and extremely threatening for white society; the Mission Indian Federation was even investigated for an alleged plot against the government.

Indeed, the 1920s saw the emergence of a new white racism in California, extending beyond Indian matters. The Ku Klux Klan suddenly appeared in both the northern and southern parts of the state, and quickly claimed 75,000 members. A crowd of five thousand people gathered to watch 2,000 Klan members sworn in at a rally in Daly City, as described in the *San Francisco Chronicle*. The Klan was reported to have recruited members in the San Francisco Police, and when Oakland authorities refused the organization permission to hold a July Fourth march in their city, veterans in Richmond, a brutal company town controlled jointly by the S.P., the Santa Fe Railway, and the Standard Oil Company of California, generously offered the Klan their own streets for a parade. The "Invisible Empire" even had a Klavern of forty students at Stanford University. But the California Klan broke up over the problem that plagued the Klan wherever it appeared: factionalism.

The passing of the grand era of radical hopes was symbolized, for many, by the death of Ricardo Flores Magón in November 1922, far from California, in a cell at Leavenworth Penitentiary. Prison officials blamed a heart attack, but Ricardo's admirers always believed he was murdered. In Leavenworth he worked in the prison library; one of his friends behind bars was Taraknath Das, a member of the Gadar Party sentenced in the 1918 San Francisco trial.

W. C. Owen continued, for his part, as a radical writer, mainly for the London anarchist paper *Freedom,* often contributing as much as three-quarters of the little weekly's content; he was, after all, a true professional. In his last years he was close to the English writer Victor Neuburg, who was also an associate of the occultist Aleister Crowley and the discoverer, much later, of the Welsh poet Dylan Thomas. William C. Owen died in a nursing home in 1929. Thomas Keell, the long-dedicated editor of *Freedom,* remembered Owen for his "knowledge of languages . . . a great help to an editor who knew hardly any," and praised him as the Anarchist movement's "best English propagandist."

Back in California even the Wobblies, their ranks expanded by the seamen, were living out the end, rather than the beginning, of an epic. In 1923, the Wobbly maritime movement took its last stand in San Pedro. On May Day of that year, the I.W.W. called for a national strike for the release of all "class war prisoners" as well as the satisfaction of economic demands. An I.W.W. historian, Fred Thompson, later recalled,

> [M]any were still in jail on wartime indictments; the number convicted under the criminal syndicalism laws in California was growing . . . [with] a number, such as Mooney . . . out of labor trials not connected to the I.W.W. Protest strikes occurred . . . but nowhere with such effectiveness as in the maritime industry. San Pedro . . . was tied up tight. . . . In most ports it was a short protest strike but won pay boosts of 15 percent. In San Pedro it developed into a lengthy free speech fight.

In the middle of the San Pedro struggle the young Slovene writer Lav Adamic arrived in the port. Landing in the United States at 14, he had worked for a Slovenian-language paper that failed, then in a silk mill in Paterson, New Jersey. He joined the Army during the World War, and fought in France on the Meuse-Argonne front. Discharged in 1920, he bummed around the country and went to sea, then came back ashore and supported himself with occasional odd jobs. He moved to Los Angeles, then to San Pedro in July 1923.

San Pedro was a logical place for him. It was home to the largest South Slavic immigrant community in California, with Slovenes and Croats particularly active on the waterfront, and as fishermen all the way up to the Bering Strait. A Croat poet, Tin Ujević, had written with lyrical irony of that diaspora, "Old is the song of the galley slave, the toiler at the oar,/new is the song of the worker in California." Adamic found employment on the docks, began writing in English, and met the Wobblies. As Mike Davis has pointed out, Adamic "record[ed] their suicidal bravery in his *Laughing in the Jungle*—an 'autobiography of an immigrant in America' that was also an extraordinary documentary of Los Angeles in the 1920s from the standpoint of its radical outcasts and defeated idealists." The liberal writer Carey

McWilliams, a virtual disciple of Adamic, later wrote that the Slovenian-American youth "thrived on Los Angeles. He reveled in its freaks, fakirs, and frauds. . . . He was its prophet, sociologist, and historian."

In 1928, while he was still working on the docks, Adamic's writings were first published by H. L. Mencken's *American Mercury.* More magazine articles appeared, and the next year Adamic published his first book, a biography of the California poet Robinson Jeffers. His works about Los Angeles, which he called "the enormous village," brought him success, and, as we shall see, influenced Nathanael West, who before his own tragic and ignominious end wrote the greatest of all Los Angeles novels, *The Day of the Locust.*

But that is to run ahead of our story. The San Pedro Wobblies' free speech fight brought the jailing of hundreds of radicals and liberals, including Upton Sinclair, who was arrested while attempting to read the Bill of Rights aloud. It became another notorious chapter in Los Angeles history, long remembered. The press continued using the I.W.W. to generate anti-radical anxieties, playing up occasional agricultural disorders and even warning in 1924 of a potential for war in San Pedro between the Wobblies and the K.K.K. But the Wobblies were finished in California, except among the "two-card" seamen, who kept their I.W.W. red cards while reentering the Sailors' Union or, typically, shipping with no union at all. Yet they were not to be forgotten, either; not by any means.

Nor was Tom Mooney forgotten, as he rotted in his cell.

PART IV

RED YEARS

All this is reportage.
—George Oppen, "Route"

*Wherein surviving California radicals are over-
taken by a wind from the Russian steppes;
Communists set up shop locally and begin spying, agitating, and organizing the least advantaged; a great strike shakes the coast, reviving
the unions; radical intellectuals gravitate between Communism and modernism; a naive but
sincere hero attempts a ballot-box revolution,
and nearly succeeds at it; labor crusading succumbs to infighting; and the California Communists, after dominating the scene, turn sour
under the impact of Stalinism*

*B*eginning in the late 1920s, the Communist Party emerged as a major force in California radicalism, which in the following decade it came to dominate. Indeed, during the Great Depression of the 1930s the influence of the California Communists was decisive not only for the Left but for the state as a whole. It is no exaggeration to say that during the 1930s the political history of California was that of the California Communists.

The greatest distinguishing element in American Communism was the sense that its adherents lived in their own world, wholly separate from the day-to-day concerns of their neighbors. Such could not be said of the old Socialists, and although the Wobblies inhabited the margin of society, with their own songs, vocabulary, methods, traditions, and martyrology, their cultural difference from those around them nonetheless reflected an organic outgrowth from the broader American culture. Such could never be said of the Communists.

One aspect of this special insularity may be seen in a psychological "disintegration" of former Socialists, Wobblies, anarchists, and other American and foreign-born radicals once they entered Communist ranks. Daring, resourceful, and charismatic individuals like Robert Minor, Anita Whitney, and James Dolsen lost their notable verve, and even their zest for combat, after they became Communists. Their personalities seemed literally to shrink; some were effectively swallowed up and disappeared, silenced.

The isolation of Communists within their special universe was reflected in many episodes of their history. From 1921, when the former Communist Labor and Communist factions merged, to 1927, the Communist Party may have had up to eight hundred members in California. (The state organization was designated, with Nevada and Arizona, as District 13 in the Party's Soviet-style structure—in which, for a long time, the states were grouped in regions.) But through most of that period the Party had no public face in California, except in a campaign to save Anita Whitney from serving time in San Quentin for her "criminal syndicalism" conviction. In addition, the Whitney effort rested almost entirely on a network of liberals who recoiled at the image of California sending a grey-haired social worker, approaching her sixties, to prison on a charge involving thought rather than deeds. In the wake of the 1917–23 lynching bee directed at the Wobblies the state's reputation for such affairs, compromised even before then by the Mooney case, was bad enough. The labor movement played almost no role in the Whitney campaign, whereas, curiously enough, the Women's Christian Temperance Union supported her.

But the fundamental truth of California Communism in those years, as of American Communism in general, was that the Party was then entirely absorbed in a complicated, arcane, and punishing internal fight among its factions, which were competing brutally for Soviet recognition as the Party leadership. This inner struggle was wholly incomprehensible to the average American worker, and even to many Communists themselves. Thus, the Communists were *in* California, but not culturally *of* it.

In structural terms, this alienation had an obvious origin: the Communist Party was externally driven, not an authentic local movement. Yet the Communists' extraordinary dedication to their own internal and rather claustrophobic discourse had other, functional aspects as well. If Communism from the outside often seemed indistinguishable from paranoid schizophrenia, from the inside it resembled nothing so much as management theory.

Revolutionaries like Bob Minor or Anita Whitney lost their original flamboyance and became, in effect, board members of a sort of corporation, "The Revolution Company," headquartered in Moscow. All decisions came from above, and required corporate obedience. Nonentities rose to the heights of power in the Party because advancement in the ranks, as in a corporation, was dependent on loyalty to the will of those above. Communist terminology, especially in internal party meetings, centered on phrases like "style of work," "concrete leadership," and "political clarification of tasks" that would have been inconceivable among the old Socialists or Wobblies. Whereas the latter kinds of radicals had as their models the imaginative and provocative exemplars of the grand revolutionary tradition, from the European peasant revolts to Zapata, the Communist ideal was one of modesty, discretion, passionlessness, subordination, and conformity, exactly as if they were so many bank clerks.

Above all, Communism was, for American Party members, a job—a job, eventually, with the Russian secret police—but a job nonetheless. That secret police, which came to be known enduringly as the KGB, even referred to the Communist Party as "the corporation" in some of its coded communications. Still, there was a compensation in this form of employment (aside from monetary payments which soon flowed), consisting in the intoxication of the Soviet experiment, enacted through unrestrained dictatorship over "a sixth of the world," with a gigantic army and limitless resources.

Lenin's "management theory of revolution" seemed to promise responsible careers as state functionaries in the service of the new enlightenment to often unemployable aspiring intellectuals, anxious to free themselves of guilt over the social and economic advances they had made over the rural and urban working classes for whom they were supposedly speaking. Further, for the younger intellectuals, workers, and students who joined the California Communists in the 1930s one must also recognize the overwhelming appeal of the *new,* of the "wave of the future," in which Communism much resembled fascism, as the crucial factor.

From 1921 to 1925 the American Communist Party, in addition to its factional preoccupations, was largely underground. The Party eventually came out in public, but the factional ordeal had left it with few California members ready for open political activity in the late 1920s, aside from a small group of Russian Jews in Los Angeles. As the Whitney case dwindled in its prominence (she was pardoned by Governor C. C. Young in 1927), an issue of truly global importance brought the Party to the attention of some Californians, as the Comintern became deeply involved with the progress of the Chinese Revolution. For the Chinese in California, the impact was predictably vast; after the World War the Chinese Revolution had entered a period of grandeur and hope that held the interest of people throughout the world.

On the second anniversary of Sun Yat-sen's death, in 1927, a San Francisco memorial publication printed praise of him and his Nationalist Party or *Guomindang* (also spelled *Kuomintang*), alongside messages of support from Munshe Singh, secretary of the Hindustan Gadar Party, and Emanuel Levin, a former instructor in English at the Jack London Memorial Institute and a "criminal syndicalism" defendant. Levin was now organizer of the Executive Committee for District 13 of the Workers [Communist] Party of America—its then title.

Addressing the Chinese Nationalists as "Dear Comrades," Levin extended "sympathy and cooperation" to the Central Executive Committee of the *Guomindang* in the United States, which happened to be headquartered in San Francisco. At that time the Communists doubtless had more to say to the Chinese in California than to any other sector of the state's population. But the marriage of the Comintern and the *Guomindang* (resulting in the transformation of the former into the "Kuomintern," according to some skeptics) proved of short duration. In July 1927 the *Guomindang* leadership under Jiang Jieshi (Chiang Kai-shek), an officer trained by Soviet Russians, massacred the Chinese Communists and their worker followers. This ghastly shock upset the worldwide Communist movement. Trotsky, Lenin's designated heir and the rival of Joseph Stalin, denounced the Comintern leadership, composed of his factional opponents, for leading the Chinese workers into slaughter. In November 1927, the tenth anniversary of the Bolshevik coup, Trotsky was expelled from the Russian Communist Party. In the last session of the Comintern to which he was allowed to speak, on September 27, anathema was pronounced on Trotsky by none other than Sen Katayama. "We have heard you and we condemn you," Katayama said coldly. The Bolshevik Revolution had entered its agony.

COMMUNIST DISTRICT ORGANIZER Levin was not the only non-Chinese Californian to become involved, at that time, in the Soviet adventure in China. While Levin intervened in the Chinese Revolution from afar, a woman who had worked for San Francisco newspapers, Rayna Simons Prohme, had gone to China via Hawaii in 1923 with her second husband, William Prohme, a *San Francisco Examiner* editorial writer and assistant managing editor. The couple threw themselves into propaganda work for the Chinese Nationalists, alongside Sun Yat-sen. In 1926, protected by their American passports, they launched a newspaper in Beijing, the *People's Tribune,* as a voice of the *Guomindang* Left. After Sun's death, Rayna Prohme had also joined his widow, Soong Qingling, in promoting feminism among Chinese women.

Rayna Prohme was a notably beautiful and charismatic woman with blazing red hair who had turned her back on the wealth of her Chicago merchant family and a marriage to Samson Raphaelson, a leftist playwright, to join William Prohme. Before they went to China, she had become well known in Hollywood as well as in California Bohemian circles, traveling between the North Beach and Russian Hill neighborhoods in San Francisco, Carmel, and a literary colony then flourishing in Ensenada, at the northern end of Baja California. One reporter recalled that she "won many friends, who enjoyed her happy moods and sympathized with her when under the somber spell of grieving for the oppressed . . . she could have led what she was wont to term the American woman's conventional semi-butterfly, semi-club life. She chose to break away from that convention, to give scope to the spirit that burned within her—the will to aid those whom she considered wronged and oppressed." Like many young women with these idealistic yearnings, Rayna Prohme also had a rough edge; she hated Jaime de Angulo, whom she met in Carmel, on sight.

An American newspaper correspondent, James Vincent Sheean, encountered Rayna Prohme in China. As described by Sheean she was an exceptionally magnetic young woman; his recollections of her, published nearly a decade afterward, were adoring. But Sheean was an able observer and his portrait of her seems accurate. Sheean described a period when

> for a few months in 1927, a little more than half a year, {Hankou] concentrated, symbolized and upheld the hope for a revolution of the world. Delegations came there from all over Europe, Asia and America to see for themselves what constituted [Hankou]'s success, the surprise and delight of a generation of thwarted Communists. . . . You could not be in [Hankou] a week without being aware of all this. French Communists, German Communists, Hindu Communists, British I.L.P. people, and numerous agitators responsible to the Komintern gave the place a fine mixed flavor of international revolt.

Sheean, the Prohmes, and other foreigners escaped the mass killing of Chinese Communists. William Prohme made his way to the Philippines. Sheean found Rayna Prohme in Moscow in September 1927; for him, in the capital of world-revolution, she had become the "sun of this solar system . . . I knew my world revolved about her," he declared. However, he insisted, "the feeble, perfumed sentiments, the romantic illusions, the limited personal desires and disappointments of boudoir 'love' had no part in the moment."

In November 1927, simultaneously with the fall of Trotsky, news came to the West that Rayna Prohme had died in Moscow of encephalitis, and had been buried with full revolutionary honors. It was reported that she was never a Communist Party member. "She might have lived easily at home, but preferred to live dangerously in China," the *San Francisco Chronicle* summarized. One of the eulogists at her funeral was Mikhail Gruzenberg, a Bolshevik functionary who cut a wide swath in China as Mikhail Borodin—his *klichka,* or revolutionary alias, to use the Russian term that entered into Comintern parlance. He praised her for having "rendered invaluable service to the oppressed Chinese people. Following the highest tradition of America, she spared no sacrifice to help slaves to freedom."

In reality her death came, according to Sheean, soon after her decision to join the Party, to enter the Lenin Institute (a training school in clandestine methods), and to commit herself to work for the Comintern in Asia through a hitherto obscure group, the Pan-Pacific Trade Union Secretariat. This was, to Sheean, "the end of Rayna Prohme." A woman he had loved because he could so profoundly believe her had surrendered to the bureaucratic expediency dictated by Leninism. Sheean badgered her, repeating the question, "Are you prepared to tell lies and forge passports and change your name and even pretend not to belong to the Party you work for?" For, after all, he wrote, "this kind of thing came nearest to affecting Rayna's certainty, for she was the soul of candor." Finally, he confronted her with a brutal insight: "You derive a personal thrill out of the idea of being a revolutionary worker. It's sheer romanticism. Far more exciting than going home to Chicago and listening to symphony concerts! That's the truth of it. Whether the idea of revolution is correct or not doesn't matter; you've got to have your thrill." A few weeks later, she died.

In 1935, her name was revived when Sheean published one of the great best-sellers of the decade, *Personal History,* in which he recounted the saga of Rayna Prohme. But her involvements with men were secondary to her role as a radical example; Sheean, for his part, had seen her as the dominant member of the Prohme couple, and he wondered if William Prohme's "presence in China in his present role was due to the accident of his marriage to Rayna." As Sheean's own prose attested, more than anybody else of her time Rayna Prohme, who combined the daring of Homer Lea with the background of Anita Whitney, was a potent symbol of the new, post-World War California generation, drawn to world revolution as defined by the Comintern.

On California ground, Emanuel Levin and his comrades had soon taken up a new area of activity: an attempt to save Nicola Sacco and Bartolomeo Vanzetti, two Italian anarchists, from the electric chair. This pair, who were associated with the ultrarevolutionary Galleani group, had been convicted of murder in a Massachusetts payroll robbery, and the campaign on their behalf loomed large in American as well as foreign radical circles. Begun by anarchists, this solidarity effort was increasingly manipulated by the Communists, but in any event Sacco and Vanzetti were executed in August 1927. San Francisco and Los Angeles saw demonstrations in their behalf; in the former city, most of the marchers were arrested, Levin excepted.

In addition to the Sacco-Vanzetti case, Communists and radicals, along with many California liberals and even some conservatives, harbored a longer-lasting concern with the fate of Tom Mooney. By now San Quentin's most famous convict, Mooney had demanded a full and public retrial, but such a proceeding never took place. In the meantime, his defense continued to expose aspects of his case that could only disgrace California. The Mooney affair, even more than the suppression of the I.W.W. or the Whitney agitation, gave the state's authorities an enduring black eye. One disclosure after another showed that then San Francisco district attorney Fickert had worked a frame-up from the beginning, aimed as much or more at Alexander Berkman than at Mooney. Liberal opinion throughout the United States clamored for Mooney's release, if not his pardon, but the state's governors, through the 1920s and most of the 1930s, refused their petitions. For his part, Mooney welcomed support from all quarters but was wary of the Communists, although not unsympathetic to the Soviet Revolution.

In 1928 the Mooney case assumed a weird direction when he was joined in San Quentin by one of the strangest figures in the history of California radicalism, a convicted burglar named Arthur Margolis, who called himself, at various times, Arthur Scott and Arthur Kent. Scott (the name he used most) was the son of a fabled San Francisco restaurateur, Pierre-Joseph Margolis, who ran an establishment called Pierre's Chateau on Baker Street near the Presidio. Arthur Scott was reputedly a gifted musician who quarrelled with his father and left home, studying in Europe and at Yale University with no support from his family. Out of filial anger, he legally changed his name. He seems to have performed in a Los Angeles orchestra and joined the Musicians' Union before he got caught robbing houses in Beverly Hills. He was sentenced to four years in San Quentin.

Once behind bars there, Scott began frequenting a rather distinguished company. He befriended Mooney, but also met J. B. McNamara and Matt Schmidt, the anarchist belatedly tried and convicted as McNamara's accomplice. Scott won Mooney's confidence to such a point that the young burglar took charge of the clandestine mimeographing of Mooney's papers, inside prison walls.

California in the 1920s had a few other prominent friends of the Soviet experiment, "fellow travelers" who fit neither the activist niche of a Whitney or Levin, nor the larger-than-life category occupied by Mooney and Rayna Prohme. One of these was Joan London. Famous although by no means flamboyant, she was the daughter of Jack London and his first wife, Bessie Maddern. The great author, who comes down to us as one of the unqualifiedly worst fathers in history, had married Maddern, an Oakland schoolteacher, in 1900. Joan was born the next year, followed by a second daughter, Becky. London left his family in Oakland while he pursued assignments as a war correspondent and worked on his books. But a worse problem for Maddern and the two girls arose from London's involvement with other women, first with the socialist Anna Strunsky and then with an adventuress, Charmian Kittredge. Bessie Maddern divorced London, naming Strunsky as respondent, but Kittredge ended up at the writer's side and remained with him until his death.

The bitterness felt by Maddern could not but affect her daughter Joan London, although a worse toll seems to have been taken by her father's outbursts of manic rage. London once threw Joan's little sister through a window; Joan, whose resemblance to her father was so exact she could not look in a mirror without being reminded of him, never resolved her feelings about this family conflict. But she made a life for herself; she married several times, first to an Oaklander, Park Abbott.

Her second husband was an assistant professor of Slavic languages at the University of California at Berkeley, Charles Malamuth. Malamuth, more than Joan London herself, seems to have felt the Soviet appeal; he also seems to have upset his academic superiors by his public statements in support of Moscow. But although the couple was a presence in the Bay Area Left of the 1920s, neither would play a major role until the middle 1930s.

Other exponents of pro-Moscow California gentility included Lincoln Steffens and his wife Ella Winter, who took up residence in Carmel. Steffens was then the most famous Sovietophile in America; returning from Russia in 1919, he uttered the most quoted (and arguably the most irresponsible) phrase about Bolshevism ever spoken by an American, "I have been over into the future, and it works." He met Winter, a young woman from Australia who worked for a peace group in Paris and had studied at the London School of Economics, and fell hard for her, even though she was much younger than he. In a gambit that would certainly have amused Sigmund Freud, he tried to repress his feelings about her by referring to her by a man's name, Peter, which stuck throughout their life together. (She was rather masculine in appearance.) They married, traveled around Europe and had a son, who was called Pete, "after his mother, Peter," as Steffens wrote guilelessly. Like the London-Malamuth ménage, Steffens and Winter may be said to have coasted through the 1920s. Similarly, Upton Sinclair, who was favorable to the Soviets but was mainly involved in writing his many books, endorsed some Comintern "front" organizations, but was otherwise inactive. In such circles, there was as yet no compelling reason to carry Bolshevik sympathies beyond the realm of theory.

But parallel with the salon existence of Sinclair, the Steffenses, and the Londons, Russian Communism had already begun to involve certain Californians in its darker side. In American Indian art, one sometimes sees representations of ritual dancers in which the last figure in line is portrayed in a different mode, perhaps colored black while the rest are red. The dancer on the edge of the dance seems not a leader but half in another world, a born child of ambivalence, a weird changeling stuck among normal humans. Native Americans seem always to have taken such beings for granted; but white society has never overcome its fear of such ambiguity.

It is in such a light that we should approach the life of Tina Modotti, artist's model, photographer, and international Communist agent. In the line of dancers beginning with Anita Whitney, Modotti is the figure at the opposite end of reality, on the border of unreality.

Tina Modotti was born in Italy in 1896. Just before the World War broke out her family moved to San Francisco, where her father ran a photography studio. She lived near the corner of Filbert and Fillmore Streets in the Marina, a fashionable San Francisco neighborhood. In her early twenties, she went to Hollywood where she worked as a silent movie actress in "exotic" Latin roles. Soon, however, she met the photographer Edward Weston, who was seven years older than she. They fell in love; but, wishing her to be more than an amorous companion, Weston also pushed her to begin working in photography. In 1923, the year Rayna Prohme abandoned Hollywood and went with her second husband to China, Modotti followed a remarkably similar path; she moved to Mexico with Weston.

She was extraordinarily lucky. Weston was among the greatest of all photographers, and was especially important in the development of a California pictorial aesthetic using the still camera. Weston returned to California in 1926, but Modotti remained in Mexico, and in 1927 she joined the Communist Party. Almost immediately, while her camera work manipulating light and shadow assumed an impressive but propagandistic cast, she seems to have been drawn into the most shadowy region of Communist activity.

In 1929 Modotti was implicated in the assassination of her new lover, a Cuban Communist, Nicanor McPartland, who called himself Julio Antonio Mella. Julio Antonio Mella seems to have been drawn to Trotsky's views. When he was shot down on a Mexico City street, some who knew him—Cuban, Mexican, and otherwise—said that Mella had been killed on orders from Moscow. Beautiful, talented Tina Modotti, from San Francisco's Marina district, was the first California radical we know to have become ensnared in Soviet political terrorism. She was not the last.

———————

THE PANORAMA CHANGED abruptly for California's Communists in 1929. Suddenly they were in the public eye in a series of aggressive and, to most ordinary observers, often baffling incidents, some of which had a clearly anti-democratic character. That year saw the stock market crash that heralded the beginning of the Great Depression, and the closing of two large Ford automobile-assembly plants in San Francisco and Los Angeles. But the new ambitiousness of the California Communists originated elsewhere, almost as far from Moscow as from the western United States.

On July 27, 1929, two years after she was pardoned for her "criminal syndicalism" conviction, Anita Whitney, along with Emanuel Levin, defied police orders and led a demonstration in front of the Chinese Nationalist consulate in San Francisco to protest the attempted seizure of the Soviet-controlled Chinese Eastern Railway. Something was in the wind, for the California Communists had adopted a new, more provocative posture. Only two months later, a "near riot" in the "Skid Row" along Third Street in San Francisco produced more arrests. In October 1929, Whitney, according to local newspapers, led five hundred Communists who "stormed" the Oakland city jail demanding the release of nine of their comrades. These included a leader of the Young Communist League, the party's youth wing, Archie Brown, arrested for unauthorized distribution of handbills. No charges were pressed.

Communist street meetings proliferated in the Bay Area, occasionally including contingents in denim uniforms, and frequently leading to riot alarms by the police. On January 5, 1930, the Communists revealed their eagerness to deny the rights of others when a group of fifty erupted into a San Francisco meeting and, battling some two hundred non-Communist Russians gathered there, rushed the podium and assaulted Viktor Chernov, the exiled leader of the Russian Social Revolutionary Party and a democrat prominent in the 1917 Revolution. Chernov, a real hero to the Russian people, suffered cuts and bruises, as did Pavel Dotsenko, an exiled Russian democrat who lived for many years after in San Francisco. Seven Communists were arrested for assault. Some of them were arrested again in demonstrations in the next few weeks, in North Beach and elsewhere in the city, where slogans focusing on growing unemployment began to dominate the Communists' placards. An anti-Chernov riot also occurred in Los Angeles.

Communists in California and throughout the world had been put on a war footing in 1928. The real immediate issue was Japan. The broader Pacific, as an area in which to divert Tokyo's attention away from Russia, now loomed larger in Moscow's thinking than China, where Russia was forced to confront Japan as a direct competitor. At first, Pacific-area tasks, both legal and illegal, were assigned to the Australian Communists, who were a small but significant component in worldwide radicalism, Australia having elected Labor governments since 1910. In 1922, the Australian delegation to the Comintern, led by a man named J. S. Garden, proposed the establishment of a Pacific regional labor grouping, eventually founded as the Pan-Pacific Trade Union Secretariat, in mid-1927.

The "Pan-Pacific" was the most extraordinary of the many international "fronts" established by the Soviet régime. With money and personnel from the Far Eastern Bureau of the Comintern and official support from the New South Wales labor federation, it was ostensibly an advocate for trade unions in China, India, Japan, the Philippines, Korea, Indochina, and Java. In reality, however, it was an espionage agency for the Soviet government. Serious uses were found, for the first time, for American Communists in international revolutionary work, both legal and illegal, through the Pan-Pacific. California became the obvious safe haven for the Comintern's Pacific schemes. The principal American continuously involved in the Pan-Pacific would be Harrison George, a former Wobbly recruited to clandestine Soviet intelligence activity.

The effects of these international intrigues were many. In late 1929 or early 1930, a pudgy young woman, Elaine Russell, was caught in a Los Angeles police raid on a local Communist office. Russell figured in the small Communist milieu of that city, most of whose members were Russian Jews or their children, like her. Faced with arrest, she spontaneously took as her *klichka* Elaine Black, which she would use long afterward. She and her then husband were on a date and she was dressed up, and they were released by an officer who warned, "Don't ever let us catch you with these red Russian Bolsheviks again." Years later she recalled, "I don't know if there were any Russians there . . . it looked to me like there were more Japanese."

For the moment, she was correct; although the Japanese Communists later dispersed from California, they were the first serious Communist cadres in the state, and their influence never completely disappeared. Through most of the 1920s the publically known California Communists amounted to little more than the handful of former Socialists in San Francisco, the group of Russian Jews in Los Angeles, and a few Finns on the north coast. But Harrison George and his comrades, who moved the Pan-Pacific to California, also encountered a Japanese-speaking network, small yet already in place and far less isolated from the larger society than the Chinese-speaking Communists on the same Pacific coast.

While the Pan-Pacific was setting up shop in San Francisco, Communist district organizer Emanuel Levin had gone to New York, where, as one of the few military veterans in American Communist ranks, he participated in founding a major "front," the Workers' Ex-Servicemen's League (W.E.S.L.). In 1930 Levin became involved in a passport fraud coordinated by Max Bedacht, who was then the top liaison in the United States for the main clandestine Soviet "organs," and left California.

Levin was replaced as California district organizer first by William Simons, an undistinguished comrade, but then by another murky figure, Samuel Dardeck, whose *klichka,* the vaguely grandiose Samuel Adams Darcy, resounded through many major events in California over the next decade. Darcy was born in 1903 and entered the Communist movement early. He went to Moscow as a militant of the Young Communist League and studied at the Lenin Institute, the Comintern's training facility. He was inducted into the Comintern bureaucracy, or *apparat,* and spoke on anticolonial movements at the 1928 Sixth Congress, as a delegate of the American party as well as of the Comintern youth arm, the Young Communist International. He served the Comintern in the Philippines before returning to the United States.

Darcy was the first leader of the California Communists who could be considered a full-fledged product of the Comintern, with no other revolutionary past and no other known life. It is psychologically as well as politically revealing that so many of his generation of American Communists became known under *klichki* rather than by their own names. As Vincent Sheean had understood when he remonstrated with Rayna Prohme a few years earlier and many miles away, such habits clashed with the rigorous sense of honesty and candor that many radicals had previously cultivated and esteemed; they at least partially reflected an addiction to the thrill of clandestinity. Perhaps in part because of his lack of an encumbering past, Darcy looked like a dynamic party functionary in the mold most appreciated by the Comintern. He took over the California party in the fullest sense, directing strategy and tactics, signing public documents, and generally putting himself at the front of Communist activity. He arrived in California just as the Party, resting on the clandestine work of the Pan-Pacific, began for the first time to successfully expand its above-ground or overt field of action. Communists in California now shifted their open, propagandistic efforts away from international issues; in 1932 a local weekly was set up, the *Western Worker.*

And then a crisis emerged in California agriculture that provided the Communists with their first local opportunity for serious "mass work," the first real test of their revolutionary program.

THE CALIFORNIA FARM upheaval of the early 1930s and the Communist involvement in it reflected a variety of phenomena in the society of the time. Unemployed men and women streamed into California seeking work as field hands and provoked occasional conflicts over hiring and pay. But equally or even more important for the Communists, discontent among farm workers coincided with the first wave of new and young recruits to the movement, impelled, no less than were the unemployed, by the anxieties of the Depression.

Agricultural labor had been a focus of radical attention in the state since the Wheatland clash of 1913, but the first farm strike in which the Communists were active agitators began toward the end of 1932 in the fruit orchards of the Vaca Valley, after growers posted a wage cut for tree pruners. Organized by the Communist-controlled Agricultural Workers Industrial

League (A.W.I.L.), the walkout gained major press coverage with a riot in Vacaville, followed by the arrest of twelve organizers, including a young woman, Nora Conklin, and a former student at the University of California, Donald Bingham. The Vacaville affair became a national scandal when six men from among the arrested were abducted from jail and flogged. The International Labor Defense (I.L.D.), a legal support agency for the Communists, was loud in its involvement, but the strike ended without further dramatic developments, and the arrested were released.

In taking their revolutionary message to California's farmlands, young Communists like Conklin and Bingham often underwent a complete change in their mode of life. They left the radical milieux of the cities, with their debates and other cultural events, bookstores and clubby cafés for a world unto itself, one that began in darkness each morning as field workers assembled, long before sunup, for their day's labor. If the young agitators toiled in the crops themselves (which was rare, for often they were prevented from actually working either by their appearance of obvious inexperience or by failure to pay off a labor contractor) they learned just how demanding farm work had always been; they fell asleep late each night too exhausted to think, much less agitate, their bodies aching as if they had been beaten. If they stayed out of the fields and orchards, serving only as organizers, they ran the risk of arrest, real-life beating, and murder. They learned to wear hats and scarves against the sun; they encountered the raw entertainments and corruptions available to farm workers in the "skid rows" of the Central Valley towns, but they also met great beauty, in the land and in the people to whom they brought their form of solidarity. They learned the ultraradical traditions of the Mexican and Filipino farm workers.

These young Communists "went to the people" as radicals in Russia and other agrarian societies had done a generation or more before them. If ever there was an element of truth in the phrase "the romance of American Communism" it was there and then in California agriculture. They had already, in that epoch, encountered the rigid discipline the Party imposed on its members. They could face an internal hearing for such infractions as leaving, without Party permission, the town or city where they lived, and Darcy and their other commanders were constantly on the lookout for signs of sympathy for Trotsky and similar Communist dissidents. But their militancy also had its intellectual rewards; they went to the fields and orchards convinced of the dialectical certainty of Comintern policy, they were inspired by Communist martyrdom in China and elsewhere, and they bore with them a sense of intellectual transcendence that had never been present among the radicals of the past. They carried in their pockets such provocative works as the writings on Hegel of the German dialectician Karl August Wittfogel, one of the most brilliant Comintern intellectuals (and an influential China scholar).

An outstanding exemplar of that generation of California Communists was a Sacramento-born man in his early twenties, Norman Lawrence Mini. Mini was the son of a Southern Pacific office clerk. Thanks to his excellent high-school record he was accepted at West Point. There he remained from 1929 to 1932, when he was expelled for drunkenness at a football game, prohibition of alcohol still being in effect. He returned to Sacramento and joined the Communists. He was also a gifted writer of fiction, and his peculiar combination of talent and "failure" was not untypical of the young Communists of his generation. In the fall of 1932 he threw himself into the Party's agricultural campaign, a child of the great valley responding to a challenge that had always been present in the community in which he grew up.

An advancing social crisis was then visible throughout the nation. The year 1932 also saw a climactic march on Washington, D.C. by veterans demanding payment of an allegedly promised "bonus" for service in the World War. Levin and the Workers' Ex-Servicemen's League had sought to manipulate the bonus marchers, but other significant maneuvers were meanwhile taking place in the California background and in the secret Communist "underground." Arthur Scott, the convicted burglar who gained the confidence of Tom Mooney in San Quentin, had joined the Communist cell within the prison in 1931; after he was paroled he assumed the task of tying the Mooney case to the Party. Scott was joined by a woman he soon married, "Titian-haired" Norma Perry. With her and a handful of comrades including Benjamin Ellisberg, a former member of the Jack London Memorial Institute in San Francisco who had become a business agent for the Plasterers' Union, Scott took over the public activity of the Tom Mooney Molders' Defense Committee, the official Mooney solidarity group.

Scott began meeting frequently with Darcy and issuing shrill pro-Communist declamations in Mooney's name, including exaggerated attacks on Paul Scharrenberg and other A.F.L. leaders for their supposed inadequacy in Mooney's behalf. To the Communist leadership, the Mooney case was as good as or better than the Sacco-Vanzetti effort had been for the capture of broad support. Mooney himself was suspicious of the Communist *apparat* but trusted Scott; however, at one point he blasted Scott and his group for excluding any mention of the anti-Soviet anarchist Berkman from their materials on the case.

Nevertheless, in February 1932, with Mooney's blessing, Scott and Norma Perry accompanied Mooney's mother, Mary Mooney, on a month-long national publicity tour sponsored by the Communist I.L.D. The trip, to fourteen cities, was vastly successful, and led to a second and more extensive national tour as well as a journey by Mother Mooney to Russia in October 1932. From then on the Communists featured Mooney throughout their literature, even though he never joined the Party.

Almost overnight, it seemed, California had become a major arena for Communist activity. As 1932 came to a close Harry Hynes, an Australian-born illegal Comintern and KGB agent, with a fraudulent U.S. passport bearing his *klichka*, Harold Hall, and a phony birthplace in Pennsylvania, began one of the most effective of all the Communist operations in California, a mimeographed bulletin (known in Communist terminology as a "shop paper"), the *Waterfront Worker*. The *Waterfront Worker* combined more or less predictable Communist rhetoric with comments on the poor working conditions of sailors and longshoremen in the port of San Francisco. West Coast seamen, as previously described, had seen their proud organization, the Sailors' Union of the Pacific, crushed in 1921; a few still held the I.W.W. "red card" but most worked without a union, and were compelled to ship out through employer-controlled hiring offices, or "fink halls" and to carry employer-issued credentials known as "fink books."

Harry Hynes was joined in producing and distributing the *Waterfront Worker* by a fellow Australian, Harry Bridges, whose family had been involved in the Australian Labor Party and who had collaborated tangentially with the Communists in San Francisco since the early 1920s. Bridges, unlike Hynes, was not a Communist cadre, but he seemed to share the pro-Moscow sympathies of many other Australian Laborites. Most importantly, Bridges was involved with a group of longshoremen who were exploring ways out of the "blue-book union," a pro-employer or "company union."

The new labor ferment on the San Francisco docks reflected more than the blandishments of Hynes and the influence of Bridges. The most significant event of 1932, the election of President Franklin Roosevelt, brought a national wave of unionization. Soon after his inauguration in March 1933 the new chief executive promulgated the National Industrial Recovery Act, or N.I.R.A., section 7A of which provided federal recognition and protection of unions as employee representatives. This step, along with an improvement in the business cycle and renewed demand for labor, stimulated mainstream union leaders to begin recruiting unorganized workers on a larger scale than at any time since the 1880s.

At the end of January 1933, two months before the accession of President Roosevelt to power, another faraway event altered the direction of world history: the takeover of Germany by Adolf Hitler. Within weeks the immense German labor movement was brutally suppressed. In the United States a national industrial strike wave occurred in 1933 in which the Communists played almost no role; but farm strikers made their mark in California. Filipino laborers struck the lettuce fields at Salinas, and in April 1933 deputy sheriffs and state police officers battled strikers and their Communist supporters in the pea and spinach fields of Alameda and Santa Clara Counties. In Hayward, deputies bombed strikers with tear gas; in a piquant response, one woman resident of the area countered by pouring boiling water from a tea kettle on the officers. Unrest spread in June to the cherry-orchard district of Sunnyvale, and in July to the canneries in San Jose, which were just beginning to process the apricot harvest. A group of Communist organizers arrested at the canneries reappeared in the apricot orchards of Sunnyvale and Saratoga within an hour of their release.

A turning point came in mid-August 1933, in Tulare County, with a walkout by peach pickers at the Tagus Ranch, a major "corporation farm," or what would today be described as an "agribusiness" enterprise. Soon the whole San Joaquin Valley peach crop was threatened, as 5,700 orchard and packing workers joined the strike. The Tagus strikers demanded a forty-hour week in addition to 35 cents per hour in wages. The movement quickly spread as far north as Tehama County. Organizers were arrested at Chico in Butte County; at Gridley, strikers reportedly destroyed thousands of cases of spinach; a thousand Filipino lettuce workers again struck at Salinas; beetfield and sugar-refinery workers threatened to walk out.

Norman Mini recalled in *The Nation,*

As each new crop came along . . . small strikes took place. . . . In August, just as the peach picking was reaching its height, the pickers on the Tagus ranch . . . walked out. . . . Then the movement began to spread; soon the whole region was out . . . the union won its demands completely. The news of the workers' first big victory spread north with amazing speed. Wherever peaches were being picked, workers walked out. . . . Without organization, without any preparation, the workers struck. And in every case they won.

Soon the Communists' Cannery and Agricultural Workers Industrial Union (C.A.W.I.U.), as it had been retitled, filled the gap. According to Mini,

[T]he union became a statewide organization: its membership grew from a few doubtful hundreds in January [1933] to around 3,000 in July, and to more than 8,000 in August. . . . The showdown came in cotton. In the last weeks of September, with more than 20,000 workers concentrated in the cotton fields, the union issued a call for a general strike when the demands for higher wages and union recognition were refused. Almost before the growers knew what was happening, more than 18,000 pickers were out solidly on a front a hundred miles long, from Bakersfield to Merced. . . . The strike ended with victory for the workers. . . . That . . . put the union solidly on its feet. As the 1933 season ended, the membership was well over 20,000.

The farm strikes stimulated newspaper reporting of Communist exploits, particularly as gallant young women in the organizers' ranks came to the fore. Lillian Monroe, who led a strike of six thousand mainly Filipino and Mexican grape pickers at Fresno, was presented in the *San Francisco Chronicle* as a "fearless and fanatic Amazon." The large-eyed, diminutive, but fetching blonde Caroline Decker, aged 21, made a magnificent advertisement for the Communist cause as executive secretary of the C.A.W.I.U. and successor to the cotton-strike leadership after the arrest of the union's state organizer, Pat Chambers, for "criminal syndicalism." The liberal *San Francisco News,* a Scripps-Howard paper, described her in Tulare, "bent over a rickety desk in a bleak, dirty office cluttered with broken chairs and boxes of supplies lighted by one feeble oil lamp that casts weird dancing shadows on walls plastered with Communist posters." She had in her hands, the paper said, "the immediate destinies of 10,000 Mexican, Negro and white cotton strikers."

The *News* evoked

> dark, gaunt faces peer[ing] at her through the dim light, watching her work, eagerly heeding her short, clipped words.
>
> "Afraid?" she was asked.
>
> "No, they are my comrades," she says simply.
>
> She clenches her tiny fist and raises it in salute.

Such reportage, even more than the martyrdom of Communists in China or in Nazi Germany, brought many more young people to the Communists.

The California growers were not without the means to fight back. Clashes with the forces of order multiplied; there were major assaults on agitators in places like Lodi, where a vineyard strike was suppressed by fire hoses, tear gas, and a mob that ran the strike leaders out of town.

The real battle came as 1934 began. According to Mini,

> In late January (1934) 3,000 lettuce pickers struck in the Imperial Valley. . . . All suspected organizers were arrested . . . the Imperial Valley "peace" officers defied Federal court injunctions and broke up all the workers' meetings. The strike was crushed. That was the beginning of the retreat. . . . In June the union made one last heroic stand . . . in the apricot orchards at Brentwood [Contra Costa county]. . . . When 400 workers turned out to picket . . . deputies calmly herded the entire group into a railroad cattle pen, picked out all the leaders, and escorted most of the rest to the county line. As a result of the strike wages were reduced from 20 cents to 15 cents an hour. After that the union folded up.

Indeed, the C.A.W.I.U. had been overtaken by events. In April 1934 the Sacramento County district attorney had begun an investigation that led to the arrest of Mini, Chambers, Decker, Nora Conklin, Donald Bingham, and thirteen other organizers on the familiar charge of "criminal syndicalism." In addition, the Communist Party leaders under Darcy had already shifted their attention to the San Francisco waterfront, where the Australian-style agitation of Harry Hynes and Harry Bridges was about to pay off in a most spectacular fashion. On May 9, 1934, some 12,000 West Coast longshoremen went out on strike, from the Pacific Northwest to San Diego. California radicalism would never be the same.

――――――――

THE GREAT WEST Coast Maritime Strike of 1934 remains an event of considerable weight in the chronicles of American labor. It marked the beginning of the recent history of San Francisco. Even more than the *Los Angeles Times* bombing of 1910, the 1934 strike had an exceptionally long-lasting impact. In its aftermath, the Communists gained enormous influence in the regional labor movement, which never completely dissipated.

The maritime strike proved to be bigger than even the most optimistic Communists expected. The striking longshoremen were joined in the walkout by thousands of seamen. The San Francisco Industrial Association, acting at the behest of the waterfront employers, rushed to hire strikebreakers and to reassure themselves and the press that port operations would soon be back to normal. *Pacific Shipper,* a trade weekly published in San Francisco, was much less sanguine. After ten days, it noted, "work accomplished by strikebreakers, many of them inexperienced and laboring under unfavorable circumstances, was by no means comparable to the numbers actually employed. In some cases, at the Northwest ports, the operators themselves ordered the workers to desist as a precaution against violence to them." The strike had caused "partial strangulation" of California commerce and a "blockade" in the Northwest, with most of the lumber industries shut down and the fruit and vegetable growers loud in their complaints.

More importantly, however, *Pacific Shipper* found evidence of deep disaffection in the struck communities: while it reported that "good order" was maintained by the police in San Francisco and Los Angeles, such efforts were "vastly less successful" in Portland and Seattle; there the police were reluctant to confront the strikers, many of whom were the officers' neighbors, friends, and relatives. (The San Francisco police, others said, were accommodating to the strikers until a riot in front of the Marine Service Bureau, the local "fink hall" employing seamen, sent two officers to the hospital.) The Northwest strikers had begun talking about a general strike if troops were called in, and dockers in British Columbia were considering joining the movement.

The strike embodied the resurgence of the Pacific Coast's mainstream labor movement rather than the efforts of Communist agitators. The (revived) Sailors' Union of the Pacific's strike committee warned the strikers against propaganda by the press and provocations by the employers. "Just remember to think for yourself," the committee insisted, concluding with a jab at the typically anonymous mimeographed handouts by the Communists: "Watch for the strike bulletin. It will be issued regularly. . . . We are not afraid to sign our names to our news, either."

Beyond the doubts about the local police originally entertained by the *Pacific Shipper*, the maritime strikers understood something that the waterfront employers and the daily press did not clearly perceive or did not want to face: by the time the strike reached the beginning of its third month, at the end of June, public opinion had moved overwhelmingly to the side of the unions. No ports had been "opened." The Northwest was completely shut down, with strikebreakers entirely gone from the scene, and in San Francisco and Oakland the strike was stronger than ever, although the work stoppage was almost "nonexistent" on the San Pedro docks.

On June 26, President Roosevelt appointed a National Longshoremen's Board to resolve the conflict. But the strikers themselves were now determined to spread the walkout by calling on the other unions on the West Coast to declare a general strike in case of further attempts to forcibly open the ports. In San Francisco, a Joint Marine Strike Committee decided that all pickets would march together, in joint lines, and each picket would be provided three meals per day. Andrew Furuseth, meanwhile, arrived in San Francisco from Washington and told a meeting of the Sailors he had "hoped and prayed for this strike for a long, long time," and was pleased that the seamen had gone "into it with our heads, instead of being dragged into it by our heels."

The "opening" of the port of San Francisco, after being put off, was rescheduled for July 2, a Monday. That day, however, 20,000 strikers and their sympathizers blocked the Embarcadero, and no attempt was made to move freight through the picket lines. On Tuesday, July 3, San Francisco police chief William J. Quinn ordered the public away from the waterfront, but the Joint Marine Strike Committee called on nonstriking unions to send their unemployed members to join the lines. At Pier 38 on the Embarcadero the Atlas Drayage Company, an entity set up by the Industrial Association, had trucks ready to move.

Nothing significant happened on the morning of July 3; then, a little after 1:00 P.M., the sound of vehicle engines was heard inside Pier 38. Police had pushed the mass of strikers back from the waterfront; but now, hearing the noise from the pier, the strikers shouted threats. Cobblestones flew, and as the huge door of the pier began to rise, the strikers pushed forward, screaming, throwing rocks, and swinging crude clubs. Police hit back, using their nightsticks at will. Maritime historian Felix Riesenberg, Jr., a witness to much of the action, wrote,

> In a cloud of dust the strikers were fighting furiously with every kind of weapon, short of firearms, forcing back the law. Police lieutenants bawled new orders; a barrage of tear-gas bombs broke in the strikers' ranks. Choking, the men fell back, shaking their fists, hurling vile epithets at the policemen. On the fringes, cars full of strikers raced off after Atlas trucks, their running boards lined with shouting sailors, longshoremen, and radicals. Beaten by the tear gas, small parties stormed along Brannan, Townsend, and King Streets. Drivers without union buttons were pulled from their seats and beaten, men in side streets were roughly questioned. Five o'clock brought temporary peace. Casualties from that first day of open fighting numbered twenty-five, thirteen of them police.

July Fourth was mainly quiet in San Francisco; the Industrial Association announced, in newspaper ads, THE PORT IS OPEN. However, on that day railroad crews who switched Embarcadero freight walked off the job.

The next morning, July 5, hundreds of pickets were in place along the waterfront, with thousands more spectators lured to the scene by newspaper headlines. "Excited, swearing groups hustled past silent pier fronts, moving along like low-flying storm-clouds," Riesenberg wrote. "Men stopped to pick up loose bricks, and strike cars raced by, carrying strategists." Policemen had donned gas masks. A little after 8:00 A.M., a truck drove out of Pier 38, and a mighty shout rose from the crowd as the strikers attacked. It was war.

Boxcars were set afire on the nearby rails as strikers descended on police, who fired tear gas and swung their clubs. Blood flowed and a haze of red seemed to settle on the battlefield. Ambulances screamed back and forth; the spectators fled as the enraged strikers were forced away from the waterfront into the downtown office district. This day would hence be known in San Francisco labor tradition as Bloody Thursday. Fighting continued until noon, and resumed after lunch(!) Dozens of strikers heaved rocks at the police from Rincon Hill, overlooking the Embarcadero. Members of the public were felled by tear gas and police clubs, and resentment was vocal, even among the bystanders. The police began showing fear, firing their weapons into the air. Everything changed at that moment: according to Riesenberg, "Protesting shrieks trembled the entire length of the waterfront. 'They're killing now! They're using guns!'" On Mission Street at Steuart, outside the longshore strike headquarters, three men were felled by police guns, and two died: a longshoreman, Howard Sperry, and a Greek Communist cook, Nick Counderakis, known as Bordoise.

But the fighting did not cease. Clerks fled the office buildings in the battle zone, sickened by tear gas and bloodshed. Nausea gas doubled men over, leaving pools of vomit. The strikers were covered with sweat and blood and dust, their clothes often in tatters. Combat continued, but Republican Governor Frank Merriam had called out the California National Guard, and by late evening its troops appeared in the streets of San Francisco.

The deaths of Sperry and Counderakis and the arrival of troops brought a pause to the Golden Gate city. The general strike was now seen not only as necessary to protest the presence of the National Guard, but also as a memorial to the dead, and as a means to force the employers to climb down. Sailors' Union leader George Larsen (who, throughout this period, was continuously attacked by the Communists with a rhetoric only slightly less brutal than that they employed against Furuseth) wrote to union officer Carl Carter in Portland, "Yesterday was the worst yet; it was real war with two killed and a number wounded, many of them seriously. It was a complete change of tactics on the part of those sworn to uphold law and order; it seems to work only one way, and for one class."

On July 9, another Monday, Sperry and Counderakis were buried in a deeply impressive funeral procession that all commentators agree played a major role in bringing wavering elements among the public over to the strikers. At the end of the week, the San Francisco Labor Council and Building Trades Council met with the maritime delegates, and a general strike was called for July 16.

The general strike began in an orderly fashion, although by this time the daily press had worked itself into full-blown hysteria over the specter of a Communist revolution. This approach helped the Communists much more than it hurt them, for it increased their credibility with the rank and file of the labor movement. However, the Communists were still a minority in the strike leadership, and the attitude of the majority of strikers was anything but pro-Soviet. On July 17, Charles Quentin, a marine fireman, wrote in a union bulletin,

> We are fighting for decent living conditions, and the right to safe liberty and the pursuit of happiness. Our adversaries are the shipowners, and the San Francisco Industrial Association. We are not fighting against innocent women and little children! A general strike is a desperate remedy, and can easily lead to unforeseen terror, misery and starvation. It is intended as a gigantic mass protest of all labor, against unjust grievances. Let us take care that we are not carried away by our enthusiasm or our bitterness, to the extent of harming the innocent. A General Strike is aimed at the capitalistic interests . . . and not at our brothers of the working classes. . . . Remember at all times to do *your own thinking*.

Quentin also listed the many things that "because of the general strike . . . you can't do in town: Go to the movies, Call a taxicab, Get your trousers pressed, Buy gasoline, Eat in a hotel dining room, Get a shave or haircut, Buy fresh vegetables, Have your automobile repaired, Board a boat for Tahiti or even Los Angeles, Move your household goods, Get your shirt washed, Go to a nightclub." Among the few union members not on strike were the railroad workers on the Southern Pacific, Santa Fe, and Western Pacific lines.

The San Francisco general strike was called off on July 19. Two days later, the Teamsters, who did not officially join the maritime strike but had honored the picket lines, returned to work. The general strike seemed to make some kind of accommodation imperative, and the Labor Council leadership acted in that spirit. In San Francisco, the Communist-Bridges group among the longshoremen agreed to a vote on the imposition of arbitration by the President's board, with the strike to end. The Communists now seemed intent on defusing the struggle, although the longshore strikers in the Northwest, who were not immediately informed of the proposed arbitration vote, and the seagoing unions favored continued resistance. Nonetheless, on July 25, the longshoremen voted by 6,388 to 1,471 to return to work. Furuseth argued that the Industrial Association had tricked the unions into the general strike, which had weakened the maritime movement.

On July 29 the longshore labor leaders appeared before a mass meeting of the Sailors' Union, and Harry Bridges warned, "I think that the longshoreman is ready to break tomorrow. I don't think that they will last. They have had enough of it." Bridges repeated several times his belief that at least a hundred striking longshoremen would return to work the next day. The Sailors then listened as a letter was read from the Shipowners' Association promising to negotiate with the union, discharge strikebreakers, employ strikers without discrimination, and seat a union representative in the "fink hall." Paul Scharrenberg had replied that the "fink halls" must shut down altogether, which the employers then accepted.

Without the longshoremen and the Teamsters, the seafaring unions could not continue the strike, and that night the Sailors voted to submit their grievances to arbitration, with one additional proviso: the hated "fink books" would be publicly burned the next day. On July 30, the Sailors' Union leadership authorized a return to work. The greatest strike in the history of the Pacific Coast was over.

Socialists have observed for generations that such mass strikes take on a life of their own and become a microcosm of revolution. Of no strike in American history is this truer than the 1934 maritime struggle. The strikers ended the walkout without full satisfaction of their demands, but with their organizations reborn and with a more combative attitude than ever before. The experience profoundly changed all and each of them, and their neighbors. In the wake of the strike, it became clear throughout the Western states that labor had propelled itself to the center of society. The maritime unions became the regional focus for labor actions in other industries, with, for example, striking miners in Alaska calling for maritime support. Through the rest of the 1930s, strikes and union organizing campaigns continued apace in California, in every industry as well as, resuscitated, in agriculture. In nearly every such instance, local labor turned to the maritime unions for help. The movement also marked the beginning of an "industrial" unionism that seemed to far exceed the hopes of the I.W.W. Above all, the movement remained a movement after the strike. The energies of the maritime workers did not immediately dissipate; rather, the movement advanced, at least temporarily, as the maritime workers recognized and utilized their new influence over the public. Indeed, the strike created a completely new political atmosphere, especially in California.

In September 1934 the "industrial" tendency in the movement produced a preliminary meeting to discuss a Maritime Federation of the Pacific

Coast, uniting all the waterfront unions, with the goal of a single contract with a single expiration date for all affiliates. This had been the great dream of the Wobblies on the coast, thwarted a generation before by craft rivalries between longshoremen and seamen. Unfortunately, however, a new competition now existed, one between the Communists and non-Communists.

The Communists, for their part, were rather overwhelmed by the whole affair. Although Darcy and his cohort took advantage of the situation to proclaim that they had led the strike from top to bottom, the revolution that had taken place actually had little in common with their conceptions.

HARRY BRIDGES AND his Communist acolytes should have been quite satisfied to emerge from the 1934 events in the ascendant in the San Francisco longshore union and with an unarguable influence in the broader ranks of West Coast labor. But the Communists lacked what they most wanted, namely control. According to David "Butch" Saunders, a seaman who became a Communist waterfront organizer, "After the 1934 strike, a struggle for power took place in the [Sailors'] Union between the Reds and the IWW faction." This split soon affected all the maritime unions, and was less a matter of the ideology of the Communist Party versus that of the Industrial Workers of the World than of the rigid "top-down" Communist bureaucracy versus the rank-and-file maritime workers. As we have seen, by that time the I.W.W. hardly existed as an organization, although many non-Communists in the maritime "class of 1934" were proud to be labeled Wobblies. Certainly, "Think for yourself"—the guiding principle of the Sailors and Marine Firemen in 1934—could no more appear in Communist Party literature than, for example, advice to buy stock in General Motors.

If the political history of California in the 1930s is that of the Communists, it may also be argued that the fate of the Communists, and of the California left, was in great part determined by the outcome of this waterfront labor rivalry. The mass strike had grown out of workplace resentments among the ordinary longshoremen and sailors, but for the Communists, even after the great conflict, the global agenda of the Comintern came far ahead of quotidian waterfront grievances. Even during the strike, whereas within the Sailors' Union and other seagoing organizations proposals for action either originated with or were fully discussed by the rank and file, Bridges and his Communist allies habitually made decisions in secret sessions away from the longshore members, and attended union meetings simply to effect their will. Indeed, Bridges and his circle had sought to call off the strike early, with the dockworkers' demands still unsatisfied, in order that the movement not escape their influence.

In the event, however, the Communists were enjoying their immense new prestige in the flush of post-strike euphoria. The main object of this sympathy was Bridges himself, whom the dailies in San Francisco had made to seem the outstanding leader of the struggle. Many aspects of the 1930s made the decade different from those before, above all in the style of the era's radicals, but nothing stands out more obviously than the fascination of the press and public of the day, perhaps influenced by the rise of cinema, with "personalities." Eugene Debs, Jack London, Alexander Berkman, and other rebel heroes of the past had been deeply loved and admired, but the level of adulation extended to the person of Harry Bridges was something novel, reminiscent of the leader-worship surrounding Mussolini, Stalin, and Hitler.

Most of this glorification was owed to the need of the daily press for a dramatic figure who would symbolize the march of events and provide a reference point in the middle of confusing developments. However, Bridges had other qualities that gave him an advantage as an up-and-coming union leader. As an Australian, he knew far more than the average American about radical labor struggles, and could think far ahead of his peers. Also as an Australian he had gained the full confidence of Harry Hynes, the Comintern agent, whose status within the Communist ranks, so long as he was present on the scene, exceeded that of almost everybody, even at times that of Darcy. Unlike other union leaders who joined the Communists, Bridges could not simply be used and tossed aside. Thus Bridges possessed an amazing degree of self-confidence.

Unfortunately, however, Bridges' Australian origin was also a liability; he was not then an American citizen, and before long, in February 1935, New York Republican congressman Hamilton Fish launched a long-running, and ultimately unsuccessful, campaign to deport him as an "alien Communist." The Communists understood very well that such an effort could be exploited and that a persecuted Bridges, following after Mooney, Sacco and Vanzetti, and other labor martyrs, could acquire even greater authority and popularity. Bridges managed, in proceeding after proceeding, as we shall see, to discredit evidence of his individual Party membership, although he freely acknowledged his close association with Communists and his enthusiasm for their line. Many, particularly at the beginning of this legal odyssey, chose to stand by Bridges.

The Communist and sympathizing milieu rallied to Bridges, although certain comrades had expressed doubts about the entire waterfront enterprise during the strike. The various *apparats* had come into conflict about how to handle it, with Harrison George, the former Wobbly in charge of the Pan-Pacific in San Francisco, issuing lengthy polemical letters denouncing Darcy and, by implication, Bridges for their alleged tactical errors. The only result of George's criticism was that he himself was removed from direction of the San Francisco branch of the Pan-Pacific in 1935 and replaced by another remarkable Comintern operative, Rudolf Blum, whose *klichki* or aliases apparently included Bradford, Betford, and, most frequently, Raymond or Rudy Baker. As Bradford, he had been chosen unanimously by top Comintern functionaries including the head of the Japanese Communist Party, Sanzo Nosaka (*klichka* Okano), to replace Harrison George in directing the Pan-Pacific and its Japanese cadre in California. Nosaka, the successor to Sen Katayama in the Comintern leadership and the most important of all these conspirators, had come to California secretly in 1934, using identification borrowed from U.S.-born Japanese, and remained here underground until 1935, directing a considerable range of Communist publications in Japanese.

By contrast with the headstrong George, Rudolf Blum or Rudy Baker was of a phlegmatic nature. Born in 1898 in what would become Yugoslavia, he emigrated to the United States as a teenager and gained U.S. citizenship through his father, a member of the Socialist Party. He had worked in factories, served prison time as a striker, been arrested for antiwar activities, and belonged to the I.W.W. A founding member of the American Communist Party, Baker joined the Soviet Communist Party while in Moscow in 1928–30. He had served as an illegal agent in Korea as well as in Canada and Britain.

Baker was, more than Harrison George, the type preferred for major Comintern responsibility. But George's removal principally demonstrated that a strain of "California localism" had appeared among the Communists, with Hynes, Darcy, Bridges, and others on the scene forging their own strategy; this separatism, traceable to the importance of the Pacific Rim in illegal Comintern work (in contrast with the European-based concerns of the above-ground American Communist leadership), remained visible throughout the rest of California Communist history.

Outside the hidden, illegal Pan-Pacific *apparat,* hundreds of fresh, young San Francisco longshoremen and seamen signed up as party members after 1934. Beyond the myth of the Communists' role in the strike other phenomena came into play. The columns of the *Western Worker* made political events in China, Spain, and other distant places seem close and comprehensible; such a practical expression of Marxist "internationalism" had been absent from radicalism before, except among the Wobblies. The new Communist adherents, while flushed with a sense of global importance, lacked both the social consciousness and the political experience of the earlier Socialists and Wobblies; indeed, they rejected the lessons of radical history. As described in another time and place by an observer of great wisdom, the Nicaraguan poet Pablo Antonio Cuadra, they believed history began with them: Communist ideology was

> presumptuously presented as an expression of the "modern." All the expensive fireworks of "progress" were set alight in its propaganda. They were advancing in every way. They represented the New. By contrast, local culture was accused of being a tradition of failure, and through a senseless and total negation of the past, what was deemed good was the new (something that has not happened yet) and the bad was defined as everything from the past.

Simultaneously with the great labor eruption of 1934, a small and varied but extremely significant group of creative intellectuals, both Communists and pro-Communist "fellow travelers," as they were called, emerged in California. The California Communists, unlike those in New York, had previously had little interest and less success in attracting radical aesthetes. Nationally, in autumn 1932, some fifty writers, artists, and similar professionals appealed to their colleagues to support the Communist candidates in that year's presidential election, William Z. Foster and James W. Ford. This campaign, although neither great in size nor enduring, nonetheless was a unique one; it was the most impressive Communist activity ever undertaken in America, at least in terms of intellectual history, for the catalogue of Foster and Ford's endorsers included such widely known and respected writers as Sherwood Anderson, Countee Cullen, John Dos Passos, Sidney Hook, Langston Hughes, Matthew Josephson, James Rorty, and Edmund Wilson.

With pro-Communist artists and writers scarce on the West Coast, it is unsurprising to find only seven California names on the Foster-Ford slate. Aside from the peripatetic Lincoln Steffens and Ella Winter, who could hardly qualify as real intellectuals in spite of their Carmel pretensions, the group included a former Socialist, the Reverend Robert Whitaker, and Miriam Allen DeFord, a labor journalist. Two Hollywood names appeared: Emjo Basshe, a Russian working in the film industry and fairly high-ranking "fellow traveler," and Samuel Badisch Ornitz, author of an "anonymous biography," *Haunch Paunch and Jowl,* published in 1923. Ornitz was also a screenwriter and seems to have been the first Communist to exercise that trade in Hollywood, having been hired by Metro-Goldwyn-Mayer in 1929. The seventh member of the group was the most significant: Henry Dixon Cowell, the "eccentric" composer who, twenty years before, had begun a friendship with Jaime de Angulo.

Like the young maritime workers who flocked into the Communist Party after 1934, Henry Cowell was enamored of the "new." But Cowell was more than an intellectual drawn into modernity by the rush of social and intellectual change; he was an authentic genius, an outstanding innovator in music, whose career stands as a quintessential example of the California intellect in every respect.

Henry Dixon Cowell was born in Menlo Park, California, in 1897. Other facts about his early life are difficult to establish; many fascinating details were put about over the years but some evade confirmation. His Irish-born father, Henry Clayton Blackwood Cowell, was a character out of the ordinary, a poet and much later a college instructor. The father temporarily deserted his family and young Henry was raised by his mother, an "other-worldly person and poetess," according to one newspaper account. She was said to have put him to work at 12, starving and pale, herding sheep in the hills of San Mateo County with a broken zither to entertain him. He had briefly studied the violin, beginning at age 5, but the gift of the zither transformed him. Young Cowell became obsessed with music; he saved his pay from sheepherding and occasional dishwashing, buying a second-hand piano for $60. He moved the piano to the log cabin in which he lived and began composing. Professor Charles Seeger of the University of California Music Department was hiking on a trail through the hills when he heard outlandish but beautiful sounds. Seeger pushed open the door of

the cabin and found, to his amazement, that a young boy was both performer and composer. Seeger introduced Cowell to a patron and arranged
for him to study at the university. A truly pioneering musicologist, Seeger
was the father of banjoist and long-faithful Communist Pete Seeger.

Whether the whole of this fascinating tale is true, it is beyond doubt
that Cowell's work as a composer began with virtually no formal training of
any kind; as the musicologist Gilbert Chase, a disciple of Charles Seeger
and admirer of Cowell, put it, the youthful composer relied "mainly on in-
tuition and experimentation." He had only a third-grade education, and in
addition to his experience in animal husbandry worked as a gardener, col-
lector of wild plants, and school janitor. But there was no lack of musical
stimulation in his environment: the organ heard in a local church, the Asian
modes that, trilling and cymbal-crashing, filled the streets of Chinatown,
and favorite Irish tunes sung by his parents. Chase has perceptively described Cowell's career as "a striking example of how beneficial it can be for
a composer to be exposed, during his formative years, to experiences that
open the way to uninhibited exploration of the varied and unorthodox
means of musical expression."

Musical history changed forever when, on March 5, 1914, Henry Cowell, still a teenager, performed on the piano at a concert in San Francisco.
Cowell played the piano with his forearm, the flat of his hands, and his fists,
producing what he called "tone clusters" including a whole octave, or two
octaves. "Tone clusters" in his later work required application of both fore-
arms to the keyboard at once; he also took to plucking the piano's strings,
and to giving combined performances on the keyboard and the piano
strings, using an assistant. At 20 he had produced almost two hundred
compositions including *The Tides of Manaunaun,* his most famous early
work, and two years later, in 1919, had probably completed a theoretical
study, *New Musical Resources.*

San Francisco was respectful, if a little uncertain, in the presence of
this prodigy. Newspaper critics tiptoed around the novelty of his methods
while comparing him, as an experimentalist who at the outset of his career
faced the world's incomprehension, with Beethoven, Wagner, and Stravin-
sky. But they also recognized his radicalism; indeed, Cowell's first finished
writings on harmony included a collaboration with Robert Luther Duffus,
one of Fremont Older's "literary fledglings," a reporter and editorial writer
at *The Bulletin* and *The Call* who not long after went to work for *The New*

York Times. In 1924 the *San Francisco Chronicle* described Cowell as "an unrepentant radical" who was "undisturbed by criticism," and his musical works as "weird and mysterious in their plangencies and provocative to the imagination."

Henry Cowell was one of those historical figures whose vision is so far ahead of his contemporaries' that he seems a throwback from the future, a beneficiary of a kind of "loop in time." In 1927, he began publishing the *New Music Quarterly* as a forum for experimental composers; he was an early partisan of Charles Ives. His fascination with non-European sources made him the great forerunner of what today we call "world music." But early in 1932, the year he endorsed the Communist presidential candidates, Cowell unveiled at events in New York and San Francisco an invention that anticipated further trends in music but also much more. Borrowing the concept of the "electronic eye," he had worked since 1929 with the Russian inventor Leon Theremin (previously the creator of the widely used electronic instrument named after himself) in building an instrument, the rhythmicon, intended to fully express the great complexity of Cowell's musical art through production of multiple simultaneous rhythms. However, the rhythmicon was extremely difficult to put to practical use and was not employed in performance until the 1970s, after Cowell's death.

Yet, as Gilbert Chase has written, Cowell "had truly become a prophet of the electronic era," not only in music, but in the broader technosocial evolution that led, not far from the hills where Cowell once herded sheep, to the growth of today's Silicon Valley. His compositions, considered bizarre in their time, were brooding but lyrical, melodious, and occasionally funny. The *New Music Quarterly* discovered and supported much younger experimentalists, including another remarkable composer, Harry Partch, born in Oakland and raised in southern Arizona. For a year, beginning in 1933, Cowell took as his student a young man born in Los Angeles, John Cage. Both Partch and Cage would contribute enormously to the reputation of California as a laboratory for American musical composition.

IN THE EARLY weeks of the 1934 maritime strike, the poet Kenneth Rexroth, a friend and admirer of Henry Cowell and a similar devotee of the "new," served as an instructor in art theory at the San Francisco Workers' School, an official Communist training center, in the Party headquarters at

121 Haight Street. The Workers' School was set up with the backing of
Steffens and Winter, along with Anita Whitney, Darcy, the former Socialist
and A.F.L. official Benjamin Ellisberg, and some other Communist functionaries. It was a typical specimen of a Communist school, such as would
come under investigation by federal and state authorities for decades afterward. It held sessions at night, mainly on the basics of Communist ideology. Introductory courses covered "Principles of Communism," "Marxian
Economics," "National and Colonial Problems," and the history of the Socialist and Communist movements. The school also offered a four-session
seminar on "Self-Defense in Courts" and an advanced class, open only to
members of the Party and the Young Communist League, in working-class
organizing.

Faculty listed in the school's literature included such prominent Communists as Darcy, Elaine Black, an American-born Japanese named Goso
Yoneda under his *klichka* of Karl Hama (although he later denied such a
role), and Sam Goodwin, speechwriter for Harry Bridges. Like the Jack
London Memorial Institute a decade and a half before, the Workers' School
also taught English and Russian, and had sections in creative arts, including
the lectures by the young poet Rexroth.

Kenneth Rexroth had come to San Francisco in mid-1927 with his wife
Andrée from Chicago, the waning capital of American Bohemia. His sharp-
imaged, beautiful verse was then published only in the littlest of "little" poetry reviews; he was younger, less gifted, and less original in his modernism
than his friend Henry Cowell. But Cowell was a precursor more than a
mentor; Rexroth, in contrast, was destined to exercise a far greater influence, in the long term, over the evolution of the California imagination. He
most resembled Cowell in that, as a young man, born in Indiana in 1905,
he had come under a wide range of nonconformist influences. Friends of
his semiradical middle-class family (his father was a pharmaceutical salesman) included Charles E. Ruthenberg, leader of the left-wing Socialists in
Ohio and the first head of the American Communist Party, who died in
1927, and Charles Fort, a fascinating creature who was once very famous as
a commentator on unexplained phenomena, such as rains of frogs and
blood, which he painstakingly inventoried and published in four compen-
dia, beginning in 1919 with *The Book of the Damned.* These personalities,
only two among a great many with whom Rexroth became acquainted either directly or at second hand, seemed to meld in his development:

Rexroth was equally a social revolutionary and a mystic, deeply curious about nature and an exceptionally acute observer of people and trends.

Synthesis was Kenneth Rexroth's great talent. Before coming West with Andrée he had enjoyed the jazzy Bohemia of Chicago until it was exhausted. The couple originally went from there to Seattle, with its small I.W.W.-oriented community of intellectuals, but they soon hitchhiked south with heavy packs on their backs. Once in San Francisco, the beauty and open spirit of the city took them over. They stayed, becoming active in the small, local experimental-poetry scene, guided by a pioneer of lesbian verse, Elsa Gidlow, who became one of Rexroth's longest-lasting friends. Soon the Rexroths had moved into the Montgomery Block, still the city's Bohemian hive as it was for *Les Jeunes* in the 1890s.

It is impossible to determine when Rexroth became a Communist. He offered conflicting accounts before his death in 1982; at one point he said he belonged to the Party from 1935 to 1938, but elsewhere he denied ever having been a member. However, he knew Emanuel Levin well, had an exceptional comprehension of Comintern activities in California, and in the early 1930s became an English-language "adviser" for *Rodo Shimbun (Workers' News),* a Japanese-language Communist paper edited by Goso Yoneda. Rexroth had a full acquaintance with a Soviet espionage ring run by a certain Richard Sorge, accurately describing the activities of the clandestine Japanese Communist cadre in a memoir written some decades later: "Inasmuch as the Japanese military government cropped the Japanese Communist Party, or rather mowed it like a lawn, the reserve echelons of the leadership were usually based in California, and unlike most representatives of foreign [Communist] parties, they mixed freely with the Japanese-American membership." Rexroth recalled, of his work with *Rodo Shimbun,* "We met in the back of a tempura parlor frequented by agricultural workers from the Sacramento-San Joaquin Valley and went over the English-language supplement word for word. . . . Of all the people around the [Communist] Movement, the Japanese and Japanese-Americans were by far the most lively, with a revolutionary ethic all their own . . . like the French anarchist youth" of a half-century ago.

Rexroth averred in his memoir that his encounter with the Japanese Communists in San Francisco had "changed his life," and he declared, "Most Japanese have a tremendous capacity for friendship, loyalty, and between the sexes . . . a great capacity for something that is passing from the

world: true erotic comradeship." He had, it seems, long been something of
a Japanophile, having been introduced while young to the poetry of Yone
Noguchi, the companion of *Les Jeunes.* But his transforming experience
with the Japanese Communists had an immense effect, for Rexroth became
the outstanding translator and interpreter of Japanese (and Chinese) poetry
into English; his versions are today an unchallengeable item of the literary
canon. His "real involvement" in Japanese language and literature began, he
later wrote, "with the young comrades of *Rodo Shimbun.*" It is extremely
unlikely that Rexroth would have been drawn into this Japanese circle, or,
for that matter, invited to teach at the Workers' School, if he had not already been a Communist.

Rexroth was also involved in other Communist activities, including front
organizations aimed at the unemployed and at San Francisco's then-small
Black population. He may even have helped produce the *Waterfront Worker.*
In the cultural area, he started the first John Reed Club, a Communist-lining
writers' association, in California, with Emjo Basshe, who counseled him
against attempting to recruit in Hollywood. Founded in New York in 1930,
the John Reed Clubs were scattered throughout the country. In 1933, soon
after Roosevelt's inauguration, Rexroth was invited to a meeting by another
friend, an expressionist painter called Bernard Baruch Zakheim.

Zakheim had summoned a group of artists, along with Rexroth, who
was an occasional painter, to discuss the desperate economic situation many
of them faced in the Depression. In an interview thirty years later, Zakheim
remembered,

> I was in Paris in 1932 having an "artist's sabbatical" when I read about the
> plight of the artists in the United States unable to find employment in their
> media. . . . When I returned to San Francisco I won a competition to do the
> fresco at the Jewish Community Center. . . . Because of my prestige with the
> Center mural, I was able to call a meeting of my fellow-artists, supported by
> Kenneth Rexroth. . . . I told the artists about local sculptor Beniamino Bu-
> fano threatening to commit suicide, and local artist Sergei Sherbakoff, who
> had an exhibit of his paintings at the Legion of Honor while he was on a
> [federal] project cleaning the toilets below the exhibit hall.

A second meeting was called at the studio of the painter Maynard Dixon,
the veteran of *Les Jeunes,* and a night telegram was sent to Washington, calling for a public works program to support painters.

Unknown to either Zakheim or Rexroth, a local businessman and artist, Edward Bruce, had been promoting the same concept, and the telegram was answered affirmatively. A pilot program, the Public Works of Art Project (P.W.A.P), had already been set up. Its first commission was for murals to decorate the Coit Tower, a monument on Telegraph Hill overlooking North Beach. Zakheim was hired for the project through another friend, the painter and sculptor Ralph Stackpole, who knew Edward Bruce.

Zakheim was, if not then a Communist, an extremely close "fellow traveler," who eventually joined the Party. Born in Poland in 1896, the son of a Hasidic Jew who became a successful wholesale butcher, Bernard was the youngest of ten children. His family hoped he would become a rabbi. When he was nine his father died; soon he began studying drawing and crafts in Warsaw, but his mother's piety forbade a career in art and he learned the upholstery trade. Nevertheless, Zakheim found a painting teacher, and then won a scholarship. By age 16 he had a studio and was working from live models. He entered the Warsaw Academy of Art, but after one year there he enlisted to fight in the World War. Captured by the Germans, he escaped after nine months and made his way to Munich.

There, in 1918, he encountered German Expressionist painting, then at its zenith. He continued to study, but, as with many of his contemporaries, the trauma of war, as well as intense anti-Semitism in the independent Poland that emerged after the World War, fortified his Expressionism. He came to the United States in 1920, proceeding almost immediately to the West Coast. Although he and his wife Eda spent time in Los Angeles they settled in San Francisco, where Zakheim gained success in custom furniture design and production. The business weathered the stock-market crash of 1929. However, he was a painter at heart and a radical, and a visit to San Francisco by Diego Rivera in 1930 led Zakheim to Mexico and work with the great revolutionary muralist.

Zakheim felt confused, torn between the academic manner of painting he had learned in Poland, the expressionism he imbibed in Munich, and the distinct "popular" style of the Mexican muralists, and it was to clear his mind that he went to Paris in 1931. When he returned he found that his furniture business, which he had left along with their two daughters in the care of his wife, had failed. Earning a living as a painter was now imperative, made somewhat easier by his contract to decorate the Jewish Community Center. Rexroth, for his part, considered Zakheim one of only two artists in

San Francisco at that time with whom he could communicate about the "new" in art.

With their P.W.A.P. commission Zakheim and Ralph Stackpole were joined by a brilliant group, chosen out of fifty applicants, to execute the Coit Tower murals. Many of them were disciples, or at least admirers, of Rivera's monumental revolutionary works. The Mexican artist's 1930 visit to San Francisco brought him a contract to paint the walls of the Stock Exchange Club, the first of three Rivera murals in the city. Rivera came with his companion, Frida Kahlo, and both developed a real love for the Bay Area, although some leading citizens objected to Rivera's attachment to Communism. (At that time Rivera was a follower of Trotsky rather than Stalin, having left the Mexican Party not long after the assassination of Julio Antonio Mella.) Of the group collaborating with Zakheim and Stackpole, Iowa-born Maxine Albro and a Russian immigrant, Victor Arnautoff, had studied with Rivera in Mexico, while a Spanish artist, José Moya del Pino, was associated with him in Europe during the World War. Another of the group, Clifford Wight, had assisted Rivera both on murals in Detroit, which Rivera had painted for a dissident Communist faction, and at Rockefeller Center in New York City on the famous—or infamous—mural with a portrait of Lenin at its center. The Rockefellers ordered the latter work covered after its completion and later had it destroyed.

This team of artistic radicals, which also included Lucien Labaudt, Ralph Chesse, Mallette Dean, and others, painted the walls of Coit Tower in a fashion that could not but inspire some and outrage others. Their themes included California's landscape, agricultural wealth, industrial power, and city life. The paintings were beautifully executed, and remain fine works of art. Here and there, however, their creators' main political orientation was clearly visible. In his lovely, Balthus-like fresco of "City Life," Arnautoff, who had a good command of light and tint, painted himself next to a newsstand with the Communist weekly *New Masses* and the *Daily Worker* on sale; John Langley Howard's "California Industrial Scenes" included May Day demonstrators, unemployed marchers, and angry gold panners glaring at rich tourists. The Hearst press in scandal-mongering articles accused Clifford Wight of attempting to include a hammer-and-sickle emblem. The worst such article fortuitously appeared on July 5, 1934, the day of the "Bloody Thursday" fighting on the waterfront! The apparent blossoming of muralistic Marxism in Coit Tower could only feed the nightmares of those who saw in the maritime strike the beginning of a Communist seizure of power.

From both a political and a historical viewpoint, however, the outstanding panel remains Zakheim's "Library," the only Expressionist work among the Coit Tower murals and a favorite of visitors. It, too, includes newspapers, here being read by library patrons, with one headline referring to a Socialist uprising in Austria and another dealing with the destruction of Rivera's mural at Rockefeller Center. Most significantly, Zakheim portrayed John Langley Howard crumpling a newspaper while pulling Marx's *Capital* off the shelf, spelling out the challenge the group believed faced their generation. At the center of the panel, shelves display books by radical authors such as John Dos Passos and the today forgotten Communist Granville Hicks, along with a volume by the sophisticated, Western-oriented Bolshevik theoretician Nikolai Bukharin, author of the program of the Russian Communist Party; his red-bound tome on *Historical Materialism* was a favorite among the young Communists of the time, but he would die at Stalin's hands four years later. In a yet more piquant and resonating detail, Zakheim painted in Rexroth, standing on the library stepladder and fingering the spines of books by authors most of whose names he had suggested to Zakheim. Zakheim even put on one of the shelves a fairly thick book bearing Rexroth's name, although Rexroth had yet to publish any books.

The Coit Tower murals were opened to the public in October 1934 after a considerable degree of bickering in the city's Art Commission, a temporary closure of the tower, some censorship, press claims that the Tower would be used as a vantage point for the waterfront strikers to attack the Embarcadero, and demonstrations by the muralists and their friends, organized in an Artists and Writers Union with Rexroth as its secretary. Most people who viewed the murals liked them quite a bit, and still do—although their presentation and upkeep today leave much to be desired.

The Communists could therefore now boast an impressive following in the arts as well as in labor. But the majority of Californians, while hurting from the Depression and jolted by the maritime strike, still looked elsewhere for political leadership. Communism also had a few revolutionary competitors under its nose, so to speak, in the shadow of Coit Tower. The North Beach district was a gathering place for an assortment of radical types; the Workers' School had an extension program there, and seamen, such as the Communist organizer "Butch" Saunders, favored the cheap restaurants and lodgings in the Italian community over the dives on the Embarcadero. Saunders regularly delivered soap-box speeches in North Beach and regularly went to jail with a band of comrades. He later recalled with amusement that after one police roundup a well-known Communist, Levon Mosgofian, whose appearance was anything but Irish, supplied an Irish alias and was threatened with a beating by an offended Irish cop.

No less a personage than Anita Whitney had moved to Russian Hill and joined the North Beach branch of the Party, appearing at street meetings where her speeches were translated into Italian and Chinese. But North Beach was never conquered by the Communists. Among the Italians, as well as in the small Spanish enclave on Broadway between Little Italy and Chinatown, the "older" anarchists had never lost their appeal. An Italian anarchist, Vincenzo Ferrero, published a monthly, *Emancipazione.* Ferrero proposed to a Romanian Jewish anarchist who had come to California, Shmuel Marcus, who called himself Marcus Graham, the launching of a new monthly in English. In January 1933 a tabloid, *MAN! (A Journal of the Anarchist Ideal and Movement),* began appearing, with no price (or better, with the hope of a donation). It was sponsored by a group of Italian, Chinese, Yiddish-speaking, and English-speaking anarchists, with Graham as its editor.

An immigrant to the United States in 1907, at 14, Graham had worked as an egg-candler and a garment cutter. A traumatic visit to a slaughterhouse as a teenager made him a vegetarian even before he heard the term. He discovered Socialism, and then the Yiddish-language anarchist press, and embarked on an illustrious career as an enemy of the established order. Arrested in New Jersey in 1918 for possession of pro-Soviet anarchist literature, he was ordered deported to Canada, where, using the name Robert Parsons, he had gone as an active pacifist earlier in the World War; but the authorities north of the border refused to admit him. Arrested in 1921 and accused of seeking to place a bomb in the New York Public Library, he was badly beaten by police and subjected to another attempt at deportation, which again did not succeed. He went voluntarily to England, believing that revolution was imminent there, and met William C. Owen, who greatly influenced him. Fifty years later Graham recalled, "He proved to be one of the most interesting men I ever had the good fortune to know. We met often and he was a fountain of knowledge in every respect. . . . Owen's spirit was that of a revolutionary."

Entering California at Yuma, Arizona, in 1930, Graham was arrested for possessing two copies of *An Anthology of Revolutionary Poetry,* which he had published in 1929, financed by his earnings as a garment cutter, and which Owen had proofread. Another effort to deport Graham, this time to Mexico from Yuma, also failed. Aside from the general indignity of such persecution, Graham was particularly outraged that in each case he had been denied vegetarian food in jail.

Graham's fearlessness was not limited to his dealings with the federal and local authorities; he also challenged the Communists to public debate, an increasingly risky undertaking after the maritime strike, when, as "Butch" Saunders admitted, the Party countered its radical rivals with "fists and baseball bats." The method used against Chernov years before was superlatively effective when applied by waterfront brawlers, something that was, obviously, old news in San Francisco. But above all, Graham was intellectually courageous; he reprinted and distributed Owen's *Anarchism Versus Socialism,* a "political testament" that is one of the boldest and bitterest indictments of state Socialism ever written. Thanks to Graham, Owen was once again read by Californians, very, very few of whom, in 1934 and thereafter, remembered Owen or indeed had ever heard of him. But Graham loved him, and was loyal to his memory.

ONE MONTH AFTER the maritime strike ended, on August 28, 1934, California showed the nature of its own authentic radicalism when the writer Upton Sinclair swept the Democratic primary for the governorship, defeating the old-guard party favorite, George Creel, and racking up nearly 100,000 votes more than the Republican incumbent, Frank Merriam. Until the year before, Californians had somewhat neglected Sinclair. Although they read his books, it was widely admitted that, rather like Jack London before him, he enjoyed a greater reputation in Europe than in America. California radicals mainly remembered his stand against the Los Angeles police alongside the Marine Transport Workers of the I.W.W. in 1923; he had been arrested for attempting to read the Bill of Rights on Liberty Hill in San Pedro, which somewhat outweighed his support for U.S. entry into the World War. In addition, he had occasionally stood as a candidate for the fading California Socialist Party.

But now, in October 1933, Sinclair issued a pamphlet entitled *I, Governor of California, And How I Ended Poverty,* which, he claimed, sold 150,000 copies in four months at 20 cents each, making it the best-selling book in the history of the state. In September 1934 more than 250,000 copies were in print, and more than 850 Upton Sinclair Clubs had been organized around the state. *I, Governor of California,* describing Sinclair's End Poverty in California or EPIC plan, made his success in the Democratic primary.

Sinclair was no enemy of Soviet Communism, having announced the EPIC concept while promoting a project by the great Soviet film director Sergei Eisenstein, who had visited Hollywood in 1930. In addition, Sinclair's books were totally banned by the Hitler régime in Germany in July 1934, which increased his stature among radicals around the world. But the California Communists were impressed neither by Sinclair's association with Eisenstein, nor by his disfavor with the Nazis, nor by the EPIC plan. By the logic of the Comintern's then-extremist line, Sinclair was a "social-fascist" who by running as a Democrat sought to bind the workers to the New Deal, which the Communists then considered, simply, a fascist scheme. The best evidence of the Communist enmity toward Sinclair consists in the absence of virtually all mention of him from the numerous memoirs of the 1930s published by Communists or former Communists, including Kenneth Rexroth, during and after the 1960s. The Communists presented Sam Darcy as their own candidate for governor of California, a decision with grave repercussions for Darcy and the party.

Sinclair's warmth, sincerity, and humor offer a complete contrast with the dour, evasive, and paranoid attitudes of the Communists. *I, Governor of California* was a polemic of an entirely different order from that employed in the feverish Communist pamphlets of the day. The occasional outbursts of social Darwinism *redux* that appeared in Communist literature were utterly absent from Sinclair's discourse, which expressed the mentality of the new enlightenment in pure form.

The simple affirmations at the core of *I, Governor of California* had an overwhelming effect on Californians in the Depression, as demonstrated by the book's multiple reprintings. Point by point, Sinclair presented the fundamentals of traditional California radicalism, only slightly updated:

> Ever since the Civil War we have been governed by a business autocracy, and there has been a continuous struggle between the autocracy and our political democracy.

He evoked a lyrical panorama of California,

> a land ready to produce almost everything which humans need . . . machines of production, marvellous creations of human ingenuity . . . roads for distributing, the finest on the whole earth.

But the pastoral is blighted:

> A strange paralysis has fallen on this land. Here are fruits rotting on the ground, and vegetables being dumped into the bays because there is no market for them . . . thousands wandering homeless, and thousands of homes which no one is allowed to occupy . . . a million people who want work and are not allowed to work . . . another million being taxed out of homes and farms to provide the money to feed those starving ones, who would be glad to earn their food but are not allowed to!

Sinclair understood the anxiety and anger of Californians at the system that had led to the Depression and, unlike the Communists, he was able to communicate in the people's own vocabulary, reflecting their own history rather than the shibboleths of distant Moscow. He harked back to the reform movement of a generation before.

> The men who have made this condition are a little band of "insiders," the masters of our chain banks, railroads, and public service corporations . . . [T]en years ago, I described them as the "Black Hand of California." . . . There is no crime these masters have stopped at. When Francis Heney, public prosecutor of San Francisco, was on the point of sending one of them to prison, they had him shot down in open court. When Fremont Older refused to desist from exposing their crimes, they had him kidnapped and spirited away on a train. These men have the mentality of birds of prey.

In analyzing the corruption of business and politics in California, he wrote, "I have felt the helplessness of a man in the presence of a forest fire, an avalanche, a tornado."

Offering his campaign slogan, END POVERTY IN CALIFORNIA! he urged Democrats to make it the program of their party, and Republicans and Socialists to support it; he did not mention Communists. He also noted that some of his associates had called on him to moderate his message, arguing that Roosevelt had been "mild in his promises; if he had announced during his campaign what he was going to do after his inauguration, he would never have been elected." But Sinclair's nature was otherwise. Although he apologized to readers for making himself the center of the EPIC concept, he could not help going as far as he could.

The bulk of *I, Governor of California* consisted of an imaginary "People's History of California, 1933–1938," outlining the measures Sinclair would put into effect after his election. That narrative began with a touching detail: the Santa Monica businessman Gilbert Stevenson, who appealed to Sinclair to join the Democrats and run for office, owned a hotel, but declared, "This is not an aristocratic place in which to hold a political conference. My rooms in this hotel are furnished in the style of our grandfathers." That is, presumably, with little more than a bed, a mirror, a chair, and a water basin; yet this image of EPIC's birthplace was imbued with the myth of California's genteel Spanish origins, the lost paradise of the missions, now doubly lost; Stevenson had owned a more luxurious hotel, the Miramar, across the street, but "the depression gave the Miramar to the bankers."

In fictional discussion with his supporters Sinclair outlined his proposals in *I, Governor of California*. First, "land colonies for the unemployed" would be established, "run by the State under expert supervision. . . . The State will set up colonies managed by trained men. It will provide adequate housing for workers, co-operative kitchens and cafeterias, and rooms for social purposes." This "third kind of agriculture" would operate alongside individual farming, which had fallen into bondage to the banks, and the large-scale agricultural industry that employed thousands of immigrant workers.

Second, idle factories would be taken over by the state and started up again, in "a new and self-maintaining world for our unemployed." The system was to be independent of the rest of the country, requiring "as few dealings as possible with our present world of speculators and exploiters."

Third, the new system would be based on a separate currency, consisting of scrip combined with $10 bonds, redeemable at 30 days' notice, serving as a state currency.

These measures were to be paid for by a state tax with a rate of 30 percent up to $50,000 per year in income and 50 percent of inherited money over $50,000. Homes occupied by their owners and farm property worked by their owners, below a valuation of $3,000, were to be exempt from land tax, but taxes would be heavier on unimproved and uncultivated property assessed at over $1,000 in value. Pensions of $50 per month would be guaranteed to the indigent over 60 years of age, to the indigent blind, to the handicapped unable to work, and to widows with two dependent children, with $25 per month more for each additional child. All such benefits would be paid only to those who had resided in California for at least three years.

The programs would be administered by three public agencies, the California Authority for Land, or CAL, the California Authority for Production, or CAP, and the California Authority for Money, or CAM. Sinclair's acronyms seem almost a caricature of the "alphabet soup" agencies, such as the National Recovery Administration (N.R.A.) and the Civil Works Administration (C.W.A.) established by Roosevelt in the "Hundred Days" of 1933 that began the New Deal. Indeed, EPIC may be described in great part as the New Deal radicalized for the California public, in a state many still considered semifeudal. *I, Governor of California* declared, "We have NIRA for the Nation; let us have EPIC for the State." The symbol of the N.R.A. was the "blue eagle," but Sinclair disliked "any kind of bird of prey" and proposed the bee as the EPIC symbol, for "she not only works hard but has means to defend herself and is willing to use them on behalf of the young." The EPIC symbol portrayed a bee with the motto, "I Produce—I Defend," which was more than a little reminiscent of the rattlesnake flag of the American Revolution and the slogan, "Don't Tread On Me."

But EPIC was more than the New Deal with a deeper socialist tinge. The writer's vision of collective farming, supplemented by a "farmers' EPIC plan," might have reminded some of the Stalinist agricultural reform just then being imposed on the Soviet peoples, but it was to be voluntary, and its spirit partook far more of the land radicalism of Henry George, W. C. Owen, and even Ricardo Flores Magón. EPIC was not a welfare scheme; Sinclair condemned the notion that "the people would be fed, but would not be allowed to grow their own food." So much of *I, Governor of California* reminds one of Owen, in particular, that one wonders if the English anarchist's *Anarchism Versus Socialism,* peddled as a pamphlet by Marcus

Graham, had not reached Sinclair. But Sinclair knew the Georgist tradition of land radicalism as well as Owen had, and Sinclair did not share Owen's suspicion of the state—quite the opposite.

In addition to beloved California radicals like Fremont Older, Sinclair's "brain trust," once he was inaugurated, was intended to include such figures as J. Stitt Wilson, the former Socialist mayor of Berkeley, and a brace of veteran Los Angeles reformers. Sinclair did not anticipate any enthusiasm for EPIC on the part of Lincoln Steffens, immobilized in the Communist straitjacket, and Steffens went unmentioned in the list of the people's champions to be recruited to Governor Sinclair's inner circle. To those who accused him of Communism, Sinclair would point to the violent polemics of the Muscovite party against him; furthermore, he argued, the Russians had borrowed his ideas, not vice versa.

Sinclair's notion of a Socialist California, self-sufficient and issuing its own money, did call to mind a specific aspect of Stalin's Communism. Stalin had imposed himself on the Bolshevik party with the slogan of "Socialism in one country," that is, an autarchic Socialist commonwealth independent from the rest of the world economy. The Reverend John Haynes Holmes, a respected religious liberal, had pointed out in reviewing an earlier Sinclair book, *The Way Out,* published in mid-1933, that the nationalist tendencies in the New Deal, and the promise of economic "success without international relations," were common to Roosevelt and Stalin, as well as Sinclair. The concept was also shared by Mussolini and Hitler; in addition to a belief in statism, the New Deal, fascism, and Stalinism all conceived of the countries where they were the law of the land as communities apart from the world. The National Socialism of Hitler and the "Socialism in one country" of Stalin were certainly mirror images of one another. Holmes's 1933 review was reprinted in copies of *I, Governor of California* in a way that fortified Sinclair's argument that the Communists were imitating him, and rather shabbily at that. However, Sinclair's call for a self-sufficient state also resonated with California's unspoken but strong tradition of cultural separatism.

Sinclair's proposals were bold; some critics claimed to see in him a demagogue and a possible dictator, and his jocular assertions that the Russians had emulated him did not make them easier to swallow. But Sinclair communicated a real hatred for fascism that just then seemed almost absent among the Communists, and his open countenance and obvious sincerity, combined with the simplicity and eloquence of *I, Governor of California,* won over thousands of people.

Sinclair's victory in the Democratic primary demonstrated the effectiveness of the candidate's entry into the party. He chose as his running mate Sheridan Downey, a Sacramento lawyer aged 50 who was born in Wyoming and came to California in 1912. Sinclair's appeal to change their registration to Democratic had been heeded by former Berkeley mayor Wilson and some others of the Socialist Party's remaining adherents, who were, in truth, few by that time.

Although viewed as a dangerous enemy by the extremist "third-period" Communists, the Socialist Party had been moribund in California since the end of the World War, and Sinclair's campaigns for the U.S. Senate in 1922 and for the governorship in 1926 and 1930 were among its only bright spots. Some of its outstanding personalities seemed to have abandoned politics: William McDevitt, once feared by the ruling powers in San Francisco for his antiwar speechmaking, had opened a bookstore. So had Jack McDonald, another former member of the Jack London Memorial Institute; McDonald's Bookstore became a haven for radicals as well as for collectors of printed literature in general. Socialist attorney Austin Lewis occasionally defended Communists while working for the American Civil Liberties Union.

A handful of Socialists chose to remain with their party and to reject Sinclair's argument for joining the Democrats; Milen Dempster, a retired minister, ran as their gubernatorial standard-bearer. Otherwise, about the only Socialist activity of significance in the state was to be found in the North Beach district of San Francisco, where an anti-Mussolini newspaper, *Il Corriere del Popolo (The People's Messenger)* came out in Italian but was ignored, of course, by the broader public. Nevertheless, Sinclair had perceived something others had not: Socialist ideas had gained a far greater influence than the party itself had ever enjoyed. It was not simply a matter of the Roosevelt New Deal's "brain trust" of Socialist-minded intellectuals, much less the attraction of Sovietism. Sinclair harked back to the presidential election of 1924, in which Socialists and Progressives had united to support Wisconsin Senator Robert M. LaFollette—who had helped Furuseth emancipate the sailors—and in which LaFollette gained five million votes nationally. In that election, according to Sinclair, the Socialists had educated the Progressives, and the experience was due to be repeated in the

EPIC movement. (It is worth noting that the American Communists had tried their best to sabotage LaFollette's candidacy.)

Finally, the Sinclair candidacy was aided by a political institution dating from the first reforms of Hiram Johnson, the "direct primary" without a convention. In addition, under then-established state practice, "cross-filing" permitted multiparty candidacies. Legally, Sinclair could have remained a Socialist and still have cross-filed as a Democrat, a Republican, or even a Prohibitionist; the latter party then offered a slate in every statewide election in California, and Sinclair was a nondrinker. But that would have conflicted with his personality; he needed to make a commitment to a mainstream party, as an expression of his typical enthusiasm for the ideas he embraced as well as of his sincerity. However, many Republicans undoubtedly voted for him as well.

AND SO THE EPIC crusade began in earnest—accurately dubbed "the campaign of the century" by author Greg Mitchell in his authoritative account of the battle (a book unfortunately of limited use for anybody aiming at a real understanding of Sinclair's program or its appeal). Sinclair's primary victory astonished the whole country, and not simply California. *The Nation* editorialized,

> If ever a revolution was due, it was due in California. Nowhere else has the battle between labor and capital been so widespread and bitter, and the casualties so large; nowhere else has there been such a flagrant denial of the personal liberties guaranteed by the Bill of Rights; nowhere else has authority been so lawless and brazen; nowhere else has the brute force of capitalism been so openly used and displayed; nowhere else has labor been so oppressed; nowhere else has there been a more false or more poisoned and poisoning press.

The EPIC primary victory came just as liberals and radicals elsewhere, and many in California, expected the state to experience a new antiradical hysteria in reaction to the maritime strike. Northern California, having lived that episode of class war most acutely, did seem, at first, less enthusiastic about EPIC than the south; yet the primary vote transformed public opinion throughout the state. The EPIC primary victory marked the second, political stage of the California revolution that had its initial, labor-based phase in the maritime strike. The strike had brought about the re-birth of militant unionism; the EPIC primary victory created the state's modern and "progressive" Democratic party.

Such a revolution, premised on the preservation of the two-party sys-tem, did not imply a violent change; yet it frightened the California busi-ness élite more than anything before or afterward, including the Wobblies of 1919. In the 1934 gubernatorial race Californians experienced an en-tirely new kind of electoral manipulation, foreshadowing broader changes in politics throughout American society. Here, more than at any other time and place, California played its role as a vanguard. The new style, however, was not reassuring to behold.

More than any candidate before him Sinclair ran on his ideas, as ex-pressed in *I, Governor of California.* Some, like the issuance of scrip, were clearly vulnerable to criticism. Once the campaign was under way, he mainly counted on the burgeoning network of EPIC Clubs, along with a weekly, the *EPIC News,* to circumvent the conservatism of the daily press and win over the unconvinced. His opponents raised the stakes in the con-test, answering him with books of their own and with much more: they used anti-Sinclair newspaper columns and cartoons, satirical papers, leaflets, billboards, radio broadcasts, and, most effective of all, faked news-reels. Sinclair's "Soviet" associations, in addition to his innovative propos-als, were predictable targets. But the *Los Angeles Times* found an especially useful weapon: its staff paged through Sinclair's works seeking, and fre-quently finding, sentences that lent themselves to an out-of-context presen-tation guaranteed to shock and disturb timid and conservative citizens. Sinclair had, after all, made himself America's most famous writer, interna-tionally, by the "frankness" (as he put it) of his books, beginning with *The Jungle* in 1906. He had successively savaged such respectable institutions as the churches, in *The Profits of Religion,* which came out in 1918; the press, in *The Brass Check,* 1919; and the school system, in *The Goose Step,* 1923. These three titles had been self-published and sold by their author through the mail, but they enjoyed a considerable readership. All of them featured a plethora of radical comments, which were soon reprinted in daily boxes on the front page of the *Times.*

In a southern California still known for its churchgoing habits, *The Profits of Religion,* as Sinclair himself later admitted, was especially suited to turn public opinion against him. A widely distributed pamphlet, produced

by a newly created California Democratic Governor's League, labeled him a
"DYNAMITER OF ALL CHURCHES AND ALL CHRISTIAN INSTITUTIONS—ACTIVE
OFFICIAL OF COMMUNIST ORGANIZATIONS—COMMUNIST WRITER—COM-
MUNIST AGITATOR—THE MAN WHO SAID THE P.T.A. HAS BEEN TAKEN OVER
BY THE BLACK HAND."

Sinclair himself compounded his problem at a press briefing on September 16, 1934, when he allowed a remark to slip from his mouth that he
had clearly not thought out. Asked whether, if EPIC was voted in, California would see a rush to its borders of jobless people from elsewhere in the
country, he replied, "I told Harry Hopkins in Washington that if I am
elected half the unemployed of the United States will come to California,
and he will have to make plans to take care of them." Of all Sinclair's naive
declarations over the years, that one did him the most harm politically, for
it was soon plastered across the front pages of the dailies, and was interpreted and reinterpreted in editorial cartoons, photo spreads, and similar
news features.

The most destructive weaponry against Sinclair was supplied by Hollywood. The newspapers printed photographs allegedly showing the unemployed heading to California in trucks and on boxcars. In one instance, the
image was a still lifted from a 1933 movie, *Wild Boys of the Road.* However,
the young genius Irving Thalberg, formerly of the Metro-Goldwyn-Mayer
studio and now working independently, produced three "newsreels" that
were destined to make campaign history: Numbers 1 through 3 of *California Election News* were shown in movie houses throughout the state. Based
on faked interviews and pseudodocumentary footage using actors, the three
shorts, employing a fraudulent "Inquiring Cameraman" to carry the action,
were extraordinary in their dishonesty, and extraordinarily effective.

The first appeared on theater screens in October and depicted working-
class and middle-class folk, some of them pro-Sinclair and others opposed
to his "socialism." The pro-Sinclair individuals all seemed poor and shifty,
while partisans of Republican gubernatorial candidate Merriam appeared to
be average, solid citizens.

The second, which came out a week later, was more venomous, offering a view of "radicals" as conceived by Hollywood: "Upton St. Clair [*sic*] is
the author of the Russian government," claimed one man. "And it worked
very well there and I think it should do so here." This subtle opinion was
followed by a similar one, from a man with a heavy foreign accent: "I have

always been a Socialist and I believe Sinclair will do best for working people." A well-dressed "workman" then presented an argument for Merriam, followed by an exchange between a Sinclairite and a supporter of Raymond Haight, running as a third, "Common Wealth" candidate. The Sinclair adherent was depicted as a mustachioed eccentric with long sideburns.

The third, shown in the last week before the November 6 election, was the most infamous: the phony "Inquiring Cameraman" was shown at a railroad yard, where a Southern Pacific switchman complained of the influx of transients into the state. Some were criminals, the railroader asserted, and his expertise was bolstered by statements from a constable and a judge, the latter also warning that many of the newcomers were Communists. A representative of the state Department of Motor Vehicles confirmed that arrivals had increased dramatically. But regardless of their past records or political orientations, there were hundreds of such hobos pouring over the state line, according to the "newsreel." The camera showed them like ants, crowding on the cars, jumping off, and swarming into the foreground.

Thalberg's involvement in the anti-Sinclair campaign reflected the candidate's own stormy relations with the film industry, and, indeed, with M.G.M. and Thalberg himself. Sinclair was fascinated by the industry and the possibility of using cinema to advance his ideas. Indeed, he had briefly gone on the M.G.M. payroll in 1932, ironically hired by Thalberg, who had bought *The Wet Parade,* a book by Sinclair on Prohibition, which was made into a successful movie. But Thalberg and Sinclair made poor collaborators, and Sinclair's reputation in Hollywood was also tainted by his association with Sergei Eisenstein. The brilliant Russian director had come to Hollywood under contract with Paramount Pictures in July 1930, acclaimed for his groundbreaking work on such films as *Strike* (1925), *The Battleship Potemkin* (1926), and *October* (1928). *Potemkin,* in particular, with its stirring depiction of a shipboard mutiny, excited filmgoers around the world and played no little role in the Communists' organizing efforts, including those aimed at seamen.

Eisenstein had great hopes for a series of "American" film projects. His first proposal to Paramount, "The Glass House," was an extremely radical project both cinematically and ideologically; it was set in a modernist apartment house with transparent walls, in which clarity of vision would break down the social conventions among its residents, leading to voyeurism and crime. But "The Glass House" could not be made into an American-style film, and Eisenstein then attempted to realize one of his favorite scenarios, an adaptation of Blaise Cendrars's *L'Or,* or *Sutter's Gold;* he had read this popular French work in a Russian translation by the Russo-Belgian anarcho-Bolshevik and anti-Stalinist Victor Serge, who at that moment was locked up as a "Trotskyist" in Siberia. This French-language classic might have made an outstanding California film. Eisenstein traveled throughout the state researching it; he first encountered authentic daguerreotypes, which enchanted him, at a tiny, neglected museum in the Gold Country. He remained obsessed with the project, and recalled, not long before his death in 1948,

> I wanted to express the disastrous role of the gold strike on Sutter's California lands, the destruction and ruin of his fertile estates and of him, through the vivid impression made on me by the California gold dredgers still at work. . . . Those mountains of waste being disgorged . . . as in Sutter's day, from the half devastated gold fields lie over the fertile green of the surrounding fields. The blossoming orchards, fields, pastures, and arable land die beneath the gray, soulless layer of stone. The rampart of stone moves implacably, ceaselessly, unrestrainably, over the green, pitilessly crushing beneath it the living shoots of life to ratify the hunger for gold.

Eisenstein filled the script with characteristic innovations, but Paramount rejected it as too expensive to make.

The *Sutter's Gold* project, it should be noted, has been the object of much unjustified derision over the years by critics who understand neither the insight of Cendrars himself nor the inspiration of Eisenstein. The latter's script might still make a wonderful film, far better than the lame version of Cendrars's book produced in 1936 by Carl Laemmle at Universal Studios and today forgotten—except insofar as its exaggerated cost contributed to the end of Laemmle's career.

Eisenstein gave up on Paramount after failing to sell David O. Selznick an adaptation of Theodore Dreiser's *An American Tragedy.* He then turned to Sinclair. But Eisenstein did not prove any easier a filmmaking partner for Sinclair than Thalberg had been. The author put up the money to produce a "Mexican" film, shot south of the border. The filmmaker worked on location from the end of 1930 to the beginning of 1932, but the 200,000 feet of film stock he exposed did not a feature make. Although the project generated much artful footage, and even some sequences capable of being shown as a film, Eisenstein and Sinclair finally broke off relations. Sinclair released part of the footage, under the title *Thunder Over Mexico,* but the film was a wholesale failure. Eisenstein then returned to Russia, where his work was under severe attack from "critics" aligned with Stalin. (The Russian dictator had even telegraphed Sinclair a denunciation of Eisenstein as a "deserter.")

Upton Sinclair, who never did anything by halves, had still more entanglements in Hollywood that enraged Irving Thalberg. In February 1933 he published one of the strangest and most interesting of his muckraking exposés, *Upton Sinclair Presents William Fox,* a book originally subsidized by the founder of Fox Studios and the gigantic Fox Theatres chain, who had been done out of his empire in the Wall Street crash of 1929. *Upton Sinclair Presents William Fox* was an elaborate rant against Fox's competitors and high finance. In it the eccentric film magnate gossiped, fantasized, and otherwise aired his dirty linen; he had even tried to stop publication of the book, but Sinclair went ahead and issued it, privately printed, from his own home, as he had so many other of his works. The enormous and permanent influence of Fox on the history of Hollywood makes the book an unknown classic; but it won no friends in Thalberg's circle. On top of all this, during the 1934 campaign Sinclair repeatedly threatened that an EPIC-ruled California would either seize the big film studios or launch its own state-controlled movie industry.

―――――――――

IT WAS, THEN, undoubtedly no surprise to the shrewd Sinclair that the three fake "newsreels," splashed on the silver screen, determined his electoral fate. His main defensive strategy was a continued but fruitless attempt to get President Roosevelt to fully endorse "production for use," the overarching principle of EPIC. But on November 6, 1934, when the votes were cast, Sinclair was beaten by Merriam. In the final tally, the EPIC candidate was credited with some 850,000 votes against 1,100,000 for Merriam. Raymond Haight, the spoiler running on the so-called Common Wealth ticket, got 300,000 votes—which, had Haight endorsed Sinclair, might have thrown the race to EPIC. The "regular" Socialist, Milen Dempster, received 2,500 votes; Sam Darcy, for the Communist Party, received 5,000.

The Communists had attacked Sinclair almost as violently as had the Merriam forces. Articles and especially cartoons in the *Western Worker* portrayed Sinclair first as a capitalist, then as a proponent of "slave labor." Although many California Communists, particularly the garrulous Darcy, later offered fanciful assertions about internal debate in the party over this policy, the claims made by some to have opposed the party leadership and to have tried to support EPIC in 1934 are largely unworthy of credence. At the height of their ultraradical "third period," fresh from the labor victory in the West Coast maritime industry, the Communists were in no mood to back a Democrat, especially a Democrat with a Socialist past. That Sinclair had, in the late 1920s, endorsed such Comintern fronts as the World Congress Against War was ignored.

Nevertheless, Party members acquired a bad conscience about the Communist anti-EPIC onslaught. Dorothy Rosenblum, a daughter of the Los Angeles Jewish cadre who achieved prominence first under her *klichka* Dorothy Ray and then, using her husband's name, as Dorothy Healey, confessed decades later that the Communists "were left on the outside, denouncing the [EPIC] movement. We called [Sinclair] a 'social fascist' . . . But we learned something from Sinclair's success. What happened had not fit our definition of what was possible or not possible."

California had changed utterly in the year 1934, but the Communists continued with their extremist and particularist line. Just how far they were willing to go in seeking to suppress rival radicals was underscored in January 1935, when seventeen of the agricultural organizers arrested for "criminal syndicalism" in Sacramento the year before, headed by Norman Mini, Pat Chambers, and Caroline Decker, were brought to trial. The proceeding, which went on into May, was a farce, yet Mini, accused of attempting to set up a revolutionary army among other absurdities, turned it into an indictment of the "three percent of the people who own 85 percent of the wealth." Responding to persistent attempts by district attorney Neil R. McAllister to twist his words into an advocacy of crime, Mini insisted on his commitment to "a movement of the producers to take back what they have produced and what has been taken from them."

Found guilty along with Chambers, Decker, Nora Conklin, and four others, Mini stood erect at his sentencing. Mini and Lorine Norman rejected probation; they said they had done nothing wrong and would admit no guilt. The eight were ordered to state prison for 14 years each. Mini declared,

> Our standing here is no accident. Our conviction is the result of the inner logic of the class struggle. But the same class struggle that results in our conviction will some day generate an irresistible wave that will sweep away forever everything this court and state represent. With this knowledge, we can face our sentences confidently; we know that the future belongs to us.

Mini's summary of the Communists' claim on the "new," with its slightly totalitarian flavor, was more than brave: Mini, alone among the defendants, faced another and more dangerous enemy in addition to the district attorney. During the trial, Mini had been denounced by the Communist Party and the I.L.D. as a "stool pigeon," literally while facing conviction. The Communists based this defamatory assault on a statement (*not* a confession) in which Mini admitted and defended his work as an organizer. Mini produced a leaflet in which he denounced Darcy: "Hoping to distract people's attention from the C.P.'s record of criminal mismanagement and wrecking in the Sacramento case, the Darcy machine broadcasts the yarn that the prosecution, which is trying to railroad me to San Quentin, has my cooperation!" Mini revealed that Darcy had dictated the statement calling him a "stool pigeon," and that it was signed under duress by the rest of the defendants, who were threatened with the loss of bail money provided by the I.L.D. According to Mini, the internationally known Communist lawyer Leo Gallagher had argued with a juror in a way that prejudiced the case against the defendants and then stated, before the jury, "I am not talking to the jury; I am talking for the people in the courtroom." Yet the jury, not the spectators, would decide whether the defendants went to prison.

The real grievance against Mini held by the "Darcy machine" originated in the trivial fact that Mini had moved away from Party orthodoxy and had contacts with a group of Trotsky supporters, the tiny Workers Party of the United States. "The C.P. . . . drove out . . . everybody who rejects the authority of the C.P.," he wrote; the Party's exclusiveness made a united defense in the Sacramento case impossible. The C.P.'s conduct was criticized by the American Civil Liberties Union and the local Socialist Party, but the Communists were unmoved: the Sacramento defense must be under their control or it would be downgraded in importance, to say the least. Caroline Decker, who had gone to the "Trotskyists" for bail money, believed that the party was satisfied to see the defendants behind bars. In a letter reprinted by Mini, Decker wrote, "Elaine [Black, now an I.L.D. official] says it's not important for us to be out. I'm definitely resigned to that now . . . So you see—here I am—in jail—ostracized by my own Party."

The group were transported to San Quentin and Tehachapi prisons, and served time; Mini was released on parole after a year, Decker and Chambers in 1937. While in prison, Mini seems to have reconciled with the Communists. But he had been taught a lesson that would be learned by many more after him: the Party would destroy people before it allowed dissent to penetrate its ranks, and would act against dissidents without concern for such action's impact on public opinion, or even on the tasks the Communists had set themselves. Nothing mattered except control; trust and mutual respect were "*bourgeois* prejudices." Mini, with plenty of time to ponder these matters as state prisoner number 57606, had become, as he himself realized, the first publicly known victim of Stalinism in California. According to his widow Kleo Apostolides, "Norman felt himself very strongly as a Californian; the realization that the farm labor activities in which he was involved were being subverted and manipulated from far away alienated him considerably" from the Communists.

THIS ENTIRE DECEITFUL performance, while doubtless appreciated by Darcy's fellow Comintern functionaries, played very poorly among California radicals. Soon, California newspapers announced that Darcy had falsified his voter registration to declare his gubernatorial candidacy in 1934, showing New York City as his birthplace when he was really born in Ukraine. In obtaining a passport for a trip to a Comintern congress then going on in Moscow, Darcy had admitted his real place of birth.

The admission that he was born in Ukraine but had stated New York as his birthplace was enough to destroy his career in California. A San Francisco judge issued a warrant for his arrest on a perjury charge. Darcy would not return to California from Moscow; he was replaced as district organizer by William Schneiderman, a Communist since 1922 when, at 16, he joined the movement after hearing the Reverend Robert Whitaker, the former Socialist turned Communist, speak. The phrase "colorless bureaucrat" could have been invented to describe Schneiderman. Darcy eventually turned up as district organizer for the party in eastern Pennsylvania, but his perjury case greatly diminished the esteem of the Communists among ordinary Californians. Other leading local Communists were already involved in similar scandals; Louise Todd, 30, had been sent to Tehachapi State Prison for falsifying signatures on ballot petitions, and even the elderly Anita Whitney was convicted of ballot fraud, although she was allowed to get off with a $600 fine.

One might wonder why the Communists involved themselves in such shenanigans. Using a false name in clandestine work, or even in a strike, might be justified to protect the Party from exposure. But the passport and electoral frauds, and the constant use of *klichki* or aliases in open Party activities, showed a distinct arrogance and recklessness. Communist motives were, however, easy to discern, and multiple: although such infractions reinforced the public image of the Communists as illegal and alien to American political standards, the Communists believed that short-term goals, such as a place on the ballot or the temporary avoidance of a "foreign" reputation for their candidate, outweighed the risks of bad publicity. After all, in their view capitalism was tottering, and bourgeois legality might be moot much sooner than most people thought; thus the Communists acted with assumed impunity, as if the fall of the American government were imminent and would leave them unpunished. In addition, for Communists the concerns of ordinary Americans about honesty and legality, especially in politics, were more "bourgeois prejudices," worthy of nothing but contempt. Few, if any of the Socialists, Wobblies, and anarchists before the World War would have agreed with them.

With the disappearance of Darcy from the local scene a new "People's Front" tactic was introduced in California, in which Communists strove to appear undemanding and cooperative in their approach to most other radicals. However, control was still their aim, especially in the labor movement, and particularly on the waterfront. That Communist psychology had not changed, regardless of their prettified demeanor, was demonstrated by an atrocious incident in a small San Francisco affiliate of the International Longshoremen's Association, the Ship Scalers' union. The Scalers were (and are today) at the bottom of the maritime heap; they did the dirtiest and most dangerous work, and had never played a prominent role in labor affairs. Most were Spanish speakers. But the Communists were determined to have their way with the Scalers' union, as they tried to do throughout the maritime movement.

On a Saturday evening, September 21, 1935, a meeting of the Ship Scalers in their hall at 32 Clay Street erupted in a wild mêlée when an anti-Communist member, Antonio Robles, was attacked while speaking from the floor. Knives, razors, and fists flew in all directions, and the battle swept into the hallway. Vicente Torres, 47, Mexican-born and an anti-Communist Scalers member, was struck with an iron pipe and propelled into the hall, then out a window and through a glass awning to the street; a rib splintered and punctured his lung. At least a dozen more men were also injured.

George Woolf, a Communist with no previous waterfront experience who had been installed as president of the Scalers, was arrested for assault with intent to commit murder, along with nine of his partisans; but charges were dismissed against all but four of them. Two weeks late, however, Vicente Torres died, and the charge became murder. Four suspects were indicted; of these only Natalio Velli was among the original arrestees. The other three were Julio Canales, Francisco Jiménez, and one of the Bay Area's best-known young Communists, Archie Brown. How Brown came to be present at a meeting of the Scalers, of which he was not a member, was one of the most interesting issues in the trial. Curiously, Brown chose to act as his own counsel.

Torres was probably killed as a warning to the anti-Communist element in the Scalers; the prosecuting attorney argued that he had been pushed out the window. Communist attorneys claimed that Torres had jumped from the window "of his own volition" and rallied the waterfront unions in protest against the trial. The defendants, Brown included, were acquitted. And what of Vicente Torres? If not shoved out a window, he was nonetheless thrown out of history, into silence; we know almost nothing of him as a person. Vicente Torres was a "rank-and-file" worker, employed at a difficult and degrading job, of the kind the Communists claimed to idolize. But when he got in the party's way, he died. Was Vicente Torres, like Norman Mini, an early victim of Stalinism in California?

The Scalers were not the only union on the West Coast waterfront to suffer the special attentions of the Communist machine. In April 1935, a labor conference in Seattle officially established the Maritime Federation of the

Pacific Coast (M.F.P.C.); that "industrial" entity had become a major goal of the 1934 strikers. Its first president was a militant patrolman, or business agent, from the Sailors' Union of the Pacific, Harry Lundeberg. Lundeberg was extremely popular in his own union and was an attractive potential recruit for the Communists. Born in Norway, he had sailed all over the world. Lundeberg was a solid "syndicalist," who, if he had not been a member of the I.W.W. (he denied actually carrying the "red card") was at least a sympathizer, in the manner common among seamen in Seattle, where he lived. In the early 1920s he had visited Australia, with its militant labor movement, and frequently shipped to Argentina, where anarchist unions held sway over the waterfront.

But Lundeberg's syndicalism involved something more than an expression of local traditions or the vagaries of life at sea. His family had been prominent in the Norwegian Labor Party. That organization, the most radical Socialist party in Europe, was influenced by Norwegian immigrants to America who had encountered the I.W.W., and it maintained a supreme degree of union militancy. They were tough, very tough; some observers said Lundeberg was the toughest man in the American labor movement. Lundeberg's commitment to labor seems to have come mainly from his mother, Alette Lundeberg, for whom he retained the tenderest of feelings. She was an outstanding Norwegian feminist, who battled for the rights of women in a just social order, according to Harry's brother Kolbjørn. She fought for free schoolbooks, free meals for students, and better instruction, as well as for vacation homes for housewives, among other demands that are still deemed highly advanced today. She became chair of the Labor Party women's organization in Oslo, Norway's capital, and was a noted, and feared, public speaker. She taught her sons well: Kolbjørn recalled proudly that Harry, "as a 14-year old boy was out fighting against the strikebreakers. He came home late at night with torn clothes from fighting with police and the strikebreakers."

The two Harrys, Bridges and Lundeberg, had much in common superficially. Both had gone to sea, and both had benefited from political education that put them far ahead of most of their peers. They could be seen as representatives, on the West Coast, of two major exemplars of world socialism: the Australian and Norwegian Labor parties, both of which drew inspiration from the I.W.W. and both of which served as political extensions of powerful union movements. But the Norwegian Labor Party, and Harry

Lundeberg, had a characteristic that set them at odds with Bridges and the Australians. The latter had always been pro-Soviet; the Norwegians had affiliated with the Comintern, but their encounter with Bolshevism made them extremely anti-Communist, although they also remained extremely radical in their Socialism. Because of this "cultural" difference, Harry Lundeberg was the only labor leader on the West Coast more sophisticated than Harry Bridges, though few perceived it at the time.

Lundeberg was at first widely believed to be a Communist, and he showed no hostility toward the Party. But a slow change began in early 1935, even before he was elected president of the M.F.P.C. The longshore strikers received an "award" from the federal government in October 1934, securing them a hiring hall operated jointly with the employers. The seagoing workers got an "award" in January 1935, and were granted union preference in hiring. However, alongside dispatching from a hiring hall to be run by the union alone, nonunion shipping "off the dock" was to continue. The sailors felt cheated. Given the influence of the "neo-Wobblies" in the shipboard unions, it could hardly have been a surprise that the sailors, firemen, and marine stewards spontaneously launched a series of unofficial "job action" strikes to impose union-only hiring. The first of the job actions was recorded on April 12, 1935, when the crew of the steamship *Cuzco* staged a walkout in San Pedro to protest the presence of nonunion stewards.

A year of such job actions followed; *"the year"* in the consciousness of the sailors. Between April 1935 and the end of March 1936, 156 such strikes, or one roughly every other day, were officially noted by the employers; it was a unique experience in American labor history. The strikes followed a uniform pattern: the crew signed on, became aware of the presence of nonunion men or of conditions to which they objected, and walked off before the ship could sail. Most of the job actions lasted only a day or so, with some occupying no more than a few hours; others went on for weeks. A handful, but no more, were called to effect the removal of Filipino seamen. But most of them were the direct expression of rank-and-file militancy. Lundeberg stood out among the union leaders in his enthusiasm for job action, and he gathered a core of "neo-Wobblies" to his side. This trend of events began to worry the Communists; they remained mortally afraid that the waterfront labor movement would slip from their grasp. In November 1935, the *Western Worker* published its first criticism of Lundeberg as an "individualist"—a code-word for anarchist, syndicalist, Wobbly. The waterfront war between "the Reds and the IWW" described by "Butch" Saunders began to take public form. But in December Lundeberg was elected secretary-treasurer of the Sailors' Union; job actions were at their height, with twenty-two strikes that month, and the Communists backed down from their criticism, at least temporarily.

Lundeberg, however, began seeking help in dealing with Communist maneuvers. He had already acquired a powerful aide in Norma Perry, the secretary of Harry Bridges since the 1934 walkout, who had parted with the burglar and Communist operative Arthur Scott. The aging Perry had seen too much as Bridges's helper; after a series of disagreements culminating in a physical assault on her by Bridges she was fired from her job and then expelled from the Communist Party. The Communists began a campaign of slander against her that lasted, amazingly, for fifty years. But Perry was a sincere, labor-minded radical. She went to work for Lundeberg and soon, in her apartment in North Beach, she introduced the Sailors' leader to some unanticipated allies: Joan London and her third husband, Barney Mass, who called himself Mayes.

London's view of Communism had changed considerably since the 1920s, when she and her second husband, Professor Charles Malamuth of the University of California's Slavic Department, were "parlor pinks." In 1932 the couple went to Moscow to see the new world for themselves, and were guided around the country by the United Press correspondent and then Communist fellow-traveler Eugene Lyons. They returned without illusions; Malamuth, who had also been subsidized as a translator of Soviet fiction, now published acerbic commentaries on the rise of Stalinism and the abandonment of the Bolshevik world-revolutionary ideal. "Compared to Lenin and Trotsky, genuinely great men and Marxian statesmen, Stalin is a great mediocrity," he wrote in the *San Francisco Chronicle*. Personally, the relationship of Joan London and Charles Malamuth was rather benevolently bizarre; they were divorced in 1930 with Malamuth complaining that she spent too much time away, lecturing on her father. They reconciled in Moscow, but were divorced again in 1934; Malamuth complained on that occasion that Joan annoyed him while he was writing by playing the radio, especially "crooners." They again reconciled, but were in divorce court for the last time in April 1935.

Joan London then took up with Mayes, a man in his thirties who had grown up in Kansas City and was a former Wobbly and a Communist leader in Detroit. Driven out of the official Party in the first purges of "Trotskyites," he had become a member of the main (but very small) Trotskyist group in America, the Communist League. Norma Perry had met a Trotskyist student, John Brum; recognizing that the Trotskyists, as critics of the Communists and Bridges, could serve as allies of Lundeberg, she arranged through Brum to meet Mayes. In an unpublished memoir that is a key document in the historiography of California labor, Mayes recalled the growth of the waterfront crisis:

> With the shipowners still refusing to hire from the seamen's union hiring halls, the [Sailors] were forced to tie up ships whose crews were partly or all nonunion. The longshoremen naturally refused to go through the picket lines, prompting the employers to put pressure on Bridges to either ignore those picket lines or lose his contract with them. Now Bridges . . . tried desperately to put an end to all job action by any union, claiming such action was a threat to all of them. . . . Bridges now stood for order on the waterfront, extolling legal action as the only solution.

But Lundeberg was determined "to win what the '34 strike did not give to the seamen—[exclusive] recognition of their own hiring halls." Mayes was soon hired to edit the *Voice of the Federation,* the weekly journal of the M.F.P.C.; he later recalled that he had been thrilled at "the chance to take on the Stalinists in what had become their most important stronghold." He was joined on the maritime front by a handful of other Trotskyists.

CALIFORNIA HAD UNDERGONE a labor revolution in the maritime strike, and a political revolution during the Sinclair campaign. Would it now produce a third, literary or artistic revolution? Many believed it would. More painters than authors had come under Communist influence, perhaps because their work, in a period marked by the great prestige of Diego Rivera, lent itself to collective enterprises, as exemplified by the Coit Tower murals. Joan London at that time made no attempt to subordinate her literary work, which still focused on her father, to her social views. Rather than attempt to emulate his career, she preferred journalism to fiction. But some writers of talent felt the appeal of the Communists.

John Steinbeck, then 32, was one such author. Like Frank Norris and

Jack London before him, Steinbeck, who grew up in the Salinas Valley, was a university dropout: he studied literature at Stanford but left without graduating. He followed a course of odd jobs and journalism, publishing his first novel, *Cup of Gold,* in 1929. Two more books followed: *The Pastures of Heaven* in 1932 and *To a God Unknown* the year after. He gained a limited success in 1935 with the publication of *Tortilla Flat,* another work steeped in the environment he considered his own. But in late 1934 he conceived a new project: "I was going to write the autobiography of a Communist," he said in a letter to a friend. He met the agricultural organizer Pat Chambers, not yet sentenced to prison for "criminal syndicalism," and studied the climactic Tagus Ranch peach strike of 1933. The result was his first major novel, *In Dubious Battle,* which he wrote in 1935 and which was published in New York in 1936.

Steinbeck was the furthest thing from a Communist himself, and his wish to write the "autobiography" of a party worker shows his naïveté as well as the extraordinary attraction the Communists exercised at that time. *In Dubious Battle,* though interesting as a period piece, failed completely as a novel and especially as a contribution to revolutionary fiction. Its main characters, the organizer Mac, based on Chambers, and his disciple Jim Nolan, are caricatures, and most of the book is taken up by their stilted discussions and by predictable, sentimentalized episodes. *In Dubious Battle* was denounced by one Communist critic as "mystical," and the charge was legitimate. Steinbeck had written an extremely personal fantasy about Communists, from which the real motivations of the young revolutionaries, as well as the personalities of the strikers, and even the landscape itself, were missing.

In a major example of writerly myopia, Steinbeck protrayed the "Torgas" strikers as entirely white, a situation virtually unknown in California agriculture at that time. But Steinbeck was not writing about social upheaval as much as the relation of Californians like himself to the soil, a theme that, if not treated overtly as in the writings of Royce or Norris, was always latent in local thinking. Although seemingly unaware of it, Steinbeck had much more in common with land radicals like Henry George, W. C. Owen, or Upton Sinclair than with someone like Pat Chambers. Thus, the name of the younger of the two protagonists of *In Dubious Battle,* Nolan, may be symbolic of "no land" in his possession.

In Dubious Battle was demolished in the pages of *The Nation* by the young critic Mary McCarthy, who called it "academic, wooden, inert. . . . The dramatic events take place for the most part off-stage and are reported, as in the Greek drama, by a breathless observer. Mr. Steinbeck for all his long and frequently pompous exchanges offers only a few rather childish, often reiterated generalizations. . . . He may be a natural story-teller; but he is certainly no philosopher, sociologist, or strike technician." McCarthy was right; although the regional and rural motifs elaborated in the pages of *In Dubious Battle* would reappear in Steinbeck's later works, in this form California's third, literary revolution had failed. No other "proletarian" works emerged that could even be compared with *In Dubious Battle.*

Yet regionalism of the kind developed by Steinbeck was, for a time, the favored medium for California radical writing. Fremont Older, the California radical *par excellence,* died in March 1935, but his wife Cora, who professed to believe in the California Indian cult of Chingichnish, published a series of mediocre books, such as *California Missions and Their Romances,* on the regional myth. This, too, was insufficient by far for a literary revolution. The Bohemians had nearly disappeared from the scene and were considered "reactionary" by the younger, pro-Communist element; but not far from Steinbeck's Salinas Jaime de Angulo stayed on in Big Sur; although he had suffered an excruciating personal tragedy, his mind continued to work in its original and fruitful way.

De Angulo, whom we last encountered on his way to Modoc County to record the language of the Pit River (Achomawi) Indians, accumulated a remarkable list of scholarly publications in anthropology and linguistics in the decade after 1921. He also quarreled with Kroeber, who blacklisted him from professional ethnology after de Angulo abandoned a job in Mexico recording Indian languages to visit his ex-wife Cary and daughter Ximena in Switzerland, where Cary was studying with Carl Jung. On his return de Angulo wrote and published a novella, *Don Bartolomeo,* and met Mabel Dodge Luhan, a patron of many radicals as well as of the writer D. H. Lawrence. Mabel Luhan and her husband Tony, a Taos Indian personality, invited de Angulo to New Mexico to meet Lawrence. According to de Angulo's daughter Gui, Mabel Luhan hoped de Angulo would instruct Lawrence in the doctrines of Jung. But the encounter with Lawrence in the summer of 1924 was unsuccessful, to say the least, and de Angulo returned to California. He then assumed a role he played for the rest of his life, as a mentor to young rebel intellectuals. About this time he wrote a novel, *The*

Reata (later retitled *The Lariat*). In 1927 he returned to ethnological field work under the patronage of the eminent anthropologist Franz Boas, who hired him to continue recording California Indian languages.

In August 1933 de Angulo was driving along the Big Sur road with his son Alvar and a woman friend, Gertrude Cothran, when their car plunged two hundred feet down a cliff. Alvar, 9 years old and de Angulo's delight, was killed; the car pinned Jaime down for seventeen hours, alongside his son's corpse, while Cothran, who freed herself after hours of effort, walked ten miles to get help. Jaime de Angulo never recovered psychologically from this ordeal; he gave up his California Indian field work for good and withdrew into seclusion at Big Sur. About this time he was visited by Bernard Zakheim, who painted a social-realist mural in the bathroom of de Angulo's house; but de Angulo found it ugly and painted it over. Steinbeck's pastoral and de Angulo's eccentricity had little more than an accident of geographical proximity in common, yet at that moment they represented the two faces of California's new literature. The third, literary revolution in California had yet to begin.

While ordinary Californians worried over headlines that seemed to describe an overwhelming world chaos, the local Communists were continuing their barely hidden campaign to dominate the waterfront labor movement. The means were physical. Barney Mayes later noted "a not-small number of unsolved murders stemming from the waterfront . . . fight for control." One of the most fascinating such cases began August 11, 1936, when a dead man wrapped in heavy chains, his nude body emptied of blood, was found in mudflats on the east side of the Bay. A rope was also tied around the victim's neck; teeth were missing in a way that demonstrated he had suffered "a terrific blow," and the lack of water in his lungs showed he had been dead when he entered the Bay.

The corpse was identified the next day as William Langley, alias Raoul Louis Cherbourg, a member of the Sailors' Union from Kentucky whose father was a judge, according to police. The newspapers said that Cherbourg, as he was generally known, had worked as an investigator on maritime cases, while Lundeberg described him as an excellent sailor who had never been in trouble aboard ship. However, in 1932 he had been jailed in Los Angeles for "criminal syndicalism." He had signed a rank-and-file statement supporting Lundeberg, and had been badly beaten by three men in a saloon in Washington state; it was then that his teeth were knocked out. He said he would have been killed in the bar fight had bystanders not come to his assistance, and expressed great fear for his life.

Lundeberg revealed that three other members of the S.U.P. had lately died under mysterious circumstances. Axel Kingstron was killed by a fall while drunk on June 13, 1936. Frank Nordlund, a seaman in his forties with a wife and child, died on July 31, two days after a shipboard and dockside fight with longshoreman Frank Nieni, in which the coroner determined Nieni acted in self-defense. Albert Skoodra, about 45, of Russian birth, was found in the bay on August 2; the San Francisco coroner held an inquest and determined that Skoodra's death was a suicide while deranged. Then Carl "Shingles" Tillman, a former Northwest sawmill worker of Swedish origin and Wobbly sympathy, now a member of the Sailors' organization and a close associate of Lundeberg, revealed that four days before his body was found, Cherbourg had asked to meet with Tillman and said he had "something very important" to tell him. Cherbourg never came to the meeting, and Tillman was convinced he had been killed to silence him. Alameda County investigators claimed that Cherbourg's blood had been drained from his body by deliberate cutting of leg arteries, and asserted that the same method was used in other waterfront deaths.

And there the case ended, at least as far as local jurisdictions were concerned. No suspect was ever arrested. Lundeberg and his men wanted desperately to find Cherbourg's killer, but the trail went cold. The only other individual interested in the case was someone Lundeberg and other unionists, as much as the Communists, considered a dangerous enemy: Harper Knowles, a local businessman and director of the Radical Research Committee of the state's American Legion. Knowles was the most knowledgeable anti-Communist investigator in the state, and remained so for the next thirty years; he kept a horrifying photograph of Cherbourg's corpse in his desk drawer for the rest of his career. In 1938, Knowles declared in public, before the newly created House Committee on Un-American Activities, that Cherbourg's death was ordered by the California Communist leadership in a meeting where Bridges was present, with the task of killing him assigned to waterfront thug "Butch" Saunders. Saunders was never arrested in the case, and said nothing about it in his memoir, published in 1995. Knowles asked the House Committee to pursue the matter, without success. Like Vicente Torres before him, William Langley, alias Raoul Louis Cherbourg, remains a person of whom we know almost nothing save that he was a son of the sea, killed and bound in chains; but we may legitimately suspect that he too was a victim of Stalinism.

However, the martyrdoms of obscure West Coast sailors were overshadowed in the fateful weeks of August 1936 by news from Moscow as disturbing as the "People's Front" turn, a year before, had been heartening. The great Soviet show trials of "old" Communists had begun. The "unhealing wound" of the purge era affected the entire world left for decades to come. However, the truth of what was happening inside Russia was difficult to ascertain; prominent Japanese and Finnish Communists from California were swept into the massacre, but their fate remains obscure even today. Radicals became even more confused when, in the wake of the trials and after some indecision, Stalin announced that the Soviet Union would aid the antifascist side in the Spanish civil war, which had begun in July; Moscow would send military officers and an international legion of volunteer troops to the battlefronts. Events seemed to have speeded up; nobody knew what would happen next, and many radicals felt caught up in the turbulence, unable to find their bearings.

Amid this storm in history, as it might be called, an old drama erupted anew in California on September 16, 1936, in no less remarkable a place than Steinbeck's Salinas. There a lettuce-shed strike by 3,200 members of the Fruit and Vegetable Workers' Union, whose leadership was resolutely anti-Communist, turned into "civil war" in the town. Strikers massed in Salinas to block transportation of nonunion lettuce. Monterey County Sheriff Carl Abbott deputized 1,000 men under the state's *posse comitatus* or "power of the county" statute (Penal Code section 723), armed 250 of them with pick-handles, and let them loose in the streets, where they gassed and beat hundreds of strikers and threatened them with guns.

Although agricultural labor turmoil never really died out in 1930s California, the Salinas strike, like the 1934 uprising on the waterfront, was a spontaneous outbreak of class conflict; indeed, like the Wheatland riot of 1913, Salinas in 1936 most resembled a traditional European peasants' revolt. The Communists were involved only as distant observers, and the *San Francisco Chronicle* described the struggle as exceptionally militant and without Muscovite interference; it had taken the Communists by surprise. The Salinas police, backed by the Highway Patrol, teargassed the Salinas Labor Temple, considered a bastion of labor conservatism, and union leader Michael Shevlin warned that if attacked again the unionists would defend themselves, implying that they would be armed. Henry Strobel, chief of the growers, was beaten by pickets, and the *Chronicle* reported that "the 'civil war' phase of the situation was exemplified by the fact that the growers' leader has two brothers who are on the side of the strikers. One, J. W. Strobel, is a teamster on strike; the other, Gilmore Strobel, is a striking vegetable worker." An attempt to mobilize the American Legion to suppress the strikers failed because too many of the strikers, most of them whites from Oklahoma and Arkansas, were themselves veterans and Legionnaires. During the street fighting, women strikers and sympathizers "screamed their determination to fight shoulder to shoulder with the men," and battled the police and Highway Patrol officers, seizing the barrels of their guns. Images fresh from newsreels of revolutionary Spain had come to Salinas, California.

Two men were shot, many heads were cracked, relatively much blood flowed, and children were felled by the gas, so that the elementary schools were closed; but, incredibly, nobody was killed. Violence soon diminished, although a series of implausible side issues intruded, keeping Salinas in the news for some weeks. An anti-Communist gadfly, Colonel Henry Sanborn, publisher of a San Rafael weekly, the *American Citizen,* had gone to Salinas to advise the police and sheriffs, and he delivered a "Red-baiting" speech after the street battle. This trivial exercise was inflated by reporters into something comparable to Mussolini's march on Rome, and a backlash against the San Francisco press, especially against the *Chronicle,* led to melodramatic charges that Salinas had, for two weeks, become a tiny fascist state. This absurd exaggeration fostered considerably more histrionics in the press, the main effect of which was to divert attention away from the strikers themselves. The next development of real significance came on September 27, when 3,000 Filipino field hands in the Salinas district, led by an extremely tenacious organizer, Crispulo D. Mensalvas of the Filipino Independent Labor Union, threatened to join the walkout. Other Filipinos were recruited as strikebreakers and a few clashes with strikers occurred on outlying roads; when seven hundred scabs, who had been housed in barricaded packing sheds, descended on Salinas with money in their pockets, some were attacked in the streets. But after a few weeks the Salinas strike was lost, and the union collapsed.

DID CALIFORNIA IN 1936 really have much in common with Spain in the fury of its civil war? Many radicals, as well as liberals frightened by

Sanbornian "fascism," thought so. Solidarity with Spain led to demonstrations in California. Support for the Spanish Left was forthcoming in San Francisco from anarchists and other radicals living in the Spanish community along Broadway, as well as from the Italian radicals in the adjacent precincts of North Beach proper. Among the former, a left-wing coalition, Acción Demócrata Española, was organized as soon as open fighting began in Spain. A founder of the group was Javier Benedet, nicknamed "*Torero*" or "Bullfighter." Benedet, 32 when the Spanish war began, was born in Spain and taken to Mexico as a child with his family. His father, a doctor of liberal views, was then caught up in the turmoil of the Mexican Revolution: Dr. Benedet was kidnapped by Pancho Villa and forced to serve his troops as a medic!

Torero Benedet earned his nickname as an apprentice bullfighter in northern Mexico, but came to San Francisco with his older brother Vicente in the mid-1920s. Both worked as waiters; Vicente later recalled a Broadway then best known for its Spanish restaurants and Basque hotels, and nights filled with political debate in cafés and bars, involving dozens of Spanish, Italian, and Mexican radicals. *Torero* Benedet found a way to continue his enthusiasm for bullfighting while in California. He fought in bloodless "Portuguese" *corridas* in Oakland and in rural towns throughout the Central Valley where bullrings were located. During the Spanish war, *Torero* Benedet appeared in bullfights to raise money for the antifascist cause, while Vicente went to Spain to fight.

Thousands of antifascist Italians in the United States also responded warmly to appeals for assistance to the beleaguered Spanish Left. In California, Italian-American liberals and socialists followed the initiatives *of Il Corriere del Popolo,* San Francisco's Italian weekly, which had been founded in 1910. The paper had struggled along until 1935, when a board that included Dr. Salvatore Schirò, a beloved North Beach physician of radical views, arranged for the paper to be taken over by Carmelo Zito, a socialist refugee from Italy.

Antifascist opinion was stronger among the Italian-Americans on the East Coast than in California, for the same reason that the Mafia was also more powerful there: the absence of an Italian-speaking industrial class in California, which would have provided antifascist recruits at the same time as, dolorously, it would have furnished victims for the gambling, prostitution, and loan-sharking controlled by the criminal syndicates.

The Marxist ethnographer Paul Radin, in a study of the North Beach Italians, recounted the tale of "An Officer from Trieste" who fought the fascists in the streets of Italy, but who was transformed "once he retired to the tranquil life of California. He was engaged in the title business and was doing very well . . . he had an adorable wife and a little boy. I asked if he still takes [an] interest in the antifascist movement, but he was evasive about it."

As Mussolini seemed to go from victory to victory, the religiosity and conservatism of the California Italians drew many to sympathize with the fascists. Soon, in San Francisco, Blackshirts took to standing outside Dr. Schirò's office, urging patients to boycott him. When Mussolini's armies invaded Ethiopia, some 10,000 California Italian housewives donated their wedding rings, and San Francisco garbage collectors amassed scrap iron, for the Italian government.

Even more than the Spanish leftists in San Francisco, the Italian group around Schirò and Zito threw themselves into the campaign for the fighters in Spain. For them antifascism became a holy cause, made even more compelling by Italy's dispatch of troops to assist the Spanish fascist leader, General Francisco Franco. An antifascist Divisione Garibaldi was organized to recruit combatants, and its commander, Randolfo Pacciardi, was brought to San Francisco to promote the effort. The Italian Socialists G. E. Modigliani (a labor leader and a brother of the artist Amedeo) and Gaetano Salvemini made similar visits. But the Italian-speaking liberals and Socialists were opposed to all forms of totalitarianism; they hated Stalinism no less than fascism.

Meanwhile, Soviet-backed International Brigade troops appeared in besieged Madrid in November 1936—saving the city, according to many accounts—and West Coast men and women began volunteering to serve in the Spanish Loyalist forces. But another, and more astute observer saw a different parallel. Ralph Chaplin, author of the "battle hymn of labor," *Solidarity Forever,* veteran Wobbly and fellow prisoner in Leavenworth Penitentiary of Ricardo Flores Magón, watched both the mass struggles in Spain and on the U.S. West Coast and saw the same menacing development in both places: an attempt at monopoly control by the Communist Party.

The hidden war on the West Coast waterfront finally exploded in a full public confrontation during the "second big strike," the Pacific maritime walkout of 1936–37. Both the longshore and seagoing contracts expired on

October 1, 1936. In the strike that followed, Harry Lundeberg and the Sailors' Union hoped to gain what they had failed to achieve in 1934—recognition of their hiring hall as the sole medium for employment. The waterfront employers announced that after October 1, all crew members would be shipped "off the dock," unless matters in dispute were submitted to arbitration. What followed was, therefore, as much an employer lockout as a strike. The strike commenced officially on October 30 and lasted ninety-nine days; it was only partly overshadowed, in the area's public consciousness, by the election of President Roosevelt to his second term.

The 1936–37 strike was peaceful on the Pacific, although attempts to widen it nationally saw violence on the East Coast. Two years after 1934, labor was a power in California, rather than a contender; the change in attitude toward the unions is wonderfully exemplified by the contemporary comments of San Francisco police chief William J. Quinn. After bragging in 1934 that his officers, who killed two men by gunfire, had saved the city from "a well-planned revolution," in the intervening period Quinn adopted the hallowed San Francisco view that the police were required, during strikes, to "maintain a strictly neutral position between the employed and the employers." Indeed, early in 1936, Quinn claimed that in 1934, "the employers were told that the police . . . would not brook the interference of any individual or set of individuals who might, in any way, attempt to usurp the powers of the chief of police. No gun men would be tolerated by the police." If not for Communist meddling, according to this convert to sweetness and light, "the labor troubles on the waterfront would undoubtedly have been adjusted without any disorders."

Quinn could afford to be benevolent in hindsight, especially since, in the 1936–37 strike, Harry Bridges came forward as the open foe of militant action. The strike was to be conducted by the Maritime Federation rather than by the individual member unions, and put forward five basic demands, the most important being hiring of all unlicensed ship crews through union halls. Soon, however, it became clear that although the "second big strike" was universally considered the Sailors' game, Bridges would seek to direct the course of negotiations. When, in December 1936, Barney Mayes published, in the *Voice of the Federation,* a report that the Sailors' Union was near an agreement with the shipowners, a gigantic uproar broke out, in which Mayes, as a Trotskyist, was accused of "undermining" the strike.

The 1936–37 strike ended with gains for both factions in the Maritime Federation. When the men returned to work in February 1937, the Sailors had won their hiring hall in permanence, along with a $10-per-month raise. The Communists then launched a campaign to "purge" Mayes from the *Voice of the Federation,* in which they succeeded; Mayes was humiliated by Bridges and removed from the editorship in an incident that the labor journalist Benjamin Stolberg later called the first "Moscow trial" in America. Fortunately, Mayes, unlike the old Bolsheviks in Moscow, could not be compelled to "confess." But the Communists issued a deranged polemic signed by Roy Hudson, then based in New York as director of party work in the maritime unions. Headed "TROTSKYITES PLOT TO DISRUPT U.S. MARITIME UNIONS," it charged that Trotskyists had "worked together with stool pigeons and fascist agents of Germany and Japan to prepare a war against the Soviet Union . . . and plotted the death of Stalin and other leaders of the Workers' Republic." Hudson claimed that "Barney Mayes and Norma Perry, his coworker" had "tried to smuggle . . . into the unions in a concealed form" an "anti-working class policy." According to Hudson, *"Mayes and other Trotskyite rats make their main task the splitting of the progressive forces by trying to mobilize and incite others against the Communists"* [emphasis in original]. Quoting fellow-Communist leader Jack Stachel, Hudson revealed the real source of such rage: the Trotskyists opposed "the great Stalin, whose stature rises with every achievement in the building of socialism, with the rising people's front the world over."

Mayes was, however, an exceedingly minor casualty of this war; the main victim was the Maritime Federation of the Pacific Coast (M.F.P.C.), which became a Communist possession. In 1938 the Sailors' Union withdrew from the federation, along with a few supporters, and the federation expired the following year. Bridges also triumphed in another realm, that of the Committee for Industrial Organization (C.I.O.), which had been established early in 1936, mainly by John L. Lewis of the United Mine Workers, to organize the unskilled workers long neglected by the A.F.L. on an industrial basis. The C.I.O., which left the A.F.L. in October 1936, grew quickly and immensely, and came to be seen as the radical wing of labor. The Communists, following the People's Front line and cultivating Lewis, gained considerable influence in the C.I.O. as it emerged as the country's second national labor federation. Late in 1937 Lundeberg and Bridges competed for Lewis's nod as California C.I.O. director, and Bridges won. This tactical victory fueled a "march inland" by the longshore union, which was already organizing warehouse and other nonmaritime employees.

From then on, Lundeberg and his Sailors were forced to chart a risky course between the conservative forces in the union movement, who were none too fond of him, and the Communists, who labeled him and his followers "reactionaries" and worse. Soon the West Coast dockworkers, who joined the C.I.O. after renaming themselves the International Longshoremen's and Warehousemen's Union (I.L.W.U.), were pushed into a fight with the Sailors' Union over jurisdiction in organizing. And finally, Bridges and his cohort led longshoremen through Sailor picket lines. After that, the waterfront labor movement that emerged from 1934 was dead. Both factions, Bridges' I.L.W.U. and Lundeberg's S.U.P., continued making labor news and remained influential in their industry. But the waterfront workers lost the élan, and with it, the credibility, that had been theirs for four years.

In the meantime, events in Spain also undermined the prestige of the Communists. Some 3,000 Americans, a great many of them Communists, had enlisted in the International Brigades fighting for the Spanish People's Front, and were formed into battalions named for Abraham Lincoln and George Washington. Many of these men were sailors. As described by the author William Herrick (the only Lincoln Battalion veteran to write at length and with full candor), they encountered a series of terrifying situations in the war zone, at the hands of their own leaders rather than those of the enemy. First, their passports were confiscated, leaving them helpless. Second, they were sent into battle without sufficient training, and since very few of the American volunteers (as compared with the Germans, French, Belgians, Italians, and East Europeans in the Brigades) had any real war experience they died in large numbers, shot down at will by the fascist troops. Third, their officers were incompetents, drawn mainly from the top ranks of the Communist Party. Their main commander, a former economics instructor from the University of California at Berkeley named Robert Hale Merriman, was nicknamed "Murderman" by his own men because of the losses under his leadership. Fourth, the American volunteers were used in firing squads against dissident Spanish radicals—revolutionary Socialists, anarchists, and members of the small anti-Stalin Workers' Party of Marxist Unification (P.O.U.M.)—whom the Communists sought to destroy as rivals. Among the P.O.U.M. victims of the Communists was the Spanish-born volunteer from San Francisco, Vicente Benedet, who, found distributing anti-Stalinist leaflets, was kidnapped and held for a time in a secret prison controlled by the KGB.

Some of the Lincoln and Washington volunteers tried to escape, but they were labeled deserters. Although they were recruited on promises that they would serve for a limited period and then be rotated out of the war zone, once they were on Spanish soil and their passports had disappeared they were informed by Earl Browder and Robert Minor (the latter having reached the depths of his political degeneration as a loud defender of the Moscow trials), that they would be kept in Spain, in combat, until the war ended. Some were executed by their fellow volunteers. The International Brigades lived apart from the Spanish people they had come to defend. But the seamen among them, who were many, could not be prevented from getting word of their abuse, and of the Communist suppression of other radicals, to the outside world, even when faced with the risk of death at Communist hands. One sailor from San Francisco, Lloyd "Sam" Usinger, played a heroic role in seeking to help get volunteers who turned against the Communists away from Spain.

Communists known in California who went to Spain to fight included Harry Hynes, who was killed there, and Archie Brown, who served as a machine gunner and survived. Hynes, the Australian-born Comintern illegal and mentor of Harry Bridges, left a notebook of undated entries that provides some of the most shocking testimony about Communist misdeeds in the Lincoln and Washington Battalions. Hynes maintained the conscientious, hard-working spirit he had shown in California; he was extremely popular, and became a temporary "political commissar" in his company, a heavy responsibility in the Soviet armed forces as well as in their imitation, the International Brigades. Archie Brown was confirmed in a similar post. But Hynes was deeply unsettled by the situation of his fellow volunteers. "Phonies and mediocrities score high here," he wrote, "a person who is sincere and unassuming is treated with indifference." While the men in the trenches went hungry, according to Hynes, "the division staff was dining off beautiful china, [with] fancy jam, sliced tomato salad."

Hynes found some of the International Brigaders inspiring in their courage: the Franco-Belgian troops, almost all of them veterans of the World War, bellowed revolutionary anthems in the heat of battle. But "the stench of the unburied dead is stifling," he wrote. The foreign volunteers had been used as "decoys to find out the strength of the fascists. So many feel the deaths were useless." Steve Nelson, a protégé of Rudy Baker, was top commissar; when the men grew tired of waiting for food and complained, he quoted to them from Stalin's speech at Lenin's funeral, a famous example of Orthodox liturgy mixed with Bolshevik piety. "But you cannot manufacture enthusiasm," Hynes noted darkly. When he protested to his superiors about the lack of food, he was told officiously that "even if we die of malnutrition because there is red tape and someone makes a mistake it is better so. We must endure. I do not become disgusted with such people as I should."

The bravery of Harry Hynes was never doubted, though he admitted in his journal, "I tried to discipline my nerves." During a bombing, he "was praying Oh God, let this pass, Oh God," when a friend was killed and the body thrown across his. An especially macabre incident of Stalinist psychology was recorded by Hynes: an officer was dying in the hospital, and "he prayed. A German Communist doctor rushed to inject him so that he passed out unconscious. It is in line with the fanatical zeal of the underdeveloped comrades who have positions of importance here," Hynes commented. He also found that "looting was common, flagrant, even indulged in by Spanish officers." He confessed, "I am very much dissatisfied . . . the officers all mediocre, got their ranks and will get extra pay. I do not want to be part of the setup here. My heart is against so much that it represents. What will be left of the I.B. . . . ? We dream of home with such desperation."

But Hynes was not completely embittered; he also wrote of the Spanish landscape, "This is a beautiful country, high and with cool breezes like the mountains of California and Arizona." Hynes was said to have died in the Brunete offensive, on July 8, 1937; his diary ended just after he told Nelson of his desire to resign as political commissar. His death was not made public until November of that year.

In Moscow the purges continued; 1937 was dreadful enough, but 1938 brought, in addition to the collapse of the West Coast maritime labor movement and disillusioning news from the Spanish war front, the trial and execution of Bukharin, the last of the major "old" Bolsheviks left in Russia. The California Communists entered a new and defining period of their history. Until 1934 they had tried, by their lights, to revolutionize California society; from 1934 to 1938 they fought for control within the reborn labor movement and then the EPIC-led Democratic party; from 1938 on, and even up to the writing of this book, their main task has been to justify the vile behavior of their Soviet rulers. All else faded into insignificance. This attitude created more opponents of the Communists than the combined forces of the American Legion, local vigilantes, federal investigative committees, and state government could have fostered in a thousand years.

The California party, in the spirit of the Moscow purges, began hunting internal enemies, real or not. In 1937 the former burglar Arthur Scott, cadre director of the Communist Party in San Francisco and head of illegal work since the 1934 strike, was suddenly removed by Schneiderman. Scott was doubtless compromised by his past association with Norma Perry, soon publicly assailed by a member of her own family as a dangerous Trotskyite. But Scott also seems to have been denounced because he had come to Communism from prison, which some elder comrades in those days saw as suspicious in itself, given that the authorities might have turned him loose to infiltrate the party. Scott found no other alternative, after that, than to return to burglary. Again caught, Scott claimed he had acted as a Robin Hood, stealing from the wealthy to financially support the party.

To escape prosecution he turned to anti-Communist investigator Harper Knowles, providing the American Legion with a very thorough picture of the California party's inner workings. Much of Arthur Scott's weird career, and many of his "revelations" to Knowles, would seem absurd and improbable were it not that the historians Harvey Klehr and John Earl Haynes have published evidence from the Moscow archives confirming them contained in a secret report from underground worker Rudy Baker on the Party's quest for purge candidates in its ranks. Baker was less than candid in recounting Scott's career; he told Moscow that the prison sentence which landed Scott in San Quentin, in contact with Tom Mooney, had been for labor activity rather than burglary. Mooney, for his part, had little further need for Scott or any other Communists. The 1938 gubernatorial election sent EPIC-lining Democrat Culbert L. Olson to the state capital, an event hailed as a victory for the people of California second only to the election of Hiram Johnson. Olson ran on a pledge to free Mooney; this time, the Communists supported the Democratic candidate, and Olson welcomed their backing.

A remarkable phenomenon occurred late in 1938. Many American Communist intellectuals were perfectly happy to play the role of loyal mouthpiece for Stalin, howling for the blood of the purge victims. They did so un-blushingly, in the wake of Moscow's 1935 proclamation of the People's Front tactic, and while trying to paint themselves as Western-style liberals in origin and character. (Party boss Earl Browder put forward the slogan "Communism is Twentieth-Century Americanism.") The ever-adaptable Lincoln Steffens died at the beginning of August 1936 and was spared the ignominy of defending the main show trials but, as blithely noted by his bi-ographer Justin Kaplan, Steffens viewed such purges as proof of the vitality of Soviet democracy: the Stalinist regime showed its "accountability," he be-lieved, by removing and executing high officials, including "old" revolu-tionaries, supposedly in response to the popular will.

The poet Kenneth Rexroth saw otherwise; he had gained preeminence among the younger Communist intelligentsia in San Francisco, but the news from abroad increasingly disturbed him. Perhaps after the purge and murder of Bukharin, which deeply affected him, he recognized that Bernard Zakheim's prank, in lettering Rexroth's and Bukharin's names on the spines of books in the Coit Tower mural, "The Library," would have led to both their deaths, as well as that of Bukharin, had the mural decorated a structure in Moscow. (Death for painting or being depicted in a picture where the name of an "enemy of the people" like Bukharin was so recorded was entirely probable in the USSR in 1937–39.) Rexroth had been reading English-language publications by the Spanish anarchists and the P.O.U.M., and he was greatly alarmed by the Stalinist drive against these Spanish revo-lutionaries. But above all, Rexroth could not stomach the judicial murders of "old" Bolsheviks in Moscow.

Rexroth had gone from his involvement in the Coit Tower murals to several years' work on the Federal Writers' Project, a major component in the New Deal under the Works Progress Administration (W.P.A.). The Writers' Project offered what would today be called "workfare" to unem-ployed poets, playwrights, and others, along with the artists employed in producing public murals and similar activities. In another such program, great photographers like Dorothea Lange, subsidized by the Farm Security Administration, traveled rural America recording the anguish of America's displaced farmers and farmworkers. But the W.P.A. was dominated by the Communist Party, partially through ideological influence over the young intellectuals, but more importantly because pre-New Deal Communist campaigns to organize the unemployed, although largely ineffectual in Cal-

ifornia, ended up securing the Communists a place in administering the
W.P.A. Beginning in 1935, Rexroth played a prominent role in the Writers'
Project in San Francisco, contributing significantly to the *WPA Guides* for
California and *San Francisco,* both of which attained notable importance,
along with much other material such as "A Field Handbook of the Sierra
Nevada" and "Camping in the Western Mountains," which was never pub-
lished. Early in 1937 he filed for divorce from Andrée, who kept herself sur-
rounded by Communist fanatics even as her health deteriorated.

In 1938, however, Rexroth withdrew from the Federal Writers' Project,
mainly to get away from the Communist atmosphere he found there. To
find his bearings, Rexroth went to the Sierra Nevada in the company of a
new love, Marie Kass, a nurse he had met in spring 1936 while assisting in
the organization of a radical nurses' group. Her background resembled his;
her father was a Hungarian Socialist. Their pilgrimage into the wilderness
was another of those events in California intellectual history that, obscure
at the time, would have great consequences, for it was then and there, in the
mind of Rexroth in Yosemite and Sequoia National Parks in 1938, that California's true literary revolution began. This revolution, based on individual
intellect and inspiration, would develop over a long time—almost twenty
years. But Rexroth, who returned from the Sierra to San Francisco and left
the Communist Party, was to become California's outstanding literary
modernist and its greatest literary radical when considered in the longer
scheme of things. In the short run, thanks to Rexroth, California saw debates over totalitarianism and the nature of the Left that were comparable,
although on a much smaller scale, to similar controversies played out in
Paris and New York, where great numbers of intellectuals broke with Stalinism.

Rexroth's departure, although not immediately reported in the radical
or the daily press, caused fury among the Communists. Zakheim, who had
just completed a series of expressionist murals at the University of California medical campus in San Francisco, declared Rexroth a "Trotskyite" and
refused otherwise to speak of or to him for many years. In certain Communist circles, Rexroth, like Norma Perry, was the subject of grotesque slander
even twenty five years later: the Communist editor Al Richmond, for example, in 1963 accused Rexroth of contributing by his alleged public cruelties
to the tragic end of his first wife Andrée, who died in 1940 from a massive
seizure. However, at least one young Communist activist and poet, George

Hitchcock, remained close to Marie Rexroth, regardless of his political differences and occasional conflict with Kenneth after the latter broke away.

During this period Rexroth wrote some of his best poems. One, "Another Early Morning Exercise," eloquently expressed not only his ambivalence about Communism but also the special relations between revolutionaries on the two sides of the Pacific that had marked the 1920s and 1930s:

> One hundred feet overhead the fog from the Pacific
> Moves swiftly over the hills and houses of San Francisco . . .
> I walk along the street at three in the morning,
> It is spring in the last year of youth . . .
> I have been sitting in Sam Wo's drinking cold aromatic liquor.
> "What did Borodin do in Canton in 1927"—
> The argument lasted five hours.
> My friend Soo sympathizes with the Left Opposition;
> He told me I had murdered forty thousand bodies on Yellow
> > Flower Hill,
> "Those bodies are on your shoulders," he said . . .

Near its end, the poem declares,

> A chill comes over me; I walk along shivering;
> Thinking of a world full of miserable lives,
> And all the men who have been tortured
> Because they believed it was possible to be happy.

In addition to its unflinching view of revolution, this poem contains a detail that, like Zakheim painting in Rexroth's name with Bukharin's, would have spelt his death in Russia and expulsion, at least, from the American Communist Party if it had been known at the time of its composition. Referring to his friend Soo's affiliation, Rexroth used the term with which the Trotskyists identified themselves, the "Left Opposition," rather than condemning them as fascist bandits. Yet Rexroth remained, in the deepest part of his being, a social revolutionary.

A counterpart to Rexroth emerged in the person of another poet, George Oppen. Oppen and Rexroth had both been published in 1932 in An "Objectivists" Anthology, printed by Oppen and edited by Louis Zukofsky, a friend of Rexroth and Ezra Pound. In contrast with Rexroth, whose verse was almost traditionally lyrical, and whose interest in the minor literary phenomenon of "Objectivism" was cursory at best, Oppen, the son of a successful San Francisco businessman, or "capitalist," of the same name, was a committed ultramodernist who cleaved to the almost meaningless "Objectivist" label. Like Pound and Zukofsky, he was dedicated to a poetry tied up in words themselves, especially, in Oppen's case, nouns—brief, ambiguous, and weighty. The young poet had gone to Oregon State University, and there met his wife, Mary Colby, in 1926; the ardor of the couple, which led them to spend a night together almost as soon as they met, brought her expulsion and his suspension from the college when the tryst was discovered. The Oppens spent two years wandering across America, then went to France, where they lived on a boat, printed books, and were visited by Zakheim.

At first the Oppens seemed impervious to Communism; but whereas the authentic rebel Rexroth began with Communism early and had worked through it by the time Stalinism reached its height, the Oppens joined only in 1935, responding to the Seventh Comintern Congress, and remained loyal to it much longer. Mary Oppen became a leading party functionary in New York State, in contact with the highest figures in clandestine Communist activity. This may partially have reflected the Comintern's pledge, in the People's Front period, to make itself the party of "defense of culture against fascism." But American Communism compelled George Oppen to stop writing poetry and give preference to political work. While some Communist poets pursued a political and populist genre of verse, many more young intellectuals, who entered the party's ranks without such credentials, were urged to abandon their creative aspirations altogether. Rather than specifying *what* to write, the party told them not to write at all.

Unlike Rexroth, the Oppens accepted this Communist-imposed silence; "Objectivism" had given way in their life to activism. Their first party assignment, as recalled by Mary Oppen forty-five years later, involved clandestine infiltration of a right-wing group. Well off and ambitious, the Oppens were indifferent to the horrors of the Stalin purges. The contradictions in personality between Rexroth and George Oppen seemed visible in their faces: Rexroth was somewhat refined looking, handsome in a "poetic" way with large and fascinating eyes, while the young Oppen, darker, aquiline, but even more classically handsome, exuded masculine aggression.

While radical poets tried to find their bearings in a turbulent time, California continued on its course of change. On January 7, 1939, during his administration's first week, California Governor Culbert L. Olson signed the pardon that released Tom Mooney from prison. Olson also commuted the sentence of Warren Billings later in the same year. An era in the history of California had ended.

PART V

CHARON'S SHORE

"Lee, you might say the fate of the working class of the world depends on us here. As Comstock goes, the West Coast goes. As the West Coast goes, the nation goes. As the nation goes, the world goes."
—Smitty, in *Lonely Crusade* by Chester Himes (1947)

Wherein World War II begins in the shadow of the Hitler-Stalin Pact; literature and music contend with deeper social issues in California; Japanese-Americans suffer a terrible injustice, but find a few white defenders; U.S. entry into the war mobilizes democratic intellectuals; other racial conflicts emerge involving Blacks and Hispanics; Soviet spies invade a California-originated project with the potential to destroy the world; Hollywood Communists test the limits of film as a propaganda medium, while hunting imaginary enemies; and a tiny group of mystical-anarchist poets, all unknowing, begins (but only begins), from California, to change the mind of America and the world forever

The election of Culbert Olson as governor and the release of Tom Mooney from San Quentin expressed the duality of the year 1939 in California. Olson's victory seemed to prove that radicalism of a kind had prevailed in the state. But Mooney's aged and exhausted condition, and his character as a survivor of a now-long-gone style of radicalism, showed up the gap between the newly triumphant left and its forebears in the state's history.

The year had serious challenges in store for California radicals and liberals—most of them, at first, coming from abroad. In April, the People's Front resistance in Spain ended, an event that caused much mourning in California. But in the last week of August, a heavier blow fell when news came from Moscow of a pact between Stalinist Russia and Nazi Germany. Less than two weeks later, Germany invaded Poland and World War II began.

The task of defending the Stalin-Hitler alliance of 1939 was not a happy one for the California Communists. With ruthless determination the Nazi army poured across the western border of Poland, and from the first bulletins announcing a trade pact between Berlin and Moscow Californians knew, or at least suspected, that the Russian army would soon deliver a fatal stab to the Warsaw government's back. Russia invaded Poland from the east on September 16, all the while proclaiming its neutrality in the German-Polish war. By the end of September Poland had disappeared as a state, carved up between the totalitarian powers.

Newspaper commentary in California was bitter. Elias Tobenkin, a correspondent for the *San Francisco Chronicle,* wrote,

Since August 23, when the Stalin-Hitler pact was signed in Moscow, the Communist movement throughout the world has been in a state of chaos. . . . The greatest blow of the Stalin coup d'état—for that is what his pact with Hitler amounts to—has been struck at the Communist parties of France and the United States, the pivotal parties of Europe and the new world. . . . The Communists in the United States have no political power and comparatively little influence in the labor movement. The membership of the [American] Communist Party is small. It has, however, a large group of "fellow-travelers." To these sympathizers, Stalin's alliance with German fascism is indefensible.

Certain pro-Communist intellectuals, however, gave the impression that, if anything, they had been prepared for the shock even before it was announced. In September 1939, *Soviet Russia Today*, then a monthly of some influence, printed one of the most outrageous of the many Stalin-loyalist declarations of that decade, an "open letter" addressed "To All Active Supporters of Democracy and Peace." Signed by four hundred public figures, the document had been released on August 14, a week before the announcement of the Berlin-Moscow alliance. It boldly insisted that "fascists" and "reactionaries" had "encouraged the fantastic falsehood that the USSR and the totalitarian states are basically alike."

Many of the four hundred names affixed to this screed remain disturbing to find on such a statement; they included, along with pulp writer Dashiell Hammett, no less a personage than Ernest Hemingway and such other cultural leaders as Lincoln Kirstein, the pioneer of the American ballet; pundit Max Lerner; Klaus Mann, son of the exiled German novelist Thomas Mann; screenwriter S. J. Perelman; anthropologist Paul Radin; newspaper correspondent Vincent Sheean; photographer Paul Strand; humorist James Thurber; even the modernist poet William Carlos Williams. Actors who signed this roster of shame included J. Edward Bromberg, Sam Jaffe, and Lionel Stander. The now shameless *Nation* magazine printed the declaration of the four hundred in the same issue that reported the signing of the pact! It was, however, the last such statement, at least in terms of the endorsers' prestige and number, to appear for some years. In revulsion at the attack on Poland many among the four hundred abandoned the Soviet cause altogether, and it was perhaps a rather dirty trick for *Soviet Russia Today* to even print the manifesto.

Only a handful of Californians joined the four hundred: Hammett, considered a San Franciscan by association for his authorship of the Sam Spade detective stories; Radin; the small group of Hollywood actors and screenwriters; professor Thomas Addis of the Stanford University Medical School; Miriam Allen deFord, labor journalist and colleague of Kenneth Rexroth on the Federal Writers' Project; Haakon Chevalier, a professor of French, and Alexander Kaun, a professor of Slavic studies at the University of California at Berkeley; ex-Socialist preacher Robert Whitaker; and the indefatigable Ella Winter. Unlike some of the East Coast intellectuals who later regretted signing the statement, the Californians were hardened, cynical partisans of Stalin who remained avid supporters of Moscow.

The *Chronicle* soon noted editorially that the expectation that "the comrades would hang their heads in silent shame over the Stalin-Hitler dis-

grace" had been disappointed. For the California Stalinists, the pact with
the Nazis was simply another scandal to be explained away, as so many had
been before: the campaign against Upton Sinclair in 1934; the passport and
electoral frauds perpetrated by the Communist leadership; the violence and
deception in the maritime labor movement; the adulation of Stalin and the
acclamation of his bloody purges. Truculence was especially evident in the
Communist faction on the waterfront: on September 13, 1939 Walter J.
Stack, a prominent Communist in the Pacific Coast Marine Firemen's
Union, wrote a letter to the *Chronicle,* denouncing the paper's "staff of condescending saviors" for an "insult to our party's intelligence." Stack quoted
California Party boss Schneiderman's claim that "Anyone who can see in
our position or the position of the Soviet Union or the non-aggression pact
anything resembling an 'alliance' with Hitler is either deliberately lying or
the victim of lies." Stack blamed the overall situation on London and Paris
and pointed to the Munich conference of 1938, at which Britain and
France sacrificed Czechoslovakia in a gambit to appease Hitler. But although Stack was hardly sophisticated enough to understand it, his references to a "second Munich, a bloody Munich" were unflattering to Stalin,
who had assumed the role of active appeaser and was about to betray Poland
in worse fashion.

Soon the inimitable Harry Bridges, backed by Stack and others, had
imposed a new line on the section of the maritime labor movement they
still controlled: "The Yanks are NOT Coming." Satirizing a popular song
from World War I, the slogan spoke for itself. The Communists described
Russia and Germany as "revolutionary states," and denounced Britain and
France insistently as rapacious imperialist powers for, as allies of Poland, declaring war on the Hitler government—in quite a contrast with Munich.
But ordinary working people and liberal intellectuals in California remained unpersuaded. More than at any other time in their history, the
Communists became an object of real revulsion among Californians. Nevertheless, impelled by Moscow, the California Communists put all their political resources on the line for the Stalin-Hitler pact. "Peace" agitation
became shrill and distasteful, deepening the rejection of the Party among
the public. Eventually, the so-called "peace" issue vitiated the influence the
Communists had with Governor Olson.

The political heir of Upton Sinclair (and the first Democratic governor
of California since 1894), Culbert Levy Olson had never been particularly

fond of Communists; he had met with them during his gubernatorial campaign, accepted their backing, and appointed some to minor offices after his inauguration—Dorothy Ray Healey, who had become a prominent agitator in agriculture, was named a state labor commissioner. Ellis Patterson, Olson's lieutenant governor, was a close fellow traveler. Patterson was an opportunist; he had switched from the Republican party to the Democrats in 1936, and was then elected to the state assembly as a write-in candidate from Monterey County. Once in office, needing friends, Patterson swung far to the Left, publicly hailing, among other such efforts, the transformation of the San Francisco Communist organ, the *Western Worker,* into the *Daily People's World* in 1938. (Patterson was joined in his endorsement by two Democratic state assemblymen from Los Angeles, Jack B. Tenney and Sam Yorty; Yorty much later was mayor of Los Angeles.)

Olson himself was of a different type altogether. Born in Utah and aged 63 when he became governor, he had as a youth worked as a cowboy, construction laborer, railroad brakeman and telegrapher and, after graduating from Brigham Young University, as a journalist and lawyer. A Democrat since the beginning of the century, he was elected to the Utah State Senate and there introduced progressive legislation, including workers' compensation, a minimum wage, the initiative and referendum, and other reforms similar to those accomplished by Hiram Johnson in California. Arriving in Southern California in 1920, Olson emerged as an active supporter of Franklin Roosevelt in 1932, and was the top vote-getter on the EPIC slate in Los Angeles in 1934, when he was elected to the California State Senate. To many, Culbert Olson was a safer version of Upton Sinclair, blessed with a more moderate and reassuring style than the novelist. In reality, Olson was never an official member of the Sinclair movement, although he embraced many EPIC principles and was chosen as the leader of the post-1934 EPIC delegation in the state legislature.

As a state senator Olson introduced EPIC bills into the 1935 lawmaking session, including a "production-for-use" plan, a massive tax bill, and other proposals that failed to pass. He campaigned for public ownership of utilities, labor-protection laws, old-age pensions, regulation of southern California oil, resettlement of the indigent on unoccupied farmland, and other visionary concepts. Governor Merriam vetoed most of such bills as passed. Olson was also known, of course, as Tom Mooney's leading champion.

EPIC had benefited, in 1934, from an influx of partisans of the numerous unorthodox radical groups that burgeoned during the Great Depression, especially in southern California. One such was the Utopian Society, which gained a considerable following for its rather vague outlook before merging with EPIC. Olson gained office in 1938 with the support of a similar group of a more bizarre and sinister kind, the "Ham-and-Eggs" pension movement. "Ham-and-Eggs" was a variant of the Townsend Old Age Pension Plan, a source of excitement among millions of elderly Americans whose proponent Francis E. Townsend, a seedy Long Beach physician, had drifted in the mid-1930s toward the fascist populism of Michigan's infamous Father Charles Coughlin.

The great upheaval of the 1930s had produced a broad gamut of protest movements in America, ranging from the labor- and intellectual-oriented Left to the center-Left reform outlook typified by Culbert Olson and beyond, to an enthusiastic right-wing radicalism pursued by Father Coughlin, Louisiana governor Huey Pierce Long, Jr., and various agrarian movements in the Midwest. This differentiation, no less than the rise of the Communists, was a novel feature, largely absent from the earlier panorama of American politics. But in California, unlike the Midwest, labor and the Left far overshadowed the right-wing radicals in public influence. Thus, California's outstanding mass-protest leader was the genial Sinclair rather than a quasi-gangster like Huey Long. Moreover, midwestern right-wing radicalism was overwhelmingly isolationist and opposed to involvement in World War II, whereas the Pacific Coast, although occasionally isolationist, in general hated totalitarianism and sympathized with the anti-Hitler Allies.

Townsend Clubs and "Ham-and-Eggs" followers shared an advocacy of government-funded pensions, to be allotted under the condition that the income must be spent within a prescribed period—allegedly to stimulate economic activity. Calling for payments of "$30 Every Thursday," and nicknamed the "Thirty-Thursday" scheme, the "Ham-and-Eggs" plan was based on a complicated issuance of scrip and stamps, and was in fact unworkable, but grew to be an inordinately popular cause. Originated by a popular Los Angeles radio personality and amateur demagogue, Robert Noble, who migrated through the EPIC milieu, the local Huey Long supporters, and another "utopian" sect, Technocracy, Inc., "Ham-and-Eggs" was taken over and run by three Southern California promoters, Willis and Lawrence Allen and Roy Owens. It had a disturbingly totalitarian feel, with giant assemblies at which participants were required to shout out the phrase "Ham-and-Eggs Everybody!" before speaking.

Olson solicited "Ham-and-Eggs" support in addition to help from the Communists. The plan, however, was defeated by the voters as an initiative on the 1938 ballot. Olson's subsequent lack of enthusiasm for the pension scheme—which he, like the Communists, viewed as a tool to be used in the advancement of his own program—led the Allen brothers and Owens to attempt to recall him. Fortunately for Olson, the organizers failed to gather enough signatures to place the recall measure on the ballot, and some of its proponents were even found guilty of fraud in circulating petitions. A second attempt to pass "Thirty-Thursday" by referendum failed late in 1939, even with the Communists lining up on its behalf. Meanwhile Olson, firmly in office, pressed his own more solid agenda.

As the greatest exponent of the authentic progressive tradition to occupy the governor's office since Hiram Johnson, Culbert Olson had as his goal "a real change, not a mere nominal or partisan change" in state government. In his campaign he seemed to have revived Johnson's own original discourse when he lashed out at the "privileged interests" and monopolies, which, he warned, had "richly profited at the State's expense. In return for their election support, they hold a controlling interest in an Administration parading as a people's government. State offices have become their agencies. State executives are their legislation lobbyists," he declared. California, he insisted, "must be freed from their domination."

His main immediate commitments included collective bargaining, tax relief, and state aid for farmers, veterans, the poor, the elderly, the jobless, small business, and women workers. Like Sinclair before him, Olson campaigned on ideas rather than personality; also like Sinclair, he offered a California version of the New Deal, but more radical and more closely identified with the aspirations of the laboring and farming classes. Olson even declared his continuing interest in "production-for-use" colonies as the best means to alleviate unemployment. There was, he said, no other means of dealing with the need for large-scale jobless relief than "by enabling the unemployed to produce for themselves."

In an address to a conclave of social workers during his first six months in office, Olson averred, "I have approached the problem of unemployment and its relief upon the principle of industrial justice—that every man and woman able and willing shall be given the right and opportunity to earn a decent living. . . . We will, if humanly possible, find [a] substitute for the dole in useful and productive employment." Private employers, he argued, could never absorb the entire pool of unemployed labor in California.

Olson was vilified by his conservative opponents as a radical, a friend of Communists, a free spender, and a "dictator" aiming to fill the state government with his own pawns. Meanwhile, Lieutenant Governor Patterson, from the beginning of Olson's term, sent out hints that he would distance himself from the governor if the option beckoned. But the California political spectacle took second place to foreign news, which was increasingly grim.

In California, the Communists maintained a "peace" propaganda line that downplayed the horrors of the same Nazism that, since 1935, they had pledged to fight to the death. This flipflop led most ordinary people to suspect that Communist and Nazi agents were working together behind the scenes, on American soil as in Europe; Communist "peace" agitation had led to the Party's legal suppression in France. The Communists then chorused that the Finns, who excited wholesale sympathy in the democratic nations when their small country was invaded by Soviet armies on November 30, 1939, were "fascist."

But in reality, in the preceding five years the Communists, and more than a few liberals, had rendered the term "fascist" almost meaningless. Already before 1935, the Roosevelt New Deal had been called "fascist" and Sinclair a "social-fascist"; afterward, excitable newspaper reporters had, as we have seen, labeled the town of Salinas "fascist" during the 1936 farm strike; college football games, as well as various movies and other entertainments, were labeled "fascist," along with anything else that the Communists disliked. Of course the Communists called Trotsky and his followers "fascist agents," and the Stalinists on the waterfront issued leaflets depicting Harry Lundeberg as a Nazi.

There were *real* fascists and Nazis in America, including California. Father Coughlin had become an open propagandist for Hitler; although the more thuggish element in his following, mostly Irish Catholics whose hatred of Britain made them sympathetic to Hitler, had little influence on the West Coast, Southern California had for years seen extensive public ructions by exotic groups like the Silver Shirts. This was probably to be expected in the same area that fostered such wild varieties of political flora and fauna as EPIC, the Utopian Society, the Townsend Clubs, and "Ham and

Eggs." In a tradition that reached back to theosophy and other mystical cults, as well as the lurid Christianity of Los Angeles evangelist Aimee Semple McPherson, Southern California in the late 1930s also hosted such weird, semitotalitarian, and mystical sects as the "Mighty I Am" commotion led by Guy W. Ballard, who claimed to have communicated with an "Ascended Master," the Count of St. Germain, on the slopes of Mount Shasta, and an equally mysterious apocalyptical swindle called Mankind United.

The Silver Shirts represented the most elaborate mix of fascism, occultism, and pure hucksterism on the California scene. Although founded and directed from the East Coast by a freelance writer in his late forties, William Dudley Pelley, the group gained its largest membership in southern California; its only stable branch in northern California was located in Oakland. "Chief Pelley," as this ludicrous figure styled himself, established the Silver Shirts in February 1933, simultaneously with Hitler's appointment as chancellor of Germany. As a youth Pelley worked in his father's successful toilet-tissue business; he then ran a series of small-town papers in New England. He went to Siberia at the end of World War I, accompanying Japanese troops fighting the Bolsheviks, as a Protestant missionary and war correspondent. During the 1920s Pelley earned a respectable income as a magazine and movie writer, living for some time near Hollywood. However, mystical preoccupations gnawed at him and in 1930, in North Carolina, he began promoting "spiritual liberation." He claimed to be in personal communication with Jesus Christ and the Almighty, and lectured on his discussions with Them.

Pelley fancied himself an American Hitler; his spiritualism became laced with anti-Semitism as soon as the Nazi régime was established in Germany. Pelley's main publication, the weekly magazine *Liberation,* was supplemented by the *Silver Legion Ranger,* published first in Oklahoma City and then, for part of 1934, in Los Angeles. In late summer of that year, California newspapers reported breathlessly that the Silver Shirts had planned a coup in San Diego, drilling with weapons stolen from military posts. Their local leader was a rancher, W. W. Kemp; allegedly the San Diego branch intended to use Communist demonstrations as a pretext to seize City Hall. At that time the Los Angeles Silver Shirt branch, the biggest in the country, typically drew as many as six hundred people to its meetings. Many adherents of the Silver Shirts were former members of the Ku Klux Klan. Some seventy-five youths, mainly German-Americans, formed a branch of the Silver Shirts in San Francisco, but it collapsed almost immediately over internal differences.

Nazi activities were predictably more substantial among German-Americans, mainly represented by the Friends of the New Germany and the German-American Bund. However anti-Nazi Germans, many of them recent exiles from the Hitler régime, also mobilized around the country. In Los Angeles the local German cultural and community societies were briefly taken over by Nazi sympathizers, but a Hollywood Anti-Nazi League showered their meetings with leaflets and eventually drove them out of public life. (The Communists maintained the Anti-Nazi League until the signing of the Stalin-Hitler pact, when it metamorphosed into the Hollywood Motion Picture Democratic [!] Committee, "opposed to diplomatic or congressional action tending to involve the U.S. in either side of a European war.") The German-American Bund announced that they would hold a convention in San Francisco in May 1938, but the labor movement, Jewish leaders, the American Legion, and anti-Nazi German refugees declared that if that happened San Francisco's streets would see opposition to the Nazis such as America had never experienced before. A handful of Bundists showed up at the San Francisco event anyway, and seven thousand pickets hemmed them in from outside the hall. The San Francisco protest demonstration broke the back of the Nazis' efforts to create an "Aryan racial bloc" on the Pacific Coast.

THE CURRENTS OF political opinion on the West Coast were stirred in November 1939 by a case involving one of the most active anti-Nazi German exiles, an ex-Communist sailor named Erich Krewet who called himself Erich Rix. Rix was arrested on November 18, 1939 in San Francisco, where he lived with his American wife and 2½-year-old son, by federal immigration inspectors. The warrant called for his immediate deportation to Germany, on a charge that in applying for American citizenship in May 1938 he had given false information by neglecting to disclose that he had once been arrested in Germany. Furthermore, Rix was alleged to have entered the United States unlawfully, after deserting a foreign vessel, and to have remained illegally on American soil. After his arrest, he was transported at midnight to Angel Island in the middle of San Francisco Bay, then an immigration processing center and jail, where he was held on $1,000 bail for "turpitude and theft."

Rix told the San Francisco dailies that his arrest was the product of his anti-Nazi activities—that he was the second most dangerous man in America, in the Nazi view, after ex-Communist playwright Ernst Toller, who was reported to have committed suicide in May 1939 in New York. Rix was a leader in the German-American League of Culture, a major force in anti-Nazi German activities that was generally aligned with the Communists. In particular, Rix agitated for the expulsion from the United States of Fritz Wiedemann, the Nazi consul in San Francisco, and he and his wife believed that Wiedemann stood behind the immigration investigation.

Rix admitted having failed to inform the U.S. authorities, on applying for citizenship, that he had been arrested in Germany in 1921 for smuggling a sack of flour ashore from a ship. This trivial infraction had, he said, been brought to the attention of the U.S. government by the Nazis; should it lead to his deportation to Germany, he would be imprisoned, tortured, and probably killed.

Harry Lundeberg and the Sailors' Union of the Pacific roared to Rix's defense. A member of the union, Rix had been waiting to ship out on a steam schooner when the immigration inspectors knocked at his door. Lundeberg's union paid Rix's bail, and Lundeberg himself came forward to praise the refugee's anti-Nazi work. According to German labor historian Dieter Nelles, Rix, "one of the seafaring profession's leading Communist cadres" before the Hitler takeover, had served two years in a Nazi concentration camp but fled to Belgium in 1935, joining the Antwerp center of the Comintern sea couriers' network, the International of Seamen and Harborworkers. In 1936, the Antwerp group broke with the Comintern and went over to the International Transportworkers Federation (I.T.F.), an anti-Communist but extremely radical organization mainly comprising seamen, based in Holland and run by a militant Social Democrat, Edo Fimmen. The Antwerp group kept more than three hundred agents operating on German international and domestic shipping. Incredibly, it proved impossible for the German secret police, the Gestapo, to infiltrate; it provided an equivalent, with a democratic aim, of the work that the Pan-Pacific Trade Union Secretariat had carried out against the Japanese on behalf of Moscow.

Rix had left a German vessel in Brazil and then sailed under the Norwegian flag to the United States, where he quit because the ship's next port was in Germany. The I.T.F. made Rix their U.S. representative and sent him to the West Coast; Lundeberg, who by now hated Nazis and Communists with equal vigor, backed the I.T.F. and Rix wholeheartedly, giving the exile space in the S.U.P. weekly, the *West Coast Sailors,* for a column of anti-totalitarian opinion called "World Voyage." Rix was sensitive to issues otherwise neglected by much of the labor press of the time. For example, in one column he criticized union members who commented negatively when their fellows could not speak English well. Such attitudes, he wrote, "automatically arouse a feeling unhealthy to the labor movement. They open the door to ridicule toward many of our members and officers." The column also included trenchant comparisons between the lot of German seafarers and those under U.S. West Coast contract, and other information from within the Nazi empire.

When Rix was arrested, Lundeberg at first suggested that the Communists had fingered the exile. The combative anti-Nazi spirit of Rix and the S.U.P. contrasted dramatically with the "peace" line then followed by the Communists, who would certainly have wanted to get rid of him. But it was soon revealed that the complaint against Rix had been turned over to the Labor Department, then responsible for immigration, by the U.S. State Department, which had received it from the German government.

Lundeberg's suspicions were, however, far from groundless. Kenneth Rexroth wrote to the ex-Communist Bertram D. Wolfe on November 13, 1939, only five days before Rix's arrest, describing the San Francisco Left at that time with mordant wit. He commented,

> The CP has come to pretty much monopolize everything to the left of Hiram Johnson, politically, socially, in every way. They control the only experimental theatre, the only ballet groups, the group of radical musicians developed by Henry Cowell, all the local artists belong to their Artists Union, most of them to their Artists Congress, most of the writers to the LAW [League of American Writers, a CP front], they run the [WPA] Writers Project (they have run that into the ground), they have tremendous influence in the Democratic Party, in fact they hold the balance of power, they control at least 200 thousand trade unionists in the state (on paper anyway), and last,

but not least . . . they monopolize the social life of the community, even the Bohemian bistros swarm with drunken comrades on the lookout for a beef.

Communist influence was so pervasive, according to Rexroth, that he found it

hard to blame anybody for being timid about manifesting himself in this milieu. Leftwing Northern California is a little Russia, completely isolated and insulated. . . . I honestly believe that, in [San Francisco], anyone who enters into open opposition to the CP, and who cannot be ignored, is gambling with his life. . . . The friends of Bridges control the public opinion of the left, any smear on Lundeberg is a smear on the [Trotskyists].

Nevertheless, regardless of Communist machinations, liberal opinion in San Francisco backed, and stood up for, Lundeberg and Rix. The *Chronicle* praised the S.U.P. for defending him, concluding, "Rix is fortunate to have the SUP alert." At the beginning of December, a group of leading lawyers joined his defense, and by the end of February 1940 the Rix case had been dropped. During the uproar, however, Lundeberg had sent a telegram to Frances Perkins, Secretary of Labor in the Roosevelt Administration, comparing the Rix proceeding, which was closed, with another immigration inquiry that then occupied far greater space in the West Coast and national press: an open and elaborate hearing that had been called, at the same facility on Angel Island, and with one of the same witnesses as in the Rix matter, to determine whether or not Harry Bridges was a Communist.

The fight for Erich Rix gained minimal coverage in the daily newspapers, but the Bridges hearing was a massive enterprise for the time, costing thousands of dollars and engaging the attention of almost a score of reporters. The proceeding originated in an immigration order in March 1938, calling for Bridges, who was still not an American citizen, to be deported to Australia for membership in the Communist Party. At the instance of Secretary Perkins, James M. Landis, Dean of the Harvard Law School, was sent to San Francisco in June 1939 to oversee an investigation in trial form, with a full complement of prosecutors and defense attorneys. Bridges's side was ordered to show cause why he should not be deported; the prosecution was required to prove that Bridges was a member or affiliate of the Communist Party and, if he was found to be so, to also prove that the Party advocated the forcible and violent overthrow of the U.S. government.

The Bridges-Landis hearing lasted nine weeks and was, both at the time and in retrospect, an unbelievable spectacle. The government's advocates were forced to prove that the works of Marx, Lenin, and Stalin, and other texts in the revolutionary curriculum of the Comintern were official publications of the Communist Party, as if this were no more than an allegation; further, they were compelled to prove to the "court" that the Communist Party sought the revolutionary overthrow of capitalism. Trotskyists and others who believed that Stalin had strayed from the correct path were amused at this situation, for they believed that the Party had indeed ceased to be revolutionary; the Communists, on the other hand, denied their past insurrectionary cant as mere rhetoric, and claimed they stood only for the peaceful evolution of society toward state socialism.

The nub of the case, however, was the question of Bridges's relation to the Party. Portraying himself as a simple but militant trade unionist whose ideas had been formed in Australia before the Communists were heard of there, the longshore leader depicted the Communists in his union as good members, whose advice was usually to be trusted but who could not and did not dictate to him. He flatly denied ever having been a Party member in any form, and his attorneys asserted that the inquiry represented a conspiracy to smash the waterfront labor movement. Several prosecution witnesses, chief among them a housepainter and purged Communist functionary named John L. Leech, who had once directed the Party apparatus in southern California, testified that Bridges had attended Party meetings as a secret member. According to Leech, Bridges was known in Party ranks as Rossi, a name obviously borrowed from the conservative mayor of San Francisco, Angelo J. Rossi. That the increasingly bumptious and arrogant Bridges would, in an expression of his peculiar sense of humor, deliberately take a *klichka* based on the name of one of his major critics seemed entirely in character. Leech even declared that as "Rossi," Bridges had been nominated to the Central Committee of the Communist Party of the U.S.A. in June 1936.

The defense strategy, as shown in the dailies, was to thoroughly discredit the prosecution witnesses, especially Leech. An affidavit was introduced in which Leech denied Bridges was ever a Communist, and claimed he had been solicited to perjure himself by waterfront employer representatives; Leech responded by describing the affidavit as a Communist concoction. Finally, the defense charged that Leech was receiving relief money from the state of Oregon under false pretenses while working as a painter. This minor sort of fraud, widespread even then, had no bearing on the matters before Dean Landis; but in the legal practice of the time, anything that could undermine the credibility of a witness was to be used. Bridges's defense team further demonstrated its willingness to use illicit means when, with apparent impunity, they introduced into the proceedings a box of documents stolen from the office of the American Legion's Harper L. Knowles.

Many liberals and unionists on the West Coast doubted that Communism alone was sufficient grounds for deportation, and many doubted that sending Bridges back to Australia would serve a useful purpose, for even with him absent the Communists could retain their grip on the longshoremen. Others, like Harry Lundeberg, whose union included many noncitizens of Scandinavian and other foreign origin, disliked the immigration authorities and were loath to appear as government witnesses against Bridges; such action would only result in the Communists labeling them "informers"—and handing the Stalinists a weapon of that caliber was not Lundeberg's style. In truth, almost nobody, in the labor movement or out of it, doubted that Bridges was subservient to the Communist line; it showed in every political position he had taken since the 1934 dock strike. Indeed, after—and only after—the signing of the Stalin-Hitler pact in August, had Bridges shifted from a position of extreme antifascism to one of loud opposition to the imperialism of Britain and France.

Before the pact the longshore union had refused to unload ships flying the Nazi German flag, and had boycotted loading scrap metal for Japan as a protest against Japan's aggression against China; Bridges himself had made provocative anti-Japanese speeches and repeatedly charged that Nazi spies had infiltrated the West Coast defense industries. But in the aftermath of Poland's destruction, Japan and Germany disappeared from Bridges's agenda; he now became the most prominent "peace" agitator in California. In mid-October 1939, three weeks after the Angel Island hearing ended, and while the country awaited Dean Landis's determination in the case, Bridges told the California state convention of the C.I.O., of which he remained regional director, that they must not "welcome a war," especially American involvement in the "age-old wars of Europe," i.e., the struggle of the Allies against the Nazis.

Antitotalitarian opinion in California deemed such statements proof that Bridges followed the Communists wherever they ordered him to go, whether actual Party membership could be proved or not. Landis, however, was indifferent to any such considerations. In the last days of 1939 his findings were turned over to Secretary Perkins and then made public. Landis decided in Bridges's favor, resoundingly so; he concurred with the defense argument that witnesses had been gathered and urged to testify falsely as part of a conspiracy by police and the shipping employers. Landis heaped obloquy on the prosecution witnesses, but reserved the full strength of his outrage for John Leech, of whose testimony he wrote, "in evasion, qualification, and contradiction it is almost unique. . . . [O]ne would be tempted to regard Leech's evasionary tactics as pathological in character, were it not that behind this screen of verbiage was a motive— Leech's desire first to conceal and later to refrain from admitting that he had fraudulently been accepting relief." Leech, Landis noted, had admitted that when he belonged to the Party he considered perjury acceptable in a capitalist court; therefore, according to Landis, Leech should be considered a perjurer thereafter as well. While Bridges was an "energetic radical," according to Landis, the government had failed to prove him a Communist.

Secretary Perkins accepted Landis's opinion, and Bridges was saved from this first attempt at his deportation. The Communists celebrated, while others gaped in awe. Thousands of ordinary union members preferred to believe in Bridges and Landis. Although the federal authorities later resumed their attempts to deport him, Bridges and his acolytes repeatedly cited Landis in his defense. The proceeding caused a great noise; still, its echoes eventually faded away, and it was forgotten except among union members, who sentimentally recalled the fight for Bridges, and a few historians. Leech disappeared from the scene.

The controversy would have remained obscure but for the research conducted by historians Harvey Klehr and John Haynes in the newly opened Moscow archives after the fall of the Soviet régime in 1991. In the files of the Comintern, Klehr and Haynes discovered a 1938 list of biographies of the twenty-four full members and fifteen candidate members of the Central Committee of the American Communist Party, prepared by a Comintern official who used the *klichka* Belov. (This alias may have been used by several individuals.) Various secret members of the Central Com-

mittee are identified in Belov's documents by their *klichki,* along with their
true names. As Klehr and Haynes have written,

> The most controversial secret union Communist is "Rossi," who is identi-
> fied in the accompanying biography as the pseudonym of Harry Bridges.
> Belov describes Bridges as "President of the Dockers' and Port Warehouse
> Workers' Union. He is a strong leader of the union movement and a mass
> worker but up till now has only limited Party experience."

Klehr and Haynes have judged the affair as follows:

> Leech . . . was a strange person; he dressed like a dandy and spoke at inter-
> minable length, frequently insisting on pursuing side issues of little relevance
> to the questions he was asked and about which he appeared to know little.
> Landis, repelled by Leech's effete manner, accused him of "verbal
> haemophilia" and doubted his honesty. On the other hand, Landis found
> Bridges's straightforward denials convincing. The Comintern's records, how-
> ever, demonstrate that Leech, weird though he was, was telling the truth.

According to the Moscow archives, Bridges's commitment to the Communist Party was "such that [he] sat on its ruling Central Committee,"
Klehr and Haynes have concluded.

Strengthened by his victory, which might have led at least to a statement of
thanks to Secretary Perkins, Bridges was, rather, encouraged to widen his attacks
on the Roosevelt Administration and its posture in favor of the anti-Nazi Allies.
The New Deal had turned "reactionary" and "anti-labor," Bridges declared.
Only a month after Landis's report was released, Bridges alleged that the very
Labor Department that secured his exoneration from the Communist charge
had failed to "live up to its promises to labor." The C.I.O., he warned, would
not necessarily support a third term for Roosevelt in the next election. In another month he had appeared at Harvard, Landis's bailiwick, to argue that "the
belief that we have a free press is ridiculous." When the I.L.W.U. held its convention in April 1940, Bridges pontificated that support for the Roosevelt Administration would "weaken the bargaining power of the ILWU and place the
CIO in the position of [e]ndorsing anti-labor and reactionary groups."

IF MOST CALIFORNIANS felt deepening dismay at the news from Europe that spring, the month of May 1940 also brought cause for local cele-

bration when the Pulitzer Prizes for fiction and drama were awarded to the state's outstanding younger writers: John Steinbeck for his novel *The Grapes of Wrath* and William Saroyan for his play *The Time of Your Life.* The latter author, a product of the large Armenian-American community clustered around Fresno in the San Joaquin Valley, had set his prize-winning work among San Francisco Bohemians, in the legendary saloon run by Izzy Gomez, and his reaction to the award was a radical one: he refused it. But in truth Saroyan was an outsider by nature, and appeared infrequently in California's ideological maelstrom.

Steinbeck's novel, however, was considered more than just another radical work. Far more than the relatively innocuous *In Dubious Battle,* in which Steinbeck had tried—and failed—to tell the story of a real Communist, *The Grapes of Wrath* was viewed by conservative farmer interests and state boosters as a Red propaganda smear—which, of course, it is not at all. Later recognized as Steinbeck's greatest work by far, *The Grapes of Wrath* is something closer to dramatized sociological research, only lightly burdened with his typical sentimentality, on the most serious social problem to affect the state in the late 1930s—the mass immigration to California of thousands of poor farmers from the "Dust Bowl" of the lower Midwest. There overcultivation had deprived the land of much of its topsoil, the remaining workable stratum had been blown away by windstorms, and the misery of the farmer had been exacerbated by abusive financial practices. At least a quarter million migrant farmers had poured into California, seeking work in the fields and orchards, and to some extent displacing the Mexicans, Filipinos, and others who had harvested most of the state's crops after the 1920s. These proud but desperate folk were known collectively as Okies because so many of them came from Oklahoma. (Even today the epithet "Okie" is as hurtful as any of America's much-used ethnic insults.)

The Grapes of Wrath was acclaimed as, and remains, a classic; it has stood the test of time. But it caused an uproar from the moment it first appeared in bookstores in spring 1939; no intellectual work before or since has ever produced such a tumult in California. Steinbeck had already published a series on migrant labor in the *San Francisco News,* and he knew what to expect. Indeed, on the first day of the year 1939 he had written to his publisher, Pascal Covici, with the same naïveté that had led him, a half decade before, to think he could write the "autobiography" of a Communist, "The fascist crowd will sabotage this book because it is revolutionary."

Revolutionary it was not, either in political sentiment or in literary technique. But it was radical, saying things that many Californians were ashamed to admit. The migrants, desperate for an opportunity to labor productively and regain their status as respectable members of society, had been lured to the state by false advertisements that exaggerated the need for harvest hands—a grievance in California agriculture since Wheatland in 1913. Having believed the ads, they were then pursued and harassed, beaten, even killed. The migrants had been twice robbed of their birthright as Americans, first in their wasted home states, then in the "promised land" west of the Colorado River.

However reminiscent of Wheatland in its origins, the crisis had not stimulated Wobbly-style or other mass radical protests by the migrants, even though such a response was presented by Steinbeck as a possibility. Those critics who sought a pretext to ban the book other than Steinbeck's presentation of a terrible economic reality attacked the book's naturalistic treatment of human relationships and its crude language.

By the end of the summer, the book had been temporarily removed from public schools and libraries by the board of supervisors in Kern County in the lower San Joaquin Valley, and the Associated Farmers, the main lobbying group for the state's agricultural employers, had discussed a statewide boycott. "The association is deeply concerned at the black eye given California in a book that has taken a few shreds of fact and built them into a story grossly unfair," trumpeted Harold Pomeroy, state secretary of the organization. The group backed off its demand for a ban. But only a month before the announcement that *Grapes* had won the Pulitzer Prize, Philip Bancroft, an orchard owner from Walnut Creek, a leader of the Associated Farmers, and a Republican politician, debated the truth or falsity of *The Grapes of Wrath* with Carey McWilliams. Only three months after *Grapes,* McWilliams published a nonfiction volume, *Factories in the Field,* on many of the same issues which also stirred the ire of the farming "interests." This Los Angeles labor lawyer and author was, in one of Governor Olson's first executive acts, appointed chief of the state Division of Immigration and Housing Administration, with responsibility for migrant issues.

The audience at the Bancroft-McWilliams debate, held in San Francisco at the Commonwealth Club, heard McWilliams vouch for Steinbeck's reliability as a reporter and ascribe the injustices outlined in the book to the large farming corporations that had papered the Dust Bowl with leaflets calling for workers. Bancroft argued in response that high wages and public relief payments had caused the exodus. The farm counties, Bancroft declared, had been "suddenly swamped by these uninvited guests who appeared on their doorsteps hungry, homeless, and destitute." California farmers, he said, "instead of having neglected or abused migrants, have done their best for them and have assumed burdens that should have been borne by the [federal] government." Bancroft assailed McWilliams and Steinbeck as pro-Communists, adding that the latter's "warped mind" led him to libel the people of the Dust Bowl as well as of California. "He transformed the inhabitants from typical God-fearing American farmers into a lot of foul-mouthed, intemperate morons," Bancroft declared, according to a report in the *San Francisco Chronicle*.

McWilliams, a gentleman as well as an important state official, refrained from personal attacks. Above all he insisted that the increasing growth of big corporate farms was the main source of social tension in California agriculture. Already, he said, 8 percent of the state's farms produced 53 percent of its crops. The two men ended the debate by shaking hands. Still, the controversy did not stop there. For Steinbeck the biggest problem created by the book's enormous success was his loss of privacy. By mid-July 1939, almost a year before receiving the Pulitzer, he had written to a friend, Elizabeth Otis, "I'm frightened at the rolling might of this damned thing. It is completely out of hand—I mean a kind of hysteria about the book is growing that is not healthy."

Similar anger, as noted, had greeted McWilliams's *Factories in the Field*. That book generated another round of debates, including one in the pages of the Sunday *Chronicle* pitting Louis Paul, an author and friend of Steinbeck as defender of McWilliams, against Ruth Comfort Mitchell, a California poet and patriot who condemned him. Paul wrote of McWilliams's "document" that its author's "sympathies [were] biased," but then noted, "Intimate acquaintance with the history of conditions existing among the agricultural workers of California is . . . conducive to bias. The harvesting of its natural wealth . . . constitutes a continuously deliberate exploitation of its field labor, as a prerogative, by the great landowning individuals and corporations of the State."

McWilliams's account of California farm labor emphasized that the state had never been hospitable to midwestern-style small farming; the semi-feudalism of the Spanish missions and the Mexican landowners had given way to the big cattle farms of the late nineteenth century. As an inspiring but failed alternative, McWilliams pointed to Burnette Haskell's Kaweah colony. Cattle had been replaced by wheat, but the absence of crop rotation farmed the land out; it was then taken over by fruit crops, leading to the emergence of industrial agriculture. The "factory in the field" was worked by imported hands, first Chinese, then Japanese, Hindu, Mexican, and Filipino. Attempts to organize the field worker, including the efforts of the Communists, as well as the non-Communist agricultural strikes exemplified by Salinas in 1936, had been met with brutality. Finally, Paul emphasized in his defense of McWilliams, "The sight of men gassed and clubbed to death in industrial warfare is conducive to traumatic and permanent bias." McWilliams suggested that only a diversification of land ownership, identified with "collectivism," would relieve the state of the migrant-labor problem, but McWilliams saw no solution in the immediate future. "His book is concerned with fact, not prophecy," Paul wrote. "Whether or not the facts themselves constitute a prophecy remains for the reader . . . to determine."

Ruth Comfort Mitchell's blast at McWilliams began by dwelling on his book's passion and combative language. "All through the book his revolutionary thinking is frankly clear. He frequently quotes Henry George and mentions Karl Marx, and refers to John Steinbeck as an authority." George and Steinbeck as insurrectionists equal to Marx—and probably better suited to accompany him than his more common iconographic associates, Engels and Lenin! McWilliams sought state protection for Communist violence, Mitchell declared; his "adolescent venom" was as inappropriate in a high government official as his "very genuine concern" for the migrant workers, whom the sensitive Mitchell compared with "noxious weeds" deposited on ranch land by floodwaters. New Deal farm policies on cotton raising had driven the Dust Bowl migrants west in search of high relief payments, Mitchell asserted—echoing Bancroft. She concluded rather hilariously with a jab at "grapes of wrath, beets of bitterness, prunes, peas, peaches of persecution and propaganda, [and] cotton of controversy." Meanwhile, her brother, Standish Mitchell, reportedly got a column by McWilliams dropped from *Westways,* the periodical of the Automobile Club of Southern California. And although abandoning calls for book-banning, farmer leader Harold Pomeroy insisted, "McWilliams' book is another of the same ilk which the Associated Farmers will fight as they will fight *The Grapes of Wrath.*"

McWilliams naturally drew sympathy from radicals and liberals throughout the state in this controversy; in retrospect, however, it must be admitted that *Factories in the Field* contains a good deal of balderdash. Communists like George Woolf, a shady sort who had made his way, in search of income, from the San Francisco waterfront to farm-labor organizing, were treated in the book as the sole legitimate champions of the rank-and-file agricultural worker. The A.F.L., which had led many farm strikes, was backhanded by McWilliams, who argued ridiculously that the California Federation of Labor "feared the democratizing effect of the organization of farm labor." In reality, the A.F.L. leaders realized that even though the allies and acolytes of Harry Bridges in the C.I.O. made flamboyant promises about organizing farm workers, the short harvest periods, the need to migrate to follow crops, and other issues of labor instability made the task of unionizing the agricultural workforce extremely difficult.

California may have seen "factories in the field" in the sense that farm work had become industrialized, but such "factories" had failed to produce the kind of close-knit, permanent working-class districts that surrounded industry in the cities and served as nurseries for infant unions; nor did they even produce authentic company towns. The Spanish-speaking *barrios* were then an insufficient base for labor organizing. However, Carey McWilliams was never one to let common sense get in the way of an impressive-sounding theory. He argued that the division between farm and factory was "artificial," "unrealistic and inaccurate." He claimed, in a breathtaking flight of sociological hallucination, that "the distinction between farm and city is practically meaningless in California today," that is, in 1939.

McWilliams also greatly overdrew his picture of anti-union repression in California agriculture, which he labeled "farm fascism." Some strikes, such as that at Salinas in 1936, had involved bloody conflicts, and violence had been applied against organizers in many localities. But to call the haphazard abuses of laborers by growers, sheriffs, vigilantes, and their supporters "fascism" was to completely misapprehend the latter phenomenon. Mussolini's movement in Italy had its origins in bands of terrorists employed to suppress rural strikes, and in Germany Adolf Hitler, an anti-union "scab" as a young man, had recruited Nazis heavily from among professional strikebreakers. But although such phenomena were continually described by the liberal and radical press as incipient in California, they never actually appeared there. The assaults on farm strikers and agitators, if sometimes fatal, were sporadic and time-specific, in contrast with the coordination and extent of the Italian *squadristi* and the German "anti-labor militia," as certain Marxists described it.

California growers produced no coordinated political or paramilitary movement comparable with the fascists in Italy or the Nazis in Germany—or even a single credible leader of a totalitarian or demagogic stripe; they gained no consistent support from the state government and were unable to impose policies favorable to their interests. In the absence of such systematic interference with and substitution for established institutions, the term *fascism* became effectively meaningless—a novelty of journalistic analysis that degenerated into a mere imprecation that was employed promiscuously by the Communists but that was also useful to them, during the Stalin-Hitler pact, to assert a specious moral equation between the real fascism of Hitler and Mussolini and ordinary agricultural capitalism in California.

The Steinbeck debate was renewed when, early in 1940, *The Grapes of Wrath* was released as a motion picture. His 1937 novel about itinerant farm workers, *Of Mice and Men,* was nonpolitical, and became a successful film in 1939. Although the *Grapes* script by Nunnally Johnson, in accord with Hollywood sensibilities of the time, censored out the book's blunt language, its harsh depiction of the migrants' odyssey west, in their broken-down jalopies, could not but further dramatize the issue. Rumors flew: the story had originally been bought by Darryl Zanuck so it could be suppressed or turned into a comedy; the state would ban it as Georgia, in 1932, had banned the legendary social reform film *I Am a Fugitive from a Chain Gang.* (This was pretty unlikely with Culbert Olson as governor.) When it came out, 20th Century-Fox warned that no children would be sold tickets to see it.

While Steinbeck was apparently quite satisfied with the film and it became a Hollywood classic, as a work of cinema *The Grapes of Wrath* was and remains a colossal and absurd failure. Given the library of praise that has grown around it over the years, this will probably be considered an outrageous opinion. Yet Hollywood has never accepted the critical standards that are taken for granted in literature and art, and the adulation accorded *The Grapes of Wrath* as a movie provides a perfect example of that willful myopia. Its pseudodocumentary photography, hailed at the time as brilliant and veridical, today seems artificial and pretentious. The cloying, tear-jerking manner that Steinbeck kept leashed and muzzled in the book ran wild in the film, making some of its scenes laughably bathetic. And the almost imperceptible "New Deal" undercurrent in the book—with government relief camps presented as a meager, if not failed, solution for the migrant problem—becomes, in the film, outright propaganda for state-sponsored rescue of the disadvantaged.

The great director John Ford had shown with *Stagecoach*, released the year before, his power as an interpreter of American myths; he was in many respects an American Eisenstein, although without the latter's technical daring. Ford's genius could not be completely expunged from *The Grapes of Wrath*, which may be why the scenes of the highway travails suffered by the migrants are more powerful than its stagey attempts at "socially conscious" composition. But Ford was no less a sentimentalist than Steinbeck. "Ma Joad," the Oklahoma Great Mother goddess portrayed by Jane Darwell (who, with Ford, won an Academy Award for the picture), spouts rhetoric that more resembles the clumsy sloganeering of People's Front Stalinism than the accurately crafted dialogue of the novel. "We'll go on forever, Pa," she croons, "because we're the people."

In the hands of San Francisco-born Mervyn LeRoy, the tough colleague of Ford who made the 1931 gangster classic *Little Caesar* as well as *I Am a Fugitive from a Chain Gang*, the film of *The Grapes of Wrath* might have become a truly immortal work. But Hollywood had changed considerably since the early 1930s, when Irving Thalberg helped beat Sinclair, but when, also, LeRoy made his magnificent "social pictures." Ford by 1939 was working in an industry filled with leftists anxious that, on screen, *The Grapes of Wrath* be made as simplistic as possible. As a result, the film succumbed to what may be best described as Stalinist mannerism. Steinbeck, fortunately, had nothing comparable to contend with in the literary field. This is why *The Grapes of Wrath* is still read but is seldom watched. But the broader phenomenon of the Hollywood Left will be taken up in due course.

Henry Fonda, sulking his way through the role of "Tom Joad," the ex-convict son of the central family in the epic, gained no Oscar but received plenty of critical praise for the film. Fonda, it should be noted, had appeared in an earlier attempt at properly leftish cinema, the 1938 picture *Blockade*, produced by Walter Wanger with a script by a moderately talented Communist playwright turned scenarist, John Howard Lawson. Set in the Spanish Civil War, and promoted as the first Hollywood feature to treat foreign events authoritatively, *Blockade* was one of the most outrageous pieces of Stalinist distortion to emerge from the Hollywood Left. Although its publicity included a smarmy disclaimer, stating that uniforms in the film had been designed so that the hero could not be identified with either the Franco or Republican forces, its main subplot dealt with a secret-police hunt for a spy made up to look like Trotsky! Critic Otis Ferguson wrote of *Blockade,* "There is achieved a deadly numb level of shameless hokum out of which anything true or decent rises only for a second to confound itself."

John Steinbeck soon turned to marine biology as a theme for his work, and never again wrote on social problems in California, although Carey McWilliams, as we shall see, continued lecturing and writing, in addition to his duties in the Olson Administration. While Steinbeck imagined *The Grapes of Wrath* to be "revolutionary"—it was far less so than Norris's *Octopus,* to say nothing of *The Iron Heel*—a true revolutionary in the arts, Henry Cowell, was just then contending with a controversy as disturbing to some as the investigations of Steinbeck and McWilliams into California's agricultural reality.

Cowell had something in common with Steinbeck's fictional Tom Joad, with whose return home from prison *The Grapes of Wrath* begins: on June 26, 1940, Cowell walked away from San Quentin prison, where he had served three and a half years for corrupting the morals of young boys. This extraordinary episode began with his arrest in May 1936. San Mateo County officials had gone to his home (and birthplace) in Menlo Park after a complaint by a female relative of a high-school student. Officers found three "young boys" in the residence, waiting for Cowell to come back. The trio claimed that six other "boys" had been given money and the loan of an automobile by the composer. When he arrived about 1:00 A.M., he confessed to the charge, and even turned over some compromising photographs to police, according to press reports.

Cowell was allowed by officers to sit at his piano and play for a half hour before he was transported to the county jail. In his cell, he was placed under a suicide watch, but as the case developed he demonstrated an exceptional aplomb. Seeking to protect the youthful victims of his desire from the public exposure that would arise from a trial, he pleaded guilty after some indecision; for this reason the actual age of the "boys" with which he was involved was never disclosed. He was sentenced to one to fifteen years in state prison. "Several women friends of Cowell were in court when sentence was passed and some wept audibly," according to the *San Francisco Chronicle.*

The journalistic and public reaction to Cowell's misfortune was worthy of note. Homosexuality was not then commonly discussed in the press; it was generally referred to, if at all, as "inversion," which sounds like a phenomenon either of weather or perhaps of international banking. Non-homosexual friends and admirers of Cowell were aghast at the case. But many observers were sympathetic, treating him as a creative genius tormented by impulses beyond his control, like Oscar Wilde a half century before. In one of the most bizarre but fascinating incidents of Cowell's unique biography, he performed two of his experimental compositions in a prison concert at the end of July 1936, only weeks after his sentencing. "His face paled when the audience sat silent after he had finished his own composition," the *Chronicle* reported. "Then came a burst of applause that lasted for several minutes. Deeply moved, Cowell raised his eyes, tried to speak, and failed. He played one more number, heard another ovation and left the stage overcome. He had won his first fight in San Quentin." On his release he proceeded to the East Coast, where he performed triumphantly with the New York Philharmonic, under Leopold Stokowski, on a program with works of Beethoven and Bach.

AS EARLIER NOTED, Henry Cowell had encouraged the work of two other experimental composers associated with California, Harry Partch and John Cage. In 1940 both were occupied with major projects. Partch was then completing a written work, *Bitter Music,* that not only embodied many of his innovative views of musical art but also addressed, in a profound and enduring way, the issues of economic deprivation, homelessness, and state relief dealt with by Steinbeck and McWilliams.

Harry Partch shared with Henry Cowell an early exposure to exotic, especially Asian, musical forms. His parents were Presbyterian missionaries in China who returned to America in 1900 after the father, Virgil F. Partch, suffered a crisis of faith, followed by the uprising of the "Boxers." Harry was born in Oakland in 1901; three years later, a combination of his mother's bad health and a new job for his father with the Immigration Service led the family to Tucson, the hot, dry, beautiful, and slightly crazy place that, since the beginning of the Spanish mission enterprise, had marked the southeast border of the California economic and cultural zone. The family soon proceeded to Benson, Arizona, a mining town close to the Mexican border, and then to Albuquerque, New Mexico. The variety of influences present in the Partch home as well as outside it included Chinese music, Mexican songs, and Native American melodies; he also learned to play the violin, mandolin, and piano. As a youth he played the piano and organ in silent movie theaters, and began composing for the piano.

Harry Partch was hardly out of high school when, in 1919, his father died and his mother took the family to Los Angeles. There she died only a year later in a streetcar accident. Harry studied music at the University of Southern California but soon quit and began wandering around the state and composing independently. He often went to Chinese-language theaters in San Francisco; he later took a job as a proofreader with the State Printing Office in Sacramento. He discovered the works of Hermann Helmholtz on acoustics in the Sacramento Public Library; they became the foundation of a life career experimenting with musical intonation. And he went to sea.

Proofreader, merchant seaman, piano teacher, or vagabond, the young Partch began modifying instruments according to his new conceptions of intonation, first by altering violin and viola fingerboards. In the early 1930s he commissioned craftsmen to assemble novel instruments according to his specifications; the first was a viola with a cello fingerboard, used to produce "just intonation" based on an octave of twenty-nine notes. This instrument, the Adapted Viola, was used in early "Partchian" compositions, combining verses from the Chinese poet Li Po with citations from the *Bible* and Shakespeare. In February 1932 he presented some of these works at a concert in San Francisco, sponsored by Henry Cowell's New Music Society. Professor Charles Seeger was another supporter of Partch's work. In June 1934 Partch received a grant from the Carnegie Corporation of $1,500, which allowed him to travel to Europe. In England he paid for the construction of a Chromatic Organ, using an octave of forty-three notes, and had it shipped home.

In spring 1935, Partch returned to the United States and to the realities of the Depression. Destitute, unfavored by patrons, he became one of the millions of male transients wandering the roads, although he obtained occasional work for the Federal Writers' Project and built new instruments. In 1936–37 he rewrote the *Arizona* volume in the American Guide Series issued by the W.P.A., and in 1939–40 he worked with Rexroth and others on the *California* Guide. Rexroth seemed not to have thought much of him; Jaime de Angulo, whom Partch visited in Big Sur and for whom he performed his music, was also unimpressed. Partch was personally diffident; to understand his genius one had to pry his ideas out of him.

The period from 1935 to the middle of World War II is known to Partch enthusiasts as his "hobo" period. The composer's experience as a transient, traveling by freight train and hitchhiking, staying in hobo jungles and relief camps, was the raw material for works that, as much or more than the fiction of Steinbeck or the sociological inquiries of Carey McWilliams, provided those who came after with a meaningful expression of what it meant to be unemployed or "on the bum" in the 1930s. Partch had developed a theory of music in which the voice in speech and the peculiarities of the American idiom were central, an "essentially vocal and verbal music." Thus Partch was doing what radical intellectuals always hoped and claimed to do: listening to, recording, and creatively transforming the daily discourse of ordinary people. This revolutionary conception, however, had no political underpinning of any kind; Partch was, if anything, a bit of a reactionary, with the traditional prejudices of white gentile America.

Nevertheless Partch's "hobo" works, although never enjoying the wide audience granted Steinbeck, are a magnificent achievement. *Bitter Music,* one of his greatest, is a journal of an eight-month period spent in state shelters for the wandering unemployed, hobo camps, and similar lodgings, complemented with songs heard on the road and conversational phrases musically notated. He wrote,

> My music still comforted and sustained me, especially because I suddenly realized that I had an inspirational and creative use for it even in a hobo jungle. I heard music in the voices all about me, and tried to notate it. . . . The nuance of inflection and thought of the lowest of our social order was a new experience in tone, and I found myself at its fountainhead, a fountainhead of pure musical Americana.

Harry Partch was unintimidated, and even attracted, by the company of convicts, the homeless, and others on society's margins. "I went south toward any god who softly whistled," he recalled, describing his progress through California. *Bitter Music* begins in Santa Rosa, in June 1935, with a traditional American tune that recurs throughout, *"Hand me down my walking cane, Oh, hand me down my walking cane, Oh, hand me down my walking cane, I'm a-goin' to leave on that midnight train, 'Cause all my sins are taken away."* The narrator then proceeds to a federal shelter for men in Stockton, obtaining a bed for one night, the next morning's breakfast, and no more, and there he notates the musical speech of an administrator who, indicating the traveler's clothing, says, *"Take 'em all off—they gotta be deloused."*

In its 125 printed pages, *Bitter Music* presents a vocal panorama of Depression California. Every detail of the life of the transient and the bum is present: the odors of many bodies, snoring, medical examinations, jail time served, and problems with the State Emergency Relief Administration or S.E.R.A., whose bureaucrats seek ways to deny eligibility by claiming that the narrator, a Californian by birth, has forfeited residence in the state. At a ranch in the San Joaquin Delta, Partch recorded a latrine inscription rich with humor; he discussed homosexuality with a companion, and later was labeled a "fruit." Indeed, among the transients male-to-male sex, and sex with animals, as well as masturbation, are constant themes: a "big palooka cups his hand out in front of him: 'Yeh—Meet the wife!' he grins," and Partch solemnly notates the words as music.

Partch never romanticized his experience as a transient: he wryly described the rejection that greeted camp residents when, in their state-issued denims lettered in white, "U.S.A.—S.E.R.A.," they entered the business districts of the California towns. He also filled *Bitter Music* with memories of his trip to Europe and his struggle to gain comprehension of his musical innovations. Continuing southward, he hitchhikes, and gets a ride from a Filipino between Santa Barbara and Ojai, recording and notating, over page after page, the soft voice of the driver preaching Christian doctrine to him on their way. He wrote, *"I rest my head against the joggling window and close my eyes, listening to the sweet music from the throat of the Filipino. He is talking so low now that he is barely audible above the motor. 'Come to Jesus, beloved! I'm telling you, brother, no man can wash your sins away . . .'"* Eventually Partch responds, "May God bless you." The narrative ends with Partch standing on the highway in the rain, sixty miles from "El-lay," drunk on Port, laughing when his thumb gains him no rides, his thoughts notated . . . *"Do you passersby know what is in my soul? Rain, rain, rain—my swift darlings—and bitter music."*

John Cage, an Angeleño by origin, was working in a similar direction in June 1940. He had just moved with his wife Xenia Kashevarova, the Alaska-born daughter of a Russian Orthodox priest, to San Francisco from Seattle, where he had worked at the experimental Cornish School, an institution that had once attracted Kenneth and Andrée Rexroth. Already in 1937 Cage had foreseen "the use of noise . . . to make music . . . [which] will continue and increase until we reach a music produced through the aid of electrical instruments . . . which will make available for musical purposes any and all sounds."

Cage had studied with Henry Cowell in New York, then with the great atonal pioneer Arnold Schoenberg in California. But Schoenberg's twelve-tone system of composition left him uninspired. Cage began introducing anvils, pieces of sheet metal, automobile brake drums, and similar unorthodox sources of sound into his compositions, along with many kinds of bells and the Javanese gamelan orchestra. His instrument of choice in 1940 was the "altered" or "prepared" piano, on which he had begun working two years before. As a student of Cowell, Cage was fascinated by the earlier composer's practice of directly plucking and otherwise sounding the strings inside the piano, along with Cowell's "tone clusters" produced by striking the keys with the forearm and fist—although Cowell had, in the meantime, turned back to a more symphonic approach.

Like Partch, Cage believed that the way forward was to reconstruct the instrument. "I decided that what was wrong was the piano, not my efforts," he later recalled. Going beyond Cowell, Cage chose to "prepare" the piano strings, first by placing such mobile objects as newspapers and ashtrays inside the instrument, then by inserting screws, bolts, and additional rough materials between two strings, so that they remained in place and expanded the tonal capabilities of the piano. He had, in effect, turned a piano into a percussion orchestra played by one performer. Most importantly, his reconstruction of the piano was such that the music produced was unpredictable. As Cage said, "The performer no longer had the impression that he would be able to hear the piece immediately on the first reading, the way it was going to sound."

The Cages were almost as poor as Partch, and as soon as they arrived in San Francisco John applied to work for the W.P.A. Music Project. But as noted by David Revill, one of his biographers, the agency administrators "did not accept he was a musician." John Cage was assigned to a recreation

318 From West to East

program, making up games to entertain children; he taught very young Chinese-Americans to make music by percussion, using flowerpots and similar items. About that time he composed his *Living Room Music,* in which four performers, using fingers and fists, produced sounds by striking any handy objects, furniture, and even walls.

The year 1940 saw musical culture in California further strengthened by the arrival of Darius Milhaud, the "bad boy" of French composers, at Mills College, a women's institution in Oakland. Born of an ancient Provençal Jewish family and famous for his invention of "polytonality" or the simultaneous playing of two keys, as well as for his innovative ballet scores, Milhaud had at age 57 been forced to flee Nazi-occupied of France. The career of Henry Cowell had conferred on the region a reputation for hospitality to the most radical music conceptions; its appeal to new composers had also been expressed by the Swiss-born Ernest Bloch, who in 1924 called San Francisco the "city of inspiration," and who spent the next five years as director of the San Francisco Conservatory of Music. Another rebel against musical conservatism, Ernst Bacon, had taught at the Conservatory and served as a supervisor and conductor of the W.P.A. Music Project.

Nevertheless, the "native Californian" revolutionaries in music, Cowell, Partch, and Cage, were much further ahead of their time than Milhaud, Bloch, or Bacon, and even though Cowell was acclaimed as a genius, it would be some years before their influence was widely felt in American musical culture. Few of the political intellectuals of the period fully understood their significance—Kenneth Rexroth, equally advanced beyond his literary contemporaries, being the great exception. Yet the search for music in foreign and popular traditions and speech, particularly as developed by Cowell and Partch, resembled, if rather remotely, a musical affectation then prevalent among the Communists: an enthusiasm for an artificial and politicized "folk music."

The great exemplar of this latter fad was Woodrow Wilson "Woody" Guthrie, a guitarist and balladeer born in Oklahoma in 1912. Guthrie had come to California in the great migrant wave from the Dust Bowl, began performing in public and on the radio, and was "discovered" by Ed Robbin, a writer for the Communist *People's World,* who arranged for him to begin publishing a column in the paper, "Woody Sez." Guthrie was probably of greater interest to the Communists for his origins than for his music, at the beginning, since the Party was extremely concerned to cultivate support among the so-called "Okies." Yet his satirical versions of old American standards—the same sources mined by Partch—made him a popular entertainer at Communist functions.

Guthrie-style singing was not real folk music; rather, it was a genre of cabaret performance that drew on folk sources. However, authentic folk music was then being studied and preserved by federally supported experts, in line with the broader cultural populism of the Roosevelt era, and folk music as a concept seemed made for the People's Front. Woody Guthrie had some talent as an author of the kind of doggerel Partch recorded among transients. But Guthrie's compositions, including a famous recension of the "Tom Joad" tale drawn from *The Grapes of Wrath,* had, at their very best, more in common with the caricatures of "the people" in Ford's film than with the powerful description of Steinbeck's written account. Of course, Guthrie's "Tom Joad" was based on the movie, not the book.

Although he may have continued to travel by freight train and thumb, by mid-1940 Woody Guthrie had driven to New York, the cynosure of all American Communist hopes, and had encountered some success there. He joined Pete Seeger, the son of the musicologist who discovered Henry Cowell, in The Almanac Singers, a group mainly remembered for their songs in support of the Stalin-Hitler pact and in opposition to American involvement in the war. The Almanacs' circle included the then-Communist writer Jim Thompson, another Oklahoman, and the actor Will Geer. The singing group's most famous, or infamous, number was an attack on Roosevelt, who, according to the Almanacs, "*said, 'I hate war, and so does Eleanor, but we won't be safe 'til everybody's dead.'*" A book could be written exclusively on the differing paths of Henry Cowell and Pete Seeger, of Harry Partch and Woody Guthrie.

While The Almanac Singers continued their "peace" propaganda via the Manhattan "café society" stage, back in California serious dissension wracked the Olson Administration and the state Democratic Party. In July 1940 the Democrats held their national convention in Chicago. Supporters of Franklin Roosevelt were looking forward to a third term, a novelty in American politics, while advocating an improved defense and greater support for embattled Britain in its war against the Nazis. The California delegation was headed by Governor Olson, and was overwhelmingly supportive of both the third term and a strong military posture. Olson himself had issued a stirring statement after the German invasion of Norway, emphasizing "the sympathy of the government of the State of California and all of its people in the struggle in which the peace-loving people of Norway are now engaged to free themselves from a ruthless invasion of their country by an imperialistic power; and our best wishes for their early and complete success in that struggle."

But if Olson's anti-Nazi views were shared by the great majority of ordinary Californians, the state Democratic Party also included a "peace" faction linked to the Communists. Lieutenant Governor Ellis Patterson came forward as the putative leader of a "Liberal" slate, both anti-third term and antiwar, in the Democratic primary. The "Patterson slate" adopted the slogan NO ARMS, NO AID, TO BRITAIN AND FRANCE, DOWN WITH IMPERIALIST WAR. Olson condemned his one-time running mate for promoting a ticket inspired by non-Californians and, even, Olson warned, "possibly from without America." Patterson responded by declaring "Labor is against war," and accusing Olson of "Red-baiting." However, Patterson's antics merely increased the suspicions of most California Democrats about him, and when it briefly appeared that Olson might be offered the vice-presidential slot under Roosevelt, many California delegates to the convention expressed alarm that this might leave the governorship in Patterson's hands.

Unfortunately, Patterson was not the only member of the Olson Administration to fall in line with Moscow; other luminaries of the "peace" Democrats included, along with Communists in both the A.F.L. and C.I.O. wings of labor, such individuals as Reuben Borough, a former associate of Upton Sinclair in the EPIC movement, and none other than Carey McWilliams—just when McWilliams's appointment by Olson as state immigration commissioner was under severe attack from conservatives. Although he was sincere in his views and conscientious in his official duties, McWilliams's manifest laziness in researching his books led him to depend excessively on Communist sources, and his considerable ego made him otherwise susceptible to Communist influence. While he seldom pursued the Party's ends, McWilliams frequently endorsed them. Olson remained loyal to McWilliams, though the favor went unreturned. Speaking before the National Conference of Social Work six weeks before the 1940 Democratic national convention, McWilliams sought to overtly link his criticism of economic injustice and the growth of industrial agriculture to the Communist "peace" line. "Entrenched interests are so strong," he declaimed, "that doubt actually exists in people's minds today as to whether we are not threatened with a breakdown of democracy itself, and should this country become involved in the present European war there is no doubt whatever that the solution of this problem will be indefinitely postponed."

———————

COMMUNIST "PEACE" INTRIGUES made most California radicals and liberals detest the Stalinists even more, and an event south of the Rio Grande confirmed the view of many that Nazi and Communist totalitarianism were indistinguishable. On August 20, 1940, a specially chosen and trained agent of the Soviet secret police attacked the exiled Leon Trotsky in the latter's study in the Mexico City suburb of Coyoacán. The next day, after emergency brain surgery, the old revolutionary died. The assassin, Ramón Mercader del Rio, was a young Catalan Communist and a veteran of the Spanish Civil War; he was found to have false passports that respectively identified him as a Canadian and a Belgian.

The Trotsky assassination resounded in California, and elsewhere, mainly as drama; the unapologetic heretic had been harassed and tracked across the planet, from Turkey to France, then to Norway and Mexico, by Stalin's agents. But San Francisco had also figured in the elaborate and extensive preparations for this supreme act of Soviet secret police terror. The mission had been entrusted by Moscow to Naum I. Eitingon, one of its most fascinating and controversial operatives. A scion of a prominent Russian Jewish family, Eitingon, like other top-secret police officials of Jewish origin, had assumed a partial *klichka,* adopting the more Russian Orthodox-sounding first name of Leonid; his other aliases included Naumov, Tom, and Pierre. Eitingon had been involved in high-level clandestine operations, including espionage in the Pacific region, since at least 1930.

In October 1939 Eitingon was dispatched to New York City to personally direct the conspiracy against Trotsky. By January 1940 Eitingon had set up a reserve structure of illegal agents in Mexico and California; clandestine Russian activities were as yet underdeveloped in Mexico itself, but agents previously emplaced in California would assist the main participants in the operation. After Trotsky was killed and the assassin arrested, Eitingon and the assassin's mother, Caridad Mercader, made their way to Los Angeles and San Francisco. Utilizing the networks he had established a decade previously, Eitingon secured passage to China for himself and Señora Mercader, in February 1941.

Stalin's savage persecution of Trotsky, although hailed by Communists and fellow-travelers with typically mindless enthusiasm, shocked antitotalitarian opinion in California, above all, for its obsessional quality, bereft of all logic or proportion. In California, the effective Trotskyists consisted of little more than Barney Mayes, the adviser to Harry Lundeberg, a few seamen working in Lundeberg's union, Mayes's wife Joan London, and her ex-husband, Charles Malamuth; the Communists by now had labeled Lundeberg the "Number One Trotskyite on the West Coast." Lundeberg was never an ideologue of that sort although he admired Trotsky personally, as did many other anti-Stalinists.

Continued support by the California Communists for the Stalin-Hitler pact made an open conflict with Governor Olson, a liberal similar to the educator John Dewey, who opposed Stalin's purges, inevitable. While the Communists and fellow-travelers shouted louder and louder for "peace," Olson endorsed compulsory military service. In September 1940 the Battle of Britain began: the *Luftwaffe* commenced uninterrupted bombing of London. The suffering and courage of England's capital city, even more than the fall of France, tore at the hearts of Californians. Meanwhile, Berlin broadcast assurances that Stalinist Russia would soon be fully integrated into the "Axis" alliance of Germany, Italy, and Japan, and Tokyo was warned that after mid-October the United States would embargo shipment of scrap iron and steel to Japan. Governor Olson called for allocation of funds to a State Defense Council, a military-preparedness institution originally set up in 1917 but abolished by the state legislature in 1935. Such a council had been newly sworn in without a financial appropriation in June 1940; it was unclear whether it could legally draw on state funds. The council was headed by University of California political scientist Samuel Chester May. (May later disinherited and denounced his son, U. C. Berkeley teaching assistant Kenneth May, for Communist activities.) Meanwhile, fresh recall attempts, based on new charges of radicalism, were bedeviling the governor.

Notwithstanding such exaggerations by his opponents the final break between Olson and the Communists came in October 1940, when the governor signed into law a legislative measure throwing the Party off the California ballot. The bill was written by then-assemblyman Jack Tenney, a Democrat from Inglewood in Los Angeles County, a member of the Musicians' Union, and coauthor of the popular song *Mexicali Rose*. First elected in 1937, Tenney originally followed a pro-Communist line; he introduced legislation into the Assembly calling for California to officially support the Spanish Republic! But Tenney was infuriated by the intrigues of Communists in the Musicians' Union, and became the Party's main local enemy as head of the legislature's Committee on Un-American Activities.

The state C.I.O., run by Harry Bridges, clamored that the removal of the Communists from the ballot was a "fascist action" and unconstitutional, while the longshore boss himself warned that unions would "become outlawed, regardless of who wins the presidential election," and that "secret police" were "scuttling the C.I.O." But Olson answered firmly that "few, if any American citizens could be found objecting to the disqualification of a party affiliated with a foreign government." He admitted that "some who would object . . . in the name of democracy and civil liberties . . . would give legal recognition to a foreign-controlled party set up for the purpose of abolishing democracy and civil liberties by any means whatsoever." But he emphasized that the new law did not disqualify an American-based party that called for the elimination of capitalism or the establishment of socialism, nor did it outlaw the Communist *per se,* or forbid the profession or advocacy of Communist doctrines. The issue was the control of the Party from abroad; regardless of its purported program, the Communist Party in California was an extension of an antidemocratic, totalitarian foreign power and so had no place on the ballot.

In reality, the law was not to come into effect until January 1941, and Communist candidates had already been certified to compete in the 1940 election. The aged Anita Whitney, who had largely faded from the scene by the late 1930s, was brought out by the Communist leadership to condemn Olson. But her arguments were feeble; Olson had, she said, been elected in 1938 with Communist support, and she asked plaintively, "You did not think we were subversive or un-American then, did you?" The poor woman ended her comments by denying the party was even "influenced by any foreign power."

In November 1940 the American people delivered their verdict: Roosevelt was elected to a third term by a popular majority of 27 million votes against 22 million for Wendell Willkie, the Republican candidate, who was then opposed to involvement in the European war. (Roosevelt's majority in the Electoral College was much higher; there he received 449 electoral votes to only 82 for Willkie.) But Olson, who had pressed both issues—involvement in Europe's war and the outlawing of the Communist Party—still had few intellectuals completely on his side. Too many wavered, like McWilliams, in the face of Communist intrigues; an outstanding exception was the screen actor Melvyn Douglas, who was prominent, with his wife Helen Gahagan Douglas, in state Democratic politics. Douglas openly fought the Communists in Hollywood, beginning his efforts upon the announcement of the Stalin-Hitler pact. But his sudden prominence as a partisan of the Allies also reflected a subtle but perceptible shift that occurred in California politics at the end of the 1930s, as the Communists increasingly focused their attention away from San Francisco to Los Angeles, and particularly to Hollywood.

The fate of *The Grapes of Wrath* as a motion picture revealed the growing influence of the Communist-oriented Left in the film industry. Yet more instructive lessons about the Hollywood radicals (if they may truly be so described) and their many contradictions, emerge from the brief career of the novelist and screenwriter Nathanael West. Hollywood had drawn many brilliant writers to work on movie scripts; although F. Scott Fitzgerald and William Faulkner were the most famous of these, West was the most significant for California history as the author of the superb novel about Los Angeles, *The Day of the Locust,* which came out in 1939. On December 22, 1940, West's life was cut short at age 36 when he and his wife, born Eileen McKenney, were killed in an automobile accident in El Centro.

Mike Davis, in *City of Quartz,* has drawn a historical line of development from Lav Adamic, who had gone east soon after the success of his book *Dynamite!,* to Carey McWilliams, who published a book on Adamic and inherited his "mantle of Los Angeles Debunker," according to Davis, and to Nathanael West. West shared the nightmare insights of Adamic and McWilliams about Los Angeles, but far more than either of them he was a creative genius, able to transmute his horror and disgust into great literature.

Born Nathan Weinstein, the author was an outsider and eccentric from very early; notwithstanding his humble Jewish origins he gave himself fraudulent airs as a gentile aristocrat, an enthusiast of fishing and hunting, of expensively tailored suits and rare first editions. Although without a high-school diploma he conned his way into Brown University, where he acquired the nickname "Pep" for his lack of initiative, and encountered S. J. Perelman, who married West's sister. West had met the poet William Carlos Williams and joined with him in publishing a little magazine, *Contact*. West also published three novels in the early 1930s, including *A Cool Million* and *Miss Lonelyhearts*. These two were bought by Hollywood, although only the latter, the unforgettable and utterly pessimistic tale of a newspaper columnist, saw production as the 1933 Fox picture *Advice to the Lovelorn*. By contrast with the novel, the film was quite forgettable. But the movie sale allowed West to dedicate himself to writing, where he previously had to work at odd jobs. (*Miss Lonelyhearts* had been highly praised by book critics but originally sold few copies.)

Perelman had become successful as a humorist, and he went to Hollywood to adapt the Marx Brothers' *Monkey Business* for the screen. He returned in 1932 to do a similar job on the Brothers' *Horse Feathers,* and "Pep" West, as he was universally known, came after him, settling for good in 1935. West's radicalism and cynicism were doubtless fed by his studio experience, for his talent gained him only assignments on mediocre second-billing or "B" pictures such as the forgotten *Ticket to Paradise* (1936). An adventure story about a plane crash in the jungle, *Five Came Back* (1939), with Lucille Ball and John Carradine, was a minor success, but much of West's film career is obviously reflected in the fictive life of Tod Hackett, the set designer and painter who is the protagonist of *The Day of the Locust*.

Both West and Perelman had frequented Communist literary circles in New York, and West in particular turned up in a similar crowd after he arrived in Los Angeles. Hollywood in 1933 was increasingly sensitive to Depression issues, as shown by "social pictures" such as *I Am a Fugitive from a Chain Gang*. But writers like West, lacking the fame and income of a Perelman, had to deal more directly with their situation as, in effect, the film industry's most exploited workers. Jay Martin, West's biographer, traces the beginning of a screenwriters' revolt to Theodore Dreiser. In 1931, dismayed that Eisenstein had been prevented from directing the film version of his novel *An American Tragedy,* Dreiser sued Paramount (unsuccessfully) over the misuse of his creation, and appealed to writers to defend their work from cinema-industry butchery. But from the beginning Hollywood was characterized by a deep suspicion of and contempt for writers, even those who were well paid. As economic and political events gave rise to ever greater uncertainty, frustrations turned into grievances; these suddenly resulted, early in 1933, in a call to organize a union.

Labor organization among screenwriters owed its main immediate stimulus to successful defiance of a proposed wage cut by members of the International Alliance of Theatrical Stage Employees (I.A.T.S.E.), the stagehands' union, soon after Roosevelt took office. When the producers attempted to cut "their" writers' pay by 50 percent, according to a memoir by Lester Cole (who would become one of the most famous Hollywood Communists), a group of scriptwriters held the inaugural meeting of what would become the Screen Writers' Guild. The pioneers included Cole, then 28, a theater professional who had first worked in the film industry six years before as a ditchdigger for Warner Brothers; the playwright Samson Raphaelson, author of the play *The Jazz Singer,* which became the first "talking picture," and former husband of Rayna Prohme; and John Howard Lawson. The organization was modeled on the Dramatists' Guild, which had gained representation in the New York theater, and in which Raphaelson and Lawson had been active.

Lawson, an author of successful Broadway plays on social themes, had come to Hollywood in 1928, finding work as a coauthor of dialogue and cowriter on such pictures as *The Ship from Shanghai* and *Our Blushing Brides,* both of which appeared in 1930. He became the Guild's first president, and the organization began its struggle for recognition as the writers' bargaining agent. The studios took little notice; their main concern was in finding talent, and competition to hire good writers took precedence over anxieties about unions, according to Lester Cole. Left-wing writers were still scarce in Hollywood; Samuel Ornitz was then probably the best known. However, late in 1934 Cole, who had become prominent in the Guild, was recruited into the Communist Party.

"Pep" West owed to Lester Cole his meeting with Eileen McKenney, who became his wife. She was the subject of *My Sister Eileen,* a popular book by her actual sister Ruth McKenney, a Communist enthusiast married to a rich San Franciscan, Richard Bransten. But Cole's friendship did not come cheap. West had, as noted, been previously associated with Communist literati, but his wife Eileen and Cole, along with Cole's then wife Jeanne, talked West into joining a "Marxist study group." In addition, whether out of the same perversity that led him to pose as a *goyishe* nobleman, or from friendship with the Communists, or simply because, along with so many others, he saw the Muscovite movement as the "wave of the future," in March 1937 Nathanael West added his signature to the most disgraceful of all the Stalinist declarations issued by fellow-traveling Americans of that epoch; a statement endorsing the Moscow purge trials and attacking a "counter-trial" launched by the educator John Dewey to inquire into the Communists' case against Trotsky. The core argument of this manifesto was this:

> Should not a country recognized as engaged in improving conditions for all its people, whether or not one agrees with all the means whereby this is brought about, be permitted to decide for itself what measures of protection are necessary against treasonable plots to assassinate and overthrow its leadership and involve it in war with foreign powers?

West was not the only Hollywoodite to sign it; others included screenwriters Ring Lardner, Jr., Samuel Ornitz, Samson Raphaelson, and Donald Ogden Stewart, and director Lewis Milestone.

But however deep his cynicism about America, "Pep" West recognized that the Communists were, in the end, no friends of his literary, as opposed to his Hollywood, ambitions. Lester Cole, in his 1981 memoir *Hollywood Red,* remembers a defining exchange between West and himself after the publication of *The Day of the Locust.*

> He gave me an autographed copy with the words, "Just don't hate me, will you?" I read the book with some uneasiness. Anticipating my criticism when I finished, he said, "I can only write one way. If I were to put into it, along with those stumblebums and phonies, the sincere, honest people who work here in Hollywood, and are making such a great fight [i.e., for unions], the whole fabric of this peculiar half world I attempted to create would be badly torn apart."
> "Okay, Pep. But if you want to know what I think. . . . "
> "I knew what you'd think months ago. That's why I didn't show you the manuscript. You would have convinced me, and I wouldn't have written anything."

This exchange has the ring of truth, even considering the more than forty years that passed between its occurrence and the writing of Cole's memoir. It is interesting, finally, more for what it says about Cole than for its view of West. Cole had no compunction about admitting that, from his viewpoint, the greatest fictional work ever conceived to expose Hollywood and its exploiters was deficient because of its failure to incorporate obvious Communist propaganda. Cole even seems to have been proud that West would hide his masterpiece from him (rather like an oppositionist under totalitarian rule), and that, if Cole had had anything to do with it, *The Day of the Locust* might never have been finished. That Cole's attitude was not exceptional is shown by the experience of Budd Schulberg, whose decision, at roughly the same time, to write his brilliant *What Makes Sammy Run?* without Party guidance led to "criticism" by the Hollywood Communists that was so overbearing it drove Schulberg out of the movement.

Remarkably enough, nearly all literary critics have perceived in *The Day of the Locust* exactly what Cole found missing: a further development, according to Mike Davis, of "Adamic's image of Los Angeles's 'spiritually and mentally starving' little people, the 'Folks.'" Indeed, the original title of the book, reflecting this reality, was "The Cheated." And of course there are no other motifs in American literature to compare, in their radical spirit, with Tod Hackett's painting, "The Burning of Los Angeles," and the riot with which *The Day of the Locust* ends. In these images West demonstrated an uncanny insight into the nature and future of Los Angeles and particularly of Hollywood, where, he wrote,

> [N]ot even the soft wash of dusk could help the houses. Only dynamite would be of any use against the Mexican ranch houses, Samoan huts, Mediterranean villas, Egyptian and Japanese temples, Swiss chalets, Tudor cottages, and every possible combination of these styles that lined the slopes of the canyon. . . . It is hard to laugh at the need for beauty and romance, no matter how tasteless, even horrible, the results of that are. But it is easy to sigh. Few things are sadder than the truly monstrous.

Lester Cole, who loved "the people" in the abstract, did not recognize humanity in its Angeleño delirium. Not long after his disturbing conversation with Cole, "Pep" West died.

———————

THE "GREAT FIGHT" for the unionization of the film industry had begun in earnest in 1937, when a series of strikes ended in victory for the Screen Actors' Guild, organized after the writers; Guild-organized "closed" shops were established at thirteen studios. "Pep" West, like Cole, Lawson, and others, became a Screen Writers' Guild official. Film employees were the highest-paid union members in America. That struggle was one of the several factors that stimulated the shift in Communist attentions from northern to southern California, although other issues are discernible as well. Dorothy Ray Healey admitted that the Los Angeles Communists always resented the authority granted to the San Francisco Communists, since from the beginning the Los Angeles group had more members. (The Russian Jewish cadre in southern California were, however, much less integrated into the area's society.)

Unfortunately for these Angeleño claims, the top Communist leaders in Moscow and New York long insisted on viewing San Francisco as the effective center of the Pacific Rim. Coincidentally San Francisco Communism, for reasons of local culture, and regardless of its contrasts with the Socialists and Wobblies of the past, had a rather historical, even "Old World" flavor, with its difficult highbrow intellectuals and its fractious union movement, somewhat reminiscent of Berlin or Paris. In the era of the People's Front, the Communists' main interest was redirected from these volatile constituencies to the broader strata of fellow travelers who were drawn from among the liberal middle class. The fellow travelers were more pliable in the face of Soviet political contortions, and obviously were a better source of cash. Further, the Communists now began avidly seeking support from the successful, the well off, the highly educated. They now recruited among those who saw themselves as an élite, who could be convinced that as Communists they were fulfilling the demands of history, whose names alone might provide the Party with immediate political gratification—and whose guilt over their class origins, as in the case of George Oppen, made them extraordinarily susceptible to demands for an extreme sacrifice and even an extinction of personality.

In addition to such alterations in their membership recruitment practices, the Party's switch in focus from San Francisco to Los Angeles reflected a cultural reorientation. The People's Front had become a relentlessly middlebrow project, and Hollywood, as the quintessence of Los Angeles, was now a fountainhead of middlebrow values in American life. This, then, was the beginning of the élitist but mediocre Left-liberalism, distant both from the labor movement and from traditional radicalism, that we know so well today, and that, through Hollywood, has come to profoundly influence

American mass culture. For the Communists, therefore, the stakes were much higher in Los Angeles than in San Francisco.

Indeed, Los Angeles radicalism had always been middle class, as harshly depicted by William C. Owen in his time, and as could be seen in the EPIC movement. Militant labor never gained a real foothold in Los Angeles, and Upton Sinclair learned, as the host of Sergei Eisenstein, that highbrow intellectuals were poison in Hollywood. Yet Hollywood provided the Communists with greater successes in the short term than San Francisco had. Hollywood was obviously a more glamorous arena than the proletarian redoubt to the north. And importantly, for many historical and demographic reasons, Los Angeles was less pro-British and interventionist than San Francisco and therefore more hospitable to the Communist "peace" line during the Stalin-Hitler pact.

"Pep" West was not middlebrow. The great influence upon his work was French Surrealism, and in *The Day of the Locust* he contributed more toward a California literary revolution than Steinbeck, or even Rexroth at that time, had ever imagined accomplishing. But the American Communists, like their Moscow mentors, had grown to dislike literary and artistic modernism, especially Surrealism. At one time their propaganda had employed Constructivist and even Dadaist styles, but they then swung over to a posture that condemned modernistic experimentation as an escape from revolutionary duties; with the advent of the People's Front they exalted, on the criterion of mass accessibility, the fake pop style of Woody Guthrie and his associates.

In the end, "Pep" West was a poet in prose, and poets, particularly those of the *avant-garde,* then counted for very little in American society; to the Communists they were dispensable. Famous authors, and practitioners of more "respectable" artistic trades such as painters, might be encouraged by the Communists to recast their work in a populist direction. But although the Party was willing to cultivate and occasionally exploit the names of well-known modernists such as William Carlos Williams, when dealing with younger recruits, as in the case of George Oppen, they counseled abnegation through creative silence and total dedication to immediate political tasks. Like Lester Cole, who would have been happier if *The Day of the Locust* had never seen the light of day, Mary Oppen, also writing more than forty years after the fact, recounted how Jacob "Pop" Mindel, an old Communist bureaucrat whom she treated with gushing admiration, advised a young Black Communist from the South to abandon drawing, in which he was gifted, for "the struggle." And like Cole, Mary Oppen saw nothing questionable about such conduct. (She also dispassionately cited Party censorship of members' reading to explain why she and George were ignorant of certain modern classics—as if accepting such strictures were perfectly normal.)

In 1940 the tension in this situation was still only latent in the case of Oppen, and had yet to blossom in that of Kenneth Rexroth. But the silence that fell on George Oppen, and which Cole would have drawn over "Pep" West, had already darkened the creative careers of other American intellectuals recruited to Communism, including the novelist Henry Roth, the poets Walter Lowenfels and Carl Rakosi (colleagues of Rexroth and Oppen), and the San Francisco writer Tillie Lerner Olsen.

Labor conflict in Hollywood broke out anew in February 1941. The Screen Cartoonists' Guild, an affiliate of the A.F.L. headed by a a 43-year-old former prizefighter and pro-Communist, Herbert K. Sorrell, called for a boycott of Walt Disney Productions, charging the studio with union-busting activities. The accusation was supported by the National Labor Relations Board (N.L.R.B.), which found that Disney had imposed a "company union" on his employees three years previously. The Screen Cartoonists' Guild struck Disney, with some seven hundred out of twelve hundred employees walking out. In May, as the N.L.R.B. was about to begin hearings on Disney, the conflict spread to the Leon Schlesinger Studio, where the Cartoonists' Guild was fighting for a wage increase. A brief strike at Schlesinger's operation was won by the Guild.

But the Disney strike became prolonged and bitter, and Sorrell later alleged that gangsters had been imported and strikers' houses bombed to break it. It seemed to have ended in the first week of August, when federal arbitration secured the employees a 10 percent hike in pay; but then, with the strike over, Disney dismissed the entire payroll and shut the studio down. After another three weeks, in September, the studio agreed to rehire five hundred workers, both strikers and nonstrikers. But Walt Disney himself was a serious anti-union combatant: he went before the N.L.R.B. to argue that the wartime collapse of the European film market, rather than the strike, had caused the dismissal of his employees. The dispute festered for years afterward.

Although Herbert Sorrell, a fellow traveler, had led the Disney strike, that was a legitimate labor fight over representation and wages rather than politics. However, the same could not be said about a bigger and more disruptive walkout that occurred at the same time in southern California, one that drew the attention of the whole country. In late May 1941, a strike began at the giant North American Aviation plant in Inglewood (the anti-Communist Tenney's assembly district), called by the C.I.O. United Auto Workers aircraft division, and involving more than 11,000 employees. The North American Aviation conflict came when the labor movement, both the A.F.L. and the C.I.O., had won notable legitimacy in southern California, and the unions at least seemed to have achieved a triumphant end to the "Forty-Year War" between capital and labor begun by "General" Otis. However, its effect was to the contrary; although the broader labor movement was not broken and the "Forty-Year War" could not be said to have resumed, the North American Aviation strike drastically undermined the influence of labor and the Left in the Los Angeles area, setting the tone for decades of far-reaching political developments.

With the Roosevelt Administration aiding Britain in its isolated fight against the Axis through Lend-Lease and other measures—but without official U.S. involvement in the war—North American Aviation, a General Motors subsidiary, held contracts in spring 1941 for $200 million worth of training and bombing planes for both the British and American forces. The gigantic plant and payroll gave an enormous lift to the local economy.

The U.A.W. Aircraft Workers were certified as the employee representative in April, and then commenced bargaining with the company under the direction, from the union side, of Detroit-based U.A.W. international representative Richard T. Frankensteen. A founder of the U.A.W., Frankensteen was renowned for having been beaten by guards in front of the Ford Motor Company's River Rouge plant in Detroit; newspaper photographs made the image of his bloodied head world-famous. Joined in the negotiations by U.A.W. West Coast director Lew Michener, Frankensteen was, like his mentor and colleague in the U.A.W. leadership, Walter Reuther, extremely militant for his union but also anti-Communist.

The Communists, who then had undeniable power within the U.A.W., were at the height of their "peace" campaign, now concentrating on the unions and aiming at "antiwar" work stoppages. In shipping, Harry Lundeberg was under Communist attack for declaring that his union would man convoys to Britain; simultaneously, the Communists blasted the F.B.I. for investigating "all 130 million Americans who want to stay out of war" (including, of course, Nazi sympathizers). A brief strike by U.A.W. employees had already occurred at the Ryan Aeronautical complex in San Diego in January 1941, and by the end of May, 24 strikes were blocking defense production around the country. On May 22, in San Francisco, Navy sailors and Marines crashed through the picket lines of a baywide shipyard strike, forcibly opening two yards. Still, the first reports of a possible strike at North American Aviation, also on May 22, emphasized that wages were the only issue over which the company and the union were at odds. Then negotiations broke off, and the membership voted to authorize a strike for a 10-cents-per-hour general increase in wages, with hourly base pay to rise from 50 to 75 cents, and a closed shop.

On May 27, 1941, President Roosevelt, in a "fireside chat" broadcast over radio, warned against defense-industry strikes. A shutdown at North American was delayed while the National Defense Mediation Board, a body parallel to the National Labor Relations Board, attempted to work out a compromise. But in the early hours of June 5, the U.A.W. local president at North American, William P. Goodman, called out all 11,500 of the company's workers. The picket line around the plant was a mile long. On the same day a strike vote was announced at Consolidated Aircraft in San Diego, which employed 16,000 workers.

Frankensteen rushed to Inglewood and sought to reopen talks, and in the next two days a national furor broke out as officials of the Navy and War (later Defense) departments threatened to take over the plant by presidential proclamation. On June 8, President Roosevelt issued an ultimatum: the strikers must return to work immediately or the federal government would seize the plant and operate it with soldiers; some Army units were already reported on their way to Inglewood. Frankensteen charged that the strike was unauthorized, and said, "I take this opportunity of serving notice on the Communists that they must keep their hands off the policies and the affairs of the aircraft division of the C.I.O. here on the West Coast." Local leaders repudiated Frankensteen, but the real problem at North American was now in the open. Strike leaders adopted an extremely provocative tone, sending a telegram to Stephen T. Early, President Roosevelt's press secretary, in which they declared, "If the Army is used to help break our strike it will mean the armed forces of the United

States will be subverted to class interests. . . . The armed forces will not break our strike!" To a great many Californians, this rhetoric seemed less characteristic of established union practice than of pro-Nazi industrial sabotage as it had been seen, particularly, in France.

Philip Murray, C.I.O. national president, and R. J. Thomas, chief executive of the U.A.W., both called on the North American strikers to return to work pending mediation. But on June 8 Harry Bridges, embroiled in his second deportation proceeding, dispatched longshore union members to join the picket line at Inglewood, and a message of support for the strike was sent by the pro-Communist leaders of the C.I.O. International Woodworkers, then conducting a lumber-industry walkout. Frankensteen had already begun to curb the Communists at North American, suspending five international organizers for the union—including his own assistant, Wyndham Mortimer, who, like Bridges, was a secret member of the Communist Party Central Committee under the *klichka* of Morgan. A mass meeting of 6,000 strikers that afternoon featured speechifying by Philip Connelly, the main Communist activist in Los Angeles labor affairs, who promised that if the U.A.W. officials refused to continue the strike Bridges would assume leadership. Frankensteen had to face a tumult of catcalls and boos, and placards depicting him as a rat and skunk, when he addressed the meeting. He did not back down, and shouted back at the crowd, "Your negotiating committee had no right to call a wildcat strike. . . . Adolf Hitler has been made the happiest man in the world by this strike." But his attempt to read a wire from R. J. Thomas was interrupted by the yelling chorus, and he was unable to read a similar telegram from Philip Murray.

On the morning of June 9, 1941, President Roosevelt signed an executive order directing the Army to seize and operate the North American Aviation plant. Before soldiers arrived at Inglewood that day, an appearance by four hundred Los Angeles police and Highway Patrol personnel resulted in a free-for-all, with officers and strikers throwing tear-gas bombs at one another. But the soldiers, bayonets fixed, imposed calm. (Within days there were 4,000 of them occupying the plant.) Meanwhile, U.S. Attorney General Robert H. Jackson denounced the walkout as "an insurrection" more than a strike, adding that "a distinction between loyal labor leaders and those who are following the Communist Party line is easy to observe. Loyal labor leaders fight for a settlement of grievances. Disloyal men who have wormed their way into the labor movement do not want settlement; they want strikes. That is the Communist Party line."

A few pickets and supporters screamed insults, identifying the soldiers with Nazis. But the next day, the strikers voted overwhelmingly to end the walkout; bargaining over the wage scale was to be resumed. Still, the Communists continued their agitation. William Pupis, a member of the negotiating committee, was suspended from work with two others after he said, at a meeting where the members voted to return, "If we had half the equipment that the boys with bayonets had we could have given them cards and spades and all the argument they wanted."

Pupis also compared the strike with the great West Coast waterfront battle of 1934; but the Communists had failed to perceive that true mass-action strikes like that maritime struggle or Salinas in 1936 were largely spontaneous upheavals, based on local conditions and traditions, and could not be artificially created to order. Federal action at North American Aviation was followed by the end of strike rumors at Consolidated Aircraft in San Diego, and the effects of Roosevelt's determined stance were felt throughout the country. On June 11 Navy Secretary Frank Knox stated that the Roosevelt Administration would not obstruct union organizing or bargaining, but would challenge "those who use those things as a cloak to attack American freedom and liberty. . . . The challenge of the subversive and communistic elements that has been flung in our teeth for months has been accepted," he said. "From here on the Government of the United States will proceed against these subversive elements in our communities as they should be proceeded against as enemies of the country."

The week of June 18 saw most of the soldiers withdrawn from North American Aviation. Turmoil festered within the U.A.W., and many observers believed a showdown between the Communists and anti-Communists within the C.I.O. would soon take place. Communist "peace" agitation continued, although the Party had clearly suffered a major setback with the American public. But the "peace" line, which had been suddenly imposed as by the push of a button, was suddenly turned off again on June 22, 1941 when thousands of German troops poured across the 1939 (or "post-Poland") border with Soviet Russia. The Stalin-Hitler alliance had ended.

For the California Communists, as well as their comrades elsewhere, the collapse of the Stalin-Hitler pact at once made it acceptable to call for

American intervention in the war. Indeed, once they had collected their wits Communists everywhere joined in the Soviet demand for an immediate Allied invasion of Europe—THE SECOND FRONT NOW!—notwithstanding that, as Winston Churchill observed, the British were already hard-pressed and had had to contend, only months before, with the specter of a full Russo-German agreement to carve up the world. But most Americans, President Roosevelt included, were glad to have the Russians on the Allied side. On June 23, Acting Secretary of State Sumner Welles announced that Russia would also be eligible for Lend-Lease or other aid. Still, in San Francisco Harry Lundeberg was unimpressed. "He felt more comfortable when the Stalinists were allies of Hitler," Barney Mayes recalled, i.e., when the war was a straight fight between democracies and dictatorships.

STALIN HAD BEEN warned of the impending Nazi betrayal. A spy ring in Japan run by Soviet agent Richard Sorge, with assistants recruited among the Japanese Communists in California, had penetrated German diplomatic and Japanese ruling circles and had transmitted top-quality military intelligence by clandestine radio to Russia. On May 20, 1941 Sorge directed an urgent message to the Kremlin, stating that the Germans would amass 170 to 190 divisions on the Soviet border and that on June 20 they would attack all along the line, driving toward Moscow. Apparently, these communications were disregarded by Stalin.

However, in the wake of the Nazi onslaught Sorge became more important than ever to his Russian bosses. In the middle of October 1941 Sorge transmitted summary messages demonstrating that the Japanese would follow an exclusively "southern" line of attack against the British and Americans, leaving Siberia as an unthreatened Russian rear area. Sorge wanted to get out of Tokyo and return to Russia; however, unknown to him, his network had already been compromised, and two of his Japanese-speaking operatives, recruited in California, were arrested. Sorge was executed by the Japanese in 1944; he has since been honored as the greatest Soviet spy of all time. But his work would have been impossible without the participation of Communists recruited in California.

Californians at home did not need the Communists to tell them that war with the Axis powers, especially Japan, was inevitable. It came early on the morning of December 7, 1941, when Japanese aircraft attacked Pearl Harbor in the Hawaiian Islands. Now America was officially in the war, a conflict in which the Pacific Coast, and California in particular, were guaranteed a central role. At the same time another, secret war had begun in American soil, for the Russians had been granted the right to establish offices throughout the United States to coordinate the acquisition and transportation of military aid. A Soviet consulate had operated in San Francisco since 1934, but during World War II the Russians, remaining at peace with Japan, transformed this facility from a base against Tokyo, as it was previously utilized, into a center for spying on American political and technological developments. In December 1941, the Soviet secret police activated (or possibly reactivated, according to American intelligence officials) a *rezidentura* or base office in San Francisco; the local KGB director, or *rezident*, was vice consul Grigory Kheifitz, *klichka* Brown, a man whose impact on California would prove exceptional.

Kheifitz's *klichka* in wartime KGB communications was *Kharon*, or Charon, borrowed from the boatman who ferried the dead across the river Styx into Hades, or hell, in Etruscan and Greek mythology. California was occasionally referred to in KGB code as "Charon's shore" *(byeryeg Kharona)*. Charon was, as we shall see, a gruesomely appropriate cover name; but the KGB seemed to have a sense of humor in such matters, for the main Western cities were also named, in the official code at that time, out of classical literature. Washington was Carthage *(Karfagen)*, the rival city destroyed by the military prowess of ancient Rome; New York was Tyre *(Tir)*, a great center of ancient Mediterranean commerce that had disappeared from the map; but San Francisco was Babylon *(Vavilon)*. Other witty items in the KGB's vocabulary included their contemptuous cover names for the FBI, known as the "hut" *(khata)*, and the new Office of Strategic Services, the forerunner of the Central Intelligence Agency, which was referred to as the "log cabin" *(izba)*. Such terms seemed to stress the primitive nature of the American security agencies when compared with the mighty KGB. The United States was "the country" *(strana)*, while Mexico was the "rural area" *(dyeryevnya)*. The U.S. State Department was "the bank"; the hated Trotskyists were "polecats" *(khorki)*.

The work of the KGB *rezidentura* in San Francisco may be studied in detail, for even before the Russians began exploiting the military alliance to spy on the United States, American authorities, during the Stalin-Hitler pact, had begun secretly recording Soviet coded messages. More than 2,900 of these communications, known by the meaningless project name VENONA, were partially or completely deciphered by American personnel after 1943, and were released by the U.S. National Security Agency beginning in 1995.

Kheifitz, the San Francisco *rezident,* was an outstanding product of the Russian secret services. According to KGB veteran and memoirist Pavel Sudoplatov, Kheifitz was a former secretary to Lenin's widow, Nadyezhda Krupskaya; he was also educated in physics, having graduated from the Jena Polytechnical Institute in Germany in 1926. He had been a Comintern functionary but was then transferred to the KGB's foreign department, working in the United States, where he cultivated American Communists, as well as working in Germany and Italy. He was KGB *rezident* in Italy in 1938, when the Stalin purges swept through the secret "organs"; his Comintern associations as well as his study in Germany made him a candidate for trial and execution, but although an arrest order was issued and he was called back to Moscow, he was spared. Sudoplatov alleges that while in Italy, Kheifitz recruited a young Communist physicist, Bruno Pontecorvo, as an active Soviet spy. Pontecorvo, who later worked on the first atomic bomb as a researcher, disappeared from the West in 1950.

Kheifitz's tasks, when he first came to San Francisco, were limited: to watch Trotskyists and to strengthen and monitor the espionage network on the West Coast waterfront. He immediately called into active service agents who had been left in place by N. I. Eitingon a decade before, as well as those remaining from the operation against Trotsky, and obtained new personnel from the ranks of the California Communists. Later Schneiderman, the state Party boss, balked at turning over local members for "special work," i.e., espionage and terrorism, but he was overruled. Local Communists, American, Mexican, or Canadian, were referred to in the wartime KGB code as "compatriots" or "fellow-countrymen" *(zemlyaki).* This detail alone shows that the American Communist Party was never independent of Moscow control.

Unfortunately, while Kheifitz was initiating his clandestine work, the California authorities became obsessed with a subversive threat that was, by comparison, trivial if not largely imaginary: that of ethnic Japanese, or *Nikkei* Californians. This panic has come to be almost invariably explained by the history of anti-Chinese agitation and "Yellow Peril" propaganda on the Pacific Coast during the late nineteenth and early twentieth centuries. But such an analysis, though both simple and satisfying to those obsessed with race as the sole cause of injustice in America, is incomplete, to say the least. Resentment against the Pearl Harbor "sneak attack" ran high among Californians, who had also been outraged throughout the 1930s by shocking news coverage of Japanese military atrocities in China. Carey McWilliams noted that anti-Chinese and anti-Japanese prejudice had greatly diminished in California by 1940. Both communities were relatively assimilated, and while the loyalty of Chinese-Americans to the United States had never been questioned, even that of Japanese-Americans was mainly taken for granted. Filipinos, rather than Chinese or Japanese, had become the chief Asian object of white prejudice in California.

During the last weeks of December 1941 and the first two months of 1942 *Nikkei* in California largely remained unmolested. Early on, Governor Olson met with Japanese-American delegations in Sacramento and expressed his belief that the majority of *Nikkei,* whose loyalty was affirmed by *Issei* (first-generation or Japan-born) and *Nisei* (second-generation or American-born) community leaders and recognized by non-Asians, would serve to keep any pro-Tokyo elements in line. Individuals of Asian origin suffered insults on the street and occasional broken windows, but no demonstrations or serious acts of violence occurred. However, white opinion began turning against the Japanese-Americans. A resurrection of "Yellow-Perilism," as well as resentment of *Nikkei* success in California agriculture, contributed to this change, but race prejudice was by no means the sole determining factor. Non-Japanese Californians were also inflamed by further setbacks for American forces after the Pearl Harbor raid, as well as by news of Japanese atrocities in the Philippines. In late January 1942, the release of a report by a commission of inquiry on the Pearl Harbor disaster, headed by U.S. Supreme Court Justice Owen Roberts, worsened the situation. The Roberts Report blamed the losses at Pearl Harbor on the local Army and Navy commands, but also described espionage activities by ethnic Japanese in Hawaii that greatly alarmed Californians.

Notwithstanding the indications of the Roberts Report the Federal Bureau of Investigation had determined, just before the Pearl Harbor attack, that Japanese espionage in California was limited, and had been thoroughly investigated and suppressed; Naval and Army Intelligence representatives agreed that no serious threat existed. However, on February 19, 1942, President Roosevelt signed Executive Order 9066, providing for military authorities to establish "exclusion" areas from which anybody could be removed or forbidden to enter or leave, with further provision for transportation, feeding, housing, and other services for evacuees. Americans of Japanese ancestry were not even mentioned in the text; but over the next ten months, a series of "exclusion orders," backed by the Congress, resulted in the confinement of virtually the entire *Nikkei* population in the Pacific states in ten "relocation centers." On March 21, President Roosevelt signed Public Law 503, establishing enforcement procedures for "exclusion." Responsibility for carrying out the program devolved on Lieutenant General John L. DeWitt, head of the Fourth Army, based at the Presidio in San Francisco.

The internment of the West Coast *Nikkei* was traumatic for the victims themselves, and its obvious parallel with the concentration camps established in the totalitarian countries was offensive to many California liberals and radicals as well. In the succeeding decades the internment has produced an array of legal, social, political, and ethnic studies dramatizing the difficulties suffered by the internees, who eventually received reparations payments from the federal government. But more germane to this book is an examination of the response by (mainly white) liberals and radicals to the violation of Japanese-American civil rights.

An interracial couple, "Karl" (Goso) Yoneda and Elaine Black, offer a microcosmic view of the internment crisis in California. Meeting in the Communist Party, they had become lovers. After several years together they were married in Washington State, which lacked California's laws on "miscegenation—which were still enforced then. Soon Elaine bore a son, Tom (named for Tom Mooney). They remained Communists throughout the period, and exemplified the unquestioning commitment to a feverish day-to-day activity for which the Stalinist generation was known—the same activism that replaced literature in the lives of the Oppens. Elaine Black had become the main California representative of the I.L.D., rushing from demonstration to demonstration, from strike to strike, and from jail to jail through the decade, often getting arrested herself. In nearly all such cases Black gained considerable publicity; in the events at Salinas in 1936, Colonel Sanborn terrified the reactionary elements by brandishing her name, even though the A.F.L. strike leaders had asked her to stay away.

The "farm fascism" claims made by McWilliams in *Factories in the Field* reflected the constant tempo of such rural conflicts, in which presumptive Communists and other agitators were often detained, beaten, and run out of town; some were murdered. Unfortunately, the Communists frequently brought such repression upon themselves and their supporters by their reckless behavior and love of headlines. But Elaine Black and the I.L.D. injected themselves into controversies that were legitimate as well. The only thing that was certain about the I.L.D. was that its activities and its aid were completely dependent on the whims of the top Communist leadership, as Norman Mini had learned; even Tom Mooney had problems with the I.L.D.

Yoneda, for his part, had spent much of the decade in related efforts, mostly in Comintern underground work aimed at Japanese sailors whose ships called at West Coast ports. Like so many other young Communists, he was admitted to the San Francisco longshore union, which facilitated these tasks; he also went to Alaska as an organizer of fish-cannery workers. *Rodo Shimbun,* the newspaper he produced with the help of Kenneth Rexroth, was replaced by a People's Front organ in Japanese, *Doho* (Brotherhood). *Doho* was published in Los Angeles, which had the largest Japanese-speaking population on the West Coast.

Yoneda was alarmed when, in a legal gambit, the American Communist Party "withdrew" from the Comintern in 1940. Party leaders dropped all noncitizens from membership, including about a hundred *Issei.* Yoneda and Shuji Fujii, a leading Communist agent under the *klichka* of Saito and the editor of *Doho,* were left to run the party's Japanese-language bureau. But a bigger shock came on the night of December 8, 1941, the day after Pearl Harbor. Late in the afternoon of the 7th, after sending a telegram to President Roosevelt pledging support to the war effort, Yoneda had been arrested by the F.B.I. on the San Francisco waterfront while laboring in a longshore gang. He was released within two days, but while he was behind bars a meeting of Japanese-American Communists was called at the Yoneda-Black residence. All of them and their non-*Nikkei* spouses, including the jailed Yoneda and Shuji Fujii, also briefly imprisoned, were summarily suspended from Party membership for the duration of the war, on the typical Stalinist pretext that allowing them to remain would make the party a haven for Japanese spies.

Elaine Black could hardly turn to the I.L.D. for help in such a situation; she reacted with "tears," and was "horrified." Yoneda, informed of the decision, was similarly "stunned and speechless," finding the action "unreal." Yoneda later recalled that no protest was made, "in spite of our shock and hurt," and wrote that "we should have registered a complaint." The *People's World* commented, in the manner they employed during the Soviet purges, that it was "preferable to inconvenience one thousand innocent persons than [to allow] one to remain in a position where he can sabotage the war effort."

Around the end of February 1942 Yoneda heard that the military would construct a "reception center" about two hundred miles northeast of Los Angeles, in the foothills near Mount Whitney—hardly as far inland as many *Nikkei* would have thought and many whites desired. The site came to be known as Manzanar (Spanish for "apple grove"). The Yoneda couple decided to move to Los Angeles; Elaine and Tommy, their son, would stay with her family. Yoneda, who had tried to enlist in the U.S. armed forces, would serve as a construction worker at the Manzanar camp. On March 17, Yoneda registered as a volunteer, and within a week he and some 830 other *Nikkei* were on their way, by Santa Fe train, to the high desert.

There was no construction work waiting for the volunteers at Manzanar; those jobs were reserved for union members—an outcome which must have left Yoneda, a labor official, bemused. Nevertheless, the group commenced cleaning and improving the barracks, even as the structures were being completed. Within a couple of days Yoneda received a strange group of visitors: Shuji Fujii, the *Doho* editor and Soviet agent, along with the modernist sculptor Isamu Noguchi, then a leading Left figure in both Japanese-American cultural life and the California arts scene, toured the camp with a team of documentary filmmakers. Yoneda soon organized a group of internees to act as "guides to meet new arrivals and to take them to their barracks," according to his memoirs.

Yoneda was a firm supporter of the Allied war against Japanese imperialism; but this posture reflected Yoneda's commitment as a Communist and experienced clandestine worker. His decisions to volunteer in the building of the camp, then to serve as a guide, led to his appointment as a "block leader." Thus Yoneda took on a role in Manzanar that somewhat resembled that assumed in the Nazi concentration camps by a stratum of collaborationist *Kapos*. Did Yoneda undertake these responsibilities because he believed in the righteousness of the Allied cause, or was he sent to Manzanar, presumably on a Soviet assignment, to spy on the rest of the prisoners? The latter possibility cannot be ignored; it should also be noted that Communists served extensively as *Kapos* in the Nazi camps. Indeed, they earned a reputation for, in effect, "administering" such camps as Dachau for the benefit of the Communist Party and its cadres rather for than the mass of prisoners. Their justification for such behavior was multiple, but mainly, Communists would do anything to safeguard the Party's interest.

After a week in Manzanar, Yoneda was astonished and angry when his wife Elaine and son Tommy suddenly appeared in the camp. Their child suffered from asthma, and Yoneda was concerned that the dust storms in the camp would make him ill; however, on March 29 Elaine Black had heard a radio bulletin ordering "all those of Japanese ancestry whose breadwinners are in the Manzanar Reception Center" to report for transportation there. She was, she said, told by army and Catholic Church officials handling the process that she would not have to go but that her child, then only 3, would. This she refused to allow; after some argument, she and her son were allowed to join her husband in the camp.

KARL YONEDA AND Elaine Black were hardly typical of either *Nikkei* or whites in their reaction to the California internment crisis. Few Japanese-Americans other than Communists would take it into their heads to collaborate in the operation as extensively as Yoneda did; fewer non-Japanese would insist on going to the camp, like Elaine Black. The great majority of *Nikkei* waited passively, day by day, to see what would happen, and then complied with the government's orders, while white society expressed relief that the issue had been, as they thought, handled.

There were, however, some *Nisei* who, as native-born Americans, refused to accept that their ancestry made them criminals or exempted them from constitutional protection, and there were whites who agreed with them. On March 28, 1942, Japanese-Americans in the Pacific states came under a 6:00 P.M. curfew ordered by General DeWitt. At about 11:00 P.M. that night, Minoru Yasui, 25, who described himself as 110 percent loyal to the United States, entered a police station in Portland, Oregon, and submitted himself to arrest, in order to challenge the curfew's legality. He was duly locked up.

Yasui's action at first did little more than enrage the Japanese-American Citizens League (J.A.C.L.), of which he was a member, and whose leadership had pledged that *Nikkei* would submit unquestioningly to the "exclusion" orders. Yet, on May 16, a second resister appeared: Gordon Hirabayashi, a 24-year-old student at the University of Washington and a Quaker, turned himself into the Seattle office of the F.B.I. in the company of an attorney, and stated his refusal to register for evacuation. His stand in defense of the constitutional rights of the *Nisei* mainly originated in his family's religious-based pacifism. He too was arrested.

Two weeks later, in San Leandro, California, a man in his twenties was arrested by local police when his identification as "Clyde Sarah," supposedly a Hawaiian of Spanish ancestry, and the story he had concocted to back it up could not be substantiated. His real name was Fred T. Korematsu, and he was a shipyard worker from Oakland. The rest of his family had gone to the Tanforan racetrack near San Francisco, which like other such facilities was being used by the government as an intake point for *Nikkei* on their way to the camps. But Korematsu refused to comply with the government's orders, and had undergone rather shoddy plastic surgery to try to Westernize his appearance. Korematsu was transferred to the county jail in San Francisco, where he was visited by a lawyer for the American Civil Liberties Union, Ernest Besig. Besig was seeking a subject for a legal test of the "exclusion" orders, and Korematsu accepted Besig's proposal.

These three—Yasui, Hirabayashi, and Korematsu—were joined by a *Nisei* woman held in a horse-stall at Tanforan: Mitsuye Endo, 22, a clerk for the state Department of Motor Vehicles. Together, Yasui in Portland, Hirabayashi in Seattle, and Korematsu and Endo in San Francisco began legal proceedings against internment that were appealed to the U.S. Supreme Court. Of these four, Korematsu and his attorney, Wayne Mortimer Collins (who later argued for Hirabayashi and Endo, as well), are the most significant.

Collins, then 42, was an authentic California liberal in background, style, and temperament as well as in conviction. He was born in Sacramento, the son of Harry Collins, the chief telegrapher for Associated Press during the 1906 earthquake and fire. Wayne Collins's law practice was small and obscure, and his personality was combative. He threw himself into the Japanese internment controversy with exceptional energy and devotion. His strategy was brilliantly improvisational; he deluged the courts with challenges and ransacked every legal authority he could find for tactical weapons to back up his filings. In his first argument on Korematsu, he assailed President Roosevelt for an unconstitutional abuse of powers in signing Executive Order 9066. As shown by Peter Irons, a historian of the cases, this approach, "radical" although nonideological—Collins had never been a leftist of any sort—proved unacceptable to the national leadership of the American Civil Liberties Union (A.C.L.U.). Based in New York, the A.C.L.U. had decided against any challenge to the constitutionality of the internment program. When Korematsu's trial began in September 1942 the San Francisco branch of the A.C.L.U. of which Collins was a member temporarily stopped answering communications from the national headquarters, which was trying to disavow Collins.

Another individual who reacted to the violation of Japanese-American rights with the feisty attitude of Wayne Collins was Morris Weisberger, then the New York port agent for the Sailors' Union of the Pacific and one of Harry Lundeberg's top assistants. Weisberger had grown up in Bellefaire, a home for disadvantaged and troubled Jewish youths in Cleveland, Ohio, then had gone to sea where he acquired radical ideas; he cleaved to the anti-Stalinists. Once an open conflict had broken out between Bridges and Lundeberg, Weisberger often found himself fighting for the union physically rather than intellectually, and sometimes ended up covered with blood. Following the "exclusion" orders, some thirty-five to forty *Nikkei* S.U.P. members were held in the horse stalls at the Santa Anita racetrack, the intake center for southern California. Weisberger went to the highest military authorities and demanded that the seamen be immediately released, insisting that they were all of proven loyalty to the United States and bore no responsibility for the criminal deeds of the Tokyo régime. After a considerable discussion, the authorities finally acceded, and S.U.P. members of Japanese ancestry were released and allowed to ship out on the Atlantic.

This effort by Weisberger and Lundeberg contrasted strongly with the anti-Asian campaign that had so long been pursued by mainstream California labor, the S.U.P. included; Weisberger closed the historic circle that began with the lone action of Coast Seamen's Union founder Sigismund Danielewicz in defending the Chinese more than fifty years before. But it also represented a dramatic difference from the policies adopted by the Communist-controlled waterfront unions. Karl Yoneda later recalled with anguish that Bridges's I.L.W.U., to which Yoneda belonged and for which he had worked long and hard, turned him down when he sought to enlist in their "Dock Battalion," soon to become a military construction (Seabee) unit. Further, although Yoneda had stood by Bridges in his many attacks on Lundeberg and the S.U.P., Yoneda and another Communist, Koji Ariyoshi, turned instead to Weisberger in August 1942, appealing for S.U.P. help in getting two Hawaiian *Nisei* sailors released from Manzanar. The seamen were successfully moved to New York and began shipping out.

Much later, both Yoneda and Elaine Black took pains to emphasize that at least one prominent Communist and leading I.L.W.U. and C.I.O. personage, Louis Goldblatt, had spoken up in defense of the interned *Nikkei*. But Goldblatt had not done much; he appeared before a commission investigating the internment scheme and warned against prejudice and hysteria, but concentrated his fire on "fascists," whom he blamed for the situation, rather than the government. More importantly, he and his comrades took little practical action to succor the victims of internment. As Vivian Raineri, the biographer of Elaine Black, wrote, "there were few who addressed the victimization—the terrorization, fears and uncertainties" of more than a hundred thousand *Nikkei* in the United States. "It was as if the question did not exist," Raineri declared. "Progressives," meaning Communists in the vocabulary of Black and Raineri, believed the "sound point of view" was "to use the patriotism of Japanese-Americans against them." The *Nisei* themselves, they claimed—presumably represented exclusively by such as Yoneda or the Japanese-American Citizens League—had recognized the military necessity of internment. Such a position was "the easy way out," Raineri averred.

Along with Wayne Collins and Morris Weisberger, Kenneth Rexroth reacted with dismay and then with bitterness to the "exclusion" program. After his break with the Communists, Rexroth had rapidly moved toward anarchism and pacifism; in 1940, the year he married Marie and his first collection of poems, *In What Hour,* was published in New York, Rexroth responded to a draft summons by registering as a conscientious objector. He went to work as a psychiatric orderly at a public hospital in San Francisco. Unlike the Communists, whose "peace" line vanished with the Nazi attack on Russia and whose cynicism and hypocrisy about the conflict he denounced, Rexroth continued to oppose the war.

Very soon after the Pearl Harbor attack, with rumors abounding of *Nikkei* removal, Kenneth and Marie Rexroth began calling friends to organize a network to obstruct any such action. They contacted the Fellowship of Reconciliation (F.O.R.), then the main American pacifist group, and the American Friends' Service Committee, and turned their four-room apartment into a station, filled with cots, on an underground railroad conveying *Nisei* out of California. Some internees asked Rexroth to guard traditional Japanese art works and other valuable possessions, which he refused to do; instead, he arranged for the California State Library to house the objects, and to set up a book service for the camps. Early in 1942 Rexroth, according to his biographer, Linda Hamalian, was introduced to Hazuko (Hazel) Takeshita through a mutual friend, Shirley Staschen, who is depicted in the Coit Tower "Library" mural in male dress. In discussions with Takeshita, Rexroth came up with a brilliant gambit to get young *Nisei* exempted from internment: registration at Eastern-U.S. correspondence schools, which would give them legitimate reason to leave the "exclusion zone" and avoid the camps. Hazuko Takeshita was one of many people the Rexroths, coordinating with the F.O.R., helped to go to Chicago, the other terminus for the anti-"exclusion" underground railroad.

If the psychological impact of internment was immense for the victims, their experiences also greatly affected Rexroth. He never forgot the suffering of aged *Issei* and other isolated internees, many speaking no English and without relatives to help them, and he never forgave the arbitrary inequity and gratuitous brutality of the operation. Years later, he condemned the J.A.C.L. as "a worse [American-] flag-waving outfit than the American Legion ever dared to be," and emphasized that the Communists had been "all in favor of crucifying the Japanese." But he also pointed out that no *Nikkei* had been physically attacked in San Francisco, Oakland, or Berkeley, most of whose residents had treated their ethnic Japanese neighbors with civility and calm. He stressed that not one case of *Nikkei* sabotage of the war effort had been recorded and, like many others, he noted that notwithstanding the Pearl Harbor horror no measure comparable to internment had been imposed in Hawaii, which had a huge Japanese population. From that moment on, Rexroth was a fervent critic of unthinking patriotism, and an enemy of the state, of all states, of all systems of government, of all coercion.

The injustice of the internments should not be used as a pretext to deny that some servants of the imperial Japanese government were engaged in spying and subversion on American soil before Pearl Harbor. They were indeed; and many *Issei,* in particular, sympathized with them. This was proven by Japanese communications traffic, decrypted by American personnel under the project name MAGIC. Americans had broken the Japanese diplomatic cipher before the Pearl Harbor attack, and the MAGIC intercepts were being read almost as soon as the messages were sent. They revealed assiduous efforts by Japanese consular and other officials to locate and recruit spies from among *Nikkei* in California; at the same time their authors recognized that overt sympathy for Japan in the war against the United States was extremely limited among these communities. Yoneda noted and others observed that the *Heimushakai* or Imperial Overseas Veterans' League had collected funds and "comfort bags" for Japanese soldiers during the invasion of China, while students in Japanese-language schools and other community groups wrote letters to soldiers and collected reusable tinfoil to support Japan's aggression on the Asian mainland. Some prominent *Issei* and *Nisei* personalities had participated in pro-imperial propaganda, and a few outspoken *Issei* had left California only a week before Pearl Harbor. In addition, during the Stalin-Hitler pact the Japanese had discussed using Communists as agents.

But few such activities had any real effect in California. Japanese subversive efforts, as opposed to espionage, were somewhat more extensive and significant, but were also ineffectual. The MAGIC traffic showed that Japanese representatives were in close contact with the America First Committee, the main advocate for antiwar isolationism after June 22. Attempts had been made by Japanese agents to put the Silver Shirts on a more serious footing, but a message from San Francisco to Tokyo, sent on June 28, 1941, described the appeals of "Chief" Pelley for backing from Japan and recommended against giving it to him.

Pelley was by then irrelevant to California, but two other pro-Japanese agitators, Robert Noble and Ellis O. Jones, although absent from the MAGIC traffic, gained the support of some Silver Shirt adherents and other such elements in Los Angeles. Noble, 42, the former pioneer of "Ham and Eggs," had founded a small organization, the Friends of Progress, with Jones. The group first promoted isolationism and then moved on to active support for the Axis powers in the war, a posture that at the time seemed utterly deranged and in retrospect still smacks of madness. Jones, 69, had been an editor of *Life* magazine; he was also a former radical, the Los Angeles director of the A.C.L.U. and a past supporter of the Communists. Jones now headed an organization, the National Copperheads, with a similar anti-Allied trajectory. At a public meeting on December 11, four days after Pearl Harbor, Noble demanded the impeachment of President Roosevelt, defended the Japanese assaults on the Philippines and Hawaii, and argued that Hitler should be allowed to dispose of European affairs. Within two days Noble and five of his associates were arrested by the F.B.I. and charged with seditious and disloyal utterances in wartime. However, U.S. Attorney General Francis Biddle ordered their release less than a month later, on the grounds that legal sanctions based on speech alone would violate their civil liberties, and that "every reasonable attempt" should be made to preserve constitutional guarantees. (Biddle had also, along with F.B.I. head J. Edgar Hoover, held similar misgivings about the constitutionality of Japanese internment, although under pressure the Attorney General gave up his objections to *Nikkei* "relocation.")

Their release led Noble and Jones to step up their activities, holding regular weekly meetings with an attendance of as many as five hundred people, but at the end of March they were rearrested with a half dozen followers and charged with sedition for interfering with the U.S. conduct of the war. In addition, state Attorney General Earl Warren ordered that they be held to answer for criminal libel against General Douglas MacArthur, who was described in a National Copperhead bulletin as having abandoned his troops in the Philippines. Noble and Jones proved to be unrepentant Axis sympathizers; Noble in particular, after three appearances, between their two arrests, before the state legislature's Un-American Activities Committee, was described in the committee's *Report* as "probably one of the most amazing witnesses to ever appear before an investigating committee." Noble cheerfully admitted all the seditious opinions and statements that had been attributed to him, and blandly offered to repeat the Nazi salute and "Heil Hitler:" greeting he had reportedly delivered at a meeting of the Friends of Progress. In July 1942 Noble and Jones were convicted of sedition and sentenced, respectively, to five and four years in federal prison.

Noble and Jones, who were finally judged to have been German rather than Japanese agents, were more a curiosity, typical of Los Angeles and its panorama of eccentrics, than a threat of consequence. But along with their interest in *Nikkei* sympathizers and white seditionists, the Japanese had pursued a much more significant propaganda campaign aimed at African-Americans and other "peoples of color." A Japanese cipher message from Rome to San Francisco only five days before the Pearl Harbor attack instructed local Japanese operatives to make contact with the old standby of international revolutionary conspiracy on the Pacific Coast, the Hindustan Gadar Party. The Tokyo authorities had authorized a Gadar leader to begin radio broadcasts promising that Japan, "protector of the world's colored peoples," would liberate India from British imperialism. Few Gadar supporters seemed to have paid any attention to these activities. But the same could not be said of American Blacks.

The MAGIC communications outlined a turn toward the use of Blacks as pro-Tokyo subversive agents once the Silver Shirts had failed to excite any enthusiasm among Japanese officials. Most of this interest focused on the East Coast, although attention was also given to Blacks in Los Angeles. The Japanese gained some success in recruiting agents and stirring sympathy for their "antiwhite" cause in African-American communities; one observer saw an expression of solidarity in the Black occupation of San Francisco's Japantown, or northern Fillmore district, after internment, with *Nikkei* turning over their homes and cars to Black friends. However, the MAGIC messages include admissions that most Blacks were oriented toward civil-rights groups supported by liberal Jews, or toward the Communists.

Indeed, during the Stalin-Hitler pact Black Los Angeles had seen considerable Communist propaganda against the war that emphasized Black grievances and demanded that the rights of African-Americans be fully guaranteed if America was to make any claim to democracy. Prior to this period, Blacks had been a minor and largely unorganized component of California society, and it may be argued that the Communist antiwar agitation of 1939–41 laid the foundation for the Black civil rights struggle in the state.

As American involvement in the war grew increasingly likely, prominent non-Communist African-Americans such as labor leader A. Philip Randolph pressed the federal government for immediate action to end discrimination in the armed services and in defense employment. The vast expansion of war-related industries greatly benefited white workers, many of whom, in southern California, were migrants from the Deep South and brought their prejudices with them. Racial tension began to emerge in the Los Angeles Basin; the president of North American Aviation, for example, declared that "regardless of training, we will not employ Negroes in the [Inglewood] plant. It is against company policy."

Beginning in December 1940, Randolph sought to organize a "March on Washington" by thousands of Black men, to protest the continued failure to employ Blacks in defense plants. The march was scheduled for July 1, 1941 but was called off after President Roosevelt issued Executive Order 8802, on June 25, barring discrimination in defense-industry employment. But as Louis Rosser, a popular young Black Communist, later recalled, the German invasion of Russia had made the Communists something more than just loyal supporters of the Allies; they were now superpatriots, unwilling to brook any action, anywhere, that they believed—or said they believed—would obstruct the war effort.

Thus the Communists, who supported *Nikkei* internment, similarly denounced any protest by Blacks, and even labeled Randolph a Nazi sympathizer, although he had supported the Allies against the Axis even when the Communists were hewing to the Stalin-Hitler pact and the "peace" line. When Randolph came to Los Angeles in 1942 to receive an award from the National Association for the Advancement of Colored People (N.A.A.C.P.), Louis Rosser and Southern California party boss Pettis Perry, also Black, were, in Rosser's words, "given the job of working out a plan [to] discredit Randolph." A well-known fellow traveler, Mrs. Charlotta Bass, publisher of a Los Angeles Black weekly, the *California Eagle,* spoke the night before the Randolph dinner. According to Rosser, Bass delivered a speech that "praised the Soviet Union, that called for the opening of the second front, and that said Randolph was a traitor to his country, that his threatened march on Washington was a march that would bring about chaos and disunite our country at a time when unity is needed."

Some Blacks believed that the vehemence of the Communists on this issue hid something other than their fanatical Soviet patriotism; the Communists continued to control unions in the aircraft industries and, it was thought, did not want to lose the support of white workers by pressing Black claims.

––––––––––

IN EXAMINING JAPANESE propaganda and its targets in the United States, it is well to return to the situation of Karl Goso Yoneda, Shuji Fujii, and their Communist comrades. Little substantial espionage, sabotage, or subversion had been carried out on behalf of the Japanese empire in California during the late 1930s. However, in the same period there had been a considerable amount of underground Japanese Communist activity in California—none of it ever, for a single instant, detected or even suspected by the American authorities. After the arrests and deportations of *Issei* Communists in the late 1920s and early 1930s, the Japanese Communists ceased working openly in California. Yoneda has written that Sanzo Nosaka, the head of the Japanese Communist Party, who left California in 1935, had reentered the United States as an "illegal" the next year and remained until 1938, provided with funds and safe houses by Communist Party members, both Japanese and white. Nosaka's main subordinate in this work was Nobumichi Ukai, *klichka* Joe Koide, who had come to California in 1933.

These names assumed a greater significance fifty years later with the opening of Soviet files. The historians Klehr and Haynes found in Moscow an exceptionally important document on secret Soviet activities in the United States, the "Brother-Son Report." "Son," none other than the ubiquitous Rudy Baker, filed this typed statement in English as a financial summary, prepared in 1943, of his agents' work in the previous year. Baker included a lengthy excursus on "Japanese cadres," including "Joe" (Koide) and "Saito" (Shuji Fujii). While Yoneda had gone to Manzanar, this pair remained free, and had been dispatched to Denver, with money and support from Communist-controlled unions, to revive *Doho,* the Japanese-language Communist paper. As the "Brother-Son Report" showed, this action was directly ordered by Baker, head of clandestine operations, who reported to Vasily Zarubin, third secretary of the Soviet embassy in Washington and a leading KGB officer under the *klichki* of Zubilin and Cooper. According to Baker, the Denver project was rejected, and Koide and Fujii went into the internment camps. Fujii/Saito, Baker wrote, had been released from internment and had gone to work for the federal Office of War Information, preparing radio broadcasts to Japan. (This was apparently an error; according to Yoneda's recollection, Fujii had joined the Office of Strategic Services.) Baker commented, "Although we have no contact with Saito it does not necessarily follow that he has betrayed the Party by accepting such a post." Baker also stated that "West Coast comrades" could be made available for secret assignments, and asked for clarification whether *Issei* or *Nisei* were preferable.

Klehr and Haynes also found and published a letter to Georgi Dimitrov, head of the Comintern, from an otherwise unknown functionary of the Soviet secret police, Plyshevsky, dated November 5, 1942, i.e., somewhat earlier than the "Brother-Son Report." Plyshevsky's letter quoted Baker, here identified by his alternate *klichka* as Betford, in high praise of Koide and Fujii: "Throughout the entire crisis Joe [Koide] held up splendidly; [he] and Saito are now the clearest thinkers around on the whole situation." Although the *Nikkei* comrades had been officially "suspended," to the pain of Yoneda and his wife, from the open American Communist organization, they continued to serve the secret Soviet apparatus. But in handling Koide and Fujii/Saito, Baker deferred to the Japanese comrades' own judgment.

Aside from its civil-liberties aspects, the internment of Pacific Coast *Nikkei* had other political and social consequences. In the 1942 gubernatorial election, Olson was thoroughly beaten by State Attorney General Earl Warren, a Republican. During the campaign the state's newspapers subjected Olson to a renewed and genuinely vicious smear offensive, accusing him of radicalism and dictatorial tendencies right up to his last day in office. "Olsonism" became a favored editorial-page insult. But Olson's alleged "weakness" on military preparedness and his flabby attitude toward *Nikkei* internment greatly contributed to his downfall.

The historian of the Olson Administration, Robert E. Burke, concluded that Olson, who was "calm and moderate," could not "be charged with any responsibility for the evacuation itself, no matter what he declared after the evacuation was begun." But while Culbert Olson had been a fainthearted friend of Californians of Japanese ethnicity, Earl Warren had distinguished himself by the viciousness and extremity of his anti-Japanese rhetoric. Warren far exceeded such Japanophobes as General DeWitt in the bigotry of his commentaries; indeed, the Attorney General seemed to incarnate the worst excesses of California's anti-Asian past, which he seemed intent on reviving. Warren had, for example, delivered himself of the opinion that *Nisei,* born in the United States, were more dangerous to the prosecution of the war than *Issei,* who had emigrated from Japan, for the mere reason that there were more of them.

This primitive mentality was displayed throughout the Olson-Warren gubernatorial race. Warren dwelt on such achievements as his survey, conducted with the assistance of local representatives, of every county with a Japanese population, charting all properties owned, occupied, or controlled by *Nikkei*. Warren suffered from a geographic phobia; he believed that

Japanese-owned farmlands had been deliberately chosen for their proximity to "vital war production and military installations," and warned that it was "more than coincidence" that, allegedly, *Nikkei* residents "completely surrounded aircraft plants." A pattern was visible, he claimed, "to lull us into a sense of false security . . . inviting another Pearl Harbor," even though the Hawaiian *Nikkei* population played virtually no role at all in the December 7 attack. Warren's obsession with land tenure greatly contributed to the suspicion among liberals that internment was no more than a property grab by non-Japanese farmers, using the war to expropriate their neighbors. This belief has entered into the collective memory of Californians and is now generally accepted as the main explanation for the state's anti-*Nikkei* policy in 1941. However, Kenneth Rexroth, as a contemporary observer, discounted this argument, pointing out that the southern San Joaquin Valley, which saw the largest transfers of former Japanese properties to new owners, experienced the fewest expressions of anti-Japanese prejudice.

Warren's strategy against Olson was, however, unquestionably effective; he beat the incumbent by 1.3 million votes to 900,000.

Pacifist organizations and individuals like Rexroth attempted to alleviate the pain inflicted on the interned; but others, including some distinguished young intellectuals, also found ways to express their principled opposition to the war, which had nothing in common with the demagogic propaganda of the Communists during the Stalin-Hitler pact, the isolationist stance of America First, or the pro-Axis sentiments of seditionists like Noble and Jones. Rexroth was not the only local author to claim conscientious objector (C.O.) status; a similar course was adopted by a 30-year-old poet named William Everson. The son of a Swedish band musician, Everson was born in Sacramento and had grown up in Selma, a farm town near Fresno, then attended Fresno State College. Drafted, he was sent to a C.O. camp on the coast at Waldport, Oregon. There Everson met a printer, Adrian Wilson; the pair launched an enterprise, the Untide Press, which issued fine poetry editions as part of an arts program in the camp. Everson had previously seen two volumes of his verse reach print.

Everson was deeply influenced by the poet Robinson Jeffers, a resident of Carmel who was an acquaintance of many California radicals and Bohemians, but whose dour outlook and pretentious verse made him anything but popular with them. Jeffers was also an opponent of the war. But the pacifism of Everson, like that of Rexroth (who loathed Jeffers) was something more than a reflection of the philosophy of Jeffers, who sought distance from all human concerns; it was, rather, an indication that something entirely new was happening in California letters, that a new generation had emerged, their preoccupations distant from the social, political, and even aesthetic attitudes of most of their immediate forebears.

Another representative of the same trend was a poet almost a decade younger than Everson, Robert Symmes, who in 1941 had begun calling himself Robert Duncan, the name of his birth family, for he had been adopted. Like Rexroth, Duncan, born in Oakland in 1919, had a remarkable early life, foreshadowed by his mother's death while giving birth to him. "She died when I was born," he wrote, "because my head was too big, tearing my way through her agony to life." He was adopted by the family of an architect who was also a devotee of Rosicrucian and theosophical mysticism, and Duncan and his work were profoundly marked by that environment, although he passed through a Trotskyist phase and then became an anarchist. At the end of the 1930s, Duncan attended the University of California at Berkeley for two years, but fled the academy for New York, where he took up with the erotic goddess Anaïs Nin and her lover, Henry Miller. A passionate lover of men, Duncan early embarked on a sensual derangement through adventuresome sex; in his youth he was almost murdered by a boy he picked up, and twice he tried to kill himself. In 1943 he (briefly) married, in an attempt to make himself "normal."

A few poets affirmed a pacifist opposition to the hostilities, but many more literary figures, as well as political intellectuals, had chosen to actively support the Allies. The Office of War Information (O.W.I.), known as "the radio station" to the KGB agents who closely surveilled it, provided many California radicals with employment that directly contributed to the war effort. Henry Cowell, for example, worked for the O.W.I.'s music division. By contrast Jaime de Angulo, Cowell's friend, was hired as a janitor in the San Francisco office of the O.W.I. De Angulo's creative work did not lend itself to propagandistic use in pursuit of the war; moreover he had experienced unremitting psychic torment since the death of his son Alvar in 1933, and his life was in disarray. In 1936 he and his wife Nancy came to the North Beach district of San Francisco and began studying the dominant local Cantonese dialect of Chinese.

He continued to migrate back and forth to Big Sur, and attempted to operate a dude ranch there, Los Pesares. This period of de Angulo's life also featured an extremely funny incident, in which he was accused of cattle rustling by a neighbor and old foe, Alejandrino Boronda, whose family had lived on the Central Coast since the arrival of the first Spanish soldiers. Boronda's cattle often wandered onto property de Angulo claimed, and finally de Angulo and his hands killed and butchered one of the animals. This resulted in a criminal charge, and the affair was described in the press as the "last cattle-rustling case in California history." Found guilty, the resourceful de Angulo, taking advantage of his medical degree, convinced the judge he should not be jailed because of claustrophobia, and avoided serving time. But although he triumphed in this dispute, other troubles awaited him. He moved back to Berkeley in 1942, and there wrote his magnificent memoir of his first linguistic fieldwork, *Indians in Overalls.* But the next year Nancy and he divorced.

Another appointee to the O.W.I., put in charge of its foreign-languages division in Washington, was a California journalist, Alan Cranston. And at the end of 1942, Karl Yoneda volunteered to leave his wife Elaine and son Tommy in Manzanar and enlist as a U.S. military-intelligence recruit. Accompanied by his comrade Koji Ariyoshi and a dozen other *Nisei,* Yoneda went to Minnesota, where he was trained in psychological warfare. After a year of preparation and waiting, Yoneda was sent with an O.W.I. team to the China-Burma-India theatre of operations to develop Japanese-language broadcasts and other means of demoralizing enemy troops.

While Yoneda, Ariyoshi, and other *Nikkei* Communists fulfilled these tasks, the KGB *resident* in San Francisco, Kheifitz or *Kharon,* was carrying out an operational agenda that eloquently justified his cover name of "Boatman of the Dead." The labors of the KGB comprised several "lines," including a technology-theft line, a "White" line directed against exiled Russian anti-Communists, the "fifth line" monitoring Soviet and foreign shipping, a "second line" aimed at nationalities from the Soviet Union such as Ukrainians, "technical line A," which engaged in the hallowed conspiratorial craft of passport and other document forgery, and the "fellow-countryman" line assigned to the American Communist Party. As might be expected, "fifth-line" activities surveilling merchant ships and sailors were a major responsibility of the San Francisco residency, given the large volume of wartime Soviet shipping to the U.S. West Coast.

Kharon organized the tracking, trapping, kidnapping, and transport back to Vladivostok of numerous Soviet mariners who had jumped ship in American ports. In this regard, his activities provide a macabre parallel to the pursuit of "runaway sailors" in nineteenth-century California. One of the first VENONA messages from San Francisco to Moscow to be decrypted, dated October 20, 1943, describes a Soviet cargo ship, the *Red October,* returning a "deserter" named Sinelnikov to Soviet territory and certain imprisonment if not immediate execution. Some sailors who left Russian vessels managed to ship out under the American flag but were still hunted by *Kharon*'s men, even while serving under the Stars and Stripes. An agent prominently featured in the VENONA traffic, Floyd Miller, *klichka* Michael Cort, infiltrated Harry Lundeberg's staff as well as the Trotskyist movement. He was suspected of spying on American sailors who, on the war-cargo run to Murmansk in arctic Russia, were allegedly interned and "disappeared" while attempting to smuggle in Trotskyist literature in Russian. The discovery of a few such leaflets aboard a Soviet tanker, the *Azerbaidzhan,* while it was docked in San Francisco led Moscow to order, via New York, special surveillance of the Bay Area Trotskyists. Miller may have reported to the KGB on "deserted" Russian seamen who were assisted by Lundeberg.

In the same period *Kharon* and his underlings were searching out other Russians in California, whom they treated as Soviet subjects regardless of their American legal status. The range of such targets was considerable: for example, *Kharon* reported an investigation into a certain Kravchenko, living in the Russian city of Rostov, who had $33 in a Bank of America account in San Francisco. But *Kharon*'s many assignments naturally focused on espionage, including the importation onto American soil of illegal agents. The saga of one of the most remarkable such operatives begins on December 31, 1942, with a message to Moscow from Naval GRU (military intelligence) in the Soviet embassy in Washington. The "illegal" was Francia Mitynin, a Soviet citizen born in Australia and known in the coded traffic as *Avstralyika* or "The Australian Woman," then as "Sally"; in her phony American role she was named Edna Margaret Patterson.

The first communication on the case, described by the National Security Agency as "one of the longest and most extraordinary messages in VENONA," presents, step by step and in exceptional detail, the fabrication of an American identity, beginning with a discussion of faking birth certifi-

cates, and continuing through notes on port security, differing styles of
dress, and related issues. It goes on to an assessment of whether San Francisco or Portland would be a better place for "The Australian Woman" to be
deposited by a Russian vessel. Although twice as many Red ships called at
Portland as at San Francisco, and Communist agents operated with impunity on the Portland waterfront, San Francisco was deemed preferable as
a larger and easier city in which to disappear, rent a room, and purchase a
train ticket. After much further preparation, "Sally" landed in San Francisco from the Russian ship *Sevastopol* on October 13, 1943. She was apparently never detected by the American authorities.

The figure of Charon appears in both Greek and Etruscan mythology.
In the latter, where his name is rendered *Charun,* he is represented as a
deathly, terrifying figure bearing a hammer. In choosing this *klichka* for
Kheifitz, the Russian secret police in part unconsciously anticipated their
own fate. The Etruscans lived as neighbors to the Romans, as did the
Carthaginians, for whom the KGB code renamed the city of Washington.
But while Carthage challenged Rome in war and lost, its culture was known
and recorded far and wide. By contrast, the Etruscans infiltrated and influenced the mighty Roman Empire and then vanished, leaving few keys to
their language and customs, which remain mysterious today. Similarly, the
Soviet empire would rival the West, but would never confront it directly in
battle; rather, it would penetrate and alter its social life. Yet the Soviet
Union was, like Etruscan civilization, destined to disappear; and at the time
of this writing, less than a decade after its fall, the task of interpreting Soviet
actions seems archaeological rather than historical. It is as if, in analyzing resources like VENONA, one is seeking to classify the most ancient remains and
fossils.

Alberto Savinio, in his book *Speaking to Clio,* narrates a trip in 1939 to
Sulmona and other Italian towns of Etruscan heritage. The war is just beginning. Savinio imagines Charun as more than the ferry operator of the
Styx, rather as a guide between worlds, and a restless wanderer. *"That morning Charun, he who escorts souls from this life to the other, awakened me and
told me it was time to go,"* Savinio writes poetically. *"I didn't even think of asking to see his arrest warrant, and followed him without saying a word."* In just
such a manner, *Kharon,* or Kheifitz, in San Francisco, overtook the lives of
Soviet subjects, Russian refugees, and California Communists. And, after
all, the hell of the ancients, the domain of the original Charon, like the hid-

den apparatus of the international Communist movement, was underground.

Almost from the beginning of his San Francisco posting in December 1941, *Kharon* was paralleled in his activities by another Soviet spy, Steve Nelson, the former commissar of the International volunteers in the Spanish Civil War, who came to San Francisco two years ahead of Kheifitz. In January 1942 Nelson assumed control of a Communist clandestine network disguised as a "trade union" branch, the local Federation of Architects, Engineers, Chemists and Technicians (F.A.E.C.T.) This group was composed of about sixty scientific researchers at two facilities: the Shell Development Company plant in Emeryville and the Radiation Laboratory at the University of California at Berkeley.

Nelson, who reported directly to Zarubin, a top KGB officer in the United States, also served a second spy network headed by Pyotr Ivanov, secretary of the San Francisco consulate, and probably serving GRU or military intelligence. According to a Central Intelligence Agency summary prepared in 1948, Nelson succeeded in "putting Ivanov in touch with a number of Communist and pro-Communist professors directly or indirectly connected with the radiation laboratory." Ivanov left the United States soon afterward and no further trace of him has been found. Nelson, in addition to being a protégé of Rudy Baker, had worked with the clandestine Japanese Communists in California since his return from Spain. In addition, Kheifitz, trained in physics, communicated with Moscow about discussions at the Rad Lab regarding a secret program to build an atomic bomb. Moscow already knew of the proposal to build such a weapon, thanks to the Russian spy Klaus Fuchs, who reported it in late 1941, and other sources. According to Pavel Sudoplatov, information was furnished to *Kharon* by the leading intellectual figure at the Rad Lab, J. Robert Oppenheimer, whom *Kharon* met as soon as he arrived in California. Nelson was also acquainted with Oppenheimer, through the physicist's wife, Katherine or Kitty, born Puening, the widow of Joe Dallet, a Communist whom Nelson called "his closest friend and comrade," and who had died in the Spanish war.

Oppenheimer, known to his intimates as "Opje" (pronounced "Oppie"), a nickname he had picked up in Holland, had been a secret Communist Party member since 1938. Like the poet George Oppen he was

Jewish, and responded to the antifascist call of the Comintern, in defense of world culture, after 1935. But also like Oppen, the physicist considered himself a member of the earth's natural élite, born to fulfill a great historical destiny. The appeal of Communism to such individuals was epitomized by the comment of Ring Lardner, Jr., son of a famous American writer and a successful Hollywood scenarist, that the Communists he knew "were brighter and more admirable and more likable than other people." Frank Oppenheimer, the brother of "Opje," was an open Party member, and Robert Oppenheimer himself paid $100 in cash dues each month to Isaac "Pop" Folkoff, financial director of the local Party. Folkoff, who came to San Francisco in 1904 at 24, operated an upholstery business for public purposes but was also a secret operative for *Kharon*. Although the Oppenheimer retinue was made up almost exclusively of people who, like himself, were fanatical Stalinists, his wife Kitty, whom he met in 1939, fell into a category of her own. Her former husband, Joe Dallet, was more than a beloved associate of Steve Nelson; after his death in Spain Dallet was transformed into a Communist demigod by the American Party, held up as the ultimate example for young Communists to prospective volunteers in Spain but also to other new adherents to the cause. A collection of Dallet's *Letters From Spain,* addressed to his wife, issued as a ten-cent pamphlet, stands as the most extraordinary example of Communist devotional literature ever produced in this country.

Joe Dallet was Stalin's Boy Scout. Born in 1907 to wealth, he had attended the private Woodmere Academy, studied at Dartmouth College, and found employment in the insurance industry before his encounter with the Communist Party, which he joined in 1929. He agitated fairly unsuccessfully among steelworkers, wrote for the Communist press, and became a Party official in Youngstown, Ohio. Once in Spain Dallet became extremely unpopular with the troops because of his limitless but also brainless activism, which involved "training" through childish games and competitions, along with inexhaustible posturing, bullying, and tantrums and a complete indifference to the real dangers the International volunteers faced on the battlefield. He was promoted to commissar but was criticized by his peers-in-command as a hated danger to morale. On October 17, 1937 Dallet was reported killed "fighting for the Spanish people," in Communist parlance; he may have been executed, or murdered by one of the men under his authority, or perhaps he committed suicide. But his attitudes toward the workers and peasants he had ostensibly come to help save from fascism reflected the arrogance typical of Stalinists; the Spanish Communists, he assured Kitty in a letter dated May 12, 1937, had promised a "cleaning out" of the anarchist movement, which then counted two million members and which had been an active revolutionary force in Spain for several generations before Bolshevism was invented.

Kitty Puening had gone from a relationship with so notable a Stalinist hero and martyr to marriage with Oppenheimer, whom physicists and Communists alike considered a rare genius. It is impossible to imagine that, consumed with her own importance, she would not have sought to convince Oppenheimer that the Russians should be informed of the atomic-bomb project, even if he did not himself want the Russians to know about it. The proposal for construction of a nuclear explosive device had been under serious discussion in Britain and the United States since 1939, when Albert Einstein wrote a celebrated letter to President Roosevelt warning that Germany had the research capacity to undertake such an enterprise. According to Sudoplatov, the still-secret Einstein letter was a topic of Oppenheimer's conversations with Kheifitz in 1941. Soon the Manhattan Engineering District, established as a cover for the project, would be in operation. *Kharon,* pilot of the dead and messenger from underground, the hammer-wielding death dealer hideous in aspect, had found a way to carry all humanity to the other side of the river Styx. He began assembling cadres on his shore; as Savinio has written, *"Charun said: 'You've rested enough. Come along now, and I'll take you to my country.'"*

IT WAS SUDDENLY a more dangerous world than ever before, although in 1942 the Allies made considerable progress in war. Nazi and imperial Japanese atrocities were not the only expression of advancing brutality. Individuals, including Americans who got in the way of Kheifitz and his KGB comrades, were risking their lives far from the battlefields. On the night of January 11, 1943, at the corner of Fifth Avenue and 15th Street in Manhattan, an Italian-American labor journalist and outspoken enemy of Stalin, Carlo Tresca, was shot to death by a then-unknown gangster, Carmine "Lilo" Galante. Even on the other side of the continent this crime featured a California element; an investigation disclosed that just before the shooting Galante had been in close proximity to Louis Goldblatt, Bridges's crony in the I.L.W.U., and another notorious Communist waterfront operator, Frederick N. "Blackie" Myers. The Tresca murder, debated for many years afterward, unsettled American radicals and liberals, who saw the Russians and their agents openly using their war alliance with the United States to fulfill their own narrow and evil ends.

Carlo Tresca, who had immigrated to the United States in 1904 at age 25, became famous in 1912, thanks to a celebrated textile workers' strike in Lawrence, Massachusetts, led by Wobblies. With powerful oratorical and publicity gifts, Tresca, nicknamed the "Bull of Lawrence," rallied the strikers. For the next quarter-century he fulfilled a unique function as the civic conscience of poorer Italian-Americans while also becoming a popular figure in Bohemian literary circles. During the 1920s he became famous once again as an enemy of fascism; after the Spanish Civil War he candidly and repeatedly denounced the Communists. He published a small anarchist-oriented weekly, *Il Martello (The Hammer),* mainly read by Italian garment workers in New York. He was gunned down after turning over copy for the next edition of the paper to his typesetter, including an editorial slashing at the hypocrisy and violence of the Stalinists. Tresca was mainly concerned about the activities of the long-serving Soviet terrorist Vittorio Vidali, who had figured in the case of Tina Modotti and Julio Antonio Mella in 1929. Modotti herself died under mysterious circumstances, very probably poisoned, in Mexico City in 1942, after reportedly breaking with Vidali.

Tresca was killed just as he was organizing a major political fight to influence the U.S. government in its wartime dealings with Italy. The Fascist régime was in crisis, an Allied invasion was clearly in the offing, and efforts were underway to coordinate the establishment of a new Italian government. These last were centered in Washington, on an entity, the Italian-American Victory Council, that had been set up by the O.W.I. The Communists, vying for a leadership role in postwar Italy, sought entry into the Victory Council, but Tresca called for the U.S. authorities to closely watch such activities, as well as those of former fascist sympathizers likely to make an opportunistic switch to the Allied outlook. Known killer Galante was arrested but was released without charge. The most significant response to the Tresca killing came from within the O.W.I.: the Californian Alan Cranston, in charge of the office's foreign-languages division, attempted to steer suspicion away from the Communists with the outlandish claim that Tresca had abandoned his anti-Stalinism and, before his death, favored collaboration with them. For this, Cranston was denounced by no less a figure than Norman Thomas, the nationally respected Socialist leader, and by many other anti-Communist radicals and Italian-American labor leaders.

Cranston was a very peculiar fellow. He had grown up on the Peninsula south of San Francisco, frequented the Cora Older circle, and reported intermittently for the Hearst International News Service (I.N.S.) in Britain and Germany during the mid-1930s. He went to Abyssinia (Ethiopia) in 1938 as a guest of the Italian occupiers and produced atrocity propaganda aimed against the Ethiopians, which landed the I.N.S. in a libel suit. In 1939 he got himself into a similar scrape when he issued a pirated booklet of excerpts from Hitler's *Mein Kampf,* a standard edition of which happened to be under copyright by the Houghton, Mifflin publishing house. In the O.W.I. his main job was to distribute press releases to foreign-language newspapers and radio broadcasters serving immigrant communities around the United States. Even before Tresca's death, Cranston played an ambiguous role in dealing with Italian antifascists. In San Francisco, the editor of *Il Corriere del Popolo,* Carmelo Zito, had repeatedly sought a post with O.W.I. and had been turned down. Cranston claimed he had supported Zito, and in an interview given fifty years later, blamed Zito's rejection on A. P. Giannini, the founder of the Bank of America, who was considered pro-Mussolini. But Zito's own archives strongly suggest that he was instead a victim of Communist hatred for his pronounced anti-Stalinism.

After his bizarre performance in the Tresca affair, Cranston again sought to suppress evidence of possible Soviet crimes by trying to distort the reportage on the discovery of a mass grave of Polish military officers at Katyn, near Smolensk, in German-occupied Russia. The Polish officers had been captured by the Russians in the 1939 invasion, and none had been heard from since 1940; forensic evidence on the corpses demonstrated that they had been killed by the Soviets. When a Polish-speaking radio commentator in Detroit read accounts of the case from the exiled Polish government in London, indicating Russian responsibility in the massacre, Cranston ordered the broadcaster muzzled and threatened to have the station's license revoked. Later he submitted a report to the O.S.S. arguing that Polish Communists operating from Russia had more support among Poles than the London government-in-exile, and suggested that the "missing" officers at Katyn were not missing at all. (The KGB chief Zarubin, then running spy operations in the U.S., was one of the organizers of the Katyn massacre!)

Such behavior by Communists and fellow travelers was the norm during World War II. They became the most bellicose propagandists and reckless treason-hunters the country had ever seen; anything critical of the Russians was subject to their outraged censure. Like anything else the Communists believed interfered with the war, all criticism of the USSR was labeled as Nazi-motivated or Nazi-controlled "fifth column" agitation.

In California, one of the most remarkable examples of this line of conduct emerged from the fascinating and still-relevant phenomenon, first seen in 1941, of youth gangs, known as "zoot suiters," in Los Angeles. The "zoot suit," condemned by the authorities as a "fantastic costume," combined a jacket with exaggeratedly long lapels and draped hem with pants that were pegged and pleated, a wide-brimmed hat, and a key chain hanging from the belt loops to the feet. In addition, "zoot suiters" usually wore heavy oxford shoes. The ensemble offered the first instance in America of a fad in dress that set the young completely apart from the rest of society; it was a "uniform" for the turbulent element in the new generation. On the West Coast the "zoot suit" was commonest among young nonwhites, Black and Spanish-speaking. And it was associated with gang affiliations and activities, which grew in Los Angeles during the war in a manner pregnant with meaning for the future of the city. The L.A. "zoot suiters" were the herald of ungovernability in the metastasized metropolis.

Spanish-speaking "zoot suiters" came to be known as *pachucos,* a term of indeterminate origin that may have originally signified an identification with El Paso, Texas, and therefore with The Border. In June 1943, the *pachucos* in Los Angeles suddenly gained public attention after an outbreak of fights with servicemen, quickly dubbed "riots" in the press. The "zoot suit" made the *pachucos* easy targets for the resentment of sailors, in particular, who viewed any young men out of military uniform as probable draft dodgers. Many non-Hispanic bystanders who joined in attacks on "zoot suiters" were pleased to have an excuse to beat up "Mexicans," whose attitudes they resented. But for their part the *pachucos* were incensed at the sailors' habit of treating all young Hispanic women as prostitutes, and the gangs soon established territories which outsiders, including servicemen, entered at the risk of their lives.

The deep frustrations of the large Hispanic minority in southern California, so long ignored and unarticulated, had inevitably found expression in the "acting out" of the *pachucos*. Octavio Paz, having observed the phenomenon firsthand, wrote, "The *pachuco* does not want to become Mexican again; at the same time he does not want to blend into the life of North America." *Pachuco* aggression had first been seen by the Los Angeles police in 1941, in gang fights. According to police investigators, gang crimes showed an exceptional degree of brutality from the beginning. In a series of early cases, a gang assaulted a 14-year-old girl, and were only stopped from raping her by a police clubbing; in several incidents couples were tied up, the girl was raped, and gang members then urinated on both. On one occasion five boys in "*pachuco* suits" raped a 56-year-old Black woman, then offered her a drink of wine, which she refused; they then drank the wine, urinated in the bottle, and forced her to drink from it. Weapons employed by the gangs included anything at hand: knives, guns, blackjacks, brass knuckles, steel bars, truck wrenches, hammers, gallon milk bottles, and, in at least one case, a car, which was driven into another car, killing two people. Beginning in late 1942, according to police, the *pachucos,* who had previously preyed exclusively on their fellow Hispanics, began attacking anybody who strayed into gang territory. Gangs spread from San Bernardino and Riverside to Ventura and Wilmington.

In the first week of June 1943 chaotic "riots" between *pachucos,* servicemen, and bystanders involved thousands of people and produced dozens of arrests. Police reported that in some clashes men and women in military uniform sided with the "zoot suiters." In a battle through the night of June 9, according to a report by Captain Richard Simon of the L.A.P.D.'s 77th Division, some two hundred servicemen armed with clubs, iron bars, hunks of lumber, and similar weapons drove in a convoy of fifty-two taxicabs into the Watts district. Without enough officers to arrest them, the rioters were herded away from the scene after forcing open the doors of two houses. A "zoot suit" wearer was seized by the rioters in a movie house but was rescued by police, who removed the attacking servicemen from the theater. At the same time, police faced a mob of about a hundred rock-throwing Black and Hispanic youths, but the officers formed a line between them and the servicemen, preventing "a violent riot." Windows were broken in many Pacific Electric interurban coaches, but nobody was injured. About a hundred servicemen were arrested and handed over to the military authorities; thirteen adults and twenty-five juveniles were detained in the Black and Hispanic gang; in addition, fifty-five juveniles were questioned and released.

Los Angeles Communists had a ready explanation for these disorders: they were provoked by the *Sinarquistas,* a political group in Mexico with a limited following in the U.S. Southwest. *Sinarquismo* was a mystical, semisecret Catholic and nationalist movement, formed in 1937 in reaction to the anticlericalism and leftism of postrevolutionary Mexican governments. It often embodied local grievances against the distant powers in Mexico City. Inside Mexico, *Sinarquistas* and their opponents occasionally attacked each other physically. On no real basis, except the hysterical propaganda of Mexican Stalinists (who claimed, of course, that the *Sinarquistas* were allied with "Trotskyites"), the Los Angeles Communists shouted that the *Sinarquistas,* as "subversive fifth columnists," were run from Berlin. The release of the VENONA KGB messages showed that much of this uproar was directed from Moscow. Articles published by the *Daily People's World* in October 1942 argued that fascists and Nazis were working secretly to corrupt Mexican-American youth in Los Angeles and incite them to violence; the Los Angeles police were blamed for exacerbating the problem by their racist abuses. Such a method, involving the literal invention of enemies and overheated rhetoric demanding their eradication, had become the main form of Communist advocacy in California, in imitation of the hunt for "Trotskyites" and "Hitler agents" in the Moscow purges.

The California legislature's Committee on Un-American Activities, under Jack Tenney, now a member of the state senate, was impelled by the *pachuco* debate to hold hearings on *Sinarquismo.* Tenney's representatives interviewed *pachucos* in the Los Angeles County Jail and called as witnesses a range of prominent Communists and fellow travelers who, having been loud in their assertions, were asked for evidence of *Sinarquista* backing by Nazi Germany. The Communists furnished no useful information of any kind about *Sinarquismo;* they admitted lacking substantial knowledge of the organization. Tenney also called representatives of the *Sinarquista* movement for lengthy interrogation. His committee's finding was that although *Sinarquismo* had authoritarian aspects and totalitarian trappings, it was not conspiratorial or subversive, had never attacked the American authorities, and was exclusively concerned with politics inside Mexico. The Communist claims about *Sinarquista* plots were imaginary.

Mexican-Americans were not the only subjects for such Communist fabrications; Karl Yoneda and his associates engaged in an elaborate campaign to convince the California authorities that a so-called "Black Dragon Society" had carried on fascist intrigues among the Japanese in the United States. No "Black Dragon Society" ever existed; it too was a product of the Communist need for enemies, real or not. But the Communist hunt for purported "Fifth Columnists" was not limited to minority groups; it was extended into the labor movement. As the war continued, union militancy had sharply increased in the United States, stoked by the visible profitability of war production and resentment of interference by federal labor boards, as well as by the democratic rhetoric of the Allies; rank-and-file workers increasingly demanded a bigger role in industry and a larger share of the national income pie.

On June 1, 1943, a half million members of the United Mine Workers under John L. Lewis struck the coal industry nationwide, demanding a $2-per-day wage hike, "portal-to-portal" pay extending throughout the shift, and other improvements. While the Roosevelt Administration reacted with moderate irritation, the rage of the Communists knew no limits. By June 7, the miners were ordered back to work by Lewis; a second strike later in the month was brief. But Harry Bridges, still in the United States under an unenforced order for his deportation to Australia, branded Lewis a "traitor"; a report signed by Bridges and four of his top I.L.W.U. officers called the miners' leader, a founder of the C.I.O., and a past patron of Bridges, "the single most effective agent of the fascist powers within the ranks of labor . . . whose entire policy and work since long before the outbreak of war has been calculated to destroy the unity of our nation, pit workers against the government, curtail production, and assist the fascist forces." Bridges's union pledged no strikes, and even no local presentation of grievances, until the war was won.

Strikers during World War II were hardly unpatriotic. In Long Beach, California, striking bus drivers, calling for a dollar-per-hour increase, refused to return to their regular jobs; but a union leader declared, backed by a unanimous vote of the members, "If the Army or Navy has any buses or trucks, we will drive them free for the purpose of transporting workers to and from all defense plants." A similar situation arose on the Santa Fe railway lines in California, where train crews seeking higher wages turned in resignation letters and petitioned the authorities for reassignment to other war-related work, or offered to enlist, but were ordered by the government to remain in their positions. A. F. Whitney, national president of the Brotherhood of Railway Trainmen, declared in June 1943,

> The mood of laboring people is not sweetened by legislative attempts to label legitimate union activities as criminal, while criminal conspiracies to violate the anti-monopoly laws are whitewashed in the name of the war effort. . . . An attempted wage and job freeze at the expense of the workers while legalized profiteering is being condoned is not conducive to morale in the factories and mills and on the rails. . . . The month of May brought to the American worker a culmination of a series of disillusionments about the economic administration of the war. The bitter truth that they are being betrayed is being driven home to them.

But to Bridges and his associates, such commonsense views were pro-Nazi treason.

Spring 1943 saw Hollywood dragged into this often baffling panorama of conflicting political interests with the release of the film *Mission to Moscow* by Warner Brothers. Based on a book of memoirs with the same title by Joseph E. Davies, former U.S. ambassador to Russia, the picture was written by Howard Koch and directed by Michael Curtiz; Walter Huston starred as Davies. Davies himself had solicited the assistance of the KGB in providing background material to support the film. An extraordinary uproar immediately ensued, for the film was the purest item of Stalinist propaganda ever to come out of the American cinema. In a letter filling two and a half columns of the *New York Times* of May 9, 1943, John Dewey and Suzanne LaFollette, his associate on the commission to investigate the Stalin purges, inventoried most of the lies included in the film: it presented Bukharin, Red Army commander Mikhail Tukhachevsky, and other purge victims as fascist agents whose guilt was unquestionable; it portrayed the Soviets as fighting the Japanese at a time when Russia and Japan remained at peace; it claimed that the Russian people wholeheartedly supported Communism, and that Soviet society during the purges was prosperous and well fed; it ignored the Stalin-Hitler pact and American Communist opposition to preparedness; it defamed American senators as unanimously isolationist, and it defended the Russian offensive against Finland.

Other commentators were equally harsh, or harsher. Dorothy Thompson, America's favorite anti-Nazi newspaper columnist, pointed out,

The famous purge trials are grossly fictionalized. These several trials stretched over two years. Here they are all telescoped into one, and in it is a figure who never appeared in any of the public trials—namely, Marshal Tukhachevsky. He was arrested, together with other Generals, secretly court-martialed, and shot. . . . I intensely resent the inference in the film that these trials established justice according to any procedure acceptable to us.

The Marxologist and philosopher Sidney Hook declared, "What we are witnessing is a propaganda buildup for conducting purges and frame-ups in this country in the Moscow style." *Mission to Moscow* was met with picket lines in front of many movie houses around the country, but Hollywood Communists considered its release to be one of the movie industry's finest moments.

IDEOLOGICAL RIVALRIES LURKING in wartime America were also dramatized by a tragedy on Monday, July 17, 1944, at 10:17 P.M., in Port Chicago, a small Navy town on the San Francisco Bay-Sacramento River Delta. Two ammunition ships, the *Quinault Victory* and *E. A. Bryan,* blew apart, killing 320 people: 250 Navy seamen, dozens of merchant mariners, and assorted naval officers, coast guardsmen, and railroad workers. Some 390 people were injured. Nothing remained of the two ships. The town was devastated. Of the Navy seamen killed in the disaster 202 were Blacks, who had been assigned duty as longshoremen.

Three weeks later, 258 Navy sailors at Mare Island on the other shore of the Delta refused to work loading munitions on the ground that the work was unsafe. Of them, fifty Blacks were arrested and charged with mutiny, convicted, and imprisoned for sixteen months each; the remaining 208 sailors received lesser discipline. The explosion and mutiny stirred Black opinion, for it seemed to many Blacks that the Black sailors had been deliberately assigned hazardous duty as a form of racial discrimination.

The Black Communist Louis Rosser came to work on the San Francisco waterfront in August 1944. He later recalled, "I went to the Communist Party headquarters. Louise Todd and Schneiderman [were] there and I said, 'Why don't we do something about this attempt to court-martial these Negro sailors?' I said, 'Ever since I have been in the Party every time something happens to a Negro the Communists say, 'Let's do something.' So Schneiderman looked out the window and said to me, 'Rosser, what is more important, loading those ships standing in the harbor for the Soviet Union or those fifty men over there who are going to jail?'" Rosser added, "Of course all the Communists did about it was write a few articles in the *Daily People's World*." Soon afterward Rosser, "tired of being a stooge for Stalin" in his words, left the Communist movement. Such experiences left many Blacks with an extreme hatred for Communists. A notable expression of this emotion is a novel by Chester Himes, *Lonely Crusade*. One of the most brilliant American writers of this century, and himself Black, Himes had come to Los Angeles at the encouragement of the successful author and film writer Louis Bromfield. Born in Missouri in 1909, Himes had been expelled from college, then entered into a criminal adventure that got him sentenced to twenty years in prison. There he began writing and, paroled in 1936, published some short stories and worked for the W.P.A. *Lonely Crusade* is a terrifying portrait of the Los Angeles Communists—based on real individuals whose identities are obvious to those who knew the environment—as hypocritical, degraded scoundrels.

In Hollywood, the need for propaganda films boosted the influence of well-established Communists like John Howard Lawson and Lester Cole, and also provided opportunities for some who had never previously worked in movies. Alvah Cecil Bessie, aged 38, was drama critic for *The New Masses,* a strident Communist weekly published in New York, when he was hired as a screenwriter by Warner Brothers in January 1943. Bessie was something of an aesthete and eccentric in his youth but had come to Communism, like other intellectuals, after 1935. He fought in the International Brigades in Spain, and produced a narrative of the experience, *Men in Battle,* which has been widely praised for its verisimilitude but which also contains sundry Communist distortions. Unfortunately, *Men in Battle* was published at the end of August 1939, and its antifascism was an embarrassment to the Party during the era of the Stalin-Hitler pact; its first printing sold almost no copies. Perhaps because of such experiences, perhaps because his early ambitions as a poet and fiction writer had been frustrated, Bessie was an extremely angry man. Although he long remained a loyal Communist, he seemed tormented by ambivalent feelings, and a tendency to play with facts and to twist the truth, visible in much of his work, may have reflected this inner conflict.

On leaving *The New Masses,* Bessie printed a warning to the fans of his theater column: "If you see any exceptionally bad moving pictures in the future, it will be reasonably certain that I've had a hand in them." This self-revelation was also extremely prescient, for the very great bulk of the war films produced by Bessie and his Communist colleagues were truly wretched. Just as they had used the war as a pretext to disavow the Black struggle for civil rights, to defame strikers, and to drum up fear of such insubstantial enemies as the *Sinarquistas,* the Communists took the opportunity to produce some of the worst exercises in cinematic superpatriotism ever seen. *Mission to Moscow,* of course, reeked of Stalinism, and other pro-Russian films such as *North Star* (1943) and *Song of Russia* (1944) were distasteful in their simple-mindedness. But films by the Hollywood Communists that dealt with ordinary American civilians and service people also offered repellent fabrications and propaganda.

One obvious exception was the 1942 production *This Gun for Hire,* perhaps the best of the wartime films made with Communist participation. With the Party-line content kept to a minimum, *This Gun for Hire* was a Hollywood landmark in several ways. It was directed for the Paramount studio by silent-movie veteran (and prominent Communist) Frank Tuttle, and its screenplay was adapted, from the Graham Greene novel *A Gun for Sale,* by W. R. Burnett and Albert Maltz. A fairly successful short-story writer in the proletarian genre of the Great Depression, Maltz, still in his early thirties, had come to Hollywood in 1941. *This Gun for Hire* anticipated the later genre of *film noir* in its presentation of Alan Ladd as "Raven," the mercenary killer who seems emotionless and conscienceless as he makes his brutal way through society: "I'm my own police," he sneers. Paired with the smoldering Veronica Lake, who seeks to find something human within him, Ladd became a major star when *This Gun for Hire* was released. One of the many interesting details of the film is the platonic relationship between Ladd and Lake, who never even kiss. Art-directed by Hans Dreier, the film includes memorable scenes in the industrial landscape of the Los Angeles rail yards.

This Gun for Hire also includes a very few, and fairly comical, political references of the kind Communist screenwriters typically sought to inject into scripts. In one ironic detail, Veronica Lake is recruited as a patriotic spy by the head of a congressional investigating committee, and responds enthusiastically. Elsewhere, the real villain of the piece is obviously modeled on John D. Rockefeller, the archetype of American corporate "fascism," yet the role is undermined by the character's goofy dialogue. Although no others could compare with *This Gun for Hire* (to say nothing of a wonderful, if flawed, propaganda film like Alfred Hitchcock's *Saboteur*, made with the participation of fellow-traveling screenwriters Peter Viertel and Dorothy Parker, and released in 1942), nearly all the war pictures made by well-known Hollywood Stalinists embodied a similarly varying mix of competence and silliness. Two 1943 Humphrey Bogart pictures, *Sahara* from Columbia and *Action in the North Atlantic* from Warner's, the first cowritten and the second entirely written by John Howard Lawson, would have been much better films had the Party lines not been so obvious.

Alvah Bessie's first assignment at Warner Brothers was to rewrite a predictably bad film, *Northern Pursuit,* starring Errol Flynn as a Canadian Mountie chasing Nazis. His next action project, released in 1945, was another Flynn vehicle for Warners, *Objective Burma!* Bessie's original story was given to Ranald McDougall and Lester Cole to be turned into a script, but Bessie received an Academy Award nomination for the film. However, although it was successful in the United States and has been praised as among Flynn's best movies, *Objective Burma!* caused an ugly controversy in Britain. Bessie, in fine Communist fashion, flouted fact in presenting the World War II campaign in Burma as in effect an American operation, when in fact Burma had been fiercely fought over by British troops, with few Yanks in sight. (The *Objective Burma!* brouhaha endured for some time, and the film was not released in Britain until 1952—and then only after an apologetic prologue was tacked on.)

But if Bessie was willing to trim reality in the interest of what seemed to be a good script idea, Lester Cole was prepared to cast aside all consideration of truth and even of decency in his enthusiasm for the war. For Cole's filmography included one of the most racist and dishonest motion pictures ever made in the United States, the 1945 film *Blood on the Sun,* produced by and starring James Cagney. This breathtaking exercise in movie manipulation regurgitated and then repeated every known cliché of American anti-Japanese prejudice, to a point of nausea; the Japanese are presented as alternately sycophantic and back-stabbing, physical and moral cowards. Asian stereotypes were nothing new for Cole, who had worked on a Charlie Chan feature; *Blood on the Sun* was also a *jiujitsu* picture, offering a caricature of Asian hand-to-hand combat that makes it a harbinger of the much later martial-arts genre. But if *Blood on the Sun* is extraordinary in its Japanophobia, it is also unrestrained in its falsification. Its main theme is the notoriously forged "Tanaka Memorial," which the film seeks to authenticate as a Japanese version of Hitler's *Mein Kampf.* Cagney plays an American journalist in prewar Japan who obtains a copy of the "Tanaka Memorial" and fights for it to be recognized as Japan's "blueprint for world domination." The "Tanaka Memorial" had no more real existence than the Black Dragon Society, but Cole, who was seemingly blind to the overwhelming racism of the film, proudly insisted for thirty years afterward that this story was based on a "real document."

While the Hollywood Communists were busy proving how easily film art could be exploited for despicable political ends, a recent arrival in California demonstrated much greater intellectual integrity: the novelist and essayist Henry Miller. After a decade in Europe and the publication of several major books, beginning with *Tropic of Cancer* in 1934, the 48-year-old Miller had returned to the United States and traveled around the country before coming to California in June 1942. In 1944 he was invited by Yanko Varda, a Greek expatriate and a fantastical artist, to visit the Central Coast—first Monterey and then Big Sur, which became Miller's home base for years.

Miller described Big Sur as "until 1937 . . . probably one of the least known regions in all America. . . . Big Sur has a climate of its own and a character all its own," he marveled. "Perhaps in the year A.D. 2000 the population may still number only a few hundred souls. Perhaps, like Andorra and Monaco, it will become a Republic all its own." Miller, who popularized Big Sur with the American intellectual public, paid homage to the region's grand pioneer: "The little community of one, begun by the fabulous 'outlander,' Jaime de Angulo, has multiplied into a dozen families," he wrote at the beginning of his *Big Sur and the Oranges of Hieronymus Bosch.* A neighbor and a peer of de Angulo, more than a friend, Miller encountered a considerable range of equally stimulating personalities at Big Sur. One of these was Norman Mini, the former farm-labor organizer and "criminal syndicalism" convict, who had apparently left the Communist Party in 1941, and whom Miller had earlier met in San Francisco at the home of Kenneth Rexroth.

Miller, in his typically hyperbolic manner when describing a friend, compared Mini with Edgar Allan Poe, who had also been expelled from West Point. Mini stayed with his wife and child near Big Sur while working on a novel—"the best first novel I have ever read," Miller enthused, echoing others' appreciation of Mini a decade before. However, according to Mini's fourth wife Kleo, his first novel, which dealt with West Point and which he had kept with him in prison, had been lost; Miller probably read his (unpublished) *To Earth Returned,* though Mini had also written a fictional treatment of California agricultural labor, *Red Cotton,* which also failed to see print. Mini, who had grown up in the Central Valley before his Communist adventure in agriculture, had at last fulfilled his bucolic destiny by becoming a fine winemaker. Miller wrote, "Norman was 'different' in that, though poor as a church mouse, he clung to his cellar, which contained some of the finest wines (native and foreign) anyone could wish for." Miller believed that Mini had promise as a writer, but saw in him "much more, indeed. He had in him the makings of a von Moltke, a Big Bill Haywood, a Kafka—and a Brillat-Savarin," Miller commented. "He impressed me immediately. I sensed that he had suffered deep humiliations. I did not look upon him then as a writer but as a strategist. A military strategist. A 'failed' strategist, who had now made life his battleground. That was Norman to me—a fascinating Norman, whom I could listen to indefinitely."

Mini, who wrote very slowly and suffered creative blocks, asked for Miller's help in revising his work. "Had his abode been Europe I doubt that Norman would have had such a struggle to express himself," Miller wrote. "For one thing, there he would have been able to make himself understood. His humility was genuine and touching. One felt that he was cut out for bigger things, that he had taken to writing in desperation, after all other avenues had been closed off. He was too sincere, too earnest, too truthful, to ever be a worldly success. His integrity was such, in fact, that it inspired fear and suspicion." After failing to place his manuscript with publishers, Mini returned from Big Sur to Berkeley and took a job as a janitor at the University of California. "Whatever Norman tackled he made an art of," Miller concluded. Such a credo was appropriate to Miller himself.

Simultaneously with the arrival of Henry Miller in Big Sur, a new intellectual tendency had emerged in Berkeley, in a little magazine called *Circle.* Edited by George Leite, who became one of Miller's associates, *Circle* produced ten issues beginning in 1944, with what Lawrence Ferlinghetti and Nancy Peters described as "antiwar, anarchist, or anti-authoritarian, civil libertarian attitudes, coupled with a new experimentation in the arts."

Henry Miller appeared in its first number; later contributors included Anaïs Nin, Kenneth Rexroth, Robert Duncan, the composers Harry Partch and Darius Milhaud, and such nationally known poets as William Carlos Williams. *Circle* also published William Everson (still in the Oregon camp for conscientious objectors), along with the Nebraska modernist poet Weldon Kees, and other experimental writers such as Thomas Parkinson, Judson Crews, and Gil Orlovitz.

The first issues of *Circle* were mimeographed, but George Leite soon secured a letterpress contract with Jack Werner Stauffacher, a printer then in his early twenties. Stauffacher had founded The Greenwood Press on his family property in San Mateo in 1934 at age 13. He was on his way to becoming a leading figure in West Coast fine printing, but with the coming of the war he, like the rest of his peers, found his assumptions about the world profoundly shaken. He served in the Army Corps of Engineers, but contracted pleurisy and was discharged. He later recalled, "my age of innocence was somehow broken. . . . We were trying to find some answers. . . . Somehow I met George Leite, maybe through Henry Miller."

Circle's second mimeographed issue had included work by a San Franciscan, Philip Lamantia, then only 16. Lamantia was a Surrealist—an authentic one, rather than an imitator—who had been published in 1943 in *VVV*, an annual printed in New York under the sponsorship of the war-exiled French Surrealist poet and theoretician André Breton. (Breton himself came as far west as Reno, but seems never to have visited San Francisco.) The son of a Sicilian-American businessman, Lamantia grew up in the Outer Mission district of San Francisco, an early refuge of gentility for successful Italian-Americans fleeing their traditional quarter of North Beach. Lamantia's verse was brilliant, romantic, and erotic; one of his most important poems begins,

> I am following her to the wavering moon
> to a bridge by the long waterfront . . .

Some thirty years later, Kenneth Rexroth described Philip Lamantia as "the best of the third generation of [international] surrealists. . . . I have never known anyone else who started out, without preliminaries, with no five-finger exercises or scales, as an achieved poet," he added. Lamantia had been sent to Rexroth by "someone I didn't know who was an English teacher" at Balboa High School, where young Philip was enrolled. Marilyn Zito, daughter of Carmelo Zito, the editor *of Il Corriere del Popolo,* was in the same class at Balboa High. She later recalled that Philip Lamantia's father had gone to Carmelo Zito and asked Zito to speak to his son about the latter's increasingly perturbing behavior. Marilyn recalls that her father came away from the meeting with Lamantia dismayed, for something was going on with the young author that was beyond the understanding of most of the older generation, even a radical like the *Corriere* editor. The meeting of Carmelo Zito and Philip Lamantia took place across a widening cultural gap. For an intellectual revolution—indeed, the long-awaited California literary revolution—had begun, with consequences beyond all expectation.

Lamantia was, like Rexroth, a pacifist; indeed, Rexroth was the first individual granted conscientious-objector status on appeal in San Francisco—and Lamantia was the second. Lamantia, Duncan, who had been discharged from the Army as a homosexual, and other new voices associated with *Circle* had something else in common beside their opposition to war: according to Rexroth, "one of the characteristics of all these new people was, to put it bluntly, mysticism." Rexroth's own poetry was increasingly concerned with occult matters as he read, for example, the seventeenth-century German shoemaker Jakob Böhme's *Signature of All Things* (*De signatura rerum*, 1622). Henry Miller, now the leader of a recognized local literary movement, had also plunged into esoteric study, including Böhme. Lamantia wrote in a poetic homage to Miller,

> just when my head is swimming in a pyramid in Mexico
> just at that time you crawl forth

The appearance of *Circle* marked the beginning of the overt phase of the California literary revolution. As Rexroth recalled, "the ideological foundations of the San Francisco Renaissance had been laid—poetry of direct speech of I to Thou, personalism, anarchism." Soon an antistatist Libertarian Circle, led by Rexroth, Lamantia, Duncan, Everson (after he left Waldport), and friends, was holding meetings, literary seminars, and dances with the support of a few surviving Italian and Spanish anarchists, and furnishing a challenge, however minor at first, to Communist domination over California radicals.

———————

THE WAR GROUND on. While Karl Yoneda had been sent to the front in Asia, back in California Yoneda's wife Elaine and their son Tommy had left the Manzanar internment camp and returned to the Bay Area. On the civil-liberties front, Wayne Collins and his colleagues continued their challenge to the legality of internment. In June 1943 the U.S. Supreme Court upheld the conviction of Minoru Yasui for curfew violation, but found that the constitutionality of the curfew for citizens, and an earlier decision that Yasui had forfeited his citizenship, merited correction by lower courts. At the same time, the Supreme Court ratified the conviction of Gordon Hirabayashi for curfew evasion. Although the Court avoided issuing an opinion on the overall constitutionality of evacuation, Chief Justice Harlan F. Stone commented negatively on the discrimination against Japanese-Americans that had been demonstrated in the program, admitting, "It is jarring to me that U.S. citizens were subjected to this treatment." In December 1944, after hearing arguments by Collins and Charles Horsky, the Court upheld the conviction of Fred Korematsu. But in their decision on the case of Mitsuye Endo, announced at the same time, the Court called for her release and that of other *Nikkei* who were "concededly loyal." In reality, a decision had already been made within the Roosevelt Administration to end "relocation." The internment of Americans of Japanese ancestry was now a moot issue, even as the war continued.

Measures were now in progress to bring the war itself to a decisive end through the atomic-bomb project, which had been nursed to fruition by J. Robert Oppenheimer and his staff in the Manhattan Engineering District. Manhattan operated through a constellation of sites at the Radiation Laboratory in Berkeley, a fabrication and testing facility at Los Alamos, New Mexico, and production plants in Washington State and Tennessee.

Almost from the beginning of Manhattan's full-time operation in January 1942, security officials were disturbed by Oppenheimer's continued association with Communists. Investigators confirmed that data from the Rad Lab had reached KGB *rezident* Kheifitz, or *Kharon,* in San Francisco. Russian spy Steve Nelson and his assistant Bernadette Doyle had been monitored in a meeting in the Berkeley apartment of Joseph Weinberg, a Rad Lab employee, in August 1943; four other Rad Lab workers, Giovanni R. Lomanitz, Irving Fox, Ken Manfred, and the very brilliant physicist David Joseph Bohm, were also present. Fox had pressed the Rad Lab branch of F.A.E.C.T., the so-called trade union, to operate out of the public eye so as to avoid surveillance by the F.B.I. (The federal authorities had requested a moratorium on union activity in the Manhattan Engineering District.)

Even more alarming, on July 2, 1944 federal agents observed a meeting at a downtown San Francisco restaurant between *Kharon,* his successor as KGB *rezident,* Grigory Kasparov (whose *klichka* was *Dar,* or Gift), and Dr. David Martin Kamen, a staff chemist at the Rad Lab and a faculty member at U.C. Berkeley since 1936. Kamen was photographed in the company of Kheifitz and Kasparov and observed as he spent two and a half hours eating and talking with the spies. A friend of Robert Oppenheimer's brother Frank and of U.C. French professor Haakon Chevalier, both well-known Communists, Kamen had met *Kharon* at the San Francisco home of Louise Rosenberg Bransten, an heiress to a dried-fruit fortune, a prominent Communist, and the paramour of Kheifitz. Kamen furnished both oral and printed, restricted and secret information on atomic research to Kheifitz and Kasparov; he was fired from the Rad Lab ten days after this meeting.

Kheifitz had been exceptionally concerned with the Rad Lab, as the VENONA intercepts later divulged. A major target of KGB espionage in the Bay Area was Boris T. Pash, a U.S. Army intelligence investigator of Russian ancestry who had interrogated "Opje" on security matters; a VENONA message of March 18, 1944 from *Kharon* to Moscow, reported (incorrectly) that Pash was en route to Iran. Other VENONA messages from *Kharon's* watch referred to Harrison George, the old Pan-Pacific functionary, who was now editor of the *Daily People's World;* also mentioned was an agent with the *klichka* of *Myasnik,* or Butcher, probably Steve Nelson, whose birth name (Mesarosh) means "butcher" in Hungarian. The KGB dispatches further commented on Harry Bridges and described contacts with "Pop" Folkoff as boss of the local Party underground.

Something was definitely wrong at the Rad Lab, if not in the whole Manhattan Engineering District. Another incident that may have had to do with atomic-bomb security occurred on January 5, 1944 when a psychiatrist, Dr. Jean Frances Tatlock, 29, was found dead in her apartment on the slopes of Telegraph Hill in San Francisco. According to a coroner's report, the young doctor had swallowed codeine, nembutal, and chloral hydrate, although death had been caused by drowning in a partly filled bathtub. Jean Tatlock, an active Communist, was the "former" mistress of "Opje." Although Oppenheimer and his wife Kitty were apparently happily married, Kitty remained at Los Alamos while Oppenheimer traveled around the country on Manhattan District business. On June 14, 1943, six months before Tatlock's death, Oppenheimer had come to San Francisco, and the pair had eaten in the little Mexican/Spanish/Basque neighborhood on Broadway between North Beach and Chinatown. They had then gone to Tatlock's apartment on Montgomery Street, where Oppenheimer spent the night with her.

The death of Jean Tatlock was mysterious, and some aspects of it have never been elucidated. Her father, Berkeley emeritus professor of English John S. P. Tatlock, had come to her apartment about 1:00 P.M. on January 5th; he had last seen his daughter on January 3rd, and she had agreed to telephone him on the 4th. When she did not call, and did not answer his calls, he waited a day before going to her apartment. He found her lying on a pile of pillows at the end of the bathtub, with her head submerged in shallow water.

Professor Tatlock then did a number of curious things. First, he did not call anybody for more than four hours. According to the coroner's sardonic notation, "Supposedly not knowing what to do, Mr. Tatlock stayed around the flat for some time and then called Halsted & Co.," an undertaker. The mortuary called the coroner. Rigor mortis was very pronounced, and the coroner determined that Jean Tatlock had died more than twelve hours before.

The *San Francisco Chronicle* of January 6 reported, "Shocked by his discovery [of the body], Dr. Tatlock kindled a blaze in the fireplace, warmed the room, and lifted his daughter's body from the tub and placed it on her studio couch." However, the condition of Jean Tatlock's body argues against her father having removed it from the tub; rather, it seems this was his way of explaining the fire he lit. The same *Chronicle* article quoted, from a note she had left, "I am disgusted with everything."

The next day, the *Chronicle,* in a follow-up article, revised its reportage on the position of the corpse, describing it "kneeling" on the pillows with her head in the water. This article included the text of a "farewell note" found on the living-room table next to some empty medication envelopes: "To those who loved me and helped me, all love and courage. I wanted to live and to give and I got paralyzed, somehow. I tried like hell to understand and I couldn't . . . At least, I could take away the burden of a paralyzed soul from a fighting world . . ." All that remained was a jagged line down the page. The note was recovered by the coroner's stewards, and was described in the coroner's report as a "purported last note (suicide)."

Professor Tatlock stated that although his daughter's medical residency at Mt. Zion Hospital was going well, she had been despondent for some time. An unpaid bill for several hundred dollars in psychiatric services was also found near her body.

Three questions emerge from this tragedy: Why did Jean Tatlock kill herself? What did Professor Tatlock burn in the fireplace? And was *Kharon*, ferryman of the dead, involved? None of these questions has yet been adequately answered. Certainly there were those who sought to follow *Kharon*, soon to return to Moscow, wherever he might lead. *"'Charun, take me with you!'"* Alberto Savinio had written. *"Charun does not listen to me. He goes away. He disappears like light extinguished in the light."* And so *Kharon* disappeared, into the light burning from the Russian battlefields, which anticipated the bright burst of the first atomic bomb, about to explode.

Another ambiguous element in the death of Jean Tatlock emerged almost fifty years later with the publication of a quasi-memoir, *Against a Field Sinister,* by Edith Arnstein Jenkins, a Communist and a close comrade of both Jean Tatlock and Haakon Chevalier. Jenkins, one of the few Communists to write candidly on "Opje," seemed mainly to recall Jean's "large breasts and thick ankles." Edith Jenkins "could not grieve" for Jean Tatlock, she later wrote. Her memory was, however, faulty, for she described Tatlock "lying in the bathtub" and added, in a rather macabre aside, "I cannot get the picture out of my mind how her large breasts must have floated on the water." But that was not possible, given the position of the corpse.

J. Robert Oppenheimer's memory was also weak; he later claimed to have barely known Edith Jenkins, and to have kept his distance from her and her husband, David, a flamboyant Communist known in the maritime labor movement as a "thug." But Jenkins's memoir describes Oppenheimer with insights that could only have been known by a close associate. Indeed, Jenkins recalled that during the worst of the Stalin purges, in 1937, "because he knew I would not be shaken in my political loyalties," Oppenheimer asked her for reassurance about the arrests of Soviet physicists. "I was scornful of what I saw as his gullibility" in believing such tales about the glorious Soviet Union, Edith Jenkins wrote. Then, again, her memory failed her: "I cannot recall where this interview took place, although I think I recall every word that Oppie spoke."

Beginning in summer 1944, David Jenkins, Edith's husband, was responsible for the most successful front operation ever seen on the West

Coast: the California Labor School (C.L.S.) This institution was nothing more than the former Workers' School of the 1930s, previously described, that had "employed" Rexroth and others in indoctrinating Communist cadres and fellow-travelers, and that imitated, very distantly, both the old Jack London Memorial Institute in San Francisco and the anarchist "Ferrer schools" established after 1910 in various countries. The San Francisco Workers' School was renamed the Tom Mooney Labor School in 1943; it was one of a network of expanded Communist training centers around the United States, modeled on the so-called Jefferson School of Social Science in New York. Communist "schools" have been the subject of considerable misrepresentation in recent years, and require a digression.

Schools of the C.L.S. type were mainly a form of evening entertainment, not unlike lecture and hobby programs held by numerous museums, community centers, and similar bodies all over America. Socialists and Trotskyists also maintained such activities, although seldom with the pretensions of the Communists, who dressed them up as if they were real schools even though they offered very little in the way of real education. The Communist "curriculum" was modeled on the seminars for Party members that first operated in Russia itself, then were exported. Core studies began with dialectical and historical materialism, the superficial "philosophy" proclaimed as the basis of Communist practice; political economy, or economics through the lens of class struggle, the history of Communism, and various courses in agitation and propaganda. Aside from elementary Russian and English, additional lectures and courses dealt with current events, and a weekly seminar interpreting the week's news according to the Party line was often the best attended of all the offerings at such schools. Tuition was minimal, and as long as the Communists had influence in the C.I.O. some of its affiliates contributed funds to the schools, leading them occasionally to run courses in basic trade union practice, public speaking, and the like.

During World War II, all the Communist schools began offering more cultural and recreation workshops in writing, art, drama, and dance, as well as in Black and Jewish history. Furthermore, the California Communists developed a relationship with the University of California that resulted in joint sponsorship of events on industrial relations and similar topics by the university and the Communist schools. The California Labor School seems to have been named to promote the belief that it was an extension of the University of California (U.C.) system into the trade-union field. (A corresponding operation in Los Angeles was titled the People's Educational Center.) However, notwithstanding the legends that have grown up around the C.L.S. and other Communist schools, they were never accredited as authentic academic institutions; if the U.C. system occasionally accepted C.L.S. courses for credit, these were limited to the field of labor sociology. The Communist schools seldom if ever included technical or vocational courses, except in the arts.

Nevertheless, when the California Labor School emerged from the former Tom Mooney Labor School, it benefited from endorsements by many Bay Area political leaders, officials of the A.F.L., and a number of respected academics. A.F.L. involvement was short-lived, as that federation, in its California branch, had become decidedly anti-Communist. But Jenkins, as its director, kept the C.L.S. going, even though he had only an eighth-grade education—a matter of considerable irritation to the A.F.L. representatives who investigated its activities before recommending that local unions steer clear of it. Dave Jenkins was indeed a piece of work.

If the California Labor School had any claim to intellectual legitimacy, it was in the arts, for although its courses in writing, painting, printmaking, and similar areas of endeavor normally consisted of little more than dogged attempts to fit all human creativity into a Stalinist straitjacket dominated by fanatics, they also attracted a few individuals who, while dedicated mainly to their literary and artistic work, cultivated fellow-traveling for social ends. As noted earlier, the California Communists had never enjoyed as much success with writers as with painters; the only author of substance involved in the C.L.S. was Muriel Rukeyser, an admired friend of Rexroth who seemed divided between excellence as a poet and confused radicalism in politics. (Rukeyser also met Octavio Paz, whose poetry she translated, in Berkeley in 1944.) Anthony Boucher, a well-known expert on mysteries and other pulp genres, also conducted a writing workshop there, but was never known as much of a leftist. A lesser figure, George Hitchcock, frequented the Rexroths while also churning out propaganda for the party, running the C.L.S. "trade union extension," and lecturing on philosophy, an area where such Soviet-approved pioneers of dialectics as the pre-Socratic Herakleitos, Plato, Bacon, Spinoza, Hume, Kant, and Hegel allowed him freedom of inspiration in the midst of Stalinist mediocrity.

Among the aspiring commissars in art were Victor Arnautoff, painter of the "City Life" panel in the Coit Tower (and by 1944 a servant of the KGB); Byron Randall and Emmy Lou Packard, who were disciples of Diego Rivera; the printmaker Giacomo Patri; and an exceptionally bad muralist, Anton Refregier. Among the "innocents" we find the greatly gifted painter Hassel Smith and the painter and merchant seaman Robert McChesney. But the latter names indicate a serious source of contradiction, for individuals like Arnautoff and Refregier were determined to make the C.L.S. and the Communist intelligentsia in general a bastion of Soviet-dictated "realism," and to prosecute an ever-more aggressive war on modernism, while Hassel Smith and McChesney were pioneers of Abstract Expressionism, a style the Communists came to denounce with incredible vituperation.

The authenticity of the California Labor School, its mission, and its legacy may be judged by its role in what was perhaps the most bizarre venture in the Communist distortion of academic life ever undertaken in America. This was the injection of the C.L.S. into a research project on "the authoritarian personality," overseen by the exiled German luminaries of the so-called Frankfurt School, Theodor W. Adorno and Max Horkheimer. The study, which began in January 1943 in the Psychology Department at the University of California at Berkeley and was financed by the American Jewish Committee, produced a book entitled *The Authoritarian Personality*. This volume concluded that the attitudes it lumped together as authoritarian, fascist, paranoid, and patriotic, including nationalism and racial prejudice, constituted a personality disorder or mental illness. For example, it equated the following statements:

> The trouble with letting Jews into a nice neighborhood is that they gradually give it a typical Jewish atmosphere.
>
> Negro musicians may sometimes be as good as white musicians, but it is a mistake to have mixed Negro-white bands.
>
> America may not be perfect, but the American Way has brought us about as close as human beings can get to a perfect society.

Thus a run-of-the-mill statement of American national pride, acceptable to many intelligent Americans, was placed in the same category with bizarre biases. The study became even more grotesque when it proposed to measure "antidemocratic trends" using the "F scale" or "fascism scale." One could hardly imagine a purer example of Stalinism than this elaborate and fundamentally dishonest labeling of political opponents as psychopaths; if anything, it appears as a remarkable example of projection.

The Authoritarian Personality has not fared well with critical writers on social psychology. In a major work on the topics it addresses—mass hatred, above all—the psychologist Neil J. Kressel has commented, "While the authors may have succeeded in identifying a right-wing type ready to follow fascists, they missed an important counterpart—authoritarianism on the Left." But this "blindness" on the part of the study's authors was willful, for their data was corrupt at its origin. The sections that allegedly sampled "working-class men and women" drew their subjects almost exclusively from the ranks of the C.L.S. and two Communist-run C.I.O. unions, the I.L.W.U. under Bridges and the United Electrical, Radio, and Machine Workers of America (U.E.) This falsification of "research" was coordinated by Berkeley professor Edward C. Tolman, a noted fellow traveler, and Rose Segure, a social worker, a former subordinate of Carey McWilliams, and a local tactician of the so-called union F.A.E.C.T. in its penetration of the Radiation Laboratory. Segure was employed as international representative by the fake union although she was neither an architect, an engineer, a chemist, nor a technician—the professions the organization supposedly represented.

———

SOME OTHERS WHO were associated with the California Labor School but who remained obscure at the time are worthy of mention here. The first of these was an anthropologist, Warren d'Azevedo, whose path to C.L.S. would seem to have been drawn by two outstanding figures in California ethnology, Robert H. Lowie, chairman of the anthropology department at U.C. Berkeley, and Paul Radin. Both were long-time Marxists and Communist supporters, if not Party members, who had, in their time, inspired Jaime de Angulo's linguistic fieldwork; d'Azevedo may be said to have followed in de Angulo's footsteps. In the late 1940s anthropologists learned of a major new development in the culture of the Washo Indians, who were living in extreme poverty on the eastern Sierra Nevada slopes of California and in western Nevada—a cult based on ingestion of the hallucinogenic cactus peyote. These Native Americans had come full circle from the *Datura*-based drug-taking that predated Spanish colonization. D'Azevedo wrote that although peyote had been used by North American Indians for at least a hundred years, the first peyote cult meetings were held among the Northern Paiute by Sam Lone Bear in the 1920s, and a Washo, Ben Lancaster, announced the revelation to his people in 1936. Joined by a former *shaman*, Sam Dick, Lancaster held meetings among both Paiute and Washo people. Some fifteen years later, d'Azevedo went among the Washo to record peyote narratives.

D'Azevedo knew George Leite, the founder of *Circle*, who sometimes appeared at the C.L.S., and the opportunity of access to peyote and its mysticism came to the attention of the Surrealist poet Philip Lamantia. Acclaimed by the literary powers on both coasts, Lamantia had journeyed to New York to work as an editor of a Surrealist-oriented monthly, *View*, but returned to San Francisco more or less unimpressed. Lamantia went to the Washo and consumed the herb, plunging into the peyote universe; he seems to have been the first white intellectual, aside from anthropologists, to have done so. This event, unnoticed when it occurred, both began the recent fascination of American writers with hallucinogenic drugs and delimited a stage in the California literary revolution, just then picking up speed.

Another personality involved with the Bay Area Communist schools was a Black student, Marguerite Johnson, who was brought to California from Missouri with her family in 1931 at age 3, but was then sent to Arkansas to live with her grandmother. In 1940 she came to San Francisco, and two years later, at 14, she "won a two-year scholarship" in theater and dance to the Labor School. She later said she "never knew why" she was given the "scholarship," which could not have amounted to very much in any case, since tuition at the "school" came to no more than a few dollars per semester. But she had a way of transforming the limitations of her environment into achievements, and of reinventing herself. Even before she graduated from high school she struggled—successfully—to become the first Black woman to work on the San Francisco streetcars. She was representative of a massive emigration of Southern Blacks to California during the war; they kept coming, to work in shipyards and other industries, and their story was partially told by Chester Himes. Blacks had, as earlier noted, taken over the former Japanese districts of California's big cities, now emptied by internment. Johnson later recalled, "In the early months of World War II, San Francisco's Fillmore District, or Western Addition, experienced a visible revolution. . . . The Japanese shops which sold products to Nisei customers were taken over by enterprising Negro businessmen, and in less than a year became permanent homes away from home for the newly arrived Southern Blacks." Marguerite Johnson had borne the nickname "Maya," coined by her brother, since childhood. She married a Greek-American sailor named Tosh Angelos; as Maya Angelou she was destined, much later, for considerable fame as a poet, even reading her work at a presidential inauguration.

The world conflict had become a war of attrition, and on all sides Americans began looking forward to peacetime. The Communist Party in the United States changed its name to the Communist Political Association and announced that class conflict would have no place in the new scheme of things. Harry Bridges proposed that the wartime no-strike pledge the longshore union had given should be extended indefinitely in peacetime. President Roosevelt, elected to a fourth term in 1944, died on April 12, 1945 and was replaced by Harry S Truman, his vice president. The Nazi Reich collapsed. The Allies—chiefly the United States—now faced the challenge of subduing a Japan believed to be committed to a suicidal defense of the home islands.

Oppenheimer and his personnel in the Manhattan project had exploded the first nuclear bomb at Alamogordo, New Mexico, on July 16, 1945, and two devastating bombs were dropped on Japan, the first at Hiroshima on August 6 and the second at Nagasaki on August 9. The Russians, who had until then maintained a cordial relationship with Tokyo, declared war against Japan on August 8, and on August 15 Emperor Hirohito broadcast by radio to his people, counseling them to accept defeat. World War II was over.

Of course, the most dramatic and problematical aspect of the war's end was the immense destructiveness of the atomic bombs. The United States was the only power in possession of military nuclear technology, or so it was believed. However, thanks to Kheifitz, Kasparov, Steve Nelson, and their many agents, the scientific fundamentals of the invention had been stolen and transmitted to Stalin. J. Robert Oppenheimer, his family and friends, and other veterans of the Manhattan Engineering District now began lobbying for nuclear-bomb technology to be officially handed over to Stalin by the Western governments. One forum for airing this demand was the California Labor School, which cohosted a conference at U.C. Berkeley where figures from Los Alamos and the Radiation Laboratory spoke. Another was a new, "Hollywood model" Communist front of well-off fellow travelers, the Independent Citizens Committee of the Arts, Sciences, and Professions, on which "Opje" openly served as a vice chairman.

San Francisco had been the site, over eight weeks in April-June 1945, of the founding conference of the United Nations. Communist spies descended on the sessions, and Stepan Apresyan, with the *klichka* of *Maj* or "May," had been sent from New York, where he had been KGB *rezident,* to take over for Kasparov, the successor to Kheifitz, in San Francisco during the conference. Apresyan called on "Pop" Folkoff and other local Communists to perform an extended list of tasks. One such local comrade was "Nat," described in VENONA messages as a local party leader; he was very likely Nat Yanish, born Noyach Yanishevsky, a Russian immigrant to the United States. Yanish was cadre chief of the Party in Alameda County, which included the Berkeley Rad Lab, and which for some years had been "probably the most powerful [Party] section outside greater New York," according to a 1948 Central Intelligence Agency analysis. Like Karl Goso Yoneda, Yanish suffered the indignity of being dropped from the Party as a noncitizen in 1940. And, beginning in 1947, Yanish was the object of a long and unsuccessful deportation attempt by the American authorities. A more prominent participant in the UN events was State Department policy expert Alger Hiss, identified by the National Security Agency as a Soviet military-intelligence agent known under the *klichka* of *Ales.*

Just after the UN conference, and a month before nuclear weapons were used against Japan, an ideological atom bomb was dropped on American Communists. A leader of the French Communist Party, Jacques Duclos, signed an article, obviously originating in Moscow, that savaged the American Communists for abandoning their Party structure (in favor of a "political association"), as well as class warfare and opposition to global American power. The California Communists had been particularly supportive of the "Browder line," as the former moderate position, associated with Earl Browder as the architect of the "Communist Political Association," was now labeled. Confusion and dismay spread through the ranks of Party organs, controlled unions, and front groups, as the tamed, Stalinized ranks awaited the next development. It was delayed for some months, but in February 1946 Browder was thrown out of the Party; he had already been stripped of his top leadership post.

The Communists restored their Party structure and their commitment to "socialist revolution," which Browder had specifically disavowed, and embarked on new adventures in the labor scene, including manipulated strikes. Some minor party bosses were purged at the same time; interestingly enough, nearly all of them were associated with the California Party. They included Harrison George and eventually Max Bedacht. It was said then that most of those who were kicked out had been on bad terms with Browder and that their ejection was intended to give an illusion of balance in the administration of party discipline. Similar explanations were offered when a group of "ultraleftist" Communists active in the Bay Area Machinists Union, including the valiant Levon Mosgofian, were driven from the Party. (Samuel Adams Darcy had been expelled as an "ultraleftist" in 1944.) But these pretexts were unlikely to have been true, and the real bases of the California Communist purges of 1946 were never clarified.

The changed Party line was particularly reflected in the labor field. With the war's end and the return home of the troops, union militancy again rose dramatically. Harry Bridges and his cohort had sought to continue the "no-strike" line they had learned to love so well, but such slogans were thrown overboard, of course, with Browder; further, the so-called "conservative" A.F.L. unions, and anti-Communist leaders within the C.I.O. such as Walter Reuther of the United Auto Workers, were suddenly on strike throughout the country. As the eminent labor reporter A. H. Raskin of the *New York Times* put it, as the end of the war "brought quiet to the fighting fronts . . . war between labor and management broke out all across the production front." In November 1945, the most significant walkout began when 175,000 workers struck the auto industry. But in the Chrysler electrical division, some 30,000 workers were represented by the Communist-controlled United Electrical Workers (U.E.), which secretly settled with Chrysler in a bid to sabotage Reuther's leadership of the U.A.W. In effect, the Communists in the U.E. broke the auto strike.

This treacherous gambit greatly discredited the Communists in labor, but the anger of the United Auto Workers led to Reuther's election as U.A.W. president; the union's California members bitterly reminded one another of the pro-Hitler "strike" the Communists had launched at North American Aviation in 1941. In the maritime field, Bridges and the longshore union, operating through a so-called "Committee for Maritime Unity" (C.M.U.) fought in the same manner against Lundeberg and the Sailors' Union of the Pacific. On the waterfront, however, Bridges and his cohort lost the competition, for in summer and fall 1946 the S.U.P., in a series of day-by-day strikes, won contract improvements and a monthly wage hike of $22.50, while the Communist C.M.U., negotiating with the shipowners in Washington, gained $5 per month less, or $17.50. Two objective observers, the West Coast maritime historians Wytze Gorter and George H. Hildebrand, declared that Lundeberg and the S.U.P. had "won the contest for prestige with the maritime rank and file."

The Communists also sought to seize and utilize A.F.L. unions for their own purposes. The main such attempt originated in Hollywood in 1945, when Herbert Knott Sorrell, now a business agent for A.F.L. Painters Local 644, which represented set painters and decorators, launched a "Conference of Studio Unions" (C.S.U.) and began leading strikes aimed at rival unions such as the A.F.L. Stagehands (I.A.T.S.E.). Sorrell portrayed himself as a campaigner against corruption and mob influence in the Hollywood unions, yet the C.S.U. strikes were clearly much more an attempt, as at North American Aviation in 1941, to create dramatic mass struggles on order. But great mass strikes cannot be fabricated.

This was demonstrated when, in December 1946, a three-day general strike was called by the A.F.L. in Oakland. A brutal confrontation, sparked by police protection of strikebreakers in a work stoppage at downtown department stores, it included demonstrations by thousands of workers, who filled the streets. Interurban street railway service shut down. Lundeberg sent members of the Sailors' Union, most of them Hawaiians, to patrol the streets against strikebreakers. A massive rally was called by the A.F.L. unions at Oakland Civic Auditorium, and, according to the S.U.P. paper, the *West Coast Sailors,* "more than 16,000 men and women drove and hitchhiked in the rain from all sections of the Bay . . . another 8,000 [were] turned away. Lundeberg was given a tremendous ovation when he addressed the massive assembly." Lundeberg declared, "The superfinks are the city administration of Oakland. . . . No ships will sail out of the East Bay." The secretary of the Alameda County Labor Council, Robert Ash, later claimed that had Lundeberg called on those present to do so, "I think they'd have taken City Hall apart, brick by brick." Meanwhile, the Brotherhood of Railway Clerks began "studying" action by Southern Pacific and Western Pacific employees in support of the strike. The Communist-controlled C.I.O. unions respected the A.F.L. picket lines in Oakland but played no major leadership role in the general strike—although, to their considerable delight, Lundeberg's Trotskyist helpers furnished important assistance. The A.F.L. won the fight.

In the California union movement, split between the A.F.L. and the C.I.O., the rank and file increasingly turned to the former, while the latter commanded the loyalty of officials as well as of hundreds of publicists, organizers, and other functionaries that the Communists had, for a decade, attached to the unions they controlled. An A.F.L. militant, whose experience merits greater examination, was Tillie Olsen Clifford (not to be confused with Tillie Lerner Olsen, a Communist intellectual). Clifford was Secretary-Treasurer of local 26 of the Laundry Workers Union, which was aligned with Lundeberg in the broader labor movement. Tillie Clifford's daughter Ruth owned The 400 Club, a bar near Lundeberg's headquarters. Many laundry workers were women; they toiled in heat, for long hours, at low wages, in a less-than-elegant job. Their union was their bulwark in the quest for dignity and self-respect, and Tillie Clifford was their beloved hero, often running for union office unopposed, repeatedly winning by big margins. On one occasion the ballots in a Laundry Workers election were counted out by Clifford's grandson, a San Francisco child born in 1942 who greatly influenced later Californians. His name was Jerry Garcia.

PART VI

IN DEFENSE OF
THE EARTH

Decent anthropologists don't associate with drunk-
ards who go rolling in ditches with shamans.
—Jaime de Angulo

*Wherein Communist influence in California
leads to division and suspicion throughout society; government investigators and Hollywood
Stalinists confuse the nation and the world with
their bad manners; painters bring about the
most profound, if the least known, of all the
California revolutions; a poet sees idols and
friends die, some horribly, and produces a manifesto of outrage; and the intersection of anti-
totalitarianism, a new poetics, and a revival of
dissidence makes California the laboratory of
an authentic worldwide revolution*

*I*n the aftermath of World War II, California was reborn as a community with greater influence on the United States and the world than it had enjoyed at any time since the Gold Rush. The invention of the atomic bomb placed California scientists in a position of responsibility for the fate of the planet. The founding of the United Nations in San Francisco seemed to express the character of California as the vanguard among the states, with a distinct identity and economic power that made it practically a country unto itself. During the war, the Pacific theater had done more to focus the attention of other Americans on the West Coast than any past military action. And in the intellectual field California was, by 1945, in the middle of a revolution that would transform the habits and mores of the globe.

Josef Stalin, the most powerful dictator in history, remained a central element in the postwar landscape, with as much influence in the Pacific Rim and on California as in Europe. The intellectual issues that wracked Paris and New York—totalitarianism versus freedom, above all—were equally present, and debated, in San Francisco and Los Angeles.

But so far only a minority of the California Left, still dominated by the Communists, perceived the reality of Stalinism. The Rexroth circle, Harry Lundeberg, and Chester Himes were widely respected, but were also susceptible to exaggerated Communist attacks. A reluctance to admit the character of the Soviet regime was visible when, as if rescued from the grave, the powerful criticisms of Stalin by Leon Trotsky were again presented to readers. In February 1946 the New York firm of Harper & Brothers announced it would publish Trotsky's biography, *Stalin: An Appraisal of the Man and His Influence.* Work on this book had occupied the last years of Trotsky's life, and fear of its contents may have impelled the KGB's agents to kill him sooner rather than later. The manuscript was unfinished at his death, but its last third was completed by the book's translator, Charles Malamuth, the ex-husband of Joan London.

As it happened, Trotsky's biography of Stalin also provoked fear in Washington and New York. With the book's publication, Harper & Brothers disclosed, rather scandalously, that although it was ready for press at the time, the title had been withdrawn from its sales list in 1941 at the request of the U.S. State Department. The legendary editor Cass Canfield, head of the publishing house, described this act of censorship as "a patriotic gesture" and blandly added, "Now that hostilities are over, Harper & Brothers feel that this biography, containing material of historical importance, should be published."

American book reviewers clucked disapprovingly at the vehemence of Trotsky's *Stalin*. Even the Trotskyists in the West, most of them intellectually bereft after their mentor's death and morally unprepared to continue an open battle with the Stalinists, were discomfited. Stalin had, during the war, become "Uncle Joe" to numbers of ordinary Americans. Few in the West articulated the fears that many felt; above all, few were willing to directly challenge the chorus of praise for Stalin sung by the Communists and the fellow travelers. One exception was Winston Churchill, who on March 5, 1946, in a speech at Fulton, Missouri, warned that "an Iron Curtain has descended across Europe." But Churchill was out of power.

The Jacques Duclos article and the reorientation of the American Communist Party had already shown that Stalin's view of the world remained suspicious, hostile, and aggressive. As always, the first overt expression of these attitudes, as opposed to the coquetry displayed in the Duclos incident, was visited on the Russian people themselves. Almost as soon as the war ended, new purges began. Russian cultural icons like the poet Anna Akhmatova, who had dedicated their talents to the national cause in wartime, were reviled and harassed. Soviet Jewish intellectuals, who had assumed special responsibilities for influencing American opinion during the war, came under attack by Stalin and his police torturers.

The California Communists, exemplified by Harry Bridges, had reveled in triumphalist rhetoric at the war's conclusion, but then wavered in confusion as Browder and others were thrown out of the Party, the line changed, and they were sent into active competition with the A.F.L. in the labor movement. In truth, the California Communist Party was dead on its feet. It had lost all capacity for initiative or inspiration, and its constituencies were either vague, like the fellow travelers, who would stand for anything but seemed to represent little as an immediate social resource, or restive, as were labor, the serious intellectuals, and Blacks. The "Negro people" had returned to the top of the Communists' agenda, even in California, since the injustices they suffered in the Deep South and elsewhere in the country made such good copy in Communist organs around the globe. But few California Blacks trusted the Communists.

Even the majority of those Californians who fondly recalled "Uncle Joe" in wartime looked askance at the local Communists, noting their obvious spinelessness in accepting the irrational contortions of the Party line. In southern California, however, resentment of the Communists had become acute. The North American Aviation strike had never been forgotten, and memories of it were revived by the antics of Herb Sorrell and the so-called Conference of Studio Unions in Hollywood. During and after the war, the Los Angeles Communists threw their weight around, bullying anybody to whom they took a dislike, especially through the C.I.O. unions they controlled. But they never understood that, unlike San Francisco, Los Angeles was too big to be cowed and manipulated by a handful of Bridges-style functionaries. Furthermore, southern California had never undergone the convulsive mass strikes that radicalized workers and their neighbors to the north and, even as they escaped the Communist grasp, provided the Party with a sympathetic environment in which to work. In Los Angeles the only such milieu consisted of the Hollywood coterie and the loose agglomeration of fellow travelers.

In the short term, however, the fellow travelers were not as important as they thought themselves to be, and nothing like what the Communists, now back in the class-warfare business, might have wanted them to be. Real intellectuals and labor militants who came under Communist influence were very often tragic cases, like J. Robert Oppenheimer. But the Hollywood hangers-on and the fellow travelers in general were, in a phrase Trotsky once used, "human dust."

The postwar California Communists were especially lacking in support from true intellectuals—accomplished writers, artists, and musicians. The film crowd hardly counted, although the party did everything possible to build dishonest mediocrities like Lester Cole and Alvah Bessie into heavyweights. The creative personalities they attracted had become cynical hacks, sunk in repetition of Party slogans; the few exceptions, like Muriel Rukeyser and George Hitchcock at the California Labor School in San Francisco, only proved the rule.

One California author prominent at the war's end, who was both gifted and a Communist, was a Filipino, Carlos Bulosan, whose autobiographical narrative, *America Is in the Heart,* became a best-seller when it was published in 1946. *America Is in the Heart* is a fascinating book, and constitutes the only substantial literary achievement by a Communist in America after 1945. Born in the Philippine province of Pangasinan in 1914, Bulosan landed in the United States in 1930. He encountered the many forms of exploitation and humiliation that afflicted Filipinos on the West Coast, from the criminality of labor contractors and loan sharks to the murder of his friends by white mobs; he eventually fell ill with tuberculosis. Like Lav Adamic before him, he transformed his experiences as a radical immigrant, questioning the American ideal, into literature; also like Adamic, he flaunted disillusion and cynicism. One serious blot on his reputation came in 1944 when he was accused of plagiarism after publication of a story of his in the *New Yorker*. (The *New Yorker* paid a small sum to settle the complaint.)

In the mid-1930s Bulosan formed a close friendship with Filipino labor organizer Crispulo Mensalvas, who had come into the public eye during the Salinas disputes of 1936. Mensalvas, born in 1909, also in the Philippines, became a Communist, but one unlike almost any other in California. His was not the genteel world of the fellow traveler or the bureaucratic Utopia of the functionary; unlike Yoneda, Mensalvas seems never to have been drawn into the clandestine apparatus, and he was never promoted to a leadership position within the broader American Communist movement. Yet if anybody in California was a real Communist, in exactly the image the Party sought to project, it was Mensalvas. He had one concern: organizing the Filipino farm and cannery workers; he went from running a Filipino ethnic union in Salinas to a succession of minor posts with a C.I.O. union that never really got off the ground, first known as the United Cannery, Agricultural, Packing and Allied Workers of America (U.C.A.P.A.W.A.) and then as the Food, Tobacco, and Agricultural Workers (F.T.A.) From time to time, Mensalvas served the branches of Bridges's I.L.W.U. that represented fish-cannery workers in the Pacific Northwest and Alaska, and in which Karl Yoneda preceded him as an organizer. Throughout, Mensalvas, dedicated and self-sacrificing, never left the rank-and-file struggle. He brought Bulosan into union organizing and publicity work.

The idealism of Mensalvas, who appears in *America Is in the Heart* as susceptible to corruption by alcohol and other vices, was inevitably deformed by his affiliation with the Communists. After 1945, the F.T.A. union, weak and disorganized, hemorrhaged cannery locals to the allegedly conservative A.F.L., which also backed, in competition with F.T.A., the National Farm Labor Union.

The gross distrust that had developed between the labor factions was eloquently revealed during a bitter strike, beginning in 1947, by 1,100 members of the N.F.L.U., against the DiGiorgio Corporation, a huge, multistate "agribusiness" enterprise of the kind Carey McWilliams had so long assailed. On the night of May 13, 1948, James Price, 32, chairman of the A.F.L. committee directing the DiGiorgio strike, then in its seventh month, was shot in the head and gravely wounded while sitting in a committee meeting in a private home at Arvin, a suburb of Bakersfield in Kern County. A car with its lights out had pulled up and poured rifle and pistol fire into the house. Republican Governor Earl Warren, then in his second term, immediately ordered an investigation, declaring, "This was obviously an attempt at assassination. Such diabolical acts call for the full force of the law being brought to bear against those responsible."

No arrests were ever made in the Price assault, but H. L. Mitchell, a veteran Socialist who headed the N.F.L.U., blamed the shooting on "strikebreakers or rival unionists"—meaning, in the latter case, F.T.A. members who, in the middle of the walkout and while strikers were facing club-swinging mob violence, deluged the Arvin district with leaflets calling on the workers to abandon the A.F.L. for the C.I.O.

THE DIGIORGIO STRIKE was more than an incident in the war between the Communists and anti-Communists in the labor movement. It revealed the persistence of wholesale injustice in California agriculture and set the tone for labor relations in the state for a generation. It also had unexpected consequences in Hollywood, and was brilliantly chronicled by one of the strike leaders, a former academic of Mexican origin, Ernesto Galarza. The account by Galarza of the strike and its extended legal accompaniment, in his book *Spiders in the House and Workers in the Field,* is the finest labor-history narrative ever composed in California.

Born in 1905, Galarza was brought up near the Mexican city of Tepic and was brought across The Border by his parents, who fled the Mexican Revolution when he was a small boy. He grew up in the Sacramento *barrio* and worked as a farm and cannery laborer and interpreter while attending school; he wrote, graduated from Occidental College with a B.A. in history, then earned an M.A. from Stanford University in history and political science and a Ph.D. in the same areas from Columbia University. Beginning in 1940 he was employed by the Foreign Policy Association in Washington, D.C., and then at the Pan American Union, the predecessor of the Organization of American States. However, in his early forties he abandoned academia and threw himself into the struggle of the National Farm Labor Union, alongside the radical but fiercely anti-Communist H. L. Mitchell. Galarza, as an intellectual, represented a diametrically opposite counterpart to Bulosan or Mensalvas.

The DiGiorgio Corporation was the creation of a Corsican immigrant, Giuseppe DiGiorgio, who immigrated to the United States in 1888 and went to work in fruit wholesaling. After failing to survive in the cutthroat banana trade on the East Coast, he came to California in 1926 and established large farms at Arvin and Delano, beginning with cultivation of plums and grapes. In twenty years his business had become the biggest produce company in America. Its headquarters was at DiGiorgio Farms, an enormous complex of large administration buildings, packing sheds, a winery, dormitories, and mess halls, with its own police and firefighters. Giuseppe DiGiorgio's other holdings were scattered through the state, and also included citrus orchards in Florida. A community center in Arvin, built with his donations, included a bust of "Mr. Joseph" on a pedestal; he provided swimming pools, baseball, and ethnic food for his workers, in a paternal fashion that was frequently cited to counter the evidence of Steinbeck and McWilliams about the squalor of farm-labor conditions.

Nevertheless, DiGiorgio's employees were dissatisfied. The influx of so-called "Okies" had changed the demographic character of Kern County, and, after years of taciturn patience, in spring 1947 the Dust Bowl refugees and their children rebelled. Bob Whatley, a one-armed man, began farm-labor organizing for Local 218, A.F.L.; he recruited a DiGiorgio shed foreman, Jim Price. DiGiorgio Farms had previously used separate dormitories and eating facilities to segregate its Filipino, Mexican, and "Anglo" (white) workers—no Blacks were then hired. However, although DiGiorgio defended its segregationist policies as a means to avoid ethnic strife, in reality the separate structures kept the three groups bidding against each other on wages, thus holding pay rates down. Furthermore, so-called *braceros,* or Mexican citizens contracted seasonally, were used to further depress wages; Ernesto Galarza had earlier been involved in planning the *bracero* program and monitoring abuses of it. The new union crossed the color barrier, and the DiGiorgio employees discovered a common interest for the first time. The great "Okie" labor upsurge that was heralded in the pages of *The Grapes of Wrath* was finally becoming possible. But as Galarza stressed, citing another observer, the migrants from the Dust Bowl had brought no traditions of civic democracy with them to California; the union meetings were the first example of community decision-making ever seen in Arvin.

Swimming pools apart, living and working conditions were unarguably bad at DiGiorgio Farms; open sewage flowed past the laborers' housing, the packing sheds were overheated, workers were fired without appeal, and there was no unemployment insurance for farm workers. Whatley wrote to Mitchell, who sent Galarza and another organizer, Henry Hasiwar, to the scene. By autumn 1947 almost nine hundred members had been enrolled in the union. The organization formulated its demands: union recognition, a wage hike of 10 cents an hour, and seniority and grievance provisions. A letter to DiGiorgio went unanswered, and on October 1, 1947, the union struck. The majority of field and shed workers, tractor drivers, and irrigators joined the walkout. As Galarza rather elegantly argued,

> [P]ractical experience in making money in a closed system had revealed to [the DiGiorgios] the alarming dangers of the Hegelian statement: "The one essential canon to make liberty deep and real is to give every business belonging to the general interests of the state a separate organization whenever they are essentially distinct." To prevent or at least delay such organization was a basic policy of the DiGiorgios.

As previously noted, the National Farm Labor Union was then involved in a serious competition with the Communist-controlled F.T.A.-C.I.O. The two organizations were described as "bitter enemies" by *San Francisco Chronicle* reporter Peter Trimble. Although the F.T.A. was in deep crisis, its Communist leadership continued to emit strident declarations about foreign policy and other issues of little immediate concern to farm and cannery workers, such as an attack on the Marshall Plan for European reconstruction, recently proposed by the Truman Administration and greeted with scorn by the Kremlin. The F.T.A. also sought to force its declining membership into a "Third Party" movement that arose in 1947 behind former vice president Henry Agard Wallace, an advocate of "peace" with Russia in the form of collaboration with Stalin. The aim of the "Third Party" was to split the Democratic party and, in California, to draw former EPIC Democrats out of their party. The possibility that a Republican might be elected president as a result was viewed as insignificant. Galarza and the other leaders of the DiGiorgio strike were concerned with completely different issues: in the dark of the humid Valley night, watching the stream of automobile headlights along the nearby Grapevine, the highway over Tejon Pass to Los Angeles (then U.S. 99 and now Interstate 5), they doggedly pursued the increasingly abstract ideal of labor solidarity. Their goal was neither an artificial mass movement to be exploited for ideological ends nor mere publicity for a scandalous social injustice; rather, they risked death for the small improvements in the workers' daily lives promised by traditional A.F.L. unionism.

But the modest demands put forward in the DiGiorgio strike loomed enormously in the minds of the strikers and their adversaries. The strike became prolonged and complicated. The strikers picketed the state Farm Labor Office in Bakersfield for sending workers to DiGiorgio Farms without informing them of the strike; the union repeatedly called on the Border Patrol to arrest and deport strikebreakers imported from Mexico, and forced state housing inspections that revealed sewage flowing under the fruit trees, filthy toilets, and workers and their families living in railroad freight cars. Strikers were evicted from company-owned homes. Kern County business rallied to DiGiorgio's cause and denounced the strike leaders as "associates of Communists." Jack Tenney and his state Un-American Activities Committee wheeled into the area repeating the same accusations, but found no evidence of Communist influence. Above all, DiGiorgio hired lawyers; they gained an injunction ordering the strike ended under the National Labor Relations Act, even though farm workers were specifically exempt from it.

Raw class conflict in the orchards, fields, and shanties was transferred to the government level, and thus dissipated, by a method Galarza described: "The scene of action shifted by stages from the picket line to the courts, to the well of the House of Representatives, to the Federal agencies and to the bureaucratic purlieus in Sacramento." This process kept the struggle alive in the press, but "could not replenish the economic resources of the workers"; unpaid and destitute, they scattered, leaving the strike still going in November 1949, after two years, with but a single picket left at the DiGiorgio shed.

However, the DiGiorgio struggle did not die easily; the conflict was historic in every way. It represented the most serious attempt yet to challenge California's agricultural labor "system." Alongside Galarza and his comrades others were palpably present in spirit: the men and women of Wheatland in 1913 and Salinas in 1936, as well as the fictional Joads. The reality exposed anew by the strike was disturbing to Californians, and the possible outcome was terrifying to DiGiorgio executives and to local authorities; the Kern County sheriff, John Loustalot, accused the union of reviving "old-time I.W.W. methods."

The DiGiorgio strike showed that postwar illusions of a suburban California of prosperity and upward mobility were deceptive, for "Okies" and other "Anglos" as well as for people of color. And the DiGiorgio confrontation spilled over into another arena when the A.F.L. Hollywood Film Council (*not* Herb Sorrell's wild-haired "Conference") produced a twenty-minute documentary film, *Poverty in the Valley of Plenty.* It was narrated by Harry Flannery, a radio newscaster who had succeeded William L. Shirer in broadcasting from Berlin in the 1930s; film star and former sports announcer Ronald Reagan, then president of the Screen Actors' Guild, was also considered for the job.

Poverty in the Valley of Plenty struck hard at DiGiorgio's paternalistic image, and the blow was not forgiven. The film emphasized the impact of "corporation farming" on the southern San Joaquin Valley. The narrator's words hammered at the viewer, revealing the hell of exploitation that disfigured the paradise of the California landscape: "Beneath this divine canopy of cleanliness and purity . . . nine or ten people live in a one-room shack." While complacent Americans grinned at the popular song *Route 66,* which offered California "kicks" to the thousands looking west for economic opportunity, the narrator of *Poverty in the Valley of Plenty* evoked "immigrant workers . . . smuggled across the Mexican border by headhunters employed by large farm interests." The film was broadcast by a Los Angeles television station and shown all over the United States. DiGiorgio responded with a libel suit against Paramount Television Productions, followed by similar filings against Flannery, the union, the Hollywood Film Council, and other entities. DiGiorgio's attorneys, Brobeck, Phleger & Harrison, demanded $1 million in general damages and an equal sum for punitive damages. The litigation was novel in that libel law, previously applied to printed or spoken expression, was here expanded to include motion-picture images and narration. The legal controversy, begun in 1949, would run for twenty years. The strike officially ended in May 1950.

The fight over *Poverty in the Valley of Plenty* intruded on a Hollywood already embroiled in a deep political crisis. In October 1947, only weeks after the DiGiorgio Farms strike started, a new series of congressional hearings began in Washington, investigating the labor chaos in Hollywood, mainly the continuing adventures of Herbert Knott Sorrell—perhaps the biggest "loose cannon" in the history of American labor, if not a whole loose battle fleet. When his "Conference of Studio Unions" (C.S.U.) commenced their strikes in 1944, the Los Angeles Communists were divided over whether to support him, since the wartime no-strike pledge by Communist labor was in force; yet Sorrell learned nothing from that. He and the Party leadership bowed and scraped and complimented one another while Sorrell himself occasionally voiced disagreement with their dictates; but by early 1947 he had thoroughly adopted the Communist agenda of attacks on the United States.

Although the C.S.U. had struck against other A.F.L. unions rather than against the employers, Sorrell charged that "a conspiracy to smash democratic unions" was at work in Hollywood. His "Conference" issued an international bulletin asserting, "If the American motion-picture monopoly can destroy our unions and depress wage rates, it will have more profits to finance its drive for control of foreign markets, which would mean displacement of thousands of film workers in other countries." The existence of such a "drive for control" outside the hysterical pages of the *People's World* was doubtful to say the least, though Sorrell comforted himself with the support of Mexican union boss Vicente Lombardo Toledano, revealed in the VENONA traffic to be a Soviet agent. Hollywood then counted 25,000 union employees out of a total payroll of 30,000; the "city of make-believe" was one of the most highly unionized in the world, according to Robert Lewin of the *Chicago Daily News*. Thus any serious attempt to break the movie-industry unions would have involved a colossal conflict. Even directors were union members, while making $200,000 per film—at that time, an inconceivably large income for most Americans. Sorrell's grandly styled "Conference" represented only 5,000 movie-industry carpenters, painters, and plumbers, and was a mere irritant to the Stagehands Union (I.A.T.S.E.), which comprised 12,500 members, or half the industry workforce, including set builders, projectionists, sound technicians, lab workers, control-camera operators, and myriad other movie-related crafts.

The unceasing uproar in the motion-picture community could not be ignored. More than any other industry Hollywood held the attention of ordinary Americans, as its products were believed to mold the national psyche. In spring 1947 the House Labor Committee conducted an inconclusive hearing in Washington on the Sorrell strikes and Communist influence over them. This session was followed in the summer by a subcommittee visit to Los Angeles, during which Sorrell, producer Samuel Goldwyn, Carey McWilliams, and other personalities were subpoenaed. A tour of the M-G-M studio by subcommittee members, in the company of Sorrell and a business agent for the Stagehands, almost turned into a brawl. Sorrell's main testimony before the House Labor subcommittee consisted of more conspiracy claims along with a fanciful description of an alleged bribe attempt.

The House Labor subcommittee returned to Washington without having accomplished much, but in October its place in the Hollywood controversy was taken by the House Committee on Un-American Activities under Congressman J. Parnell Thomas, Republican of New Jersey. The mandate of these heavier hitters was to probe deeper into Communism in Hollywood, and they began by hearing a number of interested parties in Washington. The "friendly witnesses," as they would come to be known, included producer Jack Warner, actors Gary Cooper, Adolphe Menjou, Robert Taylor, Ronald Reagan, novelist and screenwriter Ayn Rand, and nearly a dozen others. Rand rubbed in the studios' naïveté by her critique of M-G-M's wartime *Song of Russia.* Cooper and the other actors tended to downplay Communist influence in the industry, although noting its presence and occasional prominence. Reagan, as head of the Screen Actors' Guild, seconded by former Guild presidents Robert Montgomery and George Murphy, denounced the Communists in moderate tones, but cautioned, "I hope we are never prompted by fear or resentment of Communism into compromising any of our democratic principles in order to fight it." Among the studio heads, Warner accepted responsibility for the propaganda orgy of *Mission to Moscow,* and Louis B. Mayer acknowledged that he had employed writers he knew to be Communists, namely Lester Cole, Dalton Trumbo, and Donald Ogden Stewart (who had married Ella Winter, the widow of Lincoln Steffens).

Neither Cole nor Trumbo (the latter a leading antiwar propagandist during the Stalin-Hitler pact), had previously been sanctioned by the studios for their open advocacy of Communism. Indeed, they had become rich. Cole was then working on a screenplay for M-G-M on the life of Emiliano Zapata, based on a book by a long-forgotten comrade of the Flores Magòn brothers in southern California, Edgecombe Pinchon, which had been bought by the studio years before. Cole's two-year contract, he later recalled, provided for payment of $1,250 per week the first year, $1,500 the second, and, if it was renewed, $2,000 per week in the first year followed by $2,500 for the second, along with generous vacation and other benefits. Trumbo, according to Alvah Bessie, was "known to have a contract that was unique in the annals of The Industry. It was signed by M-G-M, and its provisions turned every other writer in Hollywood sick with envy: (1) a salary of $4,000 a week; (2) a complete choice of materials; (3) a minimum of one screenplay a year—or as many as he chose to write; (4) if story conferences were required, the producer had to come to Trumbo's house." Such individuals were not Communists out of victimization or even ideology; rather, they were among those whose exalted self-image led them to embrace a movement they thought would carry them to power over others. Unsurprisingly, L. B. Mayer, when asked how a writer making close to $100,000 a year could be a Communist, answered, "In my opinion, I think they're cracked."

An extremely significant comment on this phenomenon was sandwiched between appearances on October 24 by Walt Disney and Lela Rogers, the mother of actress Ginger Rogers. Disney blasted his old nemesis Herb Sorrell, but went on to label the League of Women Voters a Communist group. Lela Rogers complained that "despair and hopelessness," along with propaganda against wealth, were injected into movie scripts by Communist screenwriters. The inarticulate comments of Disney and Rogers became notorious as laughable examples of anti-Communist extremism. However, the committee also heard Oliver Carlson, a 48-year-old Swedishborn ex-Communist author, whose comments were hardly noticed at the time and have since been completely ignored. Carlson testified carefully and understatedly, and described the activities of a certain Eli Jacobson.

Jacobson, Carlson recalled, was a founding member of the Communist Party in the U.S., and had served as director of the Workers' School in New York. He had been sent to Hollywood in 1936 to build up the party "among the film folk"—not the rank-and-file workers, but "the élite . . . important film personalities." In 1938, Jacobson told Carlson he was breaking with the Party. "He was terribly agitated and was afraid he was going to be killed," Carlson said. Jacobson had disappeared from Los Angeles, and Carlson insisted, "I don't know to this day whether he is dead or alive."

The mysterious Eli Bernard Jacobson remains one of the strangest individuals to surface in the inquiry on Communism in Hollywood; however, no effort was made to follow up on Carlson's testimony. Jacobson, born in Latvia in 1894, had become a Comintern agent, like other Latvian-American Communists, and was known within the Comintern as an "underground worker." He served in the Hollywood Anti-Nazi League while a member of the Los Angeles County committee of the Communist Party. His break with the Party was gradual, and the date cannot be confirmed. He was the lover of Beryl La Cava, a prominent Hollywood fellow traveler and wife of the producer Gregory La Cava. She divorced La Cava and married Jacobson, who then trained as a lay (nonphysician) psychoanalyst. At some point, the couple met Kenneth and Marie Rexroth.

Rexroth must have been surprised to see his friend's name appear in the Hollywood hearing, and was probably relieved when the testimony went nowhere. Rexroth, at least, knew that Jacobson was still alive; they had become very close. The poet's attention was diverted by a similar proceeding closer to home, for in the same week that J. Parnell Thomas heard the "friendly witnesses," State Senator Tenney's chief investigator, R. E. Combs, was investigating Communism in the fashionable and bucolic Marin County suburb of Fairfax. His target was Elsa Gidlow, the lesbian poet who had welcomed Kenneth and Andrée Rexroth to San Francisco twenty years before, and who nursed Andrée in her final illness. In the Fairfax proceeding, Andrée Rexroth's name, like that of Eli Jacobson before the Thomas Committee, was mentioned without echo, which must have left Kenneth feeling a good deal more secure. However, the attention of just about every liberal, radical, Communist, and ex-Communist in California, if not the whole of the nation, was riveted the following week, when Congressman Thomas and the House Un-American Activities Committee heard the first ten "unfriendly witnesses." Unlike Jacobson and Andrée Rexroth, they were destined not to be overlooked.

THE "UNFRIENDLY WITNESSES" were almost all screenwriters; aside from Sorrell's operation, the Screen Writers' Guild had been the main arena of Communist agitation in the film community. On Monday, October 27, 1947, the Committee called John Howard Lawson, who had been a founder and the first president of the Guild, as a witness. Lawson was defiant and obstreperous, and his encounter with Chairman Thomas turned into a shouting match as anti-Committee liberals such as Humphrey Bogart and

Lauren Bacall, who had flown to Washington to monitor the proceedings, craned their necks to watch from the rear seats. Lawson repeatedly refused to discuss whether he was a Communist, even though he had signed many public statements favoring the Party line. Thomas ordered Lawson away from the witness stand; the chairman and the other congressmen present for the committee then voted to charge Lawson with contempt of Congress, a criminal misdemeanor.

The next day, October 28, Dalton Trumbo, Albert Maltz, and Alvah Bessie appeared as witnesses. They also were uncooperative. Trumbo was chiefly known as the author of *Johnny Got His Gun,* a novel published during the Stalin-Hitler pact and aimed against American intervention in World War II. Later, however, he authored screenplays for such patriotic epics as the fine 1944 M-G-M release *Thirty Seconds Over Tokyo,* starring Spencer Tracy as General Jimmy Doolittle. Trumbo offered to submit a pile of his scripts as proof of his loyalty to the American people, but was refused. He would not say whether he was a Communist or a member of the Screen Writers' Guild, and was excused. Following him, Maltz and Bessie were allowed to read statements, a privilege that had been denied Lawson and Trumbo. Maltz badgered Chairman Thomas, as much as accusing him of sympathy with the anti-Semitic agitator Gerald L. K. Smith, and referred to Robert Stripling, the committee's chief investigator, as "Quisling." (Quisling was the name of the hated Nazi puppet leader of Norway during World War II; the epithet then implied treason and collaboration with fascists.)

Maltz's demeanor may have reflected a personal need to compensate, in the eyes of his Communist comrades, for past sins. The cowriter on *This Gun for Hire,* he had scored high in Hollywood with *Destination Tokyo* (1944), a Cary Grant film for Warner Brothers about submarine warfare, replete with anti-Japanese racism. He also worked on the short documentary *The House I Live In* (1945), a plea for tolerance that featured popular singer Frank Sinatra (the first American entertainer to make a fortune out of mass hysteria over his sexual charisma as well as his voice), intoning a balladic accompaniment by Communist composer Earl Robinson. But Albert Maltz was an object of amusement among anti-Communists, thanks to an amazing debate that had broken out a year and a half before the current Un-American Activities hearing.

Maltz published an article titled "What Shall We Ask of Writers?" in the Communist weekly *New Masses* in February 1946, rather timidly calling for greater freedom of expression by Communist intellectuals; he expressed the heretical view that James T. Farrell, a widely known realist novelist, should be read and appreciated. But Farrell had become a Trotskyist—which Maltz did not mention—and incredible waves of Stalinist vituperation immediately crashed over the luckless Hollywoodite. Speech after speech and article after article denounced Maltz for his lack of vigilance against the counterrevolutionary Trotskyites, his deviation in the direction of bourgeois liberalism, and similar "crimes." Two months after his essay was published, Maltz recanted and "self-criticized" in groveling terms, in a widely reported display of Communist weirdness. The "Maltz affair" even made the pages of *Life* magazine, which commented, "Folding completely before Party discipline, Maltz even castigated his sympathizers, who had objected to the abusive tone in which correction was administered." According to director Edward Dmytryk, who knew whereof he spoke, Maltz's article grew out of an acrimonious controversy among the Hollywood Communists regarding Party influence over a film forgotten today, *Cornered* (1945). Of course, had Maltz resided in the Soviet Union he would simply have been shot forthwith.

Albert Maltz therefore had an incentive to prove his Communist mettle before the Committee—to demonstrate that he was not, after all, afflicted with "bourgeois-liberal" weakness. Dmytryk later noted that the "unfriendlies" had been encouraged in their behavior by the recent performance of film and aircraft-industry legend Howard Hughes, who had shouted down a Senate subcommittee investigating war profiteering. But the size of their incomes must have also induced guilt and a desire to show strength and firmness in most of the Communist screenwriters. Their appearance before J. Parnell Thomas furnished them an opportunity to prove that individuals like Trumbo had not sold out, even though receiving a salary of $4,000 per week, and that life in Hollywood had not left them "decadent," a favorite Communist reproach.

Alvah Bessie, who had barely tasted prosperity as a screenwriter, came next, and after quarreling over the committee's right to ask if he was a Communist, was excused. Trumbo, Maltz, and Bessie were also cited for contempt.

Four more "unfriendly witnesses" appeared on Wednesday, October 29: Sam Ornitz, the longest-employed Hollywood Communist, a writer of movies forgotten even then; Herbert Biberman, an arrogant and dictatorial type, married to actress Gale Sondergaard; Edward Dmytryk, and producer Adrian Scott. Ornitz and Biberman were condescending, as well as particularly loud, in their exchanges with Thomas. Dmytryk and Scott were less aggressive, although they declined to disclose whether they were Communists, and by the time their turn had come, Chairman Thomas found his patience exhausted. All four were cited for contempt.

Dmytryk and Scott had worked on *Crossfire,* a 1947 crime drama from RKO Pictures. At a number of points in the hearings *Crossfire,* which dealt with anti-Semitism, was praised as a "liberal" film, and Scott more or less implied that the committee was seeking revenge on the Hollywood Communists for producing such features. The charge was absurd, but *Crossfire* is worthy of mention, for of the films with a "message" produced in the 1940s it was one of the best. It was based on a novel, *The Brick Foxhole* by the Communist-leaning movie director Richard Brooks, that includes the murder of a homosexual by a soldier; but "queers" were still an unmentionable topic in movies, and the victim was transformed into a Jew, played by Sam Levene. The main cast members were Robert Young, as Detective Finlay, who investigates the death; Robert Ryan, as the brutal, bigoted, and drunken serviceman who kills Levene, and Robert Mitchum as a simple but fair-minded fellow-soldier who assists the police. *Crossfire* includes some daffy propaganda lines, as when a callow soldier whom the murderer tries to frame describes himself as an artist who painted a post-office mural for the W.P.A., and Levene solemnly affirms, "A lot of great artists came out of that." But the tension in the film is authentic, and the performances of all three Roberts are magnificent. Ryan, who had served in the armed forces with Brooks and lobbied hard for the role of the killer, soon regretted it, for although it was brilliantly written it left him typecast as a lout.

On October 30, the last day of the hearings, Ring Lardner, Jr., and Lester Cole appeared. Both declined to answer whether they were Communists and both were cited for contempt, making ten individuals so charged. The group became famous; indeed, as the "Hollywood Ten," they were destined for a secure place in American history even though almost nobody, even in Communist circles, knew very much about them; and most of their films, which were dreadful, were already fading from public memory.

An eleventh "unfriendly witness" also appeared on the last day: the German author Bertolt Brecht. The 49-year-old Brecht was so mouse-like in his seeming compliance with the committee that he took Chairman

Thomas by surprise. Although he was once condemned as the "poet of the Russian secret police," Brecht claimed he had never been a Communist. He left the proceeding and immediately departed for Europe. He never returned to the United States.

Cole had attempted to argue that the hearings were an assault on the Screen Writers' Guild, which was approaching a union election, but this ludicrous fantasy had little impact. However, it later became the habit of the "Ten" to claim that the investigation was an anti-union maneuver, although no such campaign ever took place in Hollywood after the 1930s. The "Ten" also referred to the hearings as an "inquisition," while a Committee for the First Amendment, made up of Bogart, Bacall, Gene Kelly, Danny Kaye, and various other stars of medium magnitude protested that the committee "persistently violated the civil liberties of American citizens." But the hearings were less an inquisition than a poker game, perhaps the greatest of all time, in which the two sides each sought to bluff the other. That aspect of the inquiry may have been most in effect on the last hearing day, when former F.B.I. agent Louis J. Russell, who had testified several times in the previous two weeks, returned to the witness stand.

Russell revealed an espionage conspiracy centered in California but at first seemingly unconnected with Hollywood. In 1942, he testified, Pyotr Ivanov, secretary of the Soviet consulate in San Francisco and confederate of Steve Nelson, had contacted George Charles Eltenton, a lecturer at the California Labor School. Eltenton, formerly affiliated with an Institute of Chemical Physics in the Soviet Union, was employed at the Shell Development Corporation in Emeryville, a facility penetrated by the F.A.E.C.T. "union." According to Russell, Ivanov offered Eltenton money for "highly secret" information on the work going on in the Berkeley Radiation Laboratory. Eltenton then contacted Haakon Chevalier, Berkeley professor of French and Communist, and told him the Russians were interested in the superweapon being developed with the participation of Rad Lab personnel. Chevalier solicited none other than his friend J. Robert Oppenheimer to assist this espionage effort but, according to F.B.I. agent Russell, "Opje" rebuffed him, warning that such action would be treason.

Russell further specified that Louise Bransten (known to have brought Kheifitz together with Martin David Kamen of the Rad Lab) had been told by Eltenton of his work to "educate a certain scientist" in a Communist direction—presumably Oppenheimer. Russell described a wide ring of Communist collaborators that included a freelance Hollywood writer and State Department employee, Charles Page, who was also associated with Louise Bransten. Page had been in contact with Vasili Zarubin/Zubilin/Cooper, the leading KGB officer in the Western Hemisphere, as well as with Chevalier, Lawson, Biberman, a veteran Comintern agent named Otto Katz (*klichka* André Simone), and two German Communist brothers, Hanns Eisler, a musician and intimate friend of Brecht, and Gerhart Eisler, an international Communist functionary. Russell also testified that in 1943 the Russians had sent an espionage operative to Hollywood, Mikhail Kalatozov.

Haakon Chevalier, curiously enough, had been named the week before in the Fairfax investigation of Elsa Gidlow. The baroque tale of Eltenton and Chevalier approaching Oppenheimer as a potential spy had been conveyed to the federal authorities by Oppenheimer himself. Both Oppenheimer and Chevalier at first refused to confirm, deny, or otherwise publicly comment on Russell's statements. Oppenheimer had taken up a post with the Institute for Advanced Study at Princeton, and Chevalier had resigned from the Berkeley faculty in January 1947. Eltenton had left Shell Development in Emeryville only three weeks before and moved to England; his house in Berkeley stood empty.

Some of the other data may have been derived from the VENONA intercepts. Chevalier, not long after Eltenton's alleged proposal, had been barred by federal authorities from an O.W.I. assignment in North Africa, on security grounds; that agency's French section, in which he sought employment, was then a major target of the KGB, as revealed in the VENONA traffic. Elsewhere in the VENONA documents we encounter Otto Katz, along with a person who may have been Brecht, and Kalatozov, the latter under the *klichka* of *Iveri,* or "Iberian," a reference (in this context) to an ancient people living in the Caucasus Mountains. (Kalatozov, later prominent as a Soviet film director, was born in Georgia.) A major selection of decrypted VENONA messages had been handed over to the F.B.I by military intelligence officers only the month before.

Journalists wondered why Russell's shocking disclosures had been injected into the Hollywood investigation; it may be that the F.B.I. and the House Committee sought to warn, or scare, the Communists by indicating that they knew much more than they were immediately revealing. That the overall intent was less a purge than a chess game seems reflected in a curious interchange between J. Parnell Thomas and Robert W. Kenny, a former attorney general of California and a lawyer for the "unfriendly witnesses." After wrangling with Thomas over his role as an advocate, Kenny commented softly, "Neither one of us is intimidating the other. Right, Mr. Chairman?"

Thomas and Stripling ran the hearings on the film industry, but a basilisk-like figure also sat as a committee member during the "friendly" testimony, rarely commenting. This was Richard Milhous Nixon, 34, elected as a Republican member of Congress from California the year before, and a Californian about whom, like William Randolph Hearst and Jack London, it seems that little new remains to be said. Nixon chose his moments, and his targets, with extreme care; representing a district in which the film industry was the dominant power, he was wary of involvement in a controversy that might negatively affect his career. At the end of July 1947 he had promised that the Un-American Activities Committee's Hollywood inquiry would be "sensational," but he opined that Communism was a bigger problem in government, labor, education, and other areas than in movies. Nixon was also instrumental in initiating a congressional investigation, beginning in 1949, into the DiGiorgio strike.

While southern California wrestled with its recent history, something far more meaningful was unfolding in the Bay region. Kenneth Rexroth's life had been brushed by the Tenney and Thomas committee investigations, but they left him largely unaffected; for Rexroth reality lay elsewhere. While J. Parnell Thomas and John Howard Lawson yelled fruitlessly at each other in the film investigation hearings, Rexroth and the other San Francisco "new poets," particularly Robert Duncan, Philip Lamantia, and William Everson, in alliance with Henry Miller at Big Sur, were reinventing American culture and bringing California to a position of worldwide literary influence such as it had never seen before. The aesthetic revolution, well under way, came to be known as "the San Francisco Renaissance."

One unarguable sign of a new historic phase came with the publication of Duncan's first book, *Heavenly City, Earthly City* in 1947. The volume was issued by Bernard Harden Porter, nicknamed Bern, a former nuclear physicist who had resigned from the Manhattan Engineering District staff after the atomic bombing of Hiroshima. While Oppenheimer and his students represented a pro-Soviet tendency among the bomb-making intelligentsia, Bern Porter single-handedly embodied a distinctly different and more fruitful form of intellectual radicalism. Born in Maine in 1910 or 1911, he received his master's degree in physics from Brown University but underwent a crisis when he realized he was more drawn to art than to science, and failed to earn his doctorate. As described by his friend and biographer, the Berkeley poet and playwright James Schevill, in 1936 Porter was conquered by the Surrealist spirit, repeatedly visiting a major exhibition at the Museum of Modern Art in New York, *Fantastic Art, Dada, Surrealism.* Porter was especially attracted by the works of the three members of the Surrealist movement born in America: Man Ray, with his experiments in photography; Alexander Calder, inventor of the mobile and the stabile; and Joseph Cornell, the fabricator of mysterious shadow-boxed dream assemblages. Working as an industrial scientist, Porter found his way into the prewar art scene in New York, attending salons held by Peggy Guggenheim and Mabel Dodge Luhan and meeting Jackson Pollock, the architect Frederick Kiesler, and other artists and intellectuals.

In 1940, Porter was "ordered by his draft board," according to his own account, to leave private employment and take up a post at Princeton University, researching the separation of the isotope uranium-235 (U_{235}), from uranium 238 (U_{238}), a major technical concern in the construction of an atomic weapon. At Princeton he met Albert Einstein and J. Robert Oppenheimer; meanwhile he continued to visit New York and to frequent *avant-garde* artists. He exhibited some photographs, sculptures, and transformed found objects, in the Surrealist style. But in 1942 he was again called by his draft board and sent to Berkeley. Schevill wrote,

> One of the three board members had been asked to look for physicists who could do research on the separation of uranium. . . . Porter was indeed qualified for the job. For his master's degree at Brown University, Porter had worked on the electromagnetic separation of radium. . . . Although there were other competing techniques for the separation of uranium isotopes, E[rnest] O. Lawrence's [electromagnetic] method developed at the University of California at Berkeley was chosen for industrial development. Porter was sent first to Lawrence's Radiation Laboratory, then to Oak Ridge, Tennessee, where a vast industrial plant designed to separate uranium on a massive scale for bomb use was established.

Bern Porter, working at the Rad Lab with Oppenheimer's pro-Communist colleagues and disciples, later described an attempt by Giovanni R.

Lomanitz and David Bohm to recruit him into F.A.E.C.T., which he re-buffed. However, he claimed that the F.B.I., spurred by the fake union's interest, pestered him with wide-ranging questions, even asking, he said, "Who was Philip Lamantia? What about Kenneth Rexroth?" Porter was deeply ambivalent about the overall Manhattan enterprise; at the beginning, in 1942, he had commented in an extremely obscure "little magazine" on his physics research:

> The fountainhead of inspiration accepts no compromise—its will is always done. While the reasons for this may seldom be evident, the resulting action is for the best. . . . Curiously the inspiration for a 6-Block Bomb is not granted anyone unless such negation has been ordained. When completed its potentialities for constructive use outweight the pernicious elements. . . .

Earlier that year he had written, in the Surrealist manner, of "everlasting purification by fire acid forever destruction with hurricane tornado eternal . . . blind deaf and dumb the written law is upon you death."

Even before the traumatic news from Hiroshima, about which he felt a profound complicity and guilt, Porter had taken an anarchist turn. He was a major partisan of Henry Miller, publishing and selling books by and about him, including an antiwar pamphlet, *Murder the Murderer* (1944). Schevill recounts Porter's concerns, at the same time as he was dealing with the heightened security regulations at the Rad Lab and at Oak Ridge, to finance publication of Miller's extremely subversive work. When, in 1945, Porter produced a *Festschrift* to honor Miller, *The Happy Rock,* he told Schevill that he "worked on it all over the country, while traveling back and forth from Berkeley to Oak Ridge, with security officials peering over my shoulder, but blissfully unaware of Miller and what he stood for."

Bern Porter also assisted George Leite in producing *Circle,* and put out Philip Lamantia's first book, *Erotic Poems,* in 1946. The Bay Area poets displayed extraordinary achievement, as well as talent, in the postwar period. Kenneth Rexroth had refined the mystical, philosophical, erotic, and social-protest strands in his verse, and was writing his best poems ever; he was finishing a major work, *The Dragon and the Unicorn,* along with exquisite love poems and fine translations from the Chinese. He was increasingly vociferous in his anti-Stalinism, however, assailing Leite for having lectured at the California Labor School, and expressed a general lack of sympathy with the Communist targets of the investigative probes. He was also in constant touch with leading anti-Stalinist and modernist writers elsewhere in the United States and in Britain, such as James T. Farrell, Dwight Macdonald, George Woodcock, and Cyril Connolly. Indeed, it may be argued that Rexroth was the first San Francisco poet with a global grasp—which he was, unfortunately, uninterested in or incapable of turning into immediate worldwide recognition such as Henry Miller enjoyed. Philip Lamantia, the "golden child" of the group, was searching for new intellectual frontiers to penetrate in anthropology, religion, and Surrealism. William Everson had become extremely cranky, arguing with Rexroth about the work of Robinson Jeffers, whom Everson still worshipped and Rexroth still hated.

Almost as fierce an anti-Stalinist as Rexroth, Robert Duncan, who later distanced himself for other reasons such as their evaluations of Ezra Pound, was a subject apart in his work and his personality, as was demonstrated by *Heavenly City, Earthly City*. Rexroth was brilliant at digesting and restating, in poetic diction, the great enduring philosophical issues; Lamantia was a unique visionary, whose relation to language was inseparable from the content of the words he employed, having dredged them from his unconscious in the cold, "scientific" manner of the Surrealists; Everson was more spontaneous than Rexroth, but drank from the same general literary stream. But Duncan was possessed of an irrefragable "auditory" linguistic gift, a sensory understanding of the music of speech and the power of lyric that is extremely rare. He stood with the outstanding French poets, Gérard de Nerval, Arthur Rimbaud, Stéphane Mallarmé, and Guillaume Apollinaire, in such experimental texts as "An Owl Is an Only Bird of Poetry":

> The vowels are physical
> corridors of the imagination
> emitting passionately
> breaths of flame. In a poem
> the vowels appear like
> the flutterings of an owl
> caught in a web and give
> aweful intimations of
> eternal life.

Duncan's personal turbulence was unrelenting. According to his biographer, Ekbert Faas, Duncan contended with the Stalinist domination of the radical student milieu at Berkeley while studying there in 1937, and his first self-published periodical, *Epitaph*, was run off on a mimeograph machine belonging to the Young People's Socialist League, a Trotskyist-dominated group. He had gone east at the end of the 1930s with the intent of studying creative writing at Black Mountain College, an ultraexperimental North Carolina institution that accepted him on the recommendation of two Berkeley professors. However, as described by Faas, "unfortunately [Duncan's] arrival at the college coincided with that of an anarchist couple on their way to Mexico. The two challenged some faculty members concerning the Stalinist betrayal of the Spanish Civil War. In the ensuing debate, Robert emerged as a lone defender of the anarchist couple and as a result was turned away the following day. He was emotionally disturbed and disturbing to the academic community, they told him," even at the supposedly nonacademic college.

Although by the time Duncan came back to Berkeley, in the mid-1940s, he had largely given up the amusements of flamboyant street and bar cruising, he was proud and open about his homosexuality, as were his younger peers, the poets Jack Spicer and Robin Blaser. (Bern Porter told James Schevill he first encountered homosexuality among Duncan and his friends.) Nevertheless, Duncan had had affairs with women, and continued to do so, and some of his best poetry is sexual but nonspecific as to orientation. One of his early poems, which ranks among the finest verse creations in English in this century, begins:

> I am a most fleshly man, and see
> in your body what stirs my spirit.
> And my spirit is intimate of my hand,
> intimate of my breast and heart,
> intimate of my parted lips
> that would seek their solace
> in your lips.

Duncan existed on the edge of "reality" in a way that represented a fulfillment of California's borderland heritage. He wrote in one of his most affecting poems, "The Song of the Borderguard":

> The man with his lion under the shed of wars
> sheds his belief as if he shed tears.

The sound of words waits—
a barbarian host at the borderline of sense.

. . .

The borderlines of sense in the morning light
are naked as a line of poetry in a war.

In *Heavenly City, Earthly City,* Duncan beautifully enunciated a central myth of the postwar "San Francisco Renaissance": that of the West Coast cities as a special environment for poetry. Near the conclusion of the poem that gave the collection its name, he wrote,

The wandering man returns to his city
as if he might return to earth a light, a joy,
and finds his rest in earthly company.

Finally, in a joint publication of Duncan and Spicer we find words that could stand as a permanent credo for California poets:

Yet this is the country of my life.
It is the westward edge of dreams,
the golden promise of our days.

—————

THE ANARCHIST, PACIFIST, theosophical, and homosexual sensibility of Robert Duncan was clearly at odds with both the shabby exigencies of the Communist intellectuals and the patriotic verities exalted by Tenney, Thomas, and other legislative defenders of postwar America. But notwithstanding the Tenney committee's Fairfax inquiry, and the F.B.I.'s alleged interference with Bern Porter, neither Duncan nor any other member of the group associated with Rexroth was harassed by investigative committees, either local or national. However, "unofficial" public attacks on Henry Miller, Rexroth, and their milieu came thick and fast in 1947, beginning with an article in *Harper's* magazine on the Big Sur "cult of sex and anarchy." This ignoble screed, by a Berkeley "freelance writer" and faculty wife of reputed Stalinist orientation, Mildred Brady, derided Miller as creator of a "potpourri of mysticism, egoism, sexualism, surrealism and anarchism." Brady also caricatured Rexroth for his devotion to anarchism and the interest, among his friends, in the ideas of the dissident psychoanalyst Wilhelm Reich. If there was an inquisition afoot in America, Mildred

Brady and her hatred of cultural unorthodoxy symbolized it as much as Tenney, Thomas, or Nixon, who at least had unarguable evidence that American Communists collaborated with Russian spies.

Miller, Rexroth, and their cohort had in common with the Communists a contempt for ordinary patriotism, though none of the former would have submitted to the patriotism of the Kremlin either. Both groups held a loyalty to a foreign ideology; but while Communists like Lester Cole or Alvah Bessie served Bolshevism, the Miller-Rexroth alliance had enlisted in the "modernist international," which fortified Western democracy rather than threatening it; they hated Stalinism just about as much as Tenney did. Unlike Tenney, the Rexroth circle knew that their anarchism was much more a Californian than a foreign phenomenon. But Duncan later recalled, in an interview with Rexroth biographer Linda Hamalian, that when he first met Kenneth and Marie in 1942, while they were running the "underground railroad" for *Nisei* to escape to the Midwest, Rexroth "didn't want anyone to know where he was. He imagined that any moment a Stalinist would come up the stairs—not that they *weren't* shooting people."

The libels of Mildred Brady were taken up and spread far and wide through the region, nationally by *Time* magazine and locally by the *San Francisco Examiner*, flagship of the Hearst chain. The *Examiner*, in particular, was oafish in its treatment of Miller; for its scribblers, staff writer Clint Mosher and columnist/blackmailer Robert Patterson, who called himself "Freddie Francisco," no ethical limits existed. The "Big Sur and San Francisco surrealists, young, angry, and loudly protesting," were turned into an outsized and menacing revolutionary movement, not all that distinct from the Communists. With unparalleled idiocy, Mosher denounced Miller:

> He is writing and talking in the surrealist manner and an important segment of the youth of the Bay area is taking his preachings as the full gospel for a better life. These anarchistic theories are being packaged and shipped to San Francisco and Berkeley and to youths across the country. . . . As a practical proposition they will undoubtedly destroy the equilibrium of many a returned veteran. . . . Certainly thousands of youngsters, without practical experience and with formative minds, will be driven into the waiting arms of the extreme leftists in politics and labor and the arts. In the general direction of the anarchist's march, the Communistic [*sic!*] Party stands as the most likely resting place for these malcontents.

Indulging in the well-known Hearst penchant for phony objectivity, Mosher conceded that Miller could not "be held personally responsible for the fact that on occasions, San Francisco youths convene in a basement apartment and pay fifty cents for the right to hear a reading of Miller-inspired poetry and for the chance to puff on a marijuana cigaret." Miller, according to these journalists, had created a cult, based on "a new youth psychology that is expressing itself in obscene writings and a general hate of everything that represents American life." One of the stupidest commentaries to appear in this avalanche of defamation was that of "Mim" Godwin, wife of the mayor of Carmel, who sought to mobilize the rich "artists" of that community against the barbarian invaders. "Mim" recalled that two young people had been seen walking down the main street of Carmel barefoot in the rain, with the legs of their jeans rolled up over their knees: "I said to them, you're not from Carmel. You're from Nob Hill in San Francisco. You ought to know better. We don't go for that kind of thing here." Her husband added moronically, "We have practically no juvenile delinquency here and we intend to keep it that way."

In reality, Jaime de Angulo, Miller, and other Bohemians at Big Sur tended to stay away from Carmel, which had lost the free-spirited atmosphere it had known as late as when Lincoln Steffens and Edward Weston were its leading residents. Mildred Brady, Clint Mosher, "Freddie Francisco," and the dimwitted Godwins did not realize that theirs was increasingly a minority opinion among those who knew anything about Miller, Rexroth, Big Sur, and the Bay Area. Other newspapers and magazines treated the phenomenon with greater detachment and insight. The *Saturday Review of Literature* took note of the noise, but concluded with exceptional perceptiveness, "It is exciting to speculate what our literature will be like in another twenty years if these sexual, anarchic, and 'philosophical' ideas should nourish another Dos Passos, Sinclair Lewis, or Hemingway." While the *Examiner* baited Miller brutally, the *San Francisco Chronicle* treated the printed assaults on him with humor, and his work and that of his friends and collaborators with understated respect. A review by *Chronicle* art critic Spencer Barefoot of *Into the Night Life,* a hand-produced book of Miller's texts with illustrations by the painter Bezalel Schatz, noted, "Miller and Schatz have said, 'This is but the beginning, a pioneer effort in a direction which may prove to be revolutionary in the making of books.' It may be that the gentlemen have something there."

The *Chronicle* had always been superior to its competitors in the seriousness of its literary, art, and music criticism, and its employees were much better informed than their counterparts about the extent of the intellectual revolution taking place in California at that time. *Into the Night Life* had been exhibited at the San Francisco Museum of Art (S.F.M.A.), which was enthusiastic about modernism in its newest forms. A similar commitment had transformed the California School of Fine Arts (C.S.F.A., later the San Francisco Art Institute) in a way that was pregnant with significance for the future of painting and sculpture in California, and which paralleled developments in New York of worldwide impact.

The true revolution in California plastic arts began administratively, with the hiring of a new director at C.S.F.A., an institution that originated in the generosity of railroad magnate Mark Hopkins. The late *Chronicle* art critic and historian Thomas Albright wrote, "The appointment of Douglas MacAgy as director of the C.S.F.A., early in 1945, was the first in a sequence of events that was to challenge traditional notions about painting in San Francisco as radically as they were being challenged in New York. The school, financially ailing since the Depression, and suffering from reduced attendance during the war, had reached such straits that in MacAgy's words the trustees 'were rather desperate' and therefore 'able to bring themselves to make concessions.'" With such concessions extending to full freedom in imposing his own curriculum and employing his own faculty, MacAgy was persuaded to take on the directorship. A Canadian by birth, MacAgy had studied at the Courtauld Institute in London as well as at other leading colleges, and had served as a curator at the Cleveland Museum. He came to the West Coast in 1941 with a job as assistant at S.F.M.A. His wife, Jermayne MacAgy, during the war had become acting director of the California Palace of the Legion of Honor, an art museum founded by Alma de Bretteville Spreckels; from that position she supported her husband's venture at C.S.F.A.

According to Albright, very early in his directorship MacAgy ordered a mural panel by Diego Rivera, which hung in the school's main gallery, to be covered with a curtain. The symbolism was, to art students, obvious: the era of realism, and particularly the social realism of the 1930s, was over. During 1945, MacAgy gave permanent contracts to younger teachers, including the painter Hassel Smith, a substitute lithography instructor at C.S.F.A. and an occasional associate of the California Labor School. As a teenager, in the early 1930s, Smith moved to California from Michigan with his family. He went to college in Chicago and acquired a considerable experience with *avant-garde* culture before returning to San Francisco in 1936. He studied at C.S.F.A. and toiled as a social worker, painted landscapes, and was employed in the lumber industry by the U.S. Forest Service. His realistic paintings had an undercurrent of keen observation, and he was, as described by Albright, "an outgoing iconoclast with the disputatiousness of a born devil's advocate."

In 1946, MacAgy hired six more new faculty members, including Edward Corbett, a painter of abstractions influenced by Piet Mondriaan. Corbett, Hassel Smith, and the merchant seaman, silkscreen artist, and painter Robert McChesney, another past denizen of the California Labor School, set up housekeeping in Point Richmond, a quiet settlement on the northeast shore of the Bay dominated by an immense Standard Oil refinery and ship terminal and the adjoining Santa Fe railway yard. MacAgy also brought into the faculty a painter and crafts teacher, Elmer Bischoff, as well as Miller's friend Yanko Varda and the photographer Ansel Adams. But the most important new hire at MacAgy's C.S.F.A. arrived in fall 1946, in circumstances dramatically recounted by Albright, when "a charismatic, patriarchal figure 'in a long black overcoat' took over as a replacement for a newly hired teacher who failed to show up." MacAgy had asked Clay Spohn, another of the new faculty, to look at two paintings. Spohn later recalled,

> They were exactly the same size, about 36 inches by 28 inches. . . . Each was done as large, bold strokes of rather dull color, more or less monochromatic with slight changes in the hue and occurring well inside the borders of the white canvas background. No attempt had been made to represent anything other than the strokes of pigment and the way they were applied—thick, heavy strokes, one into the other. . . . Frankly, I don't know what I thought.

The paintings were by Clyfford Still, a North Dakotan who was hired immediately by MacAgy. Then already 42, Still had spent much of his life in a rather splendid intellectual isolation, slowly developing his unique outlook. He taught art at a college in Washington State but went East in the mid-1930s, painting works that reflected a transition between realism and abstraction. Coming to the Bay Area during the war, he labored as a shipyard worker for the Navy, then on the assembly line in an aircraft

plant. During a time Albright characterized as one of "privation and struggle," Still completed "startlingly prophetic works," *1941-2-C* and *1943-A,*
in which his abstraction became absolute. The first consisted of "a single
dark, shaggy, monolithic shape . . . crowding an airless, deep blue field,"
according to Albright, and the second, painted on blue denim—cheaper
than canvas—presented "an organism of abstract shapes from which sym-
metry and other compositional conventions have been totally purged."
Still had a retrospective at S.F.M.A., from which these daring new works
were absent, but it was met with criticism that sent Still back east in irritation, to another teaching job. In early 1946, twelve of his paintings were
shown at Art of This Century, the major New York gallery owned by Peggy
Guggenheim, at the instance of Mark Rothko. Still's reputation was assured, and he returned to San Francisco, and applied to work at C.S.F.A.,
with considerable confidence.

Albright wrote decades afterward that Still's new style "implied an unprecedented individual freedom, and at the same time a radical commitment to the primacy of the individual, the specific, and the concrete. It all
added up to a completely new vision, which one either accepted or rejected
outright." San Francisco art students had already been exposed to the work
of Jackson Pollock, shown at S.F.M.A. in late 1945, and to Rothko, who
had a similar exhibition a year later. But the MacAgy-Still alliance, fed by an
influx of students under the G.I. Bill of Rights, which paid for World War
II veterans' education, made C.S.F.A. a center of "the revolution" in painting. Whether they were conscious of it or not—Still seems to have been—
these young artists, even though educated on the G.I. Bill, had opted for
the free art market over the government subsidies of the New Deal era. In
1947 the California Palace of the Legion of Honor sponsored a one-man
show by Still. Rexroth recalled a dozen years later, "People came up to his
vast pictures very quietly, and toppled over into them without a murmur,
and came out with nothing to say."

Perhaps inevitably, given the potential of their medium, the postwar
Bay Area artists were even more innovative than the writers. While Miller,
Lamantia, and Duncan cleaved to literary Surrealism, MacAgy and his
group rejected figurative Surrealism as no less old-fashioned than social realism. C.S.F.A. had embarked on a "'golden age' of Abstract Expressionism," according to Albright. Nevertheless, the C.S.F.A. project was not the
only attempt to test the boundaries of painting carried on in the Bay Area at

that time; an alternative effort had been launched in the aftermath of pictorial Surrealism by two younger "stars" of the European movement, who had
already greatly influenced Jackson Pollock and others in New York. These
were Gordon Onslow Ford, whom MacAgy hired as a summer lecturer in
1948, and Wolfgang Paalen. To understand what they were attempting,
however, a digression is necessary.

California had undergone a flirtation with Surrealist art in the 1930s, but
among painters, the innovation was shouted down by the Stalinist realist
school, benefiting from their W.P.A. affiliation as well as from the "hege-
mony" exercised over the Bay Area in labor and radical politics by the Communists. Art critic David Bonetti has written that

> During the early 20th century, the latest art movements . . . moved slowly
> and tended to reach California late. . . . But there was something about Sur-
> realism, the movement that explored dreams, fantasies, myths, incongruities
> and chance, that resonated with the California spirit, and it arrived here fast.
> Indeed, the first explicitly Surrealist group in the United States was formed
> in Los Angeles in 1934.

While this is true, it should be weighed against an understanding that the
Los Angeles Surrealists remained isolated and obscure. That group was
founded by Lorser Feitelson and his wife Helen Lundeberg (no relation to
the independent-minded labor leader). Bonetti has noted that Feitelson,
"calling his group 'Post-Surrealism' . . . aimed to correct Surrealism of its
morbid, chaotic and misogynist tendencies." Nonetheless, according to
Bonetti, Feitelson's best work "is steeped in eroticism."

Feitelson and Lundeberg were hardly the first California Surrealists.
Alexander Calder had lived in San Francisco as a youth—his father, the architect Alexander Stirling Calder, who designed the statuary for the Panama-
Pacific International Exposition there, had brought his family to the city in
1915. The Bay Area had already produced two successful modernist artists
associated with the Paris Surrealists: John Ferren and Charles Howard. John
Ferren was born in Oregon in 1905, the same year as Rexroth, whose friend
and "disciple" he became. He grew up in California and as a teenager, without formal art training, began sculpting heads of his friends. In the late
1920s he worked as a stonecutter and lived on Telegraph Hill in San Francisco. His encounter with Kenneth and Andrée Rexroth, although danger-

ous because of Andrée's mental problems, transformed him. Kenneth undertook to educate him in contemporary art; soon Ferren was painting figuratively, then entered into a fruitful career as an Abstractionist. He began selling his work and made enough money to study in Europe: at the Sorbonne, in Italy, and in Spain.

Ferren returned to San Francisco and held a one-man show in 1930. He began taking long walks in the Berkeley hills with Rexroth; he later commented in terms that could be described as environmentalist *avant la lettre,* "I placed my hand on a tree-trunk. I instantaneously felt that every element of the landscape was alive—the light, air, ground and trees. All were interrelated, living the same life and (this is important in my art) their forms were all interchangeable." After a hitchhiking trip with Rexroth through the southwestern and southern states, Ferren went back to Europe and lived on the island of Mallorca, painting watercolors. Soon he was fully established as an artist and his works had been acquired by leading museums. Gertrude Stein wrote of him, "He is the only American painter foreign painters in Paris consider as a painter and whose paintings interest them." During World War II he was chief of publications in the O.W.I. Psychological Warfare Division, assigned to Washington, Paris, and Algiers. Ferren remained a presence in San Francisco aesthetic life, even though he took up permanent residence on the East Coast.

A similar success abroad had been gained by Charles Howard, a son of Berkeley architect John Galen Howard and an older brother of John Langley Howard, a participant in the Coit Tower mural project. Charles Howard spent a summer in France during World War I, graduated from Berkeley in 1921, and went first to the East Coast, then back to Europe, where he spent two years. He traveled in Italy with Grant Wood, settled in New York, and held his first show, of satirical drawings, before working as a journeyman painter for a decorator. In 1927 he and his brothers, John and Robert, had a show in Berkeley, Charles Howard's first on the West Coast. He worked his way through "abstract Surrealism," and embarked on a process leading to what *San Francisco Chronicle* critic R. H. Hagan called his "smooth and brilliantly precise and beautifully balanced abstractions with mysterious names," adding, "Howard is a painter with a meticulous sense of line, pattern, and color." Unlike other Surrealist paintings, Howard's works, although often menacing and erotic, seemed to have filtered out all trace of their origins in the natural world; they offered a polished simulacrum, and powerfully anticipated later tendencies in art.

In 1932 Howard, along with Man Ray and Joseph Cornell, was chosen by New York art impresario Julien Levy for representation with the Paris Surrealists—an extremely high honor, anticipating Ferren's acceptance in Europe. In 1933 Howard moved to Britain, where he eventually became prominent in the effervescent Surrealist group there and attained a major reputation. He showed in the climactic 1936 International Surrealist Exhibition at the New Burlington Galleries in London, and collaborated in a widely read periodical, the *London Bulletin.* Back in America in 1940, he worked for the W.P.A. and exhibited his works at S.F.M.A., then, with the coming of the war, was employed as a shipfitter and an editor for the O.W.I. He created abstract murals for the federal government, won various awards, and held unquestionable stature as an American—and British—abstract artist. In 1945, he lectured at C.S.F.A., and McAgy described his work as "a moving world, of meetings and partings, gentle and cruel, austere and elegant. It is elusive, wayfaring: a drama of the mind."

Other Surrealists who visited and influenced intellectual life in California included Salvador Dalí, who arrived in Pebble Beach during World War II, caused a publicity ruckus, and then left, and Man Ray, who lived for several years in Hollywood. Man Ray had come west in the company of a salesman of men's neckwear who knew Ray's sister. Man Ray frequented Henry Miller at Big Sur, as well as the classic surrealist painter Max Ernst, then living at Sedona in Arizona, and cultivated the friendship of Los Angeles Surrealist artist William Copley. Man Ray also developed a small community of admirers in the film world, chiefly Albert Lewin, former personal assistant and intimate associate of Irving Thalberg, whose few films as director-screenwriter included *The Moon and Sixpence* (1942), *The Picture of Dorian Gray* (1945), and *The Private Affairs of Bel-Ami* (1947). However, most important in Lewin's work is *Pandora and the Flying Dutchman* (1951), a Surrealist-influenced creation for which Man Ray painted a portrait of Ava Gardner, shown in the film. In *Pandora,* Man Ray noted, "the leading man, besides being condemned to wander over the globe for eternity, is a painter who paints Pandora's portrait before he has met her—quite a Surrealist idea." Unfortunately, *Pandora and the Flying Dutchman* was not well received, and is hardly known today.

Lucien Labaudt, a painter who died in 1943, was another Coit Tower alumnus; he also maintained a design studio in San Francisco and vacillated between Surrealism and social realism in the mid-1930s, as did other, lesser figures in California art. Yet it should be kept in mind that Ferren and Howard, like Calder before them (and for that matter, like Isadora Duncan and Henry Cowell), had to leave California to gain real understanding and recognition for their work. Harry Partch, who commented bitterly on the impossibility of finding a sympathetic patron in California during the 1930s, ascribed such blindness to provincialism. However, a blossoming of Surrealism in California before 1945 had been specifically prevented by the fanaticism and bullying of the social-realist-mural crowd, who, once they gained a determining influence over the young, treated art students more or less the same way the Communist commissars on the waterfront bullied the longshoremen. It was for that reason that MacAgy's action in covering the Rivera at the C.S.F.A. was so important; aggressive, experimental modernism in the Bay Area, no less than in New York, represented an explicit rebellion against social realism.

The rearguard of Stalinist realist artists, who were mainly at the California Labor School and were led by Victor Arnautoff (revealed in the VENONA messages to be under KGB control), Bernard Zakheim, Byron Randall and Emmy Lou Packard, Giacomo Patri, and Anton Refregier, viewed the new art quite perceptively as the "counter-revolution" it indeed was. The days when Communism allied itself with artistic modernism were long past, as was emphasized by Stalin's postwar purges in Soviet cultural life. Communist propaganda throughout the world assailed abstract art in particular as "anti-human" and "nihilistic," while chromo style portraits and murals of Stalin and other Communist bosses were elevated to the status of high art.

In dealing with their former friends and colleagues who had remained faithful to the modernist impulse, the Communist artists engaged in vulgar, philistine, and personal abuse. The Abstract Expressionists were, they said, mere sellouts to the decadent rich—if they had any talent at all, which was doubtful, according to the geniuses of the California Labor School. During this period, the *Chronicle* published a polemic by Zakheim, in which he declared in a self-righteous and arrogant style reminiscent of the Moscow purge years,

The abstractionist . . . is afraid of being called a propagandist. The public must demand open forums and symposiums in the museums to question the position of these artists who avoid their responsibility to society, while mo-nopolizing the art schools and galleries and museums. . . . Fellow-artists, are you trying to build a monopoly of abstractionists, or in the affairs of this troubled world are you afraid to take sides?

Needless to say, Zakheim was not afraid to take sides—with Stalin.

SURREALISM WAS THEREFORE in the air, literarily and artistically, in California after World War II, but in a belated form, delayed in its progress by the tyranny of social realism, and already somewhat passé while MacAgy and Still were reforming art completely. Gordon Onslow Ford and Wolfgang Paalen, who landed in the Bay Area at this time, sought to surpass both figura-tive Surrealism and Abstract Expressionism, as the latter evolved stylistically.

Onslow Ford, one of the most remarkable personalities in the intel-lectual history of California, came to the Pacific as a kind of surrealist druid. The poet Philip Lamantia, who became California's most famous orthodox Surrealist, was drawn to the movement by its historic revolu-tionary, erotic, and mystical aspects. Onslow Ford had already gone be-yond that "tradition." He was the only Briton to be fully accepted into the Surrealist inner circle in Paris and the last major figure to join the Surrealists during their "heroic" period. By the time he arrived on the West Coast he had already become a guiding figure in efforts, both in Europe and in New York, to further expand the technical possibilities of plastic art and, as he put it, "to offer a deepening of consciousness in Art." Unlike some Surrealist visitors to northern California, he came to stay.

Gordon Onslow Ford was born in 1912 in England. As a youth, he en-tered into a maritime career, serving in junior grades aboard British vessels and graduating from the Royal Naval College at Dartmouth. However he decided to become a painter, and resigned from the Royal Navy in 1937 after exhibiting with the French Surrealists. He rented a studio in Paris with the Chilean painter Roberto Sebastián Matta Echaurren. Matta was one of the most gifted young acquisitions of the Surrealist movement, and the two became close and synergistic friends. In 1939, Onslow Ford was introduced to André Breton and invited to become a member of the surrealist group.

Soon Breton reproduced one of Onslow Ford's paintings in the luxurious review *Minotaure.*

Onslow Ford came to the United States the next year, and was a sparkling component of a stratum of exiled modernists whose flight from wartime Europe revolutionized the New York art world. But Onslow Ford was more than a cultivated and accomplished visitor contributing to the new universe of painting; he and Matta formed a "cell" that actively investigated the interior life of the painter. They believed, in Onslow Ford's words, "that the future of the artist lay in the unconscious *beyond* dreams—a new subject that necessitated new techniques of expression, a new subject in a new language. Matta called this direction 'psychological morphology.'" Above all, Onslow Ford was concerned with "automatism," the Surrealist method of spontaneous creation that led directly to the gestural "action painting" of certain Abstract Expressionists. When, in 1941, Onslow Ford lectured on Surrealism at the New School for Social Research, his audience included Arshile Gorky, Jackson Pollock, William Baziotes, Robert Motherwell, and other pioneers of the new style. In this period Onslow Ford produced some remarkable "biomorphic" paintings, such as *The Circuit of the Light Knight Through the Dark Queen* (1942). In this stunning work, Onslow Ford professed to have presented "a new world seen in a new way; an anthropomorphic landscape in which the painter is born and makes his circuit."

While in New York he met a California poet, Jacqueline Johnson, whom he married; the couple went to live in a village on the shores of Lake Pátzcuaro, in Mexico, in 1941. In Mexico Onslow Ford met Charles Howard and renewed his relationship with Wolfgang Paalen, whom he had met in Paris and who was now living in Mexico City and publishing an extremely heterodox art journal, *Dyn.* Onslow Ford and Johnson moved to the Bay Area in 1947, settling in San Francisco. Two years later Onslow Ford purchased the ferryboat *Vallejo,* moored at the Marinship boatyard on Richardson Bay north of Sausalito and destined to become a major monument of Bay Area intellectual life, in partnership with Yanko Varda and Forrest Wright. Onslow Ford and Johnson were joined intellectually by another California artist, Lee Mullican, and soon by Paalen, who moved to a house on Magee Street in Mill Valley, a beautiful, wooded resort town at the foot of Mount Tamalpais, just north of San Francisco, where, as sunlight penetrated the cathedral space among the redwoods, life was enacted, not merely lived.

Onslow Ford had a retrospective at S.F.M.A. in 1948, and, to accompany it, the museum published a theoretical monograph by the artist, *Towards a New Subject in Painting.* This slender volume was memorable in the local history of typography as well as in art theory, for it was designed and printed by Jack Werner Stauffacher of The Greenwood Press, along with Adrian Wilson, the typographer who had gone through the Waldport C.O. camp with William Everson. Stauffacher's brother Frank had "created the Art in Cinema program at S.F.M.A., the first film society of its kind in this country outside the Museum of Modern Art in New York," Jack Stauffacher later recalled. "The list of films that he showed was very *avant-garde* and surreal, the first time anybody in this town had seen them." Jack Stauffacher had been introduced to the Onslow Ford circle by Lee Mullican, whom he met during his Army service. "I said, 'When you get out of the Army, come and stay with me in San Mateo,' Stauffacher recalled. "He then came out and became connected with Onslow Ford and Paalen. I was the messenger." Jack Stauffacher, as a refined and restrained classicist in book design, curiously suited the tastes of Onslow Ford and other Surrealists; unlike their Dadaist forebears, the Surrealists had never done much as typographic experimentalists. Stauffacher's exquisitely tranquil page and type sensibility exemplified the highest attainment in art publishing.

In *Towards A New Subject in Painting,* which was illustrated with his own works—as well as those of Matta, Esteban Francés, Yves Tanguy, Wolfgang Paalen, Yanko Varda, Mullican, Giorgio de Chirico, Victor Brauner, Man Ray, Max Ernst, Joan Miró, Paul Delvaux, and Charles Howard—Onslow Ford sought to rationalize and clarify the formal principles that had inspired the great Surrealists, for the benefit of a fresh audience on the West Coast. The book included an essay, "Notes On My World," that begins, "I like the idea of an expanding universe and growing consciousness." Onslow Ford affirmed,

> I am a visionary. . . . In dreams I have never seen the world I paint, hence I conclude that it exists on some other level of the mind. . . . I have the feeling that everything in my world floats and that the personages and their surroundings are interactive, that their exact positions in relation to each other are determined by forces of repulsion and attraction. . . . . I no longer feel the need to decry the evils of the world, to distort or mutilate the already exist-

ing. I want to invent, to build, to love. . . . I like to think of myself as a primitive of a new civilization in the making.

Under the influence of the Mill Valley landscape, Onslow Ford's style changed drastically. He later recalled,

> I was very deeply impressed with the magnificent redwoods and the rolling hills on the Coast Range and when I first came here, I was making paintings influenced by the redwoods, a lot of paintings with parallel lines in them. I used to walk on Mt. Tamalpais . . . and it suddenly came to me, I think it was induced by the landscape, that the root of art was line, circle, and dot. . . . I came back and started making landscapes with line, circle, and dot, and I abandoned everything else.

This "environmental consciousness," similar to that of John Ferren in painting and Kenneth Rexroth in literature, was distinctly Californian.

Notwithstanding his considerable energy and intelligence, however, Onslow Ford was subordinate as an artist and thinker to Wolfgang Paalen, the central figure in this grouping as long as he was in the Bay Area. Paalen, born in Vienna in 1905, had become a Surrealist in the late 1930s, after a distinguished career in abstraction, and was immediately recognized as one of Surrealism's major talents. Prior to his affiliation with Surrealism, he was strongly influenced by a meeting in Provence with Yanko Varda, who helped liberate his outlook on the resources available to the painter. Paalen produced some of the most famous works in the Surrealist iconography, such as a series, *Combat[s] of the Saturnian Princes* (1938), widely seen as prefiguring the coming of World War II. Gustav Regler, a German ex-Communist author, a former commissar of the International Brigades in the Spanish Civil War, and a commentator on Paalen, said of the *Combat* series, "One has to go back as far as Bosch and Grünewald in order to find a vision of equal terror." *San Francisco Chronicle* art critic Alfred Frankenstein wrote in 1948 that the Austrian's surrealist paintings were "highly unorthodox . . . grim, stormy and disturbing pictures."

Paalen was fascinated by non-European art, particularly by Native American styles, both of the Northwest Coast of the United States and Canada and of Mexico. European painters beginning with the Cubists professed a fascination with African art, though most often they knew it only via images corrupted by the tourist trade in souvenirs. But Paalen's interest proved more serious. He was a pioneering scholar in the field of Northwest Native art. Described by Onslow Ford as "the last of the German romantics," he had something in common with Chamisso, who had navigated along the coast of California and Alaska in the early nineteenth century. The Surrealists were enthusiasts of the obsessional, and while still in Europe, Paalen began to fantasize a kind of alternate, interior Pacific Coast we might call "Paalenland," represented by such paintings as the magnificent *Fata Alaska* (1937), one of the most spectacular of all Surrealist paintings, and by his series of *Totemic Landscape[s] of My Childhood.* Before settling in Mexico he had traveled in 1939 by train and boat to British Columbia and Alaska in a quest for totemic art with his first wife, the Surrealist poet and painter Alice Rahon, and the Swiss photographer Eva Sulzer. The Northwest Coast was then still far off the beaten path for most Europeans, and even for many North Americans. Regler commented that Paalen was astonished "when he found with what certainty he had felt the atmosphere of the country around Sitka in his 'Fata Alaska,' before actually seeing it."

Such premonitions and supernatural awareness had always played a major role in Surrealism. Paalen wrote of that journey,

> Accustomed to travel leaning out, I would never, however, have believed it possible to forget the vehicle so completely. The rails in these woods become too abstract a hyphen, a foot-bridge too narrow and incomprehensible on the precipice of the centuries. . . . [O]n the single artery of these imponderable distances—no road yet links British Columbia to the rest of Canada—from hour to hour the acuteness of a physical sensation is so strongly sharpened that one would be tempted to stipulate the rudiments of a new sense in gestation: the sense of dimension.

The "sense of dimension" made it impossible for Paalen to remain within the confines of pictorial Surrealism, which he abandoned as he had, previously, left behind pure abstraction. Parallel with Onslow Ford and Matta, Paalen began "a more direct kind of automatism, an automatism that was not later interpreted," according to Onslow Ford. Paalen considered his 1940 painting, *Somewhere in Me,* crucial to this development; about that time, he held what he believed would be his last show of Surrealist work. According to Regler, "Even though he did not at that time foresee the rapid decline of Surrealism, he was convinced, after his stay in New York, that Surrealism had lost its revolutionary impulse." After moving to

Mexico City and launching *Dyn,* he announced his "Farewell to Surrealism," a "break" which was remarkably cordial. Belying his reputation as an intellectual tyrant, André Breton favored this "dissident" from the Surrealist ranks, trusting him, as a representative of youth, to mark out a new path. Paalen was joined by Breton and the Peruvian poet César Moro in producing an international Surrealist exhibition in Mexico City, and Paalen rejoined the "official" Surrealists in the 1950s. In the meantime, however, *Dyn* and a collection of Paalen's essays, *Form and Sense,* exercised a considerable influence in the New York art environment.

In 1939, the same year he went to Alaska, Paalen began a prescient, almost clairvoyant inquiry into post-Einsteinian physics, to learn "what is right with science and why it works—and what is wrong with art in our time and why it does not work." He perceived in Surrealism a triumph of the irrational, and in "science" (mainly as then represented in the intellectual world by Marxism) the dominance of reason. Suddenly, his goal was to merge them. He wrote,

> Science and art both have their roots in the imagination; form and sense cannot be separated since no mental concept can become intelligible without assuming a form. But it is equally false to try to poetize science (surrealist error) as to try to make a scientific art (abstract error). . . . If it is only through science that one can find the practical means to ameliorate the human condition, it is only through art that our imagination can discover the pattern of values for which these means are to be used. . . . After the failure of religion, art is, perhaps, our last chance for a new humanism.

Alfred Frankenstein observed that, in leaving figurative Surrealism, Paalen moved away from the pessimistic tone of the *Combat of the Saturnian Princes* series to a Mexican-influenced spirit that was "mystical yet positive . . . as if he had closed the sinister Pandora's box of Surrealism, made peace with himself, and devoted himself to clarification rather than turmoil." Jacqueline Johnson, Lee Mullican, Onslow Ford, and Paalen formed a movement called "the Dynaton," and showed their work at S.F.M.A. in 1951. In an accompanying essay (also printed in a beautiful pamphlet by Jack Stauffacher), Paalen defined the "Theory of the Dynaton." The concept was "not identical with, but derived from το δψνατον," Greek for *the possible,* and Paalen wrote,

> In my definition, the *Dynatón* is a limitless continuum, in which all forms of reality are potentially implicit. So that there would be no *ultimate* space-

time-continuum; spatio-temporal manifestations being only the functional conditions of *realization* of the Dynaton. Which means, the manifestations through which the potential comes within human range.

Octavio Paz wrote of Paalen, "The very nature of his work—always in motion—opposes a vision of the whole. . . . [His work], which we cannot yet see in the proper perspective," represented for Paz "a succession of spiritual battles." As his formal quest progressed, Paalen's art became "cosmic," beginning with *Space Unbound* (1941), and continuing through portraits of "cosmogons," "aerogyls," and other transdimensional beings. Albright commented that Paalen's later works "were based on short, gestural strokes of rich color that suggested the faceting of stained glass; they remained abstract, but suggested images of totems or guardian figures." Paalen's disquisitions about art and science, complementing his radical views on painterly technique, could not but attract considerable attention in postwar California, after the power of science had been dramatically illustrated by the development of the atomic bomb.

A similar interest had, unsurprisingly, seized Bern Porter, the disaffected Manhattan project participant. In 1948, while living in the bay-fishing and shipyard port of Sausalito, just south of Mill Valley, he published a text entitled *The Union of Science and Art,* later retitled the *Sciart Manifesto.* Influenced by the Dynaton, Porter declared (in a 1954 version of the manifesto), "Finite worlds of infinite reality and beauty revealed by the tools and discoveries of Science are ripe for aesthetic development." He inventoried the aspects of science he believed were best suited to art, involving light; other vibrations such as sound, electrical, and thermal waves; movement; phenomena like isotopy, relativity, and entropy; and devices such as the cyclotron and the cloud chamber, in addition to disciplines including crystallography and astrophysics. It all added up to a powerful foreshadowing, not unlike that of Henry Cowell twenty years earlier, of the rise of Silicon Valley and the information revolution. Man Ray, while in Europe, had similarly made good use of scientific and industrial processes in photography, but in general such considerations were characteristic of Surrealism only in California, where the barriers between the scientific and aesthetic intellect seemed destined to crumble, and were largely absent from Surrealist and "neo-Surrealist" activities elsewhere around the world. Wolfgang Paalen, according to Lee Mullican, "felt that there was an intellectual climate in San Francisco where something could really happen." Decades later, Onslow Ford remained fascinated by new developments in physics, including some put forward by the associate of Oppenheimer and later giant of quantum theory, David Bohm.

In the California art scene, the Communist intellectuals had been soundly repudiated. However, they continued to exercise an influence in literary life, and to capture the attention of the press as they capered before the investigating committees. Their grasp was demonstrated in 1947 when Chester Himes's *Lonely Crusade* was published; the author found on the day of publication that network radio interviews, store displays, author appearances, and other publicity arranged by his publisher, Alfred Knopf, had all been canceled. "The Communist Party had launched a real assault on the book," he later recalled. "It had some of the most terrible reviews, one of the most vicious reviews I ever read." A Communist periodical printed a cartoon of Himes as a Black man bearing a white flag, and a review compared Himes with a foul-mouthed white racist politician from Mississippi, Theodore Bilbo. An advance on his next book from Knopf vanished, and his career began disappearing, so that he was reduced to working menial jobs. His marriage broke up. Eventually he left for Europe, where he lived the rest of his life, first in France, then in Spain.

Yet, even as the Communist intelligentsia acted to silence a Black author of great genius, they continued playing the victim well. In December 1947, the "Hollywood Ten" were indicted by a federal grand jury for their refusal to tell J. Parnell Thomas and the House Committee on Un-American Activities whether or not they were Communists, and all were sentenced to short prison terms. For many Americans, the idea of such a punishment for so marginal a bunch was more than a bit absurd; the jailings proved a victory for the "Ten," not for Thomas. But the treatment of the "Hollywood Ten" had a more serious outcome for the movie industry in general: studios, employees, labor organizations, and the Communists themselves surrendered to confusion and panic. The studio management feared that Hollywood would be permanently tainted with Communist associations; actors, writers, and others who had either joined or supported the Communists faced the probability that they too could be called as witnesses. None of the "unfriendly witnesses" could be considered indispensable to the industry, notwithstanding the privileged position of such as Dalton Trumbo; as a result the so-called "Hollywood blacklist" came into existence, as studio bosses tried to discern who in their industry could be labeled a Communist and as film-industry workers sought to clear their names.

The so-called "blacklist" was a confused and tragic phenomenon; in the overall convulsion over Communism in Hollywood there were, as Trumbo himself averred many years later, "only victims." The much-alleged intention of the studio bosses to use the "blacklist" against the powerful cinema unions, as charged by the "Ten," was imaginary. Furthermore, the "suffering" imposed on screenwriters such as Trumbo, which largely consisted of their having to work under a pseudonym and at a reduced but still high fee, was mild when compared with the torture, mass imprisonment, and other punishments imposed on the Wobblies in California after World War I. Tom Mooney languished for more than twenty years in San Quentin, whereas Alvah Bessie, for example, drew a one-year sentence in a federal "white-collar" correctional institution; yet to hear the Communists tell it, the "Ten" were martyrs of the intellect comparable to Galileo, in an America that had entered inexorably on the road to fascist repression.

This was the most significant, and most unremarked, aspect of the long Hollywood controversy: the strange success with which the Communists successfully imposed their self-image as scapegoats on American (and international) opinion. The Communists had always behaved as if they were utterly above criticism; any expression of an outlook at odds with theirs or a rebuke to their posturings, however minor, they condemned as vile propaganda in the service of immoral (and, according to them, unconstitutional) attempts to suppress them. In the dispute with the Thomas Committee over Hollywood the Communists argued, in so many words, that the rest of the country was obligated to defend them whether it was in agreement with their Stalinism or not. Their "right to think unpopular thoughts" was at stake, they asserted. But in reality the only issue in question was their active and illicit service to a foreign dictatorship, of which the F.B.I. and the legislative committees had considerable reason for investigation. Few in the United States had even conceived of a "right" to be a Nazi or fascist agent. (However, Franklin Roosevelt's attorney general, Francis Biddle, had sought to protect the freedom of speech of Axis sympathizers, so long as nothing worse than speech was involved.)

Overnight, however, Americans were called on to guarantee the "rights" of Communists, who had served a foreign country's totalitarianism and expansionism far more brazenly than the American Nazis and fascists had ever thought of doing. The Communists had never hesitated to defend the worst of Stalin's atrocities; but they objected strenuously when called to account for defending them. The Communists backed up their assertion of a "right" to be protected from public scrutiny by labeling any and every opponent, but especially those who had broken with them, as "stool pigeons," "informers," and other insults borrowed from the vocabulary of the underworld. Edward Dmytryk, who broke with the rest of the "Ten," described the belief that "naming names [was] a greater crime than subversion" as the "Mafia syndrome." Of course, there could be no "informers" in the absence of some criminal activity to inform about—but this logical detail was ignored.

A truly gigantic and unending campaign ensued among American intellectuals to prevent anybody from airing any negative information or opinion on Communism; it soon required much more courage for intellectuals to testify against the Communists before the investigative committees than to keep silence, deride such investigations, or otherwise declaim as Communists did when subpoenaed. "Unfriendly witnesses" were hailed as heroes of unfettered thought, while those whose testimony reflected a real attempt to understand Communism were defamed as liars. The Communists believed that many Californians would, because of their psychology and culture, dislike "snitches" more than "Stalinists," and they proved to be right.

The propaganda campaign in favor of the "Ten" assumed a ridiculously exaggerated tone. Communist screenwriter Gordon Kahn's book on the case, *Hollywood on Trial,* described the hostile witnesses as "some of Hollywood's most distinguished authors, stars, directors, and producers." An appendix to the volume included some hysterical comments by such distinguished political scientists as Judy Garland, who pleaded, "Before every free conscience in America is subpoenaed, please speak up!" The noted public philosopher Lucille Ball added, "All of us agree that the Constitution of the United States must be defended! But the way to do this is not by shutting up the man you disagree with: you must fight for his right to speak and be heard." Myrna Loy chimed in, "We question the right of any official to abuse citizens in order to make headlines. We question the right of Congress to ask any man what he thinks on political issues." Of course, few such individuals had raised such objections when Nazis, rather than Stalinists, faced investigation.

The real aim of this strategy of the Communists was less to mobilize the American people behind them than to present to the world an image of the United States as a country of gross political persecution, virtually a fascist state, so as to divert attention from the ghastly dictatorship in Moscow, which was then carrying out fresh, bloody, and explicitly anti-Semitic purges. Such Soviet attacks on Western democracy also anticipated the new world war Stalin was preparing. Another element in this "peace offensive" was the 1948 presidential campaign of Henry Wallace and the "Independent Progressive Party" (I.P.P.), as it was called in California. Its name was an obvious misnomer (somewhat like that of the Holy Roman Empire) since it was neither independent, being an appendage of the Communists, nor "progressive," acting as it did in the interests of Stalin's fascism, and it was a conspiracy rather than a legitimate political party. As the nation approached the presidential balloting in November, debate over the Wallace candidacy among authentic liberals and in the union movement became notably bitter, particularly after the so-called "Dixiecrats" or "States' Rights Democrats," a faction of Southern white politicians violently opposed to President Truman's commitments to Black civil rights, bolted the Democratic Party and announced it would offer, as a "fourth party" candidate, Senator J. Strom Thurmond of South Carolina. Increasingly, mainstream Democrats faced the outrageous possibility that a Stalin-controlled apparatus would help put Thomas Dewey, a Republican, in the White House.

Wallace had previously been denounced by Walter Reuther, the most innovative and effective union leader in the country, as a proponent of a Communist scheme to further split the labor movement. Reuther's criticism came after Wallace, then editor of the *New Republic,* denounced Reuther's militant demand for a 23.5-cents-per-hour raise in the auto industry as impulsive and irresponsible, and falsely reported in his magazine's pages that Reuther was at odds with C.I.O. president Philip Murray. But Wallace's main concern was foreign policy, where his line was unwaveringly in favor of submission to Stalin, disguised as "understanding with Russia." Wallace was unfazed by the probability that Stalin had the means to produce an atom bomb; there was no "atomic secret," he preached, and nuclear weapons must be placed under international control, "in a sincere attempt to find world salvation." The possibility that American sincerity would not be matched by a similar attitude on the part of Stalin apparently never occurred to Wallace or other fellow travelers.

IN DECEMBER 1947 Franklin D. Roosevelt, Jr., had appealed to Wallace not to leave the Democrats, but without success. Wallace declared his candidacy for the White House, running with an amiably dumb and opportunistic politician from Idaho, ex-Democrat Senator Glen Taylor, as his vice president. A major goal of the I.P.P. was to try to lead former EPIC supporters out of the California Democratic Party, and in June 1948, Upton Sinclair himself telegraphed Wallace, calling on him to return to the party so as to avoid a Republican victory. But Sinclair had been consigned to the ranks of the reactionaries by the Communists and their "Progressive" puppets. The month before, Wallace swung through California, boasting of large donations to the I.P.P. in Hollywood by Charlie Chaplin, an egregious fellow traveler, film director Lewis Milestone, and various Communist-lining screenwriters. In the Bay Area, Wallace's campaign efforts relied on Bridges's I.L.W.U. and other Communist-run C.I.O. unions, leading Wallace to denounce the waterfront employers for seeking to abolish the maritime hiring halls—an eventuality that, somewhat like the supposed desire of the Hollywood studio bosses to break the talent guilds, never materialized in any serious form.

In a San Francisco speech, with Bridges himself presiding, Wallace brayed that "the Number One job today is a peace agreement between the United States and the Soviet Union," and claimed that opposition to Communism was really hatred of democracy, reflecting "an all-out attack on civil liberties, trade unions, individual enterprise, and the living standards of the American people." But the only civil liberties that had been questioned consisted of the freedom of American Communists to serve as Stalin's agents; individual enterprise was booming as never before; and the American people were beginning to enjoy the longest and most bountiful period of prosperity in history. Meanwhile, in the mainstream labor movement, Max Zaritsky, president of the A.F.L. Hatters Union, released a report blasting the Wallace movement as "an adventure that can serve the interests only of reaction and the Communists," and Wallace himself for "impudently" claiming to speak for labor. "Wallace talks labor and acts Communist; he talks liberal and acts reactionary," the Zaritsky document insisted.

Above all, the threat of war, actively embodied by Stalin, was used by Wallace and the I.P.P. to promote sentiments in favor of surrender to Russia. If Russia was totalitarian, according to Wallace, then resistance to Stalin's aggression would make the United States totalitarian as well. According to Wallace, Russia offered "absolutely no threat" to Western democracy, which was, rather, being undermined by American-backed fascism and atomic warmongering. The differences between the two systems were merely a matter of a failure to communicate adequately, he promised, as if the absence of competent English and Russian translators were the problem. Much of Wallace's rhetoric involved deliberate and obvious deception, as when he claimed that "the variation in Communists is as great as it is in Republicans or Democrats" and disingenuously added that since the constitution of the American Communist Party was "against overthrow of the government by force," he would be pleased to accept their support, so long as he did not have to become involved with revolutionary extremists. In reality, there had been no revolutionaries in the Communist ranks for quite a long time; a revolutionary was by no means the same thing as a KGB agent.

A "variation" such as Wallace claimed to appreciate had, it could be argued, appeared in the Soviet-dominated buffer zone of Eastern Europe at the end of June 1948, when Stalin's propaganda machine issued a public attack on the Yugoslav Communist dictator Tito. But the Wallaceites remained silent about Tito, because his situation reflected badly on the "friendly socialist cooperation" supposedly practiced between Moscow and its satellites. It must be said, however, that, particularly after the Tito-Stalin break, Wallace's constituency began to shrink visibly, as fewer and fewer Americans maintained any illusions about Wallace's delusions. In October 1948, only two weeks before the election, California congresswoman Helen Gahagan Douglas, a Democrat opposed (and smeared as a near-Red) by Richard Nixon, voiced a final appeal to Wallace to withdraw from the race in favor of Truman, even as she blasted Dewey for seeking to put atomic energy in private hands. Helen Douglas had been endorsed by the I.P.P., under the still-functioning California cross-filing system, but she spurned their backing. Within days of Helen Douglas's speech, former California attorney general Robert W. Kenny, head of a "Democrats for Wallace" front, smugly announced that Tom Dewey, the Republican candidate, would win, but that the I.P.P. would receive a half million votes in California and by 1952 the Democrat party would be controlled by the Wallaceites.

Kenny was wrong on all counts. Truman won; Wallace received only 190,000 votes in California and 1.15 million ballots nationally (yielding no electoral votes at all), compared with 24 million popular (and 303 electoral) votes for Truman and 22 million popular (189 electoral) votes for Dewey; the "Progressives" were even outpolled by the Dixiecrats, who received 1.17 million popular (and 39 electoral) votes. The *San Francisco Chronicle* editorialized that the result was "a clear and unmistakable repudiation of Soviet appeasement." The editorial added, "His watching mentors in Moscow must have gotten little comfort from their man's performance."

Few union workers or other voters who belonged to constituencies targeted by the Wallaceites—Blacks, women, and intellectuals—ended up voting for Wallace. The only layer of society in which the movement seemed to find an echo was among college youth. It could be said that the Communists had gone from focusing on the recruitment of radical workers to targeting middle-class fellow travelers, and then college students, their least sophisticated and least influential milieu for catching souls. However, in Los Angeles, where their racial agitation during the Stalin-Hitler pact had fostered the emergence of Black protest, the Wallace campaign similarly set off an unanticipated development in the form of "Bachelors for Wallace," a campaign group established by a well-known Communist, 36-year-old Harry Hay. The "bachelors" in the group's name were homosexual men, and Harry Hay was arguably the main originator of the gay rights movement.

Hay was inspired to create "Bachelors for Wallace" in August 1948, after joining John Howard Lawson, Herbert Biberman, and other movie-industry personalities in filing nomination petitions for the so-called "third party" standard-bearer. But Hay represented the other side of Hollywood Communism, counterposed to the glamorous existence of the "Ten." He was a volunteer, an "activist" at the lowest level of party work, a fixture in various fronts, and a Stalinist fanatic. An example of that attitude came to light during Herb Sorrell's early Hollywood ructions: a friend who was beaten up on a picket line in one of Sorrell's strikes found Hay completely unsympathetic, since the Party had not yet officially abandoned its wartime no-strike pledge.

Harry Hay was also then, within the community of Los Angeles Communists, thoroughly "closeted"—indeed, not only did he publicly claim to be heterosexual, he was married and, with his wife, adopted two girls.

(Thus he was not himself a bachelor, for Wallace or otherwise.) Homosexuality as an emotional affinity, to say nothing of the status of homosexuals in society, was a prohibited topic in Communist ranks (no less than in Hollywood films) and homosexuals were officially barred from joining the Party. A crude "Marxist" analysis of homosexuality presented it as a repellent feature of capitalist decadence—a prejudice that had been thoroughly repudiated in the anarchist circles of Emma Goldman and Alexander Berkman some thirty years before. Nevertheless, according to long-time *People's World* editor Al Richmond, the Communists never hesitated to recruit individual homosexuals when their strategic value to the Party outweighed the stigma of their queerdom. An additional "official" pretext for so primitive a view of human psychology was that homosexuals constituted a "security risk" for the Party, since they could presumably be blackmailed by the police into revealing Party secrets; the propriety of secret Party work, and the need to so protect it, was seldom questioned. (The U.S. State Department barred homosexuals similarly, because they could be blackmailed by foreign agents; but the State Department, at least, had legitimate secrets to keep.) Once again, the Communists demanded the right to engage in underground operations, to withhold clandestine information from the general public, and to do so under the protection of the American constitution. This was a posture never imagined by their predecessors, the Wobblies and Socialists; they dedicated their lives to their beliefs but conducted their affairs in the open and took responsibility for their radicalism. The Communists, on the other hand, claimed total innocence of treason and espionage and ascribed all accusations of such to a frame-up by the Truman Administration. They were not even "radicals," just "progressives."

Harry Hay had encountered Wobblies in his youth, but his Communist career began under the influence of Party stalwart Will Geer, actor and political leader, then known as Bill. Meeting in a theater cast, they became lovers. The pair showed up together in San Francisco in July 1934, at the height of the maritime strike. From the beginning, Hay seems to have sought to organize gays in the same fashion as the Party drew in workers, Blacks, women, and other groups. But though he submitted to Party rules, an unease gnawed at Hay for years as he tried to sort out his loyalty to the Party and his deeper drives, all the while acting in small productions, running meetings for the Film and Foto League (an organizational sibling of the "literary" John Reed Clubs), handing out leaflets for the Hollywood

Anti-Nazi League, and otherwise diffusing his energy in the repetitive tasks the Party favored. In the late 1930s Harry Hay participated in a short film that satirized Surrealism, *Even—As You and I,* and he later became a fixture in People's Songs, Inc., a front group established in the image of Woody Guthrie, Pete Seeger, and the other minstrels of Communist cabaret life. For the benefit of the latter, he developed a course in "The Historical Development of Folk Music."

Given the absymally low intellectual quality of California Communist endeavors after World War II, it should be no surprise that when Harry Hay finally "came out" with his arguments in favor of homosexuals organizing themselves, he did so under the purported aegis of none other than Josef Stalin himself. Hay's biographer, Stuart Timmons, writes blithely, "Since 1941, Harry had taught Stalin's four principles of a minority; these were a common language, a common territory, a common economy, and a common psychology and culture." Timmons then quotes Hay: "I felt we had two of the four, the language and the culture, so clearly we were a social minority." According to Chester Himes, the status of homosexuals as an oppressed minority had been argued by California Communists much earlier; but, local precedents aside, Hay's "theory" was as absurd as Stalin's was fraudulent.

It is extremely interesting that neither Hay, nor Timmons, nor the editor of Hay's (selected) writings, Will Roscoe, seems to have been aware that Robert Duncan had already dealt with many of the deeper issues which the Mattachine Society, Hay's successor organization to "Bachelors for Wallace," would eventually seek to address. It would be hard to imagine a greater difference in personality than that between Harry Hay and Robert Duncan, although it is tempting to ascribe the contrast simply to the previously noted divergence in style between radicalism in Los Angeles and in the Bay Area. Desiring their own sex, and risking the terrors of casual encounters to fulfull their passion, was about all they had in common. Both attempted "straight" marriages, but Duncan quickly abandoned the lie, whereas Hay long maintained it. Hay was typically described by his friends and lovers as intellectually fascinating and charismatic, but he lacked Duncan's really striking beauty and physical presence. Duncan, a true rebel and independent spirit, was a central figure in a highly accomplished redefinition of American poetry, while Hay was a hanger-on, a participant in superficial, pseudocultural projects such as People's Songs. Hay and his cohort performed for the "masses" as they imagined them to be, while Duncan always hewed to a superior literary ideal.

Above all, and to his great credit, Robert Duncan never fell for Stalinism or its cattle-herding manipulation of minorities, recognized or not. Duncan was no special pleader, except in favor of literature, and he hated the acceptance of a "ghetto" existence. When in 1944 he published an essay, *The Homosexual in Society,* in Dwight Macdonald's anti-Stalinist journal *Politics,* Duncan went beyond a call for the broader society to "recognize homosexuals as equals and as equals allow them neither more nor less than can be allowed any human being." He assailed the "homosexual cult of superiority," blasted the influence of this "cult" in literary and artistic life, and concluded with the remarkable affirmation that "only one devotion can be held by a human being" seeking "a creative life and expression, and that is a devotion to human freedom, toward the liberation of human love, human conflicts, human aspirations. To do this one must disown all the special groups (nations, religions, sexes, races) that would claim allegiance." He even called for "battle against the inhumanity of his own group (be it against patriotism, against bigotry, against, in this specific case, the homosexual cult)." Duncan knew his subculture, for this essay was one of the first to note the use of the term "gay" as a self-applied label; but he also knew his dialectics, and he wittily compared the exaltation of the "gay" poet Hart Crane by the "homosexual cult" to that of Lenin by the Soviet government. Encountering the legacy of Crane, reduced to "a painted mummy," Duncan wrote, "one may tiptoe by, as the visitors to Lenin's tomb tiptoe by, and, once outside, find themselves in a world that in his name has celebrated the defeat of all that he was devoted to."

Harry Hay and his admirers made a great deal of the antihomosexual discrimination by the police that led the Mattachine Society to meet secretly in Los Angeles. But the irrepressible Robert Duncan had suffered a far more substantial punishment for publishing *The Homosexual in Society.* Ekbert Faas describes how, soon after the essay appeared, Duncan received an anguished letter from John Crowe Ransom, editor of the *Kenyon Review* and then among the leading American critics. Ransom had accepted for print one of Duncan's works, "An African Elegy," influenced by the (likewise homosexual) Federico García Lorca. But after reading *The Homosexual in Society,* with its argument for a more direct articulation of homosexuality in literature, Ransom abruptly perceived in the "Elegy" an "obvious homosexual advertisement," and rejected it, even though it was already typeset. Here was yet another setback for the young Duncan, who had seen the *Kenyon Review* publication as his first access to a major journal. (The "Elegy" itself is actually too oblique in its imagery to justify Ransom's anxieties.) It is doubtful that Hay, the rigid Stalinist, would have sympathized.

WHILE MYSTICAL ANARCHISTS like Duncan and Communists like Harry Hay pondered the emergence of homosexuals as an "oppressed minority," a legal affair beginning in 1949 dramatized the old and continuing abuses suffered by Japanese-Americans on the West Coast: the treason trial of Iva Toguri d'Aquino, accused of broadcasting anti-American propaganda from Japan during World War II as "Tokyo Rose." Duncan, who despised such persecutions and had argued in defense of Ezra Pound (who had broadcast anti-Allied propaganda from Italy), would probably have sympathized with her plight. Hay, as a loyal Stalinist, would have echoed the Communists, who repeated their dismal 1941 performance on *Nikkei* rights by joining the outcry against Mrs. d'Aquino.

Mrs. d'Aquino, a *Nisei*, had in fact broadcast on Japanese radio during the war. However, rather like a figure out of a Surrealist poem, she was now accused of being someone who had never existed. "Tokyo Rose" was a generic nickname given by U.S. service personnel in the Pacific theater to any of a number of women who broadcast music and light commentary in English on Japanese radio, some of whom also spoke anti-Allied propaganda. For her part, Mrs. d'Aquino had identified herself while speaking over the radio as "Orphan Ann," and claimed she never indulged in such remarks. There was no such single person as "Tokyo Rose."

This minor factual problem did not faze Clark Lee, a Hearst newspaper reporter, and Harry Brundidge, a writer for Hearst's *Cosmopolitan* magazine. At the end of the war Lee burst into print, in the *Los Angeles Examiner*, with the claim that Mrs. d'Aquino was "the one and only Tokyo Rose." Lee and Brundidge had gone to Japan and found that of some dozens of broadcasters for Japanese radio, Mrs. d'Aquino was the only *Nisei* who had refused to accept Japanese citizenship; because of this act of American patriotism, paradoxically, she was the only Japanese wartime broadcaster who could be charged with treason against the United States. As in their earlier harassment of Henry Miller, the Hearst publications demonstrated in the "Tokyo Rose" case that truth meant nothing to them. Brundidge convinced the American military authorities in Japan that Mrs. d'Aquino should be arrested; she was jailed for a year without charges or trial, but was fully investigated by the U.S. Army, and released in May 1946 after it was concluded that she had not committed treason. A second inquiry by the U.S. Justice Department affirmed the finding of innocence.

Mrs. d'Aquino had one desire after the war: to return to her native United States. The ordeal of Iva Toguri, then in her mid-twenties and unmarried, had begun in summer 1941, when she visited Japan to attend a sick relative. She had graduated from the University of California at Los Angeles the year before, and, totally assimilated, spoke no Japanese. Caught in Japan after Pearl Harbor, she was pressured by the Japanese government to renounce her American citizenship but steadfastly refused to do so. Yet she was twice denied evacuation from Japan by ship, and the American government would not confirm her status as a citizen. Meanwhile, the rest of the Toguri family had been removed from Los Angeles to the internment camp at Gila Bend, Arizona.

Iva Toguri was considered an enemy alien by the authorities in Japan. Stranded, she searched for means to support herself—with considerable difficulty, precisely because of her loyalty to the United States. After attempting to work as a piano teacher, she was employed by the Danish legation in Tokyo; she was later hired as an English-language typist by the Domei News Agency, and in 1943 began working as a typist at Radio Tokyo. A group of Allied prisoners of war had arrived at Radio Tokyo, and were commanded to broadcast in English under threat of execution. They included an American, Captain Wallace Ince; an Australian, Major Charles Cousens; and a Filipino, Lieutenant Norman Reyes. Cousens had refused to work for the Japanese radio until directly ordered to do so by a higher-ranking prisoner of war. The trio were assigned to a program called *Zero Hour,* which would be exclusively entertainment, although Ince, Cousens, and Reyes subverted the Japanese effort through satirical references that Allied servicemen would understand but the Japanese did not. Iva Toguri was brought onto the program to function as an announcer; at first she refused, but was convinced to do so by Cousens. As noted by all commentators on the "Tokyo Rose" case, none of the hundreds of scripts for the program was written by Iva Toguri, and none of the U.S. prisoners of war who broadcast them was effectively prosecuted. Ince was never charged, and a trial of

Cousens in Australia was quashed in mid-proceeding. Iva Toguri was to become the only serious target, thanks to Lee and Brundidge, even after she was twice exonerated.

Not long before the war ended she married a Japanese-Portuguese, Felipe d'Aquino, whom she met at Domei. With the war over, Mrs. d'Aquino's eagerness to get back to California was her undoing. Her attempts to return came to the attention of a far more successful radio personality, Walter Winchell. He denounced her as "Tokyo Rose," as did the popular singer Kate Smith, known for her renditions of Irving Berlin's *God Bless America.* The controversy was renewed, and Brundidge in particular returned to the hunt. He went back to Japan to gather evidence and recruit witnesses, and wrung a signature on a faked "confession" out of Mrs. d'Aquino. The Justice Department indicted her for treason, and in September 1948 she was flown to San Francisco as a prisoner and turned over to the F.B.I. Her trial on eight counts of treason would be the first such proceeding in California since the Civil War, the Hearst papers crowed.

In the middle of this nightmare, one man stepped forward to defend Iva Toguri d'Aquino: lawyer Wayne Mortimer Collins, veteran of the Korematsu, Hirabayashi and Endo anti-internment cases. Since then, Collins had been occupied with a lesser series of *Nikkei* civil-rights matters. Just as during the war the American Civil Liberties Union was fainthearted in supporting Collins's legal campaign against internment, the A.C.L.U. now found Mrs. d'Aquino "too hot," according to San Francisco author Dean Lipton, a historian of her case. The Japanese-American Citizens League, which Collins always afterward referred to as "jackals," offered no help to Mrs. d'Aquino. Collins took the case for free, paying court costs out of his own pocket. He recruited attorneys Theodore Tamba, a conservative Republican, and George Olshausen, an occasional pro-Communist, as his assistants, also unpaid.

Collins plunged into the "Tokyo Rose" case with the same zest he had displayed in the internment cases. He and Tamba went to Japan and protested when they were denied access to prison records relevant to Mrs. d'Aquino's defense. The trial began in July 1949 and lasted almost three months. Facing special prosecutor John B. Hogan, who had gone to Japan with Brundidge to fish for evidence, and who was then added to the prosecutorial team, Collins blazed in the courtroom. The dedicated defense attorney confronted Clark Lee, then a national idol as a war correspondent, and accused him and Brundidge of bribing a Japanese witness against Mrs. d'Aquino. Collins challenged Hogan on the conditions under which he and Brundidge had gathered their "evidence," and went on to charge that Lee had conspired with Brundidge to correlate faked notes on an interview with the defendant. But Collins was no less daring outside the courtroom; at one point he broke down a door at San Francisco International Airport to rescue a witness from the F.B.I.

Cousens and Ince appeared, with others, in Mrs. d'Aquino's defense. Numerous veterans who had listened to the broadcasts insisted that "Orphan Ann" only played music and chattered in disk-jockey style, with no propaganda content. The jury returned a hung verdict (10–2 for acquittal), but was then ordered to reach a decision on the grounds of the trial's half-million-dollar cost, a considerable sum at the time. Instructions to the jurors were vague, but finally Mrs. d'Aquino was cleared of seven overt acts of treason and found guilty only of one: count number 6, "That in the fall of 1944 she broadcast, 'Orphans of the Pacific, you really are orphans now. How are you going to get home now that all of your ships are sunk?'" As noted by Dean Lipton, "If this had actually been broadcast in 1944, it would have been regarded by the [American] fighting men in the Pacific as high comedy. However, Mrs. d'Aquino denied broadcasting it. Cousens denied writing it. None of the scripts the government possessed, and none of the few recordings the government kept (it had destroyed most of them) contained these sentences."

Nevertheless, two *Nisei* witnesses who had worked at Radio Tokyo, George Nakamoto Mitsushio and Kenkichi Oki, testified the phrases had been inserted by hand into a script and that they had listened to Mrs. d'Aquino speak them. With the two witnesses necessary for a treason conviction under American constitutional law, Mrs. d'Aquino was found guilty. She was sentenced to ten years in prison and a $10,000 fine. Wayne Collins did not, however, give up; he spent the next twenty-five years fighting to clear her. She was released after six years and two months from a West Virginia women's prison and subjected to an attempted deportation to Japan, which Collins successfully blocked. "In 1949, Wayne Collins could not have realized that this case would occupy the rest of his life," Lipton wrote.

The Communists were hostile to Mrs. d'Aquino; in addition to their disregard for the situation of Japanese-Americans, especially those charged with pro-Axis sentiments, they were then much more concerned with another legal case in San Francisco, one which offered dramatic contrasts in tone with the treason trial of Iva d'Aquino. Soon after her prosecution concluded, Harry Bridges was in court again, charged in the company of two officials of the I.L.W.U., J. R. Robertson and Henry Schmidt, with conspiracy and perjury in Bridges's naturalization as a U.S. citizen in 1945. Bridges had lately been represented by a particularly obnoxious and devious Communist lawyer, Richard Gladstein, but in October 1949 Bridges announced that the firm of Gladstein, Resner, Andersen & Sawyer had been replaced as counsel by attorneys Vincent Hallinan and James Martin MacInnis.

The low-key announcement of this change in legal representation heralded much more; indeed, the sudden appearance of Hallinan as Bridges's lawyer marked the beginning of a whole new epoch in northern California's history, to be deeply influenced by the personalities of Hallinan and his family. As we shall see, the Hallinans had almost no open past associations with the Communists, yet they came to epitomize the fellow-traveling and pro-Communist mentality, particularly in the Bay Area, for the next fifty years; that is, right up until the time of writing of this narrative.

Vincent W. "Vin" Hallinan was born in San Francisco, the son of a cable-car gripman of Irish revolutionary sympathies. He obtained a law degree from St. Ignatius College, the Jesuit institution that later became the University of San Francisco. At the time Hallinan took up the law, an Irishman with a Jesuit diploma was assured of permanent political influence, if not power, in the city. He began practicing in 1919, at age 22. For much of his career, he was at odds with judges and other legal authorities, and was described in the press by adjectives like "two-fisted" and "limber-tongued." When he married Vivian Moore in 1932, he went with her to Reno while San Francisco deputies searched for him: he had only served five hours of a 24-hour sentence for contempt of court in his defense of Frank Egan, a former public defender and a convicted murderer. The soon-to-be Vivian Hallinan had sat in the courtroom during the Egan trial encouraging her fiancé in his sarcastic remarks and other stunts. She even became notoriously involved in the case, for she had driven Egan to San Francisco from a hideout at Hallinan's country cottage, and she was questioned by the Board of Supervisors in the investigation leading to Egan's removal. Hallinan himself, seemingly a devout Roman Catholic, gained a special dispensation from diocesan officials to be hastily wed in Nevada without the usual Church formalities. He faced the rest of the contempt sentence with colorful humor, commenting, according to the *San Francisco Chronicle*, "It will be tough to leave my weeping bride at the portals of the calaboose."

Through the 1930s Hallinan was known as temperamental and flamboyant, but he was no radical. Soon after his marriage he was reported by the *Chronicle* to have shot himself accidentally while "pounding the gun with a hammer." That pretty much summarized his character. As the decade dwindled he was charged with fraud, perjury, and deception, got into a fistfight with an opposing lawyer in a hallway outside a courtroom, and was accused of suborning perjury. Later he was suspended from practice by the State Supreme Court for three months after a client complained of his conduct. Meanwhile, Vivian Hallinan had become rich by investing in residential property; during World War II she was acquitted in a suit filed by the Office of Price Administration, an agency filled with Communists, for rent-gouging, failure to properly register rentals, illegal refusal of services to tenants, and unlawful evictions. "I have been so harassed and vexed by so many small bureaucrats, by conflicting interpretations of rulings, by rulings made and abrogated that I have refused to discuss the matter any further with the O.P.A.," she told the *Chronicle*. "If I try to evict a tenant for drunkenness or for nonpayment of rent, that tenant is represented in court by an O.P.A. attorney," she complained. "I know that every property owner in San Francisco is behind me in this."

Although he became involved in various legal reform controversies, until he was hired by Bridges in 1949 "Vin" Hallinan was mainly known as a picturesque advocate for accused killers and gangsters, a true San Francisco character but hardly a respected one. Then something changed; the lawyer previously known for his association with the lower end of the underworld began lending his name to Communist legal enterprises. For example, in April 1947 he confronted San Francisco District Attorney Edmund G. "Pat" Brown over an alleged racist shooting of a Black merchant seaman by a white, near the Embarcadero; Hallinan served as lead counsel for a protest group assembled by the Communists to press for the killer's prosecution. Still, past habits persisted, and only a month afterward Hallinan was hired by the widow of Nick de John (alias Vincent Rossi), a former member of Al Capone's criminal gang who had turned up dead by strangulation in San Francisco, to represent her in a coroner's inquest.

"Vin" Hallinan was no Wayne Collins, driven by sincere liberal ideals;

but whatever his motives, by the beginning of 1949 Hallinan increasingly frequented the Communists and their supporters. Perhaps he had grown bored with little imitators of Capone and decided to move up the criminal ladder to representing the accomplices of Stalin, history's worst gangster; certainly he was used to defending liars, and Bridges was a liar. Perhaps Hallinan admired and was entertained by the tumultuous and bumptious behavior the Communists and their lawyers exhibited in American courts. Perhaps he simply loved money, and was pleased to enlist Bridges and other Communists as clients. (Federal agents believed that for every court day of the Bridges-Robertson-Schmidt proceeding Hallinan received $1,000 in cash before the session opened; Hallinan also found an opportunity to acquire valuable real estate from the California Labor School during the trial.) It is hard to imagine that this ambitious and cynical man believed, with other rich fellow travelers, that Communism was inevitable in America but that collaboration with the Kremlin would preserve his wealth. His entry into their milieu and his hiring by Bridges rather showed that among the local élite in northern California (by contrast with the difficulties that had descended on the Hollywood Communists) a certain amused toleration persisted, even as the federal government attempted to hold Bridges to account. Above all, in San Francisco Bridges and the Communists retained some, although by no means a lot, of their support in the unions.

The Bridges-Robertson-Schmidt trial, which began in November 1949, furnished Hallinan with plenty of opportunities to show off, and especially to denigrate the bench, opposing counsel, prosecution witnesses, and whoever else came to mind. Repeating the Communist argument that any legal inquiry into Bridges's dishonesty constituted an attack on the West Coast longshore union, Hallinan engaged, in the words of federal judge George B. Harris, in "wholesale character assassination of Government witnesses" and "vituperation such as I have never encountered in any tribunal." Testimony against Bridges and his two comrades was, according to Hallinan, a product of an antilabor conspiracy by Hawaii's Big Five employers, who had lately undergone major I.L.W.U. strikes, and was introduced into the courtroom by "the very swill of humanity," "perjurers and stool pigeons and turncoats," and renegades who would wreck "any man's life for $100." By comparison, Wayne Collins, energetically confronting those he was convinced had paid for perjury in the "Tokyo Rose" case, was never so vicious or vulgar. But

"Vin" Hallinan had found a tune that gladdened his heart, and he proceeded to play it and sing it for the rest of his life.

After hearing Hallinan's opening arguments, Judge Harris told him "This will be a fair trial. You will have a fair trial. The Government will have a fair trial. These unfortunate characterizations may be part of your presentation, but I say to you: Leave them outside of this courtroom." Hallinan paid no heed. Bridges, Robertson, and Schmidt had been indicted for falsely declaring under oath that none of them were Communists when Bridges gained American citizenship; but Hallinan dedicated his considerable oral skills to diverting attention as far away from this simple issue as possible. Mainly Hallinan battled to substitute for the matter of whether Bridges, Robertson, and Schmidt were Communists an uproar over why such a charge might be made, as if its falsity needed no demonstration. The case against them was, he said, "a noxious, fetid, horrible growth," a remark preceded by expansive smears against more and more people as accomplices in an injustice. The F.B.I., according to Hallinan, was acting only out of pique, since Bridges had made fun of their surveillance in talks with newspaper and magazine writers. Paul Scharrenberg, an opponent of Bridges since the 1930s, was no more than a competing labor figure jealous of Bridges's popularity; Harry Lundeberg, of course, came in for special invective—Hallinan declared that the Sailors' leader, who was not a witness, was an abusive "bucko mate, a Jack London character, who has been arrested for assault in a hundred ports."

Hallinan succeeded in turning the trial into a controversy over his courtroom methods—but at the cost, after only a week, of another contempt sentence, this time for six months. In addition, his name was ordered stricken from the roll of attorneys admitted to federal practice. Hallinan responded by charging Judge Harris with personal animosity and venality. Backed up by federal prosecutor F. Joseph Donohue, Judge Harris struggled to maintain the court's dignity, telling Hallinan, "Man to man, in the alley or in the courtroom, you couldn't look me in the eye and say that." Hallinan emitted a rude noise in reply.

Bridges's defense attorney next turned to a serious attack on the prosecution's witnesses, beginning with John Schomaker, a well-known Communist functionary in the longshore union for several years, who had broken with the Party and now earned his living as a hod carrier. Schomaker knew Bridges extremely well, and testified that the union boss had been a clan destine Party member. Hallinan asked if Schomaker (like other Communists), had in the past denied his Party affiliation under oath. However, the lawyer's intention was not to so excuse Bridges and his comrades for such an action. Rather, Hallinan claimed that a court transcript in his possession showed that Schomaker had so sworn; he now attempted to portray the witness as generally inclined to perjury. Schomaker, knowing very well that such denials were a standard Communist tactic, admitted it was "possible" that he had once followed the practice. Hallinan then revealed that no such transcript and no such instance had ever occurred, but declared proudly that he had "tricked" Schomaker into admitting untruthfulness.

Schomakers's testimony was not seriously shaken, although it ended with a hilarious duel between him and Hallinan over a visit to the witness's home by a private detective, "Hal" Lipset, hired by the Bridges-Hallinan forces. Lipset, Schomaker said, had "asked me questions like a guy who was all hopped up [on drugs]. I never saw anything sillier in my life. He kept shaking his necktie at me . . . and I said, what are you, a private eye, and he said yes. I asked him when he last peeked through a keyhole and he said, 'Sir, I never peek through keyholes.'" Hallinan concluded by demanding to know if Schomaker read comic books, was an amateur detective, and expected a job with a government in payment for his services as a "professional stool pigeon." Schomaker answered negatively; he was only a hod carrier.

Schomaker was a leading witness against Bridges, but his recollections of the longshore leader's Communist activity were seconded by others. They included Henry Schrimpf, a fellow Australian and ex-Communist, still a working member of longshore Local 10; Lawrence Ross, former editor of the *Western Worker,* whom the Bridges team tried to impeach by showing that his real name was Lipman Rosenstein; and Mervyn Rathborne, a major collaborator of Bridges on the maritime labor scene until 1947 and the government's most effective witness. Rathborne testified that two women associates of Bridges had attempted to prevent him from appearing in the trial by threatening to tell his wife (falsely) that he had been unfaithful. One of these females, Jean Murray, elicited gasps in the courtroom when she told prosecutor Donohue that "his" government, which she described as a "dictatorship of the monopolies," was corrupt. (Both women were indicted for witness tampering.) Rathborne, who had served the Communists and Bridges for more than ten years, was now described by Bridges as "a drunkard, embezzler, and union-buster." The anti-Semitic overtones in the defense's treatment of Ross were paralleled by even more egregious racism when Hallinan described government witness Manning Johnson, an African-American, as "a foul, black hyena."

The defense produced a series of character witnesses, from former state attorney general Robert W. Kenny to various shipping executives, including Oscar W. Pearson, president of the Pacific Maritime Association (P.M.A.), the West Coast waterfront employers' group. Hallinan was never compelled to explain why if, as he argued, the Bridges inquiry reflected a plot by the maritime interests to frame an effective union leader, the P.M.A. chief would vouch for him. Pearson, when asked, denied that his appearance on Bridges's behalf was impelled by fear of union action.

After 81 days' commotion, in April 1950, the jury found Bridges, Robertson, and Schmidt guilty as charged. Judge Harris cited Hallinan in two instances of contempt and sentenced him to two concurrent six-month prison terms. MacInnis was also found in contempt and sentenced to three months. Judge Harris accused both attorneys of deliberately attempting to provoke a mistrial. The defendants were released on bail; the government had in reserve a civil denaturalization suit, on the argument that Bridges had obtained U.S. citizenship by fraud.

THE COMMUNISTS HAD yelled "frame-up." Other reactions to the Bridges-Robertson-Schmidt verdict by Bay Area labor revealed the degree to which support for the Communists, even among longshore workers, had diminished. The testimony of P.M.A. head Oscar W. Pearson did not go unnoticed; Harry Lundeberg declared that if Bridges was deported, "the only ones who will miss him are the shipowners and the Commies." Indeed, the prosecutors who scratched their heads in wonderment when Pearson endorsed Bridges's character did not comprehend certain aspects of life on the West Coast waterfront. One was the previously noted local acceptance of Bridges as an irritating but also entertaining phenomenon. More important, after World War II the P.M.A. adopted a so-called "new look" in dealing with him. Although Bridges, under Communist orders, had abandoned his commitment to a no-strike pledge "forever," his support for labor peace had not been forgotten. The ultramilitant Lundeberg was still the employers' main enemy on workplace issues. Put bluntly, the Communists, in the several C.I.O. unions they controlled in addition to Bridges'

I.L.W.U., had arrived at a mutually beneficial compromise with the corporations whose workers they claimed to represent: the Communist unions had become "company unions," indifferent to such issues as wages, hours, conditions, and job security in exchange for freedom to continue plying their memberships with Stalinist propaganda. Aside from the I.L.W.U., the worst offender in this regard on the Pacific Coast was the Marine Cooks' and Stewards' Union; they benefited from the high pay and improvements gained by Lundeberg's union, with which they shared jurisdiction, but they pursued few real grievances and functioned quite effectively as a full-time puppet for passenger-ship operators.

Lundeberg was not the only West Coast waterfront unionist to express disgust at this outcome. I.L.W.U. Local 10 in San Francisco, the "jewel in the crown" of the West Coast longshore labor movement, had already elected an anti-Communist administration under James Stanley Kearney, a young and extremely popular rank-and-file leader. Born in San Francisco in 1914, Kearney studied law but discovered he could make a good deal more money as a dockworker than wearing a white collar—an insight shared by quite a few others who gravitated to work in the maritime industry. Thanks to Kearney, who became Bridges's most powerful and effective critic, the San Francisco longshore union regained its soul. Kearney's election and re-election by the membership of Local 10 (which in 1947 gave him 3,100 votes against 1,400 for his opponent) was a blow to the Bay Area Communists from which, in some respects, they never recovered, and a political "scandal" that they and their legion of academic apologists have tried mightily to erase from regional history. Unlike other I.L.W.U. branches, Local 10 issued no protest against the conviction of Bridges, Robertson, and Schmidt. An official of the local who remained anonymous said, "If this had happened 20 years ago that would have suited me fine."

The authentic longshoremen of Local 10 expressed their distaste for their former Communist masters in amusing ways. When in January 1948 Kearney took office for the second time, assisted by a full "right-wing" slate that also received a landslide tally, the local's *Bulletin* suddenly sprouted an American flag, captioned "God Bless America," on its logo, and its editor, Pat O'Hannigan, announced that the local's news sheet was uninterested in issues affecting "Saudi Arabia . . . Pakistan, or Moscow," but was committed to seeing "that the brothers make a few more coconuts." The *Bulletin* reported that, after many years of uninterrupted blather, David Jenkins had been denied permission to speak to an inaugural meeting under the local's administration. Jenkins was not then a member of the local, but had been frequently allowed to address it because of his position with the California Labor School. "A vote was taken as to whether or not to hear Jenkins at that time," the *Bulletin* noted, "and with a roar that was heard down at Pier 26, the brothers voted to proceed with union business. Jenkins realized he was Joe Dundee [a waterfront term for debris] and departed." The Communists and their apologists ascribed all such actions to "cold-war hysteria," and assailed them as "repressive." But the decision of the San Francisco longshoremen to dispense with Jenkins's rhetoric was no more an act of censorship than was Douglas MacAgy's decision to cover the Rivera mural at the California School of Fine Arts; both were acts of intellectual liberation.

The Henry Wallace electoral fiasco of 1948 reduced the Communists to irrelevancy in the American labor movement, and such developments as the conviction of Bridges, Robertson, and Schmidt weakened and isolated them further. Indeed, the trial of the trio had coincided with a nongovernmental but equally serious inquiry into Communism by the national leadership of the C.I.O. Beginning in 1949, eleven Communist-dominated organizations were expelled from the national body. The first and largest was the United Electrical Workers (U.E.), which had distinguished itself by undercutting the United Auto Workers' wage offensive in 1945. At its ejection from the C.I.O. it had a half million members; 80 percent of them left it for other unions, including a new anti-Communist organization, the International Union of Electrical Workers (I.U.E.) The U.E. survived as best it could by groveling accommodation to its main bargaining partners, General Electric and Westinghouse. Another union to be expelled, the International Union of Mine, Mill and Smelter Workers, which descended from the heroic old Western Federation of Miners under "Big Bill" Haywood, had so degenerated under Communist control that its Muscovite chiefs engaged in blatant ballot-stuffing during union elections, as well as other undemocratic abuses.

On November 5, 1949, while "Vin" Hallinan was twisting and shouting and slandering in his defense of Bridges and his comrades, the C.I.O. began its investigation of the I.L.W.U. Hearings commenced in May 1950, six weeks after Bridges, Robertson, and Schmidt were convicted. Bridges, Robertson, and others of their ilk were allowed to cross-examine witnesses and offer their own in rebuttal. The C.I.O. determined that the top I.L.W.U. leadership had "consistently and without a single deviation followed the sharp turns and swerves of the Communist Party line and [had] sacrificed the economic and social interests of its membership to that line." Further, according to the C.I.O.'s official statement,

> The defense presented by Harry Bridges and his fellow officers was an evasion of the real issue involved in the trial; they objected on hypertechnical grounds to the introduction of all relevant evidence; introduced extraneous and irrelevant evidence; made unsupported and slanderous attacks upon the witnesses; and generally evidenced a hysterically evasive attitude toward the charges and toward the trial committee.

This description could be applied to virtually every instance where Communists faced public scrutiny in America. The C.I.O. rejected Bridges's claim that his Communist sycophancy represented a fulfillment of the wishes of the union's membership. The I.L.W.U. was thrown out of the C.I.O., quickly followed by its West Coast satellites, the Marine Cooks and Stewards and the International Fishermen and Allied Workers. The Food, Tobacco and Agricultural Workers (F.T.A.), with which Crispulo Mensalvas was involved, was also bounced. By that time the last two were little more than paper unions with drastically shrinking memberships, run as nearly pure Communist fronts.

The C.I.O. deliberations over the Communist-controlled entities in its fold were dramatized on June 25, 1950, when thousands of Communist troops invaded the southern half of divided Korea. For millions outside the Stalinist empire, the news was horrifying. In West Germany, American servicemen noticed that ordinary people on the streets were suddenly tense, waiting to see if the Communist offensive at the other end of the world would be supplemented with a similar assault in Europe, and whether or not South Korea would be defended by the Western powers. In 1948, Stalin had tested Western resolve by ordering a transport blockade of West Berlin, and the United States had taken the lead in organizing the "Berlin airlift" to counter it; but would the Americans so act again? Had the United States withdrawn from Korea? Would the Allies now abandon Berlin? In Yugoslavia, maverick Communist dictator Tito harbored similar anxieties after two years of incredible invective against him from Moscow.

Documents handed over to the South Korean government by the

Russian Foreign Ministry in 1994 have confirmed that the war was deliberately plotted by North Korean Communist tyrant Kim Il Sung, previously a captain in a Soviet Army intelligence unit, with the approval of
Stalin as well as that of Mao Zedong, whose Communist armies had won
control of mainland China in 1949. For most American political leaders,
to say nothing of ordinary people, the entire postwar contest with Stalin
was frightening; it underscored the unstable nature of all international relations after the atomic bombings of Hiroshima and Nagasaki. None of
the ex-Communist intellectuals who really understood Stalinism were in
positions of power in the United States, and some of the politicians who
stepped into the void of leadership that thus opened up were unsuited, not
merely for such a mental effort, but for public life in general. The career of
Richard Nixon showed that anti-Communism was popular with voters,
but such a posture often led to personal isolation and obloquy, which had
a deranging effect. In addition political anti-Communism in America was
volatile, for it often carried with it both a dizzying sense of unknown possibilities and a susceptibility to genuinely reactionary attitudes—suspicion
of intellectuals, minorities, and foreigners.

The elected official who most represented the dangers of American
anti-Communism was, of course, Republican Senator Joseph R. McCarthy
of Wisconsin. Previously known only as a legislative watchdog on government abuse, "Joe" McCarthy erupted in the Communism debate in February 1950 when he charged that 57 "card-carrying Communists" were
employed in the State Department. In the ensuing controversy, McCarthy
was effectively shown to have been bluffing about this claim, but it made
him famous, and attached his name to anti-Communism for more than a
generation after. McCarthy never dealt with California per se. But in his
personality, his methods, his blustering demeanor, and his lies, McCarthy
resembled nobody so much as Vincent Hallinan, to a degree that, in 1950
at any rate, they were mirror images of one another. That year was more
than a marker for the midcentury; a whole epoch had ended and another
was beginning, with new individuals in the forefront, McCarthy and Hallinan as well as Kim Il Sung and Mao.

The end of a historic period was also symbolized, away from the exclusively
political arena, by the death of the man who so long embodied the Bohemian intellect in California, Jaime de Angulo. De Angulo was 61 when,

in November 1948, he was diagnosed with terminal prostate cancer. The next two years saw de Angulo suffer horribly as, in Henry Miller's words, he was "mutilated, emasculated, humiliated to the very core of his being." However, as his life drew to an end de Angulo, like a firework that burns brightest in its last moments, attained and achieved much. In December 1948, from a bed in a Veterans' Administration hospital in San Francisco, he began a correspondence with Ezra Pound, the grand wizard of American verse. Pound was also institutionalized, having been locked up in St. Elizabeth's, a mental treatment facility in Washington, D.C., as an alternative to a treason trial for his wartime radio broadcasts from fascist Italy. Pound was a figure who then provoked considerable dissension among American writers, for although many were disgusted with his behavior during the war, few denied his greatness as a poet and critic, and even fewer felt that he should be tried for treason.

De Angulo had been directed to Pound by Hugh O'Neill, a neighbor at Big Sur and an associate of Henry Miller and Robert Duncan. In his first letter to St. Elizabeth's, de Angulo wrote of Pound's confinement, "I imagine you are lonely. So am I. It doesnt matter how many friends we have— some of us are always lonely. Look at Blaise Cendrars. What a life! What hasnt he done? He has been everywhere, he has known everybody . . . and he is always lonely." De Angulo also returned to his greatest love, writing to his daughter Gui, "San Francisco is a wonderful spot for doing linguistic work: Chinese, Basque, Filipino. And i want to rework all those Indian tales." At the end of 1948 he was released from the hospital, and work on his "Old-Time Stories"—a series of Indian narratives originally composed in the 1920s "for little boys and girls"—led him to an entirely new enterprise, both intellectually and technologically, in the form of Berkeley's FM-radio station KPFA. "Frequency modulation"—FM—was then a novelty that, because of its relatively low broadcasting cost, had already attracted considerable attention among radicals around the United States. KPFA was founded by a group of anarchists after a meeting of the Libertarian Circle, with Kenneth Rexroth and his cohort in attendance, was addressed by Lewis Hill, a pacifist and an enthusiast of the new medium. The project, which gained financial backing from the Rockefeller Foundation, derived its name as a nonprofit organization, the Pacifica Foundation, from its originators' pacifism.

In spring 1949 de Angulo began a year of weekly broadcasts, reading his "Old-Time Stories" over KPFA, an occasion long remembered by those who listened. He wrote to Pound describing the station as "an experiment—radio without sponsors and commercials—financed by some wealthy people." His correspondence with Pound expanded, and he began writing to Cendrars; both greatly encouraged him. Pound and his wife, notwithstanding the poet's situation, helped find a New York publisher for the "Old-Time Stories," which came out in 1953 as *Indian Tales*. De Angulo's daughter Gui wrote, "At the very end he found two people whose friendship meant more than anyone else's, Dorothy and Ezra Pound." He came to believe his cancer had gone into remission, but in February 1950 he wrote gruesomely to Pound, "Ez, hav you ever pissed blood? it's a funny sensation, first time, kind of startles you, sort of scared . . . after a while you get used to it . . . but when the blood-clots are too big to be squeezed easily thru the urethra, then WHOUCH!! . . . it hoits . . ."

If Jaime de Angulo found in Pound a special and inspiring friend, the old Bohemian played a similar role for Robert Duncan. Pound recommended Duncan, already an acquaintance of de Angulo's ex-wife Nancy, as a typist for Jaime's manuscripts, and Duncan eventually moved into de Angulo's Big Sur home. Although he was more than three decades older than Duncan, features of de Angulo's personality were extremely attractive to the Berkeley poet. De Angulo had, after his earlier good relations with Carl Jung, become exceptionally critical of the Swiss psychiatrist; Duncan hated Jung also. However, Ekbert Faas has pointed out a much more significant interest shared by de Angulo and Duncan, for the former, influenced by the androgynous tradition in Native American shamanism, had become known as a transvestite and even assumed what would today be called "transgender" characteristics. "Most important to Robert, perhaps, was Jaime's sophisticated understanding of sex," Faas writes. De Angulo had, according to Faas, "taken female hormones to the point where his distinctly male figure grew female breasts." Duncan claimed that de Angulo frequently visited San Francisco in "drag" and seduced young lesbian women, who "never discovered he was a man because his sexual activities were not of a kind that would display that little secret to them." Faas adds, "Jaime's particular excursions into shamanistic male lesbian transvestism certainly confounded all traditional Western distinctions about gender."

De Angulo's former spouse, Nancy, recalled the etiology of de Angulo's transvestism. During the early 1930s,

> There was no new woman around. . . . Jaime began to create his own excitement, going back to his old fantasies concerning women's clothes. He always said that his interest in such matters went back very far. At least to those days after his mother died, when [his sister] Pura came back from Spain to take care of [their father]. He would slip into her room when she was out, and try on her silk stockings, and be all of a jitter with excitement. . . . Somewhere along the line we acquired a copy of Virginia Woolf's *Orlando*. . . . Jaime was especially intrigued by the sex-change in the story. He began to fancy changing over himself, at least in a kind of way. He said he wanted to see what it felt like, to be a woman.

He began shaving with extra closeness, let his head of hair grow, and secured women's garments in his size by mail from Sears, Roebuck. Nancy and the rest of the ménage began referring to him as Orlando, and held *soirées* over which he presided in feminine character.

Soon he was throwing parties featuring real transvestites, and was angered when one such occasion turned into a riot of destruction and the pillage of his home. "That was the end of *that* phase," recalled Nancy. "Jaime said he detested those people. They were not his sort. They were not normal and he didn't belong with them. . . . What he really wanted, anyway, was not crazy doings like all this. It was just to be able to go about in ordinary life, dressed in women's clothes. To have just casual people see him and think of him as a woman." Nancy took Jaime on jaunts in feminine dress, to the grocery store and elsewhere, and Jaime soon began going out on his own in the evening and would drive "to service stations out in the country, stop for gas and flirt with the service-station boys," according to his daughter. These journeys, in the unsophisticated Central Coast environment before World War II, must have entailed considerable physical danger, but de Angulo kept it up until he realized he could be arrested, something he did not desire at all. However, he continued wearing women's clothes at home.

Robert Duncan began his relationship with de Angulo as a typist, but became his nurse as the old man weakened. Aside from the psychological insights to be obtained from such an experience, Duncan also gained a major understanding of linguistics from talking to de Angulo and typing up his writings on language. He began to see the English language phonologically, as a system of sounds (phonemes) rather than the letters that stood for them. He grasped the internal components of words as rhymed or counterposed, in addition to the rhyming of words. This was a staggering discovery for him, which transformed his entire outlook on verse and laid the basis for a major breakthrough in the theory of poetry:

> I began to feel, realize, one labial can rhyme with another, and it's like getting undertones and overtones on the piano. You'll anticipate it. . . . When it came back to the poem it meant that if I lost the rhyme too—now I wasn't going to lose the rhyme because I was recognizing what it was built of. The same linguistics were opening up how the language was actually moving.

Faas writes that Duncan "at first thought that nausea would overwhelm him if he'd volunteer to help Nancy in taking care of this dying man. But he finally faced the facts of it, washing him, raising or lowering him in his bed, or conducting the odd bit of ghostly dialogue with Jaime who recognized those around him with greater and greater difficulty." Jaime de Angulo died, after further hospital visits, in the last week of October 1950. His ashes were committed to San Francisco Bay. According to Duncan, cancer had left him extraordinarily emaciated, his eyes those of a maniac. Miller wrote of him as

> [A] *man,* dear Jaime de Angulo! A beloved, hated, detested, endearing, charming, cantankerous, pesky, devil-worshiping son-of-a-bitch of a man. With a proud heart and a defiant soul, filled with tenderness and compassion for all humanity, yet cruel, vicious, mean and ornery. . . . Yet even unto the end preserving his reason, his lucidity, his devil-may-care spirit, his defiance of God and man—and his great impersonal ego.

Jo Fredman, a friend of Duncan's, recalled in an interview with Faas that de Angulo, before his cancer was diagnosed, had taken her riding; de Angulo wildly costumed in purple sash and rings, brandishing a machete and lustily bellowing "Bandiera Rossa," the Italian revolutionary anthem. The man who had begun his unique intellectual career with the Socialist Labor Party, remained a radical to the end, it seems. Duncan wrote of his dying,

> How utterly ununderstandable it is that he is dead, has become something dead. Utterly ununderstandable because one has as great a faith in his im-

mortality in the mind, in the language as I argue, as one has belief, almost knowledge, of his absolute mortality.

Two months later, Duncan's life changed absolutely when he met the painter Jess Collins, who remained his companion for the rest of his life.

ON HIS DEATHBED de Angulo had written to the Pounds, in reaction to the Korean War and its effect on America,

> When a people reach a stage in culture where they can be that easily hood-winked by a press-and-radio system (obeying of course their masters, who are the banker-manufacturer-big farmer mentality—) so that the public opinion in these United states can be manufactured with a mastery worthy of the masters of the theater in Hollywood, when   people reach that stage, they are ready for fascism.

It was rather absurdly ironical for de Angulo to so write to Pound, who had embraced *real* fascism, yet the irrational mood in which America contended with the challenge of Stalinist expansionism alarmed many people besides Communists. The pitfalls of investigatorial anti-Communism were strikingly indicated in December 1950 when state senator Jack Tenney and his Fact-Finding Committee on Un-American Activities called hearings in Los Angeles to examine the death, in September 1948, of a local college student, Everitt Hudson.

The committee had begun an inquiry into Hudson's death two months after it occurred, and spent two years amassing information before calling a public hearing. Everitt Hudson, the son of an architect, was a brilliant youth, above all a gifted learner of languages. As a teenager he spoke and wrote Spanish and either French or Italian fluently; drafted in 1946, he attended the Military Intelligence Language School (later the Defense Language Institute) in Monterey, where he acquired Chinese and Japanese. He later took up Russian. His draft notice came while he was studying prelaw in his first year at Stanford University, and after his discharge he returned there. He expressed an interest in working for the State Department. He then abruptly transferred from Stanford to U.C.L.A., moved into a cooperative dormitory although his family home was nearby, and became involved in the campus activities of the Wallaceite I.P.P. He was last seen alive early on the morning of September 28, 1948 in Robinson Hall, another cooperative dormitory. He had just come there from a Communist Party meeting; at 11:45 P.M. the night before; he had run a stop sign and received a traffic ticket in Santa Monica. About 10:30 A.M. on the 28th his body was found in a pit in the Robinson Hall basement, curled around a corner of a gas furnace.

According to the Tenney Committee's report, the gas had been turned off and the furnace-room door was open, so that asphyxiation was precluded as the cause of death. Hudson's neatly folded sweater was found near him. The entire basement was dusty. There were no signs of a struggle, although a smear in the dust seemed to indicate the path of the body. Within days of the discovery the basement was, according to the committee, deliberately flooded, destroying all physical evidence. Dr. Frederick Newbarr, chief autopsy surgeon in the Los Angeles County Coroner's Office, testified before the committee that natural causes, suicide, and accident had to be excluded as causes of death, although it might have been a homicide. Superficial abrasions detected on Hudson's body may have been caused by the lowering of his body into the pit.

Committee investigators inventoried the books in Hudson's possession at his death, and found them overwhelmingly made up of Stalinist literature, including Stalin's own *Selected Writings*. He apparently had not read Trotskyist literature, which might have pointed him toward a disillusionment and conflict with the Communists. The committee also obtained Hudson's correspondence with his parents, who were ordinary Americans, religious but tolerant and politically moderate. Much of what the investigators found therein was the typical self-dramatizing agony of a young leftist at odds with his family, although not extraordinarily so. At one point while still at Stanford he wrote excitedly that he had a new academic advisor, Dr. Wayne S. Vucinich, who had fought in the O.S.S. and was attached to Tito's Yugoslav Partisans. He had also, as was later revealed, been assigned as a liaison with the Russian and Bulgarian armies. Hudson was enthusiastic about taking Russian, apparently on the advisor's urging. In February 1948, however, he added a postscript to one letter, telling his parents, "If I should die in any manner please give my body promptly to one of the college medical schools. . . . It's just something I want done in case anything should happen." Three months later Hudson's mother contacted Vucinich and expressed concern about her son's apparent surrender to Communist indoctrination. Vucinich replied neutrally, stressing that Russian was a good language for study in psychology, and describing young Hudson as "a serious and intelligent young man."

Vucinich's letter from Stanford was dated May 27, but by August 21, Hudson had moved to U.C.L.A. On that date a letter was addressed to him by a Stanford student, Andrew Syka, who had written to him earlier; in both letters Syka called Hudson by the Russian name "Kamenev"—peculiar, in that the best-known Kamenev in Russian history was the assistant of Lenin and brother-in-law of Trotsky, Lev Borisovich Kamenev. He was born Rozenfeld; "Kamenev" was a *klichka* derived from the Russian word *kamyen'* or stone, intended to parallel the names Stalin, from "steel," and Molotov, from "hammer"; all meant to convey the hardness of the bearer. However, Kamenev failed to live up to such an alias, for he briefly opposed the Bolshevik coup in 1917, and was forever after labeled "fainthearted." He was mainly remembered as one of the "sixteen" veteran Bolsheviks executed at Stalin's order in 1936. Such a nickname should hardly have been considered a joke among Communists or fellow travelers.

Yet another letter was sent to Hudson by his former Stanford roommate, a graduate student from India, Bipan Chandra, who was also a lecturer at the California Labor School. The missive, dated August 31, 1948, after Hudson had transferred to Stanford, was disturbing in that Chandra, who argued strongly that Hudson should leave U.C.L.A.—for U.C. Berkeley if not to return to Stanford—had written, "Many idealists, nonthinking individuals end up like Miss Bentley. I would never, never want anything like that to happen to you or me." Elizabeth Bentley, a former Soviet spy, had become famous after revealing the considerable extent of KGB infiltration in the American government; her name was, of course, anathema to Communists. Was Chandra warning Hudson not to do the same thing, i.e., not to defect and reveal some information he might have had about Communist espionage? Chandra also commented on "how necessary it is for all of us to steel ourselves like our friend Fuchik." Hudson seemed pretty steely as it was; he wrote letters back to Chandra and Syka in which he expressed his delight at the Communist activities at U.C.L.A., which were secret, but, according to Hudson, encompassed numerous "critical Marxists, constantly trying to weed out the idealistic garbage." The letter to Syka, in which these words were paraphrased, was still in Hudson's typewriter when he died.

The Tenney committee subpoenaed one of Hudson's Communist associates, Lola Whang, who took the predictable route of silence on grounds of possible self-incrimination. Quite a puzzle; yet the committee had an "expert witness" who they believed could elucidate the case. This was none other than Norman L. Mini, now 41, the former Communist "criminal syndicalism" prisoner, Trotskyist, and writerly friend of Rexroth and Miller. Mini appeared before the committee on December 16, 1950 and recounted his experiences as a Communist, including an association with leading Soviet spy Nathan Gregory Silvermaster, a former California state relief official who appears extensively in the VENONA traffic under the *klichka* Robert, and who was the mentor of Communist waterfront goon Louis Goldblatt. (According to Kleo Apostolides, later Mini's wife, Mini was acutely aware of Silvermaster's commanding status in Soviet clandestine operations, and his repulsion at Robert, his methods, and his attitudes, was the greatest factor in driving Mini away from the Communists. To Mini's great dismay, Silvermaster was never prosecuted by the American authorities.)

Mini then testified at length on the Hudson case. Although he had no direct knowledge of any of the principals in the affair, he had read the correspondence and had settled on two main suspects: the Stanford faculty advisor Vucinich and the mysterious Fuchik. Vucinich was unfamiliar to Mini, but this did not discourage the "expert" from describing the faculty advisor as "a person completely out of the ordinary run of individuals that Hudson has met in the radical movement before . . . in a way [Hudson] is kind of dizzy. He has met this man who is on a much higher level and the man has evidently given him to understand that he can play a very important role in the whole movement, it seems to me." Further on, Mini declared that Vucinich, "who has been in all the most dramatic parts of the war . . . this man has opened up some kind of perspective for him that he never had before." He went on to equate Vucinich with the spy boss Silvermaster. Indeed, according to Mini, "the decision to study Russian seems to me could only indicate that this man, Vucinich, who influenced Hudson so much, had some specific mission in mind for Hudson . . . for some reason or another, the idea of studying Russian becomes of terrific importance." Mini surmised that Vucinich had convinced Hudson to abandon his prelaw studies.

Mini was also concerned to "find out who this Julius Fuchik is." But that comment undermined his claims to expertise, for Julius Fuchik was not to be found anywhere in the Los Angeles Communist milieu, or even in the United States. Fuchik, a Czech Communist poet, had been executed by the Nazis in 1943. His *Notes from the Gallows,* translated into English, was an indispensable item of Communist devotional literature after World War II, known to if not read by virtually every Communist militant everywhere around the globe. Given the circumstance of Fuchik's death, Chandra's reference to him may have indicated no more than a fantasy of incipient fascism in the United States. But to fail to recognize Fuchik's name amounted to a confession that Mini, who clearly understood a great deal about California Communists in the 1930s, had kept up with very little about the Party after he left it around 1941. Still worse was his testimony on Vucinich, which was really despicable. For not only was Mini ignorant of Vucinich; his absurd, improvised comments contradicted the entire reality of Vucinich's life.

IN DECEMBER 1952 an event occurred which was of immense significance in California intellectual history, but which went completely unnoticed. The main protagonist was Kenneth Rexroth's then closest friend, the former Hollywood Communist Eli Bernard Jacobson. In a footnote to her biography of Rexroth, Linda Hamalian described the incident as follows:

> Although in a January 7, 1953, letter to [New Directions publisher James] Laughlin, Rexroth mentioned that "Eli Jacobson dropped dead recently," to others Rexroth would relate a grisly and totally unfounded story about Jacobson's death. He said that in December 1952, Jacobson's body was found floating in San Francisco Bay. His fingers had been severely beaten, as though he had been struggling to hold on to a ledge of a building, or in this case perhaps a bridge. A few days before his death, Jacobson had called Rexroth up to tell him that he was cutting his last remaining connections to the Communist Party because he had discovered at this late date that Stalin was an anti-Semite. Rexroth begged him not to break so abruptly with his comrades, and arranged to meet him in Sausalito before he took any action. Rexroth had told [San Francisco socialite] June Oppen of his proposed rendezvous, and he suspected she "warned" her brother, poet George Oppen, about Jacobson's change of heart. Rexroth absurdly speculated that Oppen was working as a "hit man" for the Party, and that he had murdered Jacobson. In an interview nearly thirty years later, Rexroth would describe Oppen as a "remarkable poet."

Had Rexroth—like his acquaintance Mini, like Tenney, and, for that matter, like Joseph McCarthy—succumbed to some form of mania in his anti-Communism? Hamalian's comments make a picturesque addition to the literature of "anti-anti-Communist" piety about the period. Unfortunately, however, she overlooked some relevant points.

To begin with, regardless of his use of the phrase "dropped dead," which could mean anything, Rexroth's oral description of his friend's demise was not "totally unfounded." The San Rafael daily *Independent-Journal,* as well as the San Francisco dailies, reported on December 5, 1952 that Jacobson, 58, had drowned, at about 1:45 P.M. on December 4, in the cold waters of a slough near the Mira Monte Fishing Club north of Novato, in Marin County. He was heard to cry for help and observed struggling in the water, and was rescued, but he died while firefighters were attempting to revive him. Marin Coroner Frank Keaton stated that Jacobson owned a houseboat, *Take It Easy,* moored in the slough and might have fallen, after a heart attack, out of a small boat that he was rowing to the houseboat; he was known to suffer from a heart condition. The *Independent-Journal* as well as the Hearst dailies said Jacobson was known to be "violently anti-Communist."

Foul play was suspected, and the newspapers noted that the sheriff had received telephone calls saying Jacobson never went out alone and, especially, that he would not have tried to row a boat because of his heart problems. Neighbors of the houseboat also pointed out that previously he had always been accompanied to and from the vessel by his wife Beryl, who, when he died, was reportedly driving to San Francisco from Los Angeles. However, Beryl Jacobson did not arrive in San Francisco, and the Marin County Sheriff, Walter B. Sellmer, had trouble finding her. After an autopsy, coroner Keaton now stated that Jacobson had died from shock after falling in the water. However, the issue of how he came to be in the water— whether he was pushed or otherwise thrown overboard intentionally—was never addressed, except by Rexroth.

The autopsy documents reveal some fascinating details: on the reverse side of the Coroner's Autopsy Surgeon's Report, a penciled notation reads "Small superficial bruise on arms + knees. Fracture left 10th ribs. Petechial hemorrhages in heart and lung." Such injuries are consistent with a struggle to get back in a boat, perhaps with an assailant wielding an oar or boathook, who might have struck the victim in the chest.

However, the investigation ended there. Could Jacobson's death have had something to do with stories that he "stole" Beryl from the film director Gregory La Cava? La Cava had remarried, and had died in Malibu in

March 1952. Remarkably, Eli Bernard Jacobson is one of the very few ex-Communists on whom the F.B.I., responding to a 1996 request under the Freedom of Information Act, reports "no record."

Was Rexroth's suspicion of the Oppens "absurd"? Certainly not, for George and Mary Oppen—the latter having been associated with the top clandestine leaders of the Party—had remained fanatical Stalinists, and were also active boaters. However, they had departed by land for a political refuge in Mexico City, along with numerous other Communists vulnerable to investigation, in 1950, while June Oppen remained in San Francisco. The fate of the Oppens' beloved sailboat is unknown, but Rexroth believed that it, if not Oppen himself, was employed in killing Jacobson. Given Rexroth's claim, if true—and there is no reason whatever to doubt it—that he had communicated only with June Oppen about Jacobson's defection, it is not outside the bounds of possibility to imagine her using the telephone to contact her brother south of The Border. In addition, certain aspects of the Oppens' self-imposed exile merit attention. They insisted that they had fled to avoid persecution, but they had never been subpoenaed by any investigative body. Mary Oppen made no attempt to seriously explain the decision to flee south; one day a Communist comrade simply told them they should leave, and they did. The full identity of the comrade is undisclosed. Her memoir, *Meaning a Life* (published in 1978), has become a canonical work among San Francisco literary scholars but also stands as one of the most opaque and unrevealing Communist recollections ever produced. In it Mary Oppen showed herself to have remained, even then, "at this late date," a completely unrepentant and uncritical defender of Stalinist Communism—although, in the customary fashion of such, Stalin and Stalinism *per se* are never mentioned in the book.

Was there something questionable about Jacobson's "late discovery" of Stalin's anti-Semitism? In reality, the extent of Stalin's fear and hatred of Jews had only been publicized in recent years, culminating in January 1953, a month after Jacobson's death, with the infamous "doctors' plot," a frame-up directed at the Jews on the Kremlin medical staff, who, in the style of tsarist anti-Semitism, were accused by the dictator of plotting blood atrocities. However, a frightful series of new purge trials in Eastern Europe following the split with Tito had, especially in Hungary and Czechoslovakia, assumed an openly anti-Semitic character. On December 3, 1952, the day before Jacobson died, Otto Katz, or "André Simone," former editor of the

Czech Communist daily *Rudé Pravo,* was hanged in Prague after a show trial in which fourteen prominent Communists, eleven of them Jews, were convicted as "Zionist Trotskyite enemies of the people." Eleven of the defendants were executed.

Katz was one of the most famous and, among underground Communists, one of the most feared of all Comintern illegals. The death of Otto Katz haunted European Communists for a generation afterward; only in 1996 was it made known in the West, through the release of the VENONA traffic, that Katz had already been under KGB suspicion during World War II, as a supposed turncoat who had sold out to British intelligence. Like Katz, Jacobson had been a clandestine Comintern agent; like Katz, Jacobson had served as a Communist in Hollywood. Given what we now know from the VENONA traffic about the extent of KGB surveillance, kidnappings, and other depredations on American soil, that Jacobson was murdered seems far from unlikely.

Certainly Otto Katz was not the only veteran of Communist clandestinity in California to fall victim to Stalin's anti-Semitism. Grigory Kheifitz, the illustrious *Kharon,* had been arrested in 1948 or 1949, according to Pavel Sudoplatov, during the main wave of anti-Jewish purges inside Russia. Kheifitz was consigned to a labor camp, from which he emerged, sick but alive, in the mid-1950s.

In 1952 George Oppen had not yet resumed writing the poetry that would gain him Rexroth's praise. But regardless of his judgment of Oppen's literary achievement, Rexroth was convinced until his death in 1982 that Oppen had played a role of some kind in Jacobson's death. Most importantly, however, the death of his close friend elicited from Rexroth one of his finest poems, *For Eli Jacobson,* in which he describes with unequaled eloquence the destruction of hope, and the heartbreak, inflicted on the radicals of his generation. It opens,

There are few of us now, soon
There will be none. We were comrades
Together, we believed we
Would see with our own eyes the new
World where man was no longer
Wolf to man, but men and women

Were all brothers and lovers
Together. We will not see it.
We will not see it, none of us.

On March 5, 1953, amid the full paroxysm of the Soviet anti-Semitic campaign, with the KGB preparing the mass deportation of Jews from Moscow and other central Russian cities, Stalin died. On March 15 a memorial meeting of a couple of hundred people in San Francisco heard William Schneiderman, California's junior Stalin since the late 1930s, say of the dictator, "Oceans of ink have been spilled to vilify him by a few detractors, but oceans of tears have been shed by people all over the world."

Juanita Wheeler, a heresy-hunting, rigid African-American Stalinist assigned to the *People's World* staff, chaired the "Stalin and Peace" meeting. "The fight against fascism will not be won until the peoples of the world can ensure peace all throughout the world," she babbled.

Holland Roberts, a querulous former academic and occasional figurehead of the California Labor School, spoke of "Stalin as a student, teacher and scholar," according to the *People's World*. "We will remember this man with a scholar's head, a worker's face, and the dress of a private soldier," he declared.

Al Richmond, an exceedingly complicated and devious man who, as editor of the *People's World*, doubtless reported directly to the KGB, commented, "The job of the people who appreciate Stalin's work is to see that the people are not deceived, entangled into lies, and thus drawn into war."

Ellis Colton, a birdlike, cadaverous figure in spectacles, then only 37 but seeming older, who managed the Communist bookstore in San Francisco, "spoke briefly about Stalin's published writings," the *People's World* noted.

Kenneth Rexroth had not written much directly referring to Stalin, but another member of his generation and a friend, the poet Kenneth Patchen, had. Indeed, while the experience of the ex-Communist was brilliantly explored in essays, memoirs, and novels in many countries, Rexroth and Patchen seem to have been the only writers in any language (except, perhaps, Russian) to produce poetry—and great poetry, at that—on the topic. As the 1930s drew to a close, the two Kenneths had appeared as the brightest young poetic lights in the American radical movement; both broke with the Stalinized milieu and denounced it, and both, as well as their wives, feared violent reprisals from the Communists. Kenneth Rexroth was known as a philosophical, love, and nature poet as well as for his political writing; Kenneth Patchen's early verse was filled with rage at militarism, fascism, and social injustice, but also with an intimacy and tenderness unsurpassed by any American poet of his time. Henry Miller had written, "The first thing one would remark on meeting Kenneth Patchen is that he is the living symbol of protest"; yet Patchen's love lyrics were and are widely admired. Robert Duncan, a great friend of Patchen, was his peer, in a different mode; where Duncan's gift was musical, Patchen's was more explosively visual—and humorous. Similarly, Philip Lamantia exceeded Patchen in the creation of startling and weighty images, but lacked Patchen's emotional intensity.

Born in 1911 in Niles, Ohio, the son of a steelworker, Kenneth Patchen wrote beautiful and enduring modernist verse on the Wobblies ("Joe Hill Listens to the Praying"), on labor in the steel mills ("May I Ask You a Question, Mr. Youngstown Sheet and Tube?"), and on racism ("Nice Day for a Lynching"). But his surrealist denunciations of the totalitarian mentality were unforgettably powerful, as in the poem "BEHOLD, ONE OF SEVERAL LITTLE CHRISTS."

Anti-Stalinism of an anarchist and pacifist tendency was a major aspect of Patchen's work, and he seemed to shoulder responsibility for the whole global attempt by revolutionary intellectuals to find a way out of the horrors of the 1930s. In a "novel," *The Journal of Albion Moonlight,* written at the beginning of World War II, he asked,

> To whom do I speak? Ah yes, to whom? To the Stalinist Communists? Debauchers of Leninism and murderers of the leaders of the October Revolution; betrayers of Spain and allies of Hitler. No, not to them. To the Trotskyist Communists? Where are they? Where are their following? Who are their leaders? What are they doing? No, surely not to them. I speak for my own kind.

Patchen had been awarded a Guggenheim fellowship in 1936, but the blunt tone of his work, his opposition to the Communists, and his status as a conscientious objector in World War II closed off his publishing opportunities, at least temporarily; during the war he began self-publication of his books. His financial situation was then already difficult. In addition he suffered from spinal problems, which began in 1935 in Los Angeles when he tried to lift the front end of a car. He underwent a series of difficult and not very successful operations, the first in 1951. On the advice of his doctor he moved with his wife, the former Miriam Oikemus, a Finnish-American radical, from New York to San Francisco, seeking a climate that might help alleviate his back pain. His arrival was a great occasion for California writers and anti-Stalinists.

Kenneth Patchen was introduced to new San Francisco readers at a series of poetry readings, including a memorable event at the San Francisco Museum of Art in 1952. The art scene was again in transition; the "revolution" of Abstract Expressionism had been halted and even, to some extent, reversed, with younger painters turning to a new "California figuration." However, there was no going back to the cloddish Stalinist realism that had preceded Douglas MacAgy's takeover of the California School of Fine Arts. MacAgy had resigned from C.S.F.A. in 1950; as noted by Tom Albright, one explanation for his disaffection that circulated around the Bay Area held that he had quit because the school's governing board refused to hire Marcel Duchamp as a teacher. MacAgy had brought Duchamp, along with Frank Lloyd Wright and the Northwest Coast Abstractionist Mark Tobey, to San Francisco in 1949 for a memorable public round table on the future of art. One must wince at the thought of how important the San Francisco art scene might have become if Duchamp, the greatest artist of the twentieth century, had come to town to live; but it was not to be.

Albright wrote that with MacAgy's departure "the curtain . . . was symbolically rung down" on the "heroic youth" of Abstract Expressionism in the Bay Area. MacAgy himself later averred, "I'd wanted Marcel there, but it never got that far." He declared his concern about the dwindling of the postwar influx of mature students and the transformation of the campus into a party school for talentless youths, among other issues. At least one observer, however, claimed MacAgy had been, in effect, forced out by the school's monied patrons after the obvious triumph of abstract and nonrepresentational art at C.S.F.A. Clyfford Still left at almost the same time, and in 1952 Hassel Smith was fired. Elmer Bischoff and David Park, another extremely influential faculty member, quit in protest.

THE BAY AREA's artists had gone further in their commitment to experiment than the poets of the San Francisco Renaissance, but the Abstract

Expressionist movement had been paralleled, and psychologically supported, by the similar scene in New York, where some former C.S.F.A. students had gone to live. *Avant-garde* music also flourished in the 1950s on the West Coast, as well as in New York. In 1947, Harry Partch had come to Gualala, north of San Francisco on the wild coast that he loved, after a difficult period at the University of Wisconsin. Most academics at that time looked on Partch, whose instrument-building had expanded in ambition and innovation, with great hostility. He moved to Mills College in Oakland, and the company of Darius Milhaud among others in 1951, then, in 1953, to a shelter at Gate 5, part of a disused wartime shipyard at Sausalito. He remained there for three and a half years, in close friendship with Gordon Onslow Ford, Yanko Varda, and a new arrival, Alan Watts, a scholar of Buddhism, while issuing records pressed on clear green Vinylite disks—cheaper than the usual technology then in use—under the Gate 5 label.

Harry Partch's return to the West Coast led to one of his most significant inventions: the "cloud-chamber bowls" (or "cloud-chamber bells," an accurate mispronunciation by some around him). These were tops and bottoms of enormous Pyrex carboys once used in "cloud-chamber" research on particle physics at the Berkeley Rad Lab; they had been thrown out, then salvaged. Partch discovered that when suspended and struck, each "bowl" emitted a unique tone. With a row of ten "bowls" the musical effect was extraordinarily beautiful; the new instrument was employed in some of Partch's most effective compositions, including his *Oedipus,* performed at Mills in 1952, and the stunning *Plectra and Percussion Dances.* The latter work was praised by the *Chronicle*'s R. H. Hagan for its "fantastically and subtly compounded rhythms" and the "peculiarly new and fascinating sound of the instruments." Hagan considered *Plectra and Percussion Dances* superior to the contemporary work of John Cage, then making a considerable sensation on the East Coast; "I doubt . . . that even John Cage . . . has produced such valid music as Mr. Partch has produced in [this] performance," Hagan wrote.

The "cloud-chamber bowls" represented an outstanding example of the merging of art and science whose coming was predicted by Bern Porter. Indeed the three great West Coast musical pioneers, Cowell, Partch, and Cage, all resembled great scientists. Although it might seem excessive to compare Cowell, elected in 1951 to the National Institute of Arts and Letters, to Einstein, both transformed the fields in which they worked by the introduction of new and unexpected elements; in addition, of course, Cowell had laid the basis for electronic music. Partch had something in common with the great astronomers, such as Johannes Kepler, who struggled to broaden human knowledge of the structure of the cosmos—and Kepler had also studied harmonics. Cage, the greatest of them in his intellectual depth and impact, calls to mind Werner Heisenberg, who theorized by way of his "uncertainty principle" that the presence of a human observer changes the nature of a phenomenon under observation. Cage had adopted silence as an element in his compositions; he savored the expectations of an audience waiting to hear music, and loved their reactions at his performance of *4'33"*, which consisted of four minutes and thirty-three seconds of silence and was first played in public in 1952.

Unconventional painters and composers, to emphasize, operated individually on both coasts. By contrast, the Bay Area poets worked as a community in a certain isolation; there was no comparable movement anywhere else in the world, nor had there been since the height of French Surrealism and its imitator groupings in the 1930s. California was provincial; but in literature, as opposed to plastic art, its very provincialism was something of an asset. Perhaps because of this continuing "implosion," the San Francisco poets grew in authority, drawing other new talents from around the country and even from abroad. Octavio Paz was deeply impressed by Rexroth, whom he met in the late 1940s, and has remained so; in 1950, and again in 1952, the Welsh poet Dylan Thomas had been welcomed at Berkeley, giving long-remembered readings on the campus. Late in the next year Thomas suddenly died, in New York, of alcoholism, aged only 39.

Rexroth had met and admired Thomas, although he was irritated when Thomas, after leaving San Francisco in 1952, went around New York spreading various inaccurate stories about him and other Bay Area writers. But Thomas's death in November 1953 hugely affected Rexroth. Victor di Suvero, an S.U.P. sailor, a poet, and a brother of the sculptor Mark di Suvero, later recalled that the night after Thomas's death he and Philip Lamantia were sitting with Rexroth in the latter's apartment "when the phone rang and it was a reporter from the *San Francisco Chronicle* wanting to know if Mr. Rexroth had anything to say about Dylan Thomas's dying. 'Why, the greatest poet writing in the English language . . . under forty!'" Rexroth exclaimed.

But Rexroth's grief about Thomas went beyond a newspaper comment.

In July 1953, with Stalin gone from the Kremlin and Eisenhower in the White House, an armistice ended the Korean War; it was, to many, a time of limited but authentic hope. However, the aging rebel Rexroth, now 48, saw around him a society that had lost its capacity to recognize and nurture the ideals and inspiration of a young genius such as Thomas had been. That society had killed his wife Andrée, and in some way it had killed Eli Jacobson, or so he may have thought. Rexroth sat down in his apartment on Eighth Avenue in San Francisco's Richmond district and composed a long, outraged manifesto in verse, "Thou Shalt Not Kill: A Memorial for Dylan Thomas." It was hardly his greatest work, yet it set out in direct and moving form a lifetime of protest, in a manner reminiscent of Patchen but with an anger so great that its quality as poetry was sometimes swamped. Yet it concluded unforgettably,

> The Gulf Stream smells of blood
> As it breaks on the sand of Iona
> And the blue rocks of Carnarvon.
> And all the birds of the deep sea rise up
> Over the luxury liners and scream,
> "You killed him! You killed him.
> In your God damned Brooks Brothers suit,
> You son of a bitch."

It was the Declaration of Independence of the California literary revolution, and it made Rexroth, and the San Francisco Renaissance, famous. Soon he was reading it publicly to jazz accompaniment, and its admirers even included some customers of Brooks Brothers.

In *Thou Shalt Not Kill* the murderers of the poet, named by Rexroth, included "Oppenheimer the million-killer." J. Robert Oppenheimer continued to generate national and international debate through the early 1950s. On leaving U.C. Berkeley in 1947 for the Institute for Advanced Study at Princeton he had addressed some five thousand faculty and students, warning them of "years of armament and years of suspicion" brought about by the very existence of the nuclear weapons he had helped to create.

A series of nuclear espionage trials and defections to Russia began in 1950, with the arrests in the West of several individuals prominent in the VENONA traffic, including a certain Rest, whose *klichka* had been changed to Charles, and Antenna, recorded as Liberal: Rest/Charles was the physicist Klaus Fuchs, and Antenna/Liberal was Julius Rosenberg. Ethel Rosenberg, the latter's spouse, appears in KGB communications in clear language, without a *klichka*. After Fuchs and the Rosenbergs were detained, Bruno Pontecorvo, a Manhattan project researcher with whose recruitment Grigory Kheifitz had begun his work among scientists, suddenly vanished from the West.

Inevitably, the suspicion of which Oppenheimer had warned fell on himself. In 1954, the Atomic Energy Commission (A.E.C.) concluded an inquiry into Oppenheimer's involvement in Manhattan District security by denying him clearance for further access to secret data. Oppenheimer's conduct at the A.E.C. hearings was problematical, to say the least; he was vague, evasive, self-contradictory, and admitted past dishonesty. He also disavowed the convoluted story of an espionage approach allegedly made to him by Eltenton and Chevalier, in a manner that simply increased the mystery surrounding his relations with Communists.

After Stalin's death and the end of the Korean War, as well as the morbidly fascinating collapse in 1954 of Joseph McCarthy's Communist-hunting campaign, even anti-Communist intellectuals began to yearn for an end to the whole ordeal. The American Communists no longer presented a threat of any kind, and Communism in general was perceived as morally defeated. Some efforts against it had been purely counterproductive, such as the adoption in California of the Levering Act, which required state employees, including college faculty, to swear a so-called "loyalty oath." By signing the oath one would attest to not belonging to any organization advocating the overthrow of the government. Some Trotskyists might have entertained themselves by pointing out that the Communist Party had long since renounced its original revolutionary intentions in America, and Communists themselves, for that very reason, might have argued that they could sign the oath in good faith. As previously noted, revolution is not the same thing as treason and espionage. However, the Levering Act oath was viewed by many as an inadmissible restriction on conscience, even though no government in the world had ever guaranteed a right to antigovernment conspiracy on the part of its citizens. Such non-Communists as Jack Spicer and Robert Penn Warren made a public issue of refusing to sign the oath.

In mid-1955 the Federal Bureau of Investigation, which had never previously paid much attention to Kenneth Rexroth, began to look into his activities in the 1930s and particularly his relations, if any, with Oppenheimer. According to documents released under the Freedom of Information Act, a certain Muriel Hortense Nicholas had, in July of that year, told the F.B.I. that within the previous two years, Rexroth had told her Oppenheimer had once been "signed up" in the Party by Dorothy Van Ghent, a poet and literary scholar with whom Rexroth had a love affair before Van Ghent gravitated to the Oppenheimer circle. Van Ghent had since moved east, to an academic post in Vermont. Muriel Nicholas also directed the Bureau agents to Wilma Belt Ghiorso, a part-time secretary in the U.C. Berkeley physics department and an employee of the Radiation Laboratory who was married to Albert Ghiorso, a Rad Lab chemist. The F.B.I. considered both of them security risks, even though Albert Ghiorso had access to restricted A.E.C. data after 1948; he was also a volunteer fund-raiser for KPFA, which now broadcast a series of popular literary talks by Rexroth. Although Mrs. Ghiorso admitted an acquaintance with Oppenheimer, she claimed no knowledge of whether he had ever joined the Communist Party, and declined to discuss her own activities in the late 1930s or those of others she knew to be Communists.

A Bureau source whose name was deleted when the relevant documents were released, but who had been a Communist from 1932 to 1935, had told the agents, according to a report dated July 15, 1955, that Rexroth had been a member until 1934 or 1935. This source also identified Andrée and Marie Rexroth as members, the latter having organized a cell of nurses. Nan R. Dunham of San Francisco, as noted in the F.B.I. files, had told the Special Committee on Un-American Activities that Rexroth and Van Ghent were Communists in the Federal Writers' Project in 1939. An "informant of questionable reliability" had (accurately) told the federal authorities of Dorothy Van Ghent's passionate relationship, while she was married to another man, with Rexroth. The F.B.I. agents visited Rexroth, who told them that "it was his impression that Van Ghent was at one time in love with [Oppenheimer]"; he later said almost the same thing in his memoirs. He downplayed his own Communist involvement, declaring that he had only attended a few meetings, found the Party distasteful, and did not join. He apparently did not mention Eli Jacobson or the Oppens to the agents. If the local agents were dissatisfied with the anarchist poet's meager cooperation, the top F.B.I. brass were doubtless irritated when other bureau investigators, soon thereafter, went to see Van Ghent.

A Bureau report of September 30, 1955, shows that Dorothy Van Ghent refused to meet with the agents except in the company of a lawyer, declined to say if she had ever been a Communist, and said she knew nothing of Oppenheimer's connection to the Party. However, she identified George Hitchcock and another man as Party members, and said Rexroth had been kicked out of the Party while working for the Writers' Project. Most importantly, the F.B.I. found out that Rexroth had written to Van Ghent warning her that the agents were about to contact her, that they knew about Muriel Nicholas, and that they were bound to question Van Ghent about her links to both Oppenheimer and Rexroth. But there the matter ended.

BEGINNING IN 1951, a series of newcomers brightened the Rexroth circle. The earliest of importance was 32-year-old Lawrence Ferling, as he then called himself, a sardonic veteran of Navy service in World War II who became an intellectual after postwar study at the Sorbonne in Paris. He was, in the beginning, mainly interested in painting; with his then wife Kirby he took over the flat on Chestnut Street in North Beach formerly occupied by Gordon Onslow Ford. He was introduced to Kenneth Rexroth by Holly Beye, a playwright, and a gifted surrealist artist, David Ruff. In mid-1953, Ferling joined Peter Martin, illegitimate son of the murdered Carlo Tresca, in opening the Pocket Book Shop. This store was located in a premises on Columbus Avenue once occupied by the Cavalli Italian book store, where crowds had, two decades before, gathered to hear Mussolini's radio speeches. The new business eventually became the City Lights Pocket Book Shop, and Ferling its sole owner. Ferling launched a series of pamphlet-sized volumes, the Pocket Poets Series, beginning with his own work under the title *Pictures of the Gone World*. Ferling's verse was light and witty, resembling the street lyricism made popular in France by writers like Jacques Prévert, whom Ferling translated. Another change came when Ferling reverted to his birth name of Ferlinghetti. The second book in the Pocket Poets Series was Rexroth's *Thirty Spanish Poems of Love and Exile*.

Late in 1953 Rexroth received a telephone call from Gareth Sherman Snyder, known to all as Gary. Born in San Francisco in 1930, he had grown up in California and the Pacific Northwest. Gary Snyder was a poet and a scholar of Buddhism; familiar with the Wobbly traditions of the West

Coast loggers and seamen, he was drawn to Rexroth's anarchist pacifism as well as to the elder poet's affinity with nature and regionality. In addition, Rexroth, the translator of Chinese and Japanese, was one of the few American intellectuals of the time who had made a sustained study of Buddhism. Snyder, a serious adherent of Zen, had shipped out to Japan, and had also worked as a U.S. Forest Service fire-watcher. When he contacted Rexroth Snyder had been in Berkeley a year, studying Chinese and Japanese. Snyder had attended Reed College in Portland, where he fell in with two older poets who, with him, ended up in San Francisco. Philip Whalen, seven years his elder, preceded him by a year, arriving in 1951, and Snyder briefly shared an apartment there with him; Lewis (Lew) Welch, born in 1926 in Phoenix, Arizona, but raised in California, did not come to San Francisco until 1957.

Allen Ginsberg was 27 years old in 1953 when he first called Rexroth's home from a Fosters Cafeteria on Sutter Street, according to the memoirist Janet Richards. Ginsberg had grown up in Paterson, New Jersey, the home of William Carlos Williams, whom he knew; indeed, Ginsberg enjoyed an advantage in the poetry scene thanks to the work of his father, Louis Ginsberg, a friend of Williams and a fairly well-known literary figure in the 1930s. Allen Ginsberg, who had met Philip Lamantia in New York in 1948, brought a letter of introduction from Williams to Rexroth when he moved to San Francisco. Like Snyder, Ginsberg introduced his friends to Rexroth, including Neal Cassady, a vagabond con man and occasional railroad worker, and Jack Kerouac, a novelist with an affection for the rails. Ginsberg and Kerouac, also like Snyder, had sailed in the merchant marine; more importantly, they shared with him a fascination with Buddhism.

Ginsberg, Kerouac, and Cassady—and the Beat Generation to which they claimed to belong—were already known in a limited way thanks to John Clellon Holmes, a friend who recorded their adventures in New York in the mid-1940s in a novel, *Go*. Holmes had been the first to put the term "Beat Generation" before the public, in a *New York Times* Sunday Magazine essay in late 1952. Beginning with an observation about marijuana use among teenagers, and the existence, in his words, of "a whole new culture where one out of five people you meet is a [drug] user," Holmes described a disaffection among the young that reached deep and broad. Kids arrested for joyriding in stolen cars and hot-rodders playing suicidal games on the highways; ex-servicemen seeking positions at the top of major corporations and advertising copywriters drinking themselves into oblivion after work; members of a "nonvirgin club" in a Midwestern high school, and models dropping names at cocktail parties; all were Beat. Holmes ascribed the term "Beat Generation" to "John Kerouac, the author of a fine, neglected novel, *The Town and the City.*"

Holmes described the Beat attitude as "an instinctive individuality, needing no Bohemianism or imposed eccentricity to express it. Brought up during the collective bad circumstances of a dreary Depression, weaned during the collective uprooting of a global war, they distrust collectivity. But they have never been able to keep the world out of their dreams," he wrote. "The fancies of their childhood inhabited the half-light of Munich, the Nazi-Soviet pact and the eventual blackout." World War II and the shaky peace that followed it stimulated their anxiety: "The peace they inherited was only as secure as the next headline." Holmes was especially insightful in perceiving that the malaise extended throughout his generation, and was not simply an affectation on the part of a clique of New Yorkers. "It is certainly a generation of extremes, including both the hipster and the 'radical' young Republican in its ranks," he commented. But he did not see such types as counterposed: "For in the wildest hipster, making a mystique of bop, drugs and the night life, there is no desire to shatter the 'square' society in which he lives, only to elude it. To get on a soapbox or write a manifesto would seem to him absurd. . . . Equally, the young Republican . . . is neither vulgar nor materialistic. . . . He conforms because he believes it is socially practical, not necessarily virtuous. Both positions, however, are the result of more or less the same conviction—namely that the valueless abyss of modern life is unbearable."

Concluding this essay, Holmes rejected a revolutionary outcome for the Beat phenomenon: "This generation may make no bombs; it will probably be asked to drop some, and have some dropped on it, however, and this fact is never far from its mind." Rather, he believed, the Beat youth would seek a spiritual renewal, "a great moral idea, conceived in desperation" based on "its ever-increasing conviction that the problem of modern life is essentially a spiritual problem." But Holmes himself was unsuited to leading such a quest; his *Go* was a conventional novel, fairly pedestrian and at times ridiculously earnest. Its protagonist, the author, sought to precisely record the frenetic but seldom productive doings of his peers, but what they were about was at once more trivial and more profound than Holmes, the literary equivalent of a deer blinded by the headlights of a car, could understand. Holmes seemed not to recognize in the Beat Generation a less vicious, more intellectualized projection into the broader, majority society of the nihilism found ten years before among the *pachucos* of Los Angeles. Octavio Paz grasped that the Hispanic zoot-suiters had gone much further than their East Coast counterparts in defying society; the Beats reflected a similar extremism, in a different time and environment.

Go fell into obscurity. Yet its failure reflected a lack not of talent but of insight. Holmes did not grasp that the sensibility of the new generation could not be described but had to be expressed; participation, rather than observation, was central to the Beat ethos. Jack Kerouac had struggled to break out of a passive, evidence-seeking mode, as in his unremarkable *Town and the City*, into a direct communication of experience. In New York, moreover, the Beat immediacy was heightened when the Ginsberg-Kerouac-Cassady crowd took up the use of an amphetamine, Benzedrine, that seemed to accommodate their yearning for an everfaster life. Once they left the restrictive environment of New York, the Beats exploded, just as the Existentialists had come to the fore in France—a new generation, with "their own manners and customs, their own entertainments and their own language," as the French Surrealist Julien Gracq had described the Parisian acolytes of Jean-Paul Sartre. Thus, transplanted to San Francisco, the Beats took over literary life rather as the Abstract Expressionists a decade before had taken over the California School of Fine Arts.

Rexroth now found the Friday night salon he had maintained as a remnant of the Libertarian Circle crowded with fresh, exciting personalities. Ginsberg visited Duncan in Berkeley and there met Michael McClure, only 21, a painter from rural Kansas and a man of considerable physical beauty and intellectual agility. Interviewed by Linda Hamalian thirty years later, McClure recalled Rexroth's devotion to the politics he had made his own. His comments on the local poets would turn into "a discussion of anarchist study groups in the city and then some thoughts about the history of anarchists would come up. He would talk about the anarchists of Barcelona. Then he would have reflections on Stalinists including our local Stalinists and condemnations and damnations and vilifi-cations and jokes and gossip."

Some time in 1955 Ginsberg began working on a poem, "Howl," that resembled Rexroth's "Thou Shalt Not Kill" in its declamatory style as well as in its corrosive view of society. Like "Thou Shalt Not Kill," "Howl" was a lament on the fate of a creative youth—in the latter case, Ginsberg's rather unremarkable mentally ill friend Carl Solomon, who had been committed to a psychiatric hospital. Solomon was no Dylan Thomas, and Ginsberg lacked the dedication to poetic structure and the tranquility that Rexroth had gained, after long and patient work, in his verse. "Howl" was a rant, rather than even a manifesto; it embodied the Benzedrine-fueled, edgy manner of the New York Beats, with language broken up and reassembled in a way that seemed to reflect brain damage. Late in 1955 Ginsberg, Lamantia, Snyder, McClure, and Whalen held a reading, with Rexroth as master of ceremonies, at the Six Gallery in the Marina district of San Francisco. Kerouac provided jugs of cheap wine as well as oral encouragement between poets, and the crowd urged Ginsberg on with shouts of "Go! Go! Go!" as he read "Howl":

> I saw the best minds of my generation destroyed by madness,
>   starving hysterical naked,
> dragging themselves through the negro streets at dawn looking
>   for an angry fix. . .

If Rexroth was the Jefferson of the California literary revolution, Ginsberg was its Thomas Paine, its pamphleteer and popularizer. In the ensuing excitement nobody seemed to notice that much of Ginsberg's unique diction, which seemed to come down to Surrealist images rehashed through Benzedrine, resulted in apparently unedited gibberish. Ginsberg and Kerouac viewed this "spontaneous bop prosody"—a phrase of Kerouac, who was better at it—as a parallel to bebop scat singing in jazz performance. But they understood neither the relationship of music to speech, which Harry Partch had explored nor that, as Duncan and Spicer learned, nonsense is valuable as a subordinate element in poetry only when it remains nonsensical and assumes no moral pretense. For example, in "Howl" we read of those "who ate fire in paint hotels or drank turpentine in Paradise Alley, death, or purgatoried their torsos night after night." This was quite a ways from Rexroth's angry but lucid style, but Ginsberg's friends thought it was marvelous. Janet Richards, in the audience at the Six Gallery reading, recollected.

> When the poets were finished we all remained fixed in our places, packed close together, until Jack and some others broke the spell by collecting money to buy more gallons of wine. Kenneth had introduced the poets; in his usual fashion of handling this position saying little himself. When it was over he was ruddy and almost continuously chuckling. He and everybody else knew we had been present at a tremendous occasion. From the night at the 6 Gallery ever afterward Allen had the devotion of everybody who knew him in San Francisco.

If Ginsberg was the Tom Paine of the California literary revolution, his capacity to inspire immediate adulation also made him resemble another popular figure then bursting into the American consciousness: Elvis Presley. The 21-year-old singer from Mississippi produced his first commercial "single" records in the spring of 1956, beginning with "That's All Right (Mama)." Like Elvis, Ginsberg was a great salesman of other people's creativity; Presley "borrowed" from such African-American musicians as Arthur "Big Boy" Crudup (who wrote "That's All Right (Mama)"), and Junior Parker (who wrote "Mystery Train," considered by most enthusiasts the quintessential rock 'n' roll song), redefining their idiom for a broader, whiter, more middle-class audience, and Ginsberg did the same with Rexroth's poetry of protest.

In the same year of 1956, Ginsberg's collection *Howl and Other Poems* was published in The Pocket Poets Series, with an incoherently anachronistic introduction signed by William Carlos Williams. The sage of Paterson described Ginsberg as someone "disturbed by the life which he had encountered about him during those first years after the First World War" and continued, "Now he turns up fifteen or twenty years later with an arresting poem." Bill Williams was 71 and his memory was poor; nobody has ever seemed to notice that "those first years after the First World War" (i.e., 1919–1925) predated the existence of Allen Ginsberg, who was born in 1926, nor did anyone count fifteen to twenty years back from 1956, which would have found the "much disturbed" Ginsberg at age 10 to 15. The spirit, not the letter, counted, a phenomenon that characterized much of what followed. Also in that year, Rexroth published one of his most important collections of verse, with the prophetic title *In Defense of the Earth.*

Was it a beginning, or an end? Robert Duncan had once compared the cult of Hart Crane with that of Lenin. Similarly, to write the history of Russia after its revolution, it is not enough to simply recount the events of the revolution itself, as if all that followed afterward was a natural and predictable outcome of those earlier events. We are now reconstructing the history of Soviet Communism following its collapse, and in doing so we are struggling to understand matters previously only partially glimpsed, or even unknown. For Communism as well as for the Beat Generation, 1956 was crucial throughout the world. On February 24–25, the Twentieth Congress of the Communist Party of the Soviet Union assembled in Moscow. There Nikita Khrushchev, the successor to the Kremlin dictatorship, rose to deliver a speech that changed world history. Its topic was "the cult of the individual and its harmful consequences." The individual in question was Stalin. The speech was a devastating indictment.

As reports of the speech appeared in the American media, loyal Communists, in California as elsewhere, at first wrote it off as a hoax perpetrated by the C.I.A. On April 28, 1956, one hundred Party leaders from all over the country, including Dorothy Ray Healey from California, assembled in New York for the first open "plenum" of the Party's national leadership in half a decade. The delegates were called into a "special session" after dinner, in which they were warned against taking notes or divulging what they were about to hear to anybody not present. Leon Wofsy, a 35-year-old who headed the Party's "youth" arm, then rose and with no introductory remarks began reading the text of Khrushchev's anti-Stalin speech to the assembly. Forty years later Wofsy, who went on to become a professor of bacteriology and immunology at Berkeley, and who played a significant role in the later student revolt there, wrote of "the shattering pain that document produced for those of us who never believed the horror tales until they finally came from a Soviet source. . . . To stretch the anguish, I was the one who read the report aloud, word for searing word, to some hundred Party leaders. . . . In the United States . . . the Communist Party had already become very weak, and the shock of a previously unaccepted reality was devastating." However, Wofsy's basic faith in "Soviet socialism" remained intact.

Dorothy Ray Healey "was convulsed with tears" after only a half hour of Wofsy's delivery, which went on for almost three more hours.

> It was unbearable . . . . Just this voice going on, piling up facts upon facts, horrible facts about what had happened in the Soviet Union. . . . At one point in his report, Khrushchev read to the delegates letters written to Stalin by some of the Old Bolsheviks he had imprisoned, who described to Stalin the tortures they were undergoing and told him that he was surrounded by enemies who were destroying the human beings who were the capital of a so-cialist society. It was like the old days of czarism, when the cossacks charged into the crowds in the streets with sabers flashing, and no one could believe that the Czar himself, that good and pious man, could possibly know what his subordinates were doing. . . . Nothing could prepare me for the magni-tude of what we were hearing. We had marched for so many years with the purity of the Soviet Union as our banner. We had believed it completely. We . . . felt we could dismiss reports of cruelty and repression in the Soviet Union as just so much propaganda. . . . And here we were, after all these years, sitting in a meeting of the Party's leaders and being told by no less an authority than the First Secretary of the Soviet Communist Party that it was not all capitalist and Trotskyist propaganda after all; that wretched, bloody crimes had been committed.

Most importantly, Healey admitted, "we bore a significant measure of responsibility for [the crimes] because we had denied the very possibility that such a thing could happen." An African-American Party leader, equally shaken, confessed to her that "had we come to power we might have com-mitted the very same crimes." Yet when Healey returned to Los Angeles and, although keeping her vow of silence about the Khrushchev revelations, alluded in a public meeting to the atrocities of Stalinism, she was met with a rebuff. "Even when the Khrushchev speech was printed, first in the *Times,* and then in the *Daily Worker* and the *People's World,* there were Commu-nists who refused to read it, who just dismissed it as capitalist propaganda," she stated.

Nevertheless, after Khrushchev's revelations Communism was as morally defeated to most of its American partisans as it had become among the general public. Fanatics, who had no place else to go, and "professional Communists" like Healey, with no other way to make a living, remained in the organization. But many, many more who had sacrificed their entire lives to the movement dropped out, fell away, and drew a cloak of silence around themselves. A handful of Party leaders, mainly in New York, tried to reorient the party in an American, democratic direction, and the *Daily Worker* and *People's World* moved from publishing Khrushchev's speech, which they would have done anyway, to frank opposition to Soviet policies. These criticisms grew more severe after the bloody suppression of a national revolt in Hungary in October 1956; certain American Communists were outstanding, within the world's pro-Soviet parties, for their forthright condemnation of the Russians' intervention.

But the New York "liberals" were soon out of the party. Many prominent fellow travelers resented the brief period of intellectual candor that marked Party life in 1956; Vincent Hallinan, for example, blasted the *Daily Worker* and *People's World,* among other leftist papers, for describing the Communist states as "all ruled by tyrannical bureaucracies." Such articles forced him, he said, to reassure himself he was not "reading a release from the State Department"; better, he warned, to "hide them from potential recruits to the socialist camp."

––––––––––––

SAINT PAUL WROTE, in Romans 8:22, "The whole creation groaneth and travaileth in pain together until now." After 1956, such a sensation was felt throughout California society. Something had ended, and something was beginning, but nobody was sure what, in either case. Internationally, a failed Anglo-French-Israeli attack on Egypt, which had nationalized the Suez Canal, simultaneously marked the last occasion when the European colonial powers tried to act as such, the beginning of a new anticolonial upheaval, and an episode of never-ending conflict in the Mideast.

A science-fiction novel, *The Body Snatchers,* set by its author, Jack Finney, in a fictional analogue of Mill Valley, was made in 1956 into a really terrifying hit movie, *Invasion of the Body Snatchers.* Starring Kevin McCarthy and Dana Wynter, and directed by Don Siegel, the picture dealt with a takeover of the fictional town by alien plant life that spawns emotionless doubles of the human population. Like other science-fiction films of the time, *Invasion of the Body Snatchers* made manifest the deep fears of Americans about the atomic age, and like other major films, it was interpreted as a parable of either Communism (a conquest by the soulless), or anti-Communism (people reduced to lifeless conformity). The author himself firmly rejected all such exotic interpretations. But the story seemed to hint at another, more poignant issue: if the "alien seed pods" were destroyed and the invasion defeated, what would become of the human replicas left behind? How would they live out their lives, waiting to die, empty of feeling?

That was the fate of the California Communists; they, too, many of them hardly into middle age, faced a vigil unto death, in which, having committed all to a horribly discredited cause, they were forced to live with the resulting void. Because of this trauma, almost none of the former Communist intellectuals participated in the main post-1956 literary and artistic ferment on the West Coast, which soon spread from San Francisco to Los Angeles and elsewhere. Among the few ex-Communists to join the new "revolt" was Rexroth's honest and kind friend George Hitchcock, who became well known as a playwright and actor in a North Beach theater company, The Interplayers; there he encountered the printer Adrian Wilson and the actor Martin Ponch, both pacifists and "graduates" of the Waldport conscientious-objector camp in World War II. Wilson had founded The Interplayers with his wife Joyce, and printed hand-set playbills for each performance.

Hitchcock met and encouraged Maya Angelou, who was then working as a nightclub singer. She described him as "a tall, shambling man with large hands and a staccato laugh, [who] doubled as an aging character actor." She "found his company easy and his intelligence exciting. He understood loving poetry. . . . We shared long walks in Golden Gate Park and picnicked in . . . Muir Woods. . . . A gentle affection, devoid of romance, grew up between us." Hitchcock introduced her to Yanko Varda, and, as Angelou later recalled, "Yanko allowed me to enter a world strange and fanciful. Although I had to cope daily with real and mundane matters, I found that some of the magic of his world stayed around my shoulders." This experience was a major episode in her emergence as a public literary personality.

George Hitchcock had left the Communist Party, but remained oriented to the Socialist Left; he did not share the phobia of a Vincent Hallinan regarding the truth about the Soviet Union, and he participated in public debates with Trotskyists and other non-Communist leftists. (Hallinan himself, it must be said, supported some collaboration between Communists and Trotskyists at that time, but only because of the extraordinary isolation of the former.)

Hitchcock's intellectual openness led, absurdly enough, to a subpoena from the House Committee on Un-American Activities, and his appearance on June 19, 1957, at a San Francisco hearing of that body that was long remembered by his friends and former comrades. The session was overshadowed by the alleged anti-committee protest of William K. Sherwood, a biochemistry researcher at Stanford, who had committed suicide after receiving a subpoena. Still, reveling in the irrelevance of both the committee and its Communist foes, Hitchcock began his testimony by identifying himself as doing "underground work with plants"; that is, he was a gardener, not an industrial agitator or a spy. Questioned about his previous associations and his involvement in Trotskyist meetings, he cited the First, Second, Third, Fourth, Fifth and Sixth Amendments as protection against such interrogation. Asked why he included the Third Amendment, which deals with billeting of soldiers in private homes, Hitchcock answered "I just throw it in." He also invited the legislators present to attend the discussion meetings he had helped to organize. He raised his hands in a boxer's gesture of victory as he left the witness stand; and he was right to do so. For, by employing the weapon of wit, he had triumphed over the committee as few other ex-Communists could claim to have done. He was not cited or otherwise sanctioned, and Bay Area liberals chuckled.

Meanwhile, Alvah Bessie, whose performance as one of the "Hollywood Ten" exemplified a less subtle approach to the House Committee, became a similar figure in San Francisco, operating stage lights at a nightclub. Bob Kaufman, a Jewish-Black poet, was another former Communist who gravitated into the new North Beach literary community. A sailor in the National Maritime Union, which had a large Communist faction but had escaped the Party's control, Kaufman had been "screened" out of seagoing work by the Coast Guard, along with thousands of other Communists, at the beginning of the 1950s. Young and gorgeous, gifted with a brilliant wit and authentic talent as a poet, Kaufman composed widely read broadsides, such as the *Abomunist Manifesto* (1959), imbued with the satirical attitude that, as embodied in the comedy of Lenny Bruce, came to be identified with the Beat Generation. Kaufman joined the Beat élite, issuing a notable mimeographed journal, *Beatitude,* from the streets of North Beach, with the support of Ginsberg and poets William Margolis and John Kelly. His poetry was recognized early on, by Ferlinghetti and others, as accomplished and important. But Kaufman took up the reckless use of amphetamines, a plague that came to ravage the San Francisco literary underground, and fell silent.

In the wake of the Khrushchev shock, a tiny number of American Communists and former Communists emerged from the intellectual freezer in which they had been kept by the Party and, operating on a promise of new creative freedom while still within the Communist milieu, sought to establish themselves as writers. While "exiled" in Mexico, George Oppen resumed writing poetry. Another such personage was an eccentric English aristocrat, the Honorable Jessica Lucy Freeman-Mitford, who had married a Communist lawyer, Robert Treuhaft, and settled in Oakland. Known far and wide as Decca, a legitimate childhood nickname rather than a *klichka*, she joined party artist Pele deLappe in producing a hilarious satire of Communist jargon, *Lifeitselfmanship*, which was circulated among the remaining comrades in mimeographed form, also in 1956. "Decca" Mitford's sudden discovery of literary ambition may have had something to do with the increasing success as an author of her sister Nancy, who in the same year scored well with a humorous but accurate book, *Noblesse Oblige*, that analyzed the distinguishing dialect of the British ruling class. Nancy Mitford divided English into "U" (upper-class) and "Non-U" usages; Decca similarly discussed "L" ("Left") and "Non-L" speech.

Lifeitselfmanship was funny to those who knew the Communists—although its fundamental conceit was lifted from Irish writer Flann O Brien's much funnier "Catechism of Cliché":

"What is Wall Street drunk with?

"Temporary but illusory success.

"List various kinds of struggles.

"All-out, political, class, cultural, principled, many-sided, one-sided, inner-Party.

"What is happening to the contradictions in the situation?

"They are sharpening and deepening. Also unfolding. (Sometimes they even gather momentum with locomotive speed.)"

Perhaps the strangest aspect of the life Decca created for herself in the Bay Area was the snobbish awe in which she was held by her fellow Communists; many of them were mesmerized by her background and early associations.

Yet another California figure who crawled from under the weight of

Stalinism at that time was Tillie Lerner Olsen, who had briefly attracted attention as a "writer of genius" in the 1930s, but then was buried in a mountain range of Communist activist tasks. Tillie Olsen had little to show for her two decades of involvement with the Cause except a sheaf of rather pale short stories, which appeared in 1961 under the title *Tell Me a Riddle*. Her works were impressionistic—little more than sketches of the lives of, for example, an aged radical couple in conflict, or an alcoholic sailor. In putting them before the public, Olsen seemed motivated, more than anything else, by a need to prove that Communists could appreciate "modernist" writing. But Olsen's work was slender, to say the least. Her story, "Hey Sailor, What Ship?" was dedicated to Jack Eggan, a popular waterfront Communist who died in the Spanish Civil War, but it conveyed very little, except that sailors were drunks. It may originally have been intended as an attack on Harry Lundeberg, who died in 1957, at 55, hounded to an early demise by the Communists.

In the last years of his life Lundeberg's union came under fire for failing to desegregate West Coast shipping, on which African-Americans were limited to working as stewards rather than deck sailors. Lundeberg had inherited this situation and could not correct it on his own. Of course it would be ridiculous to deny that the Sailors' Union, and even Lundeberg himself, were infected with anti-Black prejudice, even though the union under his leadership became multiracial, overcoming its past anti-Asian history, and Lundeberg himself had helped lead the multiracial Oakland general strike of 1946. But many West Coast unions supported by the Communists, like Bridges' I.L.W.U., were either lily-white or kept African-American members in a subordinate status. The highly unorthodox Black Trotskyist C. L. R. James, who had visited California and observed the maritime labor scene, greatly admired Lundeberg for his clear-sighted anti-Stalinism, and considered the failure to integrate his union a secondary issue at most.

Tillie Olsen, although she had sacrificed much of her life to Communism, did not write well about labor or laboring people. She later explained away her limitations by a theory of "silence" in which she argued that as a woman she had been deprived of a voice by masculine oppression. In reality, she was but one of many intellectuals silenced by their recruitment to the Party; many of them were men, like the novelist of genius Henry Roth, for whose suppression male chauvinism could not be blamed, and whose loss to American literature was much greater than the hiatus in Tillie

Olsen's career. Paradoxically, however, Jack Kerouac, who thoroughly rejected all Socialist and Communist ideology, wrote with great beauty and accomplishment about his experience as a railroad brakeman in California. Beginning with *On the Road*, which came out in 1957, Kerouac enjoyed unparalleled success as a novelist and elaborator of the California (and American) myth. Some of Kerouac's very best writing, such as his story "The Railroad Earth," grew from his immersion in and passion for railroad life. He may be the finest writer about the experience of industrial work America has ever produced; but even Allen Ginsberg's fractured poetry about the railroad surpassed in quality most of the output of Communist and fellow-traveling "proletarian" authors.

The Beats increasingly reflected an alienation in American society from the conformist values of the two Eisenhower Administrations. Even in the absence of an effective Communist social critique, the Beats were not alone. In 1957 a Chicago-born author and former plumber's assistant and engineer, John McPartland, published a novel, *No Down Payment*, that penetrated the uneasy lives of young couples in the postwar California Utopia of suburban housing developments and new professional opportunities in technology. McPartland had put out a dozen paperback novels of the quasi-pulp variety, issued with famously lurid covers by Gold Medal Books. *No Down Payment*, his first hardback volume and a best seller, was made into a highly successful movie, directed by Martin Ritt and with a cast that included Joanne Woodward, Tony Randall, Barbara Rush, and Pat Hingle. It was set in "Sunrise Acres," which epitomized the sprawling "tract" communities of the era, in which homes were available for "no money down," all of them identical right down to the barbecue pit in each backyard. The film portrayed the varied forms of desperation into which the striving suburb-dwellers descended, whether selling used cars, managing a gas station, or seeking a place as an electrical engineer: racism, alcoholism, sexual violence, police sadism. *No Down Payment* offered an insightful view of the crack-up of the "American Dream."

Its author, John McPartland, although no Beat, lived a life that could not have been more different from that described in *No Down Payment*—although he kept that life private until his death from a heart attack at 47, only a year after the film's release. He had moved to the Monterey area in 1951, and within days of his funeral, in September 1958, the dailies revealed that he had led a multiple existence, with separate wives and families scattered around the landscape. One "spouse"—whom he had never wed—and five children lived in Monterey; she had been named the town's "mother of the year" in 1956. His legal wife resided with a son in Mill Valley. The two families knew and visited each other. McPartland was soon described by newspaper reporters such as Charles McCabe of the *San Francisco Chronicle* as a "sex reformer," whose relations with his partners, more of whom came forward, constituted a grand experiment. The financial needs of his harem explained, it seemed, his need to keep churning out Gold Medal potboilers. He had written on sexual topics for *Harper's,* which had served as the forum for Mildred Brady's attacks on Henry Miller a decade before. McPartland became rich on the film of *No Down Payment,* but like Steinbeck, he was fearful of fame, especially in the less tolerant precincts of the Central Coast. Before his death he commented, perhaps disingenuously, "I don't want my wife [i.e., his Monterey companion] to get booted out of the PTA and I don't want to shock the neighbors." His consorts, according to the *Chronicle,* seemed to "spring up with the regularity of crops," with a final tally of four official marriages, plus one common-law family and at least seven and possibly nine offspring. Only Mildred Brady, crusader against "sex and anarchy," could have done this case justice, but she was not heard from.

No Down Payment was not the only saga of a distressed America then being projected on the movie screen. In 1953, Marlon Brando had appeared in *The Wild One,* based on the takeover in 1947 of another Central Coast town, Hollister, by motorcyclists, and the terror they inflicted on the locals. Produced by Stanley Kramer, the film immortalized Brando's character "Johnny" as an existential hero with a single exchange of dialogue: "What are you rebelling against, Johnny?" "Whaddaya got?" By contrast, James Dean, as "Jim," the young protagonist of the 1955 *Rebel Without a Cause,* was a less overtly rebellious character than Brando's Johnny, but *Rebel,* brilliantly directed by one-time fellow traveler Nicholas Ray, was filled with tension over the failure of a generation, represented by Jim's father (Jim Backus), to set a meaningful example in values or commitments for their children. Brando and Dean, Johnny and Jim, were cultural icons as revolutionary as Lenin and Trotsky had once been, although nobody immediately discerned it.

Hollywood Communists of the sort represented by John Howard Lawson, Lester Cole, and Alvah Bessie complained that after their expulsion from the industry American motion pictures had deteriorated into pure, mindless, escapist entertainment, gutted of all integrity, quality, and content. This critique, taken whole from the anti-American foamings of the Soviet press, was silly. The decade after the jailing of the "Hollywood Ten" saw the release, in addition to anxious science-fiction classics like *Invasion of the Body Snatchers* and "troubled youth" epics like *The Wild One* and *Rebel Without a Cause,* of such outstanding films as *Sunset Boulevard* (1950); *The Asphalt Jungle* (1950); *A Place in the Sun* (1951); *High Noon* (1952—another Stanley Kramer production); *The Night of the Hunter* (1955); *Marty* (1955); *A Face in the Crowd* (1957); *The Sweet Smell of Success* (1957); and *On the Beach* (1959; also by Kramer). All these films presented contradictory and disturbing aspects of American life; further, *film noir* flourished, and many great Westerns and war movies also appeared. The "blacklist era" constituted a great age of American cinema, and it is impossible to imagine conscienceless hacks like Lawson, Cole, or Bessie having very much to do with such a creative upsurge. Certainly Communists who had luxuriated in Japanophobia during World War II had no moral justification for disparaging the industry that in 1955 produced *Bad Day at Black Rock,* a mesmerizing cinema indictment of the anti-Japanese racism in California during World War II, starring Spencer Tracy.

Some films of the "blacklist era" presented anti-Communist actors, brutally vilified by the admirers of the "Hollywood Ten," in magnificent roles. Gary Cooper, jeered for his patriotic remarks before J. Parnell Thomas in 1947, played Marshal Will Kane in *High Noon* (1952), a Western about a lawman left to face a murderer alone. Like *Invasion of the Body Snatchers, High Noon* was also widely believed to have a hidden meaning, either Communist (the man of principle abandoned by the cowardly public) or anti-Communist (the brave man, alone, defending the law). The film is almost forgotten today; it is amazing to recall the uproar it caused among leftists when it was first shown. Unlike the later *Invasion of the Body Snatchers, High Noon* was written by a "Hollywood Red," Carl Foreman, whose Communist activities fed the rumors of a concealed message—which, of course, was the main concern of the House Committee when they went to Hollywood. In another example of excellence, Adolphe Menjou, the most hated anti-Communist in movies, played in *Paths of Glory* (1957), an extraordinary denunciation of war, the hierarchies of power, and the destruction of personal integrity. (It is worth noting that the ex-Communist pulp writer and scenarist Jim Thompson worked on the script.) As with the early social films of the 1930s, when compared with the propaganda efforts of the Hollywood Communists, *Paths of Glory* proved that the most effective American movies on social and "radical" themes were being produced without Communist guidance.

THE SADDEST VICTIMS of the Hollywood "blacklist" were not the obnoxious Lawson, Cole, Bessie, and Co., but more obscure individuals who flirted with Communism to advance their fortunes at second-rate studios or to gain influence in the Screen Writers' Guild, and who were tainted long afterward by what had, in many cases, been a youthful and temporary association. Once labeled a Communist, an actor or writer could obtain absolution by cooperating with the investigative bodies and by affirming an anti-Communist posture to the studio bosses. Some ex-Communists, Foreman included, considered such a course dishonorable, and essentially "blacklisted" themselves. But worst of all, suspicion had a ripple effect; one's current employer and close associates might be assured that one had gotten out of the Communist web, yet competition, jealousy, bigotry, fanaticism, narrow-mindedness, ignorance, and, above all, gossip kept one a victim, always anxious about the professional future. Ambiguous cases were "graylisted"—allowed to work, but never fully exonerated. Even presuming that one producer, on one film, could be convinced of an actor's or writer's loyalty, who was to say that other opportunities would be graced by equally sympathetic attitudes? Film work was never permanent, and in constantly seeking their next job those believed to be "Hollywood Reds," even if they cleared themselves, were tormented by the knowledge that the process of establishing their patriotism might have to be repeated over and over again. Furthermore, they lived in perpetual anxiety over each encounter with a new friend or lover. Many things in their past history could not be explained simply; many people avoided even minimal association with a "blacklist" victim, out of concern that the stigma might be contagious, or from sincere hatred for Communist totalitarianism. No matter how much time went by, the accusation of Communism might resurface at any moment. Only the ex-Communists themselves really understood what they had to go through.

However, if as Dalton Trumbo argued the Hollywood controversy produced "only victims," it could not be said that the only victims were alleged Reds. Edward Dmytryk was already suspended from the Communist Party when he went to jail as one of "Hollywood Ten"; while incarcerated he came to the conclusion that nothing obligated him to continue sacrificing his career to defend Stalinism. "I wanted out!" he later wrote. "Certainly not out of jail, since my sentence had only two months to run, but out of my *real* imprisonment, my association with the Hollywood Ten and . . . the Communist Party." He broke publicly with the other nine, cooperated with the House Committee on Un-American Activities, and was subsequently treated to a half-century of unbelievable defamation as a "sellout," a "snitch," etc. Elia Kazan, on the other hand, one of the real creative giants of American stage and screen, had broken with the Communists long before, and when he acted on his views by testifying accurately on Communism in the New York theater scene of twenty years past, he too was subjected to grotesque attacks. His film *On the Waterfront* (1954), a study of union corruption starring Marlon Brando, was criticized by a few diehards as a defense of "snitching"—although the Communists had never previously objected to cooperation with government in battling labor gangsterism.

Of course, the Communists saw no cause for irony in the way they, like J. Parnell Thomas and the other "inquisitors," claimed to detect such hidden propaganda in the movies. Real film people knew that propaganda could not be concealed in such a visual medium; movie propaganda was always obvious, whatever agenda it served, and its blatant character as well as its frequently esoteric idiom rendered it ineffective and sometimes laughable. Screenwriter Richard J. Collins was one of the original "unfriendly witnesses" subpoenaed by J. Parnell Thomas but was left out of the hearings after the free-for-all mounted by the "Ten"; he noted that while Communists endeavored to introduce "progressive lines" into motion pictures, these were meaningless to the moviegoer "unless you brought a code book with you." He also declared that "any real presentation of Communist material" in movies was "extremely unlikely," given the oversight of studio management.

A defining moment for the Hollywood Left took place in 1951 when the wry but combative Collins, as scenarist on the wartime film *Song of Russia,* and a Communist from 1938 to 1947, was again subpoenaed by the House Committee. He identified some twenty-five other film personalities, writers and directors, as former Communists. "Naming names" was, for those who remained pro-Communist, the ultimate act of betrayal—even though most of the names that were named in such proceedings had been proudly attached to public declarations, advertisements, and leaflets in defense of Stalin's crimes, and so were already known to investigators. Such people had once been eager to be so identified, although they decried as persecution any attempt to hold them responsible for their activities. The House Committee and other investigators were not looking for non-Communist liberals, Socialists, superficial "pinks," or the temporary Communists that made up most of the quarter-million or so people who had wandered through the California C.P. beginning in the 1920s. However, they certainly wanted to find out the identities of long-term, secret Communists whose names had not been used by the Party in public. Investigators mainly asked witnesses to "name names" to correlate them with and confirm information that was already public, and to assess how much the witness knew or had done on the Party's behalf. Abuses like that inflicted on the Stanford scholar Wayne Vucinich were rare; and even when previously unknown or obscure names came up, they did not necessarily attract much investigator interest.

Richard Collins "named names," but he did not expose anybody who had not already acted as an outright servant of Stalin, he did not degrade himself, and he did not apologize for having been a Communist. He pointed out that what later seemed to be Communist propaganda in *Song of Russia* was no more than a reflection of attitudes in wartime, when President Roosevelt's view of Russia was even more enthusiastic than that presented in the film. He denied that Communists had been active in the Screen Writers' Guild after 1947. But he also explained why, after years of defiance, he was now willing to assist the investigators. Ten days before his appearance, he had confronted his collaborator on *Song of Russia,* close friend of fourteen years, and fellow Communist Paul Jarrico, who asked him not to name names. Collins answered that he would remain silent before the inquiry if Jarrico would promise him not to support Russia in a war with the United States. According to Collins, Jarrico said, "You know my answer." Collins then decided, "Since he wouldn't give me his assurance, I wouldn't give him mine." Jarrico, of course, called Collins a liar, but would not specify just what in Collins's testimony was untrue; Jarrico "exiled" himself to Czechoslovakia, and later admitted that he remained a Communist until the late '50s.

The 1951 House Committee hearings on Hollywood had begun several days before Collins's testimony; an earlier witness was Sterling Hayden, born John Hamilton, and then 35 years old. The New Jersey-born actor, after signing his first contract with Paramount in 1940, had been promoted as "The Most Beautiful Man in the Movies" and later described himself at that time as "a male starlet." Nevertheless, until 1950, when he starred in *The Asphalt Jungle,* his acting career was humdrum, and he seemed much more passionate about the sea; he had shipped out as a youth, rose to become an officer on a schooner, and was master of a vessel at 22. He had joined the predecessor of the Office of Strategic Services (O.S.S.) in 1941, and commanded a sailing ship carrying munitions in the Caribbean, but later enlisted in the Marines before being reassigned to the O.S.S. in 1943. Like Wayne Vucinich, Hayden was assigned to Bari, Italy, from where supplies were transshipped to Tito's Communist Partisans in Yugoslavia. He went behind the German lines in Yugoslavia four times to coordinate air drops, and came under the influence of Tito's fighters, the only full-fledged guerrilla army in German-occupied Europe. He also operated a fishing boat along the wildly beautiful coasts of Dalmatia and Albania, rescuing Allied pilots whose aircraft had been shot down. Hayden was discharged from the service in 1945 with a captain's commission and the Silver Star, awarded to him by the Marines for gallantry.

Sterling Hayden revealed the name of a previously unknown Hollywood Communist: himself. When he came back to the United States on a furlough in 1944 he was "bombarded" with Communist literature by an old friend, yachtsman Ward Miller Tompkins, known as "Warwick" Tompkins, who operated a tourist schooner, the *Wander Bird,* out of the California ports. Warwick Tompkins, according to Hayden, also worked for a Soviet spy front, the Amtorg Trading Corporation; his attempted recruitment of Hayden, which the actor described to the Committee, was much more serious than was publicly perceived at the time. According to Hayden,

Tompkins introduced him to Soviet spy boss Steve Nelson, as well as to "Pop" Folkoff and Leo Baroway, featured in the San Francisco VENONA messages as KGB helpers. If the KGB was not interested in his service with the O.S.S., his skill as a boat operator might well have come in handy. However, it was in Hollywood that he joined the Party, and he seemed to have escaped the grasp of the clandestine network.

In testifying on the movie industry, Hayden said little that was new or startling. He identified Karen Morley and Abraham Polonsky as Communists, but they were already well known as such. He also indicated that so few actors had been interested in the movement that they could not even form a separate party unit, and recalled that a campaign to mobilize the Screen Actors Guild in support of Herbert Sorrell's strikes had been defeated. And he called on the H.U.A.C. legislators to assist the "graylisted" ex-Communists, whom he estimated to be in the thousands, in clearing themselves. Hayden's statements to H.U.A.C. were neither very ample nor very informative, but unlike Dmytryk and Collins, who did not regret their decision to testify, Hayden was tormented for the rest of his life by self-hatred for having been a "fink." He became a beloved eccentric in the Bay Area, sailed and acted and wrote marvelously; but he was gnawed by guilt, and drank disastrously.

Sterling Hayden, like Norman Mini, was as much a victim of anti-Communism as those he denounced. Mini was reviled as a "stool pigeon" for testifying before the Tenney Committee; his testimony lacked the accuracy of Hayden's, but he never expressed regret about it. As the 1950s wore on, Mini lived quietly, refining his skill as a winemaker, and eventually working as a tour guide at the Robert Mondavi winery in St. Helena. An early intimation that he might edit a Mondavi house organ never developed, and none of his manuscripts, which had been so highly praised by Henry Miller and others, saw print, although his wine (such as his 1977 Zinfandel, his last product) was delicious.

But Norman Mini *knew intensely* what had happened in California radicalism in the 1930s, and he passed on his knowledge of the betrayals and other intrigues of the Communists and their enemies through his talks with a young friend in Berkeley, to whom he acted as a mentor: Philip K. Dick, an aspiring writer, and the then-housemate of the poet Jack Spicer—although Dick, unlike the Spicer ménage, was not homosex-

ual. Mini and Dick worked together in a Berkeley television and radio re-
pair shop that also sold recorded music, and, according to Kleo Apostolides, who had married Philip Dick in 1950 and later married Norman
Mini, Dick was Mini's "intellectual disciple," and idolized him. Indeed, it
could be argued that nothing in the later history of California radicalism
was destined to influence the world more than the conversations about
the multiple character of ideological reality that Mini held with Dick, and
that Dick, in turn, transmuted in his exceptional science-fiction novels
and stories.

In books like *Time Out of Joint*, written in 1958, Philip K. Dick analyzed the then-latent social complexes that grew out of California Communism and anti-Communism: suspicion, manipulation, and disinformation.
His works present a landscape in which governments control individuals
through an artificial reality—sustained by drugs—in which feelings and
recollections cannot be trusted, in which nothing is what it seems to be.
Dick was neither an ideologue, nor, at the beginning, did he evince symp-
toms of mental illness, but much of his vision was derived from the experiences of Norman Lawrence Mini—revolutionary, political prisoner,
renegade—and powerfully anticipated the present-day world of mass political disaffection and increasingly sophisticated "virtual reality."

As adapted in such films as *Blade Runner* (1982) and *Total Recall*
(1990), Dick's conceptions have enormously influenced the postmodern
consciousness; like Henry Cowell, Philip K. Dick was so far ahead of his
time as to appear a "throwback from the future." His predictions about
what, at the time of this writing, is the present, are seldom comforting.
Apart from virtual reality, in August 1995, *New York Times* correspondent
Jane Perlez reported from the beautiful north Bosnian city of Banja Luka,
where several centuries-old mosques of great distinction had been entirely
obliterated by Serbian extremists who seized the town three years before.
She quoted a local Serb official, who compared the situation in Banja Luka
to that in Dick's 1964 novel *Clans of the Alphane Moon*, in which the imagined society is a giant madhouse: the paranoids, who are the brightest, are
the politicians; the very energetic manics run the military; and ideology is
in the hands of the schizophrenics.

What Norman Mini, the "elder statesman of the group around Philip
Dick" according to Kleo Apostolides, knew and conveyed to Dick—the ir-
reality of Stalinism and its impact on contemporary intellectual life—Ken-

neth Rexroth also passed on to later, younger poets, and Barney Mayes, long forgotten in a world of professional union publicity but still a friend of Mini, related to a young waterfront warrior from Hawaii, Paul Dempster. In 1958, however, these seemed little more than the whisperings of aging men, and there was no sense that the potential for rebellion had been exhausted, compromised, or extinguished.

The year before, Rexroth, Patchen, and Ferlinghetti began reading poetry to jazz accompaniment in San Francisco nightclubs, drawing big audiences. A new "West Coast" style of jazz was already popular throughout the country, and Patchen complained that his performances were handicapped by the sale of liquor, since the public most interested in poetry and jazz were under 21, college and even high-school students. At the same time, the San Francisco Beat scene leaped into the headlines when police charged Ferlinghetti and Shigeyoshi Murao, a salesclerk at the City Lights Book Shop, with selling obscene matter—in the form of Ginsberg's "Howl." A trial saw a parade of literary experts testifying to "Howl"'s status as literature rather than pornography, and the defendants were found innocent. In the jazz clubs Rexroth and Patchen continued reading their anarchist verse, while Ferlinghetti, now world famous, began composing works more oriented toward the day's headlines, such as "Tentative Description of a Dinner Given to Promote the Impeachment of President Eisenhower," printed in 1958.

At the beginning of 1959 California leftists, Ferlinghetti included, were stirred by an overseas event for the first time in years: the Cuban revolution. Fidel Castro suddenly appeared as a bearded, armed, and viscerally anti-American counterpart to the alienated, charismatic trinity of Brando, Elvis, and Kerouac, who had often been compared with each other in the press. College campuses and nightclubs began to host revivals of cabaret-type folk music in the style of Pete Seeger. The Bay Area was convulsed by protests against the execution at San Quentin of Caryl Chessman, who had been convicted for kidnapping, then a capital federal offense, under doubtful circumstances. A movement against nuclear weapons and their testing began organizing, drawing pacifists of an anarchist bent, as well as liberals and Communists. The House Committee on Un-American Activities then decided to hold new hearings on the Northern California Communist Party—which, local Party leaders asserted, had notably resisted the collapse of American Communism after the Khrushchev speech. (The California

Party, long divided between San Franciscans and Angeleños, had finally been split into two districts.)

When the House Committee got to San Francisco in May 1960 it was met with a riot at City Hall led by some two to three hundred youths, mostly from Berkeley and some of them "red-diaper babies," or children of Communists. The disruption was directed on the spot by none other than Archie Brown, Moscow's enforcer on the San Francisco waterfront and in the Spanish Civil War. On Friday, May 13, the demonstrators were washed down the City Hall steps when an excited police officer turned fire hoses on them, and dozens were arrested. Following these events, which proved to the nation that northern California, at least, was as radical as ever, House Committee investigators concluded among themselves that the action had been spurred by the serving of subpoenas on three local Communists with sinister backgrounds whom the Party did not want publicly questioned: Brown, who seemed to relish bragging about his escape from justice in the forgotten death of Vicente Torres; William Reich, a longtime resident of the Bay Area, an expert on agriculture, and a very unpleasant individual who was implicated in the conspiracy against Trotsky; and Vernon Bown, a suspended party member charged with a bombing in Louisville, Kentucky.

But whatever the immediate goal of the Communists in leading the crowd against the House Committee, numerous students were also eager to participate. The 1960 House Committee riot inaugurated a radical trend on the Berkeley campus that would gain attention again in 1964 with the Free Speech Movement. The Communist remnant in the Bay Area actively sought to reconstitute itself by recruiting the young, and for the first time in some years, an open Communist group, the W. E. B. DuBois Club— named for an African-American writer who had once been fiercely anti-Communist, but who had come to join the Party openly as his life drew to a close—appeared on the Berkeley campus. Unsurprisingly, two scions of "Vin" and Vivian, Terence Tyrone Hallinan and Conn Hallinan—"Kayo" and "Ringo"—became deeply involved in running the DuBois Club, which launched branches in San Francisco and Los Angeles.

In 1962 Terence Hallinan, then 25, observed fresh possibilities and revived, in a very modest way, the California Labor School, holding traditional Communist training classes in a conference room at his father's law office under the name of the San Francisco School for Social Science.

Terence Hallinan's School for Social Science offered its pupils the basic Marxist-Leninist curriculum that was standard in Russian "Party schools" and imitated by Communist parties around the world. Terence himself taught the fundamentals of Soviet Communism, under the philosophical rubric of "dialectical and historical materialism," using a pamphlet signed with the name of Josef Stalin. In Russia itself, Stalin's works were no longer "officially" recommended for study, a discrepancy that nobody pointed out to Kayo. In reality, Stalin's discourse on Marxist dialectics, like "his" other works, had been composed by a ghostwriter executed at Stalin's order not long after he finished writing the essay. Russian Communists under Khrushchev watched with continuing emotion as the victims of the mass purges were rehabilitated and restored to public recognition, but this dramatic process was carefully ignored by Kayo and his fellow instructors at the School. (In the same way his father had, in response to Khrushchev's speech in 1956, counseled hiding Communist self-criticisms from prospective adherents to the movement.) The School typically met twice a week, and most of those trained in it were Berkeley students; in addition to the class taught by Kayo, it featured courses on political economy, racial issues, the cold war and American strategy, and related topics. Aside from Kayo and a Castroite former professor, J. P. Morray, the faculty was made up of veteran Communists such as John Pittman, a very light-skinned African-American, once known as a promising journalist, who squandered his talent in the service of the Kremlin, and James Frederick Forest, a Party functionary of unusual intelligence and personal kindliness.

Kayo—Terence Hallinan—was a charmer as well, a great friend and companion so long as one was on his side politically. He had studied at Hastings School of Law, a San Francisco campus of the University of California, and was a light-heavyweight boxing champion at U.C. Berkeley. Getting hit on the head repeatedly seemed to have affected his speech and his memory, but he was already a focus of tumult and aggression long before joining the boxing team. In 1949, at age 12, he was dramatically rescued by helicopter from near a lake in the Sierra Nevada after fracturing his skull. Three years later the 15-year-old Kayo smashed up his car while driving with two friends, and two years after that his driver's license was suspended for three months after he, his brother Patrick Sarsfield Hallinan, or Butch, two years his elder, and a companion got in a fight with three Coast Guardsmen. That mêlée led to a further charge of strong-arm robbery when it was learned that a case of beer had been stolen from the trio. Kayo was made a ward of the juvenile court until his eighteenth birthday. (The year was 1954 and "Vin" Hallinan, their old man, was just then serving an eighteen-month jail sentence for tax evasion.) Only two months after that, Kayo and Butch were arrested again for possession of alcohol in an automobile while under the legal drinking age. When he was 18, in 1955, Kayo and three friends were jailed for battery on the owner of a ski lodge near Lake Tahoe. Two years later Kayo, now a Berkeley student, crashed a party in Marin County and was arrested again.

These donnybrooks assumed a strange regularity; two years later, in 1959, Kayo was indicted for breaking the jaw of a stranger in an unprovoked assault at a Marin bowling alley. Kayo, or his parents, paid the fines and settlements in these cases, amounting to thousands of dollars. He was still at it in 1962; while he was at Hastings, he and Butch mixed it up with two defenders of the House Committee, and the Hallinan boys got the worst of it. But Kayo was also hardly averse to battling it out fistically with leftists whose doctrines did not meet his approval, such as the Trotskyists of the Young Socialist Alliance, then benefiting in a minor way from student radicalism at Berkeley. (Some of them had "rather sweetly" looked up Norman Mini, then living in Berkeley, according to Kleo Apostolides, but he had long surpassed them.) Kayo considered the "Trots" to be irresponsible extremists, for they still talked about Marxism as a political program rather than a subject for class discussion; Kayo and his comrades, for their part, saw Marxism-Leninism as a useful intellectual tool but preferred to cultivate new faces in the local Democratic Party such as Willie L. Brown, Jr., an African-American attorney who was elected to the California Assembly in 1964 with the backing of Kayo and the DuBois Club, and who at the time of this book's publication is mayor of San Francisco.

Kayo, Butch, and the rest of the clan had extended their support to a discernible group of Democratic politicians, including the brothers Phillip and John Burton, who had been elected to state and federal legislative seats; then congressman John F. Shelley, a Communist-leaning labor leader whom they helped to elect mayor of San Francisco; and George Moscone, who was also elected to the state legislature, later becoming another mayor of San Francisco. This incipient machine had relations with a leftist faction in the state Democratic Party identified with Alan Cranston. Phil Burton, the machine's apparent boss, was somewhat suspicious of the old, orthodox

Communists but, notwithstanding occasional dissension, joined them in a united front.

Phil Burton was right to look askance at the official Communists, for if Kayo stood behind him, some genuine Stalinists stood behind Kayo. The San Francisco Communist organization was still in the hands of four of the speakers at the 1953 memorial meeting for Stalin: Holland Roberts, who helped Kayo with the School for Social Science, as he had once done for the California Labor School, Al Richmond, Juanita Wheeler, and Ellis Colton. Of those, only Richmond expressed any open criticism of the Stalin era and its legacy. For the rest of them nothing had changed. Wheeler and Colton, in particular, were always on the lookout for "agents" of the government and "deviations" in the ranks.

A GREAT REBIRTH of radicalism was in gestation, but the "old" Communists were not very popular outside their milieu; at the City Lights Book Shop, the irritable and capricious Shigeyoshi Murao—whom Janet Richards, in one of her fawning moments, praised as a master of the "Beat putdown"—refused to stock the *People's World* and other Communist Party organs, declaring that anybody who wanted to read such propaganda could go get it from the Party bookstore run by the equally irascible Ellis Colton. This was not a matter of censorship by Murao, who had been arrested for selling "Howl"; the store regularly featured the French Communist papers *L'Humanité* and *Les Lettres françaises* (which awoke Ferlinghetti's nostalgia for Paris), along with Trotskyist and anarchist journals and a few publications from a fresh movement: the American followers of Mao Zedong and the Chinese Communist party, which had broken with Moscow. For his part, Kayo Hallinan was not about to tolerate Maoists in his midst, and at 27 he threatened to throw a 15-year-old Mill Valley "red-diaper boy" out of a window for supporting the new rival faction.

Meanwhile, in Russia and Eastern Europe, Ginsberg and Ferlinghetti were becoming famous; there, even more than at home, they symbolized freedom and daring, and their verse style and public readings gained imitators in the "socialist countries." Finally, the Beats represented a beginning, whereas the Marxism embraced by Kayo was at an end. When, in 1964, the Free Speech Movement swept the Berkeley campus, the young Communists helped to initiate it, but it never followed their direction. *Tocsin*, an anti-Communist weekly of considerable wit, published in Berkeley, repeatedly called attention to the number of "red-diaper babies" active in the Berkeley student movement. But the only Stalinist to then exercise a determining influence was the attorney Robert Treuhaft, who assumed control over the students' legal defense in their successive mass arrests and trials. (His wife, Jessica Mitford, had published her best-selling assault on the funeral industry, *The American Way of Death,* in 1963.)

In the Central Valley, Crispulo Mensalvas was still involved with attempts to unionize agricultural workers; he had been joined by Louis Krainock, a former associate of Ernesto Galarza who had broken with the mainstream labor movement. Krainock and Mensalvas created a California Agricultural Workers Union (C.A.W.U.) that agitated in Filipino languages, in Spanish, and in English around Stockton, Marysville, and Porterville, California. But that union too represented a final chapter, for a competing group inspired by Galarza was also in the fields, and proved a great deal more successful at organizing; it was led by a man named César Chávez. In 1963, Galarza had been appointed to the staff of the House Committee on Education and Labor; that year, he directed a major investigation of a bus-train accident in Monterey County that killed thirty-two imported Mexican farm workers *(braceros)* and injured twenty-five more. He was also at work on his own writings, including *Barrio Boy* (1971), a masterful narrative of his origins in the Sierra Madre de Nayarit, an exotic spur of mountains in western Mexico, and his journey to the Central Valley. Galarza's home village, Jalcocotán, lay near the city of Tepic, from which Father Junípero Serra had set out more than two centuries before to establish Alta California; the San Francisco surrealist poet Philip Lamantia went there in the 1950s and encountered the *peyotl* cultures of the Cora and Huichol Indians.

In the twilight of the "old Left," as the Communists would come to be known, the West Coast waterfront continued to exercise an attraction for radicals seeking an arena. Eventually, the federal authorities had given up trying to deport Harry Bridges. In 1963 tensions inside Bridges's I.L.W.U. finally blew up when a group of eighty-two San Francisco longshoremen, 90 percent of them African-American, were thrown out of the industry. They had been hired in 1959 as "B-men" or probationary workers, without full union rights, and they naturally viewed themselves as victims of race discrimination. Their campaign for reinstatement was led by one of them,

Stanley Weir, a white intellectual, a former member of the Sailors' Union of the Pacific and a past supporter of a Trotskyist group. A child of East Los Angeles, Weir had become a friend of the novelist James Baldwin, who, to Weir's discomfort, pointed out the lack of "active novelists and writers" in the Trotskyist milieu. Baldwin issued a public statement defending the dissident dockworkers after an appeal from Weir.

Bridges reacted to the protests of the "B-men" with his usual insults, publicly branding them "drunken, lazy, 'lumpen prolo' elements" who did not belong in the I.L.W.U. What was their real offense? A court fight, which they lost, revealed that the eighty-two had been fired on Bridges's orders, to get rid of just one of them: Weir, the "Trotskyite." However, one of the Black "B-men," William Davis Edwards, then in his early forties, seemed to bear in himself much of the history of California Communism; he had been an official of the Communist-controlled Marine Cooks and Stewards Union, was "screened" off the waterfront in 1950, and was barred from the maritime industry a second time by Bridges. Weir was supported by few I.L.W.U. members except the expelled "B-men" and "right-wing" Local 10 president James Kearney; but one of Weir's closest white friends on the waterfront was a longshoreman, poet, and fiction writer, George Benet, who had also started work on the 'front in 1959.

Benet knew right from wrong in the workplace, and he stood up for Weir. The spark of solidarity that passed between these lost men, in confrontation with Harry Bridges, contained in itself the whole history and aspiration of the socialist movement. But Bridges prevailed, and the "B-men" fight in the I.L.W.U.—still a topic of bitter controversy as this book goes to press—also marked an ending. Most of the intellectuals who worked on the 'front, in that organization and others such as the Inland Boatmen's Union, remained sympathetic to the old Stalinists; the philosopher Eric Hoffer, the most famous exception, paid the price in obloquy and imposed forgetfulness about his work. Yet writers still gravitated to the docks; the poet Lew Welch began working as a ship's clerk in the I.L.W.U. not long after that, and also held membership in the I.W.W. A small Wobbly branch persisted in the East Bay, among Western Pacific Railroad workers—employees of the "Wobbly Pacific"—as the 1950s came to a close, and a few "two-card" men survived in the Sailors' Union. Some younger Wobblies had assisted Mensalvas and Krainock in the C.A.W.U. effort.

New phenomena of a radical nature were then visible throughout the

California atmosphere; only courage was needed to face them. A sedate Catholic monthly, *Ramparts,* was taken over by an enterprising if erratic journalist, Warren Hinckle III, and turned into a flamboyant muckraking organ. Marijuana smoking had become very popular, and a much stronger hallucinogen, lysergic acid diethylamide or LSD, was increasingly available. Among the enthusiasts of the latter was the young guitar musician Jerry Garcia, who was playing small clubs, with friends, in a folk and blues mode. The writer Hank Harrison (father of performer Courtney Love) has written eloquently about Garcia and his friends, whom he knew from the beginning of their adventures.

THE POET VICTOR di Suvero had perceived, in the mid-1950s, a "Sausalito-North Beach axis" along which creative energies flowed, but a decade later Hank Harrison found a similar link between Sausalito and Palo Alto, the town that had grown around Stanford University. The new Bay Area Bohemia was one where, as Harrison recalled, political lines were pacifist and anti-Stalinist, with "nothin' to do but hang out in Palo Alto, drinking coffee and letting the anxiety of how to stay alive keep your mind popping. . . . Rexroth read poetry at the Peace Center. . . . Patchen told everybody to stop making so much money."

But a historical moment was approaching when, in Harrison's words, "one day was worth a lifetime of memories." California heard loud echoes of the civil rights protests then under way in the South, and demonstrations against American involvement in the fighting in Vietnam had just begun to attract people outside the Marxist factions. Few looked beyond this situation; one who did so was Jack Spicer, who had discovered a Mediterranean republic in the Italian community of North Beach. A touching lyric poet, a foe of totalitarianism, and a serious linguist, Spicer gathered a "salon" of younger poets around him, meeting in Gino and Carlo's, a proletarian tavern, where he dispensed sarcasm while celebrating baseball, with which he was obsessed. Spicer was also absorbed in a presentiment of the future of California and the Pacific. In an interview in July 1965, at 40, he recalled to writer Tove Neville the time when "you had to be a Stalinist to be a poet," and defended Robinson Jeffers, who had been anti-Stalin. He praised the "continued tradition" emerging from the California "sea coast . . . so different from the rest of the U.S. (in climate, or economic or political interest) that it isn't really part of the rest of the U.S." He told Neville he dreamed of a Pacific commonwealth, from the Tehachapi mountains near Bakersfield to British Columbia and even to Alaska. Los Angeles would be excluded, although Spicer was born in Pasadena, because of its distinct landscape and outlook. "We were not estranged from everything until the railroad took over," he said. "I would like to be in a separate country."

On July 31, 1965, shortly after that interview, Jack Spicer collapsed on Polk Street, outside his apartment. He expired two weeks later at San Francisco General Hospital. He had drunk himself to death. On the state flag that waved above the streets of North Beach, over the rebel students at Berkeley, the longshoremen on the waterfront, and the graves of so many radicals, the legend remained: CALIFORNIA REPUBLIC, an idea whose time was yet to come.

THIRTY YEARS AFTER

*I*n the end, the amazing thing was how quickly America and the world surrendered to the California intoxication. Beginning in 1965, by leaps and bounds, the distinct California culture was successfully exported to London, New York, Amsterdam, Paris, Prague, indeed to every part of the globe. Already in 1962 the English pop-music group The Animals had indicated something in the wind when, instead of the African-American blues redone by Elvis Presley, they recorded *House of the Rising Sun,* made famous by Woody Guthrie, the "Okie"-Californian Communist cabaret minstrel. Of course their phrasing was a little different; but a similar decision was taken by a Minnesota guitarist, Robert Zimmerman, who renamed himself Bob Dylan after the poet over whose death Kenneth Rexroth had cried out, and who even went to visit Guthrie in the hospital where he lay dying.

A greater totemic figure loomed invisibly over the whole phenomenon, even though he had been dead for years and was now largely unknown: Jaime de Angulo, whose life had anticipated everything seen from 1965 on, from leftism to cross-dressing, from the defense of California Indians to the enthusiasm for Big Sur. In the late 1960s Big Sur became more famous than it had ever been before as the site of Esalen, a pseudo-Utopian workshop for endless talk and hallucination. But some saw it all coming, even from Europe. The Italian writer Italo Calvino had visited Kenneth Rexroth in San Francisco in 1959–60, and described him as

> certainly the most notable person I have encountered in America. . . . He is optimistic about the future; although there are no political or ideological movements visible, technological development, etc., will bring something new. . . . The young, he says, are in the universities where he goes for poetry readings, are part of a generation still unripe, but full of interest and revolutionary energy. The Beatniks are a superficial phenomenon. . . . But the real youth are in the universities.

The tempo of history increased dramatically simultaneously with the death of the poet Jack Spicer. On August 11–16, 1965, the district of Watts, in Los Angeles, exploded in a riot by Blacks angry at police abuse; it was not the only such riot in that epoch, but it was the least expected and the most incongruous in its image. "Ghetto riots" were, until then, considered a grim and brutal phenomenon of the industrial East. In Los Angeles, rioters frolicked on broad streets in the sun, appropriating a slogan yelled out by a radio personality: BURN, BABY! BURN! *The Burning of Los Angeles,* the ultimate surrealist premonition of Nathanael West's *Day of the Locust,* came to life.

Three weeks later, on September 8, a less flamboyant but equally significant incident occurred in the Central Valley town of Delano: Filipino grape pickers belonging to an anti-Communist A.F.L.-C.I.O. entity, the Agricultural Workers Organizing Committee (A.W.O.C.), decided to strike the fields. The walkout lasted five years; the movement brought together the mainly Filipino A.W.O.C. and a largely Hispanic (and equally anti-Communist) group, the National Farm Workers Association (N.F.W.A.) of César Chávez, in the United Farm Workers (U.F.W.). It was the biggest event in California labor history since the 1930s; but in it the Communists, including the aged Filipino organizer Crispulo Mensalvas, were irrelevant. Even among the Filipinos, leadership was now taken by men like Philip Vera Cruz, a Filipino agricultural worker who looked rather to the Wobblies—whose history he had studied in books checked out of dusty Valley libraries while he worked on the farms—as a model.

More spectacular episodes were to come, but as speedily as it seized the world's attention, so quickly did the California international revolution collapse. In 1967 San Francisco, by now the subject in itself of pop songs, hosted a "summer of love" in which thousands of "hippies," decked out in "ecstatic" clothing, avid for group sex and every known hallucinogen, and dancing to the light shows and beat of bands like Jerry Garcia's Grateful Dead, occupied a previously obscure neighborhood known as Haight-Ashbury. But already, by September 1967 and the end of that first summer, "the Haight," formerly an integrated, somewhat genteel working-class and middle-class neighborhood, had turned into a slum: mainly white, rife with users of amphetamine (then the most destructive of the drugs), and ruled, in effect, by irritable police during the day and a fascist motorcycle gang, the Hells Angels, at night. That consequence was an unperceived harbinger, for in time the liberties seized by that generation all turned back against their adherents. "Free love" developed into a massive pornography industry, such as was never seen before anywhere; in a manner not unconnected, the sudden freedom of young people to wander hitchhiking around the country became the freedom of perverts to murder hitchhiking girls and boys with impunity. Novelties in living had become fads in killing.

Except for the farm workers' movement, nearly all the radical eruptions of the fabled "Sixties" proved evanescent. In Oakland the Black Panthers appeared on the scene; but, rather than organizing the ghetto masses, they spent most of their time parading with weapons for the TV cameras and skirmishing with police; a brief campaign by the FBI to disrupt the so-called "party" destroyed it almost effortlessly. Large-scale demonstrations against the Vietnam conflict had more to do with the reluctance of young men to serve in the armed forces than with real political convictions. In the year 1968, when the whole world was convulsed by student strikes, "cultural revolution," Soviet armed intervention, and similar ructions, California, which had taken the lead in such behavior beginning in 1960, suddenly revealed another side when a man many considered its least favorite son, Richard Nixon, was elected to the presidency of the United States on a clearly antiyouth platform.

Los Angeles in 1968 suffered the ignominy of Robert Kennedy's assassination, and northern California that year gaped along with the rest of the globe at the rioting on the campus at San Francisco State University, a "struggle" then considered of tremendous moment but almost completely forgotten within a decade. The next year saw the occupation of a former federal prison on Alcatraz Island, in San Francisco Bay, by a group of American Indian protesters, but that also proved of fleeting import. A loathsome troll who recruited an army of runaway teenaged girls, Charles Manson, made himself much more famous in 1969 with his "movement" when it committed a ghastly multiple murder, the main victim of which was movie star Sharon Tate. The "Manson Family" represented neither more nor less significant a grouping than the Black Panthers; both had the characteristics of a criminal gang, and in some ways they were mirror images of one another.

An uproar driven by "the media," a term just then catching on, continued for some time. In 1970 a student mob near Santa Barbara burned down a bank in protest against the continuing Indochina war; but Santa Barbara had always been the least serious and most bourgeois of California's university towns, and it is doubtful that very many of those who joined in burning the bank actually closed their accounts with the institution. Curiously, the one element in the Vietnam controversy that really merited attention, the patriotic demonstrations of so-called "hard-hat" union members, also in 1970, was absent from California. But a Black Communist ex-professor, Angela Davis, who had made no attempt to recruit the Black populace to the Party, became involved in a bungled and messy escape attempt by some prisoners in San Rafael, leading to her arrest and trial. That, too, caused widespread commentary in its time, but it had no other outcome than the discharge of hot air, aside from the deaths of a judge and some of the conspirators.

Meanwhile, movie actress Jane Fonda distinguished herself by equally flamboyant propaganda tours to Communist North Vietnam, where she became notorious for her apparently treasonous declamations; years later she partly erased the memory of that extravagant behavior by starting her fitness business. The cycle of "revolutionary" efforts ended in 1974 when a band of marginal types that named itself the Symbionese Liberation Army slew a Black educator, Dr. Marcus Foster, and kidnapped Patricia Hearst, an heiress to the mining and media empire.

Revolutionary parties that organized nobody, riot and rebellion for the benefit of television news, and liberation armies that fought no wars—what did it all signify? California swept the world with its radical culture. But it had produced no new idea, no new movement; rather, it evinced an innovation that was radical, but on a wholly different level: the transformation of *social revolt* into *aesthetic style.*

The British poet Thom Gunn, who was to become a Californian himself, had observed in a poem written years before that Elvis Presley had turned "revolt into a style." This was not a revolution in literary and artistic style such as California had seen in the 1940s; rather, it was a change in "lifestyle," or life as a matter of style, of a pose struck, of a *posture* such as once had been common only among the dilettantes of the wealthy classes. This was California's great invention, and it explained both the suddenness with which it triumphed and the equal abruptness with which, intellectually at least, it declined.

The transformation of revolt into style had at least one antecedent: Nathanael West, in *The Day of the Locust,* had described his immortal protagonist, Tod Hackett, in Hollywood:

> [H]e walked along, [and] examined the evening crowd. A great many people wore sports clothes that were not really sports clothes. Their sweaters, knickers, slacks, blue flannel jackets with brass buttons were fancy dress. The fat lady in the yachting cap was going shopping, not boating; the man in the Norfolk jacket and Tyrolean hat was returning, not from a mountain, but an insurance office; and the girl in slacks and sneaks with a bandanna around her head had just left a switchboard, not a tennis court.

It could be argued that West's Communist comrades in the cabaret folk milieu, as well as in Hollywood, were most responsible for the spread of such simulacra throughout the culture. California radicalism, once an experiment, had become an industry.

Very little was saved or survived from this excitement. Even the farmworker movement degenerated into a cult of César Chávez, eventually fragmenting along ethnic lines between Hispanics and Filipinos. Philip Vera Cruz, a pioneer of the 1965 Delano struggle, left the United Farm Workers when Chávez began to court, of all people, the Philippine dictator Ferdinand Marcos. And of course, radical protest was eventually transformed into "political correctness," or Stalinism *redux.*

This was not what Rexroth, to cite one example, had desired. Soon he quit the Bay Area for hedonistic Santa Barbara, where he was hired by the university. He had, at the beginning, supported the Black Panthers, perhaps against his better judgment, but finally he seemed to have given up his radicalism. When he died in 1982, Octavio Paz, who had long admired him, noted that near his end Rexroth had described the main characteristic of the twentieth century as the loss of revolutionary hopes.

Rexroth's sinister shadow in poetry, George Oppen, died two years later; in 1969 he was awarded the Pulitzer Prize for his verse. Donald Davie, another British poet who had come to California (but who had not stayed), recalled him mordantly:

> Not a bit
> of help to me was George, or George's writing . . .
> I distrusted them, distrust them still.

California, after its takeover of the world, produced little of lasting value in the literary and artistic fields. The books that most effectively propagandized the revolution of the Sixties, Tom Wolfe's *Electric Kool-Aid Acid Test* and Joan Didion's *Slouching Toward Bethlehem,* shared a fundamental hollowness with the overall experience. No poets of distinction emerged to succeed Rexroth, Lamantia, Duncan, Spicer, Snyder, and company. An acolyte of their generation, Richard Brautigan, crafted a series of "hippie-surreal" novels; and a denizen of Los Angeles bars, Charles Bukowski, became a marginal literary icon (more in Europe than America) with a series of gutter epics. But strangely, these writers could not grow beyond a peculiar, almost self-caricatural prettiness (in Brautigan's case) or bluster (in Bukowski's); they formed one-member schools of a kind of genre fiction. Most of the cultural life of California during the nineteen-sixties, -seventies, and -eighties was dominated by figures from the nineteen-forties and -fifties such as Ginsberg (who flew in and out) and Ferlinghetti. While pop music, in apparent contrast, produced thousands of new bands, nearly all of their work had an ephemeral nature; the one great exception to this shallowness was Jerry Garcia's Grateful Dead.

California's literature, during this period, seemed incapable of escaping the genre trap. Its women science-fiction writers, like Ursula K. LeGuin (daughter of the anthropologist Alfred Kroeber), published novels filled with every kind of Utopian and dystopian conceit, but added nothing meaningful to the common literary legacy. Other female authors languished in forms of ethnic celebration that offered little more than the traditional "women's novel" in exotic dress. Only Philip K. Dick, who remained primarily a science-fiction author, and Maya Angelou, a voice for African-American strivings, surpassed the limits of genre literature, the former through his unique meditations on social control, and the latter with her valuable memoirs, although both were uneven in quality of output.

However, perhaps paradoxically, the movie industry showed an occasional excellence. The 1974 film *Chinatown,* written by Robert Towne and directed by Roman Polanski, the widower of Sharon Tate, is almost universally, and rightly, praised as a California classic. *Chinatown* is the third in a color trilogy of outstanding "California movies," beginning with Alfred Hitchcock's *Vertigo* in 1958 and continuing with Marlon Brando's extraordinary *One-Eyed Jacks,* a cowboy picture set on the Central Coast, in 1961. These films, along with Eric von Stroheim's immortal *Greed* (1923–25, based on Frank Norris's *McTeague*), and Billy Wilder's *Sunset Boulevard* (1950), make up a very short list of the best films about California, along with the greatest of all California films, *Blade Runner,* based on a novel of Philip K. Dick, which came out in 1982. But as the twentieth century came to a close the argument could be made, if it had not been already, that all American cinema is in some obscure way about California. The film industry also saw the emergence of a man who, at times, seemed to be the only person in California who still believed in the old Bohemian tradition: the director Francis Ford Coppola. But while he made many movies, and did good works all over the state, the creation of a great California film eluded him.

What remained? The bold experiments in music of Cowell and Partch were nearly forgotten, though both eventually gained new defenders, and a man Rexroth had greatly admired, the composer Lou Harrison, made some interesting advances. In art, the great postwar revolution of Clyfford Still and his companions had long given way to a California figurative style, and other "movements," that gained their exponents, such as Richard Diebenkorn, praise in New York and abroad, but offered little that was radical or even novel—though they could hardly be called reactionary.

A minor intellectual earthquake came in the mid-1970s with the emergence of a "punk" scene in both San Francisco and Los Angeles; this was the ultimate reduction of revolt to style, an anarchist pose that was extraordinarily well-behaved considering its nihilistic tone. The "last punk," an Angeleño named Henry Rollins, briefly excited hope in some intellectuals by reading Henry Miller from concert stages, in a revival of the old "poetry readings," known as "spoken word." But compared with Miller's writing, Rollins's own work was pretty slender. However, one major figure among the original California "punks" was a much older artist and filmmaker of genius, Bruce Conner, who had created stunning surrealist constructions in the 1950s and even more beautiful hallucinatory drawings in the psychedelic Sixties. In 1976, his short film *Crossroads,* made up of newsreel images of the atomic-test explosion at Bikini Atoll in 1946, was shown in San Francisco.

Ronald Reagan, the state's Republican governor from 1967 to 1975, made his first serious bid for the U.S. presidency in 1976; the country was at a crossroads in more ways than Bruce Conner's "punk" admirers realized. Reagan's political career, like the biographies of William Randolph Hearst and Orson Welles, has been the pretext for millions of words—though about Reagan, at least, much remains to be said. Above all, Ronald Reagan, as he showed when he was elected president in 1980, understood Communism better than any of his predecessors, precisely because of his experience with the Hollywood Stalinists of the 1940s. But although Reagan, in his own way, was as quintessentially Californian as Richard Nixon, that is another story.

And so California continued on its seeming rush toward fulfillment, but with a destiny few could perceive or predict. The radicals of the past could not have anticipated the incredible rise of homosexuals as a major political constituency; even Harry Hay had much more modest expectations. In 1992 the rioting in Los Angeles following the early acquittal—later reversed—of a group of policemen in the beating of an African-American, Rodney King, impressed Nathanael West's image of *The Burning of Los Angeles* on many minds. But it then became almost a cliché, a symptom of the decadence of California radicalism; nobody made such unholy comparisons after Watts in 1965, when most people still trembled at the thought of American decline.

What would become of California, child of modernity? Certainly its economic dynamism appeared inexhaustible, and while revived racial and ethnic divisions seemed to spell the eventual disintegration of the United States, the Golden State was gifted with exceptional powers of endurance. Revolt as style, experiment as an industry, had taken over the political and intellectual establishment, particularly on university campuses. And there could be no more striking example of the rise of California radicals to power than the composition of the San Francisco city administration as this book goes to press: Terence Tyrone "Kayo" Hallinan elected District Attorney, and an unequalled master of style, Willie L. Brown, Jr., now the mayor. And just as the California revolution of the Sixties had its counterpart in the presidencies of Nixon and Reagan, the radical demagogy of Brown and Hallinan was countered by the repeated use of Governor Hiram Johnson's great reforming tool, the initiative and referendum system, to institute changes that reversed establishment radicalism through ballot measures such as Proposition 209, which imposed an end to "affirmative action" and was approved by the electorate.

And yet . . . as Los Angeles was haunted by West's fictions, so did San Franciscans who knew their history wonder if Brown and Hallinan were not treading the same path as Ruef and Schmitz almost a hundred years before them. Would the outcome be similar? Meanwhile, on the other side of the Border, Mexico in 1997 was reaching toward a previously unimaginable democracy and stability, even as the Hispanic share of California's population grew and grew. Could some new alignment of economic and political powers emerge, running north and south between San Francisco and Mexico City?

Finally, there remained the waterfront; the turbulent maritime labor movement of the past is distant and legendary in the 1990s; the waterfront itself, once a key symbol in California's psychic landscape, has fallen into the background, appearing shabby and blighted, an obsolete remnant of industrial archaeology, on the underside of postindustrial California. Yet, almost unnoticed, Los Angeles has become the second largest container port in the world. Operating giant gleaming cranes and other ultrasophisticated technology, enjoying unprecedented high wages, the dockworkers, now including women as well as men, have begun, in a context of reinvigorated unionism in America, to launch highly effective wildcat strikes, indicating the possibility, at least, of fresh upheaval. California revolutions have always been products of rising expectations rather than of desperate oppression, and the renewed maritime union militancy fits the pattern. Who, then, can say what form this great neo-Platonist adventure, the California Republic, may take in the future?

If there is a last word, it may belong to David Joseph Bohm, the physicist of exceptional genius who had begun his career as a Stalinist disciple of J. Robert Oppenheimer. Exploring quantum reality, Bohm has described the universe in terms of a "quantum pattern of active information" basic to the cosmic structure. This challenging concept seems acutely relevant to the end of the millennium, with California, more than any other place on earth, absorbed in the "information revolution" in which Silicon Valley plays so large a role. In Bohm's universe, where all of reality is an ocean of information, we may see the ultimate Californian idea.

Bibliography

Adamic, Louis. *Dynamite*. New York: Harper & Row, 1960.

———. *Laughing in the Jungle*. New York: Harper & Brothers, 1932.

Adams, Henry. *History of the United States of America During the Administrations of Thomas Jefferson*. New York: The Library of America, 1986.

Adorno, T. W., Else Frenkel-Brunswik, Daniel J. Levinson, and R. Nevitt Sanford, in collaboration with Betty Aron, Maria Hertz Levinson, and William Morrow. *The Authoritarian Personality*. New York: The American Jewish Committee, 1950.

Alberola, Octavio. "Baja California: Attempted Insurrections." *Anarchy* (New York), Fall 1995.

Albright, Thomas. *Art in the San Francisco Bay Area, 1945–1980*. Berkeley: University of California Press, 1985.

Allen, Donald, and George F. Butterick, eds. *The Postmoderns: The New American Poetry Revised*. New York: Grove Press, 1982.

Allen, Robert L. *The Port Chicago Mutiny*. New York: Warner Books, 1989.

American Legion. Department of California. Radical Research Committee. "Agriculture Brief." Sacramento: American Legion, 1938.

———. "Alfred Renton Bridges." Sacramento: American Legion, 1938.

———. "Maritime Brief." Sacramento: American Legion, 1938.

Anderson, Jervis. "Early Voice." *The New Yorker*, December 2–16, 1972.

Anderson, Susan M. *Pursuit of the Marvelous: Stanley William Hayter, Charles Howard, Gordon Onslow Ford*. Laguna Beach: Laguna Art Museum, 1990.

Andrews, Gregg. *Shoulder to Shoulder? The American Federation of Labor, the United States, and the Mexican Revolution*. Berkeley: University of California Press, 1991.

Angelou, Maya. *I Know Why the Caged Bird Sings*. New York: Random House, 1970.

———. *Singin' and Swingin' and Gettin' Merry Like Christmas*. New York: Random House, 1976.

Anonymous. *The Deplorable History of the Catalans*. London: J. Baker, 1714.

Anonymous. "Tina Modotti." In Pierre Broué, editor, "Les Procés de Moscou dans le Monde." *Cahiers Léon Trotsky* (Grenoble, France), July–September, 1979.

Argüello, Luis. "Real Presidio de San Francisco, Cargos . . . , 30 de julio de 1818." In Enrique Arriola Woog, editor, *Sobre Rusos y Rusia: Antología Documental*. México, D.F.: Lotería Nacional, 1994.

Athearn, Robert. *The Denver and Rio Grande Western Railroad*. Lincoln: University of Nebraska Press, 1977.

Avrich, Paul. *Anarchist Portraits*. Princeton: Princeton University Press, 1988.

———. *The Haymarket Tragedy*. Princeton: Princeton University Press, 1984.

———. *Sacco and Vanzetti*. Princeton: Princeton University Press, 1991.

Balanza del comercio de España con los dominios de S.M. en América y en la India en el año de 1792. Madrid: Imprenta Real, 1805.

Banac, Ivo. *With Stalin Against Tito*. Ithaca, NY: Cornell University Press, 1988.

Barker, Tom. "The Story of the Sea." *The One Big Union Monthly/Industrial Pioneer* (Chicago), January–August 1921.

Bean, Lowell John, and Sylvia Brakke Vane. "Cults and Their Transformations." In *Handbook of North American Indians*, vol. 8, Robert F. Heizer, editor. Washington, DC: Smithsonian Institution Press, 1978.

Beatitude Anthology. San Francisco: City Lights Books, 1960.

Beck, Warren A., and Ynez D. Haase. *Historical Atlas of California*. Norman, OK: University of Oklahoma Press, 1974.

Benet, George. *A Place in Colusa*. San Pedro, CA: Singlejack Books, 1977.

Berkman, Alexander. *The Bolshevik Myth*. London: Pluto Press, 1989.

———. Correspondence seized in the office of *The Blast*. San Francisco: December 1916. Unpublished. Various dates.

Berkow, Robert, M.D., Ed. in Chief. *The Merck Manual of Diagnosis and Therapy*. Rahway, NJ: Merck & Co., 1992.

Bernhardson, Wayne, and Scott Wayne. *Baja California*. Hawthorn, Australia: Lonely Planet, 1994.

Bessie, Alvah. *Inquisition in Eden*. New York: Macmillan, 1965.

———. *Men in Battle*. San Francisco: Chandler & Sharp, 1975.

Blaisdell, Lowell L. *The Desert Revolution*. Madison: University of Wisconsin Press, 1962.

Bolton, Herbert E., ed. *Spanish Exploration in the Southwest, 1542–1706*. New York: Barnes and Noble, 1908/1963.

Bonetti, David. "California dreaming." *San Francisco Examiner*, March 10, 1995.

Boneu Companys, Fernando. *Gaspar de Portolà, Explorer and Founder of California*. Lérida, Spain: Instituto de Estudios Ilerdenses, 1983.

Bonner, Anthony, ed. *Selected Works of Ramón Llull*. 2 vols. Princeton, Princeton University Press, 1985.

Bonnet, Theodore. *The Regenerators*. San Francisco: Pacific Publishing Co., 1911.

Borob'yev, Lev. "Operatsiya 'Utka.'" *Novosti Razvyedki i Kontrrazvyedki* (Moscow), 1997.

Boscana y Mulet, P. Fray Jerónimo. *Relación histórica de la creencia, usos, costumbres y extravagancias de los indios de esta Misión de San Juan Capistrano, llamada la nación Acagchemen*. In Font Obrador, *El Padre Boscana, historiador de California*. Palma de Mallorca: Ediciones Cort, 1966.

Botkin, Benjamin A., and Alvin F. Harlow. *A Treasury of Railroad Folklore*. New York: Crown Publishers, 1953.

Bowditch, Nathaniel. *American Practical Navigator*. Washington, DC: Defense Mapping Agency, 1984.

Brinkley, Alan. *Voices of Protest*. New York: Random House, 1982.

Broué, Pierre, ed. "Les Procés de Moscou dans le Monde." *Cahiers Léon Trotsky* (Grenoble, France), July–September 1979.

Browne, Carl, and William McDevitt. *When Coxey's "Army" Marcht on Washington.* San Francisco: n.p. [McDevitt], 1944.

Buchanan, Joseph R. *The Story of a Labor Agitator.* New York: The Outlook Co., 1903.

Bulosan, Carlos. *America Is in the Heart.* Seattle: University of Washington Press, 1973.

———. *On Becoming Filipino [Selected Writings],* edited by E. San Juan, Jr. Philadelphia: Temple University Press, 1995.

Burke, Robert E. *Olson's New Deal for California.* Berkeley: University of California Press, 1953.

Cabot Rosselló, Salvador, T.O.R., editor. *El Convent de Sant Bonaventura en Llucmajor.* Llucmajor: Edició dels PP. Franciscans de la TOR de Sant Francesc, 1993.

California Senate Joint Fact-Finding Committee on Un-American Activities. *Report.* Sacramento: California Senate, 1943.

———. *Second Report.* Sacramento: California Senate, 1945.

California Senate Fact-Finding Committee on Un-American Activities, *Fourth Report.* Sacramento: California Senate, 1948.

———. *Fifth Report.* Sacramento: California Senate, 1949.

———. *Seventh Report,* Sacramento, California Senate, 1953.

———. *Twelfth Report,* Sacramento, California Senate, 1963.

Calvino, Italo. *Eremità in Parigi.* Milan: Mondadori, 1994.

Camp, William Martin. *San Francisco: Port of Gold.* New York: Doubleday, 1947.

Carlson, John Roy. *Under Cover.* New York: E. P. Dutton, 1943.

Carlson, Oliver. *A Mirror for Californians.* New York: Bobbs-Merrill, 1941.

Carner-Ribalta, J. *Contribució a una biogràfia de Gaspar Portolà.* Barcelona: Dalmau, 1966.

Castillo, Edward D. "The Impact of Euro-American Exploration and Settlement." In *Handbook of North American Indians,* vol. 8. Robert F. Heizer, editor. Washington, DC: Smithsonian Institution Press, 1978.

Cayuela Fernández, José Gregorio. "1898: el final de un Estado a ambos lados del Atlántico." In Consuelo Naranjo Orovio et al., editors, *La nación soñada: Cuba, Puerto Rico y Filipinas ante el 98.* Madrid: Doce Calles, 1996.

Cendrars, Blaise, *Hollywood: Mecca of the Movies.* Trans. Garrett White. Berkeley: University of California Press, 1995.

———. *L'Or,* Paris, Éditions Denoël, 1960.

———. *Modernities & Other Writings.* Trans. Monique Chefdor and Esther Allen. Lincoln: University of Nebraska Press, 1992.

Central Intelligence Agency. *Venona: Soviet Espionage and the American Response, 1939–1957.* Washington, DC: Central Intelligence Agency, Center for the Study of Intelligence, 1998. Published on the Internet at http://www.odci.gov/csi.

Cervantes, Miguel. *Don Quixote,* trans. by J. M. Cohen. Harmondsworth: Penguin Books, 1950.

Chamisso, Ad[e]lbert von, "The Man Without A Shadow." In J. R. Earl, editor and translator, *The Spider and the Rose.* San Francisco: Rune Mountain, 1993.

Chaplin, Ralph. *Wobbly.* Chicago: University of Chicago Press, 1948.

Chase, Gilbert. *America's Music.* Urbana and Chicago: University of Illinois Press, 1987.

Chevalier, Haakon. *Oppenheimer: The Story of a Friendship.* New York: George Braziller, 1965.

Chicago Daily News. Almanac and Year-Book. Chicago: 1884–.

Choy, Philip P., Lorraine Dong, and Marlon K. Hom. *The Coming Man: 19th-Century American Perceptions of the Chinese*. Seattle: University of Washington Press, 1994.

Clearwater, Bonnie, editor. *West Coast Duchamp*. Miami Beach, FL: Grassfield Press, 1991.

Close, Upton, pseud. [Hall, Josef Washington]. *Eminent Asians*. New York: D. Appleton & Company, 1929.

Clute, John, and Peter Nichols. *The Encyclopedia of Science Fiction*. New York: St. Martin's/ Griffin, 1993.

Cole, Lester. *Hollywood Red*. Palo Alto: Ramparts Press, 1981.

Collier, Simon, Thomas E. Skidmore, and Harold Blakemore. *The Cambridge Encyclopedia of Latin America and the Caribbean*. Cambridge: Cambridge University Press, 1992.

Combat (New York), 1968–72.

Comité Internacional de Propaganda y de Acción del Transporte. *Las Tareas del Proletariado del Transporte, Informe Leido en la Ve [sic], Conferencia Internacional de los Obreros Revolucionarios del Transporte*. Paris: Internacional Sindical Roja, n.d. [1929].

Commissió Amèrica i Catalunya 1992. *Diccionari dels Catalans d'Amèrica,* 4 vols. Barcelona: Generalitat de Catalunya, 1992.

Communist International. *Programme of the Communist International Together with the Statutes of the C.I.* New York: Workers Library Publishers, 1929.

———. *Strategy of the Communists*. A letter from the C.I. to the Mexican C.P. Chicago: Workers Party of America, 1923.

———. *The Struggle Against Imperialist War and the Tasks of the Communists*. Resolution of the VI World Congress of the C.I. [1928]. New York: Workers Library Publishers, 1932.

Communist Party of the U.S.A. *The Way Out: A Program for American Labor*. Manifesto and Principal Resolutions Adopted by the 8th Convention of the C.P. of the U.S.A. New York: Workers Library Publishers, 1934.

Congress of Industrial Organizations. *Official Reports on the Expulsion of Communist Dominated Organizations from the C.I.O.* Washington, DC: Congress of Industrial Organizations, 1954.

Conquest, Robert. *Stalin: Breaker of Nations*. New York: Viking Penguin, 1991.

Il Corriere del Popolo (San Francisco), 1910–1975.

County of Marin. Office of Frank J. Keaton, Coroner, San Rafael, California. Death Certificate and Coroner's Autopsy Surgeon's Report. Case of Eli Jacobson, 1952.

Cowan, Geoffrey. *The People v. Clarence Darrow*. New York: Times Books, 1993.

Cregg, Magda, ed. *Hey Lew*. Bolinas, CA: Magda Cregg, 1997.

Crespí Fiol, Joan. "Viaje de la Expedición de tierra de San Diego a Monterey." In Font Obrador, Bartomeu. *El P. J. Crespí, explorador de la Costa Pacífica*. [Palma]: Institut d'Estudis Balearics [with] Govern Balear, Conselleria de Cultura, Educació, i Esports, 1994.

Cross, Ira B. *History of the Labor Movement in California*. Berkeley: University of California Press, 1935.

Crouchett, Lorraine Jacobs. *Filipinos in California*. El Cerrito, CA: Downey Place Publishing House, 1982.

Cuadra, Pablo Antonio. "In Defiance of Censorship: Culture and Ideology in Nicaragua Today." In Stephen Schwartz, editor, *The Transition*. San Francisco: Institute for Contemporary Studies, 1986.

Current Biography [Yearbook] 1946. edited by Anna Rothe. New York: H. W. Wilson Co., 1947.

Current Biography Yearbook 1974, edited by Charles Moritz. New York: H. W. Wilson Co., 1975.

Cutter, Donald C. *California in 1792: A Spanish Naval Visit.* Norman, OK: University of Oklahoma Press, 1990.

———, editor. *The California Coast, A Bilingual Edition of Documents from the Sutro Collection* (1891). Norman, OK: University of Oklahoma Press, rev. ed. 1969.

Dallet, Joe. *Letters from Spain.* New York: Workers Library Publishers, 1938.

Dana, Richard Henry. *Two Years Before the Mast.* 1840. Reprinted London: The Folio Society, 1986.

Darder, Joan. "L'Entrevista amb Mn. Jordi Font." Full Dominical [de la] Església de Mallorca. [Palma]: March 31, 1996.

David, Henry M. *The History of the Haymarket Affair.* New York: Russell and Russell, 1958 (reprint).

Davie, Donald. "Recollections of George Oppen in a Letter to a Friend." *London Review of Books,* March 21, 1985.

Davis, Mike. *City of Quartz.* London: Verso, 1990.

d'Azevedo, Warren L., compiler. *Straight with the Medicine.* Berkeley: Heyday Books, 1985.

de Angulo, Gui. *The Old Coyote of Big Sur.* Berkeley: Stonegarden Press, 1995.

de Angulo, Jaime. *Indians in Overalls.* San Francisco: City Lights Books, 1990.

———. *The "Trial" of Ferrer: A Clerical-Judicial Murder.* New York: New York Labor News Co., 1920.

de Constanço, Miguel. "La defensa de la California: Informe del Señor Comandante de Artillería, México, 18 de octubre de 1794." In Enrique Arriola Woog, editor, *Sobre Rusos y Rusia: Antologia Documental.* México, D.F.: Lotería Nacional, 1994.

Dee, Dr. John. *The Hieroglyphic Monad.* London, Watkins, 1947.

Delaney, John J. *Dictionary of Saints.* Garden City, NY: Doubleday & Co., 1980.

Delgado Ribas, Josep Maria. "Bajo dos banderas (1881–1910). Sobre como sobrevivió la Compañía General de Filipinas al Desastre de 98." In Consuelo Naranjo Orovio et al., editors, *La nación soñada: Cuba, Puerto Rico y Filipinas ante el 98.* Madrid: Doce Calles, 1996.

———. "Comerç colonial i reformisme borbònic: Els decrets de lliure comerç." L'Avenç (Barcelona), April 1979.

———. and Josep Maria Fradera. "El comerç entre Catalunya i América, 1690–1898: Un intent de síntesi histórica." Typescript, n.d.

DeMarco, Gordon. *A Short History of Los Angeles.* San Francisco, Lexikos, 1988.

de Mille. Agnes George. *Henry George, Citizen of the World.* Chapel Hill, NC: University of North Carolina Press, 1950.

Denning, Michael. *The Cultural Front.* London: Verso Press, 1996.

Dennis, Peggy. *The Autobiography of An American Communist.* Westport, CT: Lawrence Hill & Co., 1977.

Dick, Philip K. *The Shifting Realities of P.K.D., Selected Literary and Philosophical Writings.* Lawrence Sutin, ed. New York: Vintage Books, 1995.

Dillon, Richard. *J. Ross Browne, Confidential Agent in Old California.* Norman, OK: University of Oklahoma Press, 1965.

Dinnean, Lawrence. *Les Jeunes.* Edited by J. R. K. Kantor. Berkeley: Bancroft Library, 1980.

Di Suvero, Victor. Untitled autobiographical essay. In *Contemporary Authors Autobiography Series,* vol. 26. Detroit: Gale Research, 1997.

Dmytryk, Edward. *It's a Hell of a Life But Not a Bad Living.* New York: Times Books, 1978.

———. *Odd Man Out.* Carbondale, IL: Southern Illinois University Press, 1996.

Draper, Theodore. *The Roots of American Communism.* New York: Viking Press, 1957.

Duncan, Robert. "The Homosexual in Society." *Politics* (New York), August 1944. Reprinted in Ekbert Faas, *Young Robert Duncan: Portrait of the Poet as Homosexual in Society.* Santa Barbara: Black Sparrow Press, 1983.

———. *Selected Poems.* New York: New Directions, 1993.

———. *The Years as Catches.* Berkeley: Oyez, 1966.

DuPlessis, Rachel Blau, ed., *The Selected Letters of George Oppen.* Durham and London: Duke University Press, 1990.

Eisenstein, Sergei M. *Immoral Memories.* Boston: Houghton Mifflin Co., 1983.

Elizalde Perez-Grueso, María Dolores. "Valor internacional de Filipinas en 1898: la perspectiva norteamericana." In Consuelo Naranjo Orovio et al., editors, *La nación soñada: Cuba, Puerto Rico y Filipinas ante el 98.* Madrid: Doce Calles, 1996.

Engelhardt, Zephyrin. *The Missions and Missionaries of California.* San Francisco: James H. Barry, 1908.

Faas, Ekbert. *Young Robert Duncan: Portrait of the Poet as Homosexual in Society.* Santa Barbara: Black Sparrow Press, 1983.

Fabre, Michel, and Robert E. Skinner, editors. *Conversations with Chester Himes.* Jackson, MS: University of Mississippi Press, 1995.

Facondo, Gabriella. *Socialismo Italiano Esiile Negli USA.* Bastogi: Editrice Italiana, 1993.

Farmer, David H. *The Oxford Dictionary of Saints.* Oxford: Oxford University Press, 1987.

Farris, Glenn J. "The Day of the Tall Strangers." *The Californians* (Sebastopol, CA), May/June 1992.

Federal Bureau of Investigation. Letter of James D. Whaley, Chief Division Counsel, to Stephen Schwartz, San Francisco, re: Eli Bernard Jacobson, May 20, 1996.

———. Reports, 1955. Released Under Freedom of Information Act. Re: J. Robert Oppenheimer, Muriel Nicholas, Kenneth Rexroth, Dorothy Van Ghent. Collection of Michael Chapman, Washington, D.C.

Ferlinghetti, Lawrence, and Nancy J. Peters. *Literary San Francisco.* San Francisco: City Lights Books and Harper & Row, Inc., 1980.

Fernández-Armesto, Felipe. Historical essays. In Andrew Eames, editor, *Mallorca & Ibiza.* Singapore, APA Publications (HK) Ltd., 1990.

Fernández Grandizo, Manuel (G. Munis). *Jalones de derrota, promesa de victoria.* México D.F.: Editorial Revolución, 1948.

Filler, Louis. *Muckraking and Progressivism in the American Tradition.* New Brunswick, NJ: Transaction Books, 1996.

Filmfront. Reprint edition annotated by Anthony Slide. Metuchen, NJ: The Scarecrow Press, 1986.

Finney, Jack. *The Body Snatchers.* New York: Dell, 1955.

Flores Magón, Ricardo [with William C. Owen and others]. *Land and Liberty,* 2nd ed. Sanday [Orkney Islands, U.K.], Cienfuegos Press, 1977.

Florescano, Enrique, and Fernando Castillo. *Controversia sobre la libertad de comercio en Nueva España, 1776–1818.* México, D.F.: I.M.C.E., 1975.

Foner, Philip S. *History of the Labor Movement in the United States.* Vol. IV: *The Industrial Workers of the World.* New York: International Publishers, 1965.

Font Obrador, Bartomeu. *Fra Juníper Serra, Les Balears i el Nou Món.* [Palma]: Caixa de Balears "Sa Nostra," n.d.

————. *Joan Crespí, Explorador i cronista franciscà a l'Alta Califòrnia.* Palma de Mallorca: Ajuntament de Palma, 1994.

————. *Juníper Serra, L'empremta mallorquina a la Califòrnia naixent.* Palma de Mallorca: Ajuntament de Palma, 1988.

————. *El Padre Boscana, historiador de California.* Palma de Mallorca: Ediciones Cort, 1966.

————. *El P. J. Crespí, explorador de la Costa Pacífica.* Palma de Mallorca: Institut d'Estudis Baleàrics (with) Govern Balear, Conselleria de Cultura, Educació, i Esports, 1994.

————. ed. *Mallorca i el Nou Món (Califòrnia).* Palma de Mallorca: Estudi General Lul.lià, 1992.

————and Norman Neuerburg. *Fr. Junípero Serra.* Palma de Mallorca: Comissió de Cultura, Consell Insular de Mallorca, 1992.

Fontana Lázaro, Josep. "Comercio colonial y crecimiento económico: Revisiones e hipótesis." Intro. to *La economía española al final del Antiguo Régimen,* vol. III: *Comercio y colonias.* Madrid: Alianza Editorial, 1983.

Forteza, Miquel. *Els descendents dels jueus conversos de Mallorca.* Palma de Mallorca: Editorial Moll, 1972.

Frost, Richard H. *The Mooney Case.* Stanford: Stanford University Press, 1968.

Fry, B. C., editor. *Tom Barker and the I. W. W.* Canberra: Australian Society for the Study of Labour History, 1965.

Fuchik, Julius. *Notes From the Gallows.* New York: New Century Publishers, 1946.

Galarza, Ernesto. *Barrio Boy.* Notre Dame, IN: University of Notre Dame Press, 1971.

————. *Spiders in the House and Workers in the Field.* Notre Dame, IN: University of Notre Dame Press, 1970.

Gallagher, Dorothy. *All the Right Enemies.* New Brunswick, NJ: Rutgers University Press, 1988.

Garcia, Jerry. *Harrington Street.* New York: Delacorte Press, 1995.

[Gardner, Meredith Knox], "Covernames in Diplomatic Traffic," Washington, DC, 30 August 1947. In Central Intelligence Agency. *Venona: Soviet Espionage and the American Response, 1939–1957.* Washington, DC: Central Intelligence Agency, Center for the Study of Intelligence, 1998. Published on the Internet at http://www.odci.gov/csi.

Garnett, Porter. *Philosophical Writings on the Ideal Book.* Compiled by Jack Werner Stauffacher. San Francisco: The Book Club of California, 1994.

Gayangos, Pascual de. *Libros de Caballerías.* In *Biblioteca de Autores Españoles.* Madrid: Ediciones Atlas, 1950.

Geoffrey of Monmouth. *History of the Kings of Britain.* Harmondsworth: Penguin Books, 1966.

Gerhard, Peter. *Pirates in the Pacific, 1575–1742.* 1960. Reprint, Lincoln: University of Nebraska Press, 1990.

German-American League for Culture. *True Answers to Nazi Claims.* n.p., 1937.

Gill, Peter B. [with Ottilie D. Markholt]. "The Sailors' Union of the Pacific, 1885–1929." Unpublished manuscript.

Ginger, Ann Fagan. *Carol Weiss King: Human Rights Lawyer.* Boulder, CO: University Press of Colorado, 1993.

Ginsberg, Allen. *Howl and Other Poems.* Introduction by William Carlos Williams. San Francisco: City Lights Books, 1956.

Gitlow, Benjamin. *I Confess.* New York: E. P. Dutton, 1940.

Glass, Fred. "'We Called It A Work Holiday': The Oakland General Strike of 1946." *Labor's Heritage* (Silver Spring, MD), Fall 1996.

Glasscock, C. B. *Bandits and the Southern Pacific.* New York: Frederick A. Stokes Co., 1929.

Goldman, Emma. *Syndicalism.* New York: Mother Earth, 1913.

Gómez Casas, Juan. *Historia del Anarcosindicalismo en España [español].* Madrid: Editorial Aguilera, 1977.

Goodchild, Peter. *J. Robert Oppenheimer: Shatterer of Worlds.* New York: Fromm, 1985.

Goodwin, James. *Eisenstein, Cinema, and History.* Urbana and Chicago: University of Illinois Press, 1993.

Gorter, Wytze, and George H. Hildebrand. *The Pacific Coast Maritime Shipping Industry, 1930–1948.* Berkeley and Los Angeles: University of California Press, 1954.

Graebner, Norman A. "The Land-Hunger Thesis Challenged." In Ramon E. Ruiz, editor, *The Mexican War: Was It Manifest Destiny?* New York: Holt, Rinehart and Winston, 1963.

Graham, Marcus. *Freedom of Thought Arraigned.* Los Angeles: *MAN!,* n.d. [1938?]

———. *Marxism and A Free Society.* London: ASP, n.d.

[Graham, Marcus]. *Free Ferrero and Sallitto.* New York: Ferrero-Sallitto Defense Committee, n.d. [1936].

Graham, Marcus, editor. *An Anthology of Revolutionary Poetry.* New York: Marcus Graham, 1929.

———. *MAN! Anthology.* London: Cienfuegos Press, 1974.

Grover, David H. *The San Francisco Shipping Conspiracies of World War One.* Napa, CA: Western Maritime Press, 1996.

Guadalupe Hidalgo Treaty of Peace 1848 and The Gadsden Treaty With Mexico 1853. Reprinted from *New Mexico Statutes 1963* Annotated Volume One. Truchas, NM: Tate Gallery, 1967.

Gudde, Erwin G. *California Place Names.* Berkeley: University of California Press, 1969.

Haas, Lisbeth. *Conquests and Historical Identities in California, 1769–1936.* Berkeley: University of California Press, 1995.

Halliwell, Leslie. *Halliwell's Filmgoer's and Video Viewer's Companion,* edited by John Walker. New York: Harper Perennial, 1993.

———. *Halliwell's Film Guide,* edited by John Walker. New York: Harper Perennial, 1995.

Hamalian, Linda. *A Life of Kenneth Rexroth.* New York: W. W. Norton & Co., 1991.

Harlow, Neal. *California Conquered.* Berkeley: University of California Press, 1982.

Harrison, Hank. *The Dead,* vol. I. San Francisco: Archives Press, 1990.

Hart, James D. *A Companion to California.* Berkeley: University of California Press, 1987.

Hatlen, Burton, editor. *George Oppen: Man and Poet.* Orono, ME: National Poetry Foundation, 1981.

Hay, Harry. *Radically Gay.* Boston: Beacon Press, 1996.

Healey, Dorothy Ray, and Maurice Isserman. *California Red.* Urbana and Chicago: University of Illinois Press, 1993.

Hedges, Elaine, and Shelley Fisher Fishkin, editors. *Listening to Silences.* New York: Oxford University Press, 1994.

Heizer, Robert F., editor. *California.* Vol. 8 in *Handbook of North American Indians.* Washington, DC: Smithsonian Institution Press, 1978.

Herrick, William. *¡Hermanos!* London: Weidenfeld and Nicolson, 1969.

Himes, Chester. *Lonely Crusade.* New York: Thunder's Mouth Press, 1994.

Hittell, Theodore H. *History of California,* vol. I. San Francisco: N.J. Stone & Co., 1897.

Hoffer, Eric. *The True Believer.* New York: Harper & Brothers, 1954.

Holmes, Clellon. "This Is the Beat Generation." *The New York Times Magazine,* November 16, 1952.

Holmes, John Clellon. *Go.* New York: Thunder's Mouth Press, 1988.

Holmstrom, David. "They Called Her Tokyo Rose." *San Francisco Examiner,* September 15, 1974.

Hynes, Harry. Journal Entries from Spanish Civil War. Collection of William Herrick.

Irons, Peter. *Justice At War.* Berkeley: University of California Press, 1993.

Jackson, Helen Hunt. *Ramona.* 1884. Reprinted New York: New American Library, 1988.

Jackson, Joseph Henry. *Anybody's Gold.* San Francisco: Chronicle Books, 1970.

James, C. L. R. Interview with Stephen Schwartz. London, February 17, 1983.

Jefferson, Thomas. *Writings.* Edited by Merrill D. Peterson. New York: The Library of America Literary Classics, 1984.

Jenkins, Edith A. *Against a Field Sinister.* San Francisco: City Lights Books, 1991.

Jepson, Willis Linn. *A Manual of the Flowering Plants of California.* Berkeley: University of California Press, 1925.

John Paul II. "Homily on the Canonization of Jesuit Fathers Roque González, Alfonso Rodríguez, and Juan del Castillo, Asunción, Paraguay, May 16, 1988." Washington, DC: National Catholic News Service.

Johnson, Jacqueline, Lee Mullican, Gordon Onslow Ford, and Wolfgang Paalen. *Dynaton 1951.* San Francisco: San Francisco Museum of Art, 1951.

Josephson, Matthew. *The Robber Barons.* London: Eyre & Spottiswoode, 1962.

Kagan, Paul. *New World Utopias.* New York: Penguin, 1975.

Kahn, Gordon. *Hollywood on Trial.* New York: Boni & Gaer, 1948.

Kaplan, Justin. *Lincoln Steffens.* New York: Simon & Schuster, 1974.

Katz, Ephraim. *The Film Encyclopedia.* New York: Harper & Row, 1979.

Kazin, Michael. *Barons of Labor.* Urbana: University of Illinois Press, 1987.

Keell, T. H. "Death of W. C. Owen." *Freedom Bulletin* (London), September 1929.

Kelly, J. N. D. *The Oxford Dictionary of Popes.* Oxford: Oxford University Press, 1986.

Kerouac, Jack. *The Dharma Bums.* New York: Viking Press, 1958.

———. *Lonesome Traveler.* New York: Grove Press, 1960.

Kim, Hakjoon. "Russian Foreign Ministry Documents on the Origins of the Korean War." *Korea and World Affairs* (Seoul), Summer 1996.

Király, Béla K. "The Aborted Soviet Military Plans Against Tito's Yugoslavia." Cited in Ivo Banac, *With Stalin Against Tito.* Ithaca, NY: Cornell University Press, 1988.

Klehr, Harvey and John E. Haynes. "Communists and the CIO: From the Soviet Archives." *Labor History* (New York), Summer 1994.

Klehr, Harvey, John Earl Haynes, and Fridrikh Igorevich Firsov. *The Secret World of American Communism.* New Haven: Yale University Press, 1995.

Knabb, Ken. *The Relevance of Rexroth.* Berkeley: Bureau of Public Secrets, 1990.

Koliqi, Ernest. "The Arbëresh in America." *Albanian Catholic Bulletin* (San Francisco), 1989.

Krauze, Enrique. *Mexico: Biography of Power.* New York: HarperCollins, 1997.

Kressel, Neil J. *Mass Hate: The Global Rise of Genocide and Terror.* New York: Plenum Press, 1996.

Kroeber, A. L. *Handbook of the Indians of California.* Washington, DC: Smithsonian Institution Press, 1925.

Lamantia, Philip. *Selected Poems 1943–1966.* San Francisco: City Lights Books, 1966.

———. "Surrealism in 1943." *VVV* (New York), 1943.

———. *Touch of the Marvelous.* Preface by Stephen Schwartz. Bolinas, CA: Four Seasons Foundation, 1974.

Landis, Arthur H. *The Abraham Lincoln Brigade.* New York: Citadel Press, 1967.

[La Pérouse, Comte de]. *Voyages and Adventures of La Pérouse.* Translated by Julius S. Gassner. Honolulu: University of Hawaii Press, 1969.

Lapp, Rudolph M. *Blacks in Gold Rush California.* New Haven: Yale University Press, 1977.

Larkin, Colin, editor. *The Guinness Encyclopedia of Popular Music.* New York: Stockton Press, 1995.

Las Casas, Bartolomé de. *In Defense of the Indians.* DeKalb, IL: Northern Illinois University Press, 1974.

Laslett, John, and Mary Tyler. *The ILGWU in Los Angeles, 1907–1988.* Inglewood, CA: Ten Star Press, 1989.

Lazitch, Branko, in collaboration with Milorad M. Drachkovitch. *Biographical Dictionary of the Comintern.* Stanford: Hoover Institution Press, 1986.

Lea, Homer. *The Valor of Ignorance.* New York: Harper & Brothers, 1942.

Lewis, Oscar. *Bay Window Bohemia.* New York: Doubleday & Co., 1956.

Libertas! (Los Angeles), April 1926.

Lie, Haakon. *En Sjømanns Saga.* Oslo: Tiden Norsk Forlag, 1993.

Lincoln, Abraham. *Speeches and Writings, 1832–1858.* New York: The Library of America, 1989.

Lipton, Dean. "Wayne M. Collins and the Case of 'Tokyo Rose.'" *Journal of Contemporary Studies* (San Francisco), Fall/Winter 1985.

London, Jack. *The Iron Heel.* Chicago: Lawrence Hill Books, n.d.

London, Joan. *Jack London and His Daughters.* Berkeley: Heyday Books, 1990.

Long, Buck, pseud. [Stephen Schwartz], and Lawrence V. Cott. "Alan Cranston's Big Lies." *The American Spectator,* April 1990.

Lovestone, Jay. *Pages From Party History.* New York, Workers Library Publishers, [1929].

Lucey, Paul A. *Lowell High School: A History of the Oldest Public High School in California.* San Francisco: Lowell Alumni Association, 1989.

Lynch, John. *Spain Under the Hapsburgs.* Vol. II: *Spain and America, 1598–1700.* Oxford: Basil Blackwell, 1969.

Lyons, Eugene. *Assignment in Utopia.* New York: Harcourt, Brace & Co., 1937.

———. *The Red Decade.* New York: Bobbs-Merrill, 1939.

Ma, L. E. A. *Revolutionaries, Monarchists, and Chinatowns.* Honolulu: University of Hawaii Press, 1990.

MacLachlan, Colin M. *Anarchism and the Mexican Revolution.* Berkeley: University of California Press, 1991.

Mahr, August C. *The Visit of the* Rurik *to San Francisco in 1816.* Stanford: Stanford University Press, 1932.

Majo Framís, Ricardo. *Vida y Hechos de Fray Junípero Serra.* Madrid: Espasa-Calpe, 1956.

Martin, Jay. *Nathanael West: The Art of His Life.* New York: Farrar, Straus & Giroux, 1970.

Martínez Albiach, Alfredo. *"Religiosidad hispana y sociedad borbónica"* (1968). Cited in Reglá, Juan, *Historia de Cataluña.* Madrid: Alianza Editorial, 1974.

Martínez Shaw, Carlos. *Cataluña en la Carrera de Indias, 1680–1756.* Barcelona, Crítica, 1981.

Marx, Karl. *The Revolutions of 1848.* Harmondsworth: Penguin Books, 1973.

Marx, Karl, and Frederick Engels. *Revolution in Spain.* New York: International Publishers, 1939.

Matthews, George T., ed. *News and Rumor in Renaissance Europe: The Fugger Newsletters.* New York: G. P. Putnam's Sons, 1959.

Mayes, Barney. Untitled memoir. Typescript. Undated. Unpublished. Collection of Paul Dempster.

Mazour, Anatole G. "Dimitriy Zavalishin: Dreamer of a Russian-American Empire." *Pacific Historical Review* (San Francisco), March 1936.

———. *The First Russian Revolution, 1825.* 2nd ed. Stanford: Stanford University Press, 1961.

McWilliams, Carey. *California: The Great Exception.* New York: A. A. Wyn, 1949.

———. *Factories in the Field.* Boston: Little, Brown, 1939.

———. *North From Mexico.* New York: Praeger, 1990.

Melville, Herman. *Typee (1846), Omoo (1847), Mardi (1849).* Reprinted in one volume. New York: The Library of America, 1982.

Mendoza, Vicente T., editor. *El Corrido Mexicano.* México, D.F.: Fondo de Cultura Económica, 1954.

Merriman, Marion, and Warren Lerude. *American Commander in Spain.* Reno: University of Nevada Press, 1986.

Meyer, Jean. *¿El sinarquismo, un fascismo mexicano?* México, D.F.: Joaquín Mortíz, 1979.

Millard, Bailey. *History of the San Francisco Bay Region.* Chicago/San Francisco/New York: American Historical Society, 1924.

Miller, Henry. *Big Sur and the Oranges of Hieronymus Bosch.* New York: New Directions, 1957.

———. *The Henry Miller Reader.* Lawrence Durrell, ed. New York: New Directions, 1959.

Milliken, Stephen F. *Chester Himes: A Critical Appraisal.* Columbia, MO: University of Missouri Press, 1976.

Mini, Norman. "That California Dictatorship." *The Nation,* February 20, 1935.

Mitchell, Greg. *The Campaign of the Century.* New York: Random House, 1992.

The Mooney-Billings Report (Suppressed by the Wickersham Commission). New York: Gotham House, 1932.

Morgan, Lewis Henry. *Ancient Society.* New York: Henry Holt and Company, 1877.

Mullen, Kevin. "Gangs Once Ruled Frisco," *San Francisco Examiner,* February 1, 1996.

Mullen, Kevin J. *Let Justice Be Done.* Reno: University of Nevada Press, 1989.

Museo de Arte Moderno. *Hommage [sic] to Wolfgang Paalen.* Mexico, D.F.: Museo de Arte Moderno, 1967.

Nadal, Jordi, and Gabriel Tortella, editors. *Agricultura, comercio colonial y crecimiento económico en la España contemporánea.* Barcelona: Ariel, 1974.

Naranjo Orovio, Consuelo, Miguel Ángel Puig-Samper, and Luis Miguel García Mora, eds. *La nación soñada: Cuba, Puerto Rico y Filipinas ante el 98.* Madrid: Doce Calles, 1996.

Nelles, Dieter. "ITF Resistance Against Nazis and Fascism in Germany and Spain." In Bob Reinalda, editor, *The International Transport Workers' Federation (ITF) 1914–1945: The Edo Fimmen Era.* Amsterdam: Stichting beheer IISG/International Institute for Social History, 1997.

Nelson, Bruce. *Workers on the Waterfront.* Urbana and Chicago: University of Illinois Press, 1988.

Nelson, Steve, with James R. Barrett and Rob Ruck. *Steve Nelson, American Radical.* Pittsburgh: University of Pittsburgh Press, 1981.

Neuburg, Victor. "William Charles Owen." *Freedom Bulletin* (London), September 1929.

Neufert, Andreas. *Gordon Onslow Ford.* Munich: Höcherl Verlag, n.d.

Newcomb, Rexford. *The Old Mission Churches and Historic Houses of California.* Philadelphia: J. P. Lippincott, 1925.

Norris, Frank. *Novels and Essays: Vandover and the Brute, McTeague, The Octopus, Essays.* New York: The Library of America, 1986.

O'Brien, Flann. *The Best of Myles.* London: HarperCollins, 1993.

Okinawa Club of America. *History of the Okinawans in North America.* Los Angeles: University of California Press and Okinawa Club of America, 1988.

Olaya, Francisco. *Genocidio Español en la España de los Austria.* México, D.F.: Editorial Ideas, 1975.

Older, Cora. *California Missions and Their Romances.* New York: Coward-McCann, 1938.

Olgin, M. J. *Why Communism? Plain Talks on Vital Problems.* With an introduction by Sam Darcy. San Francisco: Western Worker Publishers, 1934.

Oliva Melgar, Josep Maria. "La Reial Companyia de Comerç de Barcelona a les Índies." *L'Avenç* (Barcelona), April 1979.

Olsen, Tillie. *Tell Me a Riddle.* 1962. Reprint edited by Deborah Silverton Rosenfelt. New Brunswick, NJ: Rutgers University Press, 1995.

Onslow Ford, Gordon. *Ecomorphology.* Point Reyes, CA: Gordon Onslow Ford, 1993.

———. *Insights* [Petaluma, CA]: Lapis Press, 1991.

———. Notes Prepared for Stephen Schwartz. Inverness, CA: 1996.

———. *Painting in the Instant.* N.p. N.d.

———. *The Quest of the Inner-Worlds.* Curated by Fariba Bogzaran. Berkeley: John F. Kennedy University, 1996.

———. *Towards a New Subject in Painting.* San Francisco: San Francisco Museum of Art, 1948.

Oppen, George. *Collected Poems.* New York: New Directions, 1976.

Oppen, Mary. *Meaning a Life.* Santa Barbara: Black Sparrow Press, 1978.

Osio, Antonio María. *The History of Alta California.* Translated by Rose Marie Beebe and Robert M. Senkewicz. Madison, WI: University of Wisconsin Press, 1996.

Owen, William C. *Anarchism Versus Socialism.* London: Freedom Press, 1922.

———. "At Los Angeles." *Mother Earth* (New York), April 1909.

———. "The Los Angeles Times Explosion." *Mother Earth* (New York), December 1910.

Paalen, Wolfgang. *Form and Sense.* New York: Wittenborn and Co., 1945.

Palmer, Frederick. "Abe Ruef of the 'Law Offices,'" *Collier's,* January 12, 1907.

[Palou Amengual, Francesc]. *Palou's Life of Fray Junípero Serra.* Translated and edited by Maynard J. Geiger. Washington, DC: Academy of American Franciscan History, 1955.

Panikkar, Raimon. "Intercultural and Intrareligious Dialogue According to Ramon Llull." *Catalònia* (Barcelona), October 1995.

Partch, Harry. *Bitter Music: Collected Journals, Essays, Introductions, and Librettos.* Edited and with an introduction by Thomas Geary. Urbana and Chicago: University of Illinois Press, 1991.

Patchen, Kenneth. *The Journal of Albion Moonlight,* 1941. Reprinted New York: New Directions, 1961.

———. *Selected Poems.* New York: New Directions, 1957.

Paz, Octavio. "Kenneth Rexroth." In Octavio Paz, *Excursiones/Incursiones: Obras Completas,* ed. del Autor [edited by the author], *Tomo 2, Dominio Extranjero.* Barcelona: Círculo de Lectores, 1991.

———. *The Labyrinth of Solitude.* New York: Grove Press, 1961.

———. *Sor Juana, or The Traps of Faith.* Cambridge, MA: Harvard University Press, 1988.

Peat, F. David. *Infinite Potential: The Life and Times of David Bohm.* Reading, MA: Addison-Wesley Publishing Co., 1997.

People's World. Also called *Daily People's World, People's Daily World, People's Weekly World* (San Francisco, New York), 1938.

Perelman, S. J. *The Last Laugh.* New York: Simon & Schuster, 1981.

Péret, Benjamin. *Livre de Chilam Balam de Chumayel.* Paris: Editions Denoël, 1955.

Peterson, H. C. *Propaganda for War.* Norman, OK: University of Oklahoma Press, 1939.

"Philologos." "The Book of Schlemiel." *Forward* (New York), October 6, 1995.

Pilnyak, Boris. *The Volga Falls To the Caspian Sea.* Translated by Charles Malamuth. New York: Cosmopolitan Book Corp., 1931.

Pitt, Leonard. *The Decline of the Californios.* Berkeley; University of California Press, 1966.

Polito, Robert. *Savage Art: A Biography of Jim Thompson.* New York: Vintage Books, 1995.

Polk, Dora Beale. *The Island of California: A History of a Myth.* Spokane: Arthur H. Clark, 1991.

Porcel, Baltasar. *Els xuetes.* Barcelona: Edicions 62, 1983.

The Proletariat (San Francisco), May–June 1918.

Prpic, George J. *The Croatian Immigrants in America.* New York: Philosophical Library, 1971.

Quinn, William J. "The Communist Factor in Our Strikes," *Police and Peace Officers' Journal of the State of California* (San Francisco), April 1936.

[Radin, Paul]. "The Italian Dream," *City of San Francisco,* August 24, 1975. Excerpted from Paul Radin, *The Italians of San Francisco: Their Adjustment and Acculturation.* San Francisco: State [of California] Emergency Relief Administration, 1935.

Raineri, Vivian McGuckin. *The Red Angel.* New York: International Publishers, 1991.

Raskin, A. H. "Labor: Movement in Search of a Mission." In Lipset, Seymour Martin, editor, *Unions in Transition.* San Francisco: Institute for Contemporary Studies, 1986.

Rawls, James J. *Indians of California: The Changing Image.* Norman, OK: University of Oklahoma Press, 1984.

Ray, Man. *Self Portrait*. London: André Deutsch, 1963.

Reglá, Juan. *Historia de Cataluña,* Madrid: Alianza Editorial, 1974.

Regler, Gustav. *Wolfgang Paalen*. New York: Nierendorf Editions, 1946.

Reinalda, Bob, editor. *The International Transport Workers' Federation (ITF) 1914–1945: The Edo Fimmen Era*. Amsterdam: Stichting beheer IISG/International Institute for Social History, 1997.

Revill, David. *The Roaring Silence—John Cage: A Life*. New York: Arcade Publishing, 1992.

Rexroth, Kenneth. *An Autobiographical Novel,* edited by Linda Hamalian. New York: New Directions, 1991.

———. *The Collected Shorter Poems of Kenneth Rexroth*. New York: New Directions, 1966.

———. *In What Hour*. New York: Macmillan, 1940.

———. Letters to Bertram D. Wolfe, November 13, 1939 et seq. Bertram D. Wolfe Collection, Hoover Institution Archive, Stanford, CA.

Rhodes, Richard. *The Making of the Atomic Bomb*. New York: Simon & Schuster, 1986.

Rice, Richard B., William A. Bullough, and Richard J. Orsi. *The Elusive Eden: A New History of California*. New York: McGraw-Hill Book Co., 1988.

Rice, William B., *The Los Angeles Star, 1851–1864*. Berkeley: University of California Press, 1947.

Richards, Janet. *Common Soldiers*. San Francisco: Archer Press, 1979.

Richmond, Al. *A Long View From the Left*. Boston: Houghton Mifflin, 1973.

———. *Native Daughter: The Story of Anita Whitney*. San Francisco: Anita Whitney 75th Anniversary Committee, 1942.

Rideout, Walter B. *The Radical Novel in the United States, 1900–1954*. Cambridge, MA: Harvard University Press, 1956.

Rieff, David. *Los Angeles: Capital of the Third World*. New York: Simon & Schuster, 1991.

Riegel, Robert E. *The Story of the Western Railroads*. New York: Macmillan Publishing Company, 1926.

Riesenberg, Felix, Jr. *Golden Gate*. New York: Alfred A. Knopf, 1940.

Riggers' and Stevedores' Union of the Port of San Francisco. *Constitution, By-Laws, and Due Book*. 1919.

Rix, Erich. "'Sudeten-Waterloo' in U.S.A." 1939. Typescript. Unpublished.

———. "World Voyage." *West Coast Sailors* (San Francisco), March 3, June 2, and September 7, 1939.

Royce, Josiah. *California: A Study of American Character,* Boston: Houghton Mifflin Company, 1886.

Royce, Suzanne, curator. *The Years at White Gate Ranch, Stinson Beach, California 1963–1976*. Catalogue. Bolinas, CA: Bolinas Museum for the Art and History of Coastal Marin, 1995.

Roys, Ralph L., ed. *The Book of Chilam Balam of Chumayel*. Norman, OK: University of Oklahoma Press, 1967.

Rübner, Hartmut. "The International Seamen's Organisations After the First World War." In Bob Reinalda, editor, *The International Transport Workers' Federation (ITF) 1914–1945: The Edo Fimmen Era*. Amsterdam: Stichting beheer IISG/International Institute for Social History, 1997.

Ruiz, Ramón E., editor. *The Mexican War: Was It Manifest Destiny?* New York: Holt, Rinehart, and Winston, 1963.

Sainz, Fernando. *Historia de la cultura española*. Buenos Aires: Editorial Nova, n.d. [1956?].

Sánchez, Joseph P. *Spanish Bluecoats*. Albuquerque: University of New Mexico Press, 1990.

Sánchez Gómez, Luis Ángel. "Elites indígenas y política colonial en Filipinas (1847–1898)." In Consuelo Naranjo Orovio et al., editors, *La nación soñada: Cuba, Puerto Rico y Filipinas ante el 98*. Madrid: Doce Calles, 1996.

San Francisco Chronicle (San Francisco), 1865–, and *Chronicle* library files.

San Francisco Medical Examiner's Office. Coroner's Register and Necropsy. Cases of Vicente Torres, 1935, Frank Nordlund and Albert Skoodra, 1936, and Jean Tatlock, 1944.

Saunders, Donna, ed. [with David Saunders]. *A Gale-Borne Seed*. Grass Valley, CA: Wild Seed Publications, 1995.

Savinio, Alberto. *Operatic Lives,* Marlboro, VT: The Marlboro Press, 1988.

———. *Speaking to Clio*. Marlboro, VT: The Marlboro Press, 1987.

Saxton, Alexander. *The Indispensable Enemy*. Berkeley: University of California Press, 1971.

Scharlin, Craig, and Lilia V. Villanueva. *Philip Vera Cruz: A Personal History of Filipino Immigrants and the Farmworkers Movement*. Los Angeles: UCLA Labor Center, Institute of Industrial Relations, and Asian American Studies Center, 1994.

Schevill, James. *Where to Go What to Do When You Are Bern Porter: A Personal Biography*. Gardiner, ME: Tilbury House, 1992.

Schirò, Salvatore. "Commemorazione dei Venti Settembre, San Francisco 1937." Typescript. Unpublished. Claire Fraschina Collection, San Francisco.

Schneiderman, William. *Dissent on Trial*. Minneapolis: MEP Publications, 1983.

Schwartz, Nancy Lynn. *The Hollywood Writers' Wars*. New York: Alfred A. Knopf, 1982.

Schwartz, Stephen. "The Albanian Legacy of Ernest Koliqi." *Albanian Catholic Bulletin* (San Francisco), 1993.

———. *Brotherhood of the Sea: A History of the Sailors' Union of the Pacific*. New Brunswick, NJ: Transaction Books, 1985.

———. "Carmelo Zito (1899–1981): Remembering an Italian Labor Journalist." *Ralph, Official Publication of the Northern California Newspaper Guild* (San Francisco), July 1997.

———. "Cultivating the Fine Art of Printing." *San Francisco Sunday Examiner and Chronicle,* May 11, 1997.

———. "Political Murder," *Commentary,* November 1988.

———. "Proletarian Novels." *V-Search, Zines!* Vol. 2 (San Francisco), 1997.

———. "A Recollection of Lew Welch." In Magda Cregg, editor, *Hey Lew*. Bolinas, CA: Magda Cregg, 1997.

———. "Researching an Arbëresh Life: Dr. Salvatore Schirò (1876–1939)." *Illyria* (New York), April 30–May 2, 1997.

———. "The 'Tanaka Memorial': A Case Study in Soviet Disinformation." 1989. Unpublished.

———. "The Universe as Seen From North Beach." *San Francisco Sunday Examiner and Chronicle,* August 17, 1997.

———. "La Venona Mexicana." *Vuelta* (México, D.F.), August 1997.

———. "The Venona Project." *Heterodoxy* (Los Angeles), September 1996.

Schwartz, Stephen, editor. *The Transition*. San Francisco: Institute for Contemporary Studies, 1986.

———[as Buck Long] and Lawrence V. Cott. "Alan Cranston's Big Lies." *The American Spectator,* April 1990.

Second Pan-Pacific Conference of Transport Workers. *Against Imperialism on the Pacific.* [Vladivostok?]: Pan-Pacific Secretariat of Transport Workers, n.d. [1929?].

Selvin, David. *A Terrible Anger.* Detroit: Wayne State University Press, 1996.

[Serra, Junípero], *Writings of Junípero Serra.* 4 vols. Edited by Antonine Tibesar. Washington, DC: Academy of American Franciscan History, 1955.

Sevander, Mayme. *Red Exodus: Finnish-American Emigration to Russia.* Duluth: Duluth International Peace Center, 1993.

Sheean, Vincent. *Personal History.* New York: Doubleday, Doran & Co., 1935.

Shields-West, Eileen. *The World Almanac® of Presidential Campaigns.* New York: World Almanac, 1992.

Sinclair, Upton: *I, Governor of California, And How I Ended Poverty.* Los Angeles, End Poverty League, 10th printing 1934.

———. *Upton Sinclair Presents William Fox.* Los Angeles; self published, 1933.

Smith, Adam, *The Wealth of Nations.* 1776. Reprinted New York: Random House/Modern Library, 1993.

Snyder, Gary. *Mountains and Rivers Without End.* Washington, DC: Counterpoint, 1996.

Sobrequés i Callicó, Jaume. *Els Catalans en els Orígens Històrics de Califòrnia.* Barcelona: Columna, 1991.

Soler i Vidal, Josep. *Catalans als Orígens (Inicis) de San Francisco de Califòrnia.* Barcelona: Dalmau, 1988.

Solow, Herbert. *Union-Smashing in Sacramento.* New York: National Sacramento Appeal Committee, 1935.

Special Memorial Edition, Second Anniversary of Death of Dr. Sun Yat-sen. [San Francisco], March 12, 1927.

Spicer, Jack. *The Collected Books of Jack Spicer.* Edited by Robin Blaser. Los Angeles: Black Sparrow Press, 1985.

Stalin, Joseph. *Marxism and the National Question.* New York: International Publishers, 1942.

[Stalin, J.]. *Stalin's Speeches on the American Communist Party* [1929]. [New York?]: Central Committee, Communist Party, U.S.A., n.d. [1931?]. Reprinted in photo-offset by U.S. federal authorities, n.d.

Starr, Kevin. *Americans and the California Dream.* Oxford: Oxford University Press, 1973.

———. *Inventing the Dream.* Oxford: Oxford University Press, 1985.

Steffens, Lincoln. *The Autobiography of Lincoln Steffens.* New York: Harcourt, Brace & Co., 1931.

Steinbeck, Elaine, and Robert Wallsten, editors. *Steinbeck: A Life in Letters.* New York: Viking Press, 1975.

Steinbeck, John. *The Grapes of Wrath.* Harmondsworth: Penguin Books, 1992.

———. *In Dubious Battle.* Harmondsworth: Penguin Books, 1992.

Stromquist, Shelton. *A Generation of Boomers.* Urbana: University of Illinois Press, 1993.

Strong, Donald S. *Organized Anti-Semitism in America.* Washington, DC: American Council on Public Affairs, 1941.

Sudoplatov, Pavel, and Anatoli Sudoplatov. *Special Tasks.* Boston: Little, Brown, 1994.

Sugranyes de Franch, Ramon. "Ramon Llull's Missionary Work." *Catalònia* (Barcelona), October 1995.

Sutin, Lawrence. *Divine Invasions.* New York: Citadel Press, 1989.

Swift, Jonathan. *Gulliver's Travels*. 1724. Reprinted New York: Viking Penguin, 1983.

Taft, Philip. *Labor Politics American Style: The California State Federation of Labor*. Cambridge, MA: Harvard University Press, 1968.

Taylor, Paul S. *On the Ground in the Thirties*. Salt Lake City: Peregrine Smith Books, 1983.

———. *The Sailors' Union of the Pacific*. New York: Ronald Press Co., 1923.

Teggart, Frederick J., ed. *The Portola Expedition of 1769–1770, Diary of Miguel Costanso*. Berkeley: University of California, Academy of Pacific Coast History, 1911.

Temple, Richard C., editor. *The World Encompassed*. London: The Argonaut Press, 1926.

Te Paske, John, and Herbert S. Klein. "The Seventeenth-Century Crisis in New Spain: Myth or Reality?" *Past and Present,* February 1981. Cited in Josep Fontana Lazaro, "Comercio colonial y crecimiento económico: Revisiones e hipotesis," Introduction to Vol. III: *Comercio y colonias* of Josep Fontana Lazaro, *La economía española al final del Antiguo Regimen*. Madrid: Alianza Editorial, 1983.

Thompson, Fred, and Patrick Murfin. *The I.W.W.: Its First Seventy Years*. Chicago: Industrial Workers of the World, 1976.

Thorne, J. O., and T. C. Collocott, editors. *Chambers Biographical Dictionary*. London: Chambers, 1984.

Tikhmenev, P. A. *A History of the Russian-American Company*. Seattle: University of Washington Press, 1978.

Timmons, Stuart. *The Trouble With Harry Hay*. Boston: Alyson Publications, 1990.

Tocsin (Berkeley, CA; Charles Fox, publisher; Dr. George Keith, editor), 1961–67.

Togores Sánchez, Luis Eugenio. "La defensa de las Filipinas ante la estrategia de las grandes potencias en Extremo Oriente." In Consuelo Naranjo Orovio, et al., editors, *La nacion sonada: Cuba, Puerto Rico y Filipinas ante el 98*. Madrid: Doce Calles, 1996.

Trautmann, William. *How Strikes Are Lost*. Chicago: Industrial Workers of the World, [1911?].

Treutlein, Theodore E. *San Francisco Bay, Discovery and Colonization, 1769–1776*. San Francisco: California Historical Society, 1968.

Trimble, Paul C. "Economic Aspects of the Carmen's Strike Against the United Railroads of San Francisco in 1907." *Journal of the Bay Area Electric Railroad Association* (Suisun City, CA), Winter 1994–95.

Trotsky, Leon. *Stalin: An Appraisal of the Man and His Influence,* edited and translated by Charles Malamuth. New York: Harper & Brothers, n.d. [1946].

Troy, Sandy. *Captain Trips: A Biography of Jerry Garcia*. New York: Thunder's Mouth Press, 1994.

Trueta, J. *The Spirit of Catalonia*. London: Oxford University Press, 1946.

Twain, Mark. *Roughing It*. Harmondsworth: Penguin Books, 1985.

"Upton Sinclair's Victory." Editorial. *The Nation,* September 12, 1934.

Uran, Marshall, ed. *Sea-Say*. San Francisco: Muran Productions, 1995.

U.S. Department of Defense. *The "Magic" Background of Pearl Harbor*. Washington, DC: Government Printing Office, 1977.

———. *The Venona Project*. Washington,DC: National Security Agency, 1995–96. Internet publication at http://www.nsa.gov:8080.

U.S. House of Representatives, Committee on Un-American Activities, *Hearings Regarding Communist Infiltration of Radiation Laboratory and Atomic Bomb Project at the University of California, Berkeley*. Washington, DC: Government Printing Office, 1949.

————. *Hearings Regarding Steve Nelson.* Washington, DC: Government Printing Office, 1949.

————. *Hearing, Investigation of Communist Activities in the San Francisco Area.* Washington, DC: Government Printing Office, 1954.

————. *Hearing, San Francisco Area.* Testimony of Louis Rosser, December 1, 1953. Washington, DC: Government Printing Office, 1954.

————. *Hearings Held in San Francisco, Calif., June 18–21, 1957,* Washington, DC: Government Printing Office, 1957.

————. *Hearings and Appendix. The Northern California District of the Communist Party.* Washington, DC: Government Printing Office, 1960.

U.S. House of Representatives, Special Committee to Investigate Communist Activities in the U.S. *Hearings, Investigation of Communist Propaganda,* Part 5—Vol. 4. Washington, DC: Government Printing Office, 1930.

U.S. House of Representatives. Special Committee on Un-American Activities. *Hearings. Investigation of Un-American Propaganda Activities in the United States,* vol. 3. Washington, DC: Government Printing Office, 1938.

U.S. Senate. Committee on the Judiciary. Subcommittee to Investigate the Administration of the Internal Security Act and Other Internal Security Laws. *Scope of Soviet Activity in the United States.* Appendix I, Part 23-A, Washington, DC: Government Printing Office, 1957.

Venegas, Miguel. *A Natural and Civil History of California.* London: Rivington and Fletcher, 1759.

Volkogonov, Dmitri. *Stalin.* New York: Grove Weidenfeld, 1991.

————. *Trotsky.* New York: The Free Press, 1996.

Voltes i Bou, Pere. *Catalunya i la llibertat de comerç amb Amèrica.* Barcelona: Dalmau, 1964.

The Volunteer for Liberty (Barcelona), 1937–38.

Vrana, Eugene Dennis. "Salty language peppers maritime workers' stories." *The Dispatcher* (San Francisco), January 17, 1996.

Waite, Arthur Edward. *Lives of Alchemystical Philosophers.* London: Redway, 1888.

Walker, William. *The War in Nicaragua.* Tucson: University of Arizona Press, 1985.

Walter, Richard, and Benjamin Robins, editors. George Anson's *A Voyage Round the World.* Edited by Glyndwr Williams. London: Oxford University Press, 1974.

Ward, Estolv E. *The Gentle Dynamiter.* Palo Alto, CA: Ramparts Press, 1981.

Warner, Opie L. "The Police Department and the Strike." *Police and Peace Officers' Journal of the State of California* (San Francisco), August 1934.

Webb, Constance. Conversation with Stephen Schwartz. San Francisco, August 21, 1997.

"Weekend Ark Dweller Drowns in Novato Creek." San Rafael, CA, *Independent-Journal,* December 5, 1952.

Weinstein, Allen. *Perjury.* New York: Random House, 1978.

Weintraub, Hyman. "The I.W.W. in California." Unpublished graduate thesis, 1937.

Weir, Stan. "Meetings with James Baldwin." In Marshall Uran, editor, *Sea-Say.* San Francisco: Muran Productions, 1995.

————. "New Technology: A Catalyst for Crises in Collective Bargaining, Industrial Discipline, and Labor Law." *Nova Law Journal* (Fort Lauderdale), Spring 1984.

Wellman, David. *The Union Makes Us Strong.* Cambridge: Cambridge University Press, 1995.

Wells, Evelyn. *Fremont Older.* New York: Appleton-Century, 1936.

West, Nathanael. *The Day of the Locust.* 1939. Reprinted New York: Signet, 1983.

Western Worker (San Francisco), 1932–1937.

Willens, Doris. *Lonesome Traveler.* Lincoln: University of Nebraska Press, 1993.

Willoughby, Maj. Gen. Charles A. *Shanghai Conspiracy.* New York: E. P. Dutton, 1952.

Winter, Ella. *And Not to Yield.* New York: Harcourt, Brace & World, 1963.

Wofsy, Leon. *Looking for the Future.* Oakland: Institute for Social and Economic Studies, 1995.

Workers (Communist) Party of America. *The 4th National Convention of the W. (C.) P. of A.* Chicago: Daily Worker Publishing Co., 1925. Reprinted in photo-offset by U.S. federal authorities, n.d.

Workers Party of America. *Program and Constitution.* Chicago: Workers Party of America, 1924.

Works Progress Administration. *California.* American Guide Series. New York: Works Progress Administration and Hastings House, 1939.

———. *San Francisco.* American Guide Series. New York: Works Progress Administration and Hastings House, 1940.

Yanish, Nat. *Pursuit and Survival.* San Francisco: Apex Publications, 1981.

Yarmolinsky, Avrahm. *Road to Revolution.* Princeton: Princeton University Press, 1957.

Yates, Frances A. *The Art of Memory.* Chicago: University of Chicago Press, 1966.

Yoneda, Karl. "A Brief History of U.S. Asian Labor." *Political Affairs* (New York), September 1976.

———. *Ganbatte: Sixty-Year Struggle of a Kibei Worker.* Los Angeles: University of California Press, 1983.

———. "The Heritage of Sen Katayama." *Political Affairs* (New York), March 1975.

Young, Brig. Gen. Peter, editor. *The World Almanac® of World War II.* New York: Pharos Books, 1986.

Zakheim, Masha. "The Art of Medicine: Zakheim Frescoes, the University of California, San Francisco." Unpublished.

Zakheim Jewett, Masha. *Coit Tower, San Francisco: Its History and Art.* San Francisco: Volcano Press, 1983.

Zavalishin, Dmitrii. *California en 1824.* Translated into Spanish by Riña Ortíz Peralta. Mexico, D.F.: Breve Fondo Editorial, 1996.

Acknowledgments

As the author of this book, I offer my greatest thanks to Adam Bellow, my editor at The Free Press, and his associate, Chad Conway; to Jerry Roberts, managing editor of the *San Francisco Chronicle,* whose encouragement was notable and generous, and to my dear friend and irreplaceable researcher, Lawrence V. Cott.

I owe much to Richard Geiger, chief librarian of the *San Francisco Chronicle,* and to its staff of librarians, who guided me through the paper's invaluable "morgue."

I also wish to acknowledge the cooperation of the San Francisco Medical Examiner's Office.

IN DEALING WITH Spanish, Catalan, and Mallorcan sources, I owe everything to my long-standing friend and collaborator, Víctor Alba, who lives in Catalonia. Víctor put me in touch with Bartomeu Font Obrador of the Secció Juniperiana, in Palma de Mallorca, and Professor Josep Maria Delgado i Ribes of the Universitat Pompeu Fabra, in Barcelona, whose assistance was indispensable.

On Mexican issues and themes, I extend great thanks and appreciation to my colleague Aurelio Asiaín of *Vuelta,* the outstanding monthly review founded by Octavio Paz, as well as my friends Enrique Krauze and Gabriel Zaid, who assisted me during a research trip to Mexico for this book. I am also grateful to Jean Meyer of the Centro de Investigación y Docencia Económicas, the leading expert on *Sinarquismo* and other Mexican antirevolutionary movements, and especially to Antonio Saborit García Peña, Riña Ortíz Peralta, and Enrique Arriola Woog, of the Instituto Nacional de Antropología e Historia, all in Mexico City. Señor Saborit proved an invaluable aide, particularly in researching Bertram D. Wolfe and Kenneth Rexroth. In addition, I wish to thank my friend Professor Arturo Dávila of the Spanish Department of the University of California at Berkeley for his encouragement.

Paul Avrich, the outstanding historian of anarchism, was irreplaceable as a source on William C. Owen. In Britain, Stuart Christie was especially helpful in tracking Owen and Marcus Graham, whose works would be unknown today without the efforts of Christie and the late Albert Meltzer. Stuart led me to Barry Pateman of the Kate Sharpley Library in Oundle, Peterborough, Cambridgeshire, whose cooperation was also crucial for this work.

Marilyn Zito and Dora Schirò Fraschina were exceptionally generous in assisting my investigation of their fathers, Carmelo Zito and Salvatore Schirò. Wayne M. Collins, Jr., and Masha Zakheim were particularly important in my study of their parents, Wayne M. Collins, Sr., and Bernard Zakheim, as were Mariana Rexroth and John McBride in dealing with Mariana's father Kenneth, and Kleo Apostolides Mini, ex-wife of Philip K. Dick and widow of Norman Mini, whose help was truly miraculous. Finally, I thank Sandra Benedet for introducing me to her father Javier and her uncle Vicente.

My old and loyal friend Paul Dempster, former president of the Sailors' Union of the Pacific, deserves thanks not only for his support of my work but also for granting me access to the unpublished memoir of Barney Mayes.

I similarly feel great gratitude to my longtime friend and mentor William Herrick for sharing his knowledge of the tragedy of American volunteers in the Spanish Civil War, particularly the fate of Harry Hynes.

Robert Conquest, of the Hoover Institution, played his characteristic role as moral ally and model, while also assisting me in researching the Soviet secret police in general and Grigory Kheifitz in particular.

Harold and Gertrud Parker of Tiburon, California, the leading collectors in America of art by Wolfgang Paalen, encouraged this project from its earliest beginnings, and I appreciate their dedication to Paalen's work. I owe much to Suzanne Royce, art historian and assistant to Gordon Onslow Ford.

Retired deputy chief Kevin Mullen of the San Francisco Police Department assisted my investigation of the Eli Bernard Jacobson case, for which I thank him.

The physicist Jack Sarfatti, Ph.D., helped me greatly to understand scientific issues, especially in the work of David Joseph Bohm.

John Earl Haynes of the Library of Congress in Washington deserves thanks for his assistance in handling Communist archives in Moscow.

The historians Reiner Tosstorff, of the Johannes Gutenberg University in Mainz, and Dieter Nelles, of the University of Wuppertal, were exceptionally important in helping me trace German radicals in California.

I also thank Gary Tennant of the University of Bradford, West Yorkshire, for sharing his research on Julio Antonio Mella, and Michael Chapman of Eagle Publishing in Washington, who checked my research with his unparalleled archive on the Oppenheimer case.

The photographer David Gladstone, friend of Norman and Kleo Mini, served as a researcher for this book.

Robert Hawley of Ross Valley Books in Berkeley helped with out-of-print titles in California history, while John Durham of Bolerium Books in San Francisco fulfilled the same role in labor and radical history. The Freedom Bookshop in Whitechapel, London, and the New York Labor News Company, of Mountain View, California, assisted in locating extremely obscure titles in anarchist and socialist history. To them, keepers of the flame, I am especially grateful.

Finally, my thanks to Joaquín Pasos for the verse from Saint Paul, to George Melly for the quote from Thom Gunn, to Dušan Babić for helping research Mikhail Kalatozov, and to Harre W. Demoro, who was right about David Saunders.

Although most of my writing over the past thirty years has been occupied with the subject of this work, I began researching the project in an organized manner in 1976. I have herein discussed, quoted, and otherwise referred to many individuals whom I personally knew, directly observed, or reported on as a journalist. I have drawn on encounters, conversations, and (very rarely) formal interviews with the following, living and dead, to whom I express my sincere thanks, and whose mention here, in the order of their appearance in the narrative, implies neither their agreement with nor their approval of the views expressed in this book: Octavio Paz, Manuel Fernández Grandizo, Warren K. Billings, Jack McDonald, Pavel Dotsenko, Archie Brown, Elaine Black, Karl Goso Yoneda, Harry Bridges, Kenneth Rexroth, Elsa Gidlow, Marie Rexroth, Bernard Zakheim, Victor Arnautoff,

Upton Sinclair, Crispulo Mensalvas, George Hitchcock, Walter Stack, Harry Partch, Lester Cole, Alvah C. Bessie, William Everson, Robert Duncan, Jack Werner Stauffacher, Philip Lamantia, Adrian Wilson, Edith Jenkins, David Jenkins, Jerry Garcia, Edward Dmytryk, Richard Nixon, James Schevill, Robert Patterson ("Freddie Francisco"), Thomas Albright, Byron Randall, Gordon Onslow Ford, Glen Taylor, Al Richmond, Iva Toguri d'Aquino, George Olshausen, Richard Gladstein, Vincent Hallinan, Vivian Hallinan, Dean Lipton. Patrick Sarsfield "Butch" Hallinan, Terence Tyrone "Kayo" Hallinan, Conn "Ringo" Hallinan, Wayne S. Vucinich, Juanita Wheeler, Holland Roberts, Ellis Colton, Kenneth Patchen, Miriam Patchen, Alan Watts, Lawrence Ferlinghetti, Holly Beye, Gary Snyder, Philip Whalen, Lew Welch, Allen Ginsberg, Jack Finney, Martin Ponch, Bob Kaufman, Jessica Lucy Freeman-Mitford ("Decca Treuhaft"), Robert Edward Treuhaft, Tillie Lerner Olsen, C. L. R. James, Shigeyoshi Murao, William Reich, J. P. Morray, John Pittman, James Frederick Forest, Willie L. Brown, Jr., Phillip Burton, John Burton, Louis Krainock, Stanley Weir, George Benet, Warren Hinckle III, and Hank Harrison.

Index